College Majors

Second Edition

HANDBOOK

with Real Career Paths and Payoffs

The Actual Jobs, Earnings,
and Trends for Graduates
of 60 College Majors

Neeta P. Fogg, Ph.D.   Paul E. Harrington, Ed.D.   Thomas F. Harrington, Ph.D.

Foreword by Michael Farr, America's Foremost Career Author

jist *Works*
America's Career Publisher

OUACHITA TECHNICAL COLLEGE

College Majors Handbook with Real Career Paths and Payoffs, *Second Edition*
The Actual Jobs, Earnings, and Trends for Graduates of 60 College Majors

Previous edition was titled *The College Majors Handbook.*

© 2004 by JIST Publishing, Inc.

Published by JIST Works, an imprint of JIST Publishing, Inc.
8902 Otis Avenue
Indianapolis, IN 46216-1033

Phone: 1-800-648-JIST   Fax: 1-800-JIST-FAX   E-mail: info@jist.com   Web site: www.jist.com

---

Visit our Web site at www.jist.com for information on JIST, free job search information, book excerpts, and ordering information on our many products. For free information on 14,000 job titles, visit www.careeroink.com. Quantity discounts are available for JIST products. Please call our sales department at 1-800-648-JIST for a free catalog and more information.

Acquisitions Editor: Susan Pines
Development Editor: Lisa S. Williams
Editor: Stephanie Koutek
Cover Designer: Nick Anderson
Interior Designer: Aleata Howard
Interior Layout: Carolyn Newland
Proofreader: Jeanne Clark
Indexer: Henthorne House

Printed in Canada

09 08 07 06 05   9 8 7 6 5 4 3

Library of Congress Cataloging-in-Publication Data

Fogg, Neeta.
  College majors handbook with real career paths and payoffs : the actual jobs,
earnings, and trends for graduates of 60 college majors / Neeta P. Fogg, Paul E.
Harrington, Thomas F. Harrington ; foreword by Michael Farr.– 2nd ed.
      p. cm.
  Rev. ed. of: College majors handbook. c2001.
  Includes index.
  ISBN 1-59357-074-0
  1. Vocational guidance–United States. 2. Vocational interests–United States. 3.
  College majors–United States. 4. Professions–United States. I. Harrington, Paul.
  II. Harrington, Thomas F. III. Fogg, Neeta. College majors handbook. IV. Title.
  HF5382.5.U5F644 2004
  331.702'0973–dc22
                                        2004007907

ISBN 1-59357-074-0

Foreword

Where was this book when I needed it?

I went through four years of high school without any meaningful career counseling or help in selecting a college major. Fortunately, I assumed I would go to college, but I selected my first major based on little information. In college, I still didn't get any useful help in exploring career options or selecting a college major, so of course I changed my pre-med major to something impractical, English. After working a few years in unrelated jobs, I went on to a master's degree in counseling psychology with no meaningful career counseling.

Too many people make similarly important decisions with little solid information. I've turned out okay, but it sure would have been helpful back then to know more about majors that interested me and how they related to career outcomes.

I often still hear people say things like

- ▶ "Liberal arts (or whatever) is not a good degree, since you can't get a good job with it."

- ▶ "Get a degree in physical therapy (or whatever) because it pays well."

- ▶ "A college degree is a waste of time. My sister-in-law has one and is working as a waitress."

But are these and similar statements true? And are earnings and job prospects the most important things to consider when selecting a college major?

This book will help you get solid answers to these and other important questions. Instead of presenting someone's opinion, this book presents the actual employment experiences of 150,000 people who obtained four-year college degrees. It gives us the facts about the actual jobs they work in, how much they earn, and other employment-related details for graduates in 60 majors.

Finally, we know what actually happened to those who majored in the liberal arts, education, psychology, business, engineering, and so many other fields. And the results will sometimes surprise you! For example, I would not have guessed that the job most often held by psychology majors is "managers, executives, or administrators." Or that political science majors end up in the wide range of jobs that they actually do. It makes for interesting reading and will certainly help you look at some college majors in different ways.

And as for wondering whether going to college is worth it, this book answers that question with an emphatic "YES!" by laying out the compelling economic data that supports doing so. More importantly, the book will encourage you to understand how to afford going to college, as well as help you make a good decision regarding just what college majors best meet your interests, values, and employment goals.

I consider this book to be the most helpful one on its topic, and I recommend it without hesitation for anyone who is considering going to college or who is selecting or changing a college major.

I only wish the authors had written it earlier.

Michael Farr

Editor's note: Mike is an author of more than 20 books on job seeking and exploring career and learning options, including *The Very Quick Job Search, The Quick Resume & Cover Letter Book, Same-Day Resume,* and *Best Jobs for the 21st Century.* Mike also holds the position of publisher at JIST Publishing. He enthusiastically volunteered to write this foreword for a book he very much believes in.

Table of Contents

Part 1   What You Need to Know About the College Investment Decision, College Success, and Career Choice 1

Chapter 1   What Pays Off in High School: Pre-College Decisions and College and Career Choices 3

Chapter 2   The Psychology of Career Choice: Assessing Abilities, Interests, and Values 21

Chapter 3   The Economics of Career Choice 41

Part 2   Behavioral and Medical Sciences 73

Chapter 4   Audiology and Speech Pathology 75

Chapter 5   Criminal Justice and Criminology 83

Chapter 6   Health and Medical Technology 91

Chapter 7   Home Economics: Dietetics, Food, and Nutrition 101

Chapter 8   Medical Preparatory Programs 111

Chapter 9   Nursing 121

Chapter 10   Parks, Recreation, Fitness, and Leisure Studies 129

Chapter 11   Pharmacy 139

Chapter 12   Physical Therapy 145

Chapter 13   Psychology 153

Chapter 14   Social Work 165

Part 3   Business and Administration 175

Chapter 15   Accounting 177

Chapter 16   Applied Mathematics, Operations Research, and Statistics 185

Chapter 17   Economics 195

Chapter 18   Financial Management 205

Chapter 19   General Business 215

Chapter 20   General Mathematics 225

Chapter 21   Marketing 235

Chapter 22   Public Administration 243

Part 4   Education 253

Chapter 23   Elementary Teacher Education 255

Chapter 24   Mathematics and Science Teacher Education 263

Chapter 25   Physical Education and Coaching 271

Chapter 26   Secondary Teacher Education 279

Chapter 27   Special Education 289

Part 5	Engineering	297
Chapter 28	Aerospace, Aeronautical, and Astronautical Engineering	299
Chapter 29	Architecture and Environmental Design	307
Chapter 30	Chemical Engineering	315
Chapter 31	Civil Engineering	323
Chapter 32	Computer Systems Engineering	333
Chapter 33	Electrical and Electronics Engineering	343
Chapter 34	Industrial Engineering	353
Chapter 35	Mechanical Engineering	363

Part 6	Humanities and Social Sciences	373
Chapter 36	Anthropology and Archaeology	375
Chapter 37	Communications	385
Chapter 38	Dramatic Arts	393
Chapter 39	English Language, Literature, and Letters	401
Chapter 40	Foreign Languages and Literature	411
Chapter 41	Geography	421
Chapter 42	History	431
Chapter 43	Journalism	437
Chapter 44	Legal Studies and Pre-Law	445
Chapter 45	Liberal Arts and General Studies	453
Chapter 46	Music and Dance	463
Chapter 47	Philosophy	473
Chapter 48	Political Science, Government, and International Relations	483
Chapter 49	Sociology	491
Chapter 50	Visual Arts	499

Part 7	Natural Sciences	509
Chapter 51	Animal Food Sciences	511
Chapter 52	Biology and Life Sciences	519
Chapter 53	Chemistry	527
Chapter 54	Forestry and Environmental Sciences	535
Chapter 55	Geology and Geophysics	545
Chapter 56	Microbiology and Biochemistry	555
Chapter 57	Physics and Astronomy	565
Chapter 58	Plant Food Sciences	575

Part 8	Technology	583
Chapter 59	Computer Science	585
Chapter 60	Data and Information Processing	595
Chapter 61	Electrical and Electronics Engineering Technology	605
Chapter 62	Industrial Production Technology	615
Chapter 63	Mechanical Engineering Technology	625

Index		632

Preface

"What's your major?" Every first-year student entering a college or university is asked that question. A *major* is a concentration of specialized courses, usually a minimum of 24 credit hours (such as eight three-hour courses), taken during a student's third and fourth years in a four-year program.

Some colleges and universities require students to declare a major immediately upon entering their freshman year, most often in specialized technical areas such as electrical engineering, nursing, or computer science. In a liberal arts college or university, students are exposed to a spectrum of courses from different academic disciplines during the first two years for a general education. At the beginning of the third, or junior, year, most colleges require students to concentrate their studies in a particular field, such as psychology, journalism, or chemistry, as preparation for a career after graduation.

Some first-year students know exactly what they want to major in and what career they want to pursue after graduation. At the other extreme, some freshmen enter college without having made any decision about either a major or a career. Between the two extremes are most students, who have tentative or–at best–provisional ideas about possible majors and subsequent careers. Decisions for choosing one major above another are sometimes made for superficial yet practical, short-term reasons, such as which courses are less difficult and which departments have professors who give better grades. We believe that the choice of major field of study should be based on long-term career and lifestyle goals and informed by sound information.

Most of the publications offering guidance for enrolling in college contain little more than a description of the more than 3,500 colleges and universities across the nation. They provide a sketch of each college in terms of the types of students enrolled and the nature of the educational process at each college, including class sizes, student-faculty ratios, and proportion of faculty with a doctoral degree. They also provide some information on the types of programs offered. In recent years, this type of publication has provided a quality ranking of the colleges based on the admissions competitiveness of the school.

Although these publications can provide a thumbnail sketch of a large number of colleges across the country, they don't provide much insight into perhaps the most important decision that a college student will make–a decision that is even more important than the actual college selection–the choice of a major field of study.

This book provides substantive information on long-term career alternatives for bachelor's degree holders in 60 major fields of study. The basic tenet of this book is that cost of a college or university education is an investment that can yield "payoffs" in the form of economically rewarding and personally fulfilling careers. Sixty chapters–each devoted to a single major field of study–detail the economic rewards and employment experiences of graduates within each field. The chapters also discuss training opportunities at work, the types of duties performed at work, and the most common occupations in which the graduates from each of the 60 major fields of study are employed.

To be sure, salary is not the only form of payoff from a college education. Interests, values, and abilities are also personal goals in seeking job satisfaction. The information needs of guidance counselors, teachers, parents, or administrators do not neatly fall into one of the respective disciplines of the authors–economics or psychology. Rather, these educators and parents seek to understand the choices that could provide their students and children with solid opportunities yet still meet their psychological needs and personal aspirations.

This book responds to these needs by integrating the work of psychology and economics into a single comprehensive volume. The reader receives information about the personality and labor market implications of his or her choice of an undergraduate major field of study. We have tried to cross the boundaries of a single academic discipline to provide new and more meaningful information to those confronted with the task of making a college investment decision.

Recognizing that investment in a college education will yield rewards in the future, this book also provides projections of labor market demand for graduates from each of the 60 major fields of study.

For those inclined toward graduate education, this book discusses the role of graduate education in career advancement. It also presents the actual postgraduate schooling experiences of bachelor's degree holders in each of the 60 major fields, including the types of postgraduate degrees earned and the major field of study in which a degree was received.

This informative book should help anyone replace superficial, short-term assessments about a major with long-term considerations of several economic, personal, and psychological dimensions of their choice of major that should have a positive impact on a graduate's future employment and lead to a professionally rewarding career.

This book enables you to easily compare the different payoffs of each of the 60 majors on the basis of a survey of 150,000 bachelor's degree holders. For parents, students, career counselors, and anyone involved in the choice or use of a college major, this book is an enlightening and indispensable resource for choosing one major above another.

Organization of the Book

Chapter 1 starts out with the relationship between pre-college decisions on college and career choice. This chapter describes the importance of decisions made during high school on college and career outcomes. Chapters 2 and 3 provide a discussion of the psychology and economics involved in the choice of major field of study. Psychologist Thomas Harrington writes about the role that personal values, interests, personality, and abilities play in the selection of majors and career fields. Economists Neeta Fogg and Paul Harrington examine the economics of the college investment decision. We focus on the economic benefits and costs of a college diploma and the impact that the choice of a major field of study has on long-term labor market success.

The remainder of the book provides specific information on 60 major fields of study. A description of each undergraduate major and the various subfields that compose the major are provided. Next, a discussion of the skills required to enter the field successfully and the types of values, interests, personalities, and abilities that persons in the field generally possess are included.

For each major field of study, different kinds of data are provided on the employment and earnings outcomes as well as on graduates' educational pathways. Information is provided on the kinds of jobs held by graduates with a bachelor's degree in each major field of study, the activities that they undertake at work, and the sector in which they are employed. An extensive discussion of the earnings of graduates by major field of study—including their long-term earnings experiences—is provided. The level of company-supported training and the future educational activities of graduates are presented as well.

Finally, we provide data on the employment outlook—developed by the U.S. Bureau of Labor Statistics—for each of the most commonly held jobs by graduates in every major field of study. All the data and analysis included for the sixty majors pertain to college graduates who have earned a bachelor's degree only. The outcomes for persons with an earned graduate degree are not included, although information on the likelihood of earning a graduate degree of some type and the kinds of advanced degrees earned is included for each major field of study.

Sources of Information

Many of the findings and analyses included in this book are based on the results of the National Survey of College Graduates (NSCG). The NSCG is a sample of more than 148,000 respondents in the United States who completed a comprehensive questionnaire designed to gather information on the educational, employment, and earnings experiences of a cross section of college graduates across the nation. The NSCG represents the largest and most comprehensive study of college graduates ever conducted.

The NSCG allowed us to produce statistically reliable and detailed data for post-graduation outcomes of graduates in alternative major fields of study. For the first time, we have a systematic perspective on the long-term outcomes associated with choosing a particular undergraduate major field of study. Ironically, the results on which this book is based are simply a by-product of a more ambitious data collection program undertaken by the U.S. Bureau of the Census for the National Science Foundation. This larger study provides longitudinal information on college graduates in scientific, engineering, and technical fields of study.

Some information in this book was taken from U.S. Department of Labor publications and various college and university catalogs. Other materials used in the preparation of this book include *The Ability Explorer* by Joan and Thomas Harrington (Riverside Publishing Co., 1996), *The Career Decision-Making System* by Thomas Harrington and Arthur O'Shea (American Guidance Service, 1992), and *A Guide to the Development and Use of Myers-Briggs Type Indicator* by Isabel Briggs Myers and Mary H. McCaulley (Consulting Psychologist Press, 1995).

The employment projections were derived from a computer data file containing industry and occupation projections supplied by the Bureau of Labor Statistics. These projections and accompanying analyses can be found in the November 2001 issue of the *Monthly Labor Review,* published by the Bureau of Labor Statistics, U.S. Department of Labor.

Acknowledgments

The task of writing this volume was indeed daunting. The computer programming and data analysis required to accurately portray the career options and earnings experiences of college graduates for 60 individual major fields of study required sophisticated skills and great attention to detail. Kevin McCabe and Frank Tortora provided outstanding computer and research support to this endeavor. Without their abilities this volume could not have been produced. Neal Fogg read the manuscript with great care, helping us avoid errors of analysis as well as the occasional sin of omission. Joan Harrington and Linda Harrington provided tireless editing support throughout the writing of this book. Sheila Palma cheerfully handled the many administrative tasks required to bring this volume to publication.

Neeta Fogg and Paul Harrington wish to acknowledge their personal and intellectual debt to Andrew Sum, Director of the Center for Labor Market Studies at Northeastern University. Over the years Professor Sum has served as our teacher, mentor, and friend, encouraging us in our research, working with us to develop new skills and insights, and emphasizing the need for both intellectual rigor and practical meaning in our work.

What You Need to Know About the College Investment Decision, College Success, and Career Choice

CHAPTER 1

What Pays Off in High School:
Pre-College Decisions and College and Career Choices

Today's high school students, and even children leaving middle school and entering high school, are confronted with a bewildering set of choices requiring decisions that can affect their future personal well-being. The arrays of choices that today's young teens must make are far more complex than those made by their parents at the same age. Moreover, the ramifications of making the wrong choice at an early age can be much more severe than was the case even a few decades ago. As the rewards to making the right decision have become greater, the adversity associated with making the wrong decision has also become more severe. As a result, the gap between those who succeed and those who struggle has increased considerably in just the past two decades.

Middle and high school students today make decisions about schooling, sexual behavior, and drugs and alcohol use (among other things) that will shape a good part of their pathway to adulthood. While a misstep at an early age may not necessarily be fatal to long-term success, it will certainly divert a youngster from that pathway. Bearing a child while in high school does not automatically mean that a young female's chances of long-term employment and earnings success fall to zero, but it does mean that the likelihood of achieving such success will decline sharply.

Similarly, a young male abusing drugs and alcohol will likely experience a sharp reduction in his chances for life success. In both instances, a set of obstacles to personal development is created by the youth based on some bad decisions at an early age.

Certainly, all of this is unfair. Youngsters aged 13 or 14, or even 17 or 18, shouldn't have their life chances reduced because of decisions made in ignorance, on whim and caprice, or because of the teen torment of peer pressure. Yet the clear fact is that life has become increasingly unforgiving and certainly more risky for youth today than has been the case even in the recent past. Powerful economic and social forces have dramatically altered the outcomes associated with the decisions that parents and children make regarding the way the adolescent develops.

Technological change and economic growth have combined to dramatically increase the economic payoff to basic skills development, educational attainment, early work experience, and occupational proficiency. As the next chapter shows, the job content of the U.S. economy has shifted from the production of goods toward the production of services. The "new service economy," concentrated in industries such as health services, engineering and architectural services, and computer and information technology services, employs high proportions of workers with a college degree—most often in fields that require a high level of occupational knowledge, such as nursing, engineering, and computer science.

This chapter examines the set of decisions that high school students must make about the following four key issues:

- Developing basic skills—reading, writing, and mathematics

- Establishing educational goals

- Mixing work and school

- Developing occupational skills

It also provides a brief review of some of the key economic behaviors of colleges and universities when recruiting their entering undergraduate classes—including college pricing and financial aid strategies—along with a discussion of their meaning for students and parents.

Before we get into the specific questions that adolescents and parents need to consider, let's first spend a bit of time discussing the nature of the education decision-making process.

Understanding the Investment Characteristics of the Education Decision and the Need for Parental Involvement in Decision Making

Most day-to-day decisions that youngsters make are what economists think of as decisions about consumption. Consumption can be thought of as simply paying the cost for a good or service and receiving all of the benefits for that good or service immediately. There is no temporal difference between when the costs are paid and the benefits received. A good example might be the purchase of an ice cream cone. On a hot summer afternoon we might buy a double Rocky Road. When we purchase our cone from the vendor, we pay the costs at the same time that we receive the benefits of the purchase. An important implication of this is that we know with a high degree of certainty what the benefits of the ice cream cone are when we make the purchase. This means that there is relatively little risk associated with a well-informed consumption decision. When we buy the cone, we are pretty certain of what we will receive in return.

A second key category of household spending is investment goods or services. These differ from consumption goods and services in many important ways. The critical distinguishing factor between consumption and investment is time. Unlike with consumption spending, the costs and benefits of investment spending are not closely connected in time or even necessarily in space.

Investment occurs when current consumption is sacrificed toward the purchase of a good or service that is expected to yield a higher level of benefits in the future, which frequently accrue in the form of higher future income and therefore higher levels of future consumption. While many adults understand the idea of deferring current consumption for higher future consumption, it may not be an idea with which most adolescents are familiar. An 18th-century economist noted that current consumption confronts our senses, while future consumption can only be imagined. Because of their limited life experiences, adolescents may have a more limited ability than their parents to imagine the gains from delaying the gratification of their current consumption desires. This is one reason why parental involvement in schooling is so important. Middle and young high school students may have less understanding than their parents of how the abilities they develop in school will make a difference in the long run. Fundamentally, adolescents seem to have limited ability to look into the future, at least compared to parents.

Perhaps the reasons that parents better understand the difference between consumption and investment is that investment, by its very nature, involves a degree of uncertainty and therefore risk. Because the benefits of investment, by definition, occur in the future, it is not certain that they will occur at all or that all of the anticipated benefits will be produced by the investment activity. There is only a chance or a probability that the expected benefits of an investment will actually materialize. Parents,

largely through observation and experience, have a better notion than children of the uncertainty and risk associated with an investment activity, thus placing them in a better position to make investment decisions, which are usually more sophisticated than consumption decisions. For most people, especially adolescents, the preference is for current consumption. Part of being a responsible parent means pushing children to forgo current consumption (such as watching television or playing video games) to engage in activities that are investment-like in nature (for example, studying and doing extra work at school), as they are expected to yield gains in the future that exceed the value of forgone current consumption.

When individuals invest, they are in a very real sense gambling–betting that forgoing current consumption will yield higher future consumption. An individual investor's willingness to give up current consumption is in part dependent on his perception of stability and certainty of receiving the expected benefits. The more stable the investment environment, the more certain the investment will result in the expected gains or benefits. Reducing uncertainty about the future justifies placing greater weight on future benefits versus present benefits. If the future looks very uncertain, then we will not invest. For example, students with more stability in their home lives have better basic skills proficiencies than do those with less stability, so family and social stability play an important role in the investment decision. Stability in the labor market also will alter investment decisions in the labor market. If students and parents have a great degree of uncertainty about future prospects in alternative career areas, then the benefits of investing in a given field become more risky.

The problem for many students, and even parents, is that they fail to think of high school education as an investment good. For too many students, high school is a place to hang out and meet friends, but not a place to develop skills and abilities and prepare for the future. Part of the reason that students and parents treat high school matriculation somewhat cavalierly is that, in economic terms, it is often a "free good." For most students (and their parents) there are no direct out-of-pocket costs associated with a high school education. Most transactions follow the simple economic dictum that those who pay the costs receive the benefits. Transactions that are based on this rule are more likely to follow a certain sort of price discipline. Extending our ice cream example, if I pay for the ice cream, I won't throw it out, because I paid for it directly with the expectation to receive some kind of benefit for the cost incurred. But in the case of a free good, a third party pays the cost, and the beneficiaries usually undervalue the free good and waste it because they did not pay for it. A "free" good such as public high school education can frequently be badly abused by the consumer.

High school students are educational investors, and a third party–taxpayers–pays the dollar costs of their investment activity. Students make critical investment decisions over the course of the four years in school but often are unaware that they are engaged in an investment activity. The proof of this is clear. Only about 70 percent of this year's entering freshman class will graduate with a regular high school diploma four years from now. The reading, writing, and math skills of these dropouts will be markedly below those of students who complete school and earn a diploma. Those who drop out will find a labor market that is very unwelcoming to them. They will have limited employment chances, and when employed they will be more likely to find low-wage jobs with few benefits. Their long-term employment and earnings prospects are bleak. The gap in labor market success between those who choose to finish high school and those who drop out is large and has risen sharply over time.

The chances of welfare dependency, incarceration, disability, and experiencing a whole range of other social pathologies are much greater among school dropouts than among those youth who complete their high school education with a diploma. Sadly, most of the adolescents who drop out have little understanding of this. Indeed, they have very unrealistic expectations for their future and thus make a bad decision that will be quite difficult to recover from in the future. It is the role of parents to provide both the stability and knowledge for students to make solid choices when making high school education investment decisions.

Despite the fact that they can receive a free high school education that will cost taxpayers an average of about $40,000 over four years, nearly one in three students won't graduate. No second chance to access this $40,000 for schooling will come later in life. It is a cost that is unrecoverable. These dropouts have chosen current consumption, often in the form of personally and socially destructive behavior, over the uncertainty and risk associated with higher future consumption. In less technical jargon, they failed to see how education could help them. Perhaps because of unstable families or a lack of guidance, they saw little chance of future success by completing high school compared to the current gains of quitting school before completing.

Basic Skills and Economic Success

In the early 1980s a group of elected officials, educators, and business leaders published a study of elementary and secondary education titled *A Nation at Risk,* which recast the discussion of the role of education in American society. From this small volume the education reform movement was born. Reformers advocated for back-to-basics curriculum changes that emphasized reading, writing, and mathematics skills development. This emphasis was designed to correct the drift toward the "general track" course of study that increased neither students' basic skills nor occupational skills proficiencies.

The changing nature of employment opportunities in the nation has dramatically changed the role of basic skills in determining economic success. As late as 1950 almost one-half of all the workers in the best-educated state in the nation (Massachusetts) were high school dropouts. Most employment at that time was concentrated in manufacturing and other blue-collar-dominated industries, where skills (sometimes very complex ones) were learned almost exclusively on the job. Indeed, even into the 1970s some high schools in New England held "leaving ceremonies" for students (mostly boys) who dropped out at age 16 to begin their apprenticeship in a variety of trades such as machinist, tool and die maker, and many construction-related trade areas. By developing their skills on the job over the next six or seven years, those who completed their apprenticeship could have access to a very solid middle-class standard of living.

However, dramatic changes in the nature of employment since the 1970s have meant that the economic opportunities for high school dropouts have all but disappeared. Today, only about one-half of teen dropouts will find any kind of work at all. When they do work it is seldom in a full-time year-round job and almost never in a formal apprenticeship program or a job that provides any substantial on-the-job learning opportunities. Instead, dropout employment is largely relegated to very low-level service jobs, such as parking-lot attendant or kitchen helper in restaurants. Worse still for high school dropouts, the large influx of illegal immigrants into the United States in recent years (many of whom are dropouts themselves) has pushed high school dropouts out of even these very low-level jobs. Many employers say that they favor these immigrant workers (more often in their early to mid-20s) because they have better work attitudes than native-born dropouts.

Access to employment has become very strongly connected with basic skills levels. During the 1990s a large-scale study of the basic skills levels of the American workforce was sponsored by the U.S. Department of Education. This study measured the prose, document, and quantitative skills of adults and connected the results of these tests to the employment and earnings experiences of these individuals. The results of the study unequivocally demonstrated the importance of basic skills in the labor market. Basic skills affect labor market outcomes in two distinct ways—directly in the labor market and somewhat more indirectly by exerting a strong influence on the level of educational attainment completed and the kind of labor market skills developed in school.

The effect of basic skills on labor market outcomes surpasses the effect of education. Even for job seekers with the same amount of schooling, the chance that an adult will have a job is very closely connected to his or her basic skills level. Employers utilize signals of wages and unemployment in the labor market to assess the basic skills of workers quite accurately and reward those with strong basic skills. Even after accounting for the level of educational attainment, we find that those with higher basic skills have better outcomes in the job market than those with weak basic skills. Employers readily identify the considerable differences in reading, writing, and math skills that exist even among four-year college graduates. Firms are more likely to employ and try to retain and pay a higher annual salary to those college graduates with the strongest basic skills than to those graduates with the same degree level but lower basic skill proficiencies. Bachelor's degree holders with the strongest basic skills have the best employment and earnings outcomes. Those with weaker basic skills lag behind, despite holding a college degree. This kind of basic skill gap translates into labor market outcome gaps at every level of educational attainment—even among dropouts. While most dropouts have poor basic skills, dropouts with stronger basic skills have better employment and earnings outcomes than their counterparts with weak basic skills. The labor market is very good at identifying and rewarding workers with stronger basic skills with employment and higher wages—and also good at relegating those with weaker skills to either no employment or to lower-paying jobs. The rewards for basic skills in the labor market are manifested in a variety of ways, including

- Increased chance of being hired

- More hours of work over the year

- Higher hourly earnings

- Higher annual earnings

- Increased benefits offerings, such as health insurance

- Greater employment stability

- Better upward mobility

- Increased chances of employer-supported training

The lesson of the last two decades is that basic skills—reading, writing, and mathematics—are the essential ingredients for labor market success. In the absence of strong basic skills, the chances of labor market success in 21st-century America are dramatically diminished. Projections of employment growth in the future suggest that the role of basic skills in determining long-term labor market success will gain even greater importance in the future.

Basic skills not only influence the overall employment and earnings experiences of workers in the U.S. economy but also play a critical role in influencing access to career pathways across industries and occupations. The data provided in Table 1 examines the average literacy level of workers employed in various sectors of the U.S. economy. The average American worker achieved a score of 863 on this measure of prose, document, and quantitative skill. A closer look at the table reveals very large differences in average literacy scores across both industry sectors of the U.S. economy and major occupation groups within each of these industries. For example, the data reveals that workers employed in the manufacturing industry had an average literacy score of 840—modestly below the national industry average score of 863. However, the manufacturing score was nearly one standard deviation lower than that of the average worker employed in the finance, insurance and real estate, and professional services industries. Most of the difference in industry basic skills is associated with differences in the kinds of workers employed in that industry. The manufacturing sector is dominated by blue-collar jobs that have low literacy requirements. For example, routine operative, fabrication, and assembly jobs have a mean literacy score of just 741, placing the average worker in those occupations in the bottom one-sixth of the basic skills distribution of all workers. In contrast, professional specialties—such as engineering, finance, and accounting jobs—in the manufacturing industry have very high literacy requirements, with an average score among workers in those occupations of 995, placing these workers at the very highest end of the literacy proficiency distribution. Within the manufacturing industry sector, the basic skills gulf between professional workers and blue-collar workers employed in routine fabrication and operative jobs is enormous.

Table 1

Mean Combined Prose, Document, and Quantitative
Proficiencies of Employed Adults in the U.S.

Major Occupations	Manufacturing	Retail Trade	Finance, Insurance, and Real Estate	Professional Services	All Workers
Executive, Managerial	971	906	956	997	963
Professional Specialty	995	957	1,048	986	988
Technicians	926	—	—	918	925
High-Level Sales	914	885	—	—	914
Low-Level Sales	—	839	906	816	839
Clerical	881	864	686	903	890
Services	—	793	753	779	787
Craft, Precision Production	828	825	—	833	818
Operatives, Fabricators	741	808	—	788	758
Laborers and Handlers	724	794	—	—	733
All Workers	840	836	926	917	863

Over the past two decades, technological change and foreign competition have caused enormous worker dislocation (permanent job loss) and employment reorganization within the nation's manufacturing sector. Employment of workers in the professional specialties in manufacturing firms has actually increased as the remaining U.S. producers employ increasingly sophisticated production methods and organizational strategies that require high levels of professional skill. This is, in essence, replacing a large number of blue-collar workers with a new technology and a smaller, but much more productive, cadre of increasingly professional workers to produce and distribute these goods and services. Despite the fact that blue-collar workers may have many years of work experience in the manufacturing sector, they lack the basic skills needed to work in the higher-growth professional fields within the industry.

Blue collar workers dislocated from manufacturing find few alternatives in the rapidly expanding finance and professional industry sectors of the economy. First of all, these white collar industries employ almost no workers in production occupations, so skills learned by dislocated blue-collar workers from past work experiences are not transferable. The literacy skills needed to work in the high-end management and professional jobs that dominate those industries essentially preclude employment in these industry sectors for those with even average basic skill levels.

The most rapidly expanding set of industries in the U.S. is dominated by occupations that require strong basic skills proficiencies. If students fail to develop these skills by the end of high school, they will essentially be locked out of access to the best sets of employment opportunities in the nation. This is a powerful underlying factor in understanding the role of education as an investment good. Those high school students who take rigorous courses that develop their reading and analytical skills, their ability to write effectively, and their math proficiency will have much greater access to a variety of career fields. The lower a given individual's basic skills, the fewer life and career options he or she will have. A major part of life's story is written while in high school. Course selections that help develop basic skills will lead to a much wider and better set of choices after school. Failure to develop basic skills by the end of high school means many fewer options in a world that rewards those with the greatest set of alternatives.

Basic skills play a very important role in providing access to a college degree. Often when college admissions staff and high school counselors discuss access to college, the conversation turns quickly to financial aid. When elected officials talk about increasing access to college for students from various race-ethnic groups, they most often talk of increasing financial aid or reducing tuition. Two of the authors of this book are economists, and so of course we believe that money plays an important role in access to a college degree. Yet our analysis of a variety of data has led us to conclude that money is not the greatest barrier to a college degree, even for minority students. The greatest barrier to earning a college degree is poor basic skills. We find that students with high basic skills can often overcome money problems and complete a college degree. But students with low basic skills cannot overcome the barriers created by these deficiencies even if they do not have money problems.

The findings in Figure 1 compare the proportion of high school students who earned a college degree within 12 years of high school by their relative position in the basic skills distribution and the family income distribution. Unsurprisingly, students from high-income families with high basic skills (that is, family income in the highest fifth of the family income distribution and basic skills scores in the top fifth of the skills distribution) are very likely to earn a four-year college degree within 12 years after high school. The chart reveals that more than three-quarters of those from the highest-income families who also have the strongest basic skills will earn a college degree. At the other extreme, the data reveals that students from the lowest-income backgrounds who also have poor basic skills will almost never earn a college degree. Only about 1 out of 100 high school students from the lowest-income families who have basic skill scores at the bottom of the distribution will earn a bachelor's degree.

More interesting than these very predictable results are the findings about students from low-income backgrounds who have strong basic skills, as well as about their opposites—high-income students with poor basic skills. The data reveals that high-income, poor-basic-skills students are very unlikely to earn a college degree. Fewer than 3 in 100 will graduate from college within 12 years of high school. High family income seems to do little to compensate for the low basic skills of these students. In contrast, strong basic skills partially overcome low family income. Of the low-income, high-basic-skills students, more than one-third earned a college degree.

FIGURE 1

Percentage of the 14- to 17-Year-Old High School Students Who Earned a Four-Year College Degree within 12 Years, by Their Position in the Basic Skills Distribution and Their Families' Position in the Family Income Distribution

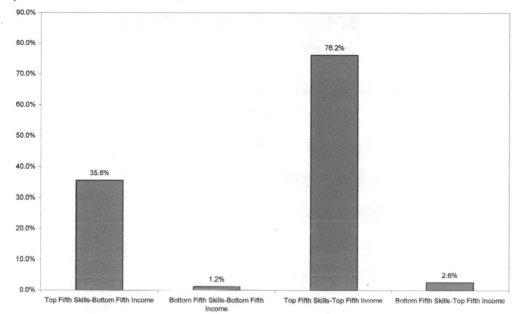

High family income in the absence of basic skills does little to enhance a student's chances of earning a four-year college degree. Yet strong basic skills substantially reduce the impact of low family income on the ability of students to earn a college degree. Of course, developing strong basic skills does not fully offset the disadvantages from growing up in a low-income family—because money does matter. However, having basic skills plays a much more important role than money does in gaining access to a college degree. It is best to have both strong basic skills and high family income, but if you can have only one, then basic skills is by far the more important.

Having poor basic skills does not just mean a lack of educational and employment opportunities for high school students. Low basic skills sharply increase the chances that high school students will suffer from a number of social pathologies by the time they enter their early

twenties. The best evidence reveals that young adults with low basic skills are at much greater risk of joblessness, poverty, welfare dependence, and a host of accompanying problems. Figure 2 provides data on the mean percentile basic skill ranking of 19- to 23-year-olds who have experienced one or more of a variety of social pathologies. The typical young adult who has been arrested scores at the 32nd percentile of the basic skills distribution. Those who were jobless scored at the 26th percentile. A young adult who had a child out of wedlock scored at the 21st percentile of the basic skills distribution, while those who were poor and welfare-dependent had a mean score that placed them at the 16th percentile. Clearly, poor basic skills mean more than diminished economic opportunity. All too often the lack of reading, writing, and math skills can result in a life pathway of dependency and criminal behavior. The choices high school students make have effects—both positive and negative—that last a lifetime.

FIGURE 2

Mean Percentile in the Basic Skills Distribution of 19- to 23-Year-Old Young Adults,
All and Subgroups with Various Social Pathologies

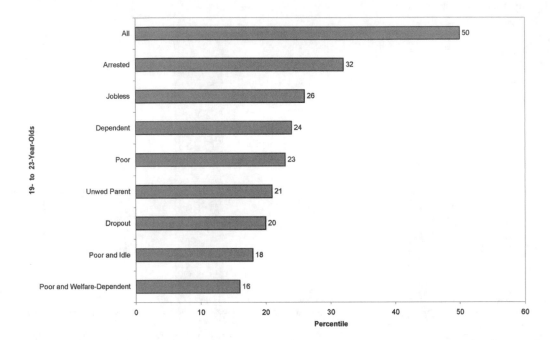

The courses that students select while in school are critically important to their basic skills development. The level and kinds of courses students take while in school have important impacts on basic skills development and on educational and labor market outcomes. Students who take courses that help develop basic skills, such as sciences, mathematics, language arts, history, and social studies, substantially increase their basic skills. Strong academic courses of study exercise reading, writing, and math skills at a high level and therefore yield strong basic skills outcomes.

Academic and college courses of study are not the only pathway to positive outcomes for high school students. High school graduates who had enrolled in focused and intensive vocational-technical programs of study that are tied to local labor demand have much better post–high school labor market experiences than those non-college-bound high school graduates who have no vocational or technical preparation. These gains are tied to finding employment in an occupation closely connected to the vocational area of specialization. More intensive vocational-technical education closely tied to local employers results in substantial long-term employment and earnings advantages. However, vocational study that is intermittent and not intensive or that is not closely tied to the local employer community yields few advantages. Thus, the quality of vocational-technical programs of local school districts, measured by their intensity and connection to the local labor market, is an essential element in the decision to enroll in these programs.

Some students may prefer to choose a "general track" course of study. The general track is dominated by courses that do little to improve either basic skills or occupational proficiencies. Consequently, such a course of study does little to improve students' educational and employment options in the future. State education reform efforts have worked to reduce the number of students in general-track courses, but many secondary programs still offer these low-quality alternatives. Courses that fail to increase educational and employment options either through emphasis on basic skills or through vocational preparation are simply a bad investment and should be avoided.

The best courses of study are ones that emphasize math and science along with strong reading and writing skills. Not only does the number of such courses taken increase basic skill levels, but also taking courses in a sequence of increasing difficulty generates higher payoffs to students, even if taking tougher courses means lower grades.

Investing in Work Experience

Frequently, one thinks of high school students who work part-time—after school, on weekends, or perhaps in a summer job—as simply earning extra money for personal consumption or perhaps, in some instances, to help support their families. Certainly, the employment of high school students does provide them with the benefits of increased income, and the earnings of high school students do alleviate the poverty problems of some families. But does it make sense for high school students to work while they are in school? Doesn't mixing work and schooling activities mean that students will have less time for studies and school-based extracurricular activities? If a bit more disposable income for teen consumption is the only benefit from work, then is it really a worthwhile activity for students?

The gains to students working in high school go well beyond the earnings they generate for themselves and their families. Working at an early age is a developmental activity akin to developing basic skills or occupational proficiencies in a school setting. Early work experience helps further enhance the productive abilities of young adults along dimensions that are not addressed by classroom-based educational activities. In economic terms, work experience during high school is an investment in developing human capital that has similar impacts as investments in education. For example, students who work more frequently during high school tend to participate in the labor market more intensively as adults, are less likely to experience a bout of unemployment as adults, and, if they become unemployed, become reemployed more quickly than those with little or no work experience while in high school. Research has estimated that high school seniors who worked 20 hours per week had annual earnings as young adults that were 25 to 30 percent higher than seniors who didn't work.

Work experience while in high school can have powerful impacts on long-term labor market outcomes. Through on-the-job learning, it provides teens and even young adults with the opportunity to develop a whole set of behavioral characteristics that are highly prized by employers. Indeed, while employers place great emphasis on basic skills and occupational knowledge and ability, these behavioral traits, sometimes known as soft skills, are their top priority when hiring and retaining workers. Willingness to learn, respectfulness for other workers and supervisors, strong work ethic, communicating effectively, and following even simple work rules like punctuality are essential to employers. Employers simply avoid those who lack these soft skills, even if they possess strong math and literacy abilities or a special sort of occupational skill.

It is no coincidence that virtually every resume submitted to employers describes the educational and work experiences of the applicant, along with a set of references. Employers use the information on the resume to assess a job applicant's strengths and weaknesses in regard to behavioral skills based on his or her record of work experience. When references are contacted, most of the conversation centers on the applicant's soft skills. Often the primary purpose of the job interview is to personally assess an individual's work attitudes, ethics, and ability to work with others.

Work experience among high school students does not seem to come at the price of less study time or fewer extracurricular activities. Our analysis of the work activities of high school students in Massachusetts found that students who worked simply watched less television than those who did not work. We found that those who worked spent about the same amount of time on homework as those who did not work at all. Virtually all researchers who have studied the connection between in-school work experiences and academic performance have concluded that working up to 20 hours per week has no adverse impacts on the academic performance of high school students.

The evidence suggests that early work experience of most kinds has a positive impact on the long-term labor market experiences of teens. However, the quality of work experience also has a positive impact on labor market outcomes. Jobs that provide the chance for students to engage in reading, writing, mathematics, and technical skills bolster long-term employment and earnings prospects, as do jobs that provide students with the chance to learn a new skill. Jobs with these characteristics are hard to find, because they are often available in industries that hire few teens, such as health, finance, insurance, and professional services. However, both parents and school systems should try hard to find employment for students in these industries because of the quality of work experience that they can provide to students and because of the career exposure that working in "adult" labor markets can provide teens.

High school students too often have little awareness of the array of career opportunities that exist in a particular industry. For example, many young people are attracted to the "helping" fields in the health arena but have little understanding of the variety of careers available in these fields or of the education and training pathways into these fields. Working in a hospital gives students exposure not only to a wide variety of health profession careers, but also to health professionals, who themselves can offer advice and information about health careers and in some instances serve as professional role models for students.

Work experience is a valuable form of human capital that is quite different from human capital developed in formal academic or occupational education settings. Work experience reduces dropout rates of students–especially among low-income and minority youth. Reductions in dropout rates can be particularly strong when work experiences are tied directly to the schooling activities of teens. Work-based learning increases the students' perception of the relevance of school-based learning. Indeed, we find high rates of enrollment in postsecondary education when work experience programs are run directly through the high schools in low-income communities. High school students engaged in the labor market see firsthand how the labor market distinguishes between those with a college degree and those with fewer years of schooling. Among students who choose not to enroll in college, prior work experience smoothes their transition into the full-time labor market after high school. Students with work experience while in school avoid long-term idleness that often characterizes the first few years after high school of non-college-bound high school graduates with no work experience.

Interestingly, there is a strong connection between the level of family income and the likelihood that a teen will be employed, but not in the way that we might expect. Most people assume that because of family income needs, students from low-income families work at higher rates than do students from higher-income backgrounds. Yet the opposite is true. The employment rate of teens rises sharply with family income. Students who live in high-poverty neighborhoods and students from low-income families are very unlikely to work, while those residing in higher-income communities or from higher-income families are more likely to be employed. Part of the difference is due to higher-income students growing up in a culture where the major activity of adults is work. The gains of work experience are clear to both parents and students, and so the children work at higher rates. Moreover, employed parents encourage their children to work and can often help their children find employment. Teens who live in high-poverty neighborhoods live in areas where the majority of adults are not employed. With adults cut off from employment, a nonworking culture takes root. Teens have fewer role models to indicate the importance of employment and have fewer resources to help them find employment. Thus, large work experience gaps are created between students from high-poverty neighborhoods and those who live in communities where work is the primary activity of adults.

It is clear that work experience produces a variety of positive outcomes for teens. Teens who do not work find themselves disadvantaged not only because of the gap in the positive outcomes associated with working, but also because of negative outcomes that are associated with not working. The facts are that teen girls who do not work are much more likely to become pregnant during their teenage years. Among boys, criminal behavior is closely associated with limited work experience. A high rate of male teen idleness makes criminal activity, especially the sale of street drugs, more attractive.

The Educational Attainment Decision

High school students must make decisions about how much education they will complete through their early adult years. A more detailed analysis of the underlying role of educational attainment on labor market outcomes is provided in the following chapters. Yet it is important to note that high school students make a set of choices about how much schooling they will undertake in their lives. The educational attainment decision is not usually made all at once. Rare is the high school student who decides that he or she will earn a doctoral degree in a particular field of study. Most often decisions to continue in school are made incrementally or, in economic terms, at the margin. For example, teens decide to finish high school or to drop out, but often the decision to finish or drop out is made on an even more incremental basis than this. Often, dropping out of high school occurs almost in a subconscious fashion, with little thought given to quitting school. Students drop out of school simply by choosing to be absent from school with increasing frequency. So the decision to drop out isn't made all at once. Instead it is often made by the choice made each morning to either stay in bed or get up and go to school.

The decision to drop out has strong adverse economic outcomes for students in terms of poor employment and earnings prospects and increasing risk of antisocial behavior. Those students who drop out are most often those with the poorest basic skills. It is obvious that poor basic skills are one effect of dropping out of school. However, it is important to understand that poor basic skills also are a key cause of dropping out. Too often students lack the reading, writing, and math skills to effectively master high-school-level material. These students are more likely to quit school than are students with stronger basic skills. The act of quitting school is much more than simply failing to complete high school; it is a way of dropping out of mainstream society and limiting life choices, resulting all too often in an existence at the margins of a community.

Students who finish high school have many more educational and employment options than do dropouts. High school graduates have much higher employment rates, are much less likely to be jobless, and have much higher annual and lifetime earnings than dropouts. Each year a large proportion of high school seniors choose to enroll in some type of postsecondary educational program. Last year about two-thirds of all graduating seniors were enrolled in school during the fall after graduation. These students enrolled in educational institutions ranging from short-term (just a few months) occupational training programs run by private, for-profit organizations to those who enrolled in full-time undergraduate programs at the nation's most prestigious educational institutions. The amount of schooling that students complete after high school has important impacts on their long-term labor market experiences. Those with more years of schooling have higher earnings than those with less. Young graduates of two-year degree programs earn 25 to 30 percent more per year than high school graduates with no degree. Young bachelor's degree holders earn about 75 percent more per year than their high-school-graduate counterparts. Large earning gaps exist between those with advanced degrees and those with a bachelor's degree only.

Not only do those with more years of schooling achieve large employment and earnings advantages compared to those with only a high school diploma, but the size of these advantages grows larger over time. The earnings of college graduates grow more rapidly for more years than the earnings of high school dropouts. The higher growth in annual earnings over the working lives of better-educated workers is in part the product of a greater set of chances for advancement for college graduates and because firms make much greater education and training investments in their college-educated staff than they do in their high-school-graduate staff. College grads have proven they can learn, so employers make their human capital investments in those staff that they believe will give them the greatest return on their investment.

Investing in Occupational Skills

The nature of employment growth in the U.S. over the past two decades has had the effect of shifting education and training costs away from firms and directly upon households and families. Colleges and universities have increasingly become a key source of labor supply for firms seeking high-level occupational skills. Indeed, whole new fields of study have been created in health, information technology, engineering, business, communications, and the arts. These new majors and degree fields were organized to meet newly emerging high-end skill demands in the American labor market.

This book provides information on the nature of expected labor market outcomes associated with earning a bachelor's degree in alternative fields of study. Our findings reveal very large employment and earnings differences for bachelor's degree holders depending on their undergraduate major field of study. These differences also are quite large at the level of master's and doctoral degrees.

The choice that students make about their major field of study is a key component of developing their career plan. Too many students opt into major fields of study by default, without giving much consideration to their choice, at least with respect to the kinds of career options this choice will both create and eliminate. The choice undergraduates make about their major will have widely varying impacts on the kinds of careers they can pursue after graduation. For example, students who choose one of the very demanding engineering majors will find they have a much broader array of employment as well as educational options than, say, a student who chooses a social science or humanities field. Engineering graduates have much better access to degrees in nontechnical or scientific fields, while graduates from social sciences and humanities are much less likely to earn a degree in a technical or scientific field. Engineers also have a somewhat wider array of employment options at the undergraduate level, including finance, insurance, and health areas. Engineering majors simply have better employment and earnings experiences across a wide variety of occupations than do majors in other fields.

The choice of major field of study is a complex one and one that will heavily influence the kind of professional career experiences that graduates will have in the future. The chapters immediately following this one explore the nature of this choice in greater detail. Before we examine this choice, however, it is useful to at least briefly discuss the last major component of the college investment decision—the cost of college.

College Prices and College Finance

Four-year college tuition and fees have risen at a very rapid pace since the early 1980s, and high tuition is often viewed as a major barrier to college access for many in American society. Congress has conducted a number of hearings related to rising college costs, and many within the higher education system itself worry that access to a four-year degree is declining for race-ethnic minorities in the nation because of sky-rocketing tuition.

Clearly understanding the potential benefits of a college education is a key element of the college investment decision. However, benefits represent only one-half of the investment equation. Parents and students need to have a clear understanding not only of the gains from a college degree, but also of the costs of earning such a degree in economic terms. The cost of college is made up of two key components:

▶ Tuition and fees, as well as other out-of-pocket costs

▶ Potential earnings that students would have earned had they not attended college

Putting aside forgone earnings for the moment, parents and students need to fully understand the costs of earning a college degree. Unfortunately, parents and students too often have a poor understanding of actual college tuitions or financial aid availability, sometimes erroneously concluding that the costs at a given college are too high for their family circumstances.

A recent survey of the parents of nearly 8,000 high school students found that only 30 percent had obtained information on college costs. Among juniors and seniors who planned to attend college, only half of all parents had obtained college cost information. More surprising still is that parents who did obtain cost information sharply overestimated the cost of the first year of tuition. Parents whose children intended to enroll at a public college overestimated the cost of first-year tuition by nearly 80 percent. Although they were much more accurate in estimating private tuition costs, there was still considerable error in estimating the first-year cost of school.

Parents and students have comparatively little knowledge of financial aid. Fewer than 60 percent of parents with high school students in their junior or senior year who intended to go to college had either spoken with someone or reviewed materials related to financial aid. Only one-third of all parents of college-bound juniors and seniors were aware of Lifetime Learning and/or HOPE scholarship tax credits. About 40 percent of the parents of these students had not begun saving or making some other kind of plan to finance their child's college education.

That high school parents and students have a limited understanding of college costs and financial aid availability is not surprising, given the degree of complexity of college finance. This complexity is in part a consequence of the very nature of colleges and universities. One highly regarded economist who has studied higher education remarked that colleges act like a cross between churches and used-car dealers. Most colleges are nonprofit organizations and as such are in fact charities of a sort. While tuition may be high, virtually every college student receives a subsidy of some type in the sense that the total of student payments never covers the cost of running a college. Other sources of income—from federal, state and local government, alumni, the business community, and other sources—pay the balance of costs of operating four-year colleges and universities. In this sense colleges are like churches in that they are the conduit through which society promotes a desired set of values, in this instance the values of knowledge, literacy, educational achievement, and the support of a wide array of social, cultural, and economic activities and objectives.

Colleges are like car dealers in the way that they operate in college enrollment markets (as well as in their growing commercial activities in sports and the commercialization of faculty research, to name just two), engaging in what college enrollment managers call "strategic packaging." Colleges and universities produce a product that is unique in that its perceived quality is largely judged by the characteristics of those who enroll in it. Rankings of college quality are largely determined by several measures of the quality of the entering freshman

class each year. Applicant SAT or ACT scores, high school class rank, and fraction of applicants admitted are frequently used measures of college quality. These measures tell us a lot about who attends a given school but reveal nothing about the quality of education these students receive once enrolled. Certainly, the most common measures of college quality now used fall far short of the rigorous measures of elementary and secondary student learning gains now required in each state under No Child Left Behind.

The level of demand for enrollment in a given college is closely connected to its perceived quality, and the quality of a college is determined by its ability to recruit a freshman class composed of the best and the brightest. So enrollment managers engage in a set of activities in the enrollment market that are designed to maximize market position by enrolling the best high school seniors possible while at the same time meeting key revenue goals for the college. One way that colleges are able to do this is to try to engage in a tuition discounting strategy whereby financial aid is used to attract those students with the best student profile as determined by the basic college quality measures. Enrollment managers try to use financial aid to entice the best and brightest students to their school while being constrained by the need to meet specific revenue targets.

The result of all of this is that the official college tuition information provided to counselors, parents, and students is really little more than a "sticker price," much like a buyer would find on the window of a car for sale. Large differences exist between the sticker price of college tuitions published by colleges and the net tuition that an average student at a given college will actually end up paying. Some analysts have found that the gap between the sticker price and the net tuition students pay in their first year may be as high as 30 to 40 percent for the average student in private, nonprofit institutions.

There also are large differences between sticker prices and net tuition costs in public four-year schools, especially among those with high tuition levels.

Colleges offer tuition discounts to those students who best meet their goals for their entering freshman class student profile. Students with high class rankings, strong basic skills as measured by the SAT or ACT, and other characteristics that suggest they will complete their degree program will receive substantial discounts, sometimes in the form of full-tuition scholarships and in some cases even the inclusion of room and board. Top students thus have a certain amount of bargaining power in establishing what their net tuition level might be. Most often college enrollment managers develop a set of criteria, based on sophisticated data analysis, to determine how much aid a student with a particular set of desirable characteristics will receive. In some cases enrollment management staff will actually negotiate net tuition, much like a car salesman will negotiate a net price from a car's sticker. The sticker is a place where the tuition discussion can begin, not where it ends.

Decisions made by parents and students on college affordability need to be based on the net tuition price, not on the sticker price. Students and parents who have multiple acceptance offers and aid packages may be in a position to negotiate larger merit aid packages (read: tuition discounts).

College enrollment managers spend a lot of time thinking through their discounting strategy and determining who among their applicants should receive financial aid, what type of aid they should receive, and how much tuition should be discounted. Top enrollment managers are able to produce high-quality entering freshman classes that further bolster the quality assessment of the institution in the enrollment market and set the stage for further gains in the near future—all the while meeting their tuition revenue objectives. This question remains (as it does for car dealers): Why don't colleges just charge the net tuition price to all students and stop all of this strategic packaging and hidden net tuition discounting? Much of the answer to this question is associated with the fact that a college degree has some of the characteristics of what economists refer to as a "snob good." A key feature of a snob good is that little is known about its real qualities, so consumers often use its price level as a measure of quality. Examples of this sort of good or service abound in liquor, fashion, retail, automobile, and many other industries, as well as in higher education. Indeed, it is one of the reasons that firms spend so much time, energy, and resources in developing a name brand—a brand that identifies certain qualities with products or services offered by that brand. Many in the higher education system believe that a high tuition sticker sends a signal of exclusivity and therefore quality.

A college degree not only has some of the characteristics of a snob good, but it is also what economists describe as a positional good. The quality of a college is not judged on the basis of its absolute level of academic excellence. Rather, parents judge colleges and universities by their position in a set of rankings of all colleges. A good education is one that is defined by most in a relative way. So when we say we want a good education for our children, we in fact mean we want a better education than that received by other students. This puts parents and students in an educational "arms race" to enroll in elite, exclusive, or the best colleges and universities. By definition, the number of top "elite" schools is limited, and these schools are careful not to raise enrollment levels in response to rising demand. Parents and students are playing a game that as a group they cannot win. There will always be only a limited supply of top 100 colleges, no matter how much parents and students strive for access to the "best." In an effort to gain access to a seat at an elite school, families send their children to exclusive preschools and grammar schools at great expense, donate extra funds to elite colleges in excess of tuition, and often try to use political and business connections to gain admission to the limited supply of seats at the top of the college pecking order. But even as more and more families try to crack into the best colleges, the number of seats at the top 100 schools remains the same. Rising demand for quality education cannot coax out additional supply, as in the case of most goods. Instead, it means a growing frenzy of parents struggling against worsening odds to get their children enrolled in an elite school.

Interestingly, there is little evidence to support the view that earning a degree from an elite college by itself markedly improves long-term employment and earnings outcomes. After accounting for basic skills proficiency and undergraduate major field of study, graduates from elite colleges earn only 2 to 3 percent more over their working lives than graduates from nonelite colleges. While parents judge colleges by their relative rankings, the labor market largely judges college graduates on the basis of their work experiences; their proficiency in reading, writing, and mathematics; and their specific occupational knowledge and skill. Chapter 3 examines the connection between the choice of college and the selection of a major field of study and provides the costs and benefits of the college investment decision.

CHAPTER 2

The Psychology of Career Choice:

Assessing Abilities, Interests, and Values

This chapter is about making informed choices. Because many of us do not allow enough time for making choices, we create stress and pressure in our lives. In this chapter, you will learn what information is important to know about yourself. You will also learn how to find this information and then organize it to make decisions that are thorough and comfortable for you. By the end of the chapter, we hope you can say, "This is my choice and my plan."

Most people think that the task of choosing a major is based simply on information and facts; therefore, the choice should be easy and straightforward. Wrong! Choosing a major–like choosing the college you will attend–takes time. You should take the time to make an informed choice about your major for the following reasons:

▶ Parents or other authority figures may have imposed their goals or wants on you. Families sometimes disapprove of a student's plans and believe they have a "say," especially when they are paying

some of the tuition. This attitude complicates the student's choices because it creates uncertainty and risks by making the parents part of the decision process. In this case, some negotiations need to occur.

▶ Several stumbling blocks may exist. These have to be dealt with first, before a decision is finalized. Consider some of these examples:

"I don't have enough money for the specific education or major I want."

"I have to work now."

"According to published information, my test scores are not good enough for the field."

"There are not many of my gender in the major."

"No colleges are in my geographic region, so I will have to leave home. This is obviously an additional cost factor."

21

If any of these scenarios are true for you, they will involve additional decisions to be made. Many people, because of their youthful inexperience, get overwhelmed. An eerie feeling emerges around choosing a major—it is a monstrous choice! "What if I pick wrong? Then I have failed." Do not subscribe to this attitude. The system forces everyone to decide, and they survive.

▶ In the process of making decisions, students may discover that they lack the perceived self-awareness that their friends have. Some people are not accustomed to being self-initiating and self-directing, so making a decision independently is a new challenge and very difficult. Some find they lack the support of others who will respect their views without imposing their judgments. Still others are lacking in self-esteem and constantly question whether they are good enough to be successful in a preferred career field. Thus, self-doubts and emotional immaturity surface to complicate the decision-making process more than was initially expected.

▶ If it is any consolation, the largest major in many colleges is "undecided," which shows that making this life-changing decision is a complex step. The choice involves work in order to complete the task correctly. Don't be afraid to take a chance or to make a decision, even if the decision may not be correct. The decision may be "incorrect" not because of what you thought would be the case, but for reasons you haven't thought about. Remember that the task of making the decision itself moves you along in a series of choices that you will be making. Take your time, check out your options, and try to make a reasonable attempt.

Knowing Yourself

Now the first step for you to review is your knowledge of yourself. Learning how to self-assess is a lifelong skill that will serve you well as you develop into the person you are meant to be. In this section, we will focus on three areas for self-assessing: your abilities, interests, and values.

Abilities

Abilities are skills, talents, or things you can do. Ability represents a degree of mastery. Occasionally the term *ability* is used interchangeably with *aptitude*. In other words, *aptitude* is the ability to do schoolwork or to reason verbally and quantitatively. Ability is not intelligence.

One last distinction: Abilities constitute broad categories of skills; that is, ability is a *macro* concept, while a skill involves doing something at a more specific *micro* level. For example, *artistic ability* is the macro term that involves *skills* of color discrimination, eye-hand coordination, and depth perception at the micro level. One person may be better at landscapes while another has portrait skills. Many people think of taking tests to learn about their abilities. We will be introducing a different methodology here: asking you to self-report your abilities.

Before proceeding, you need to know why abilities are important. Work and life satisfaction both depend on the extent to which individuals find adequate outlets for abilities, needs, values, interests, personality characteristics, and self-concepts. Ability is part of one's self-concept, according to career-development experts.

The major work-related abilities include artistic, clerical, interpersonal, language, leadership, manual, musical/dramatic, numerical/mathematical, organizational, persuasive, scientific, social, spatial, and technical/mechanical. What about athletic and dancing abilities? While athletes and dancers are very much in evidence in the media, they, in fact, do not involve large numbers of people in the work force. However, these two abilities are included under the manual and musical/dramatic categories. Reading is a basic skill and ability that is foundational to the development of many other abilities and general learning. Each of the 14 major career-related abilities are briefly defined in the following list:

- **Artistic:** Involves principles and techniques in drawing, painting, photography, sculpting, decorating, or designing.

- **Clerical:** Involves eye-hand-finger coordination to enter numbers into a computer or a form, knowledge of the operation of office and business machines, and proficiency on a computer keyboard. The skills require accuracy and attention to detail.

- **Interpersonal:** Involves the abilities to communicate well with many kinds of people; to contribute ideas and suggestions; to work cooperatively; and to demonstrate understanding, friendliness, adaptability, and politeness in a variety of settings.

- **Language:** Involves speaking clearly; understanding and responding to feedback; asking questions appropriately; and using correct grammar, spelling, and punctuation in letters and reports.

- **Leadership:** Involves making decisions that affect others; reacting quickly in emergency situations; and motivating others to work by communicating thoughts, feelings, and ideas well enough to justify a viewpoint.

- **Manual:** Involves the abilities to coordinate hands, fingers, and eyes to operate a piece of equipment, to adjust controls on machines, to manipulate hand tools, or

to assemble something that requires reading and following directions.

- **Musical or Dramatic:** Involves playing instruments; singing; reading and writing music; or interpreting roles and expressing ideas and emotions through gestures and facial expressions in comedy, plays, or movies.

- **Numerical or Mathematical:** Involves the abilities to do basic arithmetic computations or to use mathematical reasoning and concepts to solve difficult mathematics problems.

- **Organizational:** Involves maintaining written or computerized records and other forms of information in a systematic method and setting priorities that determine how to get the most important tasks completed first and on time.

- **Persuasive:** Involves the abilities to convince or motivate an individual or group of people to take a certain action, such as buying something, or to influence someone to a certain viewpoint.

- **Scientific:** Involves understanding and using scientific principles and logic to deal with different types of problems (possibly done in a technical or scientific laboratory), diagnosing and treating human and animal injuries and diseases, or studying various life forms.

- **Social:** Involves gathering, studying, and analyzing information by using logical thinking to help other people define and solve personal problems; it can include teaching others.

- **Spatial:** Involves the abilities to see differences in size, form, and shape and to visualize relationships between objects.

▶ **Technical or Mechanical:** Involves the abilities to understand technical or mechanical terms or language, to follow the proper procedures in setting up or operating equipment, to operate machines, and to understand why machines don't work and to have the capability to fix or repair them.

Self-Assessing Abilities

Each term in the preceding section defines a specific ability. Decide whether you perform the activity well, above average, below average, or not well at all. The level of mastery is important because it may communicate a person's positive self-esteem or low self-efficacy or low self-perception to perform in a specific area. Creating a table like the one in Table 1 may be helpful. Try to be honest with yourself as you do the rating. If all your abilities are high or average or low, you may find it difficult to assess yourself.

By saying, "I'm good at this task but not so good at that one," you can identify possible sources of self-esteem. You may find yourself saying, "Gee, look at that. Each ability is weak (average or great). No wonder I have trouble doing this task." Self-insights are powerful sources of self-information. Most of us are good at some things and not as good in other matters.

Table 1
Worksheet for Reality Testing Each Ability

Ability	Self-Rating (High, Above Average, Below Average, Not Well)	Grades	Work Experience	Activities/ Experiences
Artistic	_____	_____	_____	_____
Clerical	_____	_____	_____	_____
Interpersonal	_____	_____	_____	_____
Language	_____	_____	_____	_____
Leadership	_____	_____	_____	_____
Manual	_____	_____	_____	_____
Musical/Dramatic	_____	_____	_____	_____
Numerical/ Mathematical	_____	_____	_____	_____
Organizational	_____	_____	_____	_____
Persuasive	_____	_____	_____	_____
Scientific	_____	_____	_____	_____
Social	_____	_____	_____	_____
Spatial	_____	_____	_____	_____
Technical/Mechanical	_____	_____	_____	_____

Reality testing—or obtaining feedback on your performance—is an important part of self-assessment. Sources of reality testing are available to you, but frequently you must seek them out on your own. A requirement for accurate reality testing is that you know your work and have experience in the ability area in order to make an objective rating. Also, acquaintances, friends, and family members often do not want to alienate you, so the way you solicit feedback from them or the format you use to collect information is most important.

One format that people can use is to rate you in comparison to others they know in a specific ability area. For example, are you equal to the best, better than most, about the same as most, or not as good as others? In addition, grades and test information are ways of confirming a self-evaluation; many times part-time employment or an internship experience provides evaluative opportunities, and out-of-school activities definitely provide a good way to determine your proficiency in an ability. Remember, self-evaluations are subjective, so solicitation of feedback from a respected, qualified person is helpful.

Increasingly, some schools and organizations are implementing a portfolio method of assessment. A portfolio involves a collection of samples of your best work, including English papers, science projects, letters of recommendation for performing an activity, or pictures showing how you are using a specific machine or how you are being recognized for a special achievement. A concluding observation is that performing a self-assessment can identify areas in which you may want to pursue further developmental work. The structure of the self-assessment and its documentation also provide potential information for a functional resume; that is, they help to specify those activities you can do.

An additional resource for assessing abilities is the *Ability Explorer*, available from PRO-ED,

8700 Shoal Creek Boulevard, Austin, TX 78757-6897; 1-800-897-3202. This instrument is available in a hand-scored version that provides immediate feedback, shows you which occupations are related to your best abilities, and suggests ways to improve your abilities. Also, in each of the chapters that follow, there will be information about abilities that are required in the most popular jobs associated with each field of study.

Interests

Interests indicate the direction of a person's preferences; that is, your liking or disliking of an activity. Interests are important. Can you imagine working for a long time at a job that you dislike? Remember that *ability* answers the question, "What do I know and what can I do?" *Interest* answers the inquiry, "Do I like and want to do it?" Generally these are two separate questions.

An assumption of one of the major career-development theorists is that each of us can be classified according to a limited number of personality types. Work settings or work environments also can be described as uniquely accommodating to the same personality types. According to this theory, each personality type will seek out its corresponding occupational environment or job. People have a combination of personality types, so jobs also accommodate a variety of personality types. These personality types are assessed by people's interests and are described with corresponding jobs that require postsecondary education, as follows:

▶ **Artistic:** People prize independence and seek opportunities for self-expression. Some prefer lifestyles that enjoy such creative activities as art, entertainment, music, and writing.

   Sample jobs: actor/actress, advertising manager, art teacher, composer, copy writer, dancer, fashion designer, graphics designer, musician, painter, public relations specialist, radio/TV announcer, radio/TV producer, reporter, translator

▶ **Business:** People seek careers where they can lead others. They usually have good communications skills. They can persuade others to buy their products or ideas, and they gain satisfaction by convincing others to think the way they do.

Sample jobs: bank manager, buyer, farm manager, financial planner, government administrator, health care manager, hotel/food service manager, human resources manager, insurance salesperson, lawyer, marketing personnel, property manager, retail store manager, sales manager, transportation manager

▶ **Crafts:** People prefer to work with tools and things rather than with people and words. They like to build something, and they want to see practical results. They enjoy mechanical work and physical activity.

Sample jobs: airline pilot, electronics technician, forest and conservation technician, drafter, medical lab technician, technical illustrator, ship's captain

▶ **Office Operations:** People seek financial success and status with a preference for jobs that have clearly defined duties. They tend to be orderly and systematic, and they like to work with words and numbers.

Sample jobs: accountant, auditor, bank loan officer, budget analyst, insurance underwriter, market research analyst

▶ **Scientific:** People enjoy mathematics and science. They are studious, curious, and creative, and they often work with theories and unproven ideas. They may prefer to work alone.

Sample jobs: agricultural scientist, architect, actuary, biologist, chemist, computer programmer, dentist, engineer, geologist, mathematician, physician, physicist, optometrist, software engineer, statistician, systems analyst, surgeon

▶ **Social:** People provide services for others and care about the well-being of others. They have good verbal skills and get along well with people.

Sample jobs: clergy member, college administrator, counselor, dental hygienist, elementary or preschool teacher, historian, librarian, museum curator, nurse, occupational therapist, political scientist, recreation leader, school principal, secondary or vocational/technical teacher, social worker, sociologist, surgical technician

A person most often is a combination of personality types and rarely exemplifies a single personality type. For example, a common combination is social/artistic; these personality types frequently find employment in human service careers. If you feel that two types describe you, then consider reversing the types, such as artistic/social. By making this simple switch, you can expand the number of career options that are deemed appropriate for you.

Some of the common combinations of personality types are listed in Table 2 with corresponding occupations. If you notice that some combinations are missing, it may be because some combinations are not typically found among occupations requiring postsecondary education and training. According to the U.S. Department of Labor, only 20 percent of all jobs will be classified as professional in 2010.

Table 2

Employment Opportunities with Personality Type Combinations

Common Personality Type Combinations	Jobs
Crafts/Scientific	mining engineer, airline pilot
Scientific/Crafts	veterinarian, civil engineer
Scientific/Social	physician assistant, psychiatrist, pediatrician
Scientific/Business	industrial-organizational psychologist, pharmacist
Artistic/Social	art teacher, copy writer, fashion designer
Artistic/Business	comedian, motion picture camera operator, photojournalist
Social/Artistic	music therapist, speech pathologist, clergy member
Social/Business	employment relations specialist, director of special education
Social/Scientific	dietitian, clinical psychologist
Business/Crafts	park superintendent, wine maker
Business/Social	insurance sales agent, director of student affairs, legislative assistant
Office Operations/Business	tax auditor, customs inspector

As you can see, adding the second personality type brings better clarification, and the focus for a major's selection becomes more distinctive. For example, if the person is primarily scientific, he must decide whether he prefers to relate to people as a physician or to data and things as a physicist. Being aware of and sensitive to your personal characteristics is a factor in determining your satisfaction in picking a major.

An additional resource for a comprehensive interest assessment is the *Harrington-O'Shea Career Decision-Making System Revised (CDM-R),* available from American Guidance Service, 4201 Woodland Road, Circle Pines, MN 55014-1796; 1-800-328-2560. This instrument assesses and integrates a person's interests, abilities, and values and provides information about personality type and related occupations.

Another approach to assessing your interests is to use a method originally developed by the U.S. Department of Labor. The resource is entitled *Guide for Occupational Exploration*, Third Edition (M. Farr, L. L. Ludden, and L. Shatkin, 2001), and it is available from JIST Publishing by calling 1-800-648-JIST or visiting www.jist.com.

First, the U.S. Department of Labor clustered all jobs in the United States into 14 interest categories. Second, many interest survey results are based on your preferences or reactions—favorable or unfavorable—to specific job titles. So if you place a check mark in front of example occupations to indicate whether you like the job, the resulting survey may be helpful in indicating a career direction.

Several words of caution: The 14 interest categories do not all contain the same number of occupations. The artistic and scientific categories include fewer jobs than the mechanical category. Also, because this method covers all jobs in the United States, many of the jobs do not require postsecondary education. And lastly, remember that there is no activity or occupation that is only for men or for women.

Place a check mark in front of the activities you would like to do.

Arts, Entertainment, and Media

___ Editor

___ News Reporter

___ Painter

___ Actor

___ Sculptor

___ Graphic Artist

___ TV Broadcast Technician

___ Athlete

___ Musician

___ Singer

___ Dancer

Business Detail

___ Administrative Services Manager

___ Tax Preparer

___ Court Reporter

___ Medical Transcriptionist

___ Human Resources Assistant

___ Computer Operator

Construction, Mining, and Drilling

___ Construction Manager

___ Construction Worker

___ Oil and Gas Derrick Operator

Education and Social Service

___ Principal

___ Counseling Psychologist

___ Clergy

___ Social Worker

___ Teacher

___ Professor

___ Librarian

General Management and Support

___ Government Administrator

___ Public Relations Manager

___ Financial Manager

___ Human Resources Manager

___ Purchasing Manager

___ Accountant

___ Wholesale and Retail Buyer

Industrial Production

___ Industrial Production Manager

___ Metal and Plastics Machining Technologist

___ Stationary Engineer

___ Power Plant Operator

Law, Law Enforcement, and Public Safety

___ Lawyer

___ Police Officer

___ Immigration and Customs Inspector

___ Occupational Health and Safety Specialist

___ Military Service

Mechanics, Installers, and Repairers

___ Telecommunications Line Installer and Repairer

___ Automotive Master Mechanic

Medical and Health Services

___ Health Service Manager

___ Physician

___ Surgeon

___ Pharmacist

___ Dentist

___ Optometrist

___ Medical Lab Technologist

___ Radiologic Technologist

___ Physical Therapist

___ Dietitian/Nutritionist

___ Athletic Trainer

Plants and Animals

___ Farm Manager

___ Veterinarian

___ Nursery/Greenhouse Worker

___ Forest and Conservation Worker

Recreation, Travel, and Other Personal Services

___ Food Service Manager

___ Meeting and Convention Planner

___ Travel Guide

___ Flight Attendant

___ Hotel Manager

___ Chef

Sales and Marketing

___ Marketing Manager

___ Advertising Sales

___ Securities Sales

Science, Math, and Engineering

___ Information Systems Manager	___ Political Scientist
___ Physicist	___ Computer Systems Analyst
___ Chemist	___ Mathematician
___ Biologist	___ Engineer
___ Economist	___ Engineering Technician
___ Historian	

Transportation

___ Transportation Manager	___ Ship's Pilot
___ Air Traffic Controller	___ Truck Driver
___ Airplane Pilot	

This survey can be helpful when all the check marks are clustered together; however, the check marks are often scattered throughout the categories, so no clear pattern emerges. This result is a problem with this kind of survey and shows the advantage of an interest survey. Interest surveys have scales that summarize the results and indicate a focus unique to the person.

However, do not ignore the survey that is included in this chapter. If a substantial number of check marks fall under one of the 14 specific categories, this preference can provide valuable clues and meaning. For example, the survey can show that working in an office may be torture for people wanting to work with plants and animals; a paper-shuffling job may lack the excitement of physical work or the action that law enforcement work may offer. Physical activity may offer a person the opportunity to publicly perform in highly competitive events, such as an athletic event.

In summary, sometimes we are good at doing a job, but we don't enjoy doing the activities that go with the job. Other times we like or enjoy an activity, but we don't do the activity well. While there is a relationship between abilities and interests, each has unique elements. Therefore, all your interests demand examination. Don't prematurely "write off" or ignore a major without giving it due consideration. In each description of the 60 majors in this book, you will find information about the typical interests that people in the field possess.

Values

Job values, as distinguished from personal values, represent what people want to get out of work. Values bring job satisfaction. They are very personal; therefore, the same job can satisfy different values in different people. Values are viewed as cognitive representations of personal needs and are considered basic to a person's belief system. Values are fairly change-resistant. People learn values from their parents, significant others, and daily living experiences. Several examples of values are independence, working with your mind, and altruism.

A well-known expert on value clarification stated that if a belief is to be considered a value, all seven of the following standards must be met: it must be chosen freely, chosen from alternatives, chosen after due reflection, prized and cherished, publicly affirmed, acted upon, and part of a pattern of behavior that is a repeated action. Therefore, if you want to work with your mind, you should pursue a pathway of intellectual curiosity. You should wonder about the "whys" of facts rather than work with your hands. If you pursue this learning style over a period of time, however, you may have to accept that you may be perceived by others as a little "nerdy" or "techy."

People should identify personal values, study their relative importance, and tentatively prioritize them. Consider the following example of how values may help in career planning: A person expresses an interest in farming, but he finds this career blocked because of the large capital investment required to purchase land and equipment. If the person's attraction is understood in terms of valuing autonomy, alternative jobs will become immediately evident. In the current economy—where companies are downsizing, merging, outsourcing, and simply going out of business—transition to other work can more easily be accomplished if individuals have identified their work values. These economic realities are another reason why self-assessment of abilities, strengths, and weaknesses is viewed as a lifelong process.

Assessing job values and benefits is approached a little differently than assessing abilities and interests. You should consider the job values and benefits as options and weigh their importance to you in the jobs you are pursuing. You need to determine the four values and benefits that are the most important to you. Use the following list from *The Career Decision-Making System Revised* to help you determine those values. Circle your four most important values below:

- **Creativity:** Have a job where you can use your imagination and be inventive.

- **Good salary:** Be well paid for your work.

- **High achievement:** Be able to do things of importance or to succeed in a job that is difficult.

- **Independence:** Do work that lets you be your own boss and do the job the way you want without someone watching over you.

- **Job security:** Have a steady job from which you are unlikely to be fired.

- **Leadership:** Direct the work of others and make decisions affecting others.

- **Outdoor work:** Work outside most of the time.

- **Physical activity:** Do work that calls for moving about and using physical strength.

- **Prestige:** Have a job where you get respect and feel important.

- **Risk:** Work in a job that requires you to take physical risks.

- **Variety:** Do many different and interesting tasks.

- **Work with hands:** Have a job where you can use your hands, machines, or tools to make or repair things.

- **Work with people:** Work in close contact with people and be able to comfort and help others.

- **Work with mind:** Do work that requires a high level of mental ability.

What do you do now that you have indicated your four preferred values? In each description of the 60 majors in this book, you will read about values and benefits that you may receive in that field. Thus you will be able to use the information gained from rating your most desired values as you seek possible sources of work satisfaction within each major you explore.

In closing, you may be interested in knowing about the different work values that adolescents, college students, and workers have about their jobs. A high priority for adolescents is a good salary. This value decreases for workers because they value the following more: being involved in setting policy, getting recognition for work, and improving their working conditions. Also, workers do not perceive their workplaces as sources of socialization. Additional studies have noted that the values of adolescents are remarkably the same from one country to another. If you accept the idea that values are representative of needs, then many of us around the world have the same basic needs.

Collecting Information

Effective career decision making requires a multidimensional approach that involves the three domains we have already examined—abilities, interests, and values—as well as factual information about career fields. Achievement demonstrated in course work or work experience related to a specific field is obviously a source of helpful information.

While each chapter in this book is written to describe a major's uniqueness, the psychological characteristics of career fields are often very similar. Many career fields have an affinity to others, so the abilities, interests, and values associated with them may overlap. In other words, people with a certain profile of skills, likes, and desires usually have available several equally rewarding career options. Thus identifying alternative options is also an important task.

Each chapter has been written to answer the following questions about a major field of study:

▶ What is the nature of the career?

▶ What kind of work is performed by typical graduates so that I can match my abilities to the work?

▶ How is the field described so that I can assess my interest in the major?

▶ What are the major values and benefits that may emerge in this type of occupation?

▶ What are the personality characteristics of workers in this major?

▶ What kinds of work activities are in each major?

▶ Is further graduate or professional education likely to be required in this major?

▶ Will I get a job? Will it be in my major? In what part of the economy will it be? A very valuable table will show the top 10 occupations that employ graduates with a bachelor's degree in this major. The data also considers gender. With this information, you can easily determine—either through government publications, the newspaper, or the campus career-placement office—the viability of finding employment in the major when you graduate.

▶ What kind of on-the-job learning will there be, and what will it entail? Most college graduates totally ignore the fact that once they are employed, their employer will demand more learning on the job.

▶ What will I be paid, and how much can I make if I remain in this field?

▶ How does the salary in this field compare with that of other college graduates?

With the information collected from this list of questions, you are now ready to integrate the occupational information with your personal desires into a structure that will permit further analysis. The decision-making process is different for each person. Some will find the major that will make them the most money and will result in the best lifestyle. For others, this process will sound like too much work, and they will drift along and take what life dishes out.

Others will plan more and will want to have more control of their lives. For these people, such concepts as short-term goals, long-term goals, and maximizing opportunities will become a part of their formal decision-making process, which the next section discusses.

For anyone who desires more detailed information about career areas not covered by the 60 majors in this book, excellent resources are http://online.onetcenter.org and the *Occupational Outlook Handbook,* published by the U.S. Department of Labor, Washington, DC. The handbook is updated every two years, so it is the most current source readily available. It can be obtained in virtually every library or career resource center. The *Occupational Outlook Handbook* and a book version of the O*NET information are available from JIST Publishing.

Organizing the Information

The following five steps sum up the decision-making process that students must go through to determine their future work lives:

1. Set the goals.

2. Know what is most important.

3. Examine the options.

4. Assess the risks involved.

5. Establish an implementation plan.

All too frequently a solution for identifying goals is to administer a battery of tests. Presto! The results identify a person's goals and skills by offering a career cluster or occupational titles. However, using this approach exclusively misses the following important areas:

◗ Faulty assumptions, beliefs, and implications

◗ Self-improvement goals

◗ Activities that one does well and that provide personal satisfaction

◗ Future considerations of life roles and their compatibility with goals

While you can use this book as a complete self-help text, many people will find it valuable to run their ideas by others to receive feedback. At some time, almost 70 percent of students have discussed their future plans with at least one of their parents by their junior year in college. It is very valuable to dialogue about one's dreams and aspirations in the past, present, and future.

Step 1: Setting Goals

Goal setting is the logical sequel to identifying goals. Identifying goals often requires someone to cajole, nurture, and draw out a person's ideas and feelings. Goal setting requires organizational and planning skills to develop a plan of action. The first step in goal setting is to sum up the issues that were raised about your job future and major area of study. Be sure to clarify this information with people you respect, because we all know people who change their mind each time you ask.

After you sum up the issues, you need to prioritize them. This process sets up an agenda for future steps that you have to take. This prioritizing can be tricky because you have to consider motivational factors to achieve success. In other words, goal setting is based on the reinforcement theory that success is the best motivator for the student.

You need to put your goals in a certain order: The goals that are the easiest to achieve and require the least amount of time should be your first objective to pursue. When you achieve success by accomplishing these easy goals, you can then go on to the more difficult ones that may require prerequisite learning or experiences. Goal setting establishes a structure. If you have found people–friends, parents, high school counselors, or college staff members–to assist you, they may suggest some experiences to increase the likelihood that a goal can be successfully achieved.

You should give yourself enough time so that the decision-making process is less stressful. Take a look at the following true example: A high school senior knew that he was good in science and got good grades; however, he didn't know whether to major in chemistry or engineering. He talked with some people in the respective fields and chose to enter college as a chemical engineering major. He was not as lucky as his high school classmate who went to a university that did not allow freshmen to declare a specific field of engineering to study. Our person chose chemical engineering according to the college's procedures for freshmen. Despite doing well academically, he struggled for three semesters until he decided that he needed a time-out–almost two years–before he chose to return to college in the same major. He later obtained work as a chemical engineer and returned for postgraduate study in the same area. What he truly needed was time for self-examination, clarification, and reconfirmation.

You should write down each of the goals you want. Think of the written list as a contract, a statement that includes the following points: what you anticipate doing, how long each task should take, and what outcomes you expect from the activities you pursue. You should evaluate your progress based on the satisfaction you get from the outcome of your achievements.

It would be a major oversight not to mention inappropriate goals. Other people can often recognize unrealistic expectations or inappropriate goals in you because the goals are often incompatible with data from achievement, ability, personality, or interest domains. These people can use the following ways to help you determine unrealistic goals: They can tell you that you cannot reach the stated goal, they can suggest some information for you to read or a person to whom you can talk, or they can tell you to come to them for more advice. Some people don't want advice; these people may learn best by failing.

However, experience suggests that creative helpers can work with clients to make apparent mismatches actually work. For example, the introvert who wants to be a salesperson may master the computer to mount direct sales campaigns through the Internet. And a disabled person who wants to be a professional mountain climber may design a unique piece of equipment that wins the acclaim of climbers. If helpers respond to seemingly inappropriate goals without acknowledging the individual's personal needs, outcomes may be jeopardized. An individual's goal may reflect a desire for a personal need to triumph over reason.

Step 2: Knowing What Is Most Important

In this section, the values you prioritized earlier are considered in relation to other information. Frequently we like to know and compare ourselves to what other people say or to what others select as their top choices. What follows is a summary of more than 10,000 U.S. high school students' job values grouped into their top five choices, their second five choices, and the four choices least frequently chosen. The top five values include getting a good salary, having job security, holding down a job with variety, working with people, and earning high achievements. For your information, Canadian, Australian, and French youth selected these same five values in the same order as Japanese, Norwegian, and Portuguese youth.

The second tier of values includes being independent, working with your hands, gaining prestige, being creative, and working with your mind. Some variability did occur among these values in the six countries studied. The values least chosen include physical activity, leadership, outdoor work, and (physical) risk. Among the American youth, several gender differences were noted, following traditional male/female patterns. Females ranked higher than males on working with people, gaining prestige, and working with their mind; they ranked lower than males, however, on working with their hands, participating in physical activity, and being independent.

The two most frequently chosen values are good salary and job security. Often when a student initially chooses a good income as the most important value, he will adjust his thinking in the course of his work experience. What he will end up saying is, "I want the money I feel my work deserves. I don't want to be taken advantage of." Also, job security has become more important to young adults as they see that this goal is no longer a reality in today's work market. These studies and their results also worry employers from around the world when they see that the values of working with the mind and exhibiting leadership are ranked in the 10th and 12th places, respectively, out of 14 values.

Research, however, shows that the popularity of the adolescent values above changes with age. A study of one-half million employees cited 11 reasons that were more important than pay in staying with their current employer: career opportunity, challenge, feeling of making a contribution, coworkers, teamwork, a good boss, recognition, fun on the job, autonomy, and flexible hours and dress code (B. Kaye and S. Jordan-Evans, *Love 'Em or Lose 'Em: Getting Good People to Stay.* San Francisco: Berrett-Koehler Publishers, Inc., 1999, p. 6).

Realistically, job values will eventually compete with personal values. You have to be prepared to think about how the conflict between these two priorities will affect your family life and your work life as you integrate them. The following list includes some personal values:

- **Family:** Raising a family or caring for aged parents.
- **Leisure:** Having time and money for leisure.
- **Community:** Taking an active part in community affairs.
- **Personal growth:** Working on self-improvement.
- **Helping others:** Improving the quality of the lives of others.
- **Environment:** Conserving or restoring the environment.
- **Spiritual:** Doing things that follow one's personal beliefs.
- **A good life:** Achieving a comfortable and high standard of living.

Values can change as you get older and enter relationships where people come from different backgrounds. New priorities will emerge, and prior values will be replaced. Although values are important, interests may have greater influence on you when you are younger. As you develop, however, values definitely play an influential role in your life.

Step 3: Examining the Options

You can use Table 3 to consolidate the information about your education alternatives. To assess a major, record your evaluations of the 10 areas in the corresponding rows of Table 3. Indicate in the first row any major(s) you are considering.

Table 3
Evaluating Your Majors

Name of Major			
Abilities (1)			
Interests (2)			
Values (3)			
Personality Characteristics (4)			
Salary (5)			
Requires More Education (6)			
Relocation (7)			
Employment Outlook (8)			
Job Readiness (9)			
Industry Attractiveness (10)			

1. Excellent, good, fair, or poor match of your abilities with those required by the major.

2. Good, fair, or poor match of your interests with those activities and opportunities that the major can provide.

3. Very compatible, compatible, or conflicting values with people in the occupations that this major prepares you for.

4. Good, fair, or poor fit of your personality characteristics with people who enter occupations from this major.

5. Very acceptable, acceptable, or not acceptable salary.

6. Agree, do not agree, or in a quandary about whether you are willing to go back for additional schooling. Additionally, place an X on the line if you believe a source of funding is available to pay some postgraduate tuition costs.

7. Will relocate or will not relocate to find employment or to go to school in this major.

8. Excellent, good, fair, or poor outlook for jobs with this major. Additionally, put a C on the line if this is a very competitive field.

9. Yes or no that you will be fully qualified for employment with this major when you receive your bachelor's degree.

10. Attractive, fairly attractive, or not attractive, depending on whether you like the industry in which the job is or its growth potential.

The reason for using visual aids, such as Table 3, is to identify those areas that are restraining you from making a decision. You must know which areas need to be addressed if most of the other factors are valued positively. By examining the options, you can weigh the pros and cons of the consequences of a decision. Also, if some of the descriptive words from the list don't appeal to you, you can use this test as a signal to stop and question the original goal(s) set forth in Step 1.

There is fluidity to this decision-making process. Maybe you have chosen incorrect goals originally. By examining the options in Step 3, for example, you may come to the realization that you have established goals based on what your brother or sister has advised you, not your own personal goals. Or you may have been influenced by people who have said that you should be in a certain profession just because they like that profession. After assessing your own abilities, you may finally come to your own conclusion about what you like to do and how well you do it. It is okay to go back to Step 1 and select a new goal. You will be surprised how fast the process goes the second or even the third time you go through it because you have already done a lot of the work.

Step 4: Assessing the Risks

The decision model is based on the concepts of value and probability. *Value* refers to the desirability of something or to an outcome, which can be either positive or negative. A negative value means that the outcome or event is undesirable. This concept of value closely resembles the behavioral concepts of positive and negative reinforcement. In examining and evaluating the options in Step 3, you are determining the values that appear the most or least desirable.

Probability refers to the likelihood that an event or outcome will happen. Probability is related to risk, which has the following ranges:

▶ **No risk:** The outcome is known and certain.

▶ **Risky:** The outcome is known but has a specified probability factor; for example, 80 percent of people applying are accepted.

▶ **Uncertain:** The chances of the outcome occurring are unknown.

Many states have lotteries, which are examples of probabilities in action. For example, you buy a ticket for $1.00 or $2.00 with a probability of 1 million to 1 that you may win a big prize. The outcome is like a dream. On the other hand, because employers want to hire female engineers to satisfy governmental nondiscrimination laws, the probability is very high that the opportunities for employment will be excellent, because few women are studying engineering.

Probabilities are not totally controlled by the person. For example, when the economies of Southeast Asia, Japan, and Korea are in difficulty, this situation affects the world economy, with results trickling down to the individual. You encounter risk daily in driving a car or in meeting people—after all, other people may not like you!

The values you indicated while examining your options are your *expectations*—the possible outcomes that you expect to gain from each of the criteria, such as utilizing your abilities, liking the activities of the occupation, and so on. Assessing the risks is really determining the probability (high, medium, or low) that each criterion will result in the expected outcome. For example, if you get good grades in the introductory subjects, you can expect to do well in that major. If you take an internship in an area and you like what you are doing, you can expect to like the work in the future. As you can see, making a decision involves data collection. After reviewing your answers to multiple questions, you can finally make an informed choice.

Risk taking is learned. Some people simply are not risk takers, while others definitely take risks. Risk taking is not a universal quality. Some people will take many chances, including participating in such physical activity as rock climbing, which involves potential danger. Other people will take a risk in making money or in maintaining relationships or in being assertive. And others will take risks simply by expressing themselves, moving to take a new job, or traveling alone on a motorcycle across the country. Developing your talents or gifts always involves some kind of risk. Remember that each individual may have different risk-taking tendencies, depending on the situation. For this reason, you need to understand a bit about motivation.

An instructor of a college career planning course once wrote, "The most common cause of failure in college is not the lack of ability; it is the failure to establish a reason for being there." When you first establish your goals, you address this issue; however, you may not understand your motivation for going to college or choosing a major. You may not understand that college is an opportunity—both a time and a place to identify, search out, and develop your talents and gifts. Maybe you need some perspective to see that selecting a major is an opportunity in itself and can often be a motivational force.

Motivation is an internal process that drives a person to act in a purposeful manner. An individual's needs, drives, and actions are included in his motivational forces. Motives develop from needs, which are related to goals, which reflect what the individual wants. Wondering about an opportunity or a dream can be a goal and can be *articulated*. Motives are *inner drives* that cannot be seen. Only inferences can be made about a person's motives. However, goal statements and actions that are movements toward a goal are observable and can serve as the means by which the strength and understanding of the drive can be measured.

Motivation is the energy or the fuel that drives the self-development process. Motivation is the internalization of a person's drive for goal attainment. Hopefully, as a young adult you have started questioning who you are, what you want, and what your talents are, because now is the time to do these things. So goal identification and goal attainment are parts of motivation, but the creation of excitement is also part of motivation. Dreaming or envisioning yourself in a certain major can be fun. A noted career researcher said, "An individual's future is limited only by the imagination of those involved in the planning." Although thinking about the future may be scary, anxiety is also the energy that drives a person to change and to learn.

Find someone to listen to you as you describe or act out how you will perform in a specific occupation. In fact, do this exercise for several different occupations, because it may indicate adequate or inadequate job knowledge. For example, this exercise will take you from the point of saying, "I want to be a TV producer" to "This is what I would do as a TV producer." How you fill in the details about the job and how you describe the advancement opportunities for the job are critical to your success in that particular field.

Take a look at the following job history as it relates to being a TV producer. This example shows the detail that you must have as you act out each occupation that you are considering. To be a TV producer, you have to start at the bottom as a gofer, a person who runs errands for others. You probably will have to do part-time work, which is usually in the evenings for a very low salary. This low salary will prevent you from participating in many activities that your friends are doing, so you may have to get a second job just to keep up with them. After several years of this kind of work, you may get a chance at full-time work, but you will still work weekends and evenings. You will see your social life impaired in comparison with others because you finish work at midnight and leave for work at 2:00 P.M.

After examining a job in this real-world detail, you are ready to answer the question about whether you have the motivation to pursue this career. A person's motivation is often embedded in his or her self-portrayal of actually doing the job. Only you can determine the sacrifices and compromises you are willing to make to work in the kind of job you want.

In closing, this step in the development of dreams or talents can involve risks. Remember that motivation is definitely part of goal attainment.

Step 5: Establishing a Plan

You may consider this step a "no-brainer," because it is simply the mechanical process of writing down a schedule of events to do. However, it is critical to the implementation and the culmination of earlier steps.

Perhaps all that your choice of major involves is checking off a box on a class registration form. Great! Other institutions may require you to apply to be admitted and to wait for a decision

hopefully to be invited to join "the group." But what about the other issues that you raised as you explored your choice of major? How did you decide to resolve them?

Take a look at Table 4. You can use this table as a guide to plan your future. In column 1, you should list the actions to be completed–those ideas, concerns, and issues that you want to explore further. In column 2, you should list the steps you have to take to answer the questions posed in the first column. Some sample steps could include the following questions: with whom do you speak, where do you get the information or resources, where do you go or whom do you see to obtain the hands-on experience you want, and where do you take a prerequisite course? In column 3, you list your estimation of the time the activity will take. And in column 4, you list the date that you propose to do the activity.

Prolonging the completion of the action steps is not motivational; therefore, it is critical to examine your time frames for completing all your tasks. You may be able to do some of the tasks concurrently so that you can move along in your goal to choose a career.

Table 4
A Sample List of Headings for an Action Plan

Goals/Activities/Issues	What Needs to Be Done and Resources to Obtain or People to Contact	Time Estimate and Date to Be Completed

In this chapter, you have been exposed to the challenge of seeking self-knowledge, which some people only minimally achieve during their lifetime. Learning about yourself is a hard task and usually takes considerable time. Self-estimates of abilities are expressions of self-perceptions. Remember that people tend to behave in a manner consistent with their image of themselves. You have also been studying about how to make a decision. Remember that *not* making a decision is also a choice. We all have choices, and choosing to act upon them is empowering. Selecting a major is one way that you can empower yourself.

CHAPTER 3

The Economics of Career Choice

Enrolling in a college or university after graduation is widely prevalent among American high school graduates. A sizable majority of students graduating from high school choose to pursue postsecondary education. During the fall of 2002, out of 2.8 million members of that year's high school graduating class, 1.8 million, or more than 65 percent, were enrolled in colleges and universities. Year after year, a large group of high school graduates and their families make one of the most important decisions of their lives—the decision to enroll in college.

A college education is one of the costliest purchases that an individual will ever make, and completing a college education with a degree can have a lifelong impact on the individual's economic and psychological well-being and on his or her social status. Despite well-intentioned messages—from high school graduation speakers—that college is a journey to be experienced and explored, the reality is that college is a demanding, time-consuming, and expensive investment. Its status as an investment gives it a set of special properties, chief among which is that it is expected to lead to a set of benefits or desirable outcomes in the future in return for costs incurred today.

The decision to enroll in college is, in itself, not sufficient to realize the benefits of a college education. An important part of the college enrollment decision is how well the decision is made in the context of the individual's interests, aptitudes, and abilities. The quality of the decision is partly determined by the quality of the information upon which the decision is made—information about one's interests, aptitudes, and abilities balanced against the costs and expected benefits of attending college at specific institutions and in specific academic fields.

Unfortunately, for a substantial number of high school graduates whose college investment decision is not made with sufficient information, preparation, and thought, college will prove to be a failure in this regard. A substantial proportion of freshmen will fail to earn an associate's or a bachelor's degree. They will withdraw from college and try to find an alternative path through life. Others will graduate from college, but they will be unable to find meaningful work or to gain access to a lifestyle that meets their basic values. For these individuals, the college investment has simply not worked because they failed to reach a destination with value and meaning for them. Indeed, college is a journey, but as with all journeys, it has meaning only when the journey ends at the right destination.

Investment in a college education can be very lucrative. As you will learn later in this chapter, the average rate of economic return to a bachelor's degree measured by annual earnings and total earnings over a lifetime is quite high and has grown sharply over time. But before we discuss the returns to college investment, let us explore the nature of the college investment decision and compare it with other types of investment activities.

The Costs and Benefits of Investment in Higher Education

Investment is an activity in which an individual sacrifices something today in the expectation of some greater benefit that will be generated in the future. Attending college is akin to investment since college has costs that are incurred today in the expectation of benefits that will accrue in the future. Individuals who are planning to invest in a college education need to weigh the total costs of attending college with the total expected future benefits from a college education. Although many potential college enrollees are generally aware of the costs of a college education, particularly out-of-pocket costs, they are not as cognizant of the stream of future monetary benefits that will accrue to them after completing a college education. There are two major types of costs that individuals will incur when they enroll in college. The first is the out-of-pocket costs of tuition and fees that they pay to finance their education. Although these costs are large and rising, they are only a part of the total cost that students and their families pay for a college education.

A second major cost of college to the individual is the earnings they forgo while enrolled in school. Most college students do not hold down full-time jobs while they are in school. Many students hold part-time jobs for a limited number of weeks over the year, while others choose not to work at all. This reduced work effort represents "lost" earnings that college students could

have had if they opted to work full-time instead of enrolling in college. Thus, the true cost of enrolling in college includes both the out-of-pocket costs, such as tuition and fees, and the lost earnings of college students. (Most economists do not include dormitory and boarding costs in calculating the total cost of college, as individuals would have to pay these costs even if they were not enrolled in college.)

In the 2003–2004 academic year, average tuition and fee costs at private American four-year colleges were approximately $20,000 per year. At public colleges nationwide, tuition and fee costs were nearly $5,000 per year.[1] These costs are the average costs for attending a four-year college, and they vary considerably by state and by type of college. Added on to these costs are the lost earnings of students who give up full-time work. In 2003, the average young adult who obtained a high school diploma but did not enroll in postsecondary school earned about $22,000. If we assume that the typical college freshman could have had a job that paid this amount, then the average student enrolled in college gave up about $22,000 in earnings during the first year of college.

Thus, the cost for a young adult entering a private college was about $42,000, which includes the average tuition plus the lost earnings for the year—exclusive of room, board, and ancillary expenses. If we assume that students complete their education in four years, then a conservative estimate for a bachelor's degree from a private college in the 2003–2004 academic year is $168,000. This estimate is an amount sufficient to purchase a single-family home in many parts of the country or to put toward a down payment for a home in even the most expensive areas of the nation. Clearly such high costs require that substantial returns be generated in order to justify the expense!

[1] *Trends in College Pricing,* The College Board, Washington, DC, 2003

A college education does, in fact, provide substantial benefits that, on average, justify the costs of a college degree. Moreover, at least the monetary benefits of a bachelor's degree have increased over time. Table 1 presents a comparison of the earnings of young college graduates with a bachelor's degree with those of young adults who have earned only a high school diploma. The comparison is presented over the 1967 to 2001 period, and annual earnings are expressed in inflation-adjusted 2001 dollars. From the late 1960s through the early 1970s, the average young adult with a college degree earned between 22 percent and 25 percent more than high school graduates. For a brief period in the early 1970s, the earnings advantage of college graduates actually declined to the 16–17 percent range. This decline in the earnings advantage of college graduates was considered to be evidence of an oversupply of college graduates.

Table 1

Mean Annual Earnings of Employed College Graduates and
High School Graduates Aged 20 to 29, 1967–2001

Year	High School Graduates	College Graduates with a Bachelor's Degree	Absolute Difference	Relative Difference
1967	$22,081	$27,543	$5,462	24.7%
1968	$22,339	$27,738	$5,398	24.2%
1969	$23,191	$28,518	$5,328	23.0%
1970	$22,690	$28,091	$5,401	23.8%
1971	$22,061	$27,043	$4,982	22.3%
1972	$23,507	$27,182	$3,675	15.6%
1973	$23,292	$28,334	$5,043	21.6%
1974	$22,055	$25,846	$3,791	17.2%
1975	$21,050	$26,781	$5,731	27.2%
1976	$21,596	$26,903	$5,307	24.6%
1977	$21,349	$27,193	$5,843	27.4%
1978	$22,099	$27,216	$5,117	23.2%
1979	$21,957	$27,109	$5,152	23.5%
1980	$20,519	$25,800	$5,281	25.7%
1981	$19,427	$25,373	$6,918	36.9%
1983	$18,746	$26,270	$7,523	40.1%
1984	$19,370	$27,647	$8,276	42.7%
1985	$19,227	$29,163	$9,936	51.7%

(continued)

Table 1 (continued)
Mean Annual Earnings of Employed College Graduates and High School Graduates Aged 20 to 29, 1967–2001

Year	High School Graduates	College Graduates with a Bachelor's Degree	Absolute Difference	Relative Difference
1986	$19,436	$29,921	$10,486	54.0%
1987	$19,850	$30,033	$10,183	51.3%
1988	$20,109	$30,334	$10,225	50.8%
1989	$19,848	$30,857	$11,009	55.5%
1990	$19,085	$29,073	$9,988	52.3%
1991	$18,435	$27,767	$9,333	50.6%
1992	$18,085	$27,360	$9,274	51.3%
1993	$17,509	$26,678	$9,169	52.4%
1994	$18,202	$27,383	$9,181	50.4%
1995	$18,032	$28,076	$10,044	55.7%
1996	$17,993	$29,240	$11,247	62.5%
1997	$18,692	$30,423	$11,731	62.8%
1998	$19,796	$32,098	$12,302	62.1%
1999	$19,102	$32,442	$13,340	69.8%
2000	$20,506	$34,591	$14,084	68.7%
2001	$20,039	$33,382	$13,343	66.6%

Source: U.S. Bureau of the Census, Current Population Surveys, March Supplement, 1968–2002. Tabulations produced by the authors.

However, since the end of the 1970s, the size of the earnings advantage for college graduates has steadily increased. By 1981, young college graduates earned 30 percent more each year than high school graduates with no postsecondary schooling. The economic boom of the 1980s provided further advantages for college graduates. By 1990, the average young adult with a college degree earned 52 percent more per year than high school graduates.

The 1990s saw another increment in the college earnings premium. In 1999, young college graduates earned nearly 70 percent more, on average, than young adults with only a high school diploma. The onset of the recession resulted in a slight reduction of the earnings advantage of employed young college graduates. This recession saw an increase in underemployment among college graduates who were forced to shift down the employment queue and take jobs that did not fully utilize their skills and were typically filled by less-educated youth. The less-educated youth in turn were pushed further down the employment queue, leaving many of them jobless.[2] However, even during the recession the mean annual earnings of employed young college graduates were two-thirds higher than those of young employed high school graduates.

Over time, the size of the earnings advantage of college graduates relative to high school graduates has increased among young adults. But what happens to the earnings of college graduates as they age? Are college graduates able to

maintain their earnings advantage relative to high school graduates over their entire working lives, or is the earnings advantage transitory, disappearing as both college graduates and high school graduates age?

In order to answer these questions, we need to examine the earnings experience of college graduates relative to high school graduates at different ages by constructing an age-earnings profile for each group. The age-earnings profiles presented in Figure 1 trace the earnings of college graduates by age, relative to the earnings of high school graduates of the same age.

FIGURE 1

Mean Annual Earnings of Employed Persons 25 to 64 Years Old, by Educational Attainment, by Age, 2000

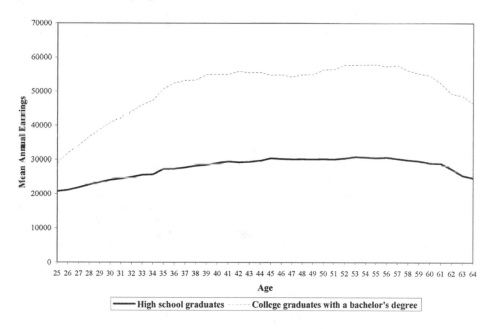

Source: U.S. Bureau of the Census, Decennial Census Public Use Micro-data Samples (PUMS) Data Files, 2000. Tabulations produced by the authors.

[2] *The recession resulted in lower earnings for many college graduates, but joblessness for many young high school graduates. Since the mean earnings presented in Table 1 excluded jobless youth, the negative impact of the recession on earnings of high school graduates was underestimated. This underlies some of the decline in the earnings premium of college graduates relative to high school graduates during the 2000–2001 period.*

Three observations are readily apparent from Figure 1. First, at every age level, college graduates earn more than high school graduates. Second, the earnings for high school graduates reach a peak much earlier than those of college graduates. Third, the relative size of the earnings advantage for college graduates increases with age. This increase indicates that the earnings advantage of a college degree increases over the life of the college graduate.

These earnings advantages of a college degree accumulate to a substantial amount over the working lifetime of these graduates. Table 2 is a comparison of the lifetime earnings of individuals with different levels of schooling. On average, individuals with a bachelor's degree earn twice as much as those with just a high school diploma over their working lifetime. A master's degree is expected to yield a lifetime earnings premium (relative to a high school diploma) of 270 percent. This means that for every dollar earned by a high school graduate, individuals with a bachelor's degree earned $2, and individuals with a master's degree or more earned $2.70 over their lifetimes. These earnings premiums result in sizable aggregate dollar amounts. In 1999, individuals with a bachelor's degree earned $942,000 more than high school graduates, and those with a master's degree or more earned $1.6 million more then high school graduates over their working lifetimes.

The return to a college degree accumulates to substantial amounts over the working lifetimes of graduates. Moreover, the lifetime earnings advantage of a college degree has grown over time. Table 3 is a comparison of the (inflation-adjusted) lifetime earnings by educational attainment between 1979 and 1999. Over the course of twenty years, between 1979 and 1999, the aggregate lifetime earnings of an individual with a bachelor's degree increased by $181,000, or nearly 11 percent. The lifetime earnings of an individual with a post-baccalaureate degree increased by nearly $375,000, or 17 percent. In contrast, the lifetime earnings of those who failed to complete high school declined by $86,000, or 12 percent, whereas high school graduates saw their lifetime earnings decline by $38,000, or nearly 4 percent.

Table 2
Lifetime Earnings of 18- to 64-Year-Old Individuals Not Enrolled in School, by Educational Attainment, 1999

Educational Attainment	Lifetime Earnings in 1999	Dollar Difference in Lifetime Earnings Compared to High School Graduates	Lifetime Earnings Premium Relative to High School Graduates
Less than high school	$624,061	–$316,971	66%
High school graduate	$941,032	NA	NA
Bachelor's degree	$1,883,060	$942,028	200%
Master's degree or more	$2,527,896	$1,586,864	269%

Source: U.S. Bureau of the Census, Decennial Census Public Use Micro-data Samples (PUMS) Data Files, 1980 and 2000. Tabulations produced by the authors.

Table 3

Changes in the Real (Inflation-Adjusted) Lifetime Earnings of 18- to 64-Year-Old Individuals Not Enrolled in School, by Educational Attainment, 1979 and 1999 (in 1999 Dollars)

Educational Attainment	1979	1999	Absolute Change	Relative Change
Less than high school	$710,431	$624,061	−$86,370	−12.2%
High school graduate	$979,051	$941,032	−$38,020	−3.9%
Bachelor's degree	$1,701,947	$1,883,060	$181,113	10.6%
Master's degree or more	$2,153,149	$2,527,896	$374,747	17.4%

Source: U.S. Bureau of the Census, Decennial Census Public Use Micro-data Samples (PUMS) Data Files, 1980 and 2000. Tabulations produced by the authors.

These divergent trends in the lifetime earnings of less-educated individuals and those with college degrees have led to a sharp increase in the lifetime earnings premium of a college education. The lifetime earnings premium of a bachelor's degree relative to a high school diploma increased from 174 percent in 1979 to 200 percent in 1999—an increase of 26 percentage points over just two decades. The lifetime earnings premium of a post-baccalaureate degree increased from 220 percent in 1979 to 270 percent in 1999, representing an increase of 49 percentage points (Table 4).

Table 4

Changes in the Lifetime Earnings Premiums of 18- to 64-Year-Old Individuals Not Enrolled in School, by Educational Attainment, 1979 and 1999

Educational Attainment	LIFETIME EARNINGS PREMIUM RELATIVE TO HIGH SCHOOL GRADUATES		Absolute Change
	1979	1999	
Less than high school	73%	66%	−7
High school graduate	100%	100%	NA
Bachelor's degree	174%	200%	+26
Master's degree or more	220%	269%	+49

Source: U.S. Bureau of the Census, Decennial Census Public Use Micro-data Samples (PUMS) Data Files, 1980 and 2000. Tabulations produced by the authors.

What underlies these divergent trends in the economic fortunes of college graduates and their poorly educated counterparts? The next section describes changes in the American economy over the past two decades and examines the relationship between the changing American economic environment and the changing employment and earnings prospects of individuals with different levels of formal education.

Changes in the American Economic Environment

Over the past twenty years, the economic fortunes of college graduates improved. Over the same time period, less-educated individuals saw a deterioration of their labor market fortunes. Underlying these divergent trends are sharp changes in labor demand. The demand for labor originates from businesses or firms, whereas labor supply originates from individuals. The exchange of labor (demand and supply) takes place in an institution that economists call the labor market. Let us first understand three terms that are commonly used to describe different aspects of the labor market: industry, occupation, and jobs.

Economists classify different types of businesses into industries based on the products or services that they provide. For example, a producer of tools is part of the manufacturing industry, a department store is classified into the retail trade industry, and an architectural services firm is classified into the professional services industry. Each industry has a certain number of positions in which they employ individuals. The total number of positions in a firm is called the total number of jobs or the total employment in the firm.

People employed in these industries work in different capacities defined by their job title. Economists classify these job titles (that describe what individuals do at work) into several different occupations. For example, a supervisor belongs to the managerial occupation, a scientist is part of professional occupations, a stockbroker is part of high-level sales occupations, and a machine tool operator is part of skilled blue-collar occupations.

Employment, or the total number of jobs, in an economy changes over time as the economy moves through economic booms and economic downturns or recessions, also known as business cycles. Employment can also change due to changes in the types of products that are demanded and produced in the economy. For example, as Internet use soared, employment in the American economy became more concentrated in computer-related industries.

Over the last two decades the industrial composition of employment in the American economy changed sharply. The most striking change occurred in employment levels in the manufacturing, or goods-producing, industry and the service industry. In 1983, more than 20 percent of the total employment in the American economy was in the manufacturing sector. By 2002, the manufacturing sector's share of total employment declined to less than 14 percent. Over the same 20-year time period, employment in the service industry increased sharply. The share of total employment in the service industry increased from 22 percent in 1983 to 32 percent in 2002, representing a 10-percentage-point increase.

Table 5
Change in Shares of Manufacturing and Services Industry Employment
in the U.S., 1983 to 2002*

Percentage of Total Employment	1983	2002	Absolute Change (Percentage Points)
Manufacturing industry	20.4%	12.8%	−7.6
Services industry	21.8%	31.5%	+9.7

Service industries consist of establishments engaged in providing a wide variety of services for individuals, businesses, government agencies, and other organizations. The fastest-growing service-sector jobs are in professional-services establishments.

Source: U.S. Bureau of the Census, Current Population Surveys Public Use Data Files, 1983 and 2002. Tabulations produced by the authors.

What does this shift of employment from the manufacturing sector to the service sector mean? These two industries require a vastly different workforce with different skill and educational levels. Members of the workforce in these two industries are concentrated in very different occupations. The service sector has a large concentration of its workforce in managerial, professional, technical, and high-level sales occupations that are frequently labeled as college labor market occupations because of the high concentration of college graduates in these occupations. These occupations are usually staffed with college-educated workers and those with high skill levels. The manufacturing industry, in contrast, has a high concentration of employees in blue-collar occupations and a small number employed in college labor market occupations.

Analysis of the occupations of workers employed in these industries reveals these differences in the occupational staffing patterns between the two industries. In 2002, more than 65 percent of service industry employees were employed in college labor market occupations, compared to only 34 percent of employees in the manufacturing sector. Blue-collar occupations accounted for only 3 percent of the service industry employees and 55 percent of the employees in the manufacturing industry.

Although the occupational staffing patterns of both industries still remain very different, changes over time in production processes and technology have resulted in an increase in the share of college labor market occupations in both industries and a decline in blue-collar employment. In the manufacturing sector, the share of college labor market occupations increased from 25 percent in 1983 to 34 percent in 2002, and the share of blue-collar occupations declined from 60 percent to 55 percent over the same time period. The share of the service industry workforce employed in college labor market occupations increased from 60 percent in 1983 to 65 percent in 2002.

Table 6

Percentage of Employees in the Manufacturing and Services Industries
in the U.S. That Were Employed in Professional, Technical, Managerial,
and High-Level Sales Occupations* and in Blue-Collar Occupations, 1983 and 2002

Percentage of Employees Working In:	1983	2002	Absolute Change
Manufacturing Industry			
Professional, technical, managerial, and high-level sales occupations	25.2%	34.0%	8.8%
Blue-collar occupations	60.2%	55.0%	−5.2%
Service Industry			
Professional, technical, managerial, and high-level sales occupations	60.1%	65.3%	5.2%
Blue-collar occupations	4.2%	3.1%	−1.1%

The following are some examples of these occupations: engineers, physicians, scientists, and teachers (professional occupations); health technicians, such as dental hygienists and laboratory technicians, electrical and electronics technicians, airplane pilots, and computer programmers (technical occupations); insurance sales, real estate sales, securities and financial services sales, and sales representatives (high-level sales occupations); managerial occupations include workers in managerial and supervisory positions.

Source: U.S. Bureau of the Census, Current Population Surveys Public Use Data Files, 1983 and 2002. Tabulations produced by the authors.

Blue-collar occupations employ individuals with skills different from those possessed by workers employed in college labor market occupations. College labor market workers acquire many of their skills in the classroom, whereas blue-collar workers are more likely to acquire skills on the job. Thus, blue-collar jobs are less likely to require a college education and are typically staffed with individuals with less than a college education. College labor market occupations usually require a college education. Clearly, the educational requirements of professional, technical, managerial, and high-level sales occupations (college labor market occupations) are very different from those of blue-collar occupations.

A comparison of the educational characteristics of workers in these occupations reveals the sharp differences between their educational attainments. In 2002, less than 2 percent of the employees in college labor market occupations were high school dropouts, compared to nearly 20 percent of blue-collar workers. The share of high school dropouts was more than 10 times higher among blue-collar workers compared to professional, technical, managerial, and high-level sales workers or college labor market workers.

Table 7

Percentage Distribution of Working-Age Adults (22–64 Years Old)
in the Professional, Technical, Managerial, and High-Level Sales Occupations
and in Blue-Collar Occupations by Their Educational Attainment, 2002

(A) Educational Attainment	(B) Professional, Technical Managerial, and High- Level Sales Occupations	(C) Blue-Collar Ocupations	(D) Ratio (C)/(B)
High school dropouts	1.9	19.6	10.22
High school graduates	14.9	47.9	3.21
Some college	25.8	26.0	1.01

*Source: U.S. Bureau of the Census, Current Population Surveys Public Use Data Files, 2000.
Tabulations produced by the authors.*

High school graduates accounted for only 15 percent of the employees working in college labor market occupations. In contrast, nearly one-half of blue-collar workers reported their highest level of education to be a high school diploma. The share of high school graduates among blue-collar workers was more than three times higher than the share of workers in college labor market occupations.

At the upper end of the educational distribution, nearly 6 out of 10 workers in professional, technical, managerial, and high-level sales occupations had earned a four-year college degree or more. The share of workers with a college degree in blue-collar occupations was less than 6 percent. The share of college graduates among blue-collar workers was only one-tenth as high as that among workers employed in college labor market occupations. This concentration of college graduates has earned these (professional, technical, managerial, and high-level sales) occupations the label "college labor market occupations."

Changes in the industry employment shares and occupational staffing patterns have had a profound effect on labor demand in the American economy. As noted previously, the manufacturing sector is more likely to employ individuals with lower levels of education, whereas employment in the service sector has a concentration of highly educated workers. A decline in the share of manufacturing employment reduced the demand for less-educated members of the workforce, while increases in the share of service industry employment resulted in an increase in the demand for workers with high levels of education.

What is the effect of these changes in labor demand? The demand and supply of different types of workers (labor) determine the level of earnings of these workers. In this regard the labor market operates like any other market. For example, if the demand for heating oil increases, holding all other factors (including supply) constant, the price of heating oil increases. Similarly, an increase in labor demand, holding all else constant, results in an increase in earnings, just as a decrease in labor demand, all else constant, results in a decline in earnings. The changes in the American economy described previously led to sharp increases in the demand for college-educated workers and a decline in the demand for less-educated workers. As a consequence, the earnings of college-educated workers increased, while the earnings of poorly educated workers declined.

When the price of a product increases, suppliers of this product usually respond with an increase in supply. Increases in the demand for college-educated workers led to increases in their earnings, signaling the American workforce and potential workforce entrants to acquire a college education. This is evident in the steady increase in college enrollment rates among high school graduates during the fall following their graduation. Adult members of the workforce also have returned to college to earn degrees. As a result, the supply of college-educated workers has increased. However, the increase in the demand for college-educated workers has outstripped the increase in the supply of these workers, resulting in a continued increase in their earnings.

The low-skills labor market witnessed the reverse. Due to a decrease in labor demand (for workers with low levels of education) that was not matched by a commensurate decrease in the supply of these workers, the lower end of the labor market has witnessed a sharp decline in earnings of poorly educated workers. Although the overall educational attainment of the American workforce has improved, there is still a substantial oversupply of low-skill workers relative to the demand for them.

The consequence of these two divergent trends in earnings is an increase in the annual earnings premiums and the lifetime earnings premiums of college graduates relative to high school graduates and high school dropouts. The demand for college-educated workers has increased sharply, and at present there are no signs of a slowdown in the demand and salary growth of well-educated workers. A college education has paid off in the past, and all indicators point to a continued increase in the payoffs to a college education.

Although it is clear that the average return to an investment in a college degree is substantial, it is important to note that these returns vary enormously by the type of college education. In order to maximize the returns within the context of the interests, abilities, aptitudes, and values of the potential student, a number of key questions must be answered. College investors are confronted with a wide array of educational choices, including decisions about what type of college to attend. Should they attend two-year or four-year schools, public or private schools, local or long-distance schools?

In addition, students must decide on the type of degree they want and whether they want to earn just a bachelor's degree or pursue postgraduate education and an advanced degree. The decision is based on a choice from dozens, if not hundreds, of alternatives. This enormous menu of choices is a major strength of American higher education. Yet this enormous array of options adds layers of complexity to the college investment decision and may seem daunting to students and parents. To better understand the degree of this complexity, it is useful to compare the nature of the investment decisions made by stock market investors to that of college investors.

Information Requirements of the College Investment Decision

The hallmark of successful Wall Street traders is their ability to obtain and process information. Each day hundreds of newspapers across the nation publish information about the earnings and profits of firms, along with information on the cost of acquiring shares of these firms. The Internet now provides up-to-the-minute information on firm performance and stock prices. Each day, newspapers and magazines publish in-depth stories about the products and future plans of a wide range of businesses. Armed with this and other information and a familiarity with the market, the Wall Street trader is in a better position to assess the benefits and costs of a host of investment alternatives.

College investors also have some general knowledge about the economic returns to their college investment. Yet the similarity ends here. While Wall Street traders have detailed information on the performance of specific companies, prospective students have little information on the stream of benefits that they can expect from a specific college investment. Students know little about the outcomes of graduates from any individual college. What they do know is derived directly from the college admissions or public relations office—hardly the sort of objective source of information upon which the Wall Street trader relies. Instead, prospective students rely on perceptions of college status as judged by friends, classmates, high school teachers and counselors, and such publications as *US News & World Report* and *Barron's*. These perceptions may have little relationship to the advantages that the college may, in fact, offer.

Limited information often forces students, parents, and counselors to rely on less-than-systematic assessments of the career pathways associated with alternative fields of study. In fact, many career counselors now advise students to avoid picking specific major fields of study. Instead, they recommend students major in the humanities and social sciences: fields that keep career options open and make students more flexible in responding to the ever-changing needs of the workplace.

Yet parents are skeptical of this advice. In a 1997 opinion survey of higher education, parents and students believed that the acquisition of specialized skills in a university setting made their children more employable in a labor market that is hungry for specific occupational and technical proficiencies.

Thus, college investors are torn between two views of the field-of-study decision. One view suggests that narrow vocational fields will lead to skills that will become increasingly obsolete. The other view suggests that the best careers in the American economy will be built on developing the specific kinds of skills required in engineering, health, computer software, and finance—the growth sectors of the American economy. Clearly the college investor is faced with a shortage of information about investment alternatives.

One way to deal with poor information and uncertainty in making an investment decision is to adopt a hedging strategy. Many casual investors on Wall Street recognize that the average return to investments in equities has been quite high in recent years, but they do not have the time to gather the information to make specific stock purchases. These investors want to tap into the earnings generated by Wall Street, but they simply do not have the resources to gather and analyze information on costs and performance of specific companies. These investors often purchase a mutual fund that is composed of a portfolio of a cross section of firms selling shares in the market. By purchasing shares in a variety of firms, the investor hedges against the failure of any single company to generate positive earnings. Despite the lack of information, the Wall Street investor minimizes the risk of substantial loss while still capturing some of the benefits of a bull market.

Although higher education is also a bull market, the educational investor does not have access to the array of hedging strategies that are available to the Wall Street investor. It is not possible to construct an educational investment portfolio that contains a mix of alternatives—each carefully balanced to provide a high rate of return while minimizing risk. The closest that an educational investor comes to adopting a hedging strategy is by choosing to major in a broad liberal arts field of study. Many college counselors, college educators, and even some business leaders contend that this approach will help hedge against the "wrong" field-of-study choice. The proponents of this strategy believe that the labor market demands a broad set of skills that provides students with a high degree of flexibility to respond to changes in the demand for skills. Moreover, proponents of this view believe that choosing a major in one of the professional fields of study—such as health, technology, or business—results in a degree of specialization that inhibits the very flexibility that is in demand in today's economy.

Evidence of earnings of individuals who graduated in different major fields of study does not support this perspective. There is a large and persistent earnings advantage that accrues to college graduates who have degrees in professional fields. A recent study prepared by one of the authors reveals large differences in the earnings of college graduates by major field of study—after accounting for other variables known to influence earnings. Graduates with degrees in such fields as engineering, computer science, health, and business have large earnings advantages compared to liberal arts graduates. These advantages persist over the entire working lives of the graduates. The study also found that the average earnings advantage of graduates from these professional fields declines sharply if they work in a job that is unrelated to the major field of study.

These advantages of choosing a professional field of study designed to prepare college graduates for a career in a specific field compared to the "educational hedging" strategy of choosing a broad liberal arts major has led to a sharp change in the major-field composition of degrees awarded. Over the past 30 years, the share of undergraduate degrees awarded in professional fields such as business, health, engineering, and computer science has grown dramatically, and the share of degrees awarded in the traditional

liberal arts fields has declined. Earnings of graduates from these professionally oriented fields strongly suggest that the specific skills that the graduates acquire while in college contribute substantially to their post-graduation earnings premiums. These findings clearly illustrate that the educational investor is not in a position to capture the benefits of a bull education market by adopting a hedging strategy. Instead, the educational investor must make a series of all-or-nothing decisions.

Another all-or-nothing decision that an educational investor must make is college choice. As with the choice of a college major, college choice is not an irreversible decision. However, changing colleges or major fields imposes high costs on the educational investor. If students enroll in a college that isn't right for them, the cost can be high in several ways: lost time, loss of credits that don't transfer, and the psychological cost of matriculating at an institution that does not reflect their values or meet their educational, social, and psychological needs.

How should a potential enrollee select a college? Proponents of selecting a college by status believe that the status of the college signals to employers something about the skills and abilities that the graduates possess. Thus, an Ivy League degree in the humanities signals to employers that the individual with such a degree possesses stronger intellectual skills than the average college graduate. This is not because Ivy League colleges necessarily instill these traits into their graduates, but because Ivy League colleges screen out students who do not possess these characteristics. These schools accept only those students who are at the very top of the nation's high school classes. Knowing this, firms that desire to hire persons of high ability hire graduates from these colleges.

Research reveals that the earnings of students who graduate from elite colleges (many of which offer only a liberal arts education) are substantially higher than the earnings of graduates from the mainstream of American higher education. However, research that examined the underlying causes of these differences reveals that after taking account of the differences between the pre-enrollment literacy skills of students of elite colleges relative to those of mainstream college students, the earnings advantage of elite students is no greater than 1 to 2 percent per year. These findings suggest that the independent effect of enrolling in an elite college is quite small and that a large part of the positive outcomes of graduates of elite colleges is attributable to the preexisting ability of students who enroll at these institutions.

In other words, students with strong academic proficiencies have a high degree of labor market success regardless of where they attend college. Thus, the earnings advantage of graduates of elite institutions is much more closely associated with their selection of only those students with above-average academic ability. Because the labor market provides substantial earnings rewards for these abilities, the average pay of graduates from these colleges is also well above average within a given field of study.

The earnings premiums of college graduates come about through a combination of solid intellectual skills, development of specific professional skills desired by employers, and access to a job that utilizes the skills learned in school. In addition to choosing the appropriate major field of study, choosing a college that has a strong record of placing its graduates in good-quality jobs is an important factor in the college investment decision.

The Educational and Labor Market Experiences of College Graduates

Depending on the choice of major, the college investment decision for 3 out of 8 graduates does not end with the receipt of the bachelor's degree. College graduates engage in an extraordinarily wide array of activities after they complete their undergraduate education. Although many graduates immediately enter career fields that become their life's work, others seek more schooling, frequently in fields of study other than that of their undergraduate specialty. Still others devote their lives to endeavors outside the paid labor market. The people in this last group often decide to meet the challenges of family life on a full-time basis.

Graduate Study

People frequently pursue graduate education after earning an undergraduate degree. More than 1 in 3 persons who earn a bachelor's degree go on to earn an advanced degree. Table 8 reveals that about one-quarter of all college graduates earn a master's degree; about 6 percent earn a doctorate; and 7 percent earn a professional degree, most often in law or medicine.

Approximately 24 percent of men and 27 percent of women with a bachelor's degree go on to earn a master's degree. Large gender gaps appear in the likelihood of earning a degree at the doctoral and professional levels. Men are more than twice as likely as women to earn a doctorate and almost three times as likely to earn a professional degree.

Table 8
Percentage of Bachelor's Degree Recipients Who Earned an Advanced Degree, by Type of Advanced Degree, by Gender

Gender	Percentage of Bachelor's Degree Holders with an Advanced Degree	TYPE OF ADVANCED DEGREE		
		Master's	Doctoral	Professional
Total	37.7%	25.2%	5.8%	6.7%
Men	38.5%	23.9%	5.3%	9.3%
Women	32.6%	26.9%	2.2%	3.5%

Source: National Science Foundation, National Survey of College Graduates, Public Use Micro-Data File, 1993. Tabulations produced by the authors.

Table 9 presents the proportion of bachelor's degree recipients in various major fields of study who eventually earn an advanced degree. The likelihood of earning a graduate degree is closely related to the undergraduate major field of study. For example, bachelor's degree holders who major in biological sciences are very likely to earn an advanced degree. Only 44 percent of the graduates in this field end their schooling at the bachelor's degree level. The remaining 56 percent go on to earn some type of advanced degree, often a professional degree in the field of medicine.

Table 9
Percentage Distribution of All College Graduates (with a Bachelor's Degree or More) Within Each Broad Undergraduate Major Field of Study, by Highest Degree Earned

Broad Undergraduate Major Field of Study	Total (All College Graduates)	Bachelor's	Master's	Doctoral	Professional
Agricultural sciences	100%	70.2%	17.8%	6.3%	5.7%
Biological sciences	100%	43.9%	26.7%	7.5%	21.9%
Business	100%	80.9%	15.2%	0.7%	3.2%
Computer science	100%	83.2%	15.4%	0.9%	0.5%
Education	100%	57.3%	39.7%	1.8%	1.2%
Engineering	100%	64.0%	30.3%	3.8%	1.9%
Health professions	100%	64.9%	21.2%	2.0%	11.9%
Mathematics	100%	58.1%	32.5%	7.1%	2.3%
Physical sciences	100%	38.9%	35.1%	16.2%	9.8%
Social sciences	100%	55.5%	31.1%	3.9%	9.5%
Humanities	100%	62.8%	27.8%	3.3%	6.1%

Source: National Science Foundation, National Survey of College Graduates, Public Use Micro-Data File, 1993. Tabulations produced by the authors.

Those who earn an undergraduate degree in one of the physical sciences, such as chemistry or physics, are even more likely to earn an advanced degree, although they more frequently earn a master's degree than a professional degree. In contrast, students who complete an undergraduate degree in business-related fields are much less likely to earn a graduate degree. Fewer than 1 out of 5 business majors eventually earn a graduate degree. Most of the graduates in these majors head directly into the labor market after graduation. Similarly, computer science majors are much less likely to earn a graduate degree. Strong labor demand and high wages make graduate school less attractive to majors from these fields.

In what fields of study are these advanced degrees earned? A look at the distribution of advanced degrees by major field of study reveals that graduate study among baccalaureate degree holders is concentrated in certain fields of study. Most often, persons who earn a master's degree

choose education as their major field of study. One-third of all master's degree holders in the country earn their degree in the education field (see Table 10). The choice of major at the advanced degree level varies greatly by gender. Women are twice as likely as men to earn a master's degree in education. Forty-four percent of all women with a master's degree majored in education, compared to 21 percent of male master's degree holders.

About one-fifth of all master's degree holders earn their degree in a business-related field; again, the gender differences are quite large. Nearly 28 percent of all master's degrees earned by men are in business, while less than 10 percent of women who earn a master's degree study business. Together, social sciences and humanities account for about one-quarter of all master's degrees earned in the country. About the same proportion of men and women earned their master's degrees in these two fields.

Table 10
Distribution of Master's Degrees Received, by Broad Major Field of Study, by Gender

Broad Major Field of Study	(A) All	(B) Men	(C) Women	(D) Ratio of Male Major Concentration and Female Major Concentration (B) / (C)
Total	100%	100%	100%	—
Agricultural sciences	0.5%	0.6%	0.3%	2.0
Biological sciences	2.2%	2.3%	2.1%	1.1
Business	19.1%	27.9%	9.8%	2.8
Computer science	2.0%	2.6%	1.3%	2.0
Education	32.3%	21.3%	43.9%	0.5
Engineering	6.4%	11.5%	1.0%	11.5
Health professions	5.4%	2.4%	8.5%	0.3
Mathematics	1.5%	1.9%	1.1%	1.7

(continued)

Table 10 (continued)
Distribution of Master's Degrees Received, by Broad Major Field of Study, by Gender

Broad Major Field of Study	(A) All	(B) Men	(C) Women	(D) Ratio of Male Major Concentration and Female Major Concentration (B) / (C)
Physical sciences	1.8%	2.7%	0.8%	3.4
Social sciences	15.3%	14.1%	16.6%	0.8
Humanities	10.0%	10.6%	9.4%	1.1
Other	3.5%	2.1%	5.2%	0.4

Source: National Science Foundation, National Survey of College Graduates, Public Use Micro-Data File, 1993. Tabulations produced by the authors.

The choice of major field of study among graduates with a doctorate degree differs sharply from the choice of major of individuals with a master's degree. At the doctoral level, the largest share of degrees is earned in the social sciences and humanities fields. More than one-third of all doctoral degrees held in the United States are earned in these two specialties (see Table 11). Women are more likely than men to earn their doctorates in social sciences, and both gender groups are roughly equally likely to earn their doctorate degree in the humanities fields. About 16 percent of all doctorates in the nation are in the education fields. The gender gap persists at the doctoral level, with women being twice as likely as men to hold degrees in this field.

Mathematics and the physical sciences account for 15 percent of doctoral degrees in the nation. In these specialties, men are twice as likely to earn degrees as women. Men who receive doctoral degrees are more than six times as likely as women to receive their degrees in engineering (12 percent of men versus 2 percent of women). Although business is the most common degree at the bachelor's degree level, few doctoral degrees are awarded in this field.

Table 11
Distribution of Doctoral Degrees Received, by Broad Major Field, by Gender

Broad Major Field of Study	(A) All	(B) Men	(C) Women	(D) Ratio of Male Major Concentration and Female Major Concentration (B) / (C)
Total	100%	100%	100%	—
Agricultural sciences	1.4%	1.6%	0.9%	1.8
Biological sciences	11.7%	11.5%	12.4%	0.9

Broad Major Field of Study	(A) All	(B) Men	(C) Women	(D) Ratio of Male Major Concentration and Female Major Concentration (B) / (C)
Business	3.1%	3.5%	1.7%	2.1
Computer science	1.2%	1.4%	0.7%	2.0
Education	15.5%	12.2%	24.8%	0.5
Engineering	9.3%	11.9%	1.9%	6.3
Health professions	5.9%	5.9%	5.9%	1.0
Mathematics	2.8%	3.4%	1.2%	2.8
Physical sciences	12.7%	15.0%	6.2%	2.4
Social sciences	20.5%	18.4%	26.4%	0.7
Humanities	14.8%	14.6%	15.3%	1.0
Other	1.1%	0.6%	2.6%	0.2

Source: National Science Foundation, National Survey of College Graduates, Public Use Micro-Data File, 1993. Tabulations produced by the authors.

Detailed information about the likelihood of completing a graduate degree and about the field in which the degree is earned is provided for 60 major fields of study discussed in chapters 4 through 63 of this book.

Labor Market Participation of College Graduates

Surveys of freshman classes at American colleges and universities consistently reveal that improved career opportunities and job access are the most important reasons for earning a bachelor's degree. For most college graduates, the economic and social rewards of a college degree are found in their work.

As noted previously, about 38 percent of all college graduates go on to earn an advanced degree of some type, but the remaining 62 percent conclude their formal schooling at the bachelor's degree level. For the graduates in the latter group, the transition into the career labor market begins at the conclusion of their undergraduate education.

Economists have developed a number of key measures of labor force activity in order to assess and compare labor force behavior of different groups. Household surveys similar to the National Survey of College Graduates are administered to gather information on the labor market activity of the working-age population, defined as individuals who are 16 years or older. Each working-age individual is assigned to one of the following three mutually exclusive labor force categories:

▶ **Employed:** persons who worked for 1 or more hours for pay or profit during the survey reference week or who worked 20 or more hours in an unpaid position in a family business

▶ **Unemployed:** persons who were jobless during the survey reference week but who had actively sought a job within the prior four weeks and were immediately available to take a position

▶ **Out of the labor force:** all persons not classified as either employed or unemployed within the scope of the survey

The first measure that economists often use to examine labor market activity is the labor force participation rate. This measure is calculated by dividing the number of persons classified as active members of the labor force (the sum of employed and unemployed persons) by the total working-age population (16 years of age and older). The labor force participation rate is thus a measure of the proportion of any group of working-age persons who are active in the labor market at a point in time.

The labor force participation rates of 16- to 64-year-old individuals classified by their highest level of education are presented in Figure 2. Findings reveal that college graduates are much more likely to participate in the job market than persons with fewer years of schooling. The participation rate is 77 percent for those with a high school diploma but no postsecondary schooling and 55 percent among adults who have not completed high school.

FIGURE 2

Labor Force Participation Rates Among Persons 16 to 64 Years Old, by Educational Attainment, March 2003

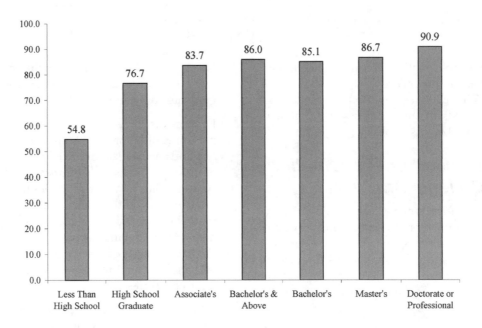

Source: U.S. Bureau of the Census, Current Population Surveys Public Use Data Files, March Supplement, 2003. Tabulations produced by the authors.

In contrast, college graduates have an overall labor force participation rate of nearly 86 percent, a level that is 9 percentage points higher than the level among high school graduates with no postsecondary schooling. Moreover, the labor force participation rates among college graduates are highest for those with advanced degrees. The participation rate for bachelor's degree holders is about 85 percent, which means that 85 out of 100 persons with only a bachelor's degree are active participants in the labor force. At the master's degree level, the participation rate is about 87 percent, while 91 percent of persons with a doctorate or a professional degree participate in the job market.

The probability that a college graduate will actively participate in the labor market is influenced by a number of key factors, including expected salary, gender, marital status, presence of children in the household, and level of educational attainment. The major field of study also has some influence over the likelihood of labor market participation, in part because of the relationship of major fields to the expected level of annual salary.

The data provided in Table 12 reveals that the participation rates of persons vary systematically by major field of study as well as by the highest degree earned. For example, at the bachelor's degree level, only about 76 percent of all persons who earned a degree in education are actively engaged in the labor market. In contrast, the participation rate of persons with a bachelor's degree in computer science is 94 percent, which means that only 6 out of 100 persons with a degree in the latter field are not actively participating in the labor market, compared to one-quarter of persons with a bachelor's degree in education.

Table 12
Labor Force Participation Rates (as percentages), by Major Field of Study and Educational Attainment

Broad Major Field of Study	Bachelor's	Master's	Doctoral or Professional
Agricultural sciences	86.0%	84.1%	86.2%
Biological sciences	82.6%	84.3%	91.0%
Business	87.2%	90.1%	89.9%
Computer science	94.2%	92.0%	93.0%
Education	75.9%	82.1%	85.3%
Engineering	83.2%	87.7%	93.1%
Health professions	84.0%	87.1%	88.5%
Mathematics	84.0%	84.1%	91.9%
Physical sciences	77.4%	83.3%	89.8%
Social sciences	84.1%	85.5%	89.9%
Humanities	77.5%	83.3%	90.3%

Source: National Science Foundation, National Survey of College Graduates, Public Use Micro-Data File, 1993. Tabulations produced by the authors.

Part of this low labor force participation rate may be because education majors are more likely to be women who may withdraw from the labor market for family reasons. Additionally, education majors have among the lowest annual salaries of all college graduates, while computer science majors work in considerably higher-paying jobs. These differences in salary expectations of graduates from the two fields also underlie the differences in their labor force participation. The choice of major field of study is closely associated with the decision to work at any given point in time. High rates of participation in the labor force, intensive employment, and the resultant accumulation of work experience significantly improve the long-term earnings prospects of college graduates.

The Employment Experiences of College Graduates

Individuals who participate in the labor market do so in order to obtain employment. Those who participate in the labor market and fail to obtain employment are considered to be unemployed. In the case of college graduates, a substantial majority of those who participate in the labor market secure employment. In 2003, more than 96 out of 100 labor force participants with a bachelor's degree were employed–the unemployment rate among this group was only 3.5 percent. The unemployment rate of master's degree holders was only 2.7 percent, while individuals with a professional or doctorate degree had an unemployment rate of only 1.5 percent. This data clearly indicates that most college graduates actively participate in the labor market and are almost always successful in securing employment.

In this section, we will examine various attributes of the jobs in which college graduates are employed. These attributes shed light on the quality of jobs held by employed college graduates across different major fields of study. The job attributes that we will examine in this section include the full-time versus part-time status of the job, the relationship of the job to undergraduate major field, and the occupation in which the graduate is employed.

The vast majority of college graduates work in full-time positions. Nearly 9 out of 10 college graduates hold full-time jobs, with only about 12 percent of college graduates working in part-time jobs. Part-time employment status varies considerably by gender. Among men, only about 6 percent hold part-time jobs, while about 20 percent of women with a college degree work in part-time positions. Persons employed in part-time positions either choose to work part-time because they prefer part-time work or are forced to work part-time because they could not obtain full-time employment. Most women who work part-time do so voluntarily for the flexibility of part-time schedules. This flexibility helps them meet other demands in their family lives. Only about 1 in 7 women holding part-time jobs do so because they cannot get access to full-time positions.

The likelihood of a woman with a college degree holding a part-time position varies considerably by major field of study. For example, fewer than 1 in 10 women with a degree in computer science work in part-time jobs (see Figure 3). In contrast, more than one-quarter of women with a degree in the health professions work in part-time jobs. Given the large share of women employed in the health fields, businesses such as hospitals and other employers of health professionals often will organize work in order to accommodate the work desires of women who possess the skills they need. In contrast, in fields such as computer science, engineering, and business, where a large fraction of all graduates are men, employers are much more likely to organize work schedules on a full-time basis.

FIGURE 3

Percentage of Employed Women Working in Part-Time Positions, by Major Field of Study

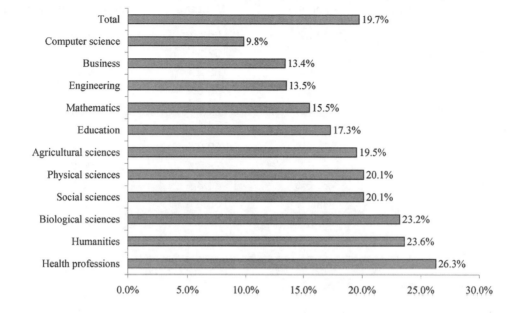

Source: National Science Foundation, National Survey of College Graduates, Public Use Micro-Data File, 1993.
Tabulations produced by the authors.

A key factor influencing the earnings experience of college graduates is the relationship between their major fields and their jobs. Graduates employed in jobs that are closely related to their major generally earn much higher annual salaries than graduates employed in jobs that are unrelated to their major. Those working in jobs that are somewhat related to their major generally have salaries that are lower than those employed in jobs closely related to the major but higher than the salaries of those working in jobs unrelated to their undergraduate field of study.

The mean annual earnings of all bachelor's degree holders employed full-time in jobs that were related to their undergraduate major field of study are $56,100 (in 2002 dollars), or 16 percent higher than the $48,400 mean annual earnings of their counterparts employed in jobs unrelated to their major. Access to jobs that utilize the skills learned in school has a strong positive impact on the earnings experience of college graduates, particularly among graduates who major in one of the professional fields of study.

One-quarter of all employed college graduates with a bachelor's degree work in a job that is not related to their undergraduate major. The likelihood of college graduates working in a job closely related to their major field of study varies sharply depending upon their major and highest degree level earned. According to data presented in Table 13, at the bachelor's degree level, 80 percent of all health sciences majors work in jobs that are closely related to their major. Similarly, three-quarters of all computer science majors do. In contrast, social science majors are much less likely to work in jobs that are closely related to their major (27 percent), as are mathematics majors with a bachelor's degree (30 percent).

Table 13
Percentage of Respondents Who Said Their Current Job Is Closely Related to Their Major

Broad Major Field of Study	Bachelor's	Master's	Doctoral or Professional
Total	44.3%	66.4%	86.0%
Agricultural sciences	39.1%	57.5%	75.0%
Biological sciences	35.6%	62.2%	85.6%
Business	43.4%	55.6%	74.5%
Computer science	73.3%	75.2%	82.6%
Education	55.9%	75.1%	77.9%
Engineering	51.9%	60.0%	72.0%
Health sciences	80.3%	78.7%	95.3%
Mathematics	29.8%	51.3%	76.9%
Physical sciences	38.1%	55.2%	73.3%
Social sciences	27.3%	57.5%	81.0%
Humanities	35.7%	70.3%	84.5%

Source: National Science Foundation, National Survey of College Graduates, Public Use Micro-Data File, 1993. Tabulations produced by the authors.

At the advanced degree level, the likelihood of graduates finding work in a job closely related to their major increases substantially. Increased specialization that accompanies advanced studies appears to increase the likelihood of finding major-field-related employment. Even in the social sciences and in mathematics, those with master's degrees, doctoral degrees, and professional degrees are much more likely to be working in a job related to their major than those with only an undergraduate degree.

College graduates find work in a wide variety of occupational areas. The annual earnings in certain occupational areas–including professional, managerial, and high-level sales occupations–are substantially above the average earnings for all occupations. Access to jobs in these key occupational clusters is the pathway through which many college graduates obtain their high annual earnings.

The data provided in Table 14 reveals that 15 percent of those with a bachelor's degree work in top- and mid-level executive and managerial jobs; 14 percent are employed in management-related positions, such as accountants and human resource professionals; and about 14 percent are employed in sales and marketing positions. These three occupational areas account for nearly 45 percent of all employment for those with only a bachelor's degree. An additional 11 percent of all bachelor's degree holders are employed in the teaching profession.

Table 14

Percentage Distribution of Employed College Graduates, by Major Occupational Category of Their Job (All Graduates and Graduates in Each Degree Category)

	Bachelor's	Master's	Doctoral	Professional	All Graduates
College Labor Market Occupations					
Executives, managers	15.0%	19.6%	15.0%	18.0%	15.4%
Management-related	14.3%	9.4%	2.4%	9.6%	11.5%
Sales and marketing	13.8%	5.6%	1.4%	2.5%	10.2%
Teachers	11.0%	24.1%	2.5%	18.1%	13.3%
Engineers	7.2%	7.0%	6.8%	1.1%	6.6%
Health occupations	6.3%	4.4%	4.1%	14.2%	8.6%
Computer occupations	5.1%	3.7%	2.0%	1.9%	4.2%
Artists, entertainers, writers	2.8%	1.8%	0.8%	4.6%	2.3%
Social workers	1.5%	2.8%	0.4%	0.0%	1.7%
Protective services	1.4%	0.4%	0.1%	1.7%	1.0%
Biological/life scientists	0.9%	1.0%	9.0%	0.8%	1.2%
Engineering technologists	0.9%	0.3%	0.2%	2.3%	0.7%
Physical scientists	0.8%	1.0%	6.4%	0.8%	1.0%
Architects	0.7%	0.5%	0.1%	9.0%	0.6%
Clergy/religious workers	0.6%	2.6%	2.6%	2.3%	1.2%
Postsecondary teachers	0.0%	3.7%	31.7%	1.0%	2.8%
Social scientists	0.6%	4.2%	8.3%	1.3%	1.8%
Non-academic teachers	0.4%	0.4%	0.2%	0.2%	0.4%
Librarians	0.3%	1.7%	0.5%	0.0%	0.6%
Lawyers	0.2%	0.5%	2.4%	0.3%	3.4%
Mathematical scientists	0.2%	0.4%	1.0%	0.0%	0.3%
Other occupations	3.2%	1.7%	1.1%	4.7%	2.5%
Non-College Labor Market Occupations	12.1%	3.3%	0.9%	5.6%	8.5%
Administrative support	5.5%	1.3%	0.2%	3.4%	3.8%
Farmers, fishermen	0.7%	0.2%	0.1%	0.2%	0.5%
Service occupations	2.1%	0.7%	0.3%	0.7%	1.5%
Blue-collar occupations	3.8%	1.1%	0.3%	1.3%	2.7%
Total	100%	100%	100%	100%	100%

Source: National Science Foundation, National Survey of College Graduates, Public Use Micro-Data File, 1993. Tabulations produced by the authors.

Most of the occupations listed in Table 14 constitute what economists term the *college labor market,* which consists of professional, technical, managerial, and high-level sales jobs that employ a large share of college graduates. However, not all persons with a bachelor's degree work in the college labor market. Administrative support, farmers, fishermen, service occupations, and blue-collar occupations are all excluded from the definition of the college labor market because people in these positions often have less than a four-year college degree. About 12 percent of all bachelor's degree holders who work in jobs outside the college labor market have much lower annual salaries than those graduates who work in the college labor market sector of the economy, even when the job is not related to their major.

A key element of success for college graduates is access to jobs in the college labor market. Graduates unable to gain access to work that utilizes their academic skills find themselves employed in occupations outside of the college labor market. These graduates are working for employers who are unwilling to pay a premium to acquire workers who possess skills that will not be utilized on the job. A college education has an impact on earnings only when the academic and professional skills that a college graduate possesses are actually utilized on the job. Failure to find a job that uses at least some of these skills translates into less advantageous long-term employment and earnings experiences, despite earning a college diploma.

College graduates are employed in a variety of industrial settings that also influence the nature of their work and the level of their earnings. While we commonly think of the American economy as dominated by employment in private, for-profit firms, less than one-half of college graduates with a bachelor's degree actually work as employees of for-profit business organizations. Large shares of college graduates work for educational organizations, government agencies, and nonprofit foundations. While 45 percent of all graduates are employed by for-profit businesses, one-quarter work in education; 11 percent work for federal, state, or local governments; and 6 percent are employed in the nonprofit sector.

FIGURE 4

Distribution of Employed College Graduates with a Bachelor's Degree, by Sector of Employment

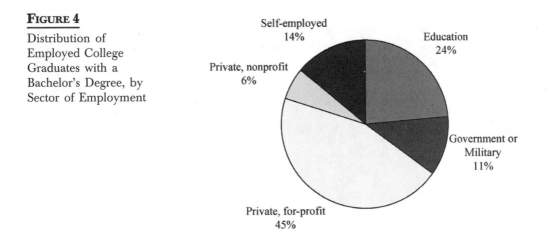

Source: National Science Foundation, National Survey of College Graduates, Public Use Micro-Data File, 1993. Tabulations produced by the authors.

Interestingly, college graduates as a group are quite entrepreneurial in nature. Approximately 1 in 7 college graduates with a bachelor's degree are self-employed; either they own and operate a business or they provide consulting services. The earnings of college graduates are substantially influenced by the industry sector in which they work. Even within the same major field of study, graduates working in private, for-profit businesses have salaries that are substantially higher than those of their counterparts who work in nonprofit organizations or educational institutions.

As may be expected, access to employment in various sectors of the economy varies sharply by major field of study. For example, private, for-profit firms employ more than 75 percent of computer science majors. In contrast, only 23 percent of those with a degree in education work in the for-profit sector of the economy. Social science majors are twice as likely as graduates with a degree in business to hold a job in a government agency.

The preceding data and analyses clearly indicate that the choice of undergraduate major does, in fact, have an important influence on career pathways of college graduates. The likelihood of completing a graduate degree, the level of advanced degree earned, and the major field in which the degree is earned are all conditional on the choice of undergraduate major field of study. The employment experience of graduates with respect to occupation and sector of employment is influenced by the major field, as is the probability of participating in the labor force. All of these factors combine to influence the long-term employment and earnings experience of college graduates. The next section presents an examination of earnings outcomes of college graduates.

The Earnings of College Graduates

A college degree provides a strong earnings advantage to those willing to make the sacrifices needed to earn it. As we have already observed, the average employed young person with a college degree earns two-thirds more per year than his or her counterpart with a high school diploma. The earnings premium of individuals with a college degree persists over their working lifetime. The lifetime earnings of an individual with a bachelor's degree are twice those of individuals with just a high school diploma ($1.9 million versus $941,000).

Furthermore, the earnings advantage of college education continues beyond the bachelor's degree. In 2002, the average annual salary of bachelor's degree holders working in full-time and year-round jobs was $60,100, while their counterparts whose highest degree was a master's degree earned $70,500 per year (see Figure 5). The earnings advantage from obtaining a doctorate or a professional degree is also quite high. Those with a doctoral degree who work full-time and year-round have mean annual salaries of $103,600, while their counterparts who possess a professional degree (usually in law or a medical specialty) earn $128,900 per year. These findings indicate that as individuals earn additional advanced degrees, they are, on average, rewarded with higher salaries.

The choice of undergraduate major field of study has an extraordinarily powerful influence on the earnings of college graduates. The annual salaries of full-time employed college graduates with a baccalaureate degree vary widely by their undergraduate major field of study. A ranking of the annual salaries of full-time employed bachelor's degree recipients for 60 major fields of study is provided in Table 15. These major fields of study are described in detail in the remaining chapters (4 through 63) of this book.

FIGURE 5

Mean Annual Earnings of Full-Time and Year-Round Employed College Graduates in 2002, by Highest Degree Earned

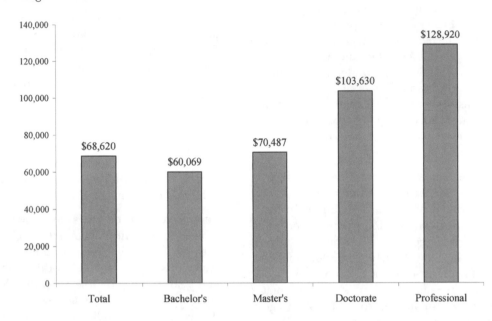

Source: U.S. Bureau of the Census, Current Population Surveys Public Use Data Files, March Supplement, 2003. Tabulations produced by the authors.

At the very top of the ranking are bachelor's degree holders with degrees in technical fields. These fields often require strong scientific and mathematical proficiencies. For example, the highest-paying field of study at the undergraduate level is chemical engineering, followed by a number of engineering fields and physics. Graduates in these majors earn between $12,000 to $21,000–or 22 percent to 40 percent–more per year than all full-time employed bachelor's degree graduates. The only social science or humanities field to make the top ten is economics, and even in this major, strong mathematics proficiencies play a key role in successfully completing an undergraduate program. Economics graduates earn nearly $10,000, or 18 percent, more per year than graduates who major in English.

At the very bottom of the earnings distribution among persons with a bachelor's degree are individuals with undergraduate degrees in the humanities and in education. Persons with degrees in these fields earn between 20 percent and 30 percent less per year than all full-time employed bachelor's degree graduates.

Table 15
Annual Earnings of Full-Time Employed College Graduates with Only a Bachelor's Degree, by Major Field of Study

	Mean Annual Earnings	Absolute Difference Relative to All	Percentage Difference Relative to All
All	$54,171	——	——
Chemical engineering	$75,579	$21,408	40%
Aerospace, aeronautical, and astronautical engineering	$73,605	$19,434	36%
Computer systems engineering	$70,084	$15,913	29%
Physics and astronomy	$69,612	$15,441	29%
Electrical and electronics engineering	$68,977	$14,806	27%
Mechanical engineering	$68,806	$14,635	27%
Industrial engineering	$68,411	$14,240	26%
Civil engineering	$66,126	$11,955	22%
Economics	$64,015	$9,844	18%
Pharmacy	$63,967	$9,796	18%
Accounting	$63,486	$9,315	17%
General mathematics	$63,376	$9,205	17%
Medical preparatory programs	$62,983	$8,812	16%
Mechanical engineering technology	$62,242	$8,071	15%
Financial management	$61,772	$7,601	14%
Chemistry	$61,619	$7,448	14%
Applied mathematics	$60,459	$6,288	12%
Computer science	$58,848	$4,677	9%
General business	$58,648	$4,477	8%
Geology and geophysics	$58,393	$4,222	8%
Electrical and electronics engineering technology	$57,927	$3,756	7%
Industrial production technology	$57,672	$3,501	6%
Marketing	$57,290	$3,119	6%
Political science	$56,971	$2,800	5%

(continued)

Table 15 (continued)
Annual Earnings of Full-Time Employed College Graduates
with Only a Bachelor's Degree, by Major Field of Study

	Mean Annual Earnings	Absolute Difference Relative to All	Percentage Difference Relative to All
Physical therapy	$56,373	$2,202	4%
Architecture and environmental design	$56,096	$1,925	4%
Legal studies and pre-law	$54,234	$63	0%
Public administration	$54,055	−$116	0%
Journalism	$52,500	−$1,671	−3%
Liberal arts/general studies	$52,203	−$1,968	−4%
Data and information processing	$52,146	−$2,025	−4%
History	$51,483	−$2,688	−5%
Biology and life sciences	$51,041	−$3,130	−6%
Nursing	$50,936	−$3,235	−6%
Plant food sciences	$50,840	−$3,331	−6%
Geography	$50,428	−$3,743	−7%
Psychology	$49,964	−$4,207	−8%
Microbiology and biochemistry	$49,524	−$4,647	−9%
Communications	$48,907	−$5,264	−10%
English	$48,890	−$5,281	−10%
Forestry and environmental sciences	$48,456	−$5,715	−11%
Sociology	$47,810	−$6,361	−12%
Health and medical technology	$47,667	−$6,504	−12%
Foreign languages and literature	$46,502	−$7,669	−14%
Animal food sciences	$46,402	−$7,769	−14%
Criminal justice and criminology	$46,104	−$8,067	−15%
Anthropology and archaeology	$45,775	−$8,396	−15%
Physical education and coaching	$45,073	−$9,098	−17%
Secondary teacher education	$44,813	−$9,358	−17%
Mathematics and science teacher education	$44,712	−$9,459	−17%
Audiology and speech pathology	$43,793	−$10,378	−19%

	Mean Annual Earnings	Absolute Difference Relative to All	Percentage Difference Relative to All
Visual arts	$43,559	−$10,612	−20%
Philosophy	$42,865	−$11,306	−21%
Parks, recreation, leisure, and fitness studies	$42,432	−$11,739	−22%
Dramatic arts	$41,580	−$12,591	−23%
Music and dance	$41,265	−$12,906	−24%
Home economics: dietetics, food, and nutrition	$38,835	−$15,336	−28%
Elementary teacher education	$38,746	−$15,425	−28%
Special education	$38,333	−$15,838	−29%
Social work	$37,836	−$16,335	−30%

Source: National Science Foundation, National Survey of College Graduates, Public Use Micro-Data File, 1993. Tabulations produced by the authors.

Clearly, the choice of undergraduate major has a powerful impact on the earnings and, ultimately, the living standards of college graduates. Analysis in this chapter has also revealed a strong relationship between the college major field of study and several labor market outcomes, including labor force participation, access to employment in certain high-level occupations, access to full-time jobs, and access to jobs that are related to undergraduate classroom training. The undergraduate major field of study also is closely associated with postgraduate education. Graduates from certain majors, such as computer science and business, are less likely to pursue postgraduate studies and more likely to enter the labor market after earning a baccalaureate degree. In contrast, graduates who major in physical sciences or mathematics are more likely to pursue postgraduate studies.

These close associations of the undergraduate major field of study with several important labor market and educational outcomes make a compelling case for a careful selection of college major by prospective college students. The idea that the choice of major field of study has little influence on the postgraduate outcomes of college graduates is *wrong*. The choice of major strongly influences the course that graduates will follow in their transition to the adult career labor market. The skills and abilities they acquire in college have lasting and even lifetime influences on their labor market outcomes, their status in the community, their happiness on the job, and their standard of living.

We do not believe that the choice of undergraduate major should be based solely or even primarily on the basis of the earnings prospect in a given field. However, because enrolling in a college or university is a costly investment decision, investors need to be well informed about important aspects of the investment alternatives available to them. The remainder of this book contains accurate, up-to-date, and detailed information on numerous aspects of 60 specific undergraduate fields of study that cover 155 study areas and careers. It is our hope that prospective college students using this manual will become better informed about what they want out of college and about the opportunities available to them after graduation.

PART 2

Behavioral and Medical Sciences

CHAPTER 4

Audiology and Speech Pathology

Speech pathology, which is a larger field than audiology, involves the assessment, treatment, and prevention of speech, language, cognitive communication, voice, swallowing, and fluency disorders.

Speech-language pathologists work with people who cannot make speech sounds, or cannot make them clearly; those with speech rhythm and fluency problems, such as stuttering; those with voice quality problems, such as inappropriate pitch or harsh voice; those with problems understanding and producing language; and those with cognitive communication impairments, such as attention, memory, and problem solving disorders. They may also work with people who have oral motor problems causing eating and swallowing difficulties.

Speech and language problems can result from hearing loss, brain injury or deterioration, cerebral palsy, stroke, cleft palate, voice pathology, mental retardation, or emotional problems. Problems can be congenital, developmental, or acquired. Speech-language pathologists use written and oral tests, as well as special instruments, to diagnose the nature and extent of impairment and to record and analyze speech, language, and swallowing irregularities. Speech-language pathologists develop an individualized plan of care tailored to each patient's needs. For individuals with little or no speech capability, speech-language pathologists select augmentative alternative communication methods, including automated devices and sign language, and teach their use. They teach these individuals how to make sounds, improve their voices, or increase their language skills to communicate more effectively. Speech-language pathologists help patients develop, or recover, reliable communication skills so that patients can fulfill their educational, vocational, and social roles.

Audiology involves the provision of direct clinical services to individuals with hearing or balance disorders. Audiologists use audiometers and other testing devices to measure the loudness at which a person begins to hear sounds, the ability to distinguish between sounds, and the nature and extent of hearing loss. They may recommend, fit, and dispense hearing aids, altering devices, and large-area amplification systems.

The educational requirement of both fields in most states is at the post-baccalaureate level. Entry into professional positions usually requires a master's degree. Speech pathology courses cover anatomy and physiology of the body areas involved in speech, language, and hearing; the development of normal speech, language, and hearing; the nature of speech and hearing disorders; acoustics; psychological aspects of communication; and evaluative methods and instrumentation. Audiology courses include anatomy; physiology; basic science; mathematics; physics; genetics; normal and abnormal communications development; auditory, balance, and neural-systems assessment and treatment; audiological rehabilitation; and ethics.

Speech-language pathologists generally possess social, language, teaching, leadership, and scientific abilities. Specifically, they must deal with people who are under stress. They need clinical skills to assess and diagnose problems and to select and carry out appropriate treatment interventions. They must master the scientific knowledge germane to this medical specialty. Using their judgment, they must make decisions. They also must have interpersonal skills to counsel parents and teachers whom they assist in their children's learning process. While both majors are classified as medical services occupations, audiologists' scientific orientation is greater, and the equipment they use requires more technological skills.

The speech pathologists' interests parallel closely the abilities above: They enjoy working therapeutically with people, often children; like to study the language and literary field; and are scientifically inclined. Audiologists' scientific and technical interests predominate, whereas the social orientation is foremost with speech pathologists.

Speech-language pathologists enjoy the satisfaction of helping people learn and adjust to problems often closely tied with an individual's self-concept. There is considerable variety and need for adaptation in this work because not everyone responds with equal effectiveness to typical treatments. With an increasing number of clients coming from diverse cultures and languages, even more creativity is required. The demanding curriculum satisfies a desire to work with one's mind and attain a sense of high achievement. Because audiologists specialize in hearing issues, including searching for reasons for the disorder, they often have a narrower focus in dealing with a person and the intellectual area of concentration.

What comes across foremost in these professionals is their respect and concern for their clients. From these relationships, they develop excellent insights, enabling them to optimally use their scientific knowledge to devise effective therapeutic interventions. They are imaginative people. They will persevere in a conscientious way in their work.

Where Do Audiology and Speech Pathology Majors Work?

At the bachelor's degree level, the majority of audiology and speech pathology majors work in the education sector of the economy, most often as special education teachers at the elementary and secondary school level and as therapy assistants and less frequently as therapists. Most persons employed as speech-language therapists or audiologists hold a master's degree in the specialty. About 3 in 10 graduates with a bachelor's degree in the field work in wage and salary positions in private-sector firms. An additional 9 percent are self-employed in their own business or provide consulting services on a self-employed basis. Few graduates of speech therapy or audiology programs work in government organizations or nonprofit charities or research foundations.

FIGURE 1

Percentage Distribution of Employed Persons with Only a Bachelor's Degree in Audiology and Speech Pathology, by Major Sector of Economic Activity

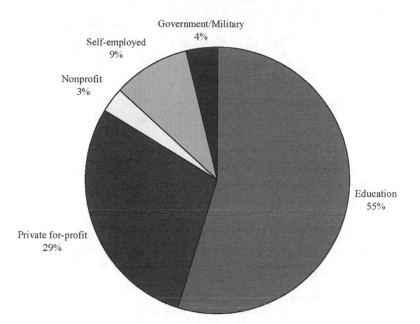

Government/Military
4%

Self-employed
9%

Nonprofit
3%

Education
55%

Private for-profit
29%

Occupations

At the bachelor's degree level, jobs that are closely related to the major field of study are relatively difficult to find. Most of the persons with only a bachelor's degree in the field work in jobs that are not closely related to the major. Those who do work in major-related positions include special education teachers and health professionals. Together, these two occupational areas employ about 43 percent of all majors at the bachelor's degree level.

Other occupations in which a substantial number of audiology and speech pathology majors have only a bachelor's degree include selected jobs in insurance, securities, and real estate sales; elementary school teachers; and some service occupations. Employment in many of these jobs is not closely connected to the undergraduate major. Those employed outside the field most often say better pay and promotion opportunities in other fields and a change in career interests were the primary reasons for employment outside the field.

Table 1

Top 10 Occupations That Employ Persons with Only a
Bachelor's Degree in Audiology and Speech Pathology

| | PERCENT OF EMPLOYED | | |
Top 10 Occupations	All	Men	Women
Special education teachers, primary and secondary	27.1	20.9	28.0
Registered nurses, pharmacists, therapists, physician assistants	16.7	25.1	15.5

(continued)

Table 1 (continued)

Top 10 Occupations That Employ Persons with Only a
Bachelor's Degree in Audiology and Speech Pathology

Top 10 Occupations	PERCENT OF EMPLOYED		
	All	Men	Women
Other service occupations, except health	8.1	0.0	9.3
Insurance, securities, real estate, business services	6.6	20.9	4.5
Elementary school teachers	5.5	0.0	6.3
Other marketing and sales occupations	5.4	0.0	6.2
Top- and mid-level managers, executives, administrators	3.7	0.0	4.3
Other administrative (e.g., records clerks, telephone operators)	3.1	0.0	3.5
Other management-related occupations	2.6	10.4	1.5
Food preparation and service occupations	2.6	0.0	3.0

Activities on the Job

▶ Teaching is the predominant work activity of persons with an undergraduate degree in audiology and speech pathology. The delivery of audiology and speech therapy services is also an important activity undertaken by graduates in this field.

▶ Most persons employed in this field also are involved in various accounting and record-keeping activities. Management and supervisory duties are also undertaken by graduates in this field.

Salaries

Audiology and speech pathology majors have annual salaries that are well below the average of all college graduates at the bachelor's degree level. Majors in this field who work in full-time jobs are paid an annual rate of $43,800, a salary that is about 25 percent below the earnings of the average college graduate with only a bachelor's degree. Salaries for persons under the age of 30 with a bachelor's degree in this field average just under $29,100 per year. Salaries increase over time as individuals accumulate more work experience and become more productive on the job. Between the ages of 45 and 49, persons with a bachelor's degree in audiology and speech pathology have average annual salaries of $51,300. Unlike the situation for most college graduates with a bachelor's degree in a professional field of study, little systematic connection exists between the earnings of graduates and the degree to which their jobs are related to their undergraduate major.

Speech pathology and audiology graduates with a bachelor's degree have earnings that vary considerably based on the occupation in which they are employed. Those who work as special education teachers have annual salaries of $44,600 per year. This rate of pay is well above that of other persons who work as special education teachers but earned a bachelor's degree in some other field outside the speech pathology field. Those majors employed in health-related fields earn only $36,100 per year, a rate of pay that is $17,000 less per year than bachelor's degree holders in other fields of study who are employed in these health fields. Part of this earnings gap is a result of license provisions that require most persons who practice at the professional level as speech therapists or audiologists to hold a master's degree in the field.

FIGURE 2

Age/Earnings Profile of Persons with Only a Bachelor's Degree in Audiology and Speech Pathology (Full-Time Workers, in 2002 Dollars)

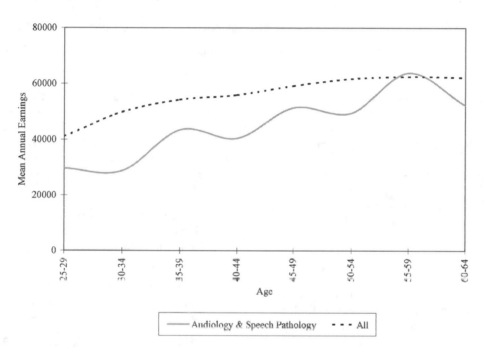

Table 2

Annual Salary of Full-Time Workers with Only a Bachelor's Degree in Audiology and Speech Pathology, Top 10 Occupations (in 2002 Dollars)

Earnings in Top 10 Occupations	All	Audiology and Speech Pathology
Total	$54,171	$43,793
Special education teachers, primary and secondary	$37,065	$44,628
Registered nurses, pharmacists, therapists, physician assistants	$53,508	$36,112
Other service occupations, except health	$39,984	$37,518
Insurance, securities, real estate, business services	$68,273	$84,095

(continued)

Table 2 (continued)
Annual Salary of Full-Time Workers with Only a Bachelor's Degree in Audiology and Speech Pathology, Top 10 Occupations (in 2002 Dollars)

Earnings in Top 10 Occupations	All	Audiology and Speech Pathology
Elementary school teachers	$39,167	$43,595
Other marketing and sales occupations	$58,208	$39,727
Top- and mid-level managers, executives, administrators	$74,051	$48,874
Other administrative (e.g., records clerks, telephone operators)	$34,547	$28,194
Other management-related occupations	$51,921	$19,424
Food preparation and service occupations	$29,506	$19,100

On-the-Job Training

Most speech pathology and audiology graduates with a bachelor's degree participate in some kind of work-related seminars or workshops over the course of the year as they seek to develop their professional skills. More than 75 percent of graduates from this major participate in such training over the course of a year.

- Most of the training taken by graduates with an audiology or speech pathology bachelor's degree is designed to improve some type of specific professional skill.

- About 1 in 4 attend courses designed to improve communication skills, including writing and public speaking.

- Few participate in management or supervisory training activities.

Post-Graduation Activities

A higher proportion of audiology or speech pathology bachelor's degree holders go on to earn an advanced degree than almost any other undergraduate major field of study. Two-thirds

of all graduates from this field eventually earn an advanced degree of some type. Most of those who go on to graduate school earn a master's degree.

- Three-quarters of those who earn a master's degree continue their studies in the field of audiology and speech pathology.

- Most of the remainder of those who are awarded master's degrees earn their degrees in some field of education.

- About 3 percent of majors in the field eventually complete a doctoral program. About one-half of these individuals continue their study in audiology or speech therapy, and an additional one-quarter earn a doctorate in education.

About 82 out of every 100 persons with a bachelor's degree only in audiology or speech pathology are employed, mostly in full-time positions. Most of those not working have chosen not to be employed, primarily to meet family responsibilities. There is little involuntary unemployment among majors in this field of study.

Employment Outlook

Future job prospects for persons with a degree in this field appear bright. Employment in several key occupations that intensively employ graduates of speech pathology and audiology programs is projected to grow at a rapid pace between 2000 and 2010.

▶ The demand for special education majors (an occupation that now employs more than 1 in 4 graduates of bachelor's programs in speech pathology) is expected to grow by nearly 30 percent through 2010. This represents a substantial slowing in overall levels of demand for special education teachers compared to earlier forecasts. Prior to the economic recession of 2001, severe labor shortages existed for special education teachers. However, state and local funding reductions for education have reduced demand for these teachers. The growth rate in the number of school-aged children is expected to slow somewhat also, slowing the rise in demand for special ed teachers. However, the overall growth rate of 30 percent is still about 50 percent higher than the expected rate of increase in the overall demand for college graduates and twice the rate of

increase in the level of overall employment expansion in the U.S. economy.

▶ Employment in health-related occupations that now employ 16 percent of graduates from this major is expected to increase by more than 790,000 jobs through 2010. Demand for these health-related professionals will increase by 27 percent, a rate of growth about one-quarter greater than that for all college graduates. Despite the national economic slowdown during the period 2001 to 2003, demand for health care professionals has remained strong. Substantial labor shortages exist in many of the health professions as colleges and universities have struggled to increase the number of graduates in the field. Some analysts expect continued long-term labor shortages in the health care fields as the nation's population ages considerably over the next decade.

▶ The rate of job growth in other occupations that often employ graduates from this field is expected to be below the average rate of increase in the demand for bachelor's degree holders. Many of these occupations are unrelated to the field of study.

Table 3

Projected Change in Employment in the Top 10 Occupations That Employ Persons with Only a Bachelor's Degree in Audiology and Speech Pathology

Top 10 Occupations	Actual Employment in 2000 (000s)	Projected Employment in 2010 (000s)	Absolute Change (000s)	Percentage Change
Special education teachers, primary and secondary	453	592	139	30.7%
Registered nurses, pharmacists, therapists, physician assistants	2,908	3,698	790	27.2%
Other service occupations, except health	9,652	11,287	1,635	21.5%

(continued)

81

Table 3 (continued)
Projected Change in Employment in the Top 10 Occupations That Employ
Persons with Only a Bachelor's Degree in Audiology and Speech Pathology

Top 10 Occupations	Actual Employment in 2000 (000s)	Projected Employment in 2010 (000s)	Absolute Change (000s)	Percentage Change
Insurance, securities, real estate, business services	1,548	1,726	178	11.5%
Elementary school teachers	1,532	1,734	202	13.2%
Other marketing and sales occupations	621	758	137	22.1%
Top- and mid-level managers, executives, administrators	10,564	11,834	1,270	12.0%
Other administrative (e.g., records clerks, telephone operators)	16,911	18,522	1,611	9.5%
Other management-related occupations	4,956	5,801	845	17.1%
Food preparation and service occupations	10,140	11,717	1,577	15.6%

CHAPTER 5

Criminal Justice and Criminology

Criminal justice involves a rich variety of concerns and problems of people from all walks of life, so its curriculum integrates social sciences, behavioral sciences, and humanities with professional courses that address topics such as terrorism, victimology, drug abuse, computer crime, criminal investigation, prison overcrowding, women in criminal justice, ethics, and legal issues. The multiple disciplinary curriculum usually permits three specializations: policing and security, legal studies, and criminology and corrections.

As times change, with the growth of violence in schools, homes, and communities with gangs, new developments in policing such as community policing also occur. Students also learn about the large field of security from a business rather than a law enforcement perspective. The legal studies concentration teaches students how to analyze the mechanics of law and the legal process and the historical and philosophical foundations of our legal system. Some students use this option as preparation for law school. In the criminology and corrections specialization, students investigate the causes of crime and assess various correctional agencies responding to criminal offending. Some people use this option for entry into parole and probation work.

Police officers are responsible for enforcing statutes, laws, and regulations. In small communities and rural areas, they have general law enforcement duties such as directing traffic at a fire scene, investigating a burglary, or giving first aid at an accident scene. In large police departments, officers may specialize and functions may change depending on their patrol area—a business district versus a residential neighborhood. Other law enforcement options such as special agents also exist—for example, FBI agents, drug enforcement officers, border patrol, customs agents, or U.S. marshals.

Legal investigators, who work in another facet of criminal justice, frequently assist lawyers in preparing criminal defenses; locating witnesses; or gathering testimonial, documentary, or physical evidence. Corporate investigators conduct internal or external investigations, usually for large companies. Their function is to prevent criminal schemes or thefts of company assets. Also, they may investigate drug use in the workplace and determine whether employees are stealing merchandise or information.

Correctional officers' duties differ with the setting in which they work. The majority of jails in the United States are operated by county governments, with about three-quarters of all jails under the jurisdiction of an elected sheriff. Prisoners come and go frequently as the American jail system processes 22 million people a year, with about one-half million inmates in jail at a given time. State and federal prisons have a much more stable population of about one million prisoners.

Educational courses that criminal justice students may take are as follows: the law and the legal process, criminology, criminal due process, introduction to criminal courts, civil liability in criminal justice, security, security management, white-collar crime, police strategy, evidence, criminal homicide, juvenile justice, probation and parole, and incarceration.

Specific abilities are being able to use a gun and other safety devices and to work with laws and regulations, including writing reports in legal terminology. Oral communicative skills are critical, whether it be so that orders are clearly understood by others or in presenting evidence to a court. Physical stamina and strength are important, as is the ability to work under stress and pressure in dangerous situations. Of course, using reasoning and practical judgment with all kinds of people is essential.

The interests of those involved in criminal justice are as follows: first, they enjoy working with people; second, they like to take charge and are not afraid to make quick decisions; and third, they have a preference for a hands-on immediate approach to resolving difficulties or problematic issues.

Criminal justice affords opportunities that involve action, risk, and excitement. There is contact with the public. Also, police represent power and authority, qualities that are satisfying to some people. On numerous occasions, having a leadership role and being in control are required in this field.

Those in criminal justice like to rely on facts in making judgments and seek immediate results. Thus, they appear to be concrete, practical, and factual, and they use their past experience to arrive at decisions in a logical and analytical way. They do not act impulsively or let their feelings bother them. They seem to live their lives according to a set of rules or judgments that they believe about the world.

Where Do Criminal Justice Majors Work?

A graduate with a degree in criminal justice is most likely to be employed in a federal, state, or local government position as a law enforcement official or in a related management position.

More than one-half of all those who earn a bachelor's degree in criminal justice are employed in a government job. About 1 in 3 graduates of criminal justice programs at the undergraduate level are wage and salary employees of a for-profit business and corporation; often these individuals work in jobs that are not closely related to the major. About 6 percent of graduates are self-employed, either as consultants or as business owners. Nonprofit and educational institutions each employ about 4 percent of the graduates of criminal justice programs.

FIGURE 1

Percentage Distribution of Employed Persons with Only a Bachelor's Degree in Criminal Justice and Criminology, by Major Sector of Economic Activity

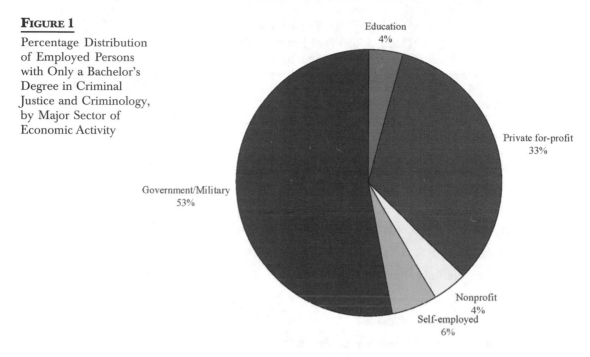

Education
4%

Private for-profit
33%

Government/Military
53%

Nonprofit
4%

Self-employed
6%

Occupations

Employment in occupations that are closely related to the field leads to substantial earnings advantages for graduates of criminal justice programs. Criminal justice majors are most likely to be employed in the government sector in protective-service occupations that are closely related to the field of study. One-third of all majors are employed in the protective-service field. These graduates work as police officers, parole officers, court officers, and prison guards and in agent positions in a number of federal agencies with law enforcement functions. Nearly 12 percent of criminal justice program graduates work in higher-paying managerial and supervisory positions that are often connected in some way to the undergraduate major. Social work is also an important avenue of employment for graduates of criminal justice programs. Eight percent of all graduates are employed in

the social work field, sometimes working with local police officials in gang control and community crime prevention activities. A number of graduates of criminal justice programs are employed in sales-related jobs that are generally not closely connected to the major. More than 8 percent of all graduates work in sales and marketing positions and in occupations related to finance, insurance, real estate, and business services. Those who work in unrelated jobs most often say that better pay and promotion opportunities in other fields, along with loss of interest in criminal justice, are the major reasons for work in a job unrelated to the field. Nearly 1 out of 10 criminal justice majors are employed in a job that does not require a college degree at all. These jobs include clerks and low-level service occupations. Those working in these jobs have poor pay and limited opportunities for advancement.

Table 1
Top 10 Occupations That Employ Persons with Only a Bachelor's Degree in Criminal Justice and Criminology

Top 10 Occupations	PERCENT OF EMPLOYED		
	All	Men	Women
Protective-service occupations	33.2	41.9	12.8
Top- and mid-level managers, executives, administrators	11.8	14.4	5.9
Social workers	8.1	5.5	14.4
Other management-related occupations	5.6	6.4	3.8
Other administrative (e.g., records clerks, telephone operators)	4.5	3.7	6.2
Other service occupations, except health	3.5	2.2	6.5
Sales occupations, including retail	3.0	2.8	3.6
Insurance, securities, real estate, business services	2.9	3.3	1.9
Other marketing and sales occupations	2.5	2.6	2.4
Personnel, training, and labor relations specialists	1.6	0.4	4.2

▶ Sharp disparities exist between the types of jobs in which men and women with a degree in criminal justice are employed. More than 40 percent of men with a degree in the field work in protective-service jobs. Only about 13 percent of women with a degree in criminal justice are employed in the protective-service occupations.

▶ One in 9 men with a degree in criminal justice is employed in a managerial or supervisory position, while only 1 in 17 women is employed in these jobs.

▶ Women with a degree in criminal justice are much more likely to work in non-college labor market jobs than their male counterparts. Six percent of men work in a job that typically does not require a college degree. Nearly 13 percent of women are employed in these occupations.

Activities on the Job

▶ Administrative and management duties are an important part of the job duties of criminal justice graduates. Report writing and record-keeping activities demand a substantial amount of time, especially among those employed in public sector jobs.

▶ The use—and, in some instances, the development—of computer applications is becoming a more important part of the work of many graduates with a degree in criminal justice.

Salaries

The annual salaries of graduates of criminal justice programs are well below the average salary of college graduates in general who have earned only a bachelor's degree. Criminal justice program graduates earn an average of $46,100, a rate of pay that is $8,000, or about 15 percent, per year less than that of the average bachelor's degree holder. Years of work experience and the development of skills learned on the job lead to relatively rapid increases in the annual pay of criminal justice graduates. The salaries of young graduates from the field aged 25 to 29 are relatively low, averaging $34,500 per year. However, as the number of years of experience in the world of work rises, the salaries of criminal justice graduates rise proportionately. By the ages 45 to 49, criminal justice graduates have annual salaries averaging $56,000, an increase of more than 60 percent relative to the salaries of younger graduates.

Unlike with most other undergraduate major fields of study, the graduates of criminal justice programs have higher annual salaries when they work in government agencies. The earnings of those working in private, for-profit companies average $44,000, while those graduates with government jobs have average salaries of $48,400 per year.

FIGURE 2

Age/Earnings Profile of Persons with Only a Bachelor's Degree in Criminal Justice and Criminology (Full-Time Workers, in 2002 Dollars)

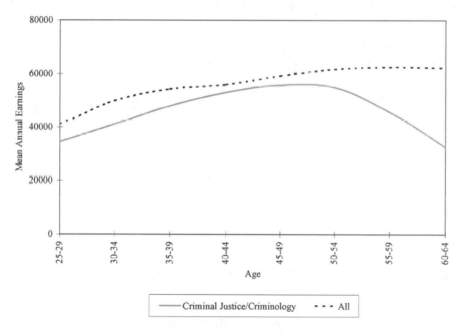

Table 2

Annual Salary of Full-Time Workers with Only a Bachelor's Degree
in Criminal Justice and Criminology, Top 10 Occupations (in 2002 Dollars)

Earnings in Top 10 Occupations	All	Criminal Justice/ Criminology
Total	$54,171	$46,104

(continued)

Table 2 (continued)
Annual Salary of Full-Time Workers with Only a Bachelor's Degree in Criminal Justice and Criminology, Top 10 Occupations (in 2002 Dollars)

Earnings in Top 10 Occupations	All	Criminal Justice/ Criminology
Protective-service occupations	$49,130	$48,734
Top- and mid-level managers, executives, administrators	$74,051	$59,968
Social workers	$36,371	$36,354
Other management-related occupations	$51,921	$42,729
Other administrative (e.g., records clerks, telephone operators)	$34,547	$40,617
Other service occupations, except health	$39,984	$35,446
Sales occupations, including retail	$52,378	$46,272
Insurance, securities, real estate, business services	$68,273	$56,130
Other marketing and sales occupations	$58,208	$45,255
Personnel, training, and labor relations specialists	$51,577	$41,216

Criminal justice majors who work in occupations that are closely related to the major field of study have annual salaries that are substantially higher than those employed in jobs not closely connected to the field. Graduates employed in one of the protective-service occupations earn an average of $48,800 per year, while those in managerial and supervisory positions that are often connected to the field earn an average of $60,000 in annual salary. However, employment in a job that is related to the field does not guarantee higher average salaries. Criminal justice majors working in social-work–related jobs earn only $36,350 per year. Employment in jobs unrelated to the field generally means lower pay. Those working in management-related jobs in accounting and personnel earn an average of $42,700 per year, while those in clerical and lower-level service occupations earn an average salary of $40,600 and $35,400, respectively. Clearly, access to employment that utilizes the skills developed within the majors provides an earnings advantage to graduates of criminal justice programs.

On-the-Job Training

The development of work-related skills on the job is an important component of the long-term career development of graduates with a degree in criminal justice. Majors from this field learn many of their skills on the job through informal learning by observation and doing, as well as through participation in training seminars and workshops. More than three-quarters of criminal justice graduates participate in a training session of some type over the course of a year. The field provides strong earnings rewards for skills learned through on-the-job experience and training programs.

▶ Much of the training is involved with the development of professional skills related to the particular occupation in which the individual is employed. Training sessions could focus on investigative techniques, new crime prevention initiatives, new equipment training, and the like.

▶ A substantial number of majors report that they participate in supervisory and management-related training over the course of a year.

▶ Communications skills are important in this field. More than 1 in 3 majors undertake training designed to improve writing or public speaking skills.

Post-Graduation Activities

Most graduates of criminal justice programs do not go on to complete an advanced degree program. Only 20 percent of all graduates eventually complete a program of advanced study. About 13 percent of majors in the field earn a master's degree, and about 6 percent earn a professional degree. Virtually no graduates from the field go on to earn a doctorate.

▶ Forty percent of the master's degrees earned are in the field of criminal justice. About 1 in 6 earn a master's degree in business, while another 14 percent also earn degrees in public affairs/administration. The education and psychology fields are the areas in which those with undergraduate degrees in criminal justice earn master's degrees.

▶ About 6 percent of criminal justice undergraduates go on to earn a law degree. Few earn a professional degree in medicine.

More than 90 percent of criminal justice graduates under the age of 65 are employed, most in full-time jobs. Only about 8 percent of graduates are jobless, and few of these individuals are involuntarily unemployed. Those not looking for work most often are at home to meet family responsibilities or because of early retirement or disability.

Employment Outlook

Overall employment levels of persons with a bachelor's degree working in the protective-service fields are expected to increase by nearly 26 percent between 2000 and 2010, according to occupational projections developed by the U.S. Bureau of Labor Statistics. This rate of growth is substantially above the overall rate of projected job demand for college graduates and sharply above the projected rate of new job creation in the nation through 2010. Growing homeland security and national security concerns will fuel the demand for well-educated protective-service professionals.

Outside of protective services, employment in most occupations that employ large proportions of criminal justice majors is expected to increase at a slower pace over this period of time. Employment levels within the protective-service occupations are expected to increase by more than 800,000 jobs over the 10-year projection period, representing a 26 percent increase in employment. Within the protective service area, employment of corrections officers is expected to increase most rapidly, growing by nearly one-third over the period. Demand for police officers is expected to rise sharply over the 10-year projection period. The number of officers is expected to increase by one-quarter between 2000 and 2010. Employment among social workers, who often provide services to offenders and ex-offenders, is projected to rise by 30 percent over the decade.

A substantial number of criminal justice graduates are also employed in managerial and administrative jobs; employment in this occupation is expected to increase by about 17 percent over the projection period. Similarly slow growth is forecast in administrative, sales, and services occupations.

Table 3

Projected Change in Employment in the Top 10 Occupations That
Employ Persons with Only a Bachelor's Degree in Criminal Justice and Criminology

Top 10 Occupations	Actual Employment in 2000 (000s)	Projected Employment in 2010 (000s)	Absolute Change (000s)	Percentage Change
Protective-service occupations	3,087	3,896	809	26.2%
Top- and mid-level managers, executives, administrators	10,564	11,834	1,270	12.0%
Social workers	468	609	141	30.1%
Other management-related occupations	4,956	5,801	845	17.1%
Other administrative (e.g., records clerks, telephone operators)	16,911	18,522	1,611	9.5%
Other service occupations, except health	9,652	11,287	1,635	16.9%
Sales occupations, including retail	15,513	17,365	1,852	11.9%
Insurance, securities, real estate, business services	1,548	1,726	178	11.5%
Other marketing and sales occupations	621	758	137	22.1%
Personnel, training, and labor relations specialists	490	578	88	18.0%

CHAPTER 6

Health and Medical Technology

This major involves the study of tissues and cells and the analysis of body fluids with the goal of detection, diagnosis, and treatment of disease. The major prepares students for the roles of medical technologist and technician and for the performance of clinical laboratory tests.

Depending on the specialization area, health and medical technologists may have different titles. For example, clinical chemistry technologists prepare specimens and analyze the chemical and hormonal contents of body fluids. Microbiological technologists examine and identify bacteria, parasites, and other microorganisms. Blood bank technologists collect, type, and match blood for transfusions. Immunology technologists examine elements and responses of the human immune system to foreign bodies that can show how a patient is responding to treatment. Cytotechnologists prepare slides of body cells and microscopically examine the cells for abnormalities that can indicate the beginning of a cancerous growth. Whatever focus the health/medical technologists have, after analyzing and evaluating their results, they all communicate the outcomes to physicians.

Technicians usually perform less-complex tests and procedures than technologists. For histology technicians, common jobs are cutting and staining tissue specimens for microscopic examination by pathologists, and for phlebotomists, common jobs are drawing and testing blood. Overall, however, the whole health and medical technology area is being affected by the development and use of new, sophisticated laboratory equipment.

Course work in this area includes chemistry, biology, microbiology, mathematics, and specialized courses in the clinical laboratory areas. In addition, computer applications, business, and management courses are also taken.

The abilities needed in these clinical laboratory technologies are scientific analytical judgment, problem solving skills, and the ability to obtain measurable and verifiable information. It must not be forgotten that medical technologists work with infectious specimens. Paying attention to following detailed procedures also is critical because small differences or changes in test substances or numerical results can be crucial for patient care. Technologists often work under pressure. Manual and finger dexterity plus color vision are needed to use delicate and sensitive equipment. Computer skills are important as automated laboratory equipment is increasingly used.

The interests of those in this field are definitely scientific, including both the chemistry and biology areas. Because of the laboratory work involved and the hands-on approach to work, medical technologists enjoy working with their hands and machines. There is an appreciation for doing detailed work and an acceptance of the fact that one's work is part of a team effort occurring within an organizational framework—generally a hospital or clinical laboratory.

Health/medical technologists must do work that requires a high level of mental ability, be able to do things of importance, and succeed in performing difficult work. They appreciate searching for new information while accepting the fact that research requires following established procedures routinely with little change.

People in this major are characterized by their thoroughness and their ability to follow a systematic approach, work hard, and have patience in doing routine and detailed activities. They are practical and prefer to be factual and have ideas stated clearly to them. Their altruistic and social feelings, however, attract them to health profession jobs such as health or medical technology that require their preferred style of precise work.

Where Do Health and Medical Technology Graduates Work?

Health and medical technology graduates are employed in different sectors of the economy. About 40 percent are employed by businesses and corporations in the private, for-profit sector of the economy. Many research laboratories, including medical testing firms, are in this sector. One-quarter of these graduates are employed in the private, nonprofit sector of the economy. Twenty-two percent of health and medical technology graduates work for educational institutions, and 7 percent are self-employed in their own business or practice. The government sector employs 6 percent of all employed health and medical technology graduates.

The skills and knowledge that health and medical technology graduates acquire during their schooling are directly applicable in the labor market. The extent of practical application of the skills of health and medical technology graduates enables many graduates to find jobs in their field. More than 75 percent are employed in jobs that are closely related to their undergraduate major field of study. More than 12 percent are employed in jobs that are somewhat related to their major. Only 12 percent of health and medical technology graduates work in jobs that are not related to their undergraduate major field of study.

Why do the latter group of health and medical technology graduates work in unrelated jobs? They cite a variety of factors as possible reasons for their employment in unrelated jobs. However, when asked to select the most important reason for employment outside their major field of study, 24 percent report that family-related reasons forced them to accept employment in unrelated jobs. One-fifth of those health and medical technology graduates who work in unrelated jobs rank better pay and promotion opportunities as the number one reason, and another one-fifth consider a change in career interests as the most important factor to influence their decision to work in an unrelated job. About 8 percent rank the general working environment as the most important factor influencing their decision to work in a job that is not related to their undergraduate major field of study.

FIGURE 1

Percentage Distribution of Employed Persons with Only a Bachelor's Degree in Health and Medical Technology, by Major Sector of Economic Activity

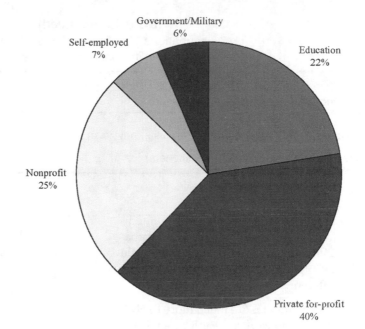

Occupations

The employment of health and medical technology graduates is concentrated in very few occupations. Two-thirds of all employed graduates work as health technologists and technicians. Five percent work as biological scientists, and another 5 percent are employed in top- to mid-level executive, administrative, and managerial occupations. Four percent work in management-related occupations as management analysts, purchasing agents, and regulatory officers, and another 4 percent are employed as nurses, pharmacists, therapists, physician assistants, or medical scientists (excluding practitioners).

Table 1

Top 7 Occupations That Employ Persons with Only a Bachelor's Degree in Health and Medical Technology

Top 7 Occupations	PERCENT OF EMPLOYED		
	All	Men	Women
Health technologists and technicians	66.6	51.2	69.7
Biological scientists	4.9	6.2	4.7
Top- and mid-level managers, executives, administrators	4.7	6.7	4.3
Sales occupations, including retail	3.8	3.2	3.9
Other management-related occupations	1.6	0.3	1.9

(continued)

Table 1 (continued)
Top 7 Occupations That Employ Persons with Only
a Bachelor's Degree in Health and Medical Technology

Top 7 Occupations	PERCENT OF EMPLOYED		
	All	Men	Women
Registered nurses, pharmacists, therapists, physician assistants	1.6	2.0	1.5
Medical scientists (excluding practitioners)	1.6	1.1	1.7

Only 17 percent of employed health and medical technology graduates are men. The occupational employment patterns of male and female health and medical technology graduates are slightly different.

▶ Female graduates are much more likely than males to work as health technologists and technicians. Nearly 70 percent of female graduates work in these occupations, compared to only 51 percent of male graduates.

▶ Male graduates, on the other hand, are slightly more likely than female graduates to work as biological scientists and in top- to mid-level executive, administrative, and managerial occupations.

Activities on the Job

The activities in which health and medical technology graduates engage at work are very closely related to the occupation in which they are employed.

▶ Seventy-seven percent of employed health and medical technology graduates spend at least 10 hours during a typical workweek in providing health services. Fifty-five percent report that they spend a majority of their typical workweek in these activities.

▶ Seven percent spend most of their time at work in management and administrative duties.

▶ Five percent engage in applied research during a major portion of their typical workweek, and another 5 percent spend most of their time at work in performing sales, purchasing, and marketing activities.

▶ Four percent of employed health and medical technology graduates spend most of their time at work in computer applications, programming, and systems-development activities.

▶ Three percent of employed graduates spend most of their workweek in teaching activities.

Salaries

The average annual salary of health and medical technology graduates with only a bachelor's degree who are employed full-time is $47,700, a level that is 12 percent lower than the average annual salary of all full-time employed college graduates. As for most college graduates, the salary of health and medical technology graduates increases with age. Skills developed through additional work experience make workers more productive, and therefore the more experienced can earn higher salaries. However, the gains from additional years of work experience do not appear as strong for graduates in health and medical technology programs compared to all college graduates. The age-earnings profile of these professionals is less steeply sloped than that for the average college graduate. More stringent credentialing requirements in the health care fields may be one part of the explanation for the reduced gains to work experience in this field.

▶ The average annual salary of health and medical technology graduates between the ages of 25 and 29 is $39,800. Graduates between the ages of 30 and 34 earn $45,200 annually.

▶ The average annual salary of health and medical technology graduates increases to $53,200 between the ages of 40 and 44 and peaks at $55,000 among 55- to 59-year-old graduates.

The average annual salary of health and medical technology graduates who work in jobs that are related to their undergraduate major field of study is higher than those who work in jobs that are not related to their major field of study. Closely related jobs pay full-time employed health and medical technology graduates $47,000 annually. Graduates employed in jobs that are unrelated to their undergraduate field of study earn $43,400 per year.

Earning an average salary of $49,200 annually, health and medical technology graduates who work in the education sector of the economy earn a higher salary than those who are employed in other sectors of the economy. The pay for health and medical technology graduates in the private, for-profit sector of the economy is $47,900 per year. The government sector and the private, nonprofit sector pay these graduates $46,100 per year.

FIGURE 2

Age/Earnings Profile of Persons with Only a Bachelor's Degree in Health and Medical Technology (Full-Time Workers, in 2002 Dollars)

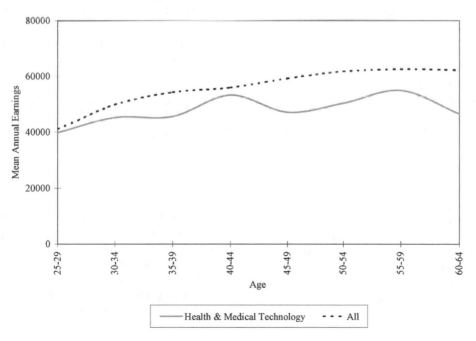

Table 2
Annual Salary of Full-Time Workers with Only a Bachelor's Degree in Health and Medical Technology, Top 7 Occupations (in 2002 Dollars)

Earnings in Top 7 Occupations	All	Health and Medical Technology
Total	$54,171	$47,667
Health technologists and technicians	$42,774	$45,580
Biological scientists	$42,794	$45,164
Top- and mid-level managers, executives, administrators	$74,051	$71,323
Sales occupations, including retail	$52,378	$45,385
Other management-related occupations	$51,921	$52,144
Registered nurses, pharmacists, therapists, physician assistants	$53,508	$67,571
Medical scientists (excluding practitioners)	$55,111	$58,896

The average annual salaries of health and medical technology graduates and all college graduates in the top 7 occupations that predominantly employ health and medical technology graduates are presented below.

▶ Health and medical technology graduates employed in high-level executive, administrative, and managerial occupations earn an average annual salary of $71,300. This occupation employs only 5 percent of the graduates and is somewhat more likely to employ male than female graduates.

▶ Nurses, pharmacists, therapists, and physician assistants with a bachelor's degree in health and medical technology earn $67,600 per year, and the annual pay for those who are employed as medical scientists (except practitioners) is $58,900.

▶ The average annual salary of graduates employed in management-related occupations is $52,100, and the annual salary of health technologist and technician occupations, which employ two-thirds of health and medical technology graduates, is $45,600.

On-the-Job Training

The career potential of a job is closely associated with the amount of work-related training on the job. Work-related training is regarded as an investment by firms because it makes workers more productive. Firms that invest in their workforce are more likely to offer pay increases and promotions to match the increasing productivity of their workers. Firms that do not invest in their workers are relatively less likely to offer pay increases and promotions. The incidence of work-related training among health and medical technology graduates is slightly higher

$41,600. Home economics majors who are employed by educational institutions earn $34,800 per year. The average annual remuneration of graduates with full-time jobs in the private, nonprofit sector is only $31,300, a level that is lower than the average salary of home economics graduates employed in other sectors of the economy.

The salaries of home economics graduates vary by the occupations in which they are employed. The average annual salary of all full-time employed home economics majors is 28 percent lower than the average salary of all college graduates. In 9 out of the top 10 occupations in which home economics graduates are employed, the salary of home economics graduates is lower than the salary of all college graduates.

▶ Home economics graduates employed in miscellaneous marketing and sales occupations earn an average annual salary of

$59,900. However, this occupation employs fewer than 5 percent of employed graduates.

▶ The second-highest earnings among home economics graduates are in top- to mid-level executive, managerial, and administrative occupations. Graduates employed in these occupations earn $48,600 per year.

▶ Graduates employed in management-related occupations earn $45,900. Sales occupations, the second-largest area of employment for home economics graduates, pay an annual salary of $38,500.

▶ The 4.7 percent of graduates employed as prekindergarten and kindergarten teachers earn the lowest salary out of the top 10 occupations in which home economics graduates are employed. The average annual salary of graduates in this group who are employed on a

FIGURE 2

Age/Earnings Profile of Persons with Only a Bachelor's Degree in Home Economics (Full-Time Workers, in 2002 Dollars)

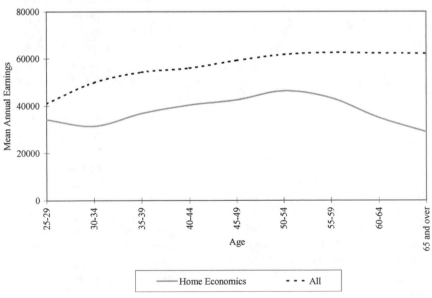

than the rate of participation in work-related training among all college graduates. While 68 percent of all college graduates acquire some kind of work-related training during a year, 74 percent of health and medical technology graduates annually engage in work-related training.

- Of those health and medical technology graduates who participate in training during the year, 91 percent receive technical training in the occupation in which they are employed.

- Twenty-eight percent of the training recipients participate in management or supervisory training.

- One-fifth receive training to improve their general professional skills, such as public speaking and business writing.

Although health and medical technology graduates decide to participate in work-related training activities, workshops, or seminars for numerous reasons, five reasons stand out as most commonly cited by graduates. Included among them are a desire to improve skills and knowledge in the occupational area of their employment, mandatory training requirements of the employer, increased opportunities for advancement in the form of a higher salary and a promotion, the need to learn new skills for a newly acquired position, and the need to acquire a professional license or certificate.

When asked to select the most important reason to acquire training, 70 percent of health and medical technology graduates who undergo training identify the need to improve their occupational skills and knowledge. Ten percent report mandatory training requirements by the employer as the most important factor underlying their involvement in work-related training. According to 6 percent of the training participants, the most important reason to participate in training activities is advancement within the firm in the form of a salary increase or a promotion, and another 6 percent rank the need to obtain a professional license or certificate as the number one reason to participate in work-related training. The need to learn skills for a newly acquired position is the number one reason to acquire training among only 3 percent of the training recipients.

Post-Graduation Activities

Of all graduates with a bachelor's degree in health and medical technology, 16 percent proceed to earn a postgraduate degree. Eleven percent earn a master's degree, 1 percent earn a doctorate degree, and 4 percent earn a professional degree.

- Twenty-six percent of all master's degrees earned by undergraduate health and medical technology majors are in the health professions. More than one-fifth of the master's degrees are earned in business management and administrative services. Fifteen percent of the degrees are earned in health and medical technology, another 15 percent in biological and life sciences, 8 percent in education, and 5 percent in psychology.

- The doctorate degrees earned by health and medical technology graduates are spread across biological and life sciences, health professions, psychology, and education.

- Most—72 percent—of the professional degrees earned by undergraduate health and medical technology majors are in the health professions, and 10 percent are earned in the field of law.

Out of all health and medical technology graduates under the age of 65, 85 percent are employed. Only 2 percent are officially unemployed; that is, they are not employed and are actively seeking employment. The remaining 13 percent are out of the labor force; that is, they are not employed and are not seeking employment. Two main reasons underlying the labor force withdrawal of health and medical technology graduates are family responsibilities and a lack of the need or desire to work. Nearly 60 percent cite family responsibilities as the reason for their labor force withdrawal, and 40 percent report their lack of a desire or need to work as one of the reasons for their withdrawal from the labor force. Additional reasons cited include retirement, schooling, and inability to work.

Employment Outlook

According to the projections by the U.S. Bureau of Labor Statistics, employment in occupations that require at least a bachelor's degree is expected to grow faster than employment in other sectors of the American labor market. Between 2000 and 2010, the U.S. economy is projected to add 22.2 million jobs, yielding an employment growth rate of 15.2 percent. The demand for college graduates is expected to increase by more than one-fifth over the same time, leading the nation in new employment opportunities. The employment growth projections in the top 7 occupations that are most likely to employ health and medical technology graduates are presented below.

▶ Health technologist and technician occupations that employ two-thirds of all health and medical technology graduates

are expected to grow rapidly over the decade. Employment in these fields is projected to increase by 26 percent, a rate of increase 1.7 times that projected for the nation as a whole. New technologies and the aging of the U.S. population are expected to fuel much of this increase in demand.

▶ Similarly high rates of job growth are projected in biological science occupations and nursing, pharmacy, therapy, and physician occupations. Employment in these occupations is projected to increase by 20 and 27 percent, respectively.

▶ Employment in high- to mid-level executive, administrative, and managerial occupations is projected to grow more slowly, increasing by just 12 percent over the decade.

▶ Employment projections for sales occupations and miscellaneous management-related occupations, such as management analysts, purchasing agents, and regulatory officers, suggest relatively slow growth in these fields. Employment in sales positions is expected to increase by about 12 percent through 2010. Management support employment levels are projected to increase at a somewhat more rapid pace of 17 percent, a rate of growth below that expected for college labor market jobs in general.

Table 3

Projected Change in Employment in the Top 7 Occupations That Employ
Persons with Only a Bachelor's Degree in Health and Medical Technology

Top 7 Occupations	Actual Employment in 2000 (000s)	Projected Employment in 2010 (000s)	Absolute Change (000s)	Percentage Change
Health technologists and technicians	2,192	2,773	581	26.5%
Biological scientists	73	88	15	20.5%
Top- and mid-level managers, executives, administrators	10,564	11,834	1,270	12.0%
Sales occupations, including retail	15,513	17,365	1,852	11.9%
Other management-related occupations	4,956	5,801	845	17.1%
Registered nurses, pharmacists, therapists, physician assistants	2,908	3,698	790	27.2%
Medical scientists (excluding practitioners)	37	47	10	27.0%

CHAPTER 7

Home Economics: Dietetics, Food, and Nutrition

This major studies the promotion of healthy eating habits to foster good health and to prevent illness. Dietitians and nutritionists plan nutrition programs and supervise the preparation and serving of meals. They help treat illness by evaluating clients' diets and suggest diet modifications regarding intake of fat, salt, and sugar and other carbohydrates.

In nursing homes and hospitals, dietitians and nutritionists can function in clinical roles and also manage the food service department. In their clinical capacity, they may also offer special group programs for diabetic or overweight patients. In public health clinics and home health agencies, they provide an educational role. For food manufacturers, they can perform food analyses, prepare reports for public dissemination, and serve as nutritional resources for marketing food products. Some function in specialized roles in wellness centers or for sport teams or perform nutritional screening—for example, monitoring cholesterol levels.

A bachelor's degree with a major in dietetics, foods and nutrition, or food service management plus supervised practice experience is required to be a dietitian or nutritionist. Students take courses in foods, nutrition, institutional management, chemistry, biology, microbiology, and physiology, as well as other courses such as statistics, business, and computer science.

The abilities required in this major cover a broad span, from being an applied scientist to being a hands-on skills person involved in directing and training food service workers to being an administrator involved in planning and possibly even budgeting and purchasing food. Scientific abilities are necessary for the required science course work. Computer skills, which will be helpful in the scientific area, also will be invaluable for the business dimensions of the field. Language and communication abilities are essential. Also, manual and finger coordination skills will be used in laboratory work, applied food and nutrition courses, and supervised practice experience.

Dietitians and nutritionists enjoy working with people in a helping capacity and like science, food, and health. The scientific interest suggests that these majors liked high school courses in mathematics, biology, and chemistry. Dietitians and nutritionists enjoy leadership roles, assuming responsibility for directing others and working to accomplish organizational goals.

The benefits for people in this field are influenced by their interpersonal orientation. They value providing services to persons with nutritional and health problems, including children and adults. They seek roles in which they will influence the opinions or decisions of others, so they willingly accept leadership roles. Satisfaction is gained in exploring new ways of doing activities.

Dietitians and nutritionists may follow different styles of operation. Some are outgoing, while others are quieter and enjoy their personal privacy. Those in more administrative positions prefer to plan their operations well in advance, defining their goals with definite expectations that their objectives will be met on schedule. They enjoy being managers but are impatient with inefficiency. Another, more introverted style of operation of some in this field still follows the underlying pattern of being thorough, hardworking, and patient in paying attention to detail, in addition to tending to be comfortable with a practical and factual orientation. However, while those in this latter group definitely are people oriented, they tend not to be gregarious or extroverted.

Where Do Home Economics Majors Work?

Only 40 percent of employed home economics graduates work for businesses and corporations in the private, for-profit sector of the economy. Another 15 percent work in the private, for-profit sector as self-employed workers in their own business or practice. Educational institutions employ large numbers of home economics graduates. About 3 out of 10 graduates work in this sector of the economy, primarily as kindergarten, elementary, and secondary school teachers. Out of all employed home economics graduates, 8 percent work in tax exempt or charitable organizations such as health clinics, nonprofit home health agencies, and wellness centers. The government sector employs 6 percent of home economics graduates.

Nearly two-thirds of all home economics graduates are employed in jobs that are closely related or somewhat related to their undergraduate major field of study. This is not surprising given the applied nature of this major field of study. Dietitians and nutritional scientists can apply their classroom knowledge in a clinical capacity or as health and nutrition scientists in various settings, such as for health clinics, food manufacturers, wellness centers, and sports teams. Nearly 37 percent work in closely related jobs, and 29 percent find that their jobs are somewhat related to their undergraduate major. A little more than one-third of all employed home economics graduates work in jobs that are not at all related to their undergraduate major field of study.

Why do home economics graduates work in jobs that are not related to their major? More than 55 percent cite the general working environment as one of the reasons for their employment outside the field of home economics. About one-half cite job location, and 49 percent report family-related factors as one of the reasons for working in unrelated jobs. A change in career interests is one of the reasons among 46 percent, and 43 percent work in unrelated jobs because of better pay and promotion opportunities. Nearly one-third of the graduates who work in unrelated jobs are forced to accept them because they cannot find related jobs.

Although home economics graduates decide to work in unrelated jobs for several reasons, when

FIGURE 1

Percentage Distribution of Employed Persons with Only a Bachelor's Degree in Home Economics, by Major Sector of Economic Activity

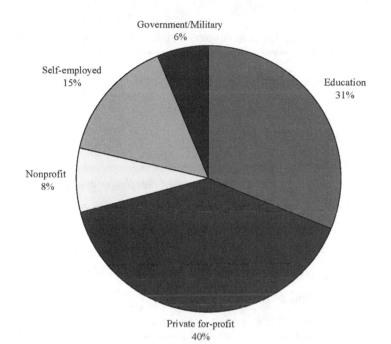

they are asked to identify the most important reason for working in an unrelated job, family-related factors are the primary reason among 23 percent of the graduates. Twenty-one percent cite a change in career choice as the number one reason, 15 percent prefer the working conditions in unrelated jobs, and 14 percent consider better pay and promotion opportunities as the most important reason for their employment choice in an unrelated field. Another 15 percent are forced to work in unrelated jobs because jobs related to their field are not available.

Occupations

Home economics graduates are employed in a variety of occupations. The top 10 occupations employ 64 percent of all employed home economics graduates. Nearly 22 percent of the graduates work in the teaching occupations: 11 percent work as secondary school teachers, 6 percent as elementary school teachers, and 5 percent as prekindergarten and kindergarten teachers. Sales and marketing occupations employ 16 percent of home economics graduates, and 11 percent are employed in clerical and secretarial occupations. More than 5 percent are employed in health occupations as clinical dietitians and nutritionists, nurses, therapists, and physician assistants. Upper-level managerial and administrative occupations employ 5 percent of the graduates, and another 5 percent are employed in management-related occupations as purchasing agents or regulatory officers.

Table 1

Top 10 Occupations That Employ Persons with Only a Bachelor's Degree in Home Economics

Top 10 Occupations	PERCENT OF EMPLOYED		
	All	Men	Women
Teachers, secondary school	11.3	0.0	11.7
Sales occupations, including retail	11.2	13.7	11.1
Teachers, elementary school	5.7	4.3	5.8
Other administrative (e.g., records clerks, telephone operators)	5.7	1.1	5.8
Registered nurses, pharmacists, therapists, physician assistants	5.3	9.3	5.2
Other management-related occupations	5.1	2.3	5.1
Top- and mid-level managers, executives, administrators	5.1	17.1	4.6
Secretaries, receptionists, typists	4.8	0.0	5.0
Other marketing and sales occupations	4.7	20.5	4.2
Teachers, prekindergarten and kindergarten	4.7	0.0	4.8

▶ Almost 97 percent of employed home economics graduates are females. Male and female graduates tend to be concentrated in different occupations.

▶ The few males who major in home economics are more likely than females to work in managerial positions and in marketing and sales occupations.

▶ Female graduates are more likely than males to work as teachers and in clerical and secretarial occupations.

Activities on the Job

The occupations in which home economics graduates are employed clearly determine the duties that they perform on their jobs. Three out of the 10 predominant employers of home economics graduates are teaching occupations. Some of the other top occupations in which home economics graduates are employed include sales, marketing, and management occupations. Unsurprisingly, teaching, sales, marketing, and management are some of the major activities that graduates typically perform on their jobs.

▶ While 44 percent of all employed home economics graduates regularly engage in teaching duties at work, nearly 30 percent spend most of their time during a typical week at work in teaching activities.

▶ About 37 percent regularly perform sales, purchasing, and marketing activities at work, and 18 percent typically spend a majority of their time in sales and marketing activities at work.

▶ Management and administrative duties are regularly performed by nearly one-half of the graduates, and 1 in 10 employed home economics graduates spends a majority of work time in these duties.

▶ One-third of home economics graduates regularly engage in employee-relations activities, including recruiting, personnel development, and training, and 8 percent conduct these duties during most of their working time.

▶ One-fifth of all employed home economics majors regularly provide professional services such as health services consultations. Only 7 percent report that they spend a majority of their time in the provision of professional services.

▶ Engagement in computer applications, programming, and systems-development activities is reported by 27 percent of all employed home economics graduates. However, only 7 percent spend most of their time on these activities.

▶ Although 84 percent of all employed home economics graduates perform accounting, finance, and contractual duties as a regular part of their jobs, only 6 percent spend most of their time in a typical workweek performing these duties.

▶ Very few home economics graduates engage in applied or basic research activities, in product design, or in development activities.

Salaries

The average annual salary of home economics graduates with only a bachelor's degree and who are employed full-time is $38,800, a level that is 28 percent lower than the average annual salary of all full-time employed college graduates. As with most college graduates, the salary of home economics majors increases as they age, albeit at a slower rate. Additionally, at different ages, home economics majors earn considerably lower salaries compared to all college graduates.

▶ The average annual salary of home economics graduates between the ages of 25 and 29 is $34,200. Graduates between the ages of 35 and 39 earn $36,900 annually.

▶ Average annual earnings of home economics graduates increase at a moderate pace as they get older. The average annual salary of 40- to 44-year-old home economics graduates who are employed full-time is $40,500. Average earnings among 45- to 49-year-olds are $42,600 per year. The salary peaks between the ages of 50 and 54, when the average salary of home economics majors is $46,300.

▶ The average annual salary of home economics graduates who work in jobs that are closely related to their major field of study is lower than those who are employed in jobs that are somewhat related to their major or not related to their undergraduate major. Graduates working in closely related jobs are employed in teaching occupations that generally pay lower salaries. Employment in closely related jobs is associated with an average salary of $36,700 per year. Those graduates who are employed in jobs that are somewhat related to their major earn $41,600 per year, and graduates employed in unrelated jobs earn an annual salary of $39,100.

▶ The average salary of self-employed home economics graduates who work full-time is $54,000 per year. The second-highest salary is among graduates employed in the private, for-profit sector working for corporations and businesses. These graduates earn an average salary of $39,100 per year. The government sector pays home economics graduates who are employed full-time an average annual salary of

Table 2

Annual Salary of Full-Time Workers with Only a Bachelor's Degree
in Home Economics, Top 10 Occupations (in 2002 Dollars)

Earnings in Top 10 Occupations	All	Home Economics
Total	$54,171	$38,835
Teachers, secondary school	$40,355	$37,334
Sales occupations, including retail	$52,378	$38,520
Teachers, elementary school	$39,167	$36,457
Other administrative (e.g., records clerks, telephone operators)	$34,547	$30,099
Registered nurses, pharmacists, therapists, physician assistants	$53,508	$35,090
Other management-related occupations	$51,921	$45,862
Top- and mid-level managers, executives, administrators	$74,051	$48,577
Secretaries, receptionists, typists	$32,246	$29,934
Other marketing and sales occupations	$58,208	$59,885
Teachers, prekindergarten and kindergarten	$33,183	$23,800

full-time basis is only $23,800. Secretarial and clerical occupations also are low-salary occupations that pay home economics graduates an average salary of about $29,900 per year.

On-the-Job Training

The career potential of a job is closely associated with the amount of work-related training on the job. Work-related training is regarded as an investment by firms because it makes workers more productive. Firms that invest in their workforce are more likely to offer pay increases and promotions to match the increasing productivity of their workers. Firms that do not invest in their workers are relatively less likely to offer pay increases and promotions. The incidence of work-related training among home economics graduates is slightly lower than the rate of participation in work-related training among all college graduates. While 68 percent of all college graduates acquire some kind of work-related training during a year, 64 percent of home economics majors annually engage in work-related training.

▶ Of those home economics graduates who receive some training during the year, 70 percent receive technical training in the occupation in which they are employed.

▶ Twenty-six percent of the training recipients receive management or supervisory training.

▶ Thirty-two percent receive training to improve their general professional skills, such as public speaking and business writing.

Although home economics graduates decide to participate in work-related training activities, workshops, or seminars for numerous reasons, four reasons stand out as most commonly cited by graduates. Included among them are a desire to improve skills and knowledge in the occupational area of their employment, a mandatory training requirement of the employer, increased opportunities for advancement in the form of a higher salary and a promotion, and the need to learn new skills for a newly acquired position. Nearly 94 percent of home economics graduates participate in work-related training to improve their occupational skills and knowledge. Another 51 percent list employer requirement as one of the reasons for their participation in work-related training. Having an increased opportunity for promotion and salary increase is one of the reasons to acquire training among 36 percent of all home economics graduates who receive work-related training. One-third cite the need to learn skills for a newly acquired position as one of the factors that underlie their decision to engage in training. One-fourth cite the need for training to acquire a professional license or certificate.

When asked to identify the most important reason to acquire training, 59 percent of home economics graduates who undergo training identify the need to improve their occupational skills and knowledge. Another 12 percent report a mandatory training requirement by the employer as the most important factor underlying their involvement in work-related training. One out of 10 considers the need to obtain a professional license or certificate as the most important reason influencing the decision to undergo work-related training. According to 7 percent of the training participants, the most important reason

is a salary increase and a promotion, and another 7 percent rank the necessity to learn skills for a newly acquired position the number one reason to acquire training.

Post-Graduation Activities

Nearly one-quarter of home economics graduates with a bachelor's degree proceed to earn a postgraduate degree: 22 percent earn a master's degree, and 2 percent graduate with a doctorate degree.

▶ Only 29 percent of the master's degrees are earned in home economics. Education is the major field of choice among 44 percent of master's degree earners, and another 5 percent of home economics graduates earn a master's degree in business management and administrative services. Master's degrees earned by undergraduate home economics majors also included psychology (4 percent) and biology and other life sciences (4 percent).

▶ One-third of the doctorate degrees among undergraduate home economics majors are earned in education, 30 percent are earned in the field of home economics, and 10 percent are earned in agricultural sciences. Psychology is the field of choice among 11 percent of the doctorate degrees earned by undergraduate home economics majors.

Out of all home economics graduates under the age of 65, 70 percent are employed. Only 2 percent are officially unemployed; that is, they are not employed and are actively seeking employment. The remaining 28 percent are out of the labor force; that is, they are not employed and are not seeking employment. Family responsibilities are the reason for labor force withdrawal among 45 percent of this group of home economics graduates, and another 48 percent voluntarily withdraw from the labor force because they do not want or need to work.

Employment Outlook

According to the projections by the U.S. Bureau of Labor Statistics, employment in occupations that require at least a bachelor's degree is expected to grow faster than employment in other sectors of the American labor market. Between 2000 and 2010, the U.S. economy is projected to add 22.2 million jobs, yielding an employment growth rate of 15.2 percent. The employment growth projections in the top 10 occupations that are most likely to employ home economics graduates are presented below.

- Secondary, elementary, kindergarten, and prekindergarten teaching occupations together employ nearly 22 percent of all home economics majors. The demand for secondary school teachers is projected to increase by 18 percent between 2000 and 2010, and employment in the elementary school teaching occupation is projected to grow by 13.2 percent, with 202,000 new jobs over the same time period. Employment projections for kindergarten and pre-kindergarten teachers are much the same as for secondary teachers. An additional 110,000 jobs and an 18 percent growth rate are projected in this occupation.

- The total employment in miscellaneous marketing and sales occupations is projected to grow very rapidly, adding 137,000 new jobs between 2000 and 2010, more than a one-fifth increase in employment levels. The second-largest area of employment for home economics graduates, sales occupations, is expected to add 1.85 million jobs, yielding an 11.9 percent growth rate.

- Health occupations for nurses, pharmacists, therapists, physician assistants, nutritionists, and the like are projected to grow by 27 percent, with an additional 790,000 new jobs between 2000 and 2010. The aging population of the nation is a major contributor to the increased demand for health care occupations.

- Employment in top- to mid-level management and administrative occupations is projected to grow by 12 percent between 2000 and 2010. The demand for management-related occupations such as human resources staff and other administrative professional jobs is projected to grow by 17 percent.

- Secretarial and clerical occupations are projected to grow at slow rates of only 10 to 11 percent. Technological advances such as fast computers, faxes, e-mail, and voice mail will reduce the demand for personnel in clerical and secretarial occupations.

Table 3

Projected Change in Employment in the Top 10 Occupations That
Employ Persons with Only a Bachelor's Degree in Home Economics

Top 10 Occupations	Actual Employment in 2000 (000s)	Projected Employment in 2010 (000s)	Absolute Change (000s)	Percentage Change
Teachers, secondary school	1,113	1,314	201	18.1%
Sales occupations, including retail	15,513	17,365	1,852	11.9%
Teachers, elementary school	1,532	1,734	202	13.2%
Other administrative (e.g., records clerks, telephone operators)	16,911	18,522	1,611	9.5%
Registered nurses, pharmacists, therapists, physician assistants	2,908	3,698	790	27.2%
Other management-related occupations	4,956	5,801	845	17.1%
Top- and mid-level managers, executives, administrators	10,564	11,834	1,270	12.0%
Secretaries, receptionists, typists	4,980	5,501	521	10.5%
Other marketing and sales occupations	621	758	137	22.1%
Teachers, prekindergarten and kindergarten	597	707	110	18.4%

CHAPTER 8

Medical Preparatory Programs

Chiropractors, dentists, optometrists, physicians, podiatrists, and veterinarians all require some undergraduate course work prior to entry into their respective programs. The prerequisites range from 45 semester hours of course work up to a four-year bachelor's degree. Most minimally require mathematics, biology, organic and inorganic chemistry, and physics course work. Medical preparation curricula are competitive and demanding programs that may result in some people changing their original goals.

Becoming a physician takes a long time, usually 11 years: 4 years of undergraduate work, 4 years of medical school, and 3 years in residency. Medical education is thus costly, requiring more than 80 percent of students to borrow money to cover expenses. A few medical schools offer 6- versus 8-year combined educational programs, and some residency specialties are longer than 3 years, taking as many as 8 years. Chiropractic college requires 4 years with at least 2 years of undergraduate college. Most dentists have at least 8 years of education beyond high school. A minimum of 3 years of under-

graduate work and 4 years for an optometry degree is required. Ninety percent of podiatrists have an undergraduate degree plus their 4-year program in podiatric medicine. While a bachelor's degree is not required, most students who are admitted possess one as they undertake the 4-year veterinary medicine program.

The practice of medicine has changed substantially in recent years. While the most recent figures show that about two-thirds of physicians are in office-based practices that include clinics and HMOs and about one-quarter are employed in hospitals, the newly trained will more likely take salaried positions in group medical practices, clinics, and HMOs. Pursuing a specialization or establishing a private practice has become too expensive for many doctors.

While there are 24 specialty boards that accommodate a broad spectrum of interests, health cost containment has created a lower demand for some of the specializations. About one-third of the physicians are referred to as being primary care physicians—that is, internists, pediatricians, and general and family practitioners.

Regarding other health care professions, chiropractic treatment of back, neck, extremities, and other joint damage has become more accepted as a result of recent research. Chiropractors do not prescribe drugs or perform surgery, which is appealing to many health-conscious Americans. Most dentists are general practitioners who run their own practice, often alone or with a small staff. Fluoridation of water supplies has decreased the incidence of tooth decay. Ophthalmologists are physicians who perform eye surgery and treat eye diseases and injuries. Dispensing opticians fit and adjust eyeglasses. Optometrists examine eyes to diagnose vision problems and eye diseases. They also provide most of the primary vision care people need, keeping in mind that more than half of the individuals in the United States wear glasses or contact lenses. Podiatrists diagnose and treat diseases and injuries of the foot and lower leg by prescribing drugs, ordering physical therapy, setting fractures, and performing surgery. Podiatrists stress the importance of our feet because the 52 bones there make up about one-fourth of all the bones in the human body. Veterinarians are involved in the health care of pets, livestock, and laboratory animals. Large animal practice is considerably different from small animal practice, which also may determine whether a veterinarian works in an urban or rural setting.

Those in the medical area typically have very good academic ability in the basic sciences, as well as the humanities and social sciences. They use logic and scientific thinking to make decisive conclusions, often done quickly in emergency situations. They have color perception, spatial ability to use new technologies and X rays, and finger dexterity to perform clinical work and surgical procedures. Physical stamina is frequently needed. Interpersonal skills are critical when dealing with both patients and families who are in pain or under stress.

The interests of those in health-diagnosing occupations in general are scientific and people oriented. In the specializations, other interests emerge. For example, a surgeon can achieve concrete immediate physical solutions through precise manual dexterity skills, whereas a psychiatrist relies on words to work with the mind of a patient. Chiropractors' involvement in sports injuries of ligaments and muscles is different from a physician treating cancer. A dentist's correction of bad-looking teeth can change a patient's total view of self. And a love for the outdoors and not liking to work indoors can give a veterinarian personal satisfaction.

The values attributed to the health professions are numerous: intellectual stimulation—thinking and reasoning; independence—deciding what has to be done and doing it; flexible work schedule—choosing one's own hours; creativity—exploring new ways to do something; the ability to help others; good salary; prestige; recognition; and variety.

In general, those in the medical area are quiet, responsible, logical, and matter-of-fact. Some are quick to arrive at their decisions and seem to ignore others' suggestions. Although others, such as those in family or chiropractic practice, may be more holistic, less reliant on immediate use of technology, and slower in collecting details, they are, however, very thorough and committed to accuracy. These different interpersonal styles can have a bearing on doctor-patient relationships. Specific specialties also differ in style; for example, psychiatrists are projected as friendly but may be absorbed and care about learning, ideas, and independent projects of their own, while pathologists might not be interested in situations for which they see no use but will do what is necessary. Dentists and optometrists tend to be very thorough, systematic, and patient with detail and routine. And some veterinarians can come across as extremely practical and impersonal, while podiatrists may project a greater social awareness and emphasize a communicative approach with their patients.

Where Do Medical Preparatory Program Graduates Work?

Medical preparatory program graduates are employed in different sectors of the economy. Businesses and corporations in the private, for-profit sector of the economy employ 46 percent. More than one-quarter work in their own practice as self-employed workers. Thirteen percent work for educational institutions, and 9 percent work in the government sector. Only 6 percent of graduates are employed in the private, nonprofit sector of the economy.

Many of the skills and much of the knowledge that medical preparatory program graduates acquire during their schooling are applicable in the labor market. Therefore, many find jobs that are related to their field. Fifty-six percent are employed in jobs that are closely related to their undergraduate major field of study. Another 18 percent are employed in jobs that are somewhat related to their major. The remaining 26 percent of medical preparatory graduates work in jobs that are not related to their undergraduate major field of study.

Why do the latter group of medical preparatory graduates work in unrelated jobs? They cite a variety of factors as possible reasons. When asked to identify one most important factor for their employment choice, one-fifth cite pay and promotion opportunities, another one-fifth work in unrelated jobs because they want to change their career track, and an additional one-fifth report their inability to find a related job or get acceptance to a medical program of their choice as the most important reason for working in an unrelated job. An additional 15 percent state that the most important reason for accepting an unrelated job is related to their family responsibilities.

FIGURE 1

Percentage Distribution of Employed Persons with Only a Bachelor's Degree in Medical Preparatory Programs, by Major Sector of Economic Activity

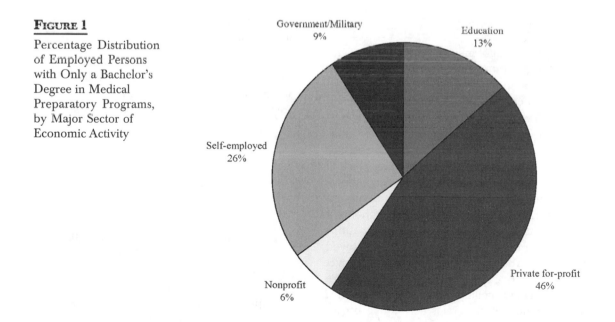

Table 1

Top 10 Occupations That Employ Persons with Only a
Bachelor's Degree in Medical Preparatory Programs

Top 10 Occupations	PERCENT OF EMPLOYED		
	All	Men	Women
Therapists, physician assistants, pharmacists, registered nurses	22.3	12.6	35.6
Diagnosing/treating practitioners (dentists, chiropractors, optometrists, physicians, psychiatrists, podiatrists, surgeons, veterinarians)	18.6	27.1	6.8
Health technologists and technicians	9.8	2.6	19.6
Top- and mid-level managers, executives, administrators	6.1	8.6	2.6
Other health occupations	4.1	4.1	4.1
Other administrative (e.g., records clerks, telephone operators)	3.7	2.4	5.5
Sales occupations, including retail	3.2	5.4	0.0
Accountants, auditors, other financial specialists	2.9	2.1	4.1
Artists, broadcasters, writers, editors, entertainers, public relations specialists	2.8	4.3	0.7
Secretaries, receptionists, typists	2.7	0.0	6.5

Occupations

The employment of medical preparatory graduates is concentrated in a few occupations. One-half work in only three occupational areas, and the top 10 occupations account for 75 percent of all employed medical preparatory graduates. Twenty-two percent of the graduates work as therapists, physician assistants, pharmacists, and nurses. Nearly one-fifth work as diagnosis and treatment practitioners who are dentists, optometrists, psychiatrists, etc. One in 10 of all employed graduates works as a health technologist or technician. The above three occupations account for more than one-half of all employed graduates. About 6 percent work in high-level managerial occupations, and 4 percent are employed in miscellaneous health occupations. The remainder work in sales, accounting, broadcasting, writing, editing, public relations, administrative support, clerical, and secretarial occupations.

Nearly 60 percent of employed medical preparatory graduates are men. The occupational employment patterns of male and female medical preparatory graduates are quite different.

 ⟩ Female graduates are more likely than males to work as nurses, therapists, and physician assistants. Thirty-six percent of female graduates are employed in these occupations, compared to only 13 percent of male graduates.

 ⟩ Female graduates also are more likely than males to work as health technologists and technicians. Nearly 20 percent of female graduates work in these occupations, compared to only 3 percent of their male counterparts.

‣ More female graduates than males are employed in administrative support and secretarial occupations.

‣ Male graduates, on the other hand, are more likely than their female counterparts (27 percent versus 7 percent) to work as diagnosis and treatment practitioners such as dentists, chiropractors, etc.

‣ A greater proportion of male graduates than female graduates are employed in top- to mid-level executive, administrative, and managerial occupations.

Activities on the Job

The activities in which medical preparatory graduates engage at work are related to their occupational employment patterns.

‣ One-half report that they spend a majority of their typical workweek in providing health services.

‣ One in 10 spends a major portion of work time in performing management and administrative duties.

‣ Eight percent spend most of their time at work in performing sales, purchasing, and marketing activities.

‣ Five percent of employed medical preparatory graduates consider teaching activities as the main part of their job.

Salaries

The average annual salary of medical preparatory graduates with only a bachelor's degree and who are employed full-time is $63,000, a level that is 16 percent higher than the average annual salary of all full-time employed college graduates. As with most college graduates, the salary of medical preparatory graduates increases with age, indicating that they get more productive and therefore can earn higher salaries as they spend more time on the job. Within each age group, the average salary of medical preparatory graduates is considerably higher than the average salary of all college graduates in those age groups.

‣ The average annual salary of medical preparatory graduates between the ages of 25 and 34 is $41,800 per year. Graduates between the ages of 35 and 44 earn $66,800 annually.

‣ The average annual salary of medical preparatory majors peaks at $79,800 among 55- to 64-year-old graduates.

The average annual salary of medical preparatory graduates who work in jobs that are closely related to their undergraduate major field of study is much higher than those who work in somewhat related jobs or jobs that are not related to their major field of study. Closely related jobs pay full-time employed medical preparatory graduates $70,900 annually. Graduates employed in somewhat related jobs earn $52,900 per year, and those whose jobs are unrelated to their undergraduate field of study earn $52,300 per year.

Earning an average salary of $89,500 annually, medical preparatory graduates working in their own practice earn a considerably higher salary than those who are employed in other sectors of the economy. The remuneration of medical preparatory graduates employed in the private, for-profit sector of the economy is $55,800 per year. Employment in educational institutions is associated with an average salary of $55,000 per year, and the government sector pays these graduates $52,300 per year.

The average annual salaries of medical preparatory graduates and all college graduates in the top 10 occupations that predominantly employ medical preparatory graduates are presented below.

▶ Health practitioners earn the highest average annual salary of $102,000 per year. This occupation is more likely to employ male than female graduates.

▶ Graduates employed in miscellaneous health occupations earn $77,700 per year.

▶ Medical preparatory graduates employed in high-level executive, administrative, and managerial occupations earn an average annual salary of $69,100. This occupation is somewhat more likely to employ male than female graduates.

▶ Nurses, pharmacists, therapists, and physician assistants with a bachelor's degree in a medical preparatory program earn $51,800 per year, and the average annual remuneration of graduates employed as health technologists and technicians is $45,400.

▶ Much like graduates from other major fields of study, medical preparatory graduates who are employed in administrative support and secretarial jobs earn less than $32,400 per year.

FIGURE 2

Age/Earnings Profile of Persons with Only a Bachelor's Degree in Medical Preparatory Programs (Full-Time Workers, in 2002 Dollars)

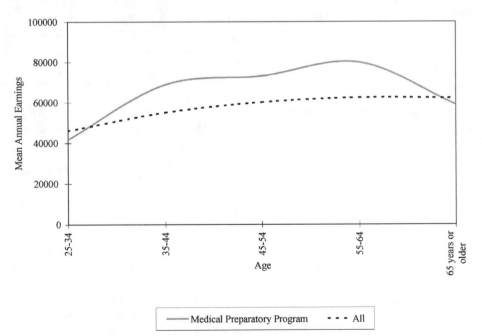

Table 2

Annual Salary of Full-Time Workers with Only a Bachelor's Degree
in Medical Preparatory Programs, Top 10 Occupations (in 2002 Dollars)

Earnings in Top 10 Occupations	All	Medical Preparatory Programs
Total	$54,171	$62,983
Registered nurses, pharmacists, therapists, physician assistants	$53,508	$51,803
Diagnosing/treating practitioners (dentists, chiropractors, optometrists, physicians, psychiatrists, podiatrists, surgeons, veterinarians)	$84,854	$101,991
Health technologists and technicians	$42,774	$45,396
Top- and mid-level managers, executives, administrators	$74,051	$69,087
Other health occupations	$39,559	$77,671
Other administrative (e.g., records clerks, telephone operators)	$34,547	$38,459
Sales occupations, including retail	$52,378	$33,244
Accountants, auditors, other financial specialists	$57,382	$57,192
Artists, broadcasters, writers, editors, entertainers, public relations specialists	$52,141	$64,744
Secretaries, receptionists, typists	$32,240	$32,372

On-the-Job Training

The career potential of a job is closely associated with the amount of work-related training on the job. Work-related training is regarded as an investment by firms because it makes workers more productive. Firms that invest in their workforce are more likely to offer pay increases and promotions to match the increasing productivity of their workers. Firms that do not invest in their workers are relatively less likely to offer pay increases and promotions. The incidence of work-related training among medical preparatory graduates is the same as the rate of participation in work-related training among all college graduates: 68 percent.

▶ Of those medical preparatory graduates who receive some training during the year, 73 percent receive technical training in the occupation in which they are employed.

▶ One-quarter of the training recipients participate in management or supervisory training.

▶ One-quarter receive training to improve their general professional skills, such as public speaking and business writing.

Although medical preparatory graduates decide to participate in work-related training activities, workshops, or seminars for numerous reasons, three reasons stand out as most commonly cited by graduates. Included among them are a desire to improve skills and knowledge in the occupational area of their employment, a need to obtain a professional license or certificate, and mandatory training requirements of the employer. When asked to select the one most important reason to acquire training, one-half of medical preparatory graduates who undergo training identify the desire to improve their occupational skills and knowledge. One-fifth cite the need to obtain a professional license or certificate, and 12 percent report mandatory training requirements by the employer as the most important factor underlying their involvement in work-related training. According to only 5 percent of the training participants, the most important reason to participate in training activities is advancement within the firm in the form of a salary increase or a promotion.

Post-Graduation Activities

Post-graduation education is high among medical preparatory graduates. Eight in 10 graduates with a bachelor's degree in a medical preparatory program proceed to earn a postgraduate degree. Only 7 percent earn a master's degree, 3 percent earn a doctorate degree, and the remaining 70 percent earn a professional degree.

- ▶ Nearly 55 percent of all master's degrees earned by undergraduate medical preparatory majors are in the health professions. Sixteen percent of the master's degrees are earned in business management and administrative services.

- ▶ Two-thirds of all doctorate degrees earned by medical preparatory graduates are in the health professions, and one-fifth are earned in biological and life sciences.

- ▶ Almost all the professional degrees earned by medical preparatory graduates

are in the medical fields—for example, MD (physicians), DDS (dentists), and the like.

Out of all medical preparatory graduates under the age of 65, 83 percent are employed. Only 3 percent are officially unemployed; that is, they are not employed and are actively seeking employment. The remaining 14 percent are out of the labor force; that is, they are not employed and are not seeking employment. The two main reasons underlying the labor force withdrawal of medical preparatory graduates are family responsibilities and enrollment in school. Nearly 35 percent cite family responsibilities as a reason for their labor force withdrawal, and 30 percent are not participating in the labor force because of their enrollment in graduate school. In addition, 12 percent suffer from a chronic illness or disabling condition, 9 percent choose early retirement, and 6 percent report their lack of a desire or need to work as one of the reasons for their withdrawal from the labor force.

Employment Outlook

According to the projections by the U.S. Bureau of Labor Statistics, employment in occupations that require at least a bachelor's degree is expected to grow faster than employment in other sectors of the American labor market. Between 2000 and 2010, the U.S. economy is projected to add 22.2 million jobs, yielding an employment growth rate of 15.2 percent. The employment growth projections in the top 10 occupations that are most likely to employ medical preparatory graduates are presented below.

- ▶ Employment in all health-related professions is projected to increase at much higher rates than the overall job growth in the economy. The demand for practitioners like dentists, chiropractors, and physicians is projected to increase by 25 percent between 2000 and 2010.

▶ Similarly high rates of job growth are projected for therapists, physician assistants, nurses, and pharmacists. Employment in these occupations is projected to increase by 27 percent.

▶ Health technologist and technician occupations that employ 10 percent of all working medical preparatory graduates are projected to add 581,000 jobs between 2000 and 2010. The demand for health technologists and technicians is projected to increase by more than one-quarter over this 10-year period.

▶ The demand for personnel in miscellaneous health occupations is projected to increase by 19 percent.

▶ Employment in high- to mid-level executive, administrative, and managerial occupations is projected to increase by 12 percent, a much slower pace of growth than that observed for health-related fields.

▶ Employment projections for sales and accounting occupations are similar to those for the overall employment in the U.S. economy. Total jobs in these occupations are projected to increase by about 12 percent.

Table 3
Projected Change in Employment in the Top 10 Occupations That Employ Persons with Only a Bachelor's Degree in Medical Preparatory Programs

Top 10 Occupations	Actual Employment in 2000 (000s)	Projected Employment in 2010 (000s)	Absolute Change (000s)	Percentage Change
Registered nurses, pharmacists, therapists, physician assistants	2,908	3,298	790	27.2%
Diagnosing/treating practitioners (dentists, chiropractors, optometrists, physicians, psychiatrists, podiatrists, surgeons, veterinarians)	3,921	4,888	967	24.7%
Health technologists and technicians	2,192	2,773	581	26.5%
Top- and mid-level managers, executives, administrators	10,564	11,834	1,270	12.0%
Other health occupations	266	317	51	19.2%
Other administrative (e.g., records clerks, telephone operators)	16,911	18,522	1,611	9.5%
Sales occupations, including retail	15,513	17,365	1,852	11.9%
Accountants, auditors, other financial specialists	2,115	2,481	366	17.3%
Artists, broadcasters, writers, editors, entertainers, public relations specialists	147	176	29	19.7%
Secretaries, receptionists, typists	4,980	5,501	521	10.5%

CHAPTER 9

Nursing

Nursing is a very broad occupational area and accommodates many opportunities for specialization, such as surgery, maternity, pediatrics, emergency room, intensive care, or involvement in specific health areas such as the heart or cancer. Some nurses work in home health agencies, schools, and public health and occupational health settings, with other directions also available for nurses who want administrative or nursing education roles. Characteristic of nurses is that they work with people who usually come to hospitals, clinics, and nursing homes with medical problems. They have close prolonged physical contact with people, touching and lifting patients. They also take blood samples, administer injections, apply dressings, and dispense medications. They become accustomed to tolerating conditions associated with mental, emotional, or physical problems or pain. These functions differentiate nursing from many careers, despite its holistic, preventive, and educational focus.

Increased medical knowledge and intensity required in rapidly expanding same-day surgery and treatments such as chemotherapy can create stressful work environments. Nursing also involves hazards from exposure to diseases such as hepatitis and AIDS, dangers from chemicals, and back injury from moving patients.

Early educational decisions require high school seniors to think of their interests as the overview suggests multiple options and career pathways. The three major educational choices are the associate degree (A.D.N.), which takes about two years to complete and is offered by community or junior colleges; a bachelor's degree (B.S.N.), which takes four to five years; and diploma programs offered by local hospitals, which take two to three years. Recently, two-thirds of nurses received an A.D.N.; one-quarter, a bachelor's degree; and an increasingly smaller number, a diploma in nursing. All students must graduate from an accredited nursing school and pass a national examination to obtain a nursing license. However, a bachelor's degree is usually necessary for administrative positions in hospitals and for community nursing. Also, a B.S.N. is required for admission to graduate nursing programs for research, teaching, clinical specialization, and, increasingly, management level positions or health services administration.

Several abilities are required in nursing: special medical skills, an understanding of technical and pharmaceutical language and information, fast and agile finger dexterity and physical coordination, strength, the ability to change rapidly from one task to another, good communications, record-keeping skills, and a willingness to follow directions exactly. Leadership is important, and this is increasingly evident when nurses must supervise other health care personnel.

Overall, nurses' interests typically follow their abilities: being social, being good communicators, and being scientifically skilled. Early in life, many entering the nursing field have had opportunities with or volunteered in caring for the elderly or sick relatives or in physical exercises with disabled persons where they have experienced scientific practices. Newer role models in the health care field–that is, physician assistants, surgical technicians, and managers in health maintenance organizations (HMOs)– present other examples of high-functioning professionals, which can be attractive career options for people with social and scientific interests. Note that social is the primary interest.

Attributes consistent across roles such as students-in-training, general staff duty nurses, nursing educators, head nurses, or directors of nursing are a desire to work with people, a desire to work with one's mind, a willingness to accept responsibility, and a desire for high achievement. Leadership is a characteristic of most staff nurses and administrators. Students-in-training, as well as nurse educators, enjoy the challenge of variety and diversity in their work.

Some nurses prefer being very logical, practical, and matter-of-fact, such as "this is what the results showed," while others come across as being friendly, offering encouragement, and being interested in what affects the individual's life, and are less interested in the technical aspects of nursing. Other qualities for nurses are the ability to make quick decisions, use good judgment, be orderly in their execution, and be goal oriented.

Where Do Nursing Majors Work?

Graduates of nursing programs work in a variety of workplace settings. About 3 out of 10 employed nursing program graduates work as wage and salary workers in private, for-profit organizations, and about the same proportion work in the nonprofit sector of the economy. One-quarter of nursing graduates work in the educational sector, while 10 percent are employed by government organizations. Few nursing majors are self-employed. Most employed graduates of undergraduate nursing programs are employed in jobs related to the major. Only 5 percent work in jobs not related to the major field of study. Those employed in unrelated jobs often say that working conditions are the primary reasons they do not work in the nursing profession.

FIGURE 1

Percentage Distribution of Employed Persons with Only a Bachelor's Degree in Nursing, by Major Sector of Economic Activity

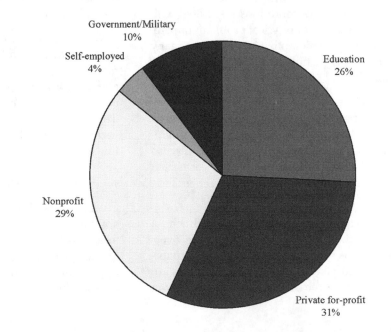

Government/Military
10%

Self-employed
4%

Education
26%

Nonprofit
29%

Private for-profit
31%

Table 1
Top 10 Occupations That Employ Persons with Only a Bachelor's Degree in Nursing

Top 10 Occupations	PERCENT OF EMPLOYED		
	All	Men	Women
Registered nurses, pharmacists, therapists, physician assistants	81.9	80.4	82.0
Top- and mid-level managers, executives, administrators	4.4	6.6	4.2
Personnel, training, and labor relations specialists	2.8	1.5	2.9
Other health occupations	1.7	3.2	1.6
Sales occupations, including retail	1.2	0.6	1.3
Postsecondary professors	1.0	0.5	1.0
Health technologists and technicians	0.9	1.9	0.8
Other management-related occupations	0.8	0.0	0.9
Insurance, securities, real estate, business services	0.6	0.0	0.6
Secretaries, receptionists, typists	0.5	0.0	0.5

Occupations

The overwhelming majority of nursing program graduates is employed in the nursing occupation. More than 80 percent of those with an undergraduate nursing degree are employed in the nursing field. An additional 4 percent are employed in managerial and supervisory positions. The remainder of employed persons with a bachelor's degree work in a variety of jobs across the economy.

Activities on the Job

▶ Most of the duties that nurses undertake involve the application of their nursing skills in various clinical settings. However, they are not the only duties involved in the nursing field.

▶ Staff supervision and employee relations are a regular part of the daily job duties of many nurses.

▶ A substantial number of nurses also engage in teaching activities, often of student nurses engaged in clinical training.

▶ Most nursing jobs involve accounting activities usually related to insurance coverage documentation.

Salaries

The salaries of persons with a bachelor's degree in nursing average $50,900 per year, a rate of pay $3,300 less than the average salary of $54,200 earned by the average college graduate working in a full-time job. The annual salaries of young nursing professionals with a bachelor's degree are much higher than their counterparts with degrees in other major fields of study. The average earnings of nursing majors between the ages of 25 to 29 is $46,800 per year, well above the earnings of other college graduates of that age.

However, nursing graduates do not experience a substantial increase in their earnings as they gain experience. For many college majors, annual earnings increase by 90 percent to 100 percent over their working lives as work experience and skill combine to raise productivity and wages. Salaries of nurses increase at a much slower rate than that observed for other bachelor's degree holders. The earnings of nursing majors rise only about 17 percent to $54,900 per year at ages 50 to 54.

Unlike in most other fields of study in which employment in the private, for-profit sector means higher pay, the earnings of persons with bachelor's degrees in nursing who work in educational, private, for-profit, or nonprofit organizations are quite similar. Nursing graduates working in educational institutions earn an average salary of $50,900. Those employed by private, for-profit companies earn $49,500 per year on average, while those employed by nonprofit organizations have annual salaries of $50,200. Persons with a nursing degree who are self-employed have much higher annual earnings than others with a bachelor's degree in the field. Earnings for self-employed nursing program graduates average about $70,600 per year, an earnings advantage of nearly 40 percent for those taking the risks of self-employment.

Graduates of nursing programs who work in jobs that are related to their major have much higher annual earnings than those employed in jobs that are not related to the nursing field. Those employed in jobs that are closely related to the field have annual salaries that are about 20 percent higher than those in unrelated positions. Graduates employed in the nursing occupation earned about $45,600 per year in 2002 dollars.

The earnings of persons with a bachelor's degree in nursing vary considerably by occupation. Graduates who gain access to mid- to upper-level management and administration jobs have salaries that average $59,600 per year, an earnings advantage of about 17 percent compared to the $50,900 average annual salary of all graduates with a nursing degree.

Those employed as registered nurses, pharmacists, therapists, and physician assistants earn an average salary of $51,100, a rate of pay about $2,400 less than the average pay of all bachelor's degree holders employed in those occupations. Nursing majors who work in sales (except insurance, finance, and real estate sales), health technology, and secretarial positions have earnings that are well below the average of other graduates from the field.

FIGURE 2

Age/Earnings Profile of Persons with Only a Bachelor's Degree in Nursing
(Full-Time Workers, in 2002 Dollars)

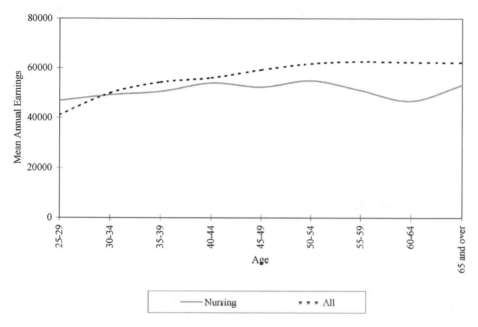

Table 2
Annual Salary of Full-Time Workers with Only a Bachelor's Degree in Nursing, Top 10 Occupations (in 2002 Dollars)

Earnings in Top 10 Occupations	All	Nursing
Total	$54,171	$50,936
Registered nurses, pharmacists, therapists, physician assistants	$53,508	$51,069
Top- and mid-level managers, executives, administrators	$74,051	$59,616
Personnel, training, and labor relations specialists	$51,577	$51,711
Other health occupations	$39,559	$52,110
Sales occupations, including retail	$52,378	$40,311
Postsecondary professors	$42,234	$48,647
Health technologists and technicians	$42,774	$36,598
Other management-related occupations	$51,921	$53,806
Insurance, securities, real estate, business services	$68,273	$60,832
Secretaries, receptionists, typists	$32,246	$27,399

On-the-Job Training

Work-based learning activities are an important part of the career development of nursing program graduates. Nearly 9 out of 10 employed persons with a degree in nursing participate in a work-based training program during the year. Most of the training that they undertake is in developing specific professional skills within the nursing profession. Frequently, nurses are required to participate in workshops and seminars related to the nursing profession in order to maintain their certification as professionals in the field.

Post-Graduation Activities

Compared to other major fields of study, persons who earn a bachelor's degree in nursing are less likely to enroll and complete a graduate program of study. Only 23 percent of all persons with an undergraduate degree in nursing eventually continue their education and earn an advanced degree. Almost all these advanced degrees are at the master's level. Only 2 percent of nursing majors at the undergraduate level go on to complete a doctorate or professional degree. Thus, undergraduate nursing programs are not a good educational pathway to becoming a physician or other medical practitioner with a doctor's degree.

▶ Among those who do earn a doctorate, most often the degree is in an education-related area or in law. Only 0.2 percent of nursing majors eventually earn a doctoral degree in a health-related area.

▶ Sixty percent of those who earn a master's degree earn an advanced degree in a nursing specialty. About 16 percent earn their master's degree in a health-related field, while about 5 percent earn a master's degree in business.

About 85 percent of those with a bachelor's degree are employed, although many of these individuals work in part-time positions. Among employed nursing graduates, nearly one-third work part-time schedules. In most instances, these individuals have decided they prefer part-time schedules. Among nursing majors who do not work, virtually none are officially classified as unemployed—that is, seeking a job but unable to find work. Rather, most nursing program graduates who are not employed have voluntarily chosen not to work. Most often these individuals do not work in order to meet family responsibilities.

Employment Outlook

Although the overall employment in the U.S. economy is projected to increase by 15.2 percent, the demand for workers with a college degree is expected to increase 22.2 percent between 2000 and 2010. The rate of job growth for the nursing occupation is projected to be considerably greater than the overall rate of growth in the demand for college graduates. Overall employment among registered nurses is expected to increase from 2,908,000 in 2000 to 3,698,000 by 2010, an increase of 790,000 jobs, or about 27 percent, over the period. The rising average age of the nation's population, along with new changes in technology and organization of health care services, is expected to cause this rise in demand. Over the past several years, shortages of registered nurses have developed across the nation. The number of graduates in the nursing field has fallen considerably in recent years despite the strong demand for skilled nurses. Many health care organizations have begun relying on graduates of overseas nursing programs to meet their staffing needs. Recent supply and demand forecasts suggest continued shortages of nurses in many states as demand rises but growth in supply lags behind need.

Employment in the managerial and administrative area, also an important source of employment opportunities for nursing majors, is expected to grow more slowly than the overall level of demand for college graduates or for persons with a degree in nursing. Slower growth rates in employment levels in the hospital industry suggest that the demand for managerial and administrative staff in that industry will slow as well. However, new opportunities for health professionals are expected in non-hospital health organizations, including skilled nursing facilities and offices of physicians. Strong job growth is expected in health occupations outside the nursing profession, including that of health technician.

Table 3
Projected Change in Employment in the Top 10 Occupations That Employ Persons with Only a Bachelor's Degree in Nursing

Top 10 Occupations	Actual Employment in 2000 (000s)	Projected Employment in 2010 (000s)	Absolute Change (000s)	Percentage Change
Registered nurses, pharmacists, therapists, physician assistants	2,908	3,698	790	27.2%
Top- and mid-level managers, executives, administrators	10,564	11,834	1,270	12.0%
Personnel, training, and labor relations specialists	490	578	88	18.0%
Other health occupations	266	317	51	19.2%
Sales occupations, including retail	15,513	17,365	1,852	11.9%
Postsecondary professors	1,344	1,659	315	23.4%
Health technologists and technicians	2,192	2,773	581	26.5%
Other management-related occupations	4,956	5,801	845	17.1%
Insurance, securities, real estate, business services	1,548	1,726	178	11.5%
Secretaries, receptionists, typists	4,980	5,501	521	10.5%

CHAPTER 10

Parks, Recreation, Fitness, and Leisure Studies

This field fits in with current interest in physical fitness, health, and leisure time. Recreation workers are activity leaders, organizers, and facility and equipment managers. By leading activities, they help people in entertainment, self-improvement, and physical fitness. They conduct classes and coach in areas such as drama, arts and crafts, tennis, water sports, gymnastics, and other sports. They plan and organize daily activities, teams, leagues, social functions, and exercise programs, whether it be at the workplace, a camp, or a recreation center. Work settings include local playgrounds, recreation areas, parks, community centers, health clubs, religious organizations, camps, tourist parks, companies, nursing homes, and park and recreation governmental commissions. Graduates of this major will usually have supervisory roles because many workers in this field are part-time, seasonal, or volunteers. Recreation workers' focus is primarily enjoyment.

Therapeutic recreation is another related major that prepares graduates to provide treatment services and recreation activities such as games, dance, and arts and crafts to people with illnesses and disabling conditions. The purpose of these activities is to reduce depression, stress, and anxiety. They help individuals to recover basic motor functioning and use resources to become integrated into the community. They work to build individuals' confidence and help them socialize better to foster more independent functioning.

Course work in the recreation field can include community organization, supervision, management, and recreation for the disabled or elderly, plus fieldwork. Specializations are park management, camp management, industrial recreation, and therapeutic recreation. Course work for therapeutic recreation includes human anatomy, physiology, medical terminology, intervention design and evaluation, and study of the characteristics of disabilities.

Attributes for persons with this major include good physical coordination and social, teaching, language, and interpersonal skills to relate to people with a wide range of skills, of different ages, and from diverse backgrounds. Leadership and organization skills are critical for planning and coordinating events, schedules, and programs. Persuasive and motivational abilities are used in instructing beginners, coaching, and working with the ill and those with disabling conditions.

Recreation workers' interests include strong people and leadership orientations. For example, a team's captain performs a leadership role. Different specializations within the field additionally involve scientific likes for those interested in knowledge about the body's anatomical functioning. Stressing athletic involvement brings an appreciation for honing the physique through practice, strength, coordination, and specific skills related to an activity or sport. The therapist sees the value of following and organizing routines.

Values are the logical sequels to the above abilities and interests—that is, believing in the worth of physical activity, working with people, and leadership. Valuing independence may seem to contradict team work. Valuing independence can represent the belief that one should be as good as one can be by doing something in one's own style.

The personality experienced on the playing field can be different when the individual assumes a leadership role. In activities, the people orientation emerges. Recreation workers enjoy talking and foster cooperation and teamwork. As administrators, they are persistent, are hard-working, and follow detail and routine. Practicality is a characteristic of a recreational leader.

Where Do Parks, Recreation, Fitness, and Leisure Studies Majors Work?

Only 43 percent of employed recreation and fitness studies graduates work for businesses and corporations in the private, for-profit sector of the economy. Another 9 percent work in the private, for-profit sector as self-employed workers in their own business or practice. Educational institutions employ large numbers of recreation and fitness studies graduates. More than one-fifth of recreation and fitness studies graduates work in this sector of the economy, primarily as elementary and secondary school teachers. The next major employer of recreation and fitness studies graduates is the government, which employs 19 percent of the graduates. Involvement with community fitness programs results in employment of 7 percent of these graduates in the private, nonprofit sector of the economy.

Only 60 percent of all recreation and fitness studies graduates are employed in jobs that are closely related or somewhat related to their undergraduate major field of study. Nearly 34 percent work in closely related jobs, and 25 percent report that their jobs are somewhat related to their undergraduate major. The remaining 41 percent of all employed recreation and fitness studies graduates work in jobs that are not at all related to their undergraduate major field of study.

FIGURE 1

Percentage Distribution of Employed Persons with Only a Bachelor's Degree in Parks, Recreation, Leisure, and Fitness Studies, by Major Sector of Economic Activity

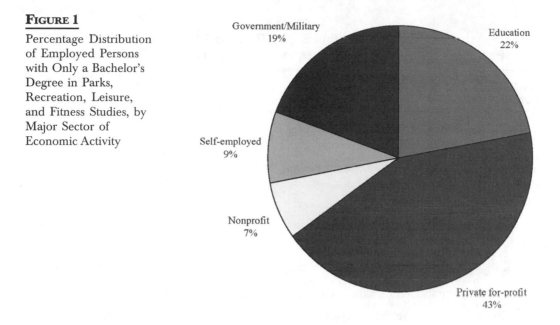

Government/Military
19%

Education
22%

Self-employed
9%

Nonprofit
7%

Private for-profit
43%

Why do recreation and fitness studies graduates work in jobs that are not related to their major? Nearly three-quarters of the graduates who work in unrelated jobs report pay and promotion opportunities as one of the factors influencing their decision to work in an unrelated job. More than one-half cite the general working environment as one of the reasons for their employment outside their field of study, and one-half are influenced by a change in their career interests. About 47 percent report job location as an influencing factor, 37 percent are unable to find a related job, and 28 percent report family-related factors as one of the reasons for working in an unrelated job.

As noted above, graduates offer several factors as influencing their decision to work in unrelated jobs. When asked to identify the most important reason for working in an unrelated job, 44 percent rank pay and promotion opportunities as number one, and 15 percent consider their inability to find a related job as the most important factor influencing their employment choice.

Twelve percent cite a change in their career track as the number one reason, and 1 out of 10 reports the general working environment as the primary reason for an employment choice in an unrelated field. Only 6 percent consider family-related factors as the most important reason for working in an unrelated job.

Occupations

Nearly 64 percent of all employed recreation and fitness studies graduates work in the top 10 occupations that predominantly employ these graduates. These occupations span across 6 major occupational areas, including teaching, managerial, sales and marketing, services, finance and real estate, and labor relations. The highest concentration is in top- to mid-level administrative and managerial occupations that employ 14 percent of recreation and fitness studies graduates. Another 7 percent are employed in management-related occupations as management analysts, purchasing agents, and regulatory officers.

Table 1

Top 10 Occupations That Employ Persons with Only a
Bachelor's Degree in Parks, Recreation, Leisure, and Fitness Studies

| | PERCENT OF EMPLOYED | | |
Top 10 Occupations	All	Men	Women
Top- and mid-level managers, executives, administrators	14.1	17.9	8.9
Teachers, secondary school	7.8	8.9	6.2
Other management-related occupations	7.4	8.0	6.7
Sales occupations, including retail	6.8	9.3	3.4
Other service occupations, except health	5.9	3.6	9.0
Insurance, securities, real estate, business services	5.2	6.3	3.8
Teachers, elementary school	4.9	3.4	6.9
Registered nurses, pharmacists, therapists, physician assistants	4.6	2.1	8.0
Personnel, training, and labor relations specialists	3.5	3.1	4.1
Other marketing and sales occupations	3.3	2.8	4.1

Teaching occupations employ 13 percent of recreation and fitness studies graduates: 8 percent as secondary school teachers and 5 percent as elementary school teachers. Sales occupations employ 7 percent of the graduates, and another 3 percent are employed in miscellaneous marketing and sales occupations. Nearly 6 percent are employed in non-health service occupations, and 5 percent work in health service occupations as physical therapists, registered nurses, and physician assistants. Slightly less than 4 percent of the graduates are employed in labor relations occupations, including personnel recruiting and training.

Fifty-eight percent of all employed recreation and fitness studies graduates are males. The occupational employment patterns of male graduates are somewhat different from the occupational employment of females.

▶ Male graduates are two times more likely than females to be employed in upper-level managerial and administrative jobs. Eighteen percent of males work in these jobs, compared to only 9 percent of employed female recreation and fitness studies graduates.

▶ There is a larger proportion of men in secondary teacher occupations than women, 9 percent versus 3 percent. Elementary teacher occupations, on the other hand, employ a larger proportion of female recreation and fitness studies graduates than males, 7 percent versus 3 percent.

▶ Insurance, financial, real estate, and business service occupations employ 6 percent of male graduates and 4 percent of female graduates.

▶ Service occupations, health and non-health, are more likely to employ female than male graduates. Non-health service occupations employ 9 percent of female graduates and fewer than 4 percent of male graduates. Health occupations, including physical therapists, nurses, and physician assistants, employ 8 percent of women and only 2 percent of male recreation and fitness studies graduates.

Activities on the Job

The occupational employment patterns of recreation and fitness studies graduates are reflected in the duties that they perform on their jobs.

▶ Teaching duties are regularly performed by 44 percent of the graduates and are considered to be a primary activity and a major portion of their jobs by 20 percent of all employed graduates.

▶ Six out of 10 employed graduates regularly engage in management and administrative duties at their jobs, and 19 percent spend a major portion of their time during a typical workweek in performing these duties.

▶ About 40 percent regularly participate in sales, purchasing, and marketing duties, and 18 percent spend most of their work time performing these duties.

▶ One-fifth of all employed recreation and fitness studies majors regularly provide professional services such as health services. Only 7 percent report that they spend a majority of their time in the provision of professional services.

▶ Nearly one-half of all employed recreation and fitness studies graduates engage in employee-relations activities, including recruiting, personnel development, and training, and 7 percent conduct these duties during most of their working time.

▶ Although 88 percent of all employed recreation and fitness studies graduates perform accounting, finance, and contractual duties as a regular part of their jobs, only 5 percent spend most of their time in a typical workweek performing these duties.

▶ Thirty-six percent of recreation and fitness studies graduates regularly perform managerial duties to oversee the quality and efficiency of the production process at their jobs, and only 3 percent spend a majority of their typical workweek engaged in these activities.

▶ Doing computer applications, programming, and systems-development activities is reported by one-quarter of all employed recreation and fitness studies graduates. However, only 3 percent spend most of their time on these activities.

▶ Very few recreation and fitness studies graduates engage in applied or basic research and in product design or development activities.

Salaries

The average annual salary of recreation and fitness studies graduates with only a bachelor's degree who are employed full-time is $42,400, a level that is only 78 percent of the average annual salary of all full-time employed college graduates. As with most college graduates, the salary of recreation and fitness studies majors increases as they age. Their age earnings profile indicates that their productivity increases as they spend more time on the job. However, the salary of recreation and fitness studies graduates in different age ranges is lower than the salaries of all college graduates in the same age groups.

▶ The average annual salary of recreation and fitness studies graduates between the ages of 25 and 29 is $34,300. Graduates between the ages of 30 and 34 earn $34,530 annually.

▶ Average annual earnings of recreation and fitness studies graduates increase as they get older. The average annual salary of 35- to 39-year-old recreation and fitness studies graduates who are employed full-time is $41,100. The average salary among 40- to 44-year-olds is $49,400 per year. The salary peaks between the ages of 45 and 49, when the average salary of recreation and fitness studies majors is $56,700.

The average annual salary of recreation and fitness studies graduates who work in jobs that are closely related to their major field of study is lower than the average salary of those who are employed in jobs that are somewhat related to their major or not related to their undergraduate major. Many graduates working in closely related jobs are employed in elementary and secondary school teaching occupations or health and non-health service occupations that generally pay these graduates lower salaries. Employment in closely related jobs is associated with an average salary of $34,980 per year. Those graduates who are employed in jobs that are somewhat related to their major earn $37,900 per year, and graduates employed in unrelated jobs earn an annual salary of $41,000.

The average salary of recreation and fitness studies graduates who work full-time in the private, for-profit sector either for businesses and corporations or as self-employed workers in their own business or practice is $41,590 per year.

Graduates employed in the government sector earn the second-highest salary. This group earns $36,700 per year. Educational institutions pay full-time employed recreation and fitness studies graduates an average salary of $33,970 per year. Graduates who work for nonprofit organizations on a full-time basis earn only $31,100 per year, a level that is lower than the average salary of recreation and fitness studies graduates employed in other sectors of the economy.

The salaries of recreation and fitness studies graduates vary by the occupations in which they are employed. The average annual salary of all full-time employed recreation and fitness studies majors is only 78 percent of the average salary of all college graduates. In 8 out of the top 10 predominant occupations, the salary of recreation and fitness studies graduates is lower than the average salary of all college graduates. In the remaining 2 (elementary and secondary school teaching occupations), recreation and fitness studies graduates earn more than the average for all college graduates employed in these occupations.

▶ Recreation and fitness studies graduates employed in finance, real estate, and business service occupations earn an average annual salary of $62,700, a level that is higher than the average salary in the remaining 9 occupations. However, these occupations employ only 5 percent of employed graduates. A greater proportion of male than female graduates is employed in these occupations.

▶ The second-highest earnings among recreation and fitness studies graduates are in jobs in top- to mid-level executive, managerial, and administrative occupations. Graduates employed in these occupations earn $55,400 per year. Male graduates are two times as likely as female graduates to be employed in these occupations.

▶ Employment in sales occupations among recreation and fitness studies graduates is associated with an average annual salary of $50,800.

▶ The average pay of recreation and fitness studies graduates employed in secondary or primary school teaching occupations is $41,600 per year.

▶ Non-health service occupations pay only $27,200 annually to recreation and fitness studies graduates. This salary is only two-thirds of the average salary of all college graduates employed in these occupations, indicating that recreation and fitness studies graduates are frequently employed in low-level service jobs. This occupation employs a larger proportion of female than male recreation and fitness studies graduates.

▶ The average salary of recreation and fitness studies graduates employed in health occupations is only 64 percent of the salary of all college graduates employed in these occupations. Graduates of recreation and fitness studies programs are employed in physical therapist and other medical assistant positions that pay lower salaries than the salary of registered nurses, pharmacists, and other high-level health services occupations.

FIGURE 2

Age/Earnings Profile of Persons with Only a Bachelor's Degree in Parks, Recreation, Leisure, and Fitness Studies (Full-Time Workers, in 2002 Dollars)

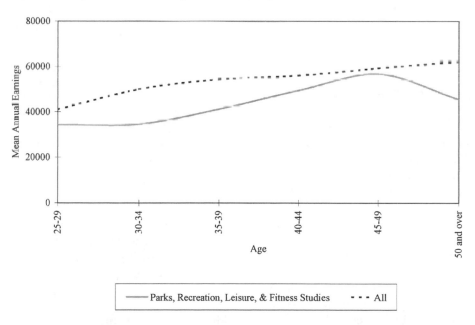

Table 2

Annual Salary of Full-Time Workers with Only a Bachelor's Degree in Parks, Recreation, Leisure, and Fitness Studies, Top 10 Occupations (in 2002 Dollars)

Earnings in Top 10 Occupations	All	Parks, Recreation, Leisure, and Fitness Studies
Total	$54,171	$42,432
Top- and mid-level managers, executives, administrators	$74,051	$55,354
Teachers, secondary school	$40,355	$41,585
Other management-related occupations	$51,921	$36,324
Sales occupations, including retail	$52,378	$50,806
Other service occupations, except health	$39,984	$27,237
Insurance, securities, real estate, business services	$68,273	$62,673
Teachers, elementary school	$39,167	$41,900
Registered nurses, pharmacists, therapists, physician assistants	$53,508	$34,466
Personnel, training, and labor relations specialists	$51,577	$40,882
Other marketing and sales occupations	$58,208	$43,866

On-the-Job Training

The career potential of a job is closely associated with the amount of work-related training on the job. Work-related training is regarded as an investment by firms because it makes workers more productive. Firms that invest in their workforce are more likely to offer pay increases and promotions to match the increasing productivity of their workers. Firms that do not invest in their workers are relatively less likely to offer pay increases and promotions. The incidence of work-related training among recreation and fitness studies graduates is about the same as the rate of participation in work-related training among all college graduates: 68 percent.

▶ Of those recreation and fitness studies graduates who receive some training during the year, 70 percent receive technical training in the occupation in which they are employed.

▶ Forty-four percent of the training recipients receive management or supervisory training.

▶ Thirty-four percent receive training to improve their general professional skills, such as public speaking and business writing.

Although recreation and fitness studies graduates decide to participate in work-related training activities, workshops, or seminars for numerous reasons, five reasons stand out as most commonly cited by graduates. Included among them is a desire to improve skills and knowledge in the occupational area of their employment, mandatory training requirements of the employer, increased opportunities for advancement in the form of a higher salary and a promotion, requirements to obtain a professional license or certificate, and the need to learn new skills for a newly acquired position.

When asked to identify the most important reason to acquire training, 65 percent of recreation and fitness studies graduates who undergo training identify the need to improve their occupational skills and knowledge. Another 13 percent report mandatory training requirements by the employer as the most important factor underlying their involvement in work-related training. Eight percent consider the need to obtain a professional license or certificate as the most important reason influencing their decision to undergo work-related training. According to 7 percent of the training participants, the most important reason is a salary increase and promotion, and 4 percent rank the necessity to learn skills for a newly acquired position as the number one reason to acquire training.

Post-Graduation Activities

Fewer than one-quarter of all recreation and fitness studies graduates with a bachelor's degree proceed to earn a postgraduate degree: 21 percent earn a master's degree, and only 1 percent graduate with a doctorate degree.

▶ One-third of the master's degrees are earned in the field of recreation and fitness studies, and another one-third of the degrees are earned in education. About 5 percent of the master's degrees earned by undergraduate recreation and fitness studies majors are in the health professions, and another 5 percent of the graduates earn a master's degree in business management and administrative services.

▶ Nearly one-half of the few doctorate degrees earned by undergraduate recreation and fitness studies majors are earned in the field of recreation and fitness studies and 45 percent are earned in the health professions. The remaining doctorate degrees are earned in education.

Out of all recreation and fitness studies graduates under the age of 65, 87 percent are employed. Only 3 percent are officially unemployed; that is, they are not employed and are actively seeking employment. The remaining 10 percent are out of the labor force; that is, they are not employed and are not seeking employment. Family responsibilities are cited as the reason for the labor force withdrawal among 45 percent of this group of recreation and fitness studies graduates, and another 39 percent voluntarily withdraw from the labor force because they do not want or need to work. Slightly over one-quarter of the labor force withdrawals of recreation and fitness studies graduates under the age of 65 are due to retirement. About 9 percent withdraw from the labor market to enroll in school, and 8 percent suffer from a chronic illness or a disabling condition.

Employment Outlook

According to the projections by the U.S. Bureau of Labor Statistics, employment in occupations that require at least a bachelor's degree is expected to grow faster than employment in other sectors of the American labor market. Between 2000 and 2010, the U.S. economy is projected to add 22.2 million jobs, yielding an employment growth rate of 15.2 percent. The employment growth projections in the top 10 occupations that are most likely to employ recreation and fitness studies graduates are presented next.

- Employment in 6 out of the top 10 occupations that are most likely to employ recreation and fitness studies graduates is projected to grow at a rate above the rate of growth of total employment in the U.S. economy.

- Employment in miscellaneous marketing and sales occupations is projected to increase by 22 percent over the same time period.

- The demand for secondary school teachers and personnel, training, and labor relations specialists is projected to increase by 18 percent between 2000 and 2010.

- An impressive job growth rate of 27 percent is projected for health occupations. Unfortunately, recreation and fitness studies graduates are more likely to get low-wage jobs in this sector of the economy. Their average salary is only 64 percent of the annual salary of all college graduates employed in these health occupations.

Table 3

Projected Change in Employment in the Top 10 Occupations That Employ Persons with Only a Bachelor's Degree in Parks, Recreation, Leisure, and Fitness Studies

Top 10 Occupations	Actual Employment in 2000 (000s)	Projected Employment in 2010 (000s)	Absolute Change (000s)	Percentage Change
Top- and mid-level managers, executives, administrators	10,564	11,834	1,270	12.0%
Teachers, secondary school	1,113	1,314	201	18.1%
Other management-related occupations	4,956	5,801	845	17.1%
Sales occupations, including retail	15,513	17,365	1,852	11.9%
Other service occupations, except health	9,652	11,287	1,635	16.9%
Insurance, securities, real estate, business services	1,548	1,726	178	11.5%
Teachers, elementary school	1,532	1,734	202	13.2%
Registered nurses, pharmacists, therapists, physician assistants	2,908	3,698	790	27.2%
Personnel, training, and labor relations specialists	490	578	88	18.0%
Other marketing and sales occupations	621	758	137	22.1%

CHAPTER 11

Pharmacy

Most people are familiar with the work of pharmacists. Most medicines today are manufactured by pharmaceutical companies in standard dosages and forms. This leaves the pharmacist's role primarily to dispense and inform consumers about a medication's use and its possible side effects. In community or retail pharmacies, a frequent function is to provide information about over-the-counter drugs and make recommendations after asking the user health-related questions. Pharmacists can become involved in drug therapy programs such as medicines for psychiatric disorders, diagnostic use of radio-pharmaceuticals, or intravenous nutrition.

Based on their choice of future employment settings, high school seniors feel a sense of immediacy in selecting a college to attend. For example, for most positions in community pharmacies, a bachelor's degree in pharmacy is generally acceptable. However, a doctor of pharmacy (Ph.D.) degree is the employer's choice for a growing number of hospitals. A bachelor of science (B.S.) degree in pharmacy, the degree most graduates receive, takes five years. A doctor of pharmacy degree normally requires at least six years, with a bachelor's degree not usually being awarded. However, more schools are offering only the Ph.D. degree, and fewer schools are offering the B.S. as the only professional degree.

All colleges of pharmacy offer courses teaching how to dispense prescriptions and practice management, leading to preparation for licensure to practice. Other entry requirements include mathematics, chemistry, biology, and social sciences courses. A license requires that the pharmacy graduate obtain a degree from an accredited college of pharmacy, pass a state licensing examination, and serve an internship under a licensed pharmacist.

Scientific ability, manual and finger dexterity to perform laboratory work, ability to recognize color and texture, and computer skills are important to the performance of pharmacy. Learning interpersonal skills is part of another major trend in pharmacists' training that emphasizes increased direct patient care and consultative services. Increasingly, pharmacists are monitoring a person's reaction to a drug or to multiple prescriptions, so collaborating with physicians requires good communication skills.

Pharmacists' interests will vary depending on whether they follow a hospital and research direction in which scientific likes predominate or a combination of scientific, business, and people orientations characterized by those in community pharmacies. Pharmacists are thorough, very accurate, and orderly. However, the pharmacy field also requires its personnel to be very alert to business changes as well as pharmaceutical advances in new available medicines.

Pharmacists value a good income, social interaction, high achievement, research work or at least a knowledge of the results of new drug studies, and the chance to work precisely. In recent years, the fact that 1 in 6 pharmacists works part-time, nights, or weekends may accommodate a better opportunity for work-family balance.

The scientific and business orientations of pharmacists bring forth practical, matter-of-fact, and organized approaches to doing things. Community or retail settings tend to increase the quality of sensitivity in pharmacists' interactions with people. Some pharmacists work in organizations in which they refer to themselves as bench scientists and where the emphasis is on data and things. Overall, pharmacists are characterized by being thorough, being accurate, and maintaining standards.

Where Do Pharmacy Majors Work?

Pharmacy program graduates work across many sectors of the American economy. Nearly 6 out of 10 pharmacy program majors work as employees of private, for-profit corporations and businesses. A substantial proportion of those with a pharmacy degree own their own businesses; more than 17 percent of all pharmacy majors are self-employed. Only a small proportion of those with a bachelor's degree in pharmacy work in educational institutions or government agencies. An extraordinarily high 90 percent of pharmacy majors are employed in jobs that are closely related to their major. However, those who do not have pharmacy-related jobs have annual salaries that are much lower.

FIGURE 1

Percentage Distribution of Employed Persons with Only a Bachelor's Degree in Pharmacy, by Major Sector of Economic Activity

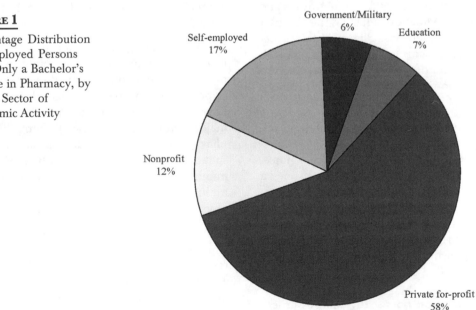

Government/Military 6%

Education 7%

Self-employed 17%

Nonprofit 12%

Private for-profit 58%

Table 1

Top 5 Occupations That Employ Persons with Only a Bachelor's Degree in Pharmacy

Top 5 Occupations	PERCENT OF EMPLOYED		
	All	**Men**	**Women**
Registered nurses, pharmacists, therapists, physician assistants	88.0	87.7	88.6
Top- and mid-level managers, executives, administrators	2.4	3.4	0.3
Other management-related occupations	1.9	2.1	1.6
Sales occupations, including retail	1.8	2.5	0.3
Health technologists and technicians	0.9	0.5	1.5

Occupations

The overwhelming majority of those who earn a bachelor's degree in the pharmacy field become employed in the health profession as pharmacists. Those not employed as pharmacists are distributed across a few occupational fields that are not closely related to the major field of study. Pharmacy graduates who work in unrelated jobs do so largely because their career interests have changed from pharmacy to some other field.

Activities on the Job

- Pharmacy majors spend the bulk of their workweek engaged in professional activities related to the major.

- A major activity of pharmacists focuses around accounting and contracting issues related to health insurance and related record-keeping activities.

- Management and administration are also a major part of the job of pharmacists, who often are responsible for the management of the pharmacy in which they work.

Salaries

Those with bachelor's degrees in pharmacy have average salaries of $64,000 per year. Pharmacy majors who are self-employed have higher salaries, averaging $71,700 per year. Those who work as wage and salary workers for private, for-profit corporations have annual earnings of $62,800. Pharmacy majors employed by educational institutions and government organizations earn $56,800 per year.

Unlike in most other fields of study, the earnings of pharmacy majors do not vary much by age. Most college graduates' salaries increase with age. Economists believe that salaries increase with age as workers become more skilled and experienced and therefore more productive on the job. However, the earnings of pharmacy majors do not seem to vary systematically with age. Rather, pharmacy majors at ages 25 to 29 earn salaries of $63,100 per year, a rate of pay sharply higher than that of college graduates of the same age in other major fields of study. Yet the earnings of persons with a pharmacy degree hover at the lower $60,000 range over their entire working lives. Like no other major field of study, the earnings of pharmacy graduates appear to be almost entirely based on the specific pharmacy-related skills and abilities learned while in college. No earnings rewards are provided to pharmacy majors for additional years of work experience and the skill normally associated with additional work experience.

Table 2 shows average earnings of pharmacy graduates and all college graduates. Pharmacy program graduates who work in pharmacy and related health occupations have annual earnings of $64,800 per year. Pharmacists at the bachelor's degree level earn 22 percent more per year in annual salaries as compared to those college graduates employed in other health professions, including nursing, and in therapy-related occupations.

FIGURE 2

Age/Earnings Profile of Persons with Only a Bachelor's Degree in Pharmacy (Full-Time Workers, in 2002 Dollars)

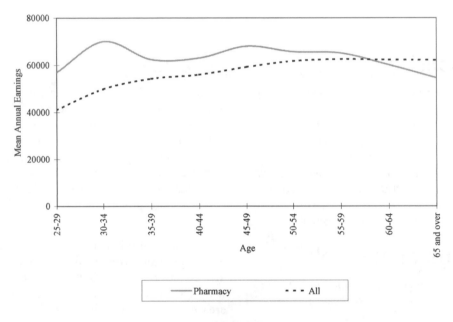

Table 2

Annual Salary of Full-Time Workers with Only a Bachelor's Degree in Pharmacy, Top 5 Occupations (in 2002 Dollars)

Earnings in Top 5 Occupations	All	Pharmacy
Total	$54,171	$63,967
Registered nurses, pharmacists, therapists, physician assistants	$53,508	$64,746
Top and mid-level managers, executives, administrators	$74,051	$70,390
Other management-related occupations	$51,921	$60,366
Sales occupations, including retail	$52,378	$72,725
Health technologists and technicians	$42,774	$61,371

Few graduates of pharmacy programs are employed in positions other than as pharmacists. Those who work as managers or supervisors (often as store managers) earn an average salary of $70,400. Some pharmacy graduates are employed in sales positions often related to the sale of pharmaceuticals and medical equipment and supplies. Pharmacy majors employed in sales occupations have salaries of $72,800 per year.

On-the-Job Training

Training workshops and seminars are an important way that persons with a degree in pharmacy stay abreast of developments in the field. More than three-quarters of pharmacists participate in training programs over the course of a year.

- Much of the work-based training that pharmacists receive is related to specific technical issues within the profession.

- Participation in training programs is a requirement for most pharmacists to maintain their license as pharmacists.

Post-Graduation Activities

Most persons who earn a bachelor's degree in pharmacy do not enroll in a graduate or professional degree program and earn an advanced degree. Only 18 percent of pharmacy majors eventually earn a graduate degree. About 7 percent earn a master's degree, 4 percent earn a doctorate, and 6 percent earn a professional degree.

- Forty percent of all master's degrees earned by pharmacy majors are in the business field, about 20 percent are earned in pharmacy, and 18 percent are in a related health field.

- About 4 percent of those with a bachelor's degree in pharmacy go on to earn a doctorate degree. One-half of all doctorates awarded to these individuals are also in the pharmacy field. About 40 percent of the doctorate degrees awarded to pharmacy majors are in the biological and related science fields.

- Nearly 6 percent of those with a bachelor's degree in pharmacy earn a professional degree. About 6 out of 10 of them are medical doctor degrees, while more than one-third are in pharmacy.

The employment rate of persons with a degree in pharmacy is very high. Ninety-five percent of all persons under the age of 65 with a degree in pharmacy are employed. However, 1 out of 6 of those working is employed in a part-time position. Most of those working part-time do not wish to work a full-time schedule. Among those not working, virtually none are involuntarily unemployed. Most often those who have decided not to work have taken an early retirement.

Employment Outlook

Employment in the health professions is expected to increase by more than one-quarter between 2000 and 2010 according to the most recent occupational projections produced by the U.S. Bureau of Labor Statistics. Job growth within the pharmacy occupation is expected to be similar to that of all health professions. The employment level of pharmacists is expected to increase by 53,000 or about 24 percent over the entire projection period. Other occupational areas of projected employment growth are presented in Table 3.

Table 3

Projected Change in Employment in the Top 5 Occupations That Employ Persons
with Only a Bachelor's Degree in Pharmacy

Top 5 Occupations	Actual Employment in 2000 (000s)	Projected Employment in 2010 (000s)	Absolute Change (000s)	Percentage Change
Registered nurses, pharmacists, therapists, physician assistants	2,908	3,698	790	27.2%
Top- and mid-level managers, executives, administrators	10,564	11,834	1,270	12.0%
Other management-related occupations	4,956	5,801	845	17.1%
Sales occupations, including retail	15,513	17,365	1,852	11.9%
Health technologists and technicians	2,192	2,773	581	26.5%

CHAPTER 12

Physical Therapy

In comparison to some of the other majors described in this book, physical therapy program entrants need a good level of self-awareness as well as knowledge of the field before entering this major. High school seniors face one of the stiffest competitions of all collegiate programs with a demanding set of science prerequisites for entry into physical therapy. In addition, the work is physically demanding, requiring strength, the need to touch individuals, and good physical agility. This major also is an emotionally demanding field when physical therapists are working with difficult medical cases. Some programs look for experiential exposure prior to admission into a program.

Physical therapists improve the mobility, relieve pain, and prevent or limit permanent physical disabilities of individuals suffering from injuries or disease. Patients can be accident victims; those with burns, heart disease, head injuries, fractures, or amputations; or people with cerebral palsy, multiple sclerosis, or nerve injuries. Work can be with the elderly, dealing with chronic debilitating conditions and arthritis. Many middle-age persons encounter trauma, strokes, and heart attacks, requiring rehabilitative services. Advances in technology enable more young children to survive birth defects, which also creates a need for care provided by physical therapists.

Evaluation of a medical history to assess strength, range of motion, and functioning is done prior to physical therapists' developing a treatment plan for a patient. Sometimes the physical therapists will implement a physician's orders or delegate to a physical therapy assistant the carrying out of a treatment strategy. Treatment can involve exercise or use of electrical stimulation, hot and cold compresses, or ultrasound to relieve pain, improve the condition of muscles, or reduce swelling. Therapists may use traction or deep tissue massage to restore function. They teach patients to use crutches, prostheses, and wheelchairs to perform daily activities and home exercises to facilitate recovery.

The field's accreditation association and requirements of the state licensure exam determine the training physical therapists receive. The program is a combination of academic courses and supervised clinical hospital experience. Course work includes biology, chemistry, physics, biochemistry, neuroanatomy, human growth and development, disease and trauma manifestations, evaluation techniques, and therapeutics procedures. Those with a biologically oriented degree desiring to enter the field can be accommodated in a master's degree program. Other health care therapy fields are occupational therapy and respiratory therapy.

Physical therapy applicants are excellent students in high school and have demonstrated scientific ability in mathematics and science courses. Classroom work and hands-on clinical applications require manual dexterity and motor coordination skills. Handling immobilized patients and their setup on machines requires mobility and physical stamina. Social and interpersonal skills are critical in motivating people and helping them understand treatments and teaching and practicing procedures. These abilities also must be used with family members of patients.

Interests are primarily scientific, followed by social or humanitarian likes. The scientific interests involve a combination of intellectual understanding with a preference for practical applications and a desire to see concrete results.

A diverse set of benefits can be achieved in physical therapy work. On the personal level, some employers accommodate flexible work schedules, and the pay is good. As well-accepted members of a medical team, physical therapists gain respect, status, and prestige within a community. On the work level, satisfaction can be gained through helping others, working with a variety of patients, and having patients recognize the therapist's use of his or her hands and machines in making them get better or offering them hope.

As with most professions, there are different styles that characterize workers. Being dedicated, considerate, and conscientious while being very precise and accurate may characterize one style. Sometimes this approach can mask an uncertainty about one's own self-knowledge. In the opposite approach, some therapists exude self-confidence along with friendliness, but they may improvise more quickly to deal with difficult cases. So along a continuum, some therapists will rely on known, documented rehabilitative approaches or technical procedures, whereas others are focused on the person and the family coping with a difficult situation. In general, having a people orientation predominates over having theoretical or technical information in dealing with a disabling or trauma case.

Where Do Physical Therapy Graduates Work?

The employment of physical therapy graduates is spread across different sectors of the economy. Businesses and corporations in the private, for-profit sector of the economy employ only 38 percent. More than one-quarter are employed in the private, nonprofit sector of the economy. Fourteen percent of all employed physical therapy graduates work for educational institutions, and 11 percent are self-employed in their own business or practice. The government sector employs 9 percent of all employed physical therapy graduates.

The skills and knowledge that physical therapy graduates acquire during their schooling are directly applicable in the labor market. Therefore, many graduates find jobs in their field. Slightly more than 84 percent are employed in jobs that are closely related to their undergraduate major field of study. Another 7 percent are employed in jobs that are somewhat related to their major. Only 9 percent of physical therapy graduates work in jobs that are not related to their undergraduate major field of study.

Why does the latter group of physical therapy graduates work in unrelated jobs? They cite a variety of factors as possible reasons for their employment in unrelated jobs. However, when asked to select the most important reason for employment outside their major field of study, 28 percent of physical therapy graduates who work in unrelated jobs rank better pay and

FIGURE 1

Percentage Distribution of Employed Persons with Only a Bachelor's Degree in Physical Therapy, by Major Sector of Economic Activity

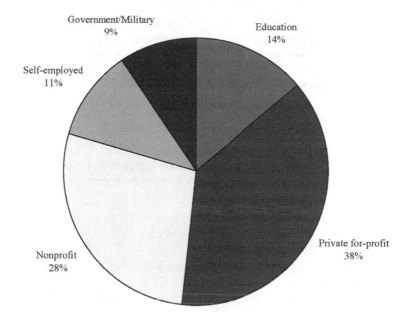

Government/Military 9%

Education 14%

Self-employed 11%

Private for-profit 38%

Nonprofit 28%

promotion opportunities as the number one reason, and 17 percent consider a change in career track as the most important factor to influence their decision to work in unrelated jobs. Another 17 percent report that family-related reasons force them to accept employment in unrelated jobs. Sixteen percent are unable to find a related job, and 13 percent rank the general working environment as the most important factor influencing their decision to work in a job that is not related to their undergraduate major field of study.

Occupations

The employment of physical therapy graduates is concentrated in very few occupations. Nearly 80 percent are employed in the health occupations, mostly as therapists but also as nurses and physician assistants. About 5 percent work as top- and mid-level executives, administrators, and managers. Two percent are employed in other miscellaneous health occupations, and 1 percent each are employed as health technologists and technicians, educational and vocational counselors, and social workers.

Table 1

Top 6 Occupations That Employ Persons with Only a Bachelor's Degree in Physical Therapy

Top 6 Occupations	PERCENT OF EMPLOYED		
	All	Men	Women
Registered nurses, pharmacists, therapists, physician assistants	78.7	79.4	78.5
Top- and mid-level managers, executives, administrators	5.1	11.5	4.1
Other health occupations	1.8	0.0	2.0

(continued)

Table 1 (continued)

Top 6 Occupations That Employ Persons with Only a Bachelor's Degree in Physical Therapy

Top 6 Occupations	PERCENT OF EMPLOYED		
	All	Men	Women
Health technologists and technicians	1.2	0.0	1.4
Counselors, educational and vocational	1.2	0.4	1.3
Social workers	1.1	0.0	1.2

Only 14 percent of employed physical therapy graduates are men. Both male and female graduates are concentrated in health occupations employed as therapists. Nearly 80 percent of both male and female physical therapy graduates are employed in these occupations.

▶ Male graduates are slightly more likely than female graduates to work in top- to mid-level executive, administrative, and managerial occupations. Nearly 12 percent of male graduates work in these occupations, compared to only 4 percent of female physical therapy graduates.

Activities on the Job

The activities in which physical therapy graduates engage at work are very closely related to the occupations in which they are employed.

▶ More than 90 percent of employed physical therapy graduates spend at least 10 hours during a typical workweek in providing health services. About 80 percent report that they spend a majority of their typical workweek in these activities.

▶ Six percent spend most of their time at work in management and administrative duties.

▶ Three percent engage in teaching activities during a major portion of their typical workweek, and 2 percent spend most of their time at work in accounting, finance, and contractual duties.

Salaries

The average annual salary of physical therapy graduates with only a bachelor's degree and who are employed full-time is $56,400, a level that is 4 percent above the average annual salary of all full-time employed college graduates. Unlike with most college graduates, the salary of physical therapy graduates increases very slowly with age, remaining in the $55,000 to $60,000 range. This indicates that additional work experience with age does not add to their productivity, and therefore their salaries increase marginally as they spend more time on the job. Within most age ranges, the average salary of physical therapy graduates is moderately higher than the average salary of all college graduates in those age groups.

▶ The average annual salary of physical therapy graduates between the ages of 25 and 29 is $50,290. Graduates between the ages of 30 and 34 earn $56,200 annually.

▶ The average annual salary of physical therapy graduates increases and peaks at $61,900 between the ages of 40 and 44.

FIGURE 2

Age/Earnings Profile of Persons with Only a Bachelor's Degree in Physical Therapy
(Full-Time Workers, in 2002 Dollars)

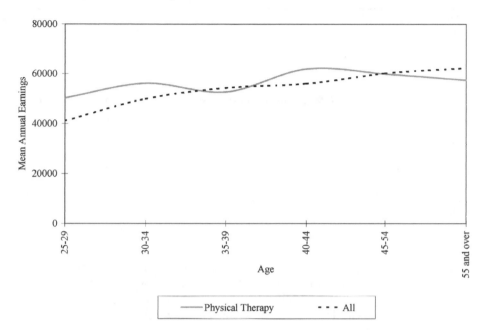

The average annual salary of physical therapy graduates who work in jobs that are related to their undergraduate major is higher than the salary of those who work in jobs that are somewhat related to their undergraduate major field of study. Graduates who are employed in jobs that are not related to their undergraduate major earn a lower salary than the salary of both groups of graduates with related jobs. Closely related jobs pay full-time employed physical therapy graduates $58,200 annually. Graduates employed in somewhat related jobs earn $47,000 per year, and those whose jobs are unrelated to their undergraduate field of study earn $42,000 per year.

Earning an average salary of $79,500 annually, the small numbers of physical therapy graduates who are self-employed in their own practice earn a higher salary than those who are employed in other sectors of the economy. The remuneration of physical therapy graduates in the private, for-profit sector of the economy is $56,400 per year. Graduates who work full-time in educational institutions earn $55,700 per year. The private, nonprofit sector pays physical therapy graduates $51,600 per year, and their average annual salary in the government sector is $46,600 per year.

The average annual salaries of physical therapy graduates and all college graduates in the top 6 occupations that predominantly employ physical therapy graduates are presented below.

▶ Physical therapy graduates employed in high-level executive, administrative, and managerial occupations earn an average annual salary of $65,100. This occupation employs only 5 percent of the graduates and is somewhat more likely to employ male than female graduates.

149

Table 2
Annual Salary of Full-Time Workers with Only a Bachelor's Degree in Physical Therapy, Top 6 Occupations (in 2002 Dollars)

Earnings in Top 6 Occupations	All	Physical Therapy
Total	$54,171	$56,373
Registered nurses, pharmacists, therapists, physician assistants	$53,508	$57,877
Top- and mid-level managers, executives, administrators	$74,051	$65,133
Other health occupations	$39,559	$40,595
Health technologists and technicians	$42,774	$31,271
Counselors, educational and vocational	$37,958	$35,077
Social workers	$36,371	$34,637

▶ Nurses, pharmacists, therapists, and physician assistants with a bachelor's degree in physical therapy earn $57,900 per year. This occupation employs nearly 80 percent of graduates.

▶ The average annual salary of graduates employed in other miscellaneous health occupations is only $40,600 per year.

▶ The average annual salary of physical therapists employed as health technologists and technicians is $31,000, and those employed as social workers and counselors earn between $34,600 and $35,100 per year. Very few graduates are employed in these low-paying occupations.

On-the-Job Training

The career potential of a job is closely associated with the amount of work-related training on the job. Work-related training is regarded as an investment by firms because it makes workers more productive. Firms that invest in their workforce are more likely to offer pay increases and promotions to match the increasing productivity of their workers. Firms that do not invest in their workers are relatively less likely to offer pay increases and promotions. The incidence of work-related training among physical therapy graduates is considerably higher than the rate of participation in work-related training among all college graduates. While 68 percent of all college graduates acquire some kind of work-related training during a year, 87 percent of physical therapy graduates engage in work-related training during a year.

▶ Of those physical therapy graduates who receive some training during the year, 89 percent receive technical training in the occupation in which they are employed.

▶ Twenty-six percent of the training recipients receive management or supervisory training.

▶ One-fifth receive training to improve their general professional skills, such as public speaking and business writing.

Physical therapy graduates decide to participate in work-related training activities, workshops, or seminars for numerous reasons. When asked to select the one most important reason to acquire training, nearly 80 percent of physical therapy graduates who undergo training identify the need to improve their occupational skills and knowledge. Nine percent report the need to obtain a professional license or certificate as the most important factor underlying their participation in work-related training. According to 4 percent of the training participants, the most important reason to participate in training activities is advancement within the firm in the form of a salary increase or a promotion.

Post-Graduation Activities

Of all graduates with a bachelor's degree in physical therapy, 20 percent proceed to earn a postgraduate degree: 18 percent earn a master's degree, and 2 percent earn a professional degree.

> ❱ Forty-three percent of all master's degrees earned by undergraduate physical therapy majors are in the field of physical therapy and other rehabilitation services. Twenty-three percent choose education as their major field of study, and 14 percent earn their master's degree in other health professions. Seven percent of the master's degrees are earned in psychology and 5 percent in business management and administrative services.

> ❱ Of all the professional degrees earned by undergraduate physical therapy majors, 56 percent are earned in the health professions and the remainder in physical therapy.

Out of all physical therapy graduates under 65 years old, 88 percent are employed. The remaining 12 percent are out of the labor force; that is, they are not employed and are not seeking employment. Almost none (0.3 percent) of the graduates are officially unemployed; that is, they are not employed and are actively seeking employment. Two main reasons underlying the labor force withdrawal of physical therapy graduates are family responsibilities and a lack of the need or desire to work. Just more than 55 percent cite family responsibilities as the reason for their labor force withdrawal, and 29 percent report their lack of a desire or need to work as one of the reasons for their withdrawal from the labor force. Additional reasons cited include retirement and schooling. Twenty-three percent of physical therapy graduates who are not in the labor force are retired, and 8 percent are enrolled in school.

Employment Outlook

According to the projections by the U.S. Bureau of Labor Statistics, employment in occupations that require at least a bachelor's degree is expected to grow faster than employment in other sectors of the American labor market. Between 2000 and 2010, the U.S. economy is projected to add 22.2 million jobs, yielding an employment growth rate of 15.2 percent. The employment growth projections in the top 6 occupations that are most likely to employ physical therapy graduates are presented here

> ❱ The demand for health occupations is projected to increase rapidly. Total employment in health occupations that include therapists, nurses, pharmacists, and physician assistants is projected to increase by 790,000 between 2000 and 2010, yielding a job growth rate of 27 percent. These occupations employ 80 percent of physical therapy graduates.

> ❱ The demand for health technologists and technicians also is projected to increase by an impressive 27 percent, adding another 581,000 jobs over the same time period. Other miscellaneous health occupations are projected to increase employment by 19 percent.

▶ Employment in high- to mid-level executive, administrative, and managerial occupations is projected to increase by 1.3 million jobs between 2000 and 2010. This represents an employment growth rate of 12 percent.

▶ The demand for social workers is expected to increase by 30 percent, and job growth is projected at a rate of 25 percent in educational and vocational counseling occupations.

Table 3
Projected Change in Employment in the Top 6 Occupations That
Employ Persons with Only a Bachelor's Degree in Physical Therapy

Top 6 Occupations	Actual Employment in 2000 (000s)	Projected Employment in 2010 (000s)	Absolute Change (000s)	Percentage Change
Registered nurses, pharmacists, therapists, physician assistants	2,908	3,698	790	27.2%
Top- and mid-level managers, executives, administrators	10,564	11,834	1,270	12.0%
Other health occupations	266	317	51	19.2%
Health technologists and technicians	2,192	2,773	581	26.5%
Counselors, educational and vocational	205	257	52	25.4%
Social workers	468	609	141	30.1%

CHAPTER 13

Psychology

Psychologists study the human mind and behavior. Research psychologists investigate the physical, cognitive, emotional, or social aspects of human behavior. Psychologists in applied fields, usually requiring post-baccalaureate study, provide mental-health care in hospitals, clinics, schools, or private settings.

Like other social scientists, psychologists formulate hypotheses and collect data to test their validity. Research methods may vary depending on the topic under study. For example, psychologists sometimes gather information through controlled laboratory experiments, as well as through administering personality, performance, aptitude, and intelligence tests. Other methods include observation, interviews, questionnaires, clinical studies, and surveys.

Psychologists apply their knowledge to a wide range of endeavors, including health and human services, management, education, law, and sports. In addition to a variety of work settings, psychologists with advanced education generally specialize in one of a number of different areas. Clinical psychologists work in counseling centers; independent or group practices; or in health maintenance organizations, hospitals, or clinics. They help mentally or emotionally disturbed clients adjust in life and may help medical and surgical patients deal with their illnesses or injuries. Some work in physical rehabilitation settings, treating patients with spinal cord injuries, chronic pain or illness, stroke, arthritis, and neurologic conditions such as multiple sclerosis. Others help people deal with times of personal crisis, such as divorce or the death of a loved one.

Cognitive psychologists deal with memory, thinking, and perceptions. Some conduct research related to computer programming and artificial intelligence.

Developmental psychologists study the physiological development that takes place throughout life. Some specialize in behavior during infancy, childhood, and adolescence; changes that take place during maturity or old age; or developmental disabilities and their effects. Increasingly, researchers are developing ways to help elderly people stay as independent as possible.

Experimental or research psychologists work in university and private research centers and in business, nonprofit, and governmental organizations. They study behavior processes with human beings and animals such as rats, monkeys, and pigeons. Prominent areas of study in experimental research include motivation, thinking, attention, learning and memory, sensory and perceptual processes, effects of substance abuse, and genetic and neurological factors affecting behavior.

Industrial-organizational (I/O) psychologists apply psychological principles and research methods to the workplace in the interest of improving productivity and the quality of work life. They conduct applicant screening, training and development, counseling, and organizational development and analysis. Industrial psychologists might work with management to reorganize the work setting to improve productivity or quality of life in the workplace.

School psychologists work in elementary and secondary schools or school district offices with students, teachers, parents, and administrators to resolve students' learning and behavior problems. They collaborate with teachers, parents, and school personnel to improve classroom management strategies or parenting skills, counter substance abuse, work with students with disabilities or gifted and talented students, and improve teaching and learning strategies.

Social psychologists examine people's interactions with others and with the social environment. They work in organizational consultation, marketing research, systems design in organizational consultation, or other applied psychology fields.

Educational course work may include learning and motivation, developmental psychology, adult development and aging, social psychology, personality, cognition, industrial/organizational psychology, abnormal psychology, sensation, perception, behavioral theory, psychopharmacology, psychology of women, and child and adolescent psychology.

Abilities involved in psychology depend on the specialization. Experimental psychology might be best viewed from a scientist's perspective with quantitative and research methodologies prominent, often similar to those used in biology. Cognitive, developmental, and social psychology may best fit in with a social research grouping, with the social science research methodology predominating. Industrial/organizational psychology with its application emphasis borders the social science research focus with the clinical personal service orientation. Clinical psychology, because of its individual service orientation in which services are mostly covered by health insurance, is a specialization completely different from traditional experimental psychology. The continuum is from experimental psychology, with abilities closer to those of a scientist, to clinical psychology, which uses people-oriented abilities that predominately represent a practitioner-scientist orientation. Thus, the abilities required in psychology all depend on the area in which one specializes.

The interests of psychologists depend on the specialization. The following three interests predominate, but their order of prominence will vary with a specific specialization. Scientific interests are involved whether the specialization focuses on the physiology of the senses or on the current belief that genetics plays a definite role in mental illness or the intellect. Clinicians rely on linguistics to communicate in their therapy, and other psychological specializations are characterized by their breadth of interests that are typified by a liberal arts education. Lastly, while clinicians may emphasize a social orientation, even the most scientific of psychologists see their work as having a social application.

The benefits of being a psychologist obviously are broad, depending on a psychologist's orientation. For example, a sampling of psychology majors valued, in descending order, working with people, having variety and diversion in their work, working with their minds, and earning a good salary. It is obvious that many human services jobs that psychology majors enter are not high paying. Perhaps respondents had more in mind with this value to seek a doctoral degree. A group of employed clinical psychologists, on the other hand, responded foremost that they valued working with their minds, followed by their sense of independence, creativity, and variety and diversion.

A caution may be that the profile of people in this field can be distorted by the largest grouping of psychologists—clinical psychologists. As a group, they look for new ways of viewing issues or practicing. Personally, they are self-confident and imaginative when it comes to their practice. They seek understanding of the behavior and motives of others. They resist routine activity, which may mean that they do not follow "the laboratory scientific methodology" of their field. Thinking that their work is important and has a greater purpose can drive them; they have a belief in the ideal. They tend to be warm, relate to others easily, are not dependent on facts, and rely on their intuition in relationships. The latter obviously would not be true of many people in the specialties.

Where Do Psychology Majors Work?

The employment of psychology graduates is spread across all major sectors of the economy. About one-half work for businesses and corporations in the private, for-profit sector. Another 13 percent are self-employed in their own business or practice. The government sector employs 16 percent, and 14 percent of psychology majors work for educational institutions. The remaining 9 percent work in the private, nonprofit sector for tax-exempt or charitable organizations.

FIGURE 1

Percentage Distribution of Employed Persons with Only a Bachelor's Degree in Psychology, by Major Sector of Economic Activity

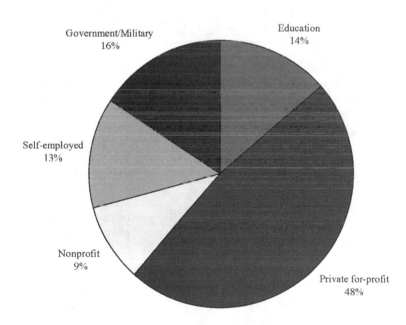

Fewer than one-quarter of psychology majors work in jobs that are closely related to the field of psychology. This is not surprising, because many jobs that are closely related to psychology require specialized skills such as those possessed by clinical, developmental, cognitive, experimental, or research psychologists with at least a master's degree or more.

A bachelor's degree does not provide these specialized skills in psychology. Rather, a bachelor's degree in psychology may provide general instruction in the field that can be utilized in marketing research, labor relations, or management and productivity improvement. These skills allow access to jobs that are somewhat related to the field of psychology. Thirty-eight percent of bachelor's degree graduates in psychology hold jobs that are somewhat related to their field, and the same number of graduates are employed in jobs that are unrelated to the field of psychology.

Although psychology majors list numerous reasons for their employment in jobs that are unrelated to their major, when asked to pick the most important factor that influenced their decision to work in an unrelated job, one-third said better pay and promotion opportunities lured them away from jobs related to psychology. Fewer than one-fifth voluntarily work in unrelated jobs because of a change in their career and professional interest. Family-related reasons are considered to be the most important factor influencing the decision to work in unrelated jobs by 13 percent, and another 13 percent are forced to work in unrelated jobs because they are unable to find related jobs.

Occupations

Psychology graduates are employed in a wide variety of occupations. The highest concentration of employed psychology gradates is in upper-level managerial occupations that employ 12 percent of the graduates. Another 8 percent are employed in sales occupations, and 7 percent work as social workers. Social workers are most likely to work in private, non-profit organizations or the government sector. Management-related occupations employ 11 percent of psychology graduates: 5 percent work as labor relations specialists, and the remaining 6 percent work in other management-related occupations as management analysts, purchasing agents, or regulatory officers. Clerical/administrative occupations employ 5 percent of the graduates, and another 5 percent of psychology majors are employed in insurance, securities, real estate, and business services occupations. These jobs are most likely unrelated to their major field of study.

Psychology majors also are employed in marketing and sales occupations, applying their skills in the marketing research area. Health occupations such as registered nurses, therapists, and physician assistants employ another 4 percent of the graduates. The top 10 occupations employ a total of 60 percent of all employed psychology graduates.

Table 1
Top 10 Occupations That Employ Persons with Only a Bachelor's Degree in Psychology

Top 10 Occupations	PERCENT OF EMPLOYED		
	All	Men	Women
Top- and mid-level managers, executives, administrators	12.0	16.1	8.8
Sales occupations, including retail	7.9	11.9	4.7
Social workers	6.9	5.3	8.0
Other management-related occupations	6.3	6.8	6.0
Personnel, training, and labor relations specialists	5.3	4.2	6.1
Other administrative (e.g., records clerks, telephone operators)	5.1	3.2	6.6
Insurance, securities, real estate, business services	5.0	5.3	4.8
Other marketing and sales occupations	4.2	3.9	4.5
Registered nurses, pharmacists, therapists, physician assistants	3.8	2.1	5.1
Accountants, auditors, other financial specialists	3.7	3.0	4.3

- Men make up less than 45 percent of all employed psychology majors. They are more than twice as likely as women graduates to be employed in high level managerial occupations and sales occupations.

- Women psychology majors are more likely than men to work as social workers in clerical/administrative occupations; personnel, training, and labor relations occupations; and health occupations.

Activities on the Job

The diversity in the occupational employment of psychology majors is reflected in the breadth of duties that they perform on their jobs.

- Nearly 55 percent said they regularly spend some time in performing management and administrative duties, whereas 18 percent of employed psychology graduates typically spend most of their work time in performing these duties.

- While 37 percent of the graduates regularly engage in sales, purchasing, and marketing duties, 16 percent say these duties typically consume most of their time at work.

- Nearly 3 out of 10 employed psychology majors regularly engage in providing health and financial consulting services at work, but only 14 percent spend most of their work time in providing professional services.

- Another activity performed by employed psychology majors is teaching. One in 10 graduates spends a majority of time at work in teaching activities.

- Eight percent of the graduates engage in labor-relations activities, including recruiting, personnel development, and training. Another 7 percent report they spend most of their work time in computer applications, programming, and systems development. An additional 7 percent spend most of their work time in performing accounting, finance, and contractual duties.

▶ Few psychology majors are engaged intensively or regularly in basic and applied research.

Salaries

The average annual salary of psychology graduates with only a bachelor's degree who are employed full-time is $49,990, a level that is 9 percent lower than the average annual salary of all full-time employed college graduates. As with most college graduates, the salary of psychology majors increases with age, indicating that they get more productive and therefore can earn higher salaries as they spend more time on the job. However, the average annual salary of psychology majors is lower than the average salary of all college graduates at every age group presented in the chart.

▶ The average annual salary of psychology majors between the ages of 25 and 29 is $35,900. Graduates between the ages of 30 and 34 earn $45,300 annually.

▶ The average annual earnings of psychology graduates increase as they get older at about the same rate as that of all college graduates. The average annual salary of 35- to 39-year-old psychology majors who are employed full-time is $51,000, and 40- to 44-year-olds earn $53,900 per year.

▶ The average annual salary continues to increase and peaks at a level of $61,100 among 50- to 54-year-old graduates.

The average annual salary of psychology majors who work in jobs that are closely related to their major field of study is lower than those who are employed in jobs that are somewhat related or not related to their major. Graduates who work in closely related jobs earn $45,400 per year. Those who work in jobs that are somewhat related to their major earn $52,600, and graduates with unrelated jobs earn an average annual salary of $50,200. Many graduates whose jobs are somewhat related to their undergraduate major are employed in health occupations; in high-level managerial, administrative, and sales jobs; labor relations occupations; and marketing jobs that are associated with higher salaries than the average salary of psychology majors in closely related jobs such as social workers or jobs in the education field. Employment in the non-college labor market occupations such as clerical/administrative occupations lowers the average annual salary in unrelated jobs compared to the average salary in jobs that are somewhat related to psychology.

The highest average annual salary of psychology majors is in the private, for-profit sector. Graduates who are self-employed in their own practice or business earn $55,500 annually, and the average salary of those who work in the private, for-profit sector for businesses and corporations is $55,000. Government sector employees with a bachelor's degree in psychology earn $45,000 per year. The lowest earnings are among psychology graduates who are employed by educational institutions—they earn $38,900—and those who work for private, non-profit institutions—they earn $39,200.

In 8 out of the 10 top occupations that employ psychology majors, the average annual salary is lower than the salary of all college graduates employed in these occupations. The average salaries of psychology majors and all college graduates in each of these 10 occupations are presented next.

▶ The average annual salary of psychology graduates in the 10 occupations varies from a high of $65,300 among top- to mid-level managers to a low of $31,700 among miscellaneous administrative occupations such as record clerks and telephone operators and $35,500 among social workers. The former is the largest employer of all psychology majors, with 12 percent of all graduates working in these occupations. However, twice as many male graduates work in these top-level managerial jobs compared to their female counterparts. In contrast, more women are likely to be employed as social workers than men psychology graduates.

▶ The average annual remuneration of psychology graduates in sales occupations is $55,400, a level that is higher than the average salary of all college graduates in these occupations. Male psychology graduates are nearly three times more likely than female graduates to be employed in these high-salary sales occupations.

▶ Labor relations specialists, personnel, and training occupations pay an average salary of $58,500 to psychology majors versus only $51,600 to all college graduates. This is a relatively lucrative field of employment for psychology majors. Females are somewhat more likely to be employed in these occupations than male psychology graduates.

▶ Psychology majors employed in insurance, securities, real estate, and business services occupations earn $62,600 annually. Male graduates are more likely than female graduates to be employed in these occupations.

FIGURE 2

Age/Earnings Profile of Persons with Only a Bachelor's Degree in Psychology (Full-Time Workers, in 2002 Dollars)

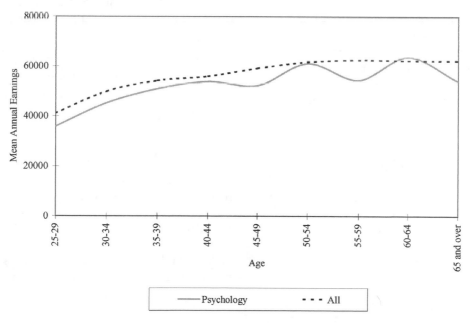

Table 2

Annual Salary of Full-Time Workers with Only a Bachelor's Degree
in Psychology, Top 10 Occupations (in 2002 Dollars)

Earnings in Top 10 Occupations	All	Psychology
Total	$54,171	$49,964
Top- and mid-level managers, executives, administrators	$74,051	$65,345
Sales occupations, including retail	$52,378	$55,408
Social workers	$36,371	$35,456
Other management-related occupations	$51,921	$48,783
Personnel, training, and labor relations specialists	$51,577	$58,488
Other administrative (e.g., records clerks, telephone operators)	$34,547	$31,667
Insurance, securities, real estate, business services	$68,273	$62,596
Other marketing and sales occupations	$58,208	$56,927
Registered nurses, pharmacists, therapists, physician assistants	$53,508	$44,978
Accountants, auditors, other financial specialists	$57,382	$52,203

On-the-Job Training

The career potential of a job is closely associated with the amount of work-related training on the job. Work-related training is regarded as an investment by firms because it makes workers more productive. Firms that invest in their workforce are more likely to offer pay increases and promotions to match the increasing productivity of their workers. Firms that do not invest in their workers are relatively less likely to offer pay increases and promotions. Nearly 7 out of 10 employed psychology majors participate in work-related training at some time during the year. This is just slightly above the 68 percent training participation rate among all employed college graduates.

▶ Of those psychology majors who received some training, 72 percent receive technical training in the occupation in which they are employed.

▶ Thirty-five percent of the training recipients receive management or supervisor training.

▶ One-third receive training to improve their general professional skills, such as public speaking and business writing.

Psychology majors decide to acquire work-related training for numerous reasons. Many training recipients commonly cite four factors. Included among them are a desire to improve skills and knowledge in the occupational area of their employment, to fulfill mandatory training requirements of the employer, to increase opportunities for promotion and salary increases, and to learn skills for a newly acquired position. More than 90 percent of psychology graduates participate in work-related training to improve their occupational skills and knowledge. Nearly 57 percent are required or expected by their employers to undergo training. Having an increased opportunity for promotion, advancement, and salary increases is the reason that 44 percent of psychology majors participate in work-related training. One-third of training recipients cite the need to learn skills for a newly acquired position as one of the reasons for their participation in work-related training. More than one-fourth of all psychology majors who participate in work-related training activities do so to acquire a professional license or certificate.

When asked to identify the single most important reason to acquire training, 60 percent of psychology majors who undergo training identify the need to improve their occupational skills and knowledge. Another 14 percent report mandatory training requirements by the employer as the most important factor for their involvement in work-related training. According to 8 percent, the most important factor for their involvement in training is to improve their opportunities for a salary increase and promotion. Seven percent, respectively, cite the need to learn skills for a newly acquired position and the need to obtain a professional license or certificate as the main factor influencing their decision to undergo work-related training.

Post-Graduation Activities

Forty-two percent of psychology graduates with a bachelor's degree proceed to earn a post-graduate degree: 29 percent earn a master's degree, 7 percent graduate with a doctorate, and 6 percent earn a professional degree.

▶ Thirty-one percent of the master's degrees are earned in the field of psychology. Many areas of practice in the field of psychology, such as clinical, developmental, cognitive, and experimental psychology, require a master's degree. Psychology majors with interests in those areas proceed to obtain a master's degree in psychology.

▶ Many in the field of psychology pursue education, business, and health interests. For example, more than 21 percent of all master's degrees held by undergraduate psychology graduates are earned in education. These graduates pursue educational psychology and counseling.

▶ In the field of business, psychology applications mainly occur in marketing research and industrial organization. Eleven percent of all master's degrees of undergraduate psychology majors are earned in business management and administrative services, and 7 percent are earned in the health sciences.

▶ Three-quarters of all doctorate degrees of undergraduate psychology majors are in the field of psychology, and another 9 percent are in the field of business management and administrative services.

▶ Forty-six percent of the professional degrees of psychology majors are earned in the field of law, and another 42 percent earn their degrees in the health professions.

Out of all psychology graduates under the age of 65, 80 percent are employed. Only 4 percent are officially unemployed; that is, they are not employed and are actively seeking employment. The remaining 16 percent are out of the labor force; that is, they are not employed and are not seeking employment. Many of the labor force withdrawals among psychology graduates are attributable to family responsibilities and a lack of the need or desire to work. Nearly 42 percent cite family responsibilities as one of the reasons for their labor force withdrawal. Another 37 percent voluntarily withdraw from the labor force because they do not have the need or desire to work. Post-graduation enrollment in school is the reason for labor force withdrawal of 15 percent of these graduates. About 8 percent are suffering from chronic illness or a disabling condition that prevents them from participating in the labor force.

Employment Outlook

According to the projections by the U.S. Bureau of Labor Statistics, employment in occupations that require at least a bachelor's degree is expected to grow faster than employment in other sectors of the American labor market. Between 2000 and 2010, the U.S. economy is projected to add 22.2 million jobs, yielding an employment growth rate of 15.2 percent. The employment growth projections in the top 10 occupations that are most likely to employ psychology graduates are presented below.

▶ The largest area of employment for psychology majors, high-level managerial and administrative occupations, is projected to add 1.27 million jobs between 2000 and 2010, yielding an employment growth rate of 12 percent.

▶ Employment in sales occupations is projected to grow by 12 percent, with an additional 1.9 million jobs between 2000 and 2010. Psychology majors employed in these occupations have above-average earnings.

▶ The demand for social workers is projected to increase rapidly between 2000 and 2010. With an additional 141,000 jobs, a 30 percent growth in employment is projected in this occupation. More females than males work in this low-wage occupation. The average salary of all college graduates employed as social workers is $36,400, and psychology majors who are employed as social workers earn $35,500 per year.

▶ The demand for registered nurses, therapists, and other health occupations is projected to grow at an above-average rate.

▶ With an additional 790,000 jobs, employment in this occupation is expected to grow by 27 percent.

▶ Above-average growth rates of employment also are projected for marketing and sales occupations and labor relations specialists. Psychology graduates employed in these occupations earn higher salaries than the average for all employed psychology majors.

Table 3
Projected Change in Employment in the Top 10 Occupations
That Employ Persons with Only a Bachelor's Degree in Psychology

Top 10 Occupations	Actual Employment in 2000 (000s)	Projected Employment in 2010 (000s)	Absolute Change (000s)	Percentage Change
Top- and mid-level managers, executives, administrators	10,564	11,834	1,270	12.0%
Sales occupations, including retail	15,513	17,365	1,852	11.9%
Social workers	468	609	141	30.1%
Other management-related occupations	4,956	5,801	845	17.1%
Personnel, training, and labor relations specialists	490	578	88	18.0%
Other administrative (e.g., records clerks, telephone operators)	16,911	18,522	1,611	9.5%
Insurance, securities, real estate, business services	1,548	1,726	178	11.5%
Other marketing and sales occupations	621	758	137	22.1%
Registered nurses, pharmacists, therapists, physician assistants	2,908	3,698	790	27.2%
Accountants, auditors, other financial specialists	2,115	2,481	366	17.3%

CHAPTER 14

Social Work

Social workers help people solve personal and family relationships or learn how to cope with community issues having an impact on their lives. They counsel their clients, identify the clients' concerns, ponder solutions, and find resources often where quick solutions are needed. Social workers work with families encountering serious conflicts, including child and spousal abuse, and issues resulting from disease of old age. A large area of specialization is gerontological services. Some of the situations social workers become involved with are housing, unemployment, lack of job skills, financial crises, disability, substance abuse, unwanted pregnancy, and disruptive social behavior.

Work settings that affect social workers' roles include general and psychiatric hospitals, schools, mental health clinics, public agencies such as public welfare, or courts. In hospitals, social workers may organize support groups if the illness is cancer, Alzheimer's disease, or AIDS. They can also be involved with finding a nursing home or arranging for home health care and obtaining specialized equipment for patients. In clinics and detoxification programs, they may lead therapy groups or plan for people's reentry into the community. In schools, the issues can be disruptive classroom behavior or truancy, and the interventions focus on working with the clients and their families. In child care

and family service agencies, the issues can involve intervening by recommending emergency shelters and monitoring situations that might eventually involve legal action such as removal of a child from the home. In prisons, a social worker can prepare pre-sentencing assessments, arrange for provision of services to a prisoner's families, or serve as a probation officer on a prisoner's release from incarceration.

Social workers are involved in preparing forms and applications, determining eligibility, arranging for services, visiting their clients, and providing support. They also focus on social or community policy and planning.

There are more than 400 accredited bachelor's degree programs in social work. Course work includes social welfare policies, human behavior and the social environment, group work, social research methods, and a supervised field experience. The master's degree in social work is another common educational credential in this field; it enables a person to enter into private practice and receive payment from insurance companies for providing psychotherapy.

A social worker needs social, teaching, language, persuasion, and leadership skills. These skills will interact with the social worker's emotional maturity and sensitivity to people and their problems. Objectivity and responsibility also are necessary because many times the social worker is confronted with two sides of a situation. Understanding the way government programs and social service organizations function is essential.

Social workers' interests involve socialization, leadership, management, and a breadth of interests commonly associated with course work in the humanities and in liberal arts programs.

Associated benefits of social work include interaction with people, mental stimulation, opportunities for variety and diverse work, and creativity. Individual problems usually have a uniqueness requiring individualized interventions, so case managers work independently.

Social workers look at each person afresh with unique concerns to be addressed. They are imaginative, extroverted, and positive in their outlook. While often working within bureaucracies, they are personally energized and seek to understand issues despite the paperwork and detail requirements of their job. Some social workers have mannerisms that initially do not

show their caring tendencies because they are more introverted. While their work style may be different, their personal drive, convictions, and intentions definitely indicate the same values and ideals of working with people, sometimes even more so than their more outgoing professional colleagues.

Where Do Social Work Graduates Work?

Social work graduates are heavily concentrated in the nonprofit sector of the economy. One-half of all employed graduates work either for the government sector or for private, nonprofit organizations. Three out of 10 are employed in the government sector of the economy, and about one-fifth are employed in private, nonprofit organizations. Educational institutions employ another 14 percent. Only 29 percent work in the private, for-profit sector for businesses and corporations, and 8 percent are self-employed in their own business or practice.

FIGURE 1

Percentage Distribution of Employed Persons with Only a Bachelor's Degree in Social Work, by Major Sector of Economic Activity

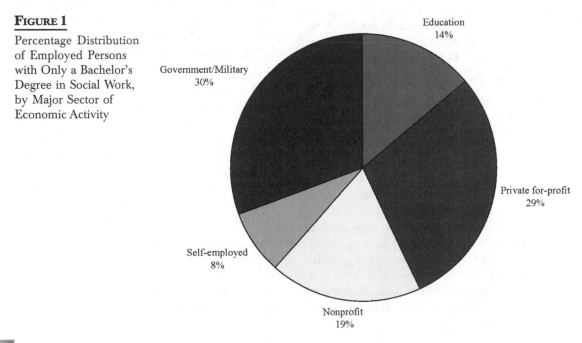

Government/Military
30%

Education
14%

Private for-profit
29%

Self-employed
8%

Nonprofit
19%

About one-half of all employed social work graduates work in jobs that are closely related to their major. Another one-quarter work in jobs that are somewhat related to their undergraduate major, and the remaining one-quarter are employed in jobs that are unrelated to their undergraduate major field of study.

Although social work majors list numerous reasons for their employment in jobs that are unrelated to their major, when asked to select the most important factor influencing their decision to work in an unrelated job, 29 percent say better pay and promotion opportunities lured them away from jobs related to social work. In fact, 54 percent of social work majors employed in unrelated jobs cite the lack of good pay and promotion opportunities in their field as one of the many reasons for their employment choice. This is not surprising given the generally lower wages in occupations related to social work. Seventeen percent cite a change in their career and professional interests as the most important factor influencing their decision to work outside their major field of study. Fifteen percent cite family-related reasons, and another 14 percent state their inability to find jobs related to social work as the most important reason for their employment shift outside their field. One in 10 workers in unrelated jobs places dissatisfaction with the general working environment as the number one reason for the decision to work in an unrelated job.

Occupations

There is a fair amount of concentration of employed social work graduates in a few occupations. Nearly one-half are employed in the top 2 occupations that employ most social work majors. Thirty-seven percent work as social workers, and 9 percent are employed in an executive, administrative, or managerial position. Clerical occupations employ another 5 percent of all employed social work graduates, and 4 percent work in miscellaneous management-related jobs as management analysts, purchasing agents, or regulatory officers, for example. More than 4 percent work in insurance, securities, real estate, and business services occupations, and another 4 percent are employed in non-health service occupations. Educational and vocational counseling, labor relations, personnel, training, miscellaneous health, and secretarial occupations are among the top 10 areas in which social work majors are employed. Each employs between 2 and 3 percent of social work graduates.

Table 1

Top 10 Occupations That Employ Persons with Only a Bachelor's Degree in Social Work

Top 10 Occupations	PERCENT OF EMPLOYED		
	All	Men	Women
Social workers	37.4	29.4	39.2
Top- and mid-level managers, executives, administrators	9.4	16.7	7.8
Other administrative (e.g., records clerks, telephone operators)	5.0	0.0	6.1
Other management-related occupations	4.3	2.4	4.7
Insurance, securities, real estate, business services	4.2	8.3	3.4
Other service occupations, except health	3.9	1.1	4.5

(continued)

Table 1 (continued)
Top 10 Occupations That Employ Persons with Only a Bachelor's Degree in Social Work

Top 10 Occupations	PERCENT OF EMPLOYED		
	All	Men	Women
Counselors, educational and vocational	2.7	2.1	2.8
Personnel, training, and labor relations specialists	2.4	4.3	2.0
Other health occupations	2.4	2.2	2.5
Secretaries, receptionists, typists	2.3	0.0	2.7

Women dominate the field of social work. Only 18 percent of employed social work graduates are men. There are sizable differences in the occupational employment patterns of male and female social work graduates.

▶ While 30 percent of male graduates are employed as social workers, 40 percent of female social work graduates are employed as social workers.

▶ Women also are more concentrated in clerical occupations. Six percent of female graduates work in clerical occupations. In contrast, none of the male social work graduates are employed in clerical jobs.

▶ Non-health service occupations employ nearly 5 percent of women but only 1 percent of male social work graduates.

▶ Male graduates are more than twice as likely as female social work graduates to work in managerial jobs. Almost 17 percent of men work in these jobs, compared to 8 percent of women.

▶ Males also are more inclined to work in the finance sector in insurance, securities, real estate, and business services occupations. Eight percent of men compared to 3 percent of women social work graduates work in these occupations.

Activities on the Job

Although many social work majors list an array of duties that they perform on the job, more than one-half say they spend most of the time at work in providing professional services, in performing managerial and administrative duties, and in teaching activities.

▶ More than one-half of all employed social work graduates regularly spend some time at work providing professional services in the form of human services like counseling and legal services to clients of social services agencies at the state and local government level. One-quarter claim that providing these services is a major part of their job.

▶ One-half of the graduates regularly engage in management and administrative duties at their jobs, and fewer than one-fifth consider these duties to be a major part of their job.

▶ Three out of 10 social work graduates regularly engage in teaching duties at work, although only 8 percent spend most of their workweek in teaching activities.

▶ More than 22 percent regularly perform sales, purchasing, and marketing duties;

however, only 7 percent of employed social work majors spend the major part of their workweek in performing these duties. Most of these are social work majors employed in clerical, administrative, and secretarial jobs who purchase various items, including office supplies.

▶ Employee-relations activities, including recruiting, personnel development, and training, are regularly performed by nearly 40 percent of the graduates; however, only 7 percent spend a large proportion of their workweek in performing these duties. Many graduates employed in labor relations, managerial, and counseling occupations are included in this group.

▶ Five percent of employed social work graduates spend most of their time at work in performing computer application, programming, and systems-development duties. More than one-quarter typically perform these duties for at least 10 hours a week at their jobs.

▶ Another 5 percent spend a majority of a typical workweek performing contractual, accounting, and finance duties. Many of these include completion of documents required to establish eligibility for receiving social services and other financial and accounting duties performed to counsel clients in their personal budgetary and eligibility matters. Although only 5 percent of all employed social work graduates intensively engage in performing these duties, nearly 9 out of 10 graduates regularly spend at least 10 hours per week on these duties.

▶ Few social work majors regularly engage in basic or applied research activities.

Salaries

Social work is a low-wage major field of study. The average annual salary of social work graduates with only a bachelor's degree and who are employed full-time is $37,800, a level that is only 70 percent of the average annual salary of all full-time employed college graduates. As with most college graduates, the age-earnings profile of social work majors increases, albeit slowly. They experience small increases in salary levels as they age. The average annual salary of social work graduates is lower than the average salary of all college graduates in every age group, and the gap between the average salary of these two groups widens as they age.

▶ Between the ages of 25 and 29, the average annual salary of social work graduates is only $30,000. Between 30 and 34 years, the average salary increases to $35,500.

▶ The average salary of 35- to 39-year-old social work graduates is somewhat higher–$39,000. The salary increases somewhat in the 40-to-45 age range, reaching $41,100.

▶ After this age, the average annual salary of social work graduates declines as they age.

The average annual salary of social work majors varies somewhat by the degree of relationship between their job and undergraduate major field of study. Graduates who work in closely related jobs earn $36,900 per year. Those who work in jobs that are somewhat related to their major earn $39,900, and graduates with unrelated jobs earn an average annual salary of $37,700. Many graduates whose jobs are somewhat related or unrelated to their undergraduate major are employed in managerial, administrative, insurance, securities, and real estate jobs. These jobs pay higher salaries than the salaries of social workers whose jobs are closely related to the undergraduate major field of study.

Self-employed social work graduates earn a higher average salary than graduates working in other sectors of the economy. The average annual salary of self-employed social work majors who work full-time in their business or practice is $43,300. The government sector pays an average annual salary of $40,000 to social work graduates who work on a full-time basis. The average salary of graduates who work for businesses or corporations in the private, for-profit sector is $37,600. The private, nonprofit sector pays social work graduates $34,900 annually. The educational sector pays full-time employed social work majors $34,400 per year.

With the exception of counseling occupations, the average annual salary of social work graduates is lower than the salary of all college graduates in the top 10 areas of employment for social work graduates. The average salaries of social work graduates and all college graduates in each of these 10 occupations are presented below.

> ▶ Social workers with a degree in social work earn an average salary of $37,800, compared to a $54,200 salary of all college graduates employed as social workers.

> ▶ The average salary of social work graduates who are employed in executive, administrative, and managerial occupations is $23,000 lower than the salary of

all college graduates employed in these occupations. However, social work graduates employed in these occupations (executive, administrative, and managerial) earn more than their counterparts employed in other occupations. This occupation predominantly employs male social work graduates rather than females.

> ▶ The difference in the salary of social work and all college graduates employed in insurance, securities, real estate, and business services occupations is nearly $26,600. Social work graduates working in these occupations, many of whom are males, earn $41,700 annually.

> ▶ Miscellaneous administrative occupations such as records clerks and telephone operators that employ only female social work graduates pay an annual salary of $29,800. All college graduates employed in these occupations earn $34,500 per year.

> ▶ Educational and vocational counselors with a social work degree earn $43,800 annually. The salary of all college graduates employed in these occupations is $37,900 per year.

> ▶ The lowest salary of social work majors is in miscellaneous health services occupations. Graduates employed in these occupations on a full-time basis earn only $19,900 per year.

FIGURE 2

Age/Earnings Profile of Persons with Only a Bachelor's Degree in Social Work
(Full-Time Workers, in 2002 Dollars)

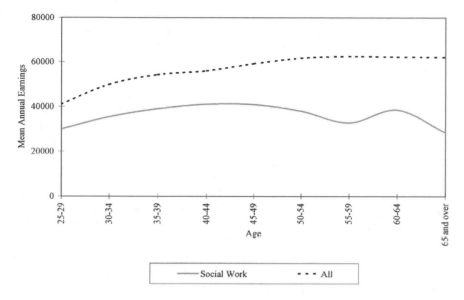

Table 2

Annual Salary of Full-Time Workers with Only a Bachelor's Degree
in Social Work, Top 10 Occupations (in 2002 Dollars)

Earnings in Top 10 Occupations	All	Social Work
Total	$54,171	$37,836
Social workers	$36,371	$35,750
Top- and mid-level managers, executives, administrators	$74,051	$50,864
Other administrative (e.g., records clerks, telephone operators)	$34,547	$29,825
Other management-related occupations	$51,921	$43,232
Insurance, securities, real estate, business services	$68,273	$41,691
Other service occupations, except health	$39,984	$34,449
Counselors, educational and vocational	$37,958	$43,809
Personnel, training, and labor relations specialists	$51,577	$43,526
Other health occupations	$39,559	$19,939
Secretaries, receptionists, typists	$32,246	$23,488

On-the-Job Training

Nearly 8 out of 10 employed social work graduates participate in work-related training at some time during the year. This rate of participation in work-related training activities is much higher than the 68 percent training participation rate among all employed college graduates.

- Of those social work graduates who receive some training, 72 percent receive technical training in the occupation in which they are employed.

- Thirty-five percent of the training recipients participate in management or supervisor training.

- Thirty-eight percent receive training to improve their general professional skills, such as public speaking and business writing.

Social work majors decide to participate in work-related training activities, workshops, or seminars for numerous reasons. Many training recipients commonly cite four factors. Included among them are a desire to improve skills and knowledge in the occupational area of their employment, mandatory training requirements of the employer, increased opportunities for advancement in the form of a promotion and a higher salary, and the need to obtain a professional license or certificate. Nearly 95 percent of social work graduates participate in work-related training to improve their occupational skills and knowledge. Another 62 percent list employer requirements as one of the reasons for their participation in training activities. Having an increased opportunity for promotion, advancement, and salary increases is the reason for 38 percent of social work majors participating in work-related training. And 32 percent of training recipients cite the need to learn skills for a newly acquired position as one of the reasons for their participation in work-related training. Another 32 percent of all social work majors who participate in work-related training

activities do so to acquire a professional license or certificate.

When asked to identify the most important reason to acquire training, 60 percent of social work majors who undergo training identify the need to improve their occupational skills and knowledge, indicating a very high commitment to their work. Another 15 percent report mandatory training requirements by the employer as the most important factor for their involvement in work-related training. According to 11 percent, the most important factor for their involvement in training is to obtain a professional license or certificate. Six percent rank an improvement in their opportunities for a salary increase and a promotion as the number one factor in influencing their decision to participate in work-related training. Another 6 percent cite the need to learn skills for a newly acquired position as the most important reason for their involvement in work-related training.

Post-Graduation Activities

Thirty-six percent of social work graduates with a bachelor's degree proceed to earn a postgraduate degree: 34 percent earn a master's degree, 1 percent graduate with a doctorate, and another 1 percent earn a professional degree.

- Sixty percent earn a master's degree in social work. Eleven percent major in education, and 8 percent earn their master's degree in psychology.

- Thirty-five percent of the doctorate degrees are earned in psychology, 28 percent in education, and 26 percent in social work.

- Seventy-seven percent of the professional degrees of undergraduate social work majors are earned in the field of law, and another 13 percent earn their degrees in the health professions.

Out of all social work graduates under the age of 65, 82 percent are employed. Only 2 percent are officially unemployed; that is, they are not employed and are actively seeking employment. The remaining 16 percent are out of the labor force; that is, they are not employed and are not seeking employment. Many of the labor force withdrawals among social work graduates are attributable to family responsibilities and a lack of the need or desire to work. Nearly 57 percent cite family responsibilities as one of the reasons for their labor force withdrawal. Another 35 percent voluntarily withdraw from the labor force because they do not have the need or desire to work. Post-graduation enrollment in school is the reason for the labor force withdrawal of 5 percent of these graduates. About 9 percent are suffering from chronic illness or a disabling condition that prevents them from participating in the labor force.

Employment Outlook

According to the projections by the U.S. Bureau of Labor Statistics, employment in occupations that require at least a bachelor's degree is expected to grow faster than employment in other sectors of the American labor market.

Between 2000 and 2010, the U.S. economy is projected to add 22.2 million jobs, yielding an employment growth rate of 15.2 percent. The employment growth projections in the top 10 occupations that are most likely to employ social work graduates are presented next.

- The demand for social workers is projected to increase rapidly between 2000 and 2010. With an additional 141,000 jobs, a 30 percent growth in employment is projected in this occupation. The aging of the population will increase the need for gerontology services. More females than males work in this low-wage occupation. The average salary of social work majors who work in social work is $35,700 per year.

- The second largest area of employment for social work majors—executive, administrative, and managerial occupations—is projected to add 1.27 million jobs between 2000 and 2010, yielding an employment growth rate of 12 percent. More male social work graduates than females are employed in this occupation.

- The demand for educational and vocational counselors is projected to grow at a healthy rate. With an additional 52,000 jobs between 2000 and 2010, the employment in this occupation is projected to grow by 25 percent.

- Miscellaneous health occupations, including aides to nurses, attendants, and orderlies, are projected to add 51,000 jobs, yielding a growth rate of 19 percent, which is above the overall rate of projected job growth. Unfortunately, the average salary of social work graduates employed in these occupations is only $19,900 per year.

Table 3

Projected Change in Employment in the Top 10 Occupations That
Employ Persons with Only a Bachelor's Degree in Social Work

Top 10 Occupations	Actual Employment in 2000 (000s)	Projected Employment in 2010 (000s)	Absolute Change (000s)	Percentage Change
Social workers	468	609	141	30.1%
Top- and mid-level managers, executives, administrators	10,564	11,834	1,270	12.0%
Other administrative (e.g., records clerks, telephone operators)	16,911	18,522	1,611	9.5%
Other management-related occupations	4,956	5,801	845	17.1%
Insurance, securities, real estate, business services	1,548	1,726	178	11.5%
Other service occupations, except health	9,652	11,287	1,635	16.9%
Counselors, educational and vocational	205	257	52	25.4%
Personnel, training, and labor relations specialists	490	578	88	18.0%
Other health occupations	266	317	51	19.2%
Secretaries, receptionists, typists	4,980	5,501	521	10.5%

Business and Administration

CHAPTER 15

Accounting

Accounting is a facet of managerial responsibility. It is the set of rules and methods by which financial and economic data are collected, processed, and summarized into reports that then can be used to make decisions. Accountants measure and communicate information about an organization's operations by recording (accountants do not perform the clerical and mechanical process of keeping records), classifying data into categories, analyzing, summarizing, and presenting information in financial terms. Accountants examine, deal with, and account for all transactions, which are any business events that are both financial and measurable. Examples of transactions are credit sales, cash receipts, tax payments, buying inventory, selling stocks, financing short- or long-term debt, and writing off uncollectable debt. Accountants touch many aspects of a business or organization, from cost or profit analysis to budgeting to involvement with management information systems.

Unlike teachers and physicians, who work mostly in the education and health care fields, respectively, accountants can work in all kinds of businesses and industries, accommodating diverse personal interests. Accounting is not a static career. Newly graduated accountants should expect job mobility. For example, beginning management accountants often start as cost accountants, junior internal auditors, or trainees for other accounting jobs before reaching a specific career goal. It is very important that accountants maintain high standards, adhering to regulations, laws, and accepted practices, because of the millions of people who rely on their main work–producing financial statements and monitoring information systems. Some accountants also fulfill multiple work roles, such as financial advising, selling insurance, and working with bankruptcy or financial services such as stocks and bonds. Those involved in preparing taxes must be prepared to encounter the stress and pressures of working overtime at certain times of the year to produce the figures needed for reports and tax returns.

In general, the level of responsibility that accountants provide is directly related to the amount of their educational experience. The field has a progressive educational system leading to certification or licensure, especially in the field of public accounting. Introductory courses include cost and tax accounting, auditing theory and procedures, finance, economics, and information systems.

Beyond the obvious mathematical skill accountants use, they also need the ability to quickly and accurately analyze, compare, and interpret facts and figures. Good oral and written communication skills are essential, whether it be to prepare financial reports or to convey information to clients and management. Using computers and software packages to incorporate work efficiencies and participating in designing financial or economic systems are requisite skills. An often forgotten skill is that accountants must purge previously learned rules and regulations and learn new and more-complex processes because of changing laws and regulations.

Accountants' interests include working with numbers and being able to categorize tasks in orderly and systematic ways to reach practical fiscal solutions. Accountants play a role in leading or influencing either an individual's or organization's fiscal decisions. They prefer to pay attention to detail and be accurate. Budgeting, financing, monitoring monetary fiscal operations, and making money are interests as well as means to afford accountants a sense of power within organizations and give them a source of satisfaction that is provided by the reactions of their individual clients.

Accountants value work that requires mental stimulation, affording a feeling of high achievement and prestige, which is rewarded with a good salary. Their practical, matter-of-fact orientation and dependability follow from a liking to organize and run things. Accountants report that important parts of their job are working with people, being involved in a variety of situations to seek fiscal solutions by creating an awareness of financial options, prioritizing choices, and being sensitive to each client's personal values as they convey their professional analysis of each client's financial situation.

Accountants are orderly, dependable, and thorough. They are steadfast in their work and are able to overcome distractions. Therefore, being organized themselves, they generally prefer organization in their lives. Accountants are business oriented and take a practical approach to many of their involvements in daily life.

Where Do Accounting Majors Work?

A large proportion of accounting majors work as wage and salary employees in private, for-profit businesses and corporations. Frequently, graduates with degrees in accounting are self-employed; 15 percent of graduates in the major own their own businesses or provide consulting services on a self-employed basis. About 12 percent of persons with an accounting degree work in government jobs. Few majors work for nonprofit charities or foundations. Most accounting majors work in jobs that are related to their undergraduate major field of study. Only 1 out of 10 accounting majors is employed in a job not related to the accounting field. Those employed in unrelated jobs have much lower earnings than those employed in jobs that use the skills they developed in their major.

FIGURE 1

Percentage Distribution of Employed Persons with Only a Bachelor's Degree in Accounting, by Major Sector of Economic Activity

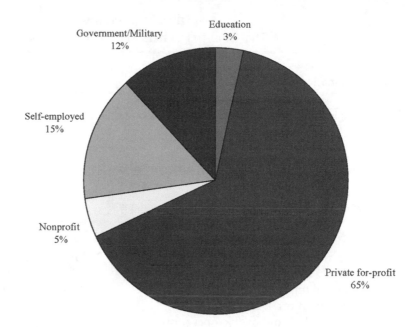

Government/Military
12%

Education
3%

Self-employed
15%

Nonprofit
5%

Private for-profit
65%

Occupations

A very large number of graduates of bachelor's degree programs in accounting are employed as accountants and auditors. More than 55 percent of all accounting graduates are employed in this occupation. Additionally, about 1 in 5 persons with a bachelor's degree in accounting are employed in management and supervisory occupations, often in a related business area. Thus, 75 percent of all those with a bachelor's degree in the field work in just two occupational areas. The remaining majors are spread out over a number of occupations, working as accounting and insurance clerks or working in stocks and bonds or real estate sales.

Table 1

Top 10 Occupations That Employ Persons with Only a Bachelor's Degree in Accounting

| | PERCENT OF EMPLOYED | | |
Top 10 Occupations	All	Men	Women
Accountants, auditors, other financial specialists	55.8	51.2	65.3
Top- and mid-level managers, executives, administrators	19.3	23.8	9.8
Accounting clerks, bookkeepers	3.5	1.8	7.1
Other management-related occupations	3.2	3.5	2.7
Insurance, securities, real estate, business services	2.8	3.6	1.1

(continued)

Table 1 (continued)
Top 10 Occupations That Employ Persons with Only a Bachelor's Degree in Accounting

Top 10 Occupations	PERCENT OF EMPLOYED		
	All	Men	Women
Other administrative (e.g., records clerks, telephone operators)	1.9	1.6	2.5
Sales occupations, including retail	1.8	1.9	1.5
Other marketing and sales occupations	1.1	1.3	0.8
Computer systems analysts	1.1	1.2	0.9
Other computer and information science occupations	0.7	0.7	0.8

▶ Women with a degree in accounting are more likely to be employed in accounting and auditing positions. They are also substantially more likely to work in accounting clerk and bookkeeper positions than men with degrees in the field.

▶ Men are much more likely to work in management and supervisory jobs than women with degrees in the field. Individuals employed in these occupations often work as accounting managers and supervisors and have salaries that are quite high relative to the average pay of an accounting degree holder.

Activities on the Job

▶ Clearly, accounting, contracting, and financial duties play a central role in the jobs of accounting program graduates, with 95 percent reporting that this is a key set of duties associated with their positions, regardless of whether they work in accounting or auditing positions.

▶ Computer skills are an important part of the skills required in these jobs, and a high number of accounting majors either develop or use various computer applications on the job.

▶ Management and administration are critical job responsibilities for many persons who graduate from college with a degree in accounting.

▶ Almost no basic or applied research is undertaken by accounting program graduates.

Salaries

Accounting program graduates at the bachelor's degree level have annual salaries of $63,500 per year, a rate of pay that is more than 17 percent above the average annual rate of pay for all full-time employed persons with a bachelor's degree. The earnings of those with a college degree in accounting vary systematically by age. Accounting program graduates aged 25 to 29 earn $45,600 per year. However, the salaries of accounting majors rise with age as they gather more experience and skill with each additional year on the job. Salaries reach an average level of $76,200 for those aged 50 to 54 with a bachelor's degree in accounting.

Accounting majors who are self-employed have average annual earnings of $80,700 per year, a rate of pay more than 27 percent higher than the average salary of all full-time employed graduates of an accounting program at the bachelor's degree level. Those who work as employees of companies earn an average salary of $63,200 per year. Employment in the education sector or in government organizations reveals a salary that averages $13,500 to $14,500 less per year than could be earned in the private sector with a bachelor's degree in accounting.

FIGURE 2

Age/Earnings Profile of Persons with Only a Bachelor's Degree in Accounting (Full-Time Workers, in 2002 Dollars)

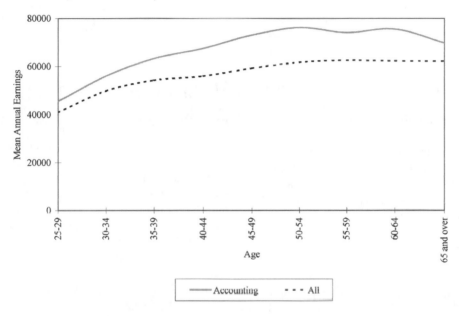

Table 2

Annual Salary of Full-Time Workers with Only a Bachelor's Degree in Accounting, Top 10 Occupations (in 2002 Dollars)

Earnings in Top 10 Occupations	All	Accounting
Total	$54,171	$63,486
Accountants, auditors, other financial specialists	$57,382	$60,734
Top- and mid-level managers, executives, administrators	$74,051	$82,946
Accounting clerks, bookkeepers	$32,380	$33,075
Other management-related occupations	$51,921	$61,937
Insurance, securities, real estate, business services	$68,273	$69,038
Other administrative (e.g., records clerks, telephone operators)	$34,547	$37,585

(continued)

Table 2 (continued)
Annual Salary of Full-Time Workers with Only a Bachelor's Degree
in Accounting, Top 10 Occupations (in 2002 Dollars)

Earnings in Top 10 Occupations	All	Accounting
Sales occupations, including retail	$52,378	$51,131
Other marketing and sales occupations	$58,208	$52,269
Computer systems analysts	$59,818	$58,599
Other computer and information science occupations	$54,228	$57,437

As with many graduates with a major in a professional field of study, access to a job that utilizes the skills acquired in the major field of study while in school results in substantially higher employment and earnings advantages. Accounting program graduates who work in jobs that are closely related to the major earn about 25 percent more per year than those employed in jobs not related to the major.

On-the-Job Training

Those who earn a degree in accounting continue to upgrade and develop work-based skills. About 70 percent of those with a degree in the field participate in some type of work-related training activity over the course of a year.

- Much of the training of persons in this field is focused on developing professional skills that enable individuals to keep current with changes in tax codes, rules and regulations, and accounting procedures.

- Majors from this field also often participate in management and supervisory training activities.

Post-Graduation Activities

Accounting majors generally do not continue their formal education after completing courses. Only 18 percent of accounting majors complete an advanced degree program at some point in their lives. Those who do go on to school usually continue in accounting or business. Sixty percent of those who earn a master's degree study business, and an additional 25 percent continue studying the accounting specialty. Few accounting majors earn any type of degree outside the business area. About 3 percent of those who earn a bachelor's degree go on to complete a law degree.

Nine out of 10 accounting majors under the age of 65 are employed, almost all in full-time positions. Of those who are not working, 70 percent have no desire to work, and many of these individuals have taken an early retirement. Only about 2 out of every 100 graduates of accounting programs are involuntarily unemployed and actively seeking work.

Employment Outlook

Employment levels in the accounting occupation are not expected to grow at a very rapid pace relative to the overall demand for college graduates. Between 2000 and 2010, the demand for accountants, auditors, and other financial specialists is expected to increase from about 2.11 million jobs to 2.48 million jobs, an increase of nearly 366,000 positions. The absolute numbers of accounting and auditor jobs are projected to increase by 181,000, representing a job growth rate of 18.5 percent for the occupation that is slightly below the rate of job growth for all bachelor's degree holders. The demand for all college graduates is forecasted to increase by 21.6 percent through 2010. Managerial and administrative occupations (other occupations in which a substantial proportion of accounting majors are employed) are expected to add 1.27 million jobs, yielding a job growth rate of 12 percent over the projections period.

Table 3
Projected Change in Employment in the Top 10 Occupations That Employ Persons with Only a Bachelor's Degree in Accounting

Top 10 Occupations	Actual Employment in 2000 (000s)	Projected Employment in 2010 (000s)	Absolute Change (000s)	Percentage Change
Accountants, auditors, other financial specialists	2,115	2,481	366	17.3%
Top- and mid-level managers, executives, administrators	10,564	11,834	1,270	12.0%
Accounting clerks, bookkeepers	1,991	2,030	39	2.0%
Other management-related occupations	4,956	5,801	845	17.1%
Insurance, securities, real estate, business services	1,548	1,726	178	11.5%
Other administrative (e.g., records clerks, telephone operators)	16,911	18,522	1,611	9.5%
Sales occupations, including retail	15,513	17,365	1,852	11.9%
Other marketing and sales occupations	621	758	137	22.1%
Computer systems analysts	431	689	258	59.9%
Other computer and information science occupations	203	326	123	60.6%

CHAPTER 16

Applied Mathematics, Operations Research, and Statistics

Here, the focus is on applied mathematics and the people involved in branches of mathematics, such as operations research analysts (sometimes called management science analysts in the workplace), actuarial scientists, and statisticians. Statisticians apply mathematics to the collection, analysis, interpretation, and presentation of numerical data. They design surveys and experiments; they also collect the data and interpret the results. They can obtain information about a group of people or things by surveying small samples of a larger group, such as to predict the winners in political elections or to determine what television programs people are watching, mostly to determine the cost of advertisements. There are many applications of statistical techniques used in almost every profession or industry—for example, to determine how much radiation exposure in a cancer treatment is harmful or to make decisions about the growth or slowdown of the economy.

Operations research analysts are problem solvers who apply mathematical principles to organizational issues such as forecasting, resource allocation, facility layout, inventory control, personnel scheduling, and distribution systems. They use a mathematical model consisting of a set of equations that explain how things work. Use of models enables analysts to break down problems into their component parts, assign numerical values to each, and determine the mathematical relationships between them. The values can be changed to examine what will happen under different circumstances to arrive at the best course of action. Consider these examples: Hospital staff examine admissions and length of patient stay, assign personnel to shifts, and monitor the use of pharmacy and laboratory services to forecast demand for added hospital services. Airline personnel study the cities served, the amount of fuel required to fly the routes, projected passenger demand, varying ticket and fuel prices, pilot schedules, and maintenance costs to produce the best flight schedules.

Actuarial scientists are mostly involved in work for insurance and investment firms dealing with risk management, pricing decisions, and investment strategies. Actuaries assemble and analyze statistics to calculate the probabilities of death, sickness, injury, retirement income level, property loss, and return on investment. For example, they can calculate the probability of claims due to automobile accidents; these claims can vary depending on the insured's age, sex, driving history, and type of car. They assure that the price of insurance will enable the company to pay the expenses of all claims. They calculate the cost of the insurance and the policy coverage so that the company will be profitable as well as competitive with other companies selling the same insurance.

Many colleges and universities urge or even require mathematics majors to take a course or even a double major in an allied field, such as computer science, engineering, economics, or one of the other sciences. The mathematics courses usually required are calculus, differential equations, and linear and abstract algebra. In the case of actuarial science, only 55 colleges and universities offer a program, but some companies will hire mathematics majors with probability and statistics course work. The actuarial science curriculum can include accounting, finance, insurance, and economics courses. Two professional societies have examinations leading to full status as actuaries.

The personal style of many mathematicians is being rational. They trust their judgment even while expressing skepticism. These individuals appear decisive and determined. Mathematicians can be original and innovative. Applied mathematicians, even though they want to see their ideas worked out in practice, must be sensitive, but equally important are people skills necessary to gain acceptance and the eventual application of their efforts and work.

Where Do Applied Mathematics Majors Work?

Nearly 8 out of 10 applied mathematics graduates work in the private, for-profit sector of the economy, either for businesses and corporations or as self-employed workers in their own businesses or practices. Nearly 70 percent work for businesses and corporations, and 9 percent are self-employed. More than 1 out of 10 graduates work in the government sector, and 8 percent are employed by educational institutions. Only 3 percent of all employed applied mathematics graduates work for private, nonprofit organizations.

FIGURE 1

Percentage Distribution of Employed Persons with Only a Bachelor's Degree in Applied Mathematics, by Major Sector of Economic Activity

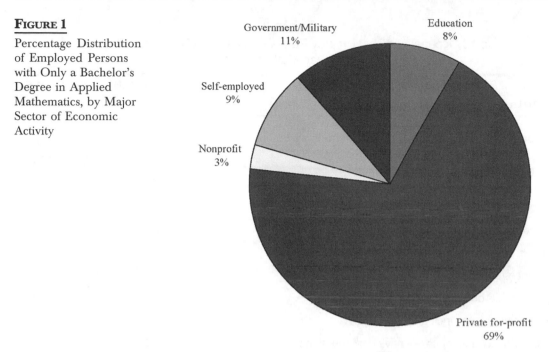

Government/Military 11%

Education 8%

Self-employed 9%

Nonprofit 3%

Private for-profit 69%

Occupations

Applied mathematics is a branch of mathematics that includes operations research analysis, actuarial science, and statistics. A number of applied mathematics graduates may not specifically use all of these skills on the job but rather the general aptitude with numbers and the ability to perform quantitative analyses. This fact is evident in the proportion of applied mathematics majors who are working in a job that is closely related to their undergraduate major and the proportion who find their jobs to be only somewhat related to their major field of study. Whereas only one-third of applied mathematics graduates consider their job to be closely related to their major, 40 percent find their job to be somewhat but not closely related to their undergraduate major. The remaining one-quarter work in jobs that are not at all related to applied mathematics.

Why do the latter group of graduates work in unrelated jobs? Graduates cite a variety of factors as possible reasons for their employment in unrelated jobs. When asked to select the most important reason for employment outside their major field of study, 19 percent of the graduates say the reason is better pay and promotion opportunities. About the same proportion find the lack of jobs in their field as the most important factor in their decision. Fifteen percent rank a change in their career interests as the number one reason. More than 10 percent of applied mathematics graduates who work in unrelated jobs consider the working environment to be the driving force behind their employment choice; another 10 percent cite job location.

Most applied mathematics graduates are employed in managerial, computer-related, finance, and insurance jobs. Nearly 65 percent of all employed applied mathematics graduates work in one of the top 10 occupations that employ

Table 1

Top 10 Occupations That Employ Persons with Only a Bachelor's Degree
in Applied Mathematics

| | PERCENT OF EMPLOYED | | |
Top 10 Occupations	All	Men	Women
Top- and mid-level managers, executives, administrators	11.6	15.8	3.4
Actuaries	8.2	6.2	12.0
Computer systems analysts	7.7	6.3	10.5
Computer programmers	7.6	8.0	6.7
Computer engineers	6.1	8.5	1.5
Other management-related occupations	5.6	4.6	7.5
Insurance, securities, real estate, business services	5.2	4.9	5.6
Other service occupations, except health	4.5	4.8	4.0
Sales occupations, including retail	3.9	4.7	2.2
Transportation and material-moving occupations	3.5	5.3	0.0

these graduates. However, within these 10 occupations, the employment of applied mathematics graduates is quite dispersed. The greatest concentration is in the high-level executive, administrative, and managerial occupations. Nearly 12 percent of the graduates work in these occupations. The second-highest concentration of applied mathematics graduates is in the actuarial field. More than 8 percent work as actuaries, a field that is closely related to this major field of study. Nearly one-fifth work in computer occupations: 8 percent as computer systems analysts, 8 percent as computer programmers, and 6 percent as computer engineers. Miscellaneous management-related occupations—for example, management analysts and purchasing agents—employ almost 6 percent of applied mathematics graduates. Insurance and securities investment occupations employ 5 percent of applied mathematics graduates. Non-health service, sales, and transportation occupations each employ between 3.5 and 4.5 percent of applied mathematics graduates.

The field of applied mathematics is somewhat dominated by men. Two-thirds of all employed applied mathematics graduates are men. The occupational employment patterns of male and female applied mathematics graduates are different.

▶ Male graduates are considerably more likely than female graduates to work as top-level executives, administrators, and managers. Nearly 16 percent of all employed male graduates work in these occupations, compared to only 3 percent of all employed female graduates.

▶ Men are also more likely than women to work as computer engineers, as computer programmers, and in transportation occupations.

▶ The employment of female applied mathematics graduates is more concentrated in actuarial occupations. Whereas 12 percent of females work in this occupation, only 6 percent of male graduates work as actuaries.

Activities on the Job

The occupational employment patterns of applied mathematics majors are reflected in the duties that they perform on their jobs.

▶ With nearly one-fifth of all mathematics majors employed in computer occupations, it is hardly surprising to find that 27 percent spend most of their time in computer applications, programming, and systems-development activities.

▶ Fourteen percent of all applied mathematics majors typically spend most of their workweek in sales, purchasing, and marketing activities.

▶ About 12 percent say that managerial and administrative duties engage them for a major part of their typical workweek.

▶ Accounting, financial, and contractual duties typically consume a major portion of the workweek of 9 percent of all employed applied mathematics graduates.

▶ Applied research duties take up the majority of work time among 7 percent of employed graduates. About 5 percent consider teaching responsibilities to be a major part of their jobs, and another 5 percent state that they spend most of their time at work in providing financial services to clients.

Salaries

The average annual salary of applied mathematics graduates with only a bachelor's degree and who are employed full-time is $60,500, a level that is nearly 12 percent higher than the average annual salary of all full-time employed college graduates. As with most college graduates, the salary of applied mathematics graduates increases with age, indicating that they get more productive and therefore can earn higher salaries as they spend more time on the job. Within most age groups, applied mathematics graduates earn higher average salaries than the salary of all college graduates in those age groups.

▶ The average annual salary of applied mathematics majors between the ages of 25 and 29 is $48,300. Graduates between the ages of 30 and 34 earn $53,700 annually.

▶ Average annual earnings of applied mathematics graduates increase at an impressive pace as they get older. The average annual salary of 35- to 44-year-old applied mathematics majors who are employed full time is $67,800, and those between the ages of 45 and 54 earn $72,600 annually.

The average annual salaries of applied mathematics majors who work in jobs that are closely related to their major field of study are higher than those who are employed in jobs that are somewhat related to their major or those whose jobs are not related to their undergraduate major field of study. Closely related jobs pay full-time employed applied mathematics graduates $62,800 annually. Graduates employed in somewhat related jobs earn $61,500 annually, and those whose jobs are unrelated to applied mathematics earn $55,500 per year.

FIGURE 2

Age/Earnings Profile of Persons with Only a Bachelor's Degree in Applied Mathematics (Full-Time Workers, in 2002 Dollars)

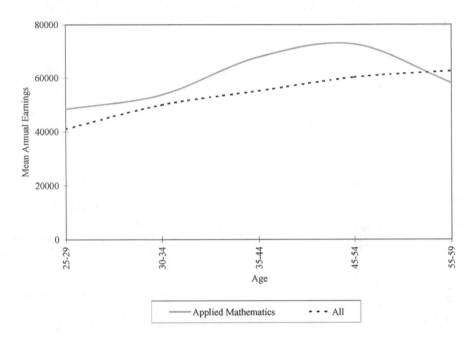

Some differences exist in the average annual salaries of applied mathematics majors by the sector in which they are employed. Graduates who work for businesses and corporations in the private, for-profit sector earn $62,800 annually. The second-highest earnings accrue to applied mathematics graduates who work in the government sector. The average annual salary of this group is $56,400. Graduates who are self-employed in their own businesses or practices earn $53,600 annually. Educational institutions pay full-time employed applied mathematics graduates $47,000 per year.

There are sizable variations in the average annual salaries of applied mathematics graduates by the occupation in which they are employed. The average annual salary of all full-time employed applied mathematics majors is 12 percent higher than the average salary of all college graduates. In 5 out of the top 10 occupations that predominantly employ applied mathematics majors, the salaries of applied mathematics majors exceed the salary of all college graduates.

▶ Applied mathematics graduates employed in high-level executive, administrative, and managerial occupations earn an average annual salary of $79,700. These occupations predominantly employ male applied mathematics graduates.

▶ Actuaries who are applied mathematics majors earn $73,500 annually. This high-paying occupation predominantly employs female applied mathematics graduates.

Table 2

Annual Salary of Full-Time Workers with Only a Bachelor's Degree in Applied Mathematics, Top 10 Occupations (in 2002 Dollars)

Earnings in Top 10 Occupations	All	Applied Mathematics
Total	$54,171	$60,459
Top- and mid-level managers, executives, administrators	$74,051	$79,742
Actuaries	$87,450	$73,498
Computer systems analysts	$59,818	$61,091
Computer programmers	$55,715	$61,207
Computer engineers	$66,859	$70,576
Other management-related occupations	$51,921	$68,752
Insurance, securities, real estate, business services	$68,273	$45,312
Other service occupations, except health	$39,984	$32,302
Sales occupations, including retail	$52,378	$51,757
Transportation and material-moving occupations	$64,088	$56,840

▶ Computer systems analysts and computer programmers with a degree in applied mathematics earn about $61,100 annually.

▶ Computer engineer occupations that employ more male than female applied mathematics graduates pay an average salary of $70,600 annually.

▶ The lowest-paying out of the top 10 occupations that predominantly employ applied mathematics graduates is non-health service occupations. While it employs only 4.5 percent of applied mathematics graduates, the average salary of these workers is only $32,300 per year.

On-the-Job Training

The career potential of a job is closely associated with the amount of work-related training on the job. Work-related training is regarded as an investment by firms because it makes workers more productive. Firms that invest in their workforce are more likely to offer pay increases and promotions to match the increasing productivity of their workers. Firms that do not invest in their workers are relatively less likely to offer pay increases and promotions. The incidence of work-related training among applied mathematics graduates is higher than the rate of participation in work-related training among all college graduates. While 68 percent of all college graduates acquire some kind of work-related training during a year, 71 percent of applied mathematics majors engage in work-related training.

- Of those applied mathematics graduates who receive some training, 75 percent receive technical training in the occupation in which they are employed.

- Forty-one percent of the training recipients participate in management or supervisory training.

- One-third receive training to improve their general professional skills, such as public speaking and business writing.

Although applied mathematics graduates decide to participate in work-related training activities, workshops, or seminars for numerous reasons, four reasons stand out as most commonly cited by graduates. These are a desire to improve skills and knowledge in the occupational area of their employment, mandatory training requirements of the employer, increased opportunities for advancement in the form of a higher salary and a promotion, and the need to learn new skills for a newly acquired position. Nearly 92 percent of applied mathematics graduates participate in work-related training to improve their occupational skills and knowledge. Another 58 percent list employer requirements as one of the reasons for their participation in work-related training. Having an increased opportunity for promotion and salary increase is one of the reasons to acquire training among one-half of all recipients of applied mathematics training. Nearly one-third cite the need to learn skills for a newly acquired position as one of the factors that underlie their decision to engage in training. One-fifth cite the need for training to acquire a professional license or certificate.

When asked to identify the most important reason to acquire training, 52 percent of applied mathematics graduates who undergo training identify the need to improve their occupational skills and knowledge. Another 16 percent report mandatory training requirements by the employer as the most important factor underlying their involvement in work-related training.

According to 13 percent of the training participants, the most important reason is a salary increase and promotion. Eight percent rank the necessity to learn skills for a newly acquired position as the number one reason to acquire training, and about 7 percent consider the need to obtain a professional license or certificate as the most important reason influencing their decision to undergo work-related training.

Post-Graduation Activities

Of all graduates with a bachelor's degree in applied mathematics, 31 percent proceed to earn a postgraduate degree: 26 percent earn a master's degree, and the remaining 5 percent earn a doctorate degree.

Twenty-nine percent of all master's degrees earned by undergraduate applied mathematics majors are in the field of applied mathematics. One-quarter of the master's degrees are earned in the field of business administration and management. A number of these graduates choose operations management as their specialty to apply mathematical principles to organization and allocation of resources, inventory control, and personnel scheduling. About 16 percent of the degrees are earned in the field of computer and information sciences. The skills required in the field of computer sciences, such as logical reasoning and abstract thinking, are also some of the main skills required in applied mathematics. In fact, one-fifth of employed applied mathematics undergraduate majors work in computer-related jobs as systems analysts, programmers, and computer engineers. Applied mathematics skills also overlap with the aptitude and skills required in the engineering field. Sixteen percent of the master's degrees earned by applied mathematics undergraduate majors are in the engineering field: 9 percent in engineering and the remaining 7 percent in the field of engineering-related technology.

One-half of all the doctorate degrees earned by undergraduate applied mathematics majors are in the field of applied mathematics. The rest are spread across an array of fields, some of which include engineering, computer sciences, and other physical sciences.

Out of all applied mathematics graduates under the age of 65, 92 percent are employed. Only 2 percent are officially unemployed; that is, they are not employed and are actively seeking employment. The remaining 6 percent are out of the labor force; that is, they are not employed and are not seeking employment. Three main reasons underlie the labor force withdrawal of applied mathematics graduates: 45 percent are retired, 43 percent cite family responsibilities as the reason for labor force withdrawal, and one-quarter lack the desire or the need to work. Additionally, 16 percent have chronic illness or a disabling condition.

Employment Outlook

According to the projections by the U.S. Bureau of Labor Statistics, employment in occupations that require at least a bachelor's degree is expected to grow faster than employment in other sectors of the American labor market. Between 2000 and 2010, the U.S. economy is projected to add 22.2 million jobs, yielding an employment growth rate of 15.2 percent. The employment growth projections in 6 out of the top 10 occupations that are most likely to employ applied mathematics graduates are at or above the average rate of growth for the entire U.S. economy.

> The fastest growth in demand is projected in the computer-related occupations. The demand for computer engineers, including hardware and software engineers, is projected to grow by 679,000 jobs, or nearly 90 percent, between 2000 and 2010. Computer systems analysts will see employment increase by 60 percent, with an additional 258,000 jobs between 2000 and 2010. Employment in computer programming is projected to grow slightly above average, with the addition of 95,000 jobs; a 16 percent growth is projected in the demand for computer programmers.

> The top area of employment for applied mathematics majors—upper-level executive, administrative, and managerial occupations—is projected to add 1.27 million jobs between 2000 and 2010. This represents an employment growth rate of 12 percent.

> Insurance, securities, real estate, and business services occupations are projected to add 178,000 jobs over the same time period, yielding an employment growth rate of 11.5 percent. Miscellaneous non-health service occupations, the occupations with the lowest salary among applied mathematics graduates, are projected to increase employment by nearly 17 percent.

> The slowest-growing occupation is actuaries. A major source of employment for female applied mathematics graduates, this occupation is expected to add only 1,000 jobs between 2000 and 2010, yielding a growth rate of just 7 percent. Access to jobs in this high-paying occupation will become increasingly difficult, given the weak growth projected for this occupation.

Table 3
Projected Change in Employment in the Top 10 Occupations That
Employ Persons with Only a Bachelor's Degree in Applied Mathematics

Top 10 Occupations	Actual Employment in 2000 (000s)	Projected Employment in 2010 (000s)	Absolute Change (000s)	Percentage Change
Top- and mid-level managers, executives, administrators	10,564	11,834	1,270	12.0%
Actuaries	14	15	1	7.1%
Computer systems analysts	431	689	258	59.9%
Computer programmers	585	680	95	16.2%
Computer engineers	757	1,436	679	89.7%
Other management-related occupations	4,956	5,801	845	17.1%
Insurance, securities, real estate, business services	1,548	1,726	178	11.5%
Other service occupations, except health	9,652	11,287	1,635	16.9%
Sales occupations, including retail	15,513	17,365	1,852	11.9%
Transportation and material-moving occupations	10,088	11,618	1,530	15.2%

CHAPTER 17

Economics

Economics is the study of the allocation of resources and the production, distribution, and consumption of goods and services. Economists examine how societies produce and exchange goods and services to satisfy material needs. They also analyze the process of economic growth and change and identify policies that contribute to its success or failure. Most economists are concerned with the applications of economic policy in a particular area such as finance, labor, agriculture, transportation, energy, or health. Others develop theories to explain phenomena such as unemployment or inflation.

Economists conduct research, collect and analyze data, monitor economic trends, and develop forecasts such as energy costs, interest rates, and the amount of imports. They use their understanding of economic relationships to advise businesses and other organizations, including insurance companies, banks, securities firms, industry and trade associations, labor unions, and government agencies such as Agriculture or Labor. Economists use mathematical models to develop programs predicting answers to questions such as the nature and length of business cycles, the effects of a specific rate of inflation on the economy, or the effects of tax legislation on unemployment levels.

Economists devise methods and procedures for obtaining the data they need. For example, sampling techniques may be used to conduct a survey, and various mathematical modeling techniques may be used to develop forecasts. Preparing reports on the results of their research is an important part of the economist's job. Relevant data must be reviewed and analyzed, applicable tables and charts prepared, and the results presented in clear, concise language that can be understood by non-economists. Presenting economic and statistical concepts in a meaningful way is particularly important for economists whose research is directed toward making policies for an organization. For example, an economist working in state or local government might analyze data on the growth of school-aged populations, prison growth, and employment and unemployment rates to project spending needs for future years.

Education course work may include macroeconomics, microeconomics, medical economics, economics of crime, labor economics, women in the labor market, income inequalities and discrimination, environmental economics, comparative economics, financing government: taxation and debt, and managerial economics. Quantitative skills are very important, so mathematics, statistics, econometrics, sampling theory, and survey design courses are often taken.

Undergraduate economics students report that they have interpersonal, leadership, mathematical, and computational abilities. Job analyses also mention understanding and use of appropriate theories and methods, as well as accuracy in processing data. Persistence is required because much time is spent independently, and analysis does involve problem solving. Verbal and oral communication skills are necessary so that economists can present findings in a clear and meaningful way.

The quantitative emphasis predominates economists' interests. Whether it be mathematical modeling or the presentation of research findings numerically, mathematical interests are high. Economists also are noted by their breadth of interests and should not be pigeon-holed as entirely business oriented. Economics as a discipline fits well within the breadth and diversity of a liberal arts tradition. Economics is a social science that searches for answers to societal issues.

Economists value earning a good salary and gaining a sense of high achievement when they do difficult tasks very well. Job security is a priority; economists want to work where they will not lose their positions. Also, they differentiate themselves from mathematicians by their desire to work on social problems. They value working independently but accept the routine of research and working with numbers.

Objectivity, open-mindedness, and systematic work habits characterize those in the social sciences. However, economists accept the necessity of performing detailed work about which other social scientists may show a disdain. The quantitative orientation of economists, including heavy use of the computer, modeling applications, and use of large databases, may create for some an independence, an orientation toward prediction, and a determination "to prove" their viewpoint.

Where Do Economics Majors Work?

A large majority of economics graduates work in the private, for-profit sector of the economy for businesses and corporations or in their own business or consulting practice as self-employed workers. Sixty-four percent are employed by businesses and corporations in the private, for-profit sector, and nearly one-fifth are self-employed. Economics graduates also work in the government sector for various governmental agencies such as the Labor Department, the Commerce Department, the Treasury, federal reserve banks, and the like. Nearly 1 in 10 economics graduates with a bachelor's degree work in the government sector. The education sector employs only 5 percent of these graduates, and 3 percent work in the private, nonprofit sector for tax-exempt or charitable organizations.

Nearly 7 out of 10 economics graduates are employed in jobs that are related to their undergraduate major field of study. Twenty-one percent consider their jobs to be closely related to economics, and nearly one-half are employed in jobs that they consider to be somewhat related to their undergraduate major field of study. The latter group of graduates generally work in the business or finance fields performing duties that, although not directly related to their classroom training, do bear some relationship to what they learned in their undergraduate economics curriculum. The remaining 30 percent work in jobs that are not related to economics.

Why do economics graduates work in jobs that are not related to their undergraduate major field of study? The 3 out of 10 graduates who fall in this category offer a variety of reasons for their employment choice. When asked to select the one most important factor influencing their choice to work in an unrelated job, one-third of the graduates employed in unrelated jobs cite

FIGURE 1

Percentage Distribution of Employed Persons with Only a Bachelor's Degree in Economics, by Major Sector of Economic Activity

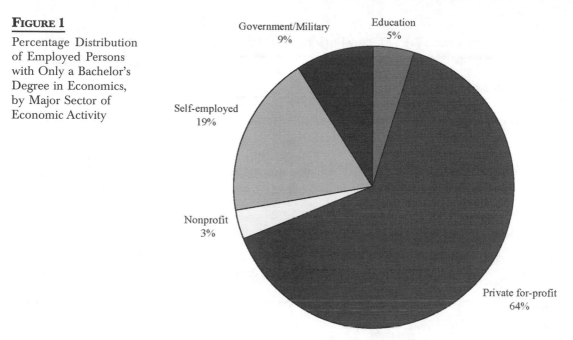

Government/Military 9%

Education 5%

Self-employed 19%

Nonprofit 3%

Private for-profit 64%

pay and promotion opportunities, and 17 percent report a change in their career and professional interests. More than 15 percent are forced to work outside their field because of a lack of related jobs, 10 percent cite family-related reasons, and 9 percent report that the most important factor that influenced their employment in an unrelated job is the overall work environment.

Occupations

A large number of economics graduates are employed in managerial, finance, insurance, real estate, marketing, and sales sectors of the economy. Six out of the top 10 occupations that predominantly employ economics graduates belong to these sectors of the economy. A little more than 63 percent of employed economics graduates work in these 6 occupations. Employment of economics graduates is fairly concentrated. Nearly 73 percent of all employed economics graduates work in the top 10 occupations.

Graduates are most concentrated in top- to mid-level executive, administrative, and managerial occupations. Nearly 21 percent work in these occupations. Insurance, finance, real estate, and business services occupations employ 11 percent of economics graduates, and another 11 percent are employed as accountants, auditors, and financial specialists. One out of 10 works in a sales occupation, and 5 percent work in miscellaneous marketing and sales occupations. Nearly 7 percent work in management-related occupations as management analysts, purchasing agents, or regulatory officers. Among the top 10 occupations that employ economics graduates are non-health service, clerical, agricultural, and forestry occupations. However, these occupations together employ fewer than 10 percent of the graduates.

Table 1
Top 10 Occupations That Employ Persons with Only a Bachelor's Degree in Economics

Top 10 Occupations	PERCENT OF EMPLOYED		
	All	Men	Women
Top- and mid-level managers, executives, administrators	20.8	23.6	10.2
Insurance, securities, real estate, business services	11.0	12.3	6.2
Accountants, auditors, other financial specialists	10.5	10.0	12.2
Sales occupations, including retail	10.0	11.3	5.3
Other management-related occupations	6.5	6.2	7.4
Other marketing and sales occupations	4.5	4.3	5.3
Other service occupations, except health	2.8	2.2	5.3
Agriculture, forestry, fishing, and related occupations	2.6	3.3	0.0
Other administrative (e.g., records clerks, telephone operators)	2.4	1.4	6.3
Construction trades, miners, well drillers	1.6	2.1	0.0

Nearly 8 out of 10 economics graduates are men. The occupational employment patterns of male and female graduates are very different. The employment of female graduates is dispersed across different occupations, while male graduates tend to be more concentrated in a few occupations. The top 10 occupations employ 77 percent of male graduates compared to only 58 percent of female economics graduates.

- Male economics graduates are more than two times as likely as females to work in upper level executive, administrative, and managerial occupations. 24 percent of male graduates work in these occupations, compared to only 10 percent of their female counterparts.

- Men also are 2 times (12 percent versus 6 percent) more likely than women to work in insurance, securities, real estate, and business services occupations.

- Sales occupations also are more likely to employ male economics graduates. More than 11 percent of male graduates are employed in sales occupations that employ only 5 percent of female economics graduates.

- Women are slightly more likely than men to work in accounting, auditing, and financial specialties occupations (12 percent versus 11 percent).

- Clerical and non-health service occupations together employ 12 percent of female economics graduates and only 4 percent of their male counterparts.

Activities on the Job

The activities of economics graduates on their jobs reflect their occupational employment. Nearly 6 out of 10 employed graduates spend most of their time during a typical workweek performing sales, marketing, purchasing, managerial, accounting, and finance duties.

▶ More than one-half of employed economics graduates regularly engage in sales, purchasing, and marketing activities, and 22 percent spend most of their time during a typical week in performing these duties.

▶ Two-thirds of the graduates spend at least 10 hours per week at their jobs in performing management and administrative tasks, and 22 percent consider management and administration to be a major part of their job.

▶ Eighty-four percent of all employed economics graduates regularly spend at least 10 hours per week in accounting, finance, and contractual duties, and 14 percent of the graduates report that these duties consume most of their time at work.

▶ Nearly 3 out of 10 graduates regularly provide professional services like financial consulting to their clients, and 7 percent spend most of their typical workweek in providing these services.

▶ Economics graduates are very quantitatively inclined. They use large databases to estimate and test economic theory for its validity in the "real world." Given this quantitative orientation and the use of large databases, computers are widely used by graduates. About 40 percent regularly perform computer application, programming, and systems-development duties, and 7 percent spend most of their time at work in these activities.

▶ Another 40 percent regularly spend time at work in employee-relations activities, including recruiting, personnel development, and training; however, only 4 percent consider these duties to be a major portion of their job.

▶ Only 4 percent of economics graduates spend most of their time in teaching activities, and 3 percent devote a majority of their typical workweek to applied research activities.

Salaries

The average annual salary of economics graduates with only a bachelor's degree who are employed full-time is $64,000, a level that is 18 percent higher than the average annual salary of all full-time employed college graduates. As with most college graduates, the salary of economics graduates increases with age, indicating that they get more productive and therefore can earn higher salaries as they spend more time on the job. The average annual salary of economics majors increases at a faster pace as they age, and their average salary exceeds the average salary of all college graduates in every age range.

▶ The average annual salary of 25- to 29-year-old economics graduates is $45,400. Between the ages of 30 and 34, the average annual salary rises to $59,200, followed by another increase to $61,800 in the next age range of 35- to 39-year-old graduates.

▶ Between the ages of 40 and 44, graduates' average annual salary is $68,400, rising to $71,100 in the 45-to-49 age group. The average salary of economics graduates peaks at $81,400 between the ages of 50 and 54.

Securing employment in a job that is closely related or somewhat related to their undergraduate major is associated with sizable salary advantages among economics graduates. The average annual salary of graduates who work in closely related jobs is $68,300. Graduates with employment in jobs that are somewhat related to their major earn $65,600 per year. In contrast, the average salary of graduates employed

FIGURE 2

Age/Earnings Profile of Persons with Only a Bachelor's Degree in Economics
(Full-Time Workers, in 2002 Dollars)

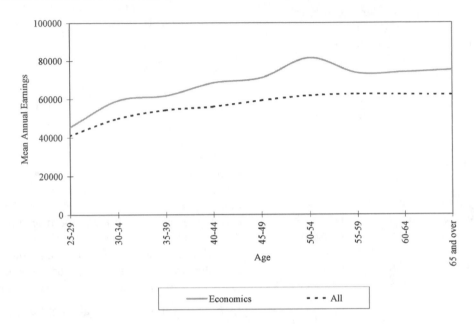

full-time in a job that is not related to their field of study is $53,200.

Economics graduates who work for businesses and corporations in the private, for-profit sector earn a higher average salary, $64,800, than graduates working in other sectors of the economy. The average annual salary of self-employed economics graduates who work full-time in their businesses or practices is $63,800. The government sector pays an average annual salary of $51,200 to economics graduates who work on a full-time basis. Like most other college graduates from different majors, the educational sector, which pays full-time employed economics graduates $39,800 per year, is the lowest-paying sector in the economy.

The average salaries of economics graduates in 7 out of the top 10 occupations that predominantly employ economics graduates are considerably higher than the average salary of all college graduates. The average salaries of economics graduates and all college graduates in each of these 10 occupations are presented below.

▶ The highest earnings of economics graduates are in the top- to mid-level managerial and administrative occupations. The average salary of economics graduates in these occupations, $85,800, is 16 percent higher than the average salary of all college graduates employed in these occupations. These occupations are more likely to employ male economics graduates than female graduates.

▶ The annual salary of economics graduates employed in insurance, finance, and real estate occupations, another area that predominantly employs male economics graduates, is $75,600.

Table 2
Annual Salary of Full-Time Workers with Only a Bachelor's Degree in Economics, Top 10 Occupations (in 2002 Dollars)

Earnings in Top 10 Occupations	All	Economics
Total	$54,171	$64,015
Top- and mid-level managers, executives, administrators	$74,051	$85,854
Insurance, securities, real estate, business services	$68,273	$75,644
Accountants, auditors, other financial specialists	$57,382	$61,433
Sales occupations, including retail	$52,378	$56,087
Other management-related occupations	$51,921	$56,477
Other marketing and sales occupations	$58,208	$64,555
Other service occupations, except health	$39,984	$48,228
Agriculture, forestry, fishing, and related occupations	$45,437	$45,055
Other administrative (e.g., records clerks, telephone operators)	$34,547	$31,950
Construction trades, miners, well drillers	$50,531	$48,307

- The average salary in miscellaneous marketing and sales occupations is $64,600 per year, and the pay of economics graduates employed in sales occupations and management-related occupations—for example, management analysts, purchasing agents, or regulatory officers—is $56,000 per year.

- Non-health service occupations, which are more likely to employ female than male economics graduates, pay an average salary of $48,200 per year.

- The lowest average salary of economics graduates out of the top 10 occupations is in clerical jobs. The annual salary of graduates in this occupation is only $31,900 per year. This occupation is more likely to employ female graduates than male economics graduates.

On-the-Job Training

The career potential of a job is closely associated with the amount of work-related training on the job. Work-related training is regarded as an investment by firms because it makes workers more productive. Firms that invest in their workforce are more likely to offer pay increases and promotions to match the increasing productivity of their workers. Firms that do not invest in their workers are relatively less likely to offer pay increases and promotions. The rate of participation in work-related training during a year among employed economics graduates is the same as the training participation rate of all college graduates: 68 percent.

- Of those economics graduates who receive some training during a year, 74 percent receive technical training in the occupation in which they are employed.

▶ Forty-two percent of the training recipients receive management or supervisor training.

▶ Thirty-one percent receive training to improve their general professional skills, such as public speaking and business writing.

Although economics majors decide to participate in work-related training activities, workshops, or seminars for numerous reasons, five factors stand out as the most commonly cited. Included among them are a need to improve skills and knowledge in the occupational area of their employment, mandatory training requirements of the employer, increased opportunities for advancement in the form of a promotion and a higher salary, a need to obtain a professional license or certificate, and a need to acquire skills for a new position.

When asked to select the one most important reason to acquire training, 60 percent of economics majors who undergo training identify the need to improve their occupational skills and knowledge. Another 14 percent report a mandatory training requirement by employers as the most important factor for their involvement in work-related training. Nearly 10 percent rank an improvement in their opportunities for a salary increase or a promotion as the number one factor in influencing their decision to participate in work-related training. According to 8 percent, the most important factor for their involvement in training is the need to obtain a professional license or certificate, and 5 percent consider the need to learn skills for a recently acquired job to be the number one reason for their participation in work-related training.

Post-Graduation Activities

More than 35 percent of economics graduates with a bachelor's degree proceed to earn a postgraduate degree: 24 percent earn a master's degree, 4 percent graduate with a doctorate, and another 9 percent earn a professional degree.

▶ More than 53 percent earn their master's degree in business management and administrative services. Only one-fifth choose economics as their major field of study for their master's degree. Another 8 percent secure their master's degree in education. The rest are dispersed across different major fields.

▶ Nearly 60 percent of all doctorate degrees of undergraduate economics majors are earned in economics. A little more than 9 percent are earned in business administration and management, and another 9 percent are earned in education.

▶ Nearly 9 out of 10 (87 percent) professional degrees among undergraduate economics majors are earned in law, and 9 percent are earned in the health professions.

Out of all economics graduates under the age of 65, 88 percent are employed. Only 3 percent are officially unemployed; that is, they are not employed and are actively seeking employment. The remaining 9 percent are out of the labor force; that is, they are not employed and are not seeking employment. Many of the labor force withdrawals among economics graduates are attributable to family responsibilities, retirement, and a lack of the need or desire to work. Nearly 38 percent cite family responsibilities as one of the reasons for their labor force withdrawal. Another 38 percent cite retirement as the reason for their labor force withdrawal, and 27 percent withdraw from the labor force because they do not have the need or desire to work. One out of 10 labor force withdrawals is attributable to chronic illness or a disabling condition, and 5 percent of these withdrawals are because of postgraduate school enrollment.

Employment Outlook

According to the projections by the U.S. Bureau of Labor Statistics, employment in occupations that require at least a bachelor's degree is expected to grow faster than employment in other sectors of the American labor market. Between 2000 and 2010, the U.S. economy is projected to add 22.2 million jobs, yielding an employment growth rate of 15.2 percent. The employment growth projections in the top 10 occupations that are most likely to employ economics graduates are presented in this section.

▶ The fastest growth in demand is projected in miscellaneous marketing and sales occupations. Adding 137,000 jobs between 2000 and 2010, the employment in these occupations is projected to grow by 22 percent. Only 5 percent of economics graduates are employed in these occupations.

▶ The area of largest employment for economics graduates—upper-level executive, administrative, and managerial occupations—is projected to add 1.27 million jobs between 2000 and 2010, yielding an employment growth rate of 12 percent. More than twice as many male economics graduates as females are employed in this occupation. This occupation also is associated with the highest salary among economics graduates.

▶ The demand for personnel in insurance, finance, and real estate occupations is projected to increase at a rate of 12 percent between 2000 and 2010. This occupation also is more likely to employ male than female economics graduates.

▶ The employment projections for accountants, auditors, and financial specialists, and for other management-related occupations such as management analysts, purchasing agents, and regulatory officers, are slightly higher that the projected growth of overall employment. Total jobs in both occupations are projected to increase by about 17 percent.

Table 3

Projected Change in Employment in the Top 10 Occupations That Employ Persons with Only a Bachelor's Degree in Economics

Top 10 Occupations	Actual Employment in 2000 (000s)	Projected Employment in 2010 (000s)	Absolute Change (000s)	Percentage Change
Top- and mid-level managers, executives, administrators	10,564	11,834	1,270	12.0%
Insurance, securities, real estate, business services	1,548	1,726	178	11.5%
Accountants, auditors, other financial specialists	2,115	2,481	366	17.3%
Sales occupations, including retail	15,513	17,365	1,852	11.9%
Other management-related occupations	4,956	5,801	845	17.1%

(continued)

Table 3 (continued)
Projected Change in Employment in the Top 10 Occupations That
Employ Persons with Only a Bachelor's Degree in Economics

Top 10 Occupations	Actual Employment in 2000 (000s)	Projected Employment in 2010 (000s)	Absolute Change (000s)	Percentage Change
Other marketing and sales occupations	621	758	137	22.1%
Other service occupations, except health	9,652	11,287	1,635	16.9%
Agriculture, forestry, fishing, and related occupations	1,429	1,480	51	3.6%
Other administrative (e.g., records clerks, telephone operators)	16,911	18,522	1,611	9.5%
Construction trades, miners, well drillers	7,451	8,439	988	13.3%

CHAPTER 18

Financial Management

Financial managers oversee the flow of cash and financial instruments, monitor the extension of credit, assess the risk of transactions, raise capital, analyze investments, prepare reports to satisfy tax and regulatory requirements, develop information to assess a firm's present and future financial status, and communicate with investors or stockholders. In a small firm, one or two people may do all the above functions, but in larger companies, each function may represent an area with a separate manager whose title may be treasurer, controller, cash and credit manager, risk and insurance manager, reserve officer, or financial analyst.

Banks are not the only places where financial managers work. Practically every company employs at least one person with a financial management background. Different industries, such as insurance, securities, and health care, offer a variety of interests to people working in financial management.

This field can also be very dynamic, with the expansion of global trade; shifting federal and state laws and regulations; and a proliferation of new, complex financial instruments. Some people enjoy this field because they often work with top management in developing the financial information these executives require in their leadership roles. They are close to the power brokers.

A degree in accounting, finance, or business administration is the educational preparation for typical entry into the field of financial management.

Obviously, good computational skills are fundamental, as is facility in the use and understanding of sophisticated computerized software in the financial management field. Key is the ability to make independent analyses of collected quantitative data and its interpretation to make judgments that others might refer to as laden with risks. Financial managers make weighty decisions, often within situations that are well regulated by laws and standard accounting practices. They are both consumers and producers of fiscal reports presented mathematically and diagrammatically. Important is the ability to communicate effectively both in speaking and in writing.

Interests are focused on business, money, numbers, analytical thinking, and a company's or institution's type of organization and operation. Tact is also required in dealing with people. Flexibility to both be independent and work on varied projects and in groups will characterize many financial managers. They play influential leadership roles within organizations.

Financial managers value jobs in which a large amount of money can be earned and that provide the challenge of giving considerable amounts of thorough, concentrated thought and reasoning to situations. They seek the prestige gained through public recognition of "having made it," as well as having others acknowledge their prowess with numbers.

Financial managers are goal oriented and matter-of-fact pragmatists who are guided by those things which seem useful. They enjoy seriousness and the ability to remain focused at times on set objectives that possibly may be at odds with other departments within a company, such as sales and marketing, which are much more people oriented.

Where Do Financial Management Majors Work?

Nearly 9 out of 10 persons who graduate in the field of financial management work in the private, for-profit sector of the economy, either for businesses and corporations or in their own business or practice as self-employed workers. Three-quarters work for businesses and corporations in the private, for-profit sector, and another 13 percent work as self-employed workers in their own businesses or practices. The government sector employs 8 percent of financial management graduates. Only 2 percent work for educational institutions, and another 2 percent work for private, nonprofit organizations.

Financial management graduates possess skills and knowledge that are applicable in a diverse array of industries. In addition to banks, financial management graduates have job opportunities in health, securities, and insurance industries, to name a few. Nearly every firm requires some type of financial management. The extent of practical application of the skills of financial management enables many graduates to find jobs in their field. Eight out of 10 financial management graduates work in jobs that are related to

their undergraduate major field of study. About 40 percent are employed in jobs that are closely related to their major, and another 40 percent consider their jobs to be somewhat related to their undergraduate major. Only 20 percent of financial management graduates work in jobs that are not at all related to their undergraduate major.

Why do the latter group of financial management graduates work in unrelated jobs? They cite a variety of factors as possible reasons for their employment in unrelated jobs. More than 60 percent consider better pay and promotion opportunities outside their field as one of the reasons to work in those jobs, and 40 percent work in unrelated jobs to change their career track. The same proportion cite the general working environment—for example, hours of work, equipment at work, or the general working conditions—as one of the factors to influence their decision, and an equal number of financial management graduates report that one of the reasons for working in unrelated jobs is their inability to find related jobs. One-third are forced to work in unrelated jobs because of the more convenient location of those jobs. And one-quarter cite family-related factors as one of the reasons to choose employment outside their undergraduate major field of study.

When asked to pick the most important reason for employment outside their major field of study, 34 percent of the graduates point to better pay and promotion opportunities, and 21 percent rank the lack of available related jobs as the number one reason for their employment in an unrelated job. About 15 percent consider a change in career track as the most important factor to influence their decision to work in an unrelated job, and 9 percent consider the general working environment as the top-ranking factor in their employment choice outside the field of financial management. Family-related reasons are the most important factor influencing the employment choice for 8 percent of the graduates who work in unrelated jobs.

FIGURE 1

Percentage Distribution of Employed Persons with Only a Bachelor's Degree in Financial Management, by Major Sector of Economic Activity

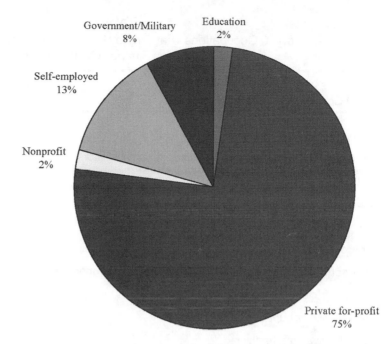

Occupations

The employment of financial management graduates is very concentrated in a few occupations. Nearly 60 percent are employed in only 3 occupations, and the top 6 occupations account for nearly three-fourths of all employed financial management graduates. Employment of financial management graduates is mainly concentrated in high-level accounting, managerial, finance, insurance, real estate, and sales and marketing occupations. Twenty-three percent are employed as accountants, auditors, and financial specialists. Another 20 percent are employed in high-level executive, administrative, and managerial positions. Nearly 16 percent of financial management graduates work in insurance, finance, and real estate occupations, and 6 percent work in management-related occupations as management analysts, purchasing agents, and regulatory officers. More than 4 percent of employed financial management graduates work in marketing occupations, and another 4 percent work in sales occupations. Clerical occupations employ another 4 percent of financial management graduates, and 3 percent work as accounting clerks and bookkeepers.

Table 1
Top 10 Occupations That Employ Persons with Only a Bachelor's Degree in Financial Management

Top 10 Occupations	PERCENT OF EMPLOYED		
	All	Men	Women
Accountants, auditors, other financial specialists	23.0	21.4	28.2
Top- and mid-level managers, executives, administrators	20.1	23.6	9.1
Insurance, securities, real estate, business services	15.8	18.7	7.1
Other management-related occupations	6.4	5.9	8.1
Other marketing and sales occupations	4.5	4.5	4.5
Sales occupations, including retail	4.2	4.5	2.9
Other administrative (e.g., records clerks, telephone operators)	4.1	2.0	10.7
Accounting clerks, bookkeepers	2.9	1.3	8.1
Other service occupations, except health	1.5	1.6	0.9
Computer systems analysts	1.3	1.4	1.0

Nearly 76 percent of employed financial management graduates are men. The occupational employment patterns of male and female financial management graduates are quite different.

- ▶ Female graduates are more likely than males to work as accountants, auditors, and financial specialists. More than 28 percent of female graduates work in these occupations, compared to only 21 percent of employed male financial management graduates.

- ▶ Female graduates also are much more likely than male graduates to work as accounting clerks and bookkeepers and in clerical/administrative occupations. Whereas 11 percent of employed female financial management graduates work in clerical occupations such as record clerks and telephone operators, only

2 percent of male graduates are employed in these occupations. Similarly, 8 percent of female graduates work as accounting clerks and bookkeepers compared to only 1 percent of male financial management graduates.

- ▶ Male graduates are considerably more likely than female graduates to work as top-level executives, administrators, and managers. Nearly 24 percent of all employed male graduates work in these occupations compared to only 9 percent of employed female graduates.

- ▶ Men with a bachelor's degree in financial management also are more likely than female graduates to work in insurance, finance, and real estate occupations (19 percent versus 7 percent).

Activities on the Job

The activities in which financial management graduates engage at work are very closely related to the occupations in which they are employed.

- More than 9 out of 10 employed financial management graduates report that they spend at least 10 hours per week in accounting, financial, and contractual duties at work, and 31 percent indicate that they spend a majority of their time at work on these activities. This is not surprising, given the large proportion of graduates who are employed as accountants, auditors, and financial specialists.

- Nearly 70 percent regularly perform management and administration duties at work, and 16 percent spend most of their time at work in performing these duties. Performance of these duties is related to the high rates of employment in managerial and administrative occupations.

- Sales, marketing, and purchasing activities regularly engage 46 percent of employed financial management graduates, and one-fifth engage in these activities for a major part of their typical workweek.

- Forty-five percent regularly spend time at work in computer applications, programming, and systems-development activities, while 8 percent spend a major part of their typical workweek in performing computer application duties. Widespread use of computers in many sectors of the economy, particularly the finance sector, results in a high rate of computer use among financial management graduates.

- Professional services, mainly financial services, are regularly provided to clients by 36 percent of employed financial management graduates. About 8 percent spend most of their time during a typical workweek in providing these services.

Salaries

The average annual salary of financial management graduates with only a bachelor's degree who are employed full-time is $61,800, a level that is more than 14 percent higher than the average annual salary of all full-time employed college graduates. As with most college graduates, the salary of financial management graduates increases with age, indicating that they get more productive and therefore can earn higher salaries as they spend more time on the job. Within each age range, financial management graduates earn considerably higher average salaries than the salary of all college graduates in those age groups.

- The average annual salary of financial management graduates between the ages of 25 and 29 is $45,100. Graduates between the ages of 30 and 34 earn $57,500 annually.

- Average annual earnings of financial management graduates increase at an impressive pace as they get older. The average annual salary of 35- to 39-year-old financial management graduates who are employed full-time is $68,200, increasing to $70,800 for 40- to 44-year-old graduates, followed by another increase to $76,000 among graduates between the ages of 45 and 49. After increasing to $78,100 among 50- to 54-year-old graduates, the average annual salary of financial management graduates peaks at a high level of $81,600 per year at the ages of 55 to 59.

▶ The average annual salary of financial management graduates who work in jobs that are related to their major field of study is considerably higher than the salary of graduates who work in jobs that are not related to their undergraduate major field of study. Closely related jobs pay full-time employed financial management graduates $67,700 annually. Graduates employed in somewhat related jobs earn $63,200 per year, and those whose jobs are unrelated to their undergraduate field of study earn $46,100 per year.

▶ Earning an average salary of $67,100 annually, financial management graduates who are self-employed in their own businesses or practices earn a higher salary than those who are employed in other sectors of the economy. The average salary of graduates who work for businesses and corporations in the private, for-profit sector of the economy is $62,800 per year. The pay of financial management graduates for their employment in the government sector is $52,200 per year. The lowest salary among financial management graduates occurs in the education sector, where full-time employed graduates earn $36,800 per year.

The average annual salaries in most of the top 10 occupations that predominantly employ financial management graduates are above the salary of all college graduates employed in those occupations. There are sizable variations in the average annual salaries of financial management graduates by the occupation in which they are employed. Just within the top 10 occupations, the average annual salaries among full-time workers range from a high of $78,400 to a low of $31,600 among full-time workers.

▶ Financial management graduates employed in high-level executive, administrative, and managerial occupations earn an average annual salary of $78,400. This occupation predominantly employs male graduates.

▶ Other areas that predominantly employ male financial management graduates—insurance, finance, and real estate occupations—pay graduates an average annual salary of $76,900.

▶ The average salary in management-related occupations such as management analysts, purchasing agents, and regulatory officers is $60,200 per year.

▶ Accounting occupations, which are the top employers of financial management graduates, particularly female graduates, pay graduates an average annual salary of $57,100.

▶ Clerical and administrative occupations and accounting clerks and bookkeeping occupations pay financial management graduates the lowest salary out of the top 10 occupations, $31,600 per year.

FIGURE 2

Age/Earnings Profile of Persons with Only a Bachelor's Degree in Financial Management (Full-Time Workers, in 2002 Dollars)

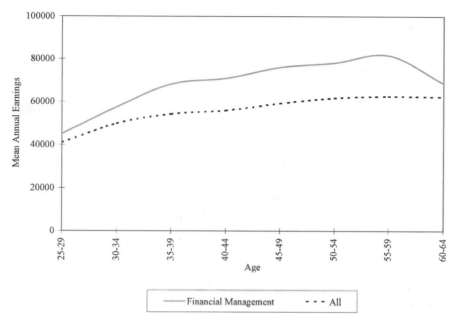

Table 2

Annual Salary of Full-Time Workers with Only a Bachelor's Degree in Financial Management, Top 10 Occupations (in 2002 Dollars)

Earnings In Top 10 Occupations	All	Financial Management
Total	$54,171	$61,772
Accountants, auditors, other financial specialists	$57,382	$57,130
Top- and mid-level managers, executives, administrators	$74,051	$78,377
Insurance, securities, real estate, business services	$68,273	$76,925
Other management-related occupations	$51,921	$60,254
Other marketing and sales occupations	$58,208	$59,203
Sales occupations, including retail	$52,378	$55,186
Other administrative (e.g., records clerks, telephone operators)	$34,547	$31,583
Accounting clerks, bookkeepers	$32,380	$31,714
Other service occupations, except health	$39,984	$45,636
Computer systems analysts	$59,818	$53,652

On-the-Job Training

The career potential of a job is closely associated with the amount of work-related training on the job. Work-related training is regarded as an investment by firms because it makes workers more productive. Firms that invest in their workforce are more likely to offer pay increases and promotions to match the increasing productivity of their workers. Firms that do not invest in their workers are relatively less likely to offer pay increases and promotions. The incidence of work-related training among financial management graduates is slightly higher than the rate of participation in work-related training among all college graduates. While 68 percent of all college graduates acquire some kind of work-related training during a year, nearly 70 percent of financial management graduates annually engage in work-related training.

- Of those financial management graduates who receive some training during the year, 79 percent are engaged in technical training in the occupation in which they are employed.

- Forty-four percent of the training recipients participate in management or supervisory training.

- Thirty-three percent receive training to improve their general professional skills, such as public speaking and business writing.

Although financial management graduates decide to participate in work-related training activities, workshops, or seminars for numerous reasons, four reasons stand out as most commonly cited by graduates. Included among them are a need to improve skills and knowledge in the occupational area of their employment, mandatory training requirements of the employer, increased opportunities for advancement in the form of a higher salary and a promotion, and the need to learn new skills for a newly acquired position.

When asked to select the one most important reason to acquire training, 58 percent of financial management graduates who undergo training identify the need to improve their occupational skills and knowledge. Thirteen percent report mandatory training requirements by the employer as the most important factor underlying their involvement in work-related training. According to another 13 percent of the training participants, the most important reason is a salary increase and a promotion. The need to obtain a professional license is the number one reason to acquire training among 7 percent of graduates, and 6 percent rank the necessity to learn skills for a newly acquired position as the number one reason to acquire training.

Post-Graduation Activities

Of all graduates with a bachelor's degree in financial management, 23 percent proceed to earn a postgraduate degree: 18 percent earn a master's degree, and the remaining 5 percent earn a professional degree.

- Forty percent of all master's degrees earned by undergraduate financial management majors are in the field of financial management, and 49 percent are earned in the field of business administration and management.

- Almost all professional degrees earned by undergraduate financial management majors are in the field of law.

Out of all financial management graduates under the age of 65, 91 percent are employed. Only 3 percent are officially unemployed; that is, they are not employed and are actively seeking employment. The remaining 6 percent are out of the labor force; that is, they are not employed and are not seeking employment. The labor force withdrawal of one-half of financial management graduates who are out of the labor force is attributable to family responsibilities, and another 29 percent indicate that they lack the desire or the need to work in the labor market. Nearly 12 percent of financial management graduates who withdraw from the labor force are retired, and another 12 percent suffer from a chronic illness or a disabling condition. Postgraduate education activities among financial management majors account for only 8 percent of the labor force withdrawals.

Employment Outlook

According to the projections by the U.S. Bureau of Labor Statistics, employment in occupations that require at least a bachelor's degree is expected to grow faster than employment in other sectors of the American labor market. Between 2000 and 2010, the U.S. economy is projected to add 22.2 million jobs, yielding an employment growth rate of 15.2 percent. The employment growth projections in 5 out of the top 10 occupations that are most likely to employ financial management graduates are at or above the average rate of growth for the entire U.S. economy.

- The fastest growth in demand is projected in the occupation that is the tenth-largest employer of financial management graduates—computer systems analyst. Adding 258,000 jobs

between 2000 and 2010, the employment in this occupation is projected to grow by nearly 60 percent.

- Employment projections for accountants, auditors, and financial specialists and for other management-related occupations such as management analysts, purchasing agents, and regulatory officers, are both projected to increase by about 17 percent.

- The demand for personnel in upper-level managerial occupations, as well as in insurance, finance, and real estate occupations, is projected to increase at a rate of 12 percent between 2000 and 2010. Both occupations are more likely to employ male financial management graduates than female graduates.

- The 2 occupations that are more likely to employ women graduates than male graduates—miscellaneous administrative occupations such as record clerks and telephone operators, and accounting clerks and bookkeepers—are projected to grow at below-average rates between 2000 and 2010. Widespread use of high-technology equipment, such as voice mail, e-mail, faxes, and particularly computers, is largely responsible for only a 10 percent increase in the clerical jobs and a 2 percent increase in the number of jobs in the accounting clerk and bookkeeping occupations.

Table 3
Projected Change in Employment in the Top 10 Occupations That
Employ Persons with Only a Bachelor's Degree in Financial Management

Top 10 Occupations	Actual Employment in 2000 (000s)	Projected Employment in 2010 (000s)	Absolute Change (000s)	Percentage Change
Accountants, auditors, other financial specialists	2,115	2,481	366	17.3%
Top- and mid-level managers, executives, administrators	10,564	11,834	1,270	12.0%
Insurance, securities, real estate, business services	1,548	1,726	178	11.5%
Other management-related occupations	4,956	5,801	845	17.1%
Other marketing and sales occupations	621	758	137	22.1%
Sales occupations, including retail	15,513	17,365	1,852	11.9%
Other administrative (e.g., records clerks, telephone operators)	16,911	18,522	1,611	9.5%
Accounting clerks, bookkeepers	1,991	2,030	39	2.0%
Other service occupations, except health	9,652	11,287	1,635	16.9%
Computer systems analysts	431	689	258	59.9%

CHAPTER 19

General Business

Business is about making money or achieving the best with given resources. Every enterprise, business, or organization, including nonprofit ones, is administered and managed. Of course, some enterprises, businesses, or organizations are administered and managed better than others. Thus, effective principles and practices of business administration and management are applicable to everyone in business, whatever their self-expressed professional identity. By necessity, the majors covered under the business category are delimited considering the very large number of job titles: 320 alone are listed under the general heading of managers and administrators, according to the U.S. Department of Labor.

Business Management/ Administrative Services

This major encompasses a very broad field. It involves leading, running things, and/or supervising people. There are managers in the nonprofit as well as the for-profit sector; business owners, large or small; and administrators, including government administrators. Military officers also administrate and manage. Work areas range from construction, engineering and science, health care, advertising, hotels, restaurants, farming, real estate, employment, banking,

and industrial production to sales or television program production. All organizations are managed and administered.

There is a difference between administration and management positions. The U.S. Department of Labor's distinction is that business administrators direct, through lower-level personnel, all or part of the activities in business establishments, government agencies, and labor unions. Administrators set policies, make important decisions, and determine priorities. Administrators in service areas that provide health care (such as hospitals), safety, recreation, and social services (such as welfare, schools, churches, libraries, and museums) manage, through lower-level personnel, all or part of their activities. Administrators are usually responsible to a board of directors or government agency that sets overall policies and goals for their organization or institution. Within established guidelines, administrators plan and oversee programs and activities that are carried out by others. On the other hand, managers direct the operations of various kinds of establishments such as stores, hotels, food service facilities, distribution warehouses, transportation and airline terminals, and automobile service stations. Managers usually carry out their activities according to policies and procedures determined by owners, administrators, or other persons with higher authority.

Educational requirements typically include foundational course work in accounting, finance, marketing, economics, management, organizational behavior, business policy, computer-based information systems, and statistics, plus courses in the humanities, mathematics, and social sciences. Most people, in addition, have a concentration area with more courses in accounting, management-information systems, marketing, transportation, international business, human resources, finance and insurance, or small business entrepreneurship.

The ability to recognize and solve business and organizational problems with sound and ethical judgment is critical. Being able to understand the role of a business or organization's social responsibilities within a community or region or around the world can be valuable. Qualities important for success include leadership, self-confidence, motivation, decisiveness, and flexibility. Managers and administrators do encounter stress that will require stamina when they are under pressure. The ability to communicate effectively is essential to manage effectively.

Those working in this area like to understand how to function effectively within an organization or group, be involved in interpersonal interactions, and be careful to pay attention to details. While it sounds good to be the boss, it is hard work to take full responsibility for something. While interacting with people can be fun socially, getting them to produce efficiently and perform quality work can be difficult at times. Managers and administrators must accept, at least, that they evaluate performance by the numbers and results "on the bottom line."

High salaries attract people to management and administration positions. There is power also in being boss, especially if one is successful and receives public recognition. As stated earlier, every organization needs to be administered and managed, and often, the people in these positions receive public recognition, especially in the numerous small towns across our nation where so many people live. Obviously, possessing wisdom and intelligence is viewed as important to having achieved success; however, luck must be acknowledged. Managers and administrators also value having autonomy, being independent, and having diverse opportunities.

Managers and administrators can either be extroverted or introverted. They are thinkers who organize their facts and data and plan their goals well in advance. They also are logical, analytical, and practical; can be impersonal; and do not like confusion. They have to work at accepting the opinions of others, which is easier if the opinions are clearly stated and well supported by information. They are very comfortable and patient with getting all the facts and then can be very decisive. Most in this field do not and prefer not to make decisions intuitively or impulsively.

Where Do General Business Majors Work?

More than two-thirds of all employed general business graduates work for businesses and corporations in the private, for-profit sector of the economy. Another 15 percent are self-employed, working in their own businesses or practices. The government sector employs 1 out of 10 general business graduates, and 4 percent work for educational institutions. The remaining 3 percent of employed general business graduates work for private, nonprofit organizations.

FIGURE 1

Percentage Distribution of Employed Persons with Only a Bachelor's Degree in General Business, by Major Sector of Economic Activity

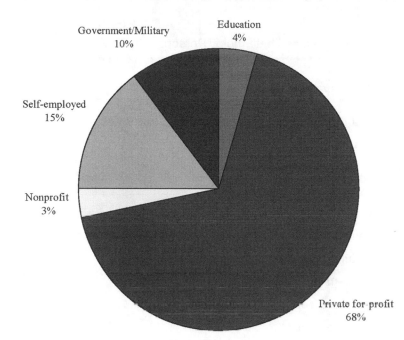

General business graduates possess a broad array of skills that are useful in performing management and administrative functions in a variety of industries and occupations. The extent of practical application of the general business skills enables many graduates to find jobs in their field. More than 8 out of 10 general business graduates work in jobs that are related to their undergraduate major field of study. About 35 percent are employed in jobs that are closely related to their major, and another 47 percent consider their jobs to be somewhat related to their undergraduate major. Only 18 percent of general business graduates work in jobs that are not at all related to their undergraduate major.

Why do the latter group of general business graduates work in unrelated jobs? They cite a variety of factors as possible reasons for their employment in unrelated jobs. When asked to select the one most important reason for employment outside their major field of study,

28 percent of the graduates point to better pay and promotion opportunities, and 14 percent rank the lack of available related jobs as the number one reason for their employment in unrelated jobs. About 13 percent consider a change in career interests as the most important factor to influence their decision to work in unrelated jobs, and 12 percent consider the general working environment as the top-ranking factor in their employment choice outside the field of general business. Family-related reasons are the most important factor influencing the employment choice for 10 percent of the graduates who work in unrelated jobs. About 7 percent rank job location as the key factor in their decision to work in unrelated jobs.

Occupations

The employment of general business graduates is concentrated in a few occupations. More than one-half are employed in only 4 occupations, and nearly 70 percent are employed in the top

Table 1

Top 10 Occupations That Employ Persons with Only a Bachelor's Degree in General Business

Top 10 Occupations	PERCENT OF EMPLOYED		
	All	Men	Women
Top- and mid-level managers, executives, administrators	23.6	27.8	11.9
Other management-related occupations	10.2	10.0	10.8
Accountants, auditors, other financial specialists	9.2	8.1	12.0
Sales occupations, including retail	9.1	10.0	6.5
Insurance, securities, real estate, business services	8.3	9.1	6.1
Other administrative (e.g., records clerks, telephone operators)	4.5	3.0	8.6
Other marketing and sales occupations	4.4	4.8	3.4
Personnel, training, and labor relations specialists	3.1	2.5	4.5
Secretaries, receptionists, typists	2.1	0.0	8.0
Other service occupations, except health	1.8	1.5	2.5

7 occupations. The top 10 occupations that predominantly employ general business graduates account for more than 76 percent of all employed general business graduates. Employment of general business graduates is mainly concentrated in high-level managerial, administrative, accounting, finance, insurance, real estate, and sales and marketing occupations. Twenty-four percent are employed as top- to mid-level executives, managers, and administrators. Another 10 percent are employed in management-related occupations—for example, management analysts, purchasing agents, or regulatory officers. More than 9 percent work as accountants, auditors, and financial specialists, and another 9 percent of general business graduates work in sales occupations. Insurance, finance, and real estate occupations employ 8 percent of the graduates, and 5 percent work in clerical jobs—for example, as records clerks and telephone operators.

A little more than 73 percent of employed general business graduates are men. The occupational employment patterns of male and female general business graduates are quite different.

▶ Female graduates are more likely than males to work as accountants, auditors, and financial specialists. Exactly 12 percent of female graduates work in these occupations, compared to 8 percent of employed male general business graduates.

▶ Female graduates also are much more likely than male graduates to work in clerical/administrative occupations. Whereas 9 percent of employed female general business graduates work in clerical occupations as records clerks and telephone operators, for example, only 3 percent of male graduates are employed in these occupations.

- Female general business graduates are more likely to work as secretaries, receptionists, and typists (8 percent versus none of the male graduates).

- Male graduates are considerably more likely than female graduates to work as top-level executives, administrators, and managers. Nearly 29 percent of all employed male graduates work in these occupations, compared to only 12 percent of employed female graduates.

- Men with a bachelor's degree in general business also are more likely than female graduates to work in insurance, finance, and real estate occupations (9 percent versus 6 percent) and in sales occupations (10 percent versus 7 percent among female graduates).

Activities on the Job

The activities in which general business graduates engage at work are very closely related to the occupations in which they are employed.

- More than 70 percent regularly perform management and administration duties at work, and 25 percent spend most of their time at work in performing these duties. Performance of these duties is related to the high proportion of employment of general business graduates in managerial and administrative occupations.

- Sales, marketing, and purchasing activities regularly engage one-half of all employed general business graduates, and 22 percent spend a majority of their time at work performing these duties.

- More than 8 out of 10 employed general business graduates report that they spend at least 10 hours per week in accounting, financial, and contractual duties at work,

and 13 percent indicate that they spend a majority of their time at work on these activities.

- Forty-one percent regularly spend time at work in computer applications, programming, and systems-development activities, while 8 percent spend a major part of their typical work week in performing computer application duties. Widespread use of computers in almost every sector of the economy results in a high rate of computer use among many college graduates, including general business graduates.

- Nearly one-half of all employed general business graduates engage in employee-relations activities, including recruiting, personnel development, and training, and 6 percent spend a majority of their typical workweek in these activities.

- Professional services like financial and other consulting services are regularly provided to clients by 22 percent of employed general business graduates. About 5 percent spend most of their time during a typical workweek in providing these services.

Salaries

The average annual salary of general business graduates with only a bachelor's degree who are employed full-time is $58,600, a level that is 8 percent higher than the average annual salary of all full-time employed college graduates. As with most college graduates, the salary of general business graduates increases with age, indicating that they get more productive and therefore can earn higher salaries as they spend more time on the job. Within each age range, the average salary of general business graduates is higher than the average salary of all college graduates in those age groups.

- The average annual salary of general business graduates between the ages of 25 and 29 is $41,500. Graduates between the ages of 30 and 34 earn $50,700 annually.

- The average annual earnings of general business graduates increase as they get older. The average annual salary of 35- to 39-year-old general business graduates who are employed full-time is $59,100, increasing to $62,200 for 40- to 44-year-old graduates, followed by another increase to $64,200 among graduates between the ages of 45 and 49. After increasing to $67,300 among 50- to 54-year-old graduates, the average annual salary of general business graduates peaks at a high level of $69,700 per year at the ages of 55 to 59.

The average annual salary of general business graduates who work in jobs that are related to their major field of study is considerably higher than the salary of graduates who work in jobs that are not related to their undergraduate major field of study. Closely related jobs pay full-time employed general business graduates $64,500 annually. Graduates employed in somewhat related jobs earn $58,600 per year, and those whose jobs are unrelated to their undergraduate field of study earn $46,200 per year.

Earning an average salary of $67,700 annually, general business graduates who are self-employed in their own businesses or practices earn a higher salary than those who are employed in other sectors of the economy. The average salary of graduates who work for businesses and corporations in the private, for-profit sector of the economy is $59,500 per year. The pay of general business graduates in the government sector is $51,700 per year. The lowest salary among general business graduates is in the education sector, where full-time employed graduates earn $42,700 per year.

The average annual salaries in 8 out of the top 10 occupations that predominantly employ general business graduates are above the salary of all college graduates employed in those occupations. There are sizable variations in the average annual salaries of general business graduates by the occupation in which they are employed. Just within the top 10 occupations, the average annual salaries of full-time workers range from a high of $74,200 to a low of $34,000.

- General business graduates employed in high-level executive, administrative, and managerial occupations earn an average annual salary of $74,200. These occupations predominantly employ male graduates.

- Other occupations that predominantly employ male general business graduates—insurance, finance, and real estate—pay graduates an average annual salary of $73,500.

- The average annual salary of general business graduates who are employed full-time in marketing and sales occupations is $62,700.

- Graduates employed in labor relations, personnel, and training occupations earn $59,700 per year.

- The lowest salary among the top 10 occupations is in clerical and secretarial occupations that, respectively, pay general business graduates an average salary of $35,300 and $33,900 per year. Both of these occupations are more likely to employ female than male general business graduates.

FIGURE 2

Age/Earnings Profile of Persons with Only a Bachelor's Degree in General Business
(Full-Time Workers, in 2002 Dollars)

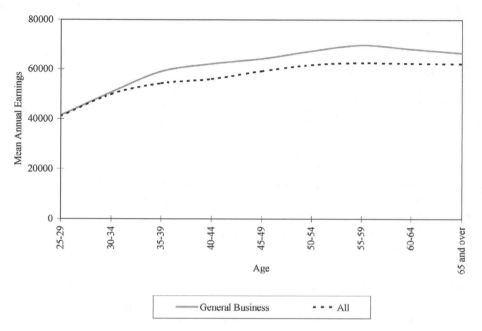

Table 2

Annual Salary of Full-Time Workers with Only a Bachelor's Degree
in General Business, Top 10 Occupations (In 2002 Dollars)

Earnings in Top 10 Occupations	All	General Business
Total	$54,171	$58,648
Top- and mid-level managers, executives, administrators	$74,051	$74,168
Other management-related occupations	$51,921	$50,881
Accountants, auditors, other financial specialists	$57,382	$54,223
Sales occupations, including retail	$52,378	$56,253
Insurance, securities, real estate, business services	$68,273	$73,506
Other administrative (e.g., record clerks, telephone operators)	$34,547	$35,326
Other marketing and sales occupations	$58,208	$62,658
Personnel, training, and labor relations specialists	$51,577	$59,747
Secretaries, receptionists, typists	$32,246	$33,946
Other service occupations, except health	$39,984	$41,202

On-the-Job Training

The career potential of a job is closely associated with the amount of work-related training on the job. Work-related training is regarded as an investment by firms because it makes workers more productive. Firms that invest in their workforce are more likely to offer pay increases and promotions to match the increasing productivity of their workers. Firms that do not invest in their workers are relatively less likely to offer pay increases and promotions. The incidence of work-related training among general business graduates is about the same as the rate of participation in work-related training among all college graduates. While 68 percent of all college graduates acquire some kind of work-related training during a year, 67 percent of general business graduates annually engage in work-related training.

- Of those general business graduates who receive some training during the year, 71 percent receive technical training in the occupation in which they are employed.

- One-half of the training recipients receive management or supervisory training.

- Thirty-two percent receive training to improve their general professional skills, such as public speaking and business writing.

Although general business graduates decide to participate in work-related training activities, workshops, or seminars for numerous reasons, four reasons stand out as most commonly cited by graduates. These are a desire to improve skills and knowledge in the occupational area of their employment, mandatory training requirements of the employer, increased opportunities for advancement in the form of a higher salary and promotion, and the need to learn new skills for a newly acquired position. Nearly 93 percent of general business graduates participate in work-related training to improve their occupational skills and knowledge. Another 53 percent list employer requirements as one of the reasons for their participation in work-related training. Having an increased opportunity for promotion and salary increase is one of the reasons to acquire training among 49 percent of all general business graduates who receive work-related training. Nearly 29 percent cite the need to learn skills for a newly acquired position as one of the factors that underlie their decision to engage in training. More than one-fifth cite the need for training to acquire a professional license or certificate.

When asked to select the one most important reason to acquire training, 62 percent of general business graduates who undergo training identify the need to improve their occupational skills and knowledge, and 13 percent report mandatory training requirements by the employer as the most important factor underlying their involvement in work-related training. According to another 10 percent of the training participants, the most important reason is a salary increase and promotion. The need to obtain a professional license is the number one reason to acquire training among 7 percent of graduates with training, and 5 percent rank the necessity to learn skills for a newly acquired position as the number one reason to acquire training.

Post-Graduation Activities

Of all graduates with a bachelor's degree in general business, only 16 percent proceed to earn a postgraduate degree: 13 percent earn a master's degree, and the remaining 3 percent earn a professional degree.

- Forty percent of all master's degrees earned by undergraduate general business majors are in the field of general business, and 25 percent are earned in the other fields within the business administration and management major. Nearly 14 percent choose to earn a master's degree in education.

- Almost 90 percent of the professional degrees earned by undergraduate general business majors are in the field of law, and another 7 percent are earned in the health professions.

Out of all general business graduates under the age of 65, 88 percent are employed. Only 3 percent are officially unemployed; that is, they are not employed and are actively seeking employment. The remaining 9 percent are out of the labor force; that is, they are not employed and are not seeking employment. Nearly 41 percent of general business graduates who withdraw from the labor force say they are retired, and 11 percent suffer from a chronic illness or disabling condition. The labor force withdrawal of 32 percent of general business graduates is attributable to family responsibilities, and one-quarter indicate that they lack the desire or the need to work in the labor market. Pursuing postgraduate education among general business majors is the reason for only 4 percent of the labor force withdrawals.

Employment Outlook

According to the projections by the U.S. Bureau of Labor Statistics, employment in occupations that require at least a bachelor's degree is expected to grow faster than employment in other sectors of the American labor market. Between 2000 and 2010, the U.S. economy is projected to add 22.2 million jobs, yielding an employment growth rate of 15.2 percent. The employment growth projections in 5 out of the top 10 occupations that are most likely to employ general business graduates are at or above the average rate of growth for the entire U.S. economy.

- The fastest growth in demand is projected in miscellaneous marketing and sales occupations. Adding 137,000 jobs between 2000 and 2010, the employment in these occupations is projected to grow by 22 percent.

- Projections for accountants, auditors, and financial specialists and for other management-related occupations such as management analysts, purchasing agents, and regulatory officers indicate that employment in these occupations will grow by 17 percent between 2000 and 2010.

- The demand for personnel in upper-level managerial occupations and in insurance, finance, and real estate occupations is projected to increase by 12 percent between 2000 and 2010. Both occupations are more likely to employ male general business graduates than female graduates.

- The two occupations that are more likely to employ women general business graduates than their male counterparts are projected to grow at a slower rate than the job growth projected for the U.S. economy. Widespread use of high-technology equipment, such as voice mail, e-mail, fax, and particularly computers, is largely responsible for only a 10 percent increase in the clerical jobs and secretaries, typists, and receptionist occupations.

Table 3

Projected Change in Employment in the Top 10 Occupations That
Employ Persons with Only a Bachelor's Degree in General Business

Top 10 Occupations	Actual Employment in 2000 (000s)	Projected Employment in 2010 (000s)	Absolute Change (000s)	Percentage Change
Top- and mid-level managers, executives, administrators	10,564	11,834	1,270	12.0%
Other management-related occupations	4,956	5,801	845	17.1%
Accountants, auditors, other financial specialists	2,115	2,481	366	17.3%
Sales occupations, including retail	15,513	17,365	1,852	11.9%
Insurance, securities, real estate, business services	1,548	1,726	178	11.5%
Other administrative (e.g., records clerks, telephone operators)	16,911	18,522	1,611	9.5%
Other marketing and sales occupations	621	758	137	22.1%
Personnel, training, and labor relations specialists	490	578	88	18.0%
Secretaries, receptionists, typists	4,980	5,501	521	10.5%
Other service occupations, except health	9,652	11,287	1,635	16.9%

CHAPTER 20

General Mathematics

Mathematics, a basic science, is the foundation upon which many other disciplines are built. The number of workers using mathematical techniques is many times greater than the number of persons actually called mathematicians. For example, those in engineering, computer science, physics, and economics all use mathematics extensively, but they are not called mathematicians.

Mathematicians speak of their field as being theoretical or applied, but overlap does exist. Theoretical mathematics concerns developing new principles or new relationships between existing mathematical principles without considering practical uses. Applied mathematicians, for example, use theories and techniques for analyzing the mathematical aspects of computer and communication networks, effects of new drugs on disease, aerodynamic characteristics of aircraft, or distribution costs of businesses.

Mathematics involves conducting research and testing hypotheses and alternative theories in algebra, geometry, number theory, and logic. It involves performing computations and applying methods of numerical analysis by using computers and plotters in solving problems. Mathematicians use computers extensively to analyze relationships to solve complex problems, develop models, and process large amounts of data. A high degree of proficiency in computer database collection and use of sophisticated software programs is expected. Mathematicians conceive and develop ideas for application of mathematics in other sciences, engineering, defense work, computers, and business.

Most colleges and universities offer a mathematics degree. Common courses offered are calculus, differential equations, linear and abstract algebra, probability theory, numerical analysis, topology, modern algebra, discrete mathematics, mathematical logic, and statistics. Some institutions urge or even require mathematics majors to take course work or even a double major in an allied field such as computer science, engineering, or economics.

Mathematicians value working with their minds, researching, reasoning, using numbers to solve problems, and being creative. Many prefer to be independent and critical and to follow an impersonal logic in examining events. Earning a good salary and having prestige are also important to them.

FIGURE 1

Percentage Distribution of Employed Persons with Only a Bachelor's Degree in General Mathematics, by Major Sector of Economic Activity

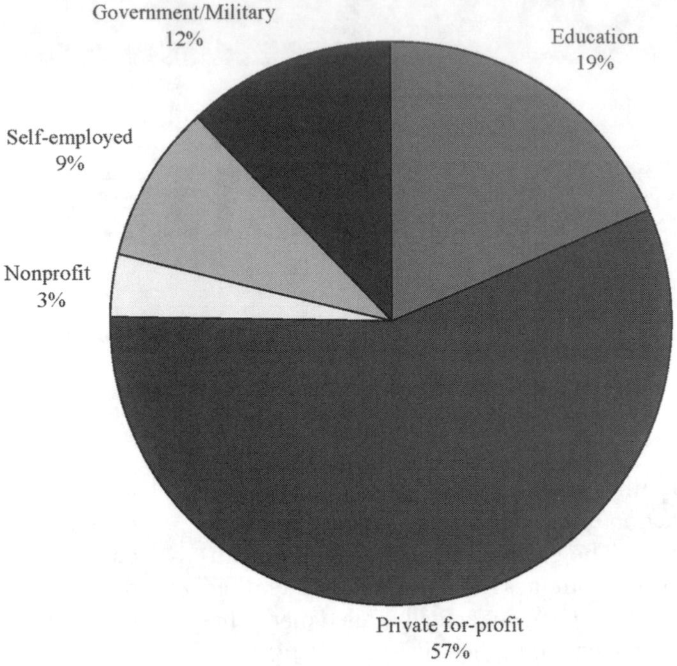

Government/Military
12%

Education
19%

Self-employed
9%

Nonprofit
3%

Private for-profit
57%

Where Do General Mathematics Majors Work?

Persons who graduate in the field of general mathematics are less likely to work in the private, for-profit sector of the economy than applied mathematics graduates. Fewer than 70 percent of general mathematics graduates work in the private, for-profit sector of the economy: 57 percent work for businesses and corporations, and 9 percent are self-employed in their own businesses or practices. Mathematicians who major in applied mathematics are more likely than their counterparts who major in general mathematics to secure jobs in the private, for-profit sector because the former acquire skills that are more directly applicable to the corporate and business world. Those who major in general mathematics, on the other hand, are less likely to secure jobs in the private sector and much more likely to enter the field of education than applied mathematics graduates. One-fifth of all employed general mathematics majors are employed by educational institutions, and another 12 percent work for the government sector. Only 3 percent of all employed general mathematics graduates work for private, nonprofit organizations.

Occupations

Only 20 percent of general mathematics graduates work in jobs that are closely related to their undergraduate major. About 43 percent consider their jobs to be somewhat related to general mathematics, and the remaining 27 percent of general mathematics graduates work in jobs that are not at all related to their undergraduate major field of study. General mathematics graduates may not specifically use their general mathematics skills on the job but rather a whole grouping of skills associated with mathematics. Hence, a larger proportion consider what they do at work as being somewhat but not closely related to their field of study.

Why do the latter group of general mathematics graduates work in unrelated jobs? They cite a variety of factors as possible reasons for their employment in unrelated jobs. Little less than one-half consider better pay and promotion opportunities outside their field as one of the reasons to work in those jobs. The same proportion cite the general working environment, such as hours of work, equipment at work, or the general working conditions, as one of the factors to influence their decision. An equal proportion work in unrelated jobs because of the more convenient location of available jobs. And another one-half consider their desire to change their career and professional interests as one of the reasons to work in unrelated jobs. One-third are unable to find jobs in their field, and another one-third cite family-related reasons to choose employment outside their undergraduate major field of study.

When asked to select the most important reason for employment outside their major field of study, 22 percent of the graduates pick better pay and promotion opportunities, and 19 percent rank a change in their career interests as the number one reason for their employment in unrelated jobs. Family-related reasons are the most important factor influencing the employment choice in unrelated jobs for 15 percent, and about the same proportion find the lack of jobs in their field as the most important factor in their decision. The general working environment is the top-ranking factor for 8 percent of general mathematics graduates working in unrelated jobs, and 6 percent are strongly motivated by job location in their decision to work outside their undergraduate major field of study.

Most general mathematics graduates are employed in managerial, teaching, and computer jobs. Nearly two-thirds of all employed general mathematics graduates work in 1 of the top 10 occupations that employ these graduates. However, within these 10 occupations, the employment of general mathematics graduates is somewhat dispersed. One of the 2 occupations with the greatest concentration is high-level executive, administrative, and managerial occupations. More than 13 percent of the graduates work in these occupations. The second-highest concentration of general mathematics graduates is in the secondary school teacher occupation; nearly 13 percent work in this occupation. Four computer and information science occupations together employ nearly one-quarter of general mathematics graduates. More than 8 percent work as computer systems analysts, and another 8 percent are employed as computer programmers. The computer engineering occupation employs 4 percent, and another 4 percent are employed in miscellaneous computer science occupations.

Table 1

Top 10 Occupations That Employ Persons with Only a Bachelor's Degree in General Mathematics

Top 10 Occupations	PERCENT OF EMPLOYED		
	All	Men	Women
Top- and mid-level managers, executives, administrators	13.4	16.8	7.8
Teachers, secondary school	12.7	7.1	21.7

(continued)

Table 1 (continued)

Top 10 Occupations That Employ Persons with Only a Bachelor's
Degree in General Mathematics

Top 10 Occupations	PERCENT OF EMPLOYED		
	All	Men	Women
Computer systems analysts	8.2	9.5	6.2
Computer programmers	7.8	7.1	8.9
Other management-related occupations	5.3	5.9	4.3
Computer engineers	4.3	4.6	3.8
Other computer and information science occupations	4.2	4.8	3.1
Sales occupations, including retail	3.6	3.7	3.5
Other administrative (e.g., records clerks, telephone operators)	3.3	2.3	5.0
Insurance, securities, real estate, business services	3.2	3.7	2.4

Sixty-two percent of all employed general mathematics graduates are men. The occupational employment patterns of male and female general mathematics graduates are different.

▶ Male graduates are considerably more likely than female graduates to work as top-level executives, administrators, and managers. Nearly 16 percent of all employed male graduates work in these occupations, compared to 8 percent of employed female graduates.

▶ Female general mathematics graduates are concentrated in the teaching occupation. Nearly 22 percent are employed as secondary school teachers, compared to only 6 percent of male graduates.

Activities on the Job

The activities on which general mathematics graduates spend most of their time at work are very closely related to the occupations in which they are employed.

▶ One-fourth spend a majority of their time at work in computer applications, programming, and systems-development activities. With nearly one-fourth of all general mathematics majors employed in computer occupations, it is hardly surprising to find such a prevalence of computer-related activities among general mathematics graduates. More than one-half of all employed graduates regularly spend at least 10 hours per week in these activities.

▶ Management and administration activities typically consume most work time among 17 percent of general mathematics graduates. More than one-half regularly perform these duties at work.

▶ Sixteen percent of all employed graduates typically engage in teaching activities for a major part of their workweek. More than one-quarter regularly perform some teaching function at work.

- Although two-thirds regularly perform some accounting, financial, and contractual duties at work, only 8 percent spend more hours in that activity than any other activity at work.

- Sales, purchasing, and marketing duties typically use up most of the workweek among 7 percent of all employed general mathematics graduates, and 5 percent spend most of their time at work in providing financial services to clients.

Salaries

The average annual salary of general mathematics graduates with only a bachelor's degree who are employed full-time is $63,400, a level that is more than 17 percent higher than the average annual salary of all full-time employed college graduates. As with most college graduates, the salary of general mathematics graduates increases with age, indicating that they get more productive and therefore can earn higher salaries as they spend more time on the job. Within each age group, general mathematics graduates earn higher average salaries than the salary of all college graduates in those age groups.

- The annual average salary of general mathematics majors between the ages of 30 and 34 is $60,400.

- Average annual earnings of general mathematics graduates increase at an impressive pace as they get older. The average annual salary of 35- to 39-year-old general mathematics majors who are employed full-time is $67,000. The average salary peaks at the age of 50 to 54, when graduates earn $69,000 per year.

The average annual salary of general mathematics majors who work in jobs that are closely related to their major field of study is lower than the salary of those who are employed in jobs that are somewhat related to their major. Part of the cause for a lower salary in closely related jobs is attributable to the low salary in teaching positions. Most of the general mathematics graduates in teaching positions consider their jobs to be closely related to their major. Closely related jobs pay full-time employed general mathematics graduates $58,900 annually. Graduates employed in related jobs earn $72,000 annually, and those whose jobs are unrelated to general mathematics earn $53,500 per year.

General mathematics graduates working in the private, for-profit sector earn more than their counterparts working in other sectors of the economy. Graduates who work for businesses and corporations in the private, for-profit sector earn $73,100 per year. Self-employed general mathematics graduates earn an average salary of $62,700 annually. Those in government sector jobs among general mathematics graduates earn an average salary of $56,100 per year. Educational institutions pay full-time employed general mathematics graduates $39,700 per year.

There are sizable variations in the average annual salaries of general mathematics graduates by the occupations in which they are employed. The average annual salary of all full-time employed general mathematics majors is 17 percent higher than the average salary of all college graduates. In 8 out of the top 10 occupations that predominantly employ general mathematics majors, the salaries of general mathematics majors exceed the salary of all college graduates. In the remaining 2 occupations, the average salaries of general mathematics graduates are almost the same as the average salaries of all college graduates employed in those 2 occupations. These 2 occupations include secondary school teachers and clerical occupations.

FIGURE 2

Age/Earnings Profile of Persons with Only a Bachelor's Degree in General Mathematics
(Full-Time Workers, in 2002 Dollars)

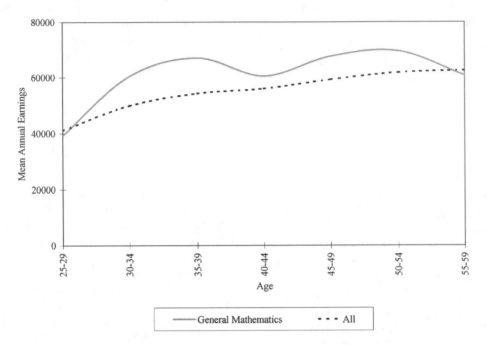

- General mathematics graduates employed in high-level executive, administrative, and managerial occupations earn an average annual salary of $90,100. These occupations predominantly employ male graduates.

- All 4 computer-related occupations pay high salaries to general mathematics graduates. Computer systems analysts with a degree in general mathematics earn $72,800 annually; miscellaneous computer science occupations pay $72,100 to general mathematics

graduates, and the salary of general mathematics graduates working as computer engineers is $70,200. Graduates who are employed as computer programmers earn $63,100 annually.

- One of the lowest-paying of the top 10 occupations, which predominantly employs female general mathematics graduates, is secondary school teaching. While it employs 22 percent of female general mathematics graduates, the average salary of these workers is $38,900 per year.

Table 2

Annual Salary of Full-Time Workers with Only a Bachelor's Degree
in General Mathematics, Top 10 Occupations (in 2002 Dollars)

Earnings in Top 10 Occupations	All	General Mathematics
Total	$54,171	$63,376
Top- and mid-level managers, executives, administrators	$74,051	$90,136
Teachers, secondary school	$40,355	$38,873
Computer systems analysts	$59,818	$72,845
Computer programmers	$55,715	$63,101
Other management-related occupations	$51,921	$61,183
Computer engineers	$66,859	$70,172
Other computer and information science occupations	$54,228	$72,092
Sales occupations, including retail	$52,378	$56,139
Other administrative (e.g., records clerks, telephone operators)	$34,547	$32,654
Insurance, securities, real estate, business services	$68,273	$82,035

On-the-Job Training

The career potential of a job is closely associated with the amount of work-related training on the job. Work-related training is regarded as an investment by firms because it makes workers more productive. Firms that invest in their workforce are more likely to offer pay increases and promotions to match the increasing productivity of their workers. Firms that do not invest in their workers are relatively less likely to offer pay increases and promotions. The incidence of work-related training among general mathematics graduates is slightly lower than the rate of participation in work-related training among all college graduates. While 68 percent of all college graduates acquire some kind of work-related training during a year, 66 percent of general mathematics majors annually engage in work-related training.

▶ Of those general mathematics graduates who receive some training, 79 percent receive technical training in the occupation in which they are employed.

▶ Thirty-six percent of the training recipients participate in management or supervisory training.

▶ Twenty-nine percent receive training to improve their general professional skills, such as public speaking and business writing.

Although general mathematics graduates decide to participate in work-related training activities, workshops, or seminars for numerous reasons, four reasons stand out as most commonly cited by graduates. These are a desire to improve skills and knowledge in the occupational area of their employment, mandatory training requirements of the employer, increased opportunities for advancement in the form of a higher salary and promotion, and the need to learn new skills for a newly acquired position.

When asked to identify the most important reason to acquire training, 64 percent of general mathematics graduates who undergo training identify the need to improve their occupational skills and knowledge. Another 14 percent report mandatory training requirements by the employer as the most important factor underlying their involvement in work-related training. According to 8 percent of the training participants, the most important reason is a salary increase and promotion, and 6 percent rank the necessity to learn skills for a newly acquired position as the number one reason to acquire training. Only 5 percent consider the need to obtain a professional license or certificate as the most important reason influencing their decision to undergo work-related training.

Post-Graduation Activities

Of all graduates with a bachelor's degree in general mathematics, 45 percent proceed to earn a postgraduate degree: 34 percent earn a master's degree, 8 percent earn a doctorate degree, and the remaining 3 percent earn a professional degree.

- ▶ Only one-quarter of all master's degrees earned by undergraduate general mathematics majors are earned in the field of general mathematics. About 23 percent are earned in education, 17 percent in business administration and management, and 10 percent of the master's degrees are earned in computer and information sciences. Applied mathematics is the field of choice for a master's degree among 8 percent of undergraduate general mathematics majors.

- ▶ Almost 30 percent of the doctorate degrees earned by undergraduate general mathematics majors are in the field of general mathematics. The next most preferred major in the doctorate degrees of undergraduate general mathematics majors is applied mathematics (16 percent). Fourteen percent earn their doctorate in education, and 10 percent choose the field of computer and information sciences.

- ▶ Out of the few professional degrees earned by general mathematics bachelor's degree holders, one-half are in the health professions, and 40 percent in law.

Out of all general mathematics graduates under the age of 65, 85 percent are employed. Only 4 percent are officially unemployed; that is, they are not employed and are actively seeking employment. The remaining 11 percent are out of the labor force; that is, they are not employed and are not seeking employment. Three main reasons that underlie the labor force withdrawal of general mathematics graduates are family responsibilities, a lack of the need or desire to work, and retirement. Forty-two percent cite family responsibilities as the reason for labor force withdrawal, 30 percent lack the need or desire to work, and 28 percent are retired. Additionally, 8 percent cite school enrollment as the reason for their labor force withdrawal, and 5 percent suffer from a chronic illness or disabling condition.

Employment Outlook

According to the projections by the U.S. Bureau of Labor Statistics, employment in occupations that require at least a bachelor's degree is expected to grow faster than employment in other sectors of the American labor market. Between 2000 and 2010, the U.S. economy is projected

to add 22.2 million jobs, yielding an employment growth rate of 15.2 percent. With one exception, the employment growth projections in the top 10 occupations that are most likely to employ general mathematics graduates are mixed. Employment in technical fields that employ mathematicians is projected to grow very rapidly. Other occupations that employ large numbers of mathematicians are projected to grow at a pace much closer to the average of all occupations.

▶ The fastest growth in demand for mathematicians is projected in the computer-related occupations. Employment in the computer systems analyst occupation is expected to increase by 60 percent, with nearly an additional one-quarter million jobs between 2000 and 2010. The demand for computer engineers is projected to grow by 90 percent. With an additional 679,000 jobs, employment in this occupation is expected to nearly double between 2000 and 2010. Miscellaneous computer and information sciences occupations will see employment increase by 123,000 jobs, or 60 percent, during the same time period. Some observers are more skeptical of these high projected rates of new job creation in information technology fields. Employment levels in IT have declined since 2000 as the national economy's business cycle entered into a period of recession. Unemployment increased substantially among IT workers. Increasingly, firms are employing workers in other nations in computer, mathematics, and other occupations where much of the work is expressed in mathematics and is easily

digitized. As the national economy recovers, the demand for mathematicians in the IT areas will be impacted by this offshoring phenomenon.

▶ The top area of employment for general mathematics majors—upper-level executive, administrative, and managerial occupations—is projected to add 1.2 million jobs between 2000 and 2010. This represents an employment growth rate of nearly 12 percent.

▶ The demand for secondary school teachers, the second largest area of employment for general mathematics graduates, is projected to increase by 18 percent, with an additional 201,000 jobs between 2000 and 2010. However, this occupation, which predominantly employs women graduates, is a low-paying occupation, with the second-lowest salary out of the top 10 employers of general mathematics graduates.

▶ Insurance, securities, real estate, and business services occupations are projected to add 178,000 jobs over the same time period, yielding an employment growth rate of 11.5 percent. Employment in sales and miscellaneous management-related occupations is projected to grow at a somewhat slower pace than overall employment growth in the economy.

▶ Clerical occupations are projected to add 1.6 million jobs, yielding a below-average growth of 9.5 percent. This group of occupations is associated with the lowest annual salary out of the 10 top employers of general mathematics graduates.

Table 3
Projected Change in Employment in the Top 10 Occupations That
Employ Persons with Only a Bachelor's Degree in General Mathematics

Top 10 Occupations	Actual Employment in 2000 (000s)	Projected Employment in 2010 (000s)	Absolute Change (000s)	Percentage Change
Top- and mid-level managers, executives, administrators	10,564	11,834	1,270	12.0%
Teachers, secondary school	1,113	1,314	201	18.1%
Computer systems analysts	431	689	258	59.9%
Computer programmers	585	680	95	16.2%
Other management-related occupations	4,956	5,801	845	17.1%
Computer engineers	757	1,436	679	89.7%
Other computer and information science occupations	203	326	123	60.6%
Sales occupations, including retail	15,513	17,365	1,852	11.9%
Other administrative (e.g., records clerks, telephone operators)	16,911	18,522	1,611	9.5%
Insurance, securities, real estate, business services	1,548	1,726	178	11.5%

CHAPTER 21

Marketing

Marketing is closely related to advertising and sales. Marketing involves marketing research, marketing strategy, sales, promotions, pricing, product development, and public relations. In small firms, the marketing function may be subsumed by another manager, administrator, or the owner. Because marketing is a subspecialization within a business administration or management program, the focus here will be that of marketing management.

Marketing managers develop the organization's detailed marketing strategy. With the help of subordinates, including product development managers and market research managers, they determine the demand for products and services offered by the firm and its competitors and identify potential consumers—for example, business firms, wholesalers, retailers, government, or the general public. Mass markets are further categorized according to various demographics, such as region, age, income, and lifestyle. Marketing managers develop pricing strategy with an eye toward maximizing the organization's share of the market and its profits while ensuring that the organization's customers are satisfied. In collaboration with sales, product development, and other managers, marketing managers monitor trends that indicate the need for new products and services and oversee product development. They work with advertising and promotion managers to best promote the organization's products and services and to attract potential users.

Sales managers direct the firm's sales program. They assign sales territories and goals and establish training programs for their sales representatives. Managers advise their sales representatives on ways to improve their sales performance. In large, multiproduct firms, they oversee regional and local sales managers and their staffs. Sales managers maintain contact with dealers and distributors. They analyze sales statistics gathered by their staffs to determine sales potential and inventory requirements and monitor the preferences of customers. Such information is vital to develop products and maximize profits.

Except in the largest organizations, advertising and promotion staffs generally are small and serve as liaisons between the organization and the advertising or promotion agency to which many advertising or promotional functions are contracted out. Advertising managers oversee the account services, creative services, and media services departments. The account services department is managed by account executives, who assess the need for advertising and, in advertising agencies, maintain the accounts of clients. The creative services department develops the subject matter and presentation of advertising. A creative director, who oversees the copy chief and art director and their staffs, supervises the department. The media services department is supervised by the media director, who oversees planning groups that select the communication media—for example, radio, television, newspapers, magazines, or outdoor signs—to disseminate the advertising.

Promotion managers supervise staffs of promotion specialists. They direct promotion programs combining advertising with purchase incentives to increase sales. In an effort to establish closer contact with purchasers—dealers, distributors, or consumers—promotion programs may involve direct mail, telemarketing, television or radio advertising, catalogs, exhibits, inserts in newspapers, in-store displays and product endorsements, and special events. Purchase incentives may include discounts, samples, gifts, rebates, coupons, sweepstakes, and contents.

The education of those in marketing and sales is varied, but some of the course work may include marketing, sales, advertising management, retailing, market research, telemarketing, accounting, finance, and statistics. Entrants to the advertising field may take course work in journalism or advertising programs in which courses might include creative and technical writing, communications methods and technology, visual arts, and public relations. Database applications, word processing, and computer skills are important.

A key ability in marketing is to create new ways of presenting information that will attract people's attention. This can be related to understanding how people react to words, pictures, and colors. The ability to speak and write clearly and convincingly is part of capturing the minds of all kinds of people and influencing their opinions. People with low energy levels are not found in marketing. Good interpersonal and computer skills are expected requirements. Tact and good judgment are necessary.

Marketing personnel like to work in groups, be people-oriented, and be involved in organizational and planning activities. This field requires excellent interpersonal relations to effectively maintain relationships with a broad scope of people having different needs. Those in this field tend to like the breadth of learning associated with liberal arts in which reading and writing, intellectual, and artistic interests can be nurtured.

Many benefits can be gained in marketing. The field pays well, offers variety, and allows for creative self-expression. There is a mental challenge to promotional-type work, as well as a competitive mind-set. Major goals are to reach out to persuade and influence other people's decisions. While marketing research is the systematic collection of data, marketing managers usually have considerable public contact where they meet and get "hands-on" impressions of products and services needed from customers.

Marketing managers usually possess openness to new ideas, are quick to react, and are not afraid to follow their hunches. They enjoy using their intellectual curiosity and reasoning to search for new insights. This approach affords them the variety, diversion, and challenges they enjoy. They usually are good talkers, are well informed, and can be good company.

Where Do Marketing Majors Work?

The overwhelming majority of graduates with a bachelor's degree in marketing work in the private, for-profit sector of the American economy, mostly in sales and marketing positions. Nearly 75 percent work as wage and salary employees in businesses and corporations. However, many marketing majors opt to become self-employed. Fifteen percent of all marketing majors either work as self-employed consultants to other businesses or own and operate companies. Marketing majors rarely work in educational institutions or government organizations.

FIGURE 1

Percentage Distribution
of Employed Persons
with Only a Bachelor's
Degree in Marketing,
by Major Sector of
Economic Activity

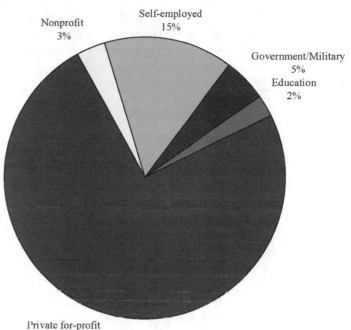

Nonprofit
3%

Self-employed
15%

Government/Military
5%

Education
2%

Private for-profit
75%

Occupations

Graduates of marketing programs are heavily employed in a few sales, marketing, administrative, and managerial positions and other jobs that are related to the field of study. In fact, more than 80 percent of all marketing majors work in jobs related to their undergraduate major. More than 40 percent of marketing graduates work in sales, including retail sales jobs, insurance, stocks and bonds, real estate sales, and marketing positions. An additional 19 percent are employed in managerial and administrative jobs, often overseeing sales and marketing organizations. Less than 1 in 5 graduates work in a job unrelated to the major. Better pay and promotion and a desire to change careers are the major reasons that graduates work in jobs unrelated to the marketing and sales field.

Table 1

Top 10 Occupations That Employ Persons with Only a Bachelor's Degree in Marketing

Top 10 Occupations	PERCENT OF EMPLOYED		
	All	Men	Women
Sales occupations, including retail	20.9	23.0	16.8
Top- and mid-level managers, executives, administrators	18.8	22.9	10.5
Other marketing and sales occupations	11.8	9.9	15.5

(continued)

237

Table 1 (continued)

Top 10 Occupations That Employ Persons with Only a Bachelor's Degree in Marketing

Top 10 Occupations	PERCENT OF EMPLOYED		
	All	Men	Women
Insurance, securities, real estate, business services	11.6	13.3	8.1
Other management-related occupations	7.8	8.0	7.5
Accountants, auditors, other financial specialists	4.6	3.0	7.8
Other administrative (e.g., records clerks, telephone operators)	3.4	2.0	6.1
Other service occupations, except health	1.4	1.2	1.8
Personnel, training, and labor-relations specialists	1.3	0.6	2.7
Artists, broadcasters, writers, editors, entertainers, public relations specialists	1.2	0.2	3.1

▶ Men are more likely to be employed in managerial and administrative positions than women with a marketing degree. Nearly 23 percent of men with a marketing degree are employed in these high-wage jobs, while only 10 percent of women with a degree in the field work in these positions.

▶ Women are somewhat more likely to work in occupations not closely related to the field, including accounting-related jobs as well as in clerical positions.

Activities on the Job

▶ Accounting, finance, and contracting tasks are a part of the work of most graduates in the marketing field.

▶ Sales and marketing are the primary activities that graduates in this major undertake.

▶ Little basic or applied research is undertaken on the job by graduates in this major.

▶ Many marketing graduates utilize computer applications as a regular part of their work activities.

Salaries

Marketing graduates employed in full-time jobs have annual salaries that are higher than the average salary of all college graduates who are employed in full-time jobs. The average bachelor's degree holder earns $54,200 per year, while the annual salary for marketing majors is $57,300, an earnings advantage of $3,100, or about 6 percent, per year. The size of the earnings advantage of marketing majors relative to the average college graduate increases with years of work experience after graduation. Marketing majors aged 25 to 30 earn a salary of about $40,900. By ages 45 to 54, their earnings rise above $75,000. Thus, in 20 years, the earnings of marketing majors increase by more than 80 percent in inflation-adjusted terms. The sharp increase in the earnings of marketing majors over time is the result of the central role that real-world experience plays in the sales and marketing professions. Marketing and sales professionals develop many of their skills on the job through both informal on-the-job learning and observation and participation in training programs. As they develop a set of skills and professional relationships over time, their productivity and earnings rise as well.

Graduates with degrees in marketing who are employed in various sales and marketing positions all have earnings that are above the average of college graduates. Those who work in managerial and administrative jobs have annual salaries of $71,400 per year. Those employed in occupations outside sales and management jobs earn less. Marketing graduates employed in jobs not related to the field have annual salaries that are $11,400–or 22 percent–lower per year than those employed in jobs closely related to the field.

FIGURE 2

Age/Earnings Profile of Persons with Only a Bachelor's Degree in Marketing (Full-Time Workers, in 2002 Dollars)

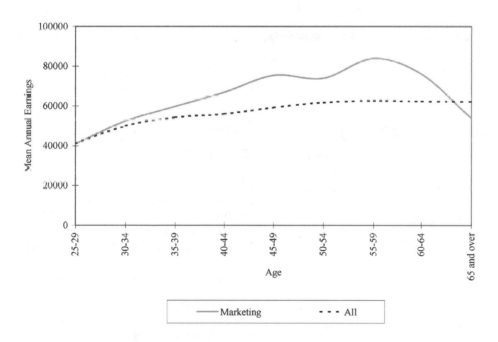

Table 2
Annual Salary of Full-Time Workers with Only a Bachelor's Degree in Marketing, Top 10 Occupations (in 2002 Dollars)

Earnings in Top 10 Occupations	All	Marketing
Total	$54,171	$57,290
Sales occupations, including retail	$52,378	$57,093
Top- and mid-level managers, executives, administrators	$74,051	$71,422
Other marketing and sales occupations	$58,208	$58,980
Insurance, securities, real estate, business services	$68,273	$64,443
Other management-related occupations	$51,921	$49,855
Accountants, auditors, other financial specialists	$57,382	$51,619
Other administrative (e.g., records clerks, telephone operators)	$34,547	$36,603
Other service occupations, except health	$39,984	$36,076
Personnel, training, and labor relations specialists	$51,577	$41,749
Artists, broadcasters, writers, editors, entertainers, public relations specialists	$52,141	$60,580

On-the-Job Training

The development of skills on the job is a critical feature in the career development of marketing majors. While on-the-job learning is an important method of skill development, the majority of marketing majors participate in some type of formal work-based training activity over the course of the year. Nearly two-thirds of majors with a degree in this field participate in workshops or seminars sometime during the year.

> ▶ Much of the training is oriented to developing professional sales and marketing skills. Nearly one-half of all majors engage in some type of management or supervisory training.

Post-Graduation Activities

Marketing majors are less likely to complete an advanced degree program than graduates from almost any other undergraduate field of study. Fewer than 15 percent of all those with a bachelor's degree in marketing eventually earn some type of degree beyond the bachelor's degree major. Most earn a master's degree.

> ▶ Eleven percent of all marketing majors earn a master's degree, about three-quarters in a business field.

> ▶ Almost no marketing degree holders earn a doctoral degree.

> ▶ About 1 percent of marketing majors go on to earn a law degree.

Nearly 90 percent of all marketing majors under the age of 65 are employed, almost all in full-time jobs. About 3 percent are unemployed and actively seeking a job. About 8 percent have chosen not to work; many stay at home in order to meet family obligations.

Employment Outlook

Demand for college graduates is expected to increase more rapidly than overall labor demand between 2000 and 2010, according to employment projections produced by the U.S. Bureau of Labor Statistics. Total employment of persons with a bachelor's degree is expected to increase by more than one-fifth through 2010. The demand for many key occupations that employ marketing majors is mixed. Overall demand for sales workers is expected to increase by about 12 percent between 2000 and 2010, a rate of growth well below the average for college graduates.

Table 3
Projected Change in Employment in the Top 10 Occupations That Employ Persons with Only a Bachelor's Degree in Marketing

Top 10 Occupations	Actual Employment in 2000 (000s)	Projected Employment in 2010 (000s)	Absolute Change (000s)	Percentage Change
Sales occupations, including retail	15,513	17,365	1,852	11.9%
Top- and mid-level managers, executives, administrators	10,564	11,834	1,270	12.0%
Other marketing and sales occupations	621	758	137	22.1%
Insurance, securities, real estate, business services	1,548	1,726	178	11.5%
Other management-related occupations	4,956	5,801	845	17.1%
Accountants, auditors, other financial specialists	2,115	2,481	366	17.3%
Other administrative (e.g., records clerks, telephone operators)	16,911	18,522	1,611	9.5%
Other service occupations, except health	9,652	11,287	1,635	16.9%
Personnel, training, and labor relations specialists	490	578	88	18.0%
Artists, broadcasters, writers, editors, entertainers, public relations specialists	2,371	2,864	493	20.8%

CHAPTER 22

Public Administration

This field covers those government administrators not elected by their constituents. This is a large area because it includes all the managers, except appointees, who are hired to be responsible for running the federal, state, county, city, town, and district government functions.

Public administrators, like business managers, have overall responsibility for the performance of their organizations. Working in conjunction with elected officials, they set goals and then organize programs to attain them. They appoint department heads who oversee the work of the civil servants who carry out programs or enforce laws enacted by their legislative bodies. They plan budgets, specify how government funds will be used, and ensure that resources are used properly and programs are carried out as planned.

Because public administrators administer for the public, they meet with elected officials and confer with other government leaders and constituents to discuss proposed programs and determine citizens' level of support. They may nominate citizens to boards and commissions, solicit bids from and select contractors to do work for the government, encourage business investment and economic development in their jurisdictions, and seek federal or state funds. The size of the jurisdiction determines the use of aides and assistants or requires doing much of the work by oneself.

Educational course work may include introduction to politics, public policy analysis, public administration, organization theory, public personnel administration, public budgeting and finance, politics and the mass media, techniques and practices of public management, civil liberties, business and government relations, intergovernmental relations, and legal issues in public administration. Obviously, government involves many areas for specialization, some of which are finance, personnel matters, legal areas, and civil engineering.

The abilities required in public administration are developing plans, organizing people and their work, and solving problems. Decision-making skills, sometimes on limited or contradictory information, are needed. This task can create pressure and stress. Public speaking and communication skills are prerequisites, as well as being able to get along with others. Negotiating and budget skills are critical.

Public administrators like and appreciate the functions of organizations. They are people oriented. They enjoy being in positions of power, control, and status. Since in the end they are assessed on their ability to perform, they get satisfaction in being very practical in doing things and delivering services.

The benefits gained in this type of work may vary based on the type and level of government function involved. For example, in rural areas, there may be a lot of public recognition, such as being written up in the newspapers and having public contact, because the issues involved may have a direct impact on people's lives. Some public administrators have a high public profile and thus gain prestige from their leadership. The work of planning, organizing, and budgeting requires working with one's mind and often calls for creative solutions. Public administrators, while they may not make as much money as business managers, usually are well paid.

People in this field, whether extroverted or introverted, seek outcomes with a preference for immediate and visible results. Also, because of their involvement with the public, they tend to be conservative. They are characterized by being thorough, dependable, and well-organized workers. They process and analyze information and decisions in a logical and systematic way. They are pragmatic and practical people.

Where Do Public Administration Graduates Work?

Nearly 40 percent of employed public administration graduates work in the government sector of the economy. One-half work in the private, for-profit sector of the economy, a majority of whom are employed in wage and salary jobs for businesses and corporations. Only 5 percent are self-employed in their own professional businesses or practices. Training in administration, management, organization, and budgeting provide public administration graduates with skills to work in the private sector as managers, administrators, and the like. One in 10 public administration graduates works for an educational institution, and the remaining 3 percent are employed in the nonprofit sector.

A large fraction of public administration graduates—43 percent—work in jobs that are only somewhat related to their undergraduate major. Only 27 percent consider their jobs to be closely related to their major field of study. The remaining 30 percent work in jobs that are unrelated to their undergraduate major. Nearly 60 percent report that they choose to work outside their field of study because of better pay and promotion opportunities. Another 20 percent do so because of a change in their career and professional interests.

FIGURE 1

Percentage Distribution of Employed Persons with Only a Bachelor's Degree in Public Administration, by Major Sector of Economic Activity

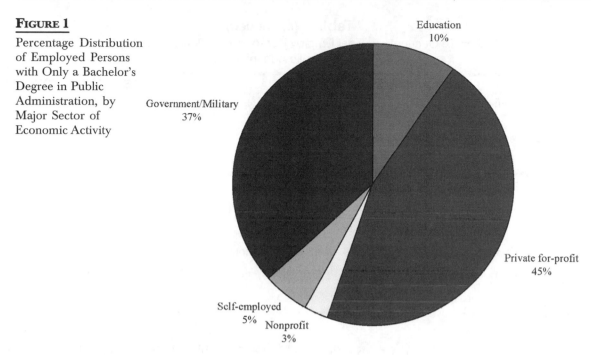

Education 10%

Government/Military 37%

Private for-profit 45%

Self-employed 5%

Nonprofit 3%

Occupations

The occupational employment of public administration graduates reveals that more than one-quarter work as top- to mid-level managers, executives, and administrators. Nine percent work in occupations concerned with insurance, real estate, buying and selling securities, and providing business services such as management, consulting, and public relations. Another 9 percent work in protective-service occupations, which are concerned with protecting the public against crime, fire, and acts of war. People in these occupations include police officers and detective correction officers, fire department workers, and personnel of the armed forces. Other predominant occupations of employment for public administration graduates are miscellaneous management occupations such as management analysts, purchasing agents, inspectors, and other regulatory officers.

Table 1

Top 10 Occupations That Employ Persons with Only a Bachelor's Degree in Public Administration

Top 10 Occupations	PERCENT OF EMPLOYED		
	All	Men	Women
Top- and mid-level managers, executives, administrators	26.0	28.0	20.5
Insurance, securities, real estate, business services	8.9	9.6	6.8

(continued)

Table 1 (continued)

Top 10 Occupations That Employ Persons with Only a Bachelor's
Degree in Public Administration

Top 10 Occupations	PERCENT OF EMPLOYED		
	All	Men	Women
Protective-service occupations	8.7	11.9	0.0
Other management-related occupations	8.3	8.9	6.6
Sales occupations, including retail	3.8	4.1	2.9
Social workers	3.5	3.0	4.9
Other service occupations, except health	3.5	4.0	2.2
Other administrative (e.g., records clerks, telephone operators)	3.2	1.5	7.8
Other health occupations	3.1	4.2	0.0
Postsecondary professors	3.0	2.1	5.6

▶ A substantial number of persons with an undergraduate degree in public administration are employed as managers and administrators, particularly men, 28 percent of whom secure managerial and administrative employment, compared to only 21 percent of women public administration graduates.

▶ Employment in insurance, real estate, securities, and business services also is somewhat more prevalent among male than among female public administration graduates (9.6 percent versus 6.8 percent).

▶ Women are more than 5 times more likely than men to be employed in administrative/clerical occupations.

▶ All public administration majors who are employed in protective-service occupations are males. Nearly 12 percent of males secure employment in protective-service occupations.

Activities on the Job

▶ More than 80 percent of public administration graduates perform accounting, financial, and contractual duties in a typical workweek as a regular part of their job.

▶ Management and administrative functions regularly take up at least 10 hours during a typical workweek of two-thirds of all employed public administration graduates.

▶ More than one-half regularly perform employee-relations duties, including recruitment, personnel development, and training.

▶ Forty percent regularly engage in computer applications, programming, and systems-development activities, and an equal proportion report that management of quality and productivity occupies at least some part of their typical workweek at the job.

▶ Thirty-eight percent say their duties in a typical workweek consist of providing professional services such as financial and legal services.

▶ One-third of public administration graduates perform purchasing, marketing, and sales activities at their jobs on a regular basis, and 23 percent engage in teaching activities.

▶ Fewer than 1 in 10 public administration graduates are engaged in basic or applied research, product development, or equipment design on a regular basis.

Salaries

The average annual salary of public administration graduates with a bachelor's degree who are employed full-time is $54,000. As with most college graduates, the salary of public administration graduates increases with age, indicating that they get more productive and therefore earn higher salaries as they spend more time on the job. The salary of public administration graduates, however, rises quite steeply until the age of 55, after which the average annual salary declines quite rapidly.

▶ At two ends of the age distribution—25 to 39 and 55 years and older—the annual salary of public administration graduates is below the average level for all college graduates. Between the ages of 40 and 54, however, the average annual salary of public administration graduates outpaces the average earnings of all college graduates by a wide margin.

▶ Public administration graduates between the ages of 40 and 44 earn $65,800, which is 17 percent more than the average of all college graduates in that age group. Those who are 45 to 49 years old earn $66,000, or 11 percent above the average earnings of all 45- to 49-year-old college graduates. The average annual salary of 50- to 54-year-old public administration graduates—$74,100—exceeds that of all college graduates in the same age group by 20 percent.

▶ Public administration graduates between the ages of 25 and 29 on average earn $36,100 per year. The average annual salary of 30- to 34-year-old graduates is $45,100, whereas those graduates who are 35 to 39 years old earn an average annual salary of $49,500.

Public administration graduates who work in the government sector earn an average annual salary of $56,200. The private, for-profit sector pays an average annual salary of $55,600 to public administration graduates who work full-time. Employment in the education sector secures much lower earnings among public administration majors with only a bachelor's degree. Their average annual salary is $38,900, a level that is only 72 percent of the average annual salary of all employed public administration graduates.

FIGURE 2

Age/Earnings Profile of Persons with Only a Bachelor's Degree in Public Administration
(Full-Time Workers, in 2002 Dollars)

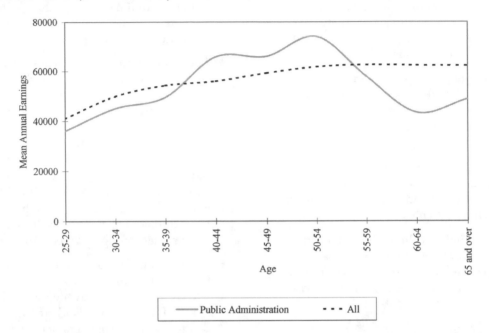

Obtaining a job that is either closely or somewhat related to the undergraduate major field of study is, on average, associated with a sizable salary premium relative to the average annual salary in jobs that are unrelated to the major field of study. Public administration graduates who secure jobs that are related to their major earn $56,300, or 19 percent more than their counterparts with unrelated jobs, who earn $47,400. Graduates whose jobs are somewhat related to their major earn an average annual salary of $57,200, yielding a salary premium of 20 percent more than jobs that are not at all related to public administration.

The salaries of public administration graduates vary widely by occupation. Out of the top 10 occupations that employ public administration graduates, the highest average salary accrues to those who are employed as top- to mid-level managers and administrators. The average annual salary in administrative/clerical occupations, which employ a disproportionate number of female public administration graduates, is only $30,300.

Table 2

Annual Salary of Full-Time Workers with Only a Bachelor's Degree
in Public Administration, Top 10 Occupations (in 2002 Dollars)

Earnings in Top 10 Occupations	All	Public Administration
Total	$54,171	$54,055

Earnings in Top 10 Occupations	All	Public Administration
Top- and mid-level managers, executives, administrators	$74,051	$73,986
Insurance, securities, real estate, business services	$68,273	$47,275
Protective-service occupations	$49,130	$50,998
Other management-related occupations	$51,921	$56,474
Sales occupations, including retail	$52,378	$44,866
Social workers	$36,371	$34,803
Other service occupations, except health	$39,984	$40,856
Other administrative (e.g., records clerks, telephone operators)	$34,547	$30,030
Other health occupations	$39,559	$29,266
Postsecondary professors	$42,234	$42,333

On-the-Job Training

Work-related training is an important indicator of the long-term career potential of a job. Firms that invest in their workers at high rates are much more likely to offer pay increases and promotions than firms that do not invest in their workers. Out of all public administration graduates who are employed, 78 percent receive some type of work-related training. Participation in work-related training activities is 91 percent among those public administration graduates who are employed in the government sector. The training rate of public administration graduates working in the private, for-profit sector also is high: 75 percent.

▶ Two-thirds of public administration graduates who receive some training are engaged in technical training in their occupations.

▶ Participation in management or supervisor training is reported by 46 percent of those public administration graduates who receive some kind of training.

▶ Three in 10 public administration graduates report receiving training in communication skills, such as public speaking and business writing.

Sixty percent of employed public administration graduates participate in training to acquire additional skills and to increase their occupational knowledge. About 14 percent are required to participate in work-related training by their employers. According to 12 percent of public administration graduates, the most important reason for their participation in work-related training is to increase their salary and to improve their opportunities to secure a promotion.

Post-Graduation Activities

Nearly 70 percent of all public administration graduates have only a bachelor's degree. A large majority of the postgraduate degrees earned are master's degrees. Only 7 percent earn a doctorate or a professional degree.

▶ Of all public administration graduates who earn a master's degree, 37 percent continue with public administration as their major field of study at the master's level. Nearly one-quarter choose business management and administrative services as their major field of study. About 11 percent earn their master's degree in one of the social sciences, such as history.

▶ Only 1.4 percent of all public administration graduates earn a doctorate degree, of whom two-thirds choose to major in law, 27 percent in public administration, and the rest in education.

▶ Six percent of all undergraduate public administration majors earn a professional degree, and all the degrees are earned in the field of law.

Almost 93 percent of all public administration graduates with only a bachelor's degree who are under 65 years old are employed. Fewer than 1 percent are not employed but looking for employment. The remaining 7 percent of all public administration graduates are out of the labor force; that is, they are neither working nor looking for work. More than 70 percent of those public administration graduates who withdraw from the labor force do so because of family responsibilities. One-fifth withdraw from the labor force because they do not desire or need to work.

Employment Outlook

The U.S. Bureau of Labor Statistics projects employment in occupations that require at least a bachelor's degree to grow faster than employment in other sectors of the American labor market. Between 2000 and 2010, the U.S. economy is projected to add 22.2 million jobs, yielding an employment growth rate of 15.2 percent. The employment outlook for occupations that employ public administration graduates is strong in protective services, social work, and academic positions. Slower growth is forecast in management and insurance and related business services.

▶ Total employment in top- to mid-level executive, managerial, and administrative occupations that employ 26 percent of public administration graduates is expected to grow by 12 percent between 2000 and 2010.

▶ Insurance, real estate, stocks and bonds, and business services employment is expected to rise by 178,000 jobs, or about 11.5 percent, over the decade.

Table 3

Projected Change in Employment in the Top 10 Occupations That Employ Persons with Only a Bachelor's Degree in Public Administration

Top 10 Occupations	Actual Employment in 2000 (000s)	Projected Employment in 2010 (000s)	Absolute Change (000s)	Percentage Change
Top- and mid-level managers, executives, administrators	10,564	11,834	1,270	12.0%
Insurance, securities, real estate, business services	1,548	1,726	178	11.5%

Top 10 Occupations	Actual Employment in 2000 (000s)	Projected Employment in 2010 (000s)	Absolute Change (000s)	Percentage Change
Protective-service occupations	3,087	3,896	809	26.2%
Other management-related occupations	4,956	5,801	845	17.1%
Sales occupations, including retail	15,513	17,365	1,852	11.9%
Social workers	468	609	141	30.1%
Other service occupations, except health	9,652	11,287	1,635	16.9%
Other administrative (e.g., records clerks, telephone operators)	16,911	18,522	1,611	9.5%
Other health occupations	266	317	51	19.2%
Postsecondary professors	1,344	1,659	315	23.4%

PART 4

Education

CHAPTER 23

Elementary Teacher Education

I nclusive in this major's description are pre-school, kindergarten, and elementary school teachers. Some teachers may work in private schools, while others are employed within public school systems.

People entering elementary education know the field well through models they have personally experienced. But what some people considering the field of education may not have experienced is the difficulty in working with unmotivated students, the stress of working with self-doubt, the frustration of working with children with difficulties or from different cultures, and the lack of family or institutional support.

The learning process in schools has become less structured and more group oriented in recent years. For example, to help students understand concepts, educators use problem-solving experiments with apparatus. Distance learning, computers, and visual aids create more realistic situations for teachers to demonstrate applications. While a de-emphasis on memorization and drill has occurred, reading, writing, speaking, and working with mathematics and science problems remain critical. A newer emphasis on the development of critical and logical thinking is being encouraged through creatively exploring the environment. Reading remains a foundational specialization.

Teachers are licensed in all states, but the variation in course work requirements from state to state must be examined.

Kindergarten, preschool, and elementary teachers have a talent for working with children, plus possessing organizational, administrative, and record-keeping abilities. Besides being patient, they can be creative, communicative, influential, and motivational. In addition to language proficiency and leadership skills, they have a breadth of artistic, linguistic, and musical likes.

Elementary teachers enjoy young children and must have an idea of the age with which they prefer to work: preschool; the primary grades, ages 5 through 8; or with 9- to 13-year-olds, where there are opportunities for teaching more subject-oriented specializations. The motivation of working with this latter group may be in seeing students develop new specific content skills so that they experience a feeling of self-satisfaction. Also, some aspiring to elementary education enjoy a young age group because they like the independence of working alone with a group in a classroom and the freedom to choose and experiment with different teaching styles and methods. Teaching involves leading and influencing roles.

The qualities that elementary teachers and students in training value are similar for both elementary and early childhood education. Both feel that working with people, being creative, working with one's mind, having variety and diversion, and being independent are equally important. Overall, teachers at this level are characterized as being friendly, concerned with the feelings of others, and conscientious to fulfill a set of obligations.

This very large occupation includes both quiet and talkative, outgoing people. These external characteristics nevertheless do not take away

from the general tendencies to be warm, friendly, and considerate. These educators work to meet their obligations despite the fact that many pre-school and elementary teachers are not technically oriented themselves. Educational policies that push mathematics and science are problematic for some teachers who do not personally avow valuing and following logical systematic thinking required by these subjects.

Where Do Elementary Teacher Education Majors Work?

Unsurprisingly, the great majority of employed persons with a degree in elementary education work in the education sector of the American economy. While almost 70 percent of college graduates in this field work in education, private, for-profit firms employ 16 percent, and about 7 percent are self-employed. Only rarely do elementary education majors work in government jobs outside the education field.

FIGURE 1

Percentage Distribution of Employed Persons with Only a Bachelor's Degree in Elementary Teacher Education, by Major Sector of Economic Activity

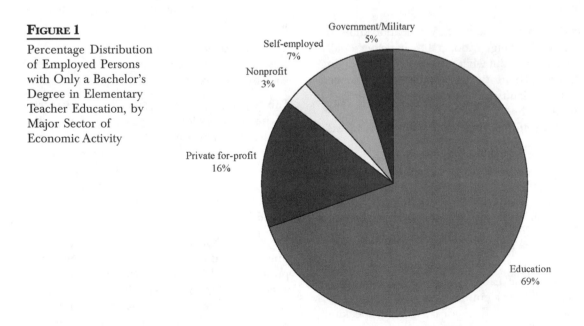

Government/Military 5%

Self-employed 7%

Nonprofit 3%

Private for-profit 16%

Education 69%

Table 1
Top 10 Occupations That Employ Persons with Only a Bachelor's Degree in Elementary Teacher Education

Top 10 Occupations	PERCENT OF EMPLOYED		
	All	Men	Women
Teachers, elementary school	47.7	37.9	48.7
Teachers, prekindergarten and kindergarten	10.0	1.4	10.9
Teachers, secondary school	3.9	9.0	3.4
Special education teachers, primary and secondary	3.5	3.7	3.5
Top- and mid-level managers, executives, administrators	3.5	8.9	2.9
Other administrative (e.g., records clerks, telephone operators)	3.1	2.3	3.2
Sales occupations, including retail	3.1	3.6	3.1
Other service occupations, except health	2.9	0.8	3.1
Secretaries, receptionists, typists	2.8	0.0	3.1
Other management-related occupations	2.2	4.9	1.9

Occupations

Elementary education majors generally are employed in jobs that are closely related to their undergraduate major field of study. Two-thirds of those working consider their jobs to be closely related to their college major. Virtually all of those in jobs that are closely related to the major are employed as teachers. Nearly one-half of all majors are employed as elementary school teachers, with an additional 10 percent working as preschool and kindergarten teachers. Thus, nearly 60 percent are working as teachers with young children. An additional 4 percent of elementary education majors are employed as high school teachers, and 3.5 percent are special education teachers. Elementary teacher education is not a good starting point in which to develop an administrative or managerial career in education. Only 3.5 percent of all graduates in this field eventually rise to a mid- to upper-level administrative or managerial position.

Nearly one-quarter of all elementary education majors work in jobs that are unrelated to the field. These individuals work in clerical, sales, and service occupations, jobs that often do not require a college degree.

Activities on the Job

▶ Unsurprisingly, teaching comprises the major activity that graduates in this major undertake; however, they are also involved in many record-keeping and administrative tasks as well.

▶ About one-fifth of graduates in the field employ computer applications on their jobs.

▶ Few elementary education majors are engaged in either applied or basic research activities.

Salaries

The annual salaries of elementary education majors are quite low compared to other college graduates. Salaries for those with a bachelor's degree in the field averaged $38,700 per year in 2002-dollar terms. The average person with a bachelor's degree earns $54,200 per year, or about 40 percent more than elementary education majors. Part of this large difference is a result of teachers working fewer weeks over the course of the year than the typical college graduate.

Majors in the field aged 25 to 29 earn an average salary of only $30,300 per year. This rate of pay rises to $41,900 by ages 50 to 54. The wage gains that teachers receive over time are largely the result of collective bargaining agreements that emphasize seniority in establishing pay scales. Majors who work in the education sector earn $37,800, while those employed by for-profit companies make an average salary of $41,000. Self-employed graduates earn an average of $44,800 per year. Graduates employed in jobs unrelated to the elementary education field earn about 6 percent more than those employed in closely related jobs, but likely work more weeks over the year.

The earnings of elementary education majors vary somewhat on the basis of the type of job in which they are employed. Majors who work as elementary school teachers earn $38,800 per year, while those who work as kindergarten and preschool teachers earn less, averaging $34,300 annually. Majors employed as high school teachers earn $37,100, and special education teachers earn $37,600. Majors who work in clerical and secretarial occupations that generally do not require a college degree have annual salaries that are well below the average of graduates in the field.

FIGURE 2

Age/Earnings Profile of Persons with Only a Bachelor's Degree in Elementary Teacher Education (Full-Time Workers, in 2002 Dollars)

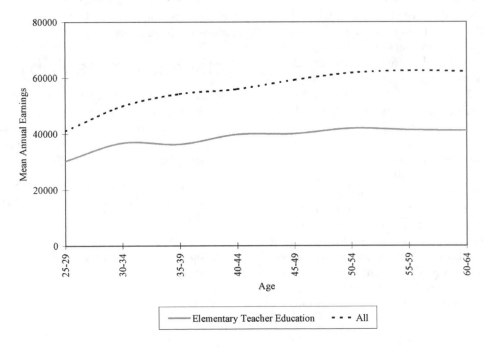

Table 2
Annual Salary of Full-Time Workers with Only a Bachelor's Degree in Elementary Teacher Education, Top 10 Occupations (in 2002 Dollars)

Earnings in Top 10 Occupations	All	Elementary Teacher Education
Total	$54,171	$38,746
Teachers, elementary school	$39,167	$38,789
Teachers, prekindergarten and kindergarten	$33,183	$34,350
Teachers, secondary school	$40,355	$37,074
Special education teachers, primary and secondary	$37,065	$37,550
Top- and mid-level managers, executives, administrators	$74,051	$54,369
Other administrative (e.g., records clerks, telephone operators)	$34,547	$31,345
Sales occupations, including retail	$52,378	$37,717
Other service occupations, except health	$39,984	$33,905
Secretaries, receptionists, typists	$32,246	$29,730
Other management-related occupations	$51,921	$52,769

On-the-Job Training

Opportunities for informal on-the-job learning are limited in the teaching profession. Instead, teachers must participate in professional development activities in order to maintain or improve their teaching skills. About three-quarters of all graduates of elementary education programs participate in training workshops and seminars designed to impart a variety of work-based skills.

▶ The majority of those participating in training enroll in workshops and seminars designed to bolster a specific professional skill in teaching or other areas related to their specific job duties.

▶ More than one-third participate in training sessions designed to enhance communications skills, including writing and public speaking skills.

Post-Graduation Activities

More than one-third of all elementary education majors go on to earn an advanced degree after completing college. Virtually all of those who do study at the graduate level earn a master's degree. Only 1 percent continue their education through the completion of a doctorate. Rarely do majors from this field earn a professional degree in law or medicine.

- Nearly 90 percent of all master's degrees earned by elementary education majors are in the education field. About one-half of them are in elementary education and the other one-half are in some other education specialty.

- Most of those who earn a doctorate continue in the education field.

Employment rates of elementary education majors are low. Only about three-quarters of all graduates in the field are employed. Of this group, 1 in 5 holds a part-time position. Involuntary unemployment occurs infrequently among graduates in this major. Only about 2 percent are jobless and actively seeking work. About one-fifth of elementary education graduates choose not to work. Most often these persons say that they do not work in order to meet family responsibilities.

Employment Outlook

The rate of increase in the demand for elementary school teachers is expected to be much slower than that for college graduates in general. According to the U.S. Bureau of Labor Statistics, the employment among persons with a bachelor's degree is expected to increase by 22.2 percent between 2000 and 2010, while economy-wide employment levels are expected to grow by only 15.2 percent. However, employment in the elementary teacher occupation is expected to increase by only 13 percent over the forecast period. The demand for prekindergarten and kindergarten teachers is expected to increase by 18 percent over the decade. Employment in secondary and preschool teacher occupations is expected to grow more rapidly over this period and may provide a larger share of all employment opportunities for those with a degree in elementary education. The demand for special education teachers is expected to increase very rapidly, expanding by more than 30 percent in just 10 years. The slow rate of projected employment increase in the elementary teaching fields may be viewed as conservative. The number of school-aged children and trends in pupil/teacher ratios heavily influences elementary teacher demand. Because of unexpectedly large foreign immigration, the demand for elementary teachers remained strong during the 1990s. Foreign immigration is expected to continue at very high rates in the foreseeable future and thus will bolster demand for teachers in many states.

Table 3
Projected Change in Employment in the Top 10 Occupations That
Employ Persons with Only a Bachelor's Degree in Elementary Teacher Education

Top 10 Occupations	Actual Employment in 2000 (000s)	Projected Employment in 2010 (000s)	Absolute Change (000s)	Percentage Change
Teachers, elementary school	1,532	1,734	202	13.2%
Teachers, prekindergarten and kindergarten	597	707	110	18.4%
Teachers, secondary school	1,113	1,314	201	18.1%
Special education teachers, primary and secondary	453	592	139	30.7%

Top 10 Occupations	Actual Employment in 2000 (000s)	Projected Employment in 2010 (000s)	Absolute Change (000s)	Percentage Change
Top- and mid-level managers, executives, administrators	10,564	11,834	1,270	12.0%
Other administrative (e.g., records clerks, telephone operators)	16,911	18,522	1,611	9.5%
Sales occupations, including retail	15,513	17,365	1,852	11.9%
Other service occupations, except health	9,652	11,287	1,635	16.9%
Secretaries, receptionists, typists	4,980	5,501	521	10.5%
Other management-related occupations	4,956	5,801	845	17.1%

CHAPTER 24

Mathematics and Science Teacher Education

The mathematics and science subject areas traditionally have been separated for specific attention from secondary education. The practice originally may have arisen because of the belief that a strong knowledge of these content areas was fundamental before one could teach. In fact, the U.S. Congress set mathematics and science education as a high national priority in post–World War II years when science and technology were part of the national security race with Communist Russia. Another reason for focusing on these teacher education areas is that when the interest and personality profiles of teachers were researched, the analysis showed that mathematics and science teachers clustered with scientists, while other teachers clustered primarily with those in social occupations.

As with all education, teaching in these areas increasingly is being geared to having students achieve mastery performance of standards in every subject at each grade level. The aim also is to have students understand abstract concepts, learn problem solving, and develop critical-thinking thought processes. Techniques of evaluating student progress have moved to the use of portfolios from total reliance on grades, where an A grade of performance by one teacher may mean something different from another teacher's assignment of an A grade. This newer assessment method presents individual mastery by displaying actual samples of learning results, such as pictures of projects and best examples of writing. Also, new technology, including the use of computers, is improving teaching methodology by offering a more realistic presentation of information.

Each state has its own certification requirements that everyone is advised to examine for the state in which one wants to teach. In general, for those working in middle and high schools, course work is required in adolescent development, introduction to special education, the learning process, curriculum theory, methods and materials for instruction, and student practice teaching. In addition, the following teachers must demonstrate knowledge in these specific areas:

- Mathematics: algebra, geometry, calculus, number theory, probability and statistics, and discrete mathematics.

- Biology: botany, zoology, human biology, genetics, ecology, and chemistry.

- Chemistry: organic, analytical, and physical chemistry; physics; and related aspects of mathematics.

- Earth Sciences: geology; oceanography; astronomy; ecology; meteorology; and related aspects of chemistry, physics, and biology.

- Physics: mechanics, heat, light, sound; modern physics; and related aspects of mathematics.

- Also, all mathematics and science teachers must know the modes of inquiry and methods of research and experimentation in mathematics and science, including laboratory techniques and the use of computers.

The interests of mathematics and science teachers are scientific, including liking to probe natural phenomena, work with numbers, and solve technical problems. Also, they appreciate the value and role of equipment and machines in the exploration and discovery process. They also have a people orientation that serves as the attraction to teaching rather than other applications for their mathematics and science knowledge.

Those in this major value the opportunity to work with adolescents in a developmental way. The teaching process provides the chance to be creative in motivating youth to learn. Teachers are also leaders and do influence their students about subjects they personally like and value. Also, there is mental stimulation in working with numbers and keeping current with scientific knowledge.

Overall, people in this field like to keep everything factual, stressing analytical thinking, logic, and organization. In their personal lives, they are thorough, systematic, patient, hard working, and persevering. But there are different preferences for interacting noted within the group, although both have a concern for students. One group may appear to be impersonal. Thus, students who attempt to get special attention by appealing to the teacher's feelings may not get results, whereas students who present the facts behind a request may receive a successful response to an appeal. The other group is seen as those who are supportive of people and their projects and project sympathy, tactfulness, and kindness.

Where Do Mathematics and Science Teacher Education Graduates Work?

While the expectation for persons who major in an education field at the undergraduate level is that they will work in some capacity in education, only about one-half of all mathematics and science teacher education majors actually end up working in an educational institution. Relatively low pay in the teaching profession and strong demand for persons with technical skills in mathematics-related fields mean that many majors from this area are eventually employed in higher-paying jobs in private, for-profit companies or the government. Private, for-profit firms employ 30 percent of majors from this field, while an additional 9 percent are self-employed either as consultants to other organizations or through their own companies. An additional 9 percent work for a government agency. Only rarely are these majors employed by a nonprofit charity or research foundation.

FIGURE 1

Percentage Distribution
of Employed Persons
with Only a Bachelor's
Degree in Mathematics
and Science Teacher
Education, by Major
Sector of Economic
Activity

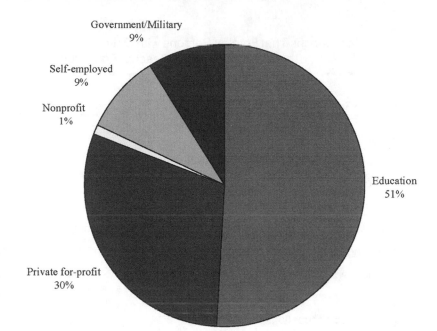

Government/Military
9%

Self-employed
9%

Nonprofit
1%

Education
51%

Private for-profit
30%

Occupations

A substantial number of all majors from this field are employed in jobs that are closely related to the major field of study. Nearly 40 percent of all graduates with a degree in mathematics and science teacher education are employed as secondary school teachers, and 4.5 percent work as elementary school teachers. An additional 7.7 percent of all majors in this field work as mid- or upper-level managers or administrators, often in leadership positions in local school districts. However, 30 percent of all graduates work in jobs that are unrelated to the major, and an additional 22 percent say their current jobs are only somewhat related to the field. About 8 percent of all majors work in sales- and marketing-related jobs, and about 3 percent work as computer systems analysts. Graduates in this field employed in jobs unrelated to the field most often said that working conditions, pay, and promotion potential are the most important reasons that they chose to work in jobs unrelated to the field. Strong math and science skills are in demand in many sectors of the economy. Thus, those with a bachelor's degree in math and science education work outside the education industry more often than do others with undergraduate degrees in education.

A substantial number of mathematics and science teacher education majors work in jobs that generally do not require a college degree, including secretarial and related clerical positions. Graduates from this field who work in jobs that do not require a degree have very low annual earnings; economists refer to these graduates as underemployed. This poor earnings experience is the result of employment in jobs that do not utilize the skills and abilities associated with a college degree.

Table 1
Top 10 Occupations That Employ Persons with Only a Bachelor's Degree in Mathematics and Science Teacher Education

Top 10 Occupations	PERCENT OF EMPLOYED		
	All	Men	Women
Teachers, secondary school	39.6	37.8	41.1
Top- and mid-level managers, executives, administrators	7.7	11.6	4.4
Sales occupations, including retail	5.2	5.3	5.0
Teachers, elementary school	4.5	2.7	6.0
Other administrative (e.g., records clerks, telephone operators)	3.8	1.3	5.9
Accounting clerks, bookkeepers	3.1	0.0	5.8
Computer systems analysts	3.1	4.6	1.8
Secretaries, receptionists, typists	2.6	0.0	4.9
Other service occupations, except health	2.5	1.3	3.5
Other marketing and sales occupations	2.5	5.0	0.3

▌ Men and women with bachelor's degrees in mathematics and science teacher education are about equally likely to be employed as secondary school teachers. However, women are twice as likely to work as elementary school teachers relative to men in the same degree field.

▌ Jobs in upper- and mid-level management are much more likely to employ men with a degree in the field than women.

▌ Women with a degree in mathematics and science teacher education are 5 to 6 times more likely to be employed in secretarial and clerical positions than men in the same major.

Activities on the Job

▌ Most persons with a degree in mathematics and science teacher education have accounting, finance, or contract functions as part of their job duties.

▌ About one-half of all graduates in the field engage in teaching activities. For one-half of all graduates in the field, teaching is the predominant job duty.

▌ Managerial and supervisory duties are undertaken by 36 percent of majors from the field.

▌ One-third of all majors develop or use computer applications on the job. About 1 in 10 majors say that this is the most important duty at work.

FIGURE 2

Age/Earnings Profile of Persons with Only a Bachelor's Degree in Mathematics and Science Teacher Education (Full-Time Workers, in 2002 Dollars)

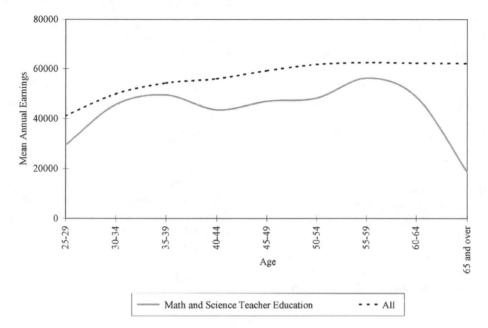

Salaries

Persons employed in full-time jobs with a bachelor's degree in mathematics and science teacher education earn an average salary of $44,700 per year in 2002-dollar terms. College graduates with a bachelor's degree earn an average salary of $54,200. Thus, graduates with a major in this field can expect to earn about 18 percent less per year than the average college graduate. Persons aged 25 to 29 with a degree in the major earn only $29,400 per year, yet by age 50 to 54, the earnings of majors rise to $48,300 per year, an earnings increase of 65 percent in terms of real inflation-adjusted dollars. This sharp increase in the earnings of graduates in this major is the result of two separate factors. First, teacher contracts across the nation base teacher compensation scales largely on seniority. Thus, almost by definition, older teachers receive higher pay than younger ones.

However, nearly one-half of all graduates from the field work outside the education sector. The earnings of these individuals also rise sharply with age. Most of these graduates work in jobs that are not closely related to the undergraduate major; thus, many skills have to be acquired on the job. Through a combination of informal learning on the job and through participation in formal work-based training workshops and seminars, those employed outside education develop their skills and become more valuable to employers over time. With increasing years of skill development and work experience, the real wages of these individuals increase as their value to employers rises.

Sharp disparities exist in the earnings of persons with a bachelor's degree on the basis of the sector of the economy in which they are employed. Majors who work for private, for-profit businesses earn an average salary of

$54,600 per year, a rate of pay 36.5 percent higher than the $40,100 salary of those who work for an educational institution. Strong demand in the private sector for employees with mathematics and computer skills contributes substantially to this large earnings differential. Graduates with teaching degrees in these fields also have substantially higher salaries when they work for government organizations. Salaries for those who work in government average $47,900 per year in 2002-dollar terms. Those who are self-employed have earnings that are well below the average of all those with a degree in the technical teaching area.

Given the relatively low pay of mathematics and science teacher education majors who work in the education sector, it is not surprising that those majors employed in jobs that are closely related to their undergraduate field of study have annual salaries that are well below those of persons in jobs that are unrelated to the major. Those who report that their work is closely tied to the undergraduate major field of study earn an average of $36,900, while those who work in jobs unrelated to the field report an annual salary of $43,800. Top-paying jobs are in top- to mid-level management positions, where salaries average $61,900. Mathematics and science teacher education majors who work as computer systems analysts also have high earnings, with an average annual salary of $57,500. Majors working in sales occupations earn relatively high salaries, averaging between $47,900 and $49,000 per year. Mathematics and science teacher education majors working in elementary or secondary education have earnings of $41,100 and $38,800, respectively. Those majors unable to find employment in a job that normally requires a college degree have very low annual salaries. Majors employed in secretarial and clerical fields have average salary levels that range from $19,800 to $29,000.

Table 2
Annual Salary of Full-Time Workers with Only a Bachelor's Degree in Mathematics and Science Teacher Education, Top 10 Occupations (in 2002 Dollars)

Earnings in Top 10 Occupations	All	Mathematics and Science Teacher Education
Total	$54,171	$44,712
Teachers, secondary school	$40,355	$38,829
Top- and mid-level managers, executives, administrators	$74,051	$61,848
Sales occupations, including retail	$52,378	$49,010
Teachers, elementary school	$39,167	$41,151
Other administrative (e.g., records clerks, telephone operators)	$34,547	$25,770
Accounting clerks, bookkeepers	$32,380	$29,051
Computer systems analysts	$59,818	$57,549
Secretaries, receptionists, typists	$32,246	$19,826
Other service occupations, except health	$39,984	$39,505
Other marketing and sales occupations	$58,208	$47,955

On-the-Job Learning

More than 7 out of 10 graduates with a degree in mathematics and science teacher education participate in some type of formal training program related to their job over the course of a year. Those employed as teachers are more likely than those working in other occupations to engage in this type of training. The teaching profession relies heavily on formal classroom training to develop professional skills rather than informal on-the-job learning. Teacher certification requirements often demand regular participation in professional development seminars and workshops.

▶ More than three-quarters of graduates with degrees in mathematics and science education participate in training designed to enhance specific occupational skills ranging from teaching methods to computer programming innovations.

▶ Thirty percent of the graduates in this major field engage in training designed to enhance their communications skills by participating in public speaking and business writing programs over the course of a year.

▶ More than one-fourth of all graduates in the major attend supervisory and management workshops. Most often these sessions are related to personnel, industrial relations, and human resource issues.

▶ Graduates in the field do not participate in training programs because they believe it will help them receive pay increases or promotions. Rather, their participation is motivated by the need to keep abreast of developments in the field and further sharpen their work-based skills.

Post-Graduation Activities

Like other teacher education majors, those who earn a bachelor's degree in mathematics and science teacher education are more likely to earn an advanced degree of some type compared to other college graduates. More than one-half of all those who earn a degree in this field go on to earn a graduate degree. About 45 percent of all graduates in the field earn a master's degree, while an additional 3 percent earn a doctorate, and 2 percent earn a professional degree.

▶ Among mathematics and science teacher education majors who earn a master's degree, 75 percent continue their studies at the graduate level in an education-related field. Ten percent of those with a master's earn their degrees in mathematics, a scientific field, or in computer science. About 6 percent earn a master's degree in business.

▶ Only a small number of those who earn an undergraduate degree in mathematics and science teacher education earn a doctorate. About three-quarters of these degrees are in the education field. The remaining doctorates are mostly awarded in a computer-, mathematics-, or science-related field.

The employment rate of persons with bachelor's degrees in the mathematics and science teacher education field is 85 percent. Among the 15 percent not working, almost none are involuntarily unemployed. Most of those not working have chosen not to work primarily in order to meet family responsibilities at home.

Employment Outlook

Overall demand for persons with a bachelor's degree is expected to increase by 22.2 percent between 2000 and 2010, a rate of growth much more rapid than the 15.2 percent increase forecast in the overall level of demand for labor in the American economy. A more mixed picture emerges when analyzing the demand for workers in the specific occupational areas that are most likely to employ those with a degree in mathematics and science teacher education. Overall employment levels for secondary school teachers are expected to increase by 18 percent between 2000 and 2010. However, given the increased emphasis on mathematics, science, and computer curricula in American high schools, it is likely that demand for graduates in this field will outstrip the rate of overall increase in the demand for secondary school teachers.

Employment levels among elementary school teachers are expected to increase by only 13 percent over the projection period, a rate of growth equal to only about 60 percent of that of all college graduates. In contrast, job prospects for graduates in the computer systems analyst position appear quite bright. Employment is expected to increase by 60 percent over the next decade, adding nearly 258,000 jobs over the projection period. Demand for sales workers, an important source of jobs for majors in this field, will likely increase by between 12 and 22 percent.

Table 3
Projected Change in Employment in the Top 10 Occupations That Employ
Persons with Only a Bachelor's Degree in Mathematics and Science Teacher Education

Top 10 Occupations	Actual Employment in 2000 (000s)	Projected Employment in 2010 (000s)	Absolute Change (000s)	Percentage Change
Teachers, secondary school	1,113	1,314	201	18.1%
Top- and mid-level managers, executives, administrators	10,564	11,834	1,270	12.0%
Sales occupations, including retail	15,513	17,365	1,852	11.9%
Teachers, elementary school	1,532	1,734	202	13.2%
Other administrative (e.g., records clerks, telephone operators)	16,911	18,522	1,611	9.5%
Accounting clerks, bookkeepers	1,991	2,030	39	2.0%
Computer systems analysts	431	689	258	59.9%
Secretaries, receptionists, typists	4,980	5,501	521	10.5%
Other service occupations, except health	9,652	11,287	1,635	16.9%
Other marketing and sales occupations	621	758	137	22.1%

CHAPTER 25

Physical Education and Coaching

Physical education is an attractive major because students themselves often were athletes, enjoyed sports, took part in athletic activities, or enjoy teaching people physical activities. Physical education provides students with the skills to offer others the opportunity to learn physical conditioning, to teach others to be able to play a particular sport, or to engage in activities that some individuals consider fun, even including learning to dance.

Physical education teachers plan and conduct activities to build strength, develop coordination, and test physical endurance. They explore with students the concept of wellness and examine behaviors that lead to a high level of physical and emotional well being. They help people learn self-assessment techniques to assess health risks, life-cycle issues, and stress management. They instruct people concerning proper nutrition, drug use and abuse, and human sexuality.

Coaching is a function many teachers, not just physical education teachers, perform. Many people who have varying levels of skill in a specific sport take part in coaching. Therefore, the development of skill proficiency and amount of teaching, including knowing the rules and playing strategy, may differ for various coaches. Conditioning and motivating athletes are part of the job, as are planning schedules and activities and arranging for availability of equipment.

Coaches usually specialize in specific sports. Modeling activities and practicing plays are typical coaching functions.

Physical education teachers work in elementary schools (grades 1 through 6 or 8), middle schools (grades 5 through 8), or secondary or high schools (grades 7 through 12). While their subject area remains constant, the content and activities are adapted to the developmental levels of students. Generally, the course work of those preparing to work at the elementary level is broader, with more specialized courses in athletic areas and sports being offered for those preparing to work with older students. However, physical education departments have encountered fiscal cutbacks as schools have reduced community educational budgets. Physical education teachers, as a result, have adapted by often covering all grade levels and traveling to various schools on different days of the week. This phenomenon has affected some of the training preparation of physical education teachers. Common courses are anatomy and physiology, motor development, physical conditioning, kinesiology, and theory of coaching.

The abilities of physical education teachers are primarily social and communicative ones. They work to inspire personal confidence and motivate students. They actively participate in the learning process of the unique skills of a specific sport and its rules and strategies of play. They also help students through exercises of physiological development. Leadership and organizational skills are definitely requirements. Obviously, physical education teachers need physical skills, motor coordination, strength, stamina, and physical agility because they typically teach using modeling and one-on-one, hands-on demonstration.

The interests of these majors follow the abilities cited above. While in some events, people may compete individually, generally there is a social element to athletics. Planning, organizing, and assuming leadership roles are involved. And, whether or not liking physical involvement is the primary motivation, those in physical education and coaching appreciate activity and action.

Numerous benefits can be derived from physical education teaching and coaching. Competition, public attention, and possibly recognition from successful performance or winning provide one type of satisfaction. Another type of satisfaction is derived from the leadership and authority gained from a position of control. Still another area of enjoyment comes from physical activity and outdoor involvement.

Pragmatism and a realistic approach characterize people in this area. As persons in charge, they influence others; they rely on memory of facts, past events, and games to make judgments, leading to a conservative style. They pay close attention to details and accuracy. They enjoy an administrative role, deciding what has to be done and giving orders, but they do not appreciate inefficiency on the part of others. They believe in the value of hard work, patience, and thoroughness.

Where Do Physical Education Majors Work?

Typically, physical education program graduates are employed in some aspect of primary and secondary education. However, the majority of graduates work in jobs in other sectors of the American economy. More than 30 percent of physical education graduates work as employees in private, for-profit businesses and corporations. About 11 percent are self-employed, and 8 percent work for government agencies at the federal, state, and local level. Many of those who work outside education are employed in positions that are largely unrelated to the physical education field.

FIGURE 1

Percentage Distribution of Employed Persons with Only a Bachelor's Degree in Physical Education and Coaching, by Major Sector of Economic Activity

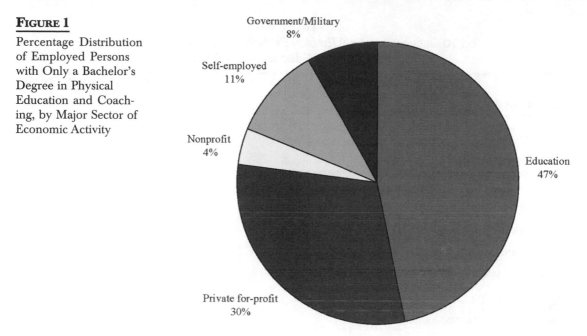

Government/Military
8%

Self-employed
11%

Nonprofit
4%

Education
47%

Private for-profit
30%

Occupations

Physical education majors with a bachelor's degree most often work as elementary and secondary school teachers. More than 36 percent of all majors are employed as elementary or secondary school teachers. About two-thirds of those employed as teachers work at the high school level, and the rest work with younger children in elementary schools. A small number of majors are involved in pre-elementary education activities. Nearly 9 percent of physical education majors are employed in managerial and administrative positions, often within the educational system. Although these jobs are not directly related to the major, those employed in these jobs often work their way into management positions after working as teachers for a number of years. Those not employed in education often work in sales occupations, including insurance, stocks and bonds, and real estate sales. Forty percent of physical education majors work in jobs unrelated to the field of study. Most often these individuals decide to work outside the field because of what they view as relatively poor pay and promotion opportunities of jobs related to the physical education major.

Table 1
Top 10 Occupations That Employ Persons with Only a Bachelor's Degree in Physical Education and Coaching

Top 10 Occupations	PERCENT OF EMPLOYED		
	All	Men	Women
Teachers, secondary school	24.6	24.1	25.2
Teachers, elementary school	11.9	9.2	15.1
Top- and mid-level managers, executives, administrators	8.9	11.7	5.5
Sales occupations, including retail	6.0	6.0	6.0
Insurance, securities, real estate, business services	4.3	6.0	2.1
Other management-related occupations	4.1	4.7	3.4
Other service occupations, except health	2.8	1.8	4.0
Personnel, training, and labor relations specialists	2.5	1.8	3.2
Protective-service occupations	2.3	2.9	1.6
Postsecondary professors	2.2	2.1	2.4

▶ Women with degrees in the field are substantially more likely to work as elementary school teachers than men.

▶ Men with degrees in physical education are twice as likely to work in high-level management and administrative jobs than are women with bachelor's degrees in the field.

Activities on the Job

▶ Among a substantial proportion of physical education majors, teaching is a central element of the tasks they undertake on a daily basis on their job.

▶ Many majors employed outside the teaching profession are engaged in sales and marketing activities as part of their daily job duties.

▶ Personnel and employee relations are also key elements in the duties of persons employed outside the teaching profession.

Salaries

The salaries of all college graduates with a bachelor's degree average about $54,200 per year in 2002-dollar terms. Graduates of undergraduate physical education programs earn an average of only $45,100 per year, a rate of pay about $9,100, or about 17 percent, below that of their college-educated counterparts. The earnings of physical education graduates aged 25 to 29 averages about $33,900 per year. By the time these graduates reach age 50 to 54, these earnings rise to $55,800 per year, an increase of more than 60 percent in inflation-adjusted dollars. The increase in earnings with age is associated with two distinct developments among this group of graduates. Among those physical education majors who enter the teaching professions, the contracts under which they work are designed to reward job tenure. Thus, while entry wages are low, teacher contracts provide substantial wage increments for each additional year of work. Among those outside the teaching field, no contract exists to automatically reward years on the job with pay increases. Nonetheless, the earnings levels of those outside education also increase rapidly with age. Majors working outside teaching are employed in sales management and other occupations in which their college training is largely not applicable to many job duties. Instead, many of the skills required for success in these fields are learned through experience and acquired on the job. For these individuals, earnings increase with age because employers value the additional experience and skills that employees acquire on the job over time.

The salaries of physical education majors vary considerably by sector of the economy. Those employed in private, for-profit businesses earn an average salary of $49,900 per year. Those employed by educational institutions earn only $40,500. Majors employed in education

have lower annual salaries in part because they work substantially fewer weeks over the course of the year than those employed in the private sector.

The earnings of physical education majors vary somewhat by occupation. The best-paying positions among these individuals are found in the high-level sales area, including the sales of real estate, insurance, and stocks and bonds. Earnings of physical education majors employed in these sales areas average $74,500 per year. Majors employed in managerial and administrative positions earn $58,900. These individuals are largely employed in the education sector and therefore are paid substantially less than other college graduates in similar jobs, most of whom work in the higher-paying private, for-profit sector. Physical education majors who work in jobs unrelated to the field of study have salaries that are 12 percent lower than those who are employed in positions that are closely related to the field.

FIGURE 2

Age/Earnings Profile of Persons with Only a Bachelor's Degree in Physical Education and Coaching (Full-Time Workers, in 2002 Dollars)

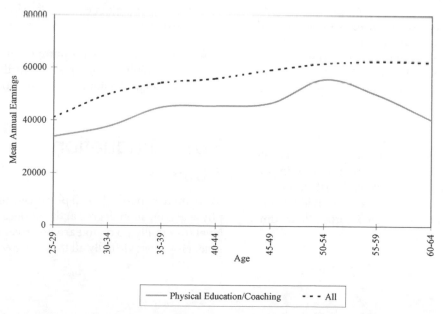

Table 2
Annual Salary of Full-Time Workers with Only a Bachelor's Degree
in Physical Education and Coaching, Top 10 Occupations (in 2002 Dollars)

Earnings in Top 10 Occupations	All	Physical Education/Coaching
Total	$54,171	$45,073
Teachers, secondary school	$40,355	$41,349
Teachers, elementary school	$39,167	$37,277
Top- and mid-level managers, executives, administrators	$74,051	$58,940
Sales occupations, including retail	$52,378	$43,371
Insurance, securities, real estate, business services	$68,273	$74,513
Other management-related occupations	$51,921	$45,731
Other service occupations, except health	$39,984	$45,087
Personnel, training, and labor relations specialists	$51,577	$51,959
Protective-service occupations	$49,130	$47,038
Postsecondary professors	$42,234	$52,977

On-the-Job Training

Among physical education program graduates who become teachers, formal workshops and training seminars are the primary means by which these individuals develop their professional teaching skills. More than 80 percent of majors who work as teachers participate in these formal work-based training programs. However, among majors employed outside education, informal, on-the-job learning is a relatively more important method of skills development. Fewer than 60 percent of the majors employed in private, for-profit companies participate in formal training activities. Often these individuals engage in training designed to improve their communications skills.

▶ About 30 percent of all majors participate in formal training programs in order to maintain their professional certifications.

▶ The major motive for participation in these training programs is to further develop professional skills and knowledge.

Post-Graduation Activities

More than 40 percent of all persons who earn a physical education degree at the undergraduate level eventually go on to earn an advanced degree. However, virtually all these degrees are at the master's level. Only infrequently do physical education majors continue their schooling to the doctoral level or earn a professional degree in law or medicine.

- Eighty percent of all master's degrees earned by graduates in this field are in physical education or some other education field. Incentives to earn advanced degrees among those working in the educational system are strong because most teacher contracts reward additional degrees earned along with seniority.

- Only rarely does graduate study for these majors deviate from the education field. Those who earn master's degrees outside education most often study a health- or business-related field.

- Only about 1 percent of all those with a bachelor's degree in physical education eventually earn a doctoral degree. Virtually all these doctorates are in the education field.

Among physical education majors under the age of 65, more than 85 percent are employed, most in full-time positions. About 2 percent are jobless and actively seeking work. However, about 11 percent of all majors choose not to work. Most often these individuals have taken an early retirement or have chosen to stay at home in order to better meet family responsibilities.

Employment Outlook

The long-term job prospects for college graduates in the American economy appear to remain strong. U.S. Bureau of Labor Statistics projections of employment suggest that the demand for workers with a bachelor's degree will increase by about 21 percent between 2000 and 2010, a rate of increase that is much more rapid than the expected 15 percent increase in overall employment levels within the economy. The demand for workers in the secondary teaching profession is expected to increase by about 18 percent, a rate of change somewhat below the average change in the demand for college graduates. The demand for elementary teachers is expected to rise at a considerably slower pace. Most other occupations that employ graduates with a physical education degree are expected to increase demand at a relatively slow rate compared to the change in the level of demand for college graduates overall.

Table 3
Projected Change in Employment in the Top 10 Occupations That Employ Persons with Only a Bachelor's Degree in Physical Education and Coaching

Top 10 Occupations	Actual Employment in 2000 (000s)	Projected Employment in 2010 (000s)	Absolute Change (000s)	Percentage Change
Teachers, secondary school	1,113	1,314	201	18.1%
Teachers, elementary	1,532	1,734	202	13.2%
Top- and mid-level managers, executives, administrators	10,564	11,834	1,270	12.0%
Sales occupations, including retail	15,513	17,365	1,852	11.9%

(continued)

Table 3 (continued)
Projected Change in Employment in the Top 10 Occupations That Employ Persons with Only a Bachelor's Degree in Physical Education and Coaching

Top 10 Occupations	Actual Employment in 2000 (000s)	Projected Employment in 2010 (000s)	Absolute Change (000s)	Percentage Change
Insurance, securities, real estate, business services	1,548	1,726	178	11.5%
Other management-related occupations	4,956	5,801	845	17.1%
Other service occupations, except health	9,652	11,287	1,635	16.9%
Personnel, training, and labor relations specialists	490	578	88	18.0%
Protective-service occupations	3,087	3,896	809	26.2%
Postsecondary professors	1,344	1,659	315	23.4%

CHAPTER 26

Secondary Teacher Education

Secondary teacher education is one of the broadest majors, covering English to social science, language to geography or chemistry. People do not enter secondary teaching blindly, because they personally have experienced the field during their own education. What may be novel is the different community support for schools, size, cultural composition, academic rigor, and student commitment to study. Other differences may be the type of school board control. For example, almost all religious groups support and operate schools according to their philosophy of education. Another organizational variation could be working in a middle or junior high school where the grades range from 5 to 9. Some people enjoy working with this volatile developmental age group and feel these students are easier to teach than older students because of their greater motivation to learn.

Teachers prepare group presentations and must adapt to students individually. They assign readings in textbooks, use exercises to develop skill proficiency, listen to oral presentations, and assess students' progress. They also must maintain an environment conducive to learning, which means maintaining discipline. They may collaborate with other teachers to articulate a curriculum across grades. Teachers prepare tests, grade papers, assign grades, oversee study halls and homerooms, meet with parents or guardians to discuss achievement and personal development, and may participate in extracurricular activities.

All states license their public school teachers. Those entering teaching need to check out specific state requirements. Teacher certification may require a master's degree after developing competency first in an academic discipline.

In general, course work is required for those teaching in middle and high schools in adolescent development, introduction to special education, the learning process, curriculum theory, methods and materials for instruction, and student practice teaching. In addition, the following specific requirements are used as examples of the knowledge required in specific content areas:

- English: History and study of language; English, American, and world literature; theories of language acquisition; written and oral composition; drama; speech communication; literary criticism and techniques of research in the field of English; writing, including techniques for evaluating writing; relationships of English to other fields of knowledge

- History: Methods of historical research; physical, economic, political, intellectual, and social forces that shape civilizations, including sex, race, and ethnicity; origin and development of world cultures; the economic, political, social, and cultural history of the United States; relationships between history and related fields, such as geography, political science, economics, sociology, anthropology, psychology, literature, and the arts

In addition to the ability to master their specialty area, teachers exhibit language and leadership skills. Critical are interpersonal and communication abilities, both verbal and oral, to convey information and to facilitate expressive language development in students.

Interests universal to all teachers are being social and people oriented and enjoying communicating and reading. Teaching involves leading and influencing roles. In addition, those who enter teaching need to examine the content of a specialized teaching major, such as foreign languages, for more information as well as related abilities and interests to best understand the career of a foreign language teacher.

As a group, secondary teachers value working with their minds, working with people, expressing their creativity, experiencing variety, and having the opportunity for diversion.

Secondary school educators are a very diverse group. For example, middle school teachers' personality styles may show them to be nice, more talkative than high school teachers, more active in the school's curriculum, and less interested in technical subject areas but committed to those areas that affect people's lives. Some teachers like to be well organized, serious, and demanding of students who, in turn, actually perform very well, verifying the personal axiom that if one works hard, one will be successful. Many others are friendly and concerned with people's feelings but still project a commitment to high standards of performance. This group of teachers generally is not in mathematics and sciences. Other teachers enjoy being imaginative and enthusiastic. They will improvise but also are prone to changes in their own interests. Reading about a specific major in this book will provide additional information.

Where Do Secondary Teacher Education Majors Work?

Only 39 percent of secondary teacher education graduates work in the education sector of the economy. About the same number work in the private, for-profit sector of the economy for businesses and corporations. Eleven percent are self-employed, and 7 percent of secondary teacher education graduates are employed in the government sector. The remaining 5 percent work for nonprofit organizations in the private, nonprofit sector of the economy.

The distribution of employed secondary teacher education graduates by sector of the economy indicates that many graduates are not employed in jobs that are closely related to their undergraduate education. Only 38 percent work in jobs that are closely related to their undergraduate major. Another 26 percent are employed in jobs that are somewhat related to their undergraduate major field of study. The remaining 36 percent of secondary teacher education graduates work in jobs that are not related to their field of study.

FIGURE 1

Percentage Distribution of Employed Persons with Only a Bachelor's Degree in Secondary Teacher Education, by Major Sector of Economic Activity

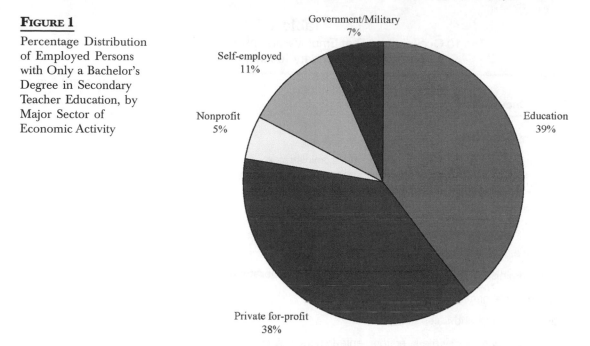

Government/Military
7%

Self-employed
11%

Nonprofit
5%

Education
39%

Private for-profit
38%

Why do so many secondary teacher education graduates work in jobs that are unrelated to their major? Although they cite a number of different reasons for their employment choice in an unrelated field, when asked to select the most important reason, 31 percent of the graduates cite better pay and promotion opportunities outside their field as the most important factor underlying their employment decision. Nearly one-fifth are forced to work in unrelated jobs because they are unable to find related jobs. Sixteen percent of secondary teacher education graduates who work in unrelated jobs do so to change their career track. About 13 percent do not like the general working conditions in related jobs, and 11 percent consider family-related reasons to be the most important factor influencing their decision to work in unrelated jobs.

Occupations

The employment of secondary teacher education graduates is quite dispersed across different occupations. Fewer than one-quarter are employed as secondary school teachers, and 4 percent work as elementary school teachers. One in 10 is employed as a top- to mid-level manager or administrator. Secretarial jobs employ 5 percent of graduates, and 4 percent work in clerical and administrative support occupations. Sales occupations employ 5 percent of the graduates, and finance and real estate occupations employ 4 percent of all secondary teacher education graduates.

Table 1
Top 10 Occupations That Employ Persons with Only a Bachelor's Degree in Secondary Teacher Education

Top 10 Occupations	PERCENT OF EMPLOYED		
	All	Men	Women
Teachers, secondary school	23.7	23.5	23.8
Top- and mid-level managers, executives, administrators	9.4	15.9	5.3
Secretaries, receptionists, typists	5.2	0.0	8.5
Sales occupations, including retail	5.1	6.6	4.2
Other management-related occupations	4.2	3.7	4.6
Insurance, securities, real estate, business services	4.2	5.7	3.2
Other administrative (e.g., records clerks, telephone operators)	4.1	1.5	5.8
Teachers, elementary school	4.0	2.4	5.0
Other marketing and sales occupations	3.3	3.5	3.2
Artists, broadcasters, writers, editors, entertainers, public relations specialists	3.3	4.0	2.9

The field of secondary teacher education is somewhat dominated by women. Only 39 percent of all employed graduates are men. Some differences exist in the occupational employment patterns of male and female secondary teacher education graduates.

> Male graduates are considerably more likely than female graduates to work as top-level executives, administrators, and managers. Nearly 16 percent of all employed male graduates work in these occupations, compared to only 5 percent of all employed female graduates.

> Men are also more likely than women to work in finance sector occupations and in sales occupations.

> Female secondary teacher education graduates tend to be more concentrated than male graduates in secretarial and administrative support occupations. Women graduates also are more likely than males to work as elementary school teachers.

Activities on the Job

The activities that secondary teacher education graduates perform at work are reflective of the occupations in which they work.

> Teaching activities take up a major portion of the typical workweek of 34 percent of all employed graduates.

> Twelve percent report that management and administration duties take up most of their time at work, and another 12 percent spend most of their time in sales, purchasing, and marketing duties.

▶ About 8 percent spend most of their workweek in performing accounting, finance, and contractual duties, and 6 percent mostly engage in computer applications, programming, and systems-development activities at work.

Salaries

The average annual salary of secondary teacher education graduates with only a bachelor's degree who are employed full-time is $44,800, a level that is only 83 percent of the average annual salary of all full-time employed college graduates. As with most college graduates, the salary of secondary teacher education graduates increases with age. Most secondary teachers work under contracts that increase pay based on years of work experience and number of courses taken beyond the graduate level. Within every age group, the average salaries of secondary teacher education graduates are considerably lower than the average salaries of all college graduates in those age groups.

▶ Graduates between the ages of 25 and 29 earn an average annual salary of $29,300. As they age, the average salary of graduates increases to $35,100 between the ages of 30 and 34 and to $44,500 among 35- to 39-year-old graduates.

▶ Graduates between 45 and 49 earn $48,400 per year, and the salary of secondary teacher education graduates peaks to $54,300 among 55- to 59-year-olds.

The average annual salaries of secondary teacher education majors who work in jobs that are related to their major field of study are lower than the salaries of those who work in jobs that are not related to their undergraduate major field of study. The average annual salary of graduates employed in closely related jobs is $40,900. Most of these closely related jobs are in the education sector, which is typically associated with lower salaries. Graduates who work in somewhat related jobs earn $45,600 per year, and the average salary in unrelated jobs of secondary teacher education majors is $48,500 per year. The latter are more likely to work in high-level managerial occupations, finance sector occupations, or high-level sales jobs.

The average salary of secondary teacher education graduates also varies by the sector in which they are employed. Graduates who work for businesses and corporations in the private, for-profit sector earn $51,500 annually. The second highest earnings accrue to self-employed graduates, whose average salary is $45,000 per year. Graduates who work in the government sector annually earn $41,600. The education sector and nonprofit organizations in the private sector pay secondary teacher education graduates an average salary of $39,300 per year.

The earnings of secondary teacher education majors vary somewhat based on the types of jobs in which they are employed.

FIGURE 2

Age/Earnings Profile of Persons with Only a Bachelor's Degree in Secondary Teacher Education (Full-Time Workers, in 2002 Dollars)

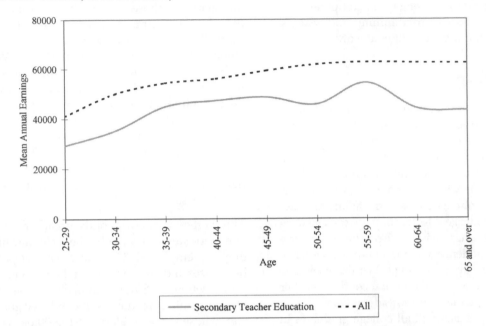

- ▶ Graduates who work in insurance and finance occupations earn a higher average salary than those employed in the top 10 occupations that predominantly employ secondary teacher education graduates. Many more male than female graduates are employed in these occupations.

- ▶ The average salary of graduates who work as top- to mid-level managers and administrators is $66,100 per year. These occupations are much more likely to employ male than female graduates. Management-related occupations like management analysts, purchasing agents, and regulatory officers pay graduates an average salary of $53,600 per year.

- ▶ Employment as secondary school teachers pays a salary of $40,000 annually, and graduates who are elementary school teachers earn $38,700 per year. These occupations together employ more than one-quarter of all working secondary teacher education graduates.

- ▶ Employment in secretarial and administrative support occupations is associated with low average salaries. These occupations are more likely to employ female than male graduates.

Table 2
Annual Salary of Full-Time Workers with Only a Bachelor's Degree in Secondary Teacher Education, Top 10 Occupations (in 2002 Dollars)

Earnings in Top 10 Occupations	All	Secondary Teacher Education
Total	$54,171	$44,813
Teachers, secondary school	$40,355	$39,984
Top- and mid-level managers, executives, administrators	$74,051	$66,081
Secretaries, receptionists, typists	$32,246	$28,672
Sales occupations, including retail	$52,378	$48,656
Other management-related occupations	$51,921	$53,574
Insurance, securities, real estate, business services	$68,273	$69,867
Other administrative (e.g., records clerks, telephone operators)	$34,547	$35,314
Teachers, elementary school	$39,167	$38,675
Other marketing and sales occupations	$58,208	$40,577
Artists, broadcasters, writers, editors, entertainers, public relations specialists	$52,141	$52,779

On-the-Job Training

The career potential of a job is closely associated with the amount of work-related training on the job. Work-related training is regarded as an investment by firms because it makes workers more productive. Firms that invest in their workforce are more likely to offer pay increases and promotions to match the increasing productivity of their workers. Firms that do not invest in their workers are relatively less likely to offer pay increases and promotions. The incidence of work-related training among secondary teacher education graduates is the same as the rate of participation in work-related training among all college graduates. The rate of participation during one year in work-related training, including workshops and seminars, among all employed college graduates and secondary teacher education graduates is 68 percent.

▶ Of those secondary teacher education graduates who receive some training during the year, 71 percent participate in technical training in the occupation in which they are employed.

▶ Thirty-one percent of the training recipients participate in management or supervisory training.

▶ Thirty-six percent receive training to improve their general professional skills, such as public speaking and business writing.

Although secondary teacher education graduates decide to participate in work-related training activities, workshops, or seminars for numerous reasons, four reasons stand out as most commonly cited by graduates. These are a desire to improve skills and knowledge in the occupational area of their employment, mandatory training requirements of the employer, increased opportunities for advancement in the form of a higher salary and promotion, and the need to obtain a professional license or certificate. Two-thirds of graduates who acquire some training consider the desire to improve skills and knowledge in the occupational area of their employment as the most important factor underlying their decision to undergo training. Fourteen percent select mandatory requirements of the employer to be the most important factor influencing their participation in training activities. Among 7 percent of the training recipients, the most important reason to participate in work-related training activities is the need to obtain a professional license or certificate. Only 5 percent of all secondary teacher education graduates who receive training consider the number one reason for their training endeavor to be improved pay and promotion opportunities.

Post-Graduation Activities

Post-graduation education is very common among secondary teacher education graduates. Of all graduates with a bachelor's degree in secondary teacher education, 46 percent proceed to earn a postgraduate degree: 40 percent earn a master's degree, 3 percent secure a doctorate degree, and another 3 percent receive a professional degree.

▶ Three-quarters of all master's degrees earned by undergraduate secondary teacher education majors are in the field of education. The rest are spread across an array of majors, including business, psychology, and English language and literature.

▶ A similar distribution of the major field of study is observed among doctorate degrees earned by undergraduate secondary teacher education majors. Three-quarters are earned in the field of education.

▶ More than 60 percent of all professional degrees earned by graduates are in the field of law, and one-fifth are earned in the health professions.

Out of all secondary teacher education graduates under the age of 65, 83 percent are employed. Only 2 percent are officially unemployed; that is, they are not employed and are actively seeking employment. The remaining 16 percent are out of the labor force; that is, they are not employed and are not seeking employment. Three main reasons underlie the labor force withdrawal of secondary teacher education graduates: 30 percent retire early, 42 percent cite family responsibilities as the reason for labor force withdrawal, and 36 percent lack the desire or the need to work. Additionally, 9 percent have a chronic illness or a disabling condition that prevents their participation in the labor market.

Employment Outlook

Employment in occupations that require at least a bachelor's degree is projected to grow faster than employment in other sectors of the American labor market. Between 2000 and 2010, the U.S. economy is projected to add 22.2 million jobs, yielding an employment growth rate of 15.2 percent. The employment growth projections in the top 10 occupations that are most likely to employ secondary teacher education graduates are presented next.

▶ Secondary teacher occupations are projected to grow at a rate somewhat above the average rate of all jobs, but below the growth rate in demand for college graduates. With 201,000 additional jobs, the employment in this occupation is projected to increase by 18 percent between 2000 and 2010.

▶ Employment in upper-level executive, administrative, and managerial occupations and in insurance and finance occupations is projected to increase by 12 percent over the same time period. Both these occupations are more likely to employ male than female secondary teacher education graduates.

▶ Employment levels in sales occupations are expected to rise by about 12 percent between 2000 and 2010. Employment in management-related occupations is forecast to rise by 17 percent over the decade.

▶ The demand for elementary school teachers is expected to increase at a below-average pace of 13 percent between 2000 and 2010. Employment in administrative support and clerical jobs is projected to grow by only 10 percent over the decade.

Table 3
Projected Change in Employment in the Top 10 Occupations That Employ Persons with Only a Bachelor's Degree in Secondary Teacher Education

Top 10 Occupations	Actual Employment In 2000 (000s)	Projected Employment In 2010 (000s)	Absolute Change (000s)	Percentage Change
Teachers, secondary school	1,113	1,314	201	18.1%
Top- and mid-level managers, executives, administrators	10,564	11,834	1,270	12.0%
Secretaries, receptionists, typists	4,980	5,501	521	10.5%
Sales occupations, including retail	15,513	17,365	1,852	11.9%
Other management-related occupations	4,956	5,801	845	17.1%
Insurance, securities, real estate, business services	1,548	1,726	178	11.5%
Other administrative (e.g., records clerks, telephone operators)	16,911	18,522	1,611	9.5%
Teachers, elementary school	1,532	1,734	202	13.2%
Other marketing and sales occupations	621	758	137	22.1%
Artists, broadcasters, writers, editors, entertainers, public relations specialists	2,371	2,864	493	20.8%

CHAPTER 27

Special Education

The special education major is a subspecialty of either elementary or secondary teacher education that prepares students to work with individuals with special needs. Specific special education programs in which students can specialize during their preparation period are specific learning disabilities, mental retardation, speech or language impairment, emotional disturbance, visual and hearing impairment, orthopedic impairment, autism, brain impairment, multiple disabilities, and the gifted and talented. Special education training helps to design learning experiences and modify instruction for the above populations at either the pre-school, elementary, middle, or secondary school level.

Special education teachers are legally required to help develop with other educational specialists an Individualized Education Program (IEP) for each special education student. The IEP considers the student's ability and learning style in specifying learning objectives and recommending strategies to reach achievement goals. The IEP then becomes a plan that special education teachers follow.

The organizational pattern of special education is varied. Some special education teachers have their own classrooms and teach classes with all special needs students. Others work as resource room teachers, providing individualized help for several hours a day to students in regular education classes, while others teach along with regular education teachers in classes composed of both general and special education students. There also are residential schools or hospitals that offer educational programs that usually include individuals having more complex and difficult needs to address.

The educational requirements in special education are changing in that some institutions are requiring a fifth year or post-baccalaureate preparation. In general, special education teachers usually spend longer in preparation than general education teachers. Courses include educational psychology, legal issues of special education, child growth and development, and methodology courses for teaching specific disabilities.

Communication ability is a crucial skill because special education teachers work with students and interact frequently with parents, other faculty, and administrators. Language and mathematical skills are needed because they are usually areas that special education instructors teach, especially at the elementary level. Social and persuasive abilities are additional skills that teachers possess and use daily. Knowledge of medical terminology and human anatomy are required in understanding the affected areas of the various disabling conditions.

The interests involved in teaching those with special needs focus on the social area and especially liking to work with children. Often, people entering this field have had direct personal contact with a child with a specific disability. Teaching also involves an organizational approach to learning. This specific field of education calls for paying close attention to details, even following some repetitive and routine activities in the implementation of their functions.

Values satisfied in this career field include creativity, where teachers can use their imagination and be resourceful. There can be a sense of achievement in performing a difficult and important task. There will be opportunities for variety and trying out new educational approaches as new specialized equipment is introduced to the field. There is satisfaction in working in close contact with people in a helping relationship. Some teachers enjoy the independence of working with a class of students without someone watching how they do their work.

People in this area tend to benefit from hands-on learning more than study. They perform better on the job than on school exams. They like to make their decisions based on their feelings. This feeling orientation helps them to be tactful and provide warmth in relations with others.

They enjoy variety but typically adapt very well to routine. They show compassion and have empathy in offering care to others.

Where Do Special Education Majors Work?

Special education majors, regardless of whether they work as special education teachers, most often work in the educational sector of the economy. More than 7 out of 10 persons with a bachelor's degree in special education work in some part of the nation's educational system. However, a substantial share of graduates of special education programs become self-employed, some providing freelance services to school districts or sometimes to families who want extra help for their children. However, many self-employed graduates of special education programs are engaged in activities that are unrelated to their major field of study while in school. About 1 out of 6 special education majors are employed in a private, for-profit corporation. Most often these individuals work in jobs that are not closely connected to their undergraduate major field of study. Few special education majors work for nonprofit organizations outside the educational field.

FIGURE 1

Percentage Distribution of Employed Persons with Only a Bachelor's Degree in Special Education, by Major Sector of Economic Activity

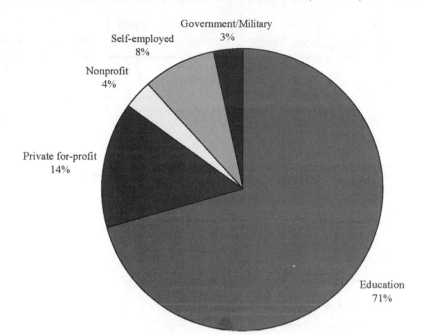

Occupations

College graduates with an undergraduate degree in special education are very likely to be employed in a job that is closely related to their undergraduate major. More than 70 percent of all employed persons with a bachelor's degree in special education say that their current job is closely related to their college major. Nearly one-half of all special education graduates with a bachelor's degree only are employed as special education teachers. About 11 percent work as elementary school teachers, and an additional 5 percent are employed as prekindergarten or kindergarten teachers. Thus, about two-thirds of employed special education graduates work as teachers. An additional 3 percent of graduates work in managerial and administrative positions, some within the educational sector.

About 1 in 5 special education majors are employed in a job that is unrelated to the undergraduate major field of study. Most often these individuals are employed in unrelated jobs because of what they perceive as limited pay and promotion potential in special education teaching. Others leave the field because their career interests have changed. Few work outside the field because they are unable to get a job related to special education.

Table 1
Top 10 Occupations That Employ Persons with Only a Bachelor's Degree in Special Education

Top 10 Occupations	PERCENT OF EMPLOYED		
	All	Men	Women
Special education teachers, primary and secondary	49.6	42.0	50.8
Teachers, elementary school	11.4	3.1	12.7
Teachers, prekindergarten and kindergarten	4.8	3.1	5.0
Accounting clerks, bookkeepers	3.1	0.0	3.6
Top- and mid-level managers, executives, administrators	3.1	6.1	2.7
Insurance, securities, real estate, business services	3.0	9.3	2.0
Other service occupations, except health	2.9	3.1	2.9
Other management-related occupations	2.4	4.9	2.0
Social workers	1.9	0.0	2.2
Secretaries, receptionists, typists	1.6	0.0	1.9

- Men with degrees in special education are somewhat less likely to work as special education teachers in primary and secondary schools than are women.

- Men are twice as likely to hold managerial or administrative positions as women with bachelor's degrees in special education.

- Nearly 1 in 10 men with a degree in special education work in insurance, stocks and bonds, or real estate sales. Women with special education degrees rarely work in these fields.

Activities on the Job

- Unsurprisingly, graduates of special education programs spend the greatest amount of time during the workweek engaged in teaching activities. Teaching, however, is not the sole task of special education program graduates.

- More than 90 percent report that they spend at least some part of the workweek engaged in some type of accounting or finance activity.

- About 1 in 3 special education graduates with a bachelor's degree are engaged in some type of managerial or administrative activity on the job.

▶ One in 4 special education graduates reports being engaged in some type of computer programming activity while on the job.

▶ Few special education graduates at the bachelor's degree level report that they are engaged in basic research activities.

Salaries

Special education majors have annual salaries that are among the lowest of all college graduates with only a bachelor's degree. The mean annual salary of persons with a bachelor's degree in special education is $38,300, while the average person with a bachelor's degree earns $54,100. This represents an annual earnings deficit for special education program graduates of about 30 percent in comparison to the average college baccalaureate holder. The relatively low annual pay of special education majors is the product in part of working fewer weeks over the course of the year. Most special education majors who work in the educational sector of the economy do not work as teachers during the summer and have a number of weeks off during the school year as well. Many persons who choose special education as a major do so with the knowledge that while their earnings are lower, they will have much more time off over the course of the year than other employed bachelor's degree holders. Thus, special education majors place a premium on this time that is not shared by other college graduates.

Over their working lives, special education majors earn considerably less each year than the average graduate with a bachelor's degree only. Between the ages of 25 and 29, special education majors earn about $27,700 per year. Because most teacher contracts provide pay increments on the basis of year of seniority and college credits earned above the bachelor's degree, the earnings of special education majors continue to increase through the pre-retirement years. By the time these majors reach the ages of 55 to 59, their earnings rise to $52,400 per year. Thus, the annual salary of graduates in the field increases by nearly 90 percent in inflation-adjusted terms over their working lives. Earnings are highest for special education majors who work in the private, for-profit sector of the economy; they report annual salaries of $46,500. Those employed in educational institutions earn $36,700 in salary per year.

Special education graduates who work in jobs outside the field have annual salaries that are well above those working in occupations closely related to their undergraduate major field of study. Those with a bachelor's degree in special education who work outside the field earn about 30 percent more per year than those employed in jobs that are closely related. However, a substantial part of this difference is attributable to differences in the number of weeks of work those in education-related jobs actually work over the year relative to those outside the education field.

FIGURE 2

Age/Earnings Profile of Persons with Only a Bachelor's Degree in Special Education
(Full-Time Workers, in 2002 Dollars)

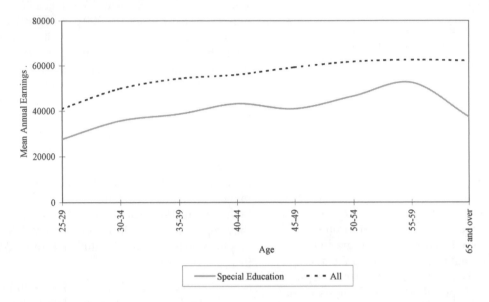

Table 2

Annual Salary of Full-Time Workers with Only a Bachelor's Degree in Special Education, Top 10 Occupations (in 2002 Dollars)

Earnings in Top 10 Occupations	All	Special Education
Total	$54,171	$38,333
Special education teachers, primary and secondary	$37,065	$37,145
Teachers, elementary school	$39,167	$37,668
Teachers, prekindergarten and kindergarten	$33,183	$26,474
Accounting clerks, bookkeepers	$32,380	$24,912
Top- and mid-level managers, executives, administrators	$74,051	$56,059
Insurance, securities, real estate, business services	$68,273	$70,923
Other service occupations, except health	$39,984	$35,020
Other management-related occupations	$51,921	$47,184
Social workers	$36,371	$29,314
Secretaries, receptionists, typists	$32,246	$21,042

- Top-paying occupations for special education majors include stocks and bonds and real estate sales jobs. Most special education majors employed in this area are men.

- Management and administration occupations also are relatively high-paying jobs that employ a substantial number of special education bachelor's degree holders. Although they are among the highest-paid of special education graduates, majors employed in these occupations earn considerably less than other college graduates employed in jobs with managerial or administrative titles.

- Special education majors employed as special education teachers earn an average salary of $37,100 per year. Those employed as elementary teachers earn $37,700, while those working as preschool or kindergarten teachers earn an average pay of only $26,500 per year, a rate of pay less than one-half that of the average pay of all employed bachelor's degree holders.

On-the-Job Training

Professional development is an important part of the career development of persons who earn a bachelor's degree in special education. Over the course of a year, nearly 80 percent of all those with a degree in special education participate in some type of work-related professional development activity including seminars, workshops, and other work-related training activity.

- About 70 percent of those who participate in a training activity say that they receive training in a specific skill or technique that is related to their immediate job duties.

- About one-third receive training that is designed to improve public speaking, writing, and communications skills.

- Most of those who participate in a training session of some type do so out of a desire to develop additional skills related to their field. Some see training as a way to advance within the field.

Post-Graduation Activities

Special education majors who earn a bachelor's degree are quite likely to continue their education and earn an advanced degree of some type. More than 4 out of 10 special education bachelor's degree recipients eventually earn an advanced degree of some type. The motivation for obtaining such a degree is closely tied to teachers' compensation systems across the nation that, in addition to seniority, base pay increments on additional degrees earned above the bachelor's level. Almost all the advanced degrees earned are at the master's degree level. Few special education majors go on to earn a doctorate or professional degree.

- Nearly 60 percent of those who earn a master's degree continue their studies in the field of special education. An additional 30 percent earn their master's degree in some other education-related graduate field of study.

- Few special education majors earn degrees outside the educational field. Those who earn a degree outside education most often earn a master's degree in a health-related field. Rarely do special education majors earn a graduate degree in business or a technical/scientific field.

The employment rate of persons with a special education degree is below the average of all bachelor's degree holders. Two out of 10 special education majors under the age of 65 are not employed. Most of these individuals are not looking for work. Instead, they have chosen not to work primarily because of family responsibilities. Almost none are jobless because they were unable to find suitable jobs.

Employment Outlook

Special education teachers are expected to be in great demand over the next decade as the demand for special education services rises sharply. While the number of employed bachelor's degree holders is expected to increase by just more than one-fifth through 2010, the number of employed special education teachers is forecast to increase by more than 30 percent, according to the most recent employment projections produced by the U.S. Bureau of Labor Statistics. Thus, special education teachers are projected to be one of the most rapidly expanding occupations in the American economy. Access to jobs closely related to the major field of study should remain strong for special education program graduates. Employment of non–special education teachers is expected to increase at a slower pace, especially for elementary teachers, although the demand for preschool teachers will grow at an above-average pace compared to all occupations in the economy.

Table 3

Projected Change in Employment in the Top 10 Occupations That
Employ Persons with Only a Bachelor's Degree in Special Education

Top 10 Occupations	Actual Employment in 2000 (000s)	Projected Employment in 2010 (000s)	Absolute Change (000s)	Percentage Change
Special education teachers, primary and secondary	453	592	139	30.7%
Teachers, elementary school	1,532	1,734	202	13.2%
Teachers, prekindergarten and kindergarten	597	707	110	18.4%
Accounting clerks, bookkeepers	1,991	2,030	39	2.0%
Top- and mid-level managers, executives, administrators	10,564	11,834	1,270	12.0%
Insurance, securities, real estate, business services	1,548	1,726	178	11.5%
Other service occupations, except health	9,652	11,287	1,635	16.9%
Other management-related occupations	4,956	5,801	845	17.1%
Social workers	468	609	141	30.1%
Secretaries, receptionists, typists	4,980	5,501	521	10.5%

Engineering

CHAPTER 28

Aerospace, Aeronautical, and Astronautical Engineering

Like all engineering, the aerospace field involves design, development, testing, and involvement in the manufacturing process. Aeronautical engineers develop new technologies for use in commercial aviation, air defense systems, and space exploration. They often specialize in such areas as structural design, guidance navigation and control, instrumentation, communications, or production methods. Or they specialize in such products as commercial planes, helicopters, spacecrafts, or rockets. Further specialization can involve aerodynamics, propulsion, thermodynamics, celestial mechanics, or acoustics.

Most jobs exist in California, Washington, Texas, and Florida. U.S. Defense Department expenditures play a major role in the availability of work in this highly competitive field. The expenditures also control the size of the field. If one desires to enter aerospace, the applicant needs to seek out institutions with a recognized accredited program and a good placement record for its graduates. A sound academic preparation in the fundamentals is what some employers want because these companies often prefer to give their own specific formal training. Specialized courses are applied aerodynamics, flight vehicle design, trajectory dynamics, and aerospace propulsion systems.

A person's interests follow the same ability patterns: the enjoyment of science, the conceptualization of design, and the institution of practical outcomes. As in many fields, some people seek concrete, immediate solutions; some enjoy forming more conceptual and abstract ideas; and others are challenged and respond creatively to brainstorming the solutions for research problems in groups. Teamwork may be a new orientation for some high school students and an important criterion in selecting a college or university where the teaching methodology follows a collective achievement orientation.

Aeronautical engineers value creativity, a good salary, prestige, intellectual stimulation, research, mathematics, and the opportunity to encounter varied scientific problems.

Many aeronautical engineers claim that teamwork is a critical skill. They prefer friendly work environments and are willing to work with others in using their ingenuity, imagination, and improvisation skills to arrive at quick solutions. They do, however, recognize different work styles of colleagues who may search for the answers through detailed probing and the need to be correct. Personal responsibility and conscientiousness are positive influences on a team and are valued by individuals.

Where Do Aerospace, Aeronautical, and Astronautical Engineering Majors Work?

Three-quarters of all employed aerospace, aeronautical, and astronautical engineering majors work as wage and salary workers in the private, for-profit sector of the economy. Two-thirds work in the private, for-profit sector of the economy as wage and salary workers for businesses and corporations, and 8 percent are self-employed in their own incorporated or non-incorporated business or practice. The government sector employs one-fifth of all aerospace, aeronautical, and astronautical engineering majors with a bachelor's degree. Only 1 in 20 works for educational institutions or for private, nonprofit organizations.

FIGURE 1

Percentage Distribution of Employed Persons with Only a Bachelor's Degree in Aerospace, Aeronautical, and Astronautical Engineering, by Major Sector of Economic Activity

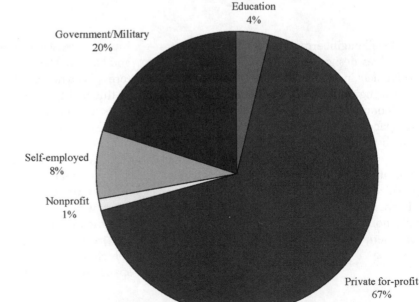

Occupations

Out of all employed aerospace, aeronautical, and astronautical engineering graduates, 46 percent work in jobs that are closely related to their undergraduate major, and another 31 percent are employed in jobs that are somewhat related to their field of study. The remaining 23 percent work in jobs that are not related to their undergraduate major field of study. Aerospace engineering majors cite a diverse array of reasons for working in jobs that are not related to their undergraduate major field of study.

When asked to list the most important reason for working in an area outside their field, nearly one-third said that jobs related to aerospace engineering are not available. A number of the jobs of aerospace, aeronautical, and astronautical engineering majors are contingent upon the level of defense spending by the government. The post–Cold War decline in defense spending by the federal government reduced the number of jobs for aerospace and aeronautical engineering majors in the government sector and in the private, for-profit sector in businesses, companies, and corporations that rely on defense contracts. About 22 percent of aerospace, aeronautical, and astronautical engineering majors cite pay and promotion opportunities, and another 15 percent say that a change in their career interests is the most important reason for working in an area outside their undergraduate major field of study.

Nearly 60 percent of aerospace, aeronautical, and astronautical engineering graduates are concentrated in 3 occupations. About 30 percent are employed as aeronautical, aerospace, and astronautical engineers. Another 15 percent are employed in transportation occupations, mainly in the air transportation sector. Top- to mid-level management, executive, and administration occupations are the source of jobs to 12 percent of aerospace engineering majors. Another 9 percent are employed in mechanical and other miscellaneous engineering occupations.

Table 1
Top 10 Occupations That Employ Persons with Only a Bachelor's Degree in Aerospace, Aeronautical, and Astronautical Engineering

Top 10 Occupations	PERCENT OF EMPLOYED		
	All	Men	Women
Aeronautical, aerospace, and astronautical engineers	30.3	30.0	34.5
Transportation and material-moving occupations	14.9	14.3	28.1
Top- and mid-level managers, executives, administrators	11.8	12.0	7.6
Mechanical engineers	5.0	5.3	0.0
All other engineers	3.9	4.1	0.0
Sales occupations, including retail	3.6	3.8	0.0
Other marketing and sales occupations	2.4	2.5	0.0
Construction trades, miners, well drillers	2.1	2.2	0.0
Personnel, training, and labor relations specialists	1.9	1.7	6.7
Electrical and electronics engineers	1.9	2.0	0.0

- Only 5 percent of all employed aerospace, aeronautical, and astronautical engineering majors are women. Women are somewhat more likely to be employed as aerospace, astronautical, and aeronautical engineers than men: 35 percent versus 30 percent.

- Women are twice as likely as men to be employed in transportation occupations. Whereas 14 percent of male aerospace engineering majors are employed in transportation occupations, 28 percent of women work in transportation occupations.

- Male aerospace engineering majors are more likely than female majors to work in top- to mid-level managerial, executive, and administration occupations and in mechanical and other miscellaneous engineering occupations.

Activities on the Job

- Fifty-three percent of all employed aerospace, aeronautical, and astronautical engineering graduates perform accounting, finance, and contractual duties as a regular part of their jobs.

- The same proportion—53 percent—engage in management and administration on a regular basis.

- About 45 percent perform computer applications, programming, and systems-development duties regularly.

- Thirty percent are regularly involved in activities related to employee relations, including recruiting, personnel development, and training.

- Applied research is performed regularly by 28 percent of aerospace, aeronautical, and astronautical engineering graduates.

The same proportion spend at least some time regularly on their jobs in product development by using knowledge gained from research for production of materials and devices.

- More than one-quarter are engaged in sales, purchasing, and marketing activities as a regular part of their jobs.

- Few aerospace, aeronautical, and astronautical engineering majors are regularly engaged in basic research activities, teaching, or professional services such as health care, finances, and legal services.

Salaries

The average annual salary of full-time aerospace, aeronautical, and astronautical majors with only a bachelor's degree is $73,600, a level that is 36 percent higher than the average annual salary of all full-time employed college graduates. Like most college graduates, the salary of aerospace engineering majors increases with age. This increase indicates that they get more productive and they earn higher salaries as they spend more time on the job. However, the salary increase of aerospace, aeronautical, and astronautical engineering majors is much steeper than the rate of increase among all college graduates. Their productivity rises more rapidly with age than the increase in productivity of all college graduates. Within all age groups, the average annual salary of aerospace engineering majors is considerably higher than the average annual salary of all college graduates.

- The annual average salary of aerospace, aeronautical, and astronautical engineering majors between the ages of 25 and 29 is $50,100. Graduates between the ages of 30 and 34 earn $60,000 annually.

▶ The average annual salary increases at a rapid pace as these engineers get older. The average annual salary between the ages of 45 and 49 is $94,500, and the salary between the ages of 55 and 59 is $98,200 per year.

▶ The average annual salary of aerospace, aeronautical, and astronautical engineering majors who work in jobs that are closely related to their major field of study is $77,600. Graduates whose jobs are somewhat related to their major earn $42,800 per year. The average annual salary of graduates whose jobs are unrelated to the major is $60,400.

▶ The average annual salary of self-employed aerospace engineering majors is $88,100. Government employees earn an average annual salary of $68,900.

Graduates employed in the private, for-profit sector earn an average annual salary of $74,200.

Except for sales and construction occupations that employ fewer than 6 percent of all aerospace, aeronautical, and astronautical engineering majors, the average annual earnings of these graduates are much higher than the earnings of all college graduates in each of the 10 occupations that are predominant employers of aerospace engineering majors. When employed as aerospace, aeronautical, and astronautical engineers, graduates earn an average salary of $69,700. The average annual salary of graduates employed in transportation occupations is $106,500, and graduates employed in top- to mid-level management, executive, and administrative jobs earn $89,800.

FIGURE 2

Age/Earnings Profile of Persons with Only a Bachelor's Degree in Aerospace, Aeronautical, and Astronautical Engineering (Full-Time Workers, in 2002 Dollars)

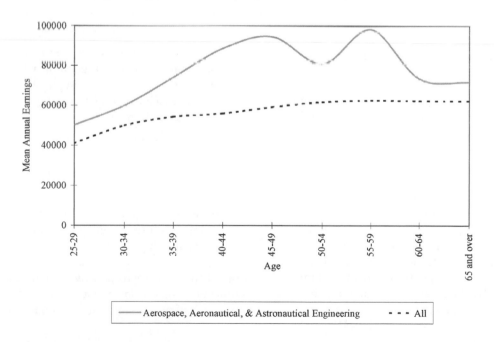

Table 2
Annual Salary of Full-Time Workers with Only a Bachelor's Degree in Aerospace, Aeronautical, and Astronautical Engineering, Top 10 Occupations (in 2002 Dollars)

Earnings in Top 10 Occupations	All	Aerospace, Aeronautical, and Astronautical Engineering
Total	$54,171	$73,605
Aeronautical, aerospace, and astronautical engineers	$68,111	$69,676
Transportation and material-moving occupations	$64,088	$106,464
Top- and mid-level managers, executives, administrators	$74,051	$89,781
Mechanical engineers	$64,905	$64,936
All other engineers	$62,544	$65,988
Sales occupations, including retail	$52,378	$41,653
Other marketing and sales occupations	$58,208	$99,927
Construction trades, miners, well drillers	$50,531	$24,883
Personnel, training, and labor relations specialists	$51,577	$52,262
Electrical and electronics engineers	$66,404	$66,735

On-the-Job Training

The career potential of a job is closely associated with the amount of work-related training on the job. Work-related training is regarded as an investment by firms because the training makes workers more productive. Firms that invest in their work force are more likely to offer pay increases and promotions to match the increasing productivity of their workers. Firms that do not invest in their workers are relatively less likely to offer pay increases and promotions. Nearly two-thirds of all employed aerospace, aeronautical, and astronautical engineering majors receive some type of work-related training on their jobs. The training rate among all college graduates is 68 percent.

▶ Of those aerospace, aeronautical, and astronautical engineering majors who receive some training during a year, 79 percent receive technical training in their occupational field.

▶ Only 22 percent receive training to improve their general professional skills, such as public speaking and business writing.

▶ Fewer than 40 percent of the training recipients receive management or supervisory training.

Nearly 90 percent of aerospace, aeronautical, and astronautical engineering majors who participate in some work-related training do so to improve their occupational skills and knowledge. About 56 percent are required or expected by their employers to undergo training. Increased opportunity for promotion, advancement, and salary increases is the reason for 51 percent of aerospace, aeronautical, and astronautical engineering majors to participate in work-related training. One-quarter participate in training to obtain a professional license or certificate.

Post-Graduation Activities

After graduating with a bachelor's degree, 35 percent of aerospace, aeronautical, and astronautical engineering majors proceed to earn a post-graduate degree: 31 percent earn a master's degree; 3 percent graduate with a doctorate; and only 1 percent earn a professional degree.

- Thirty-six percent of all master's degrees are earned in aerospace, aeronautical, and astronautical engineering. Another 36 percent of aerospace, aeronautical, and astronautical engineering graduates earn a master's degree in business management and administration. About 18 percent earn a master's degree in other major and miscellaneous engineering fields.

- Among those who earn doctoral degrees, 58 percent major in aerospace, aeronautical, and astronautical engineering and one-quarter earn their doctoral degrees in other engineering fields.

- About 48 percent of professional degrees by aerospace, aeronautical, and astronautical engineering graduates are earned in the field of law. Another 45 percent are earned in health-related fields.

Out of all aerospace, aeronautical, and astronautical engineering graduates less than 65 years old, 90 percent are employed. Only 4 percent are officially unemployed; that is, they are not employed and are actively seeking employment. The remaining 6 percent are out of the labor force; that is, they are not employed and are not seeking employment. Retirement is the reason for labor force withdrawal among 59 percent of aerospace, aeronautical, and astronautical engineering majors who are out of the labor force; 22 percent withdraw to enroll in school; and 21 percent of all labor force withdrawals among aerospace, aeronautical, and astronautical engineering majors are due to chronic illness or permanent disability.

Employment Outlook

According to the projections by the U.S. Bureau of Labor Statistics, employment in occupations that require at least a bachelor's degree is expected to grow faster than employment in other sectors of the American labor market. Between 2000 and 2010, the U.S. economy is projected to add 22.1 million jobs, yielding an employment growth rate of 15 percent. The employment growth projections in the top 10 occupations that are most likely to employ aerospace, aeronautical, and astronautical engineering graduates are presented in Table 3.

- The demand for aerospace, aeronautical, and astronautical engineering occupations is expected to grow by 14 percent between 2000 and 2010. Unless the supply of aerospace engineering majors declines, graduates will experience more than their current level of difficulty in finding employment in their undergraduate major field of study.

- Employment in transportation occupations—the second-largest employer of aerospace, aeronautical, and astronautical engineering majors—is projected to grow by 15 percent.

▶ The demand for top- to mid-level managers, executives, and administrators is projected to grow by 12 percent, a somewhat lower rate than the rate of growth projected for total employment in the U.S. economy between 2000 and 2010.

▶ The demand for mechanical engineers is projected to increase by 14 percent.

Table 3
Projected Change in Employment in the Top 10 Occupations That Employ Persons with Only a Bachelor's Degree in Aerospace, Aeronautical, and Astronautical Engineering

Top 10 Occupations	Actual Employment in 2000 (000s)	Projected Employment in 2010 (000s)	Absolute Change (000s)	Percentage Change
Aeronautical, aerospace, and astronautical engineers	50	57	7	14.0%
Transportation and material-moving occupations	10,088	11,618	1,530	15.2%
Top- and mid-level managers, executives, administrators	10,564	11,834	1,270	12.0%
Mechanical engineers	221	251	30	13.6%
All other engineers	253	254	1	0.4%
Sales occupations, including retail	15,513	17,365	1,852	11.9%
Other marketing and sales occupations	621	758	137	22.1%
Construction trades, miners, well drillers	7,451	8,439	988	13.3%
Personnel, training, and labor relations specialists	490	578	88	18.0%
Electrical and electronics engineers	288	319	31	10.8%

CHAPTER 29

Architecture and Environmental Design

Architects build ideas. They work in steps. First they listen to a client's ideas, requirements, and budget of what he or she wants to build or develop. Next they produce drawings, a report with environmental impact, and ideas about site selection for their client's review. After discussion with the client, alterations follow. Eventually, drawings are developed for construction with details of structural systems that include air conditioning, heating, electricity, and plumbing, as well as site and landscape plans. The plans can specify building materials. Architects follow building codes, zoning laws, fire regulations, and disability-access concerns and requirements. Buildings also must be functional, safe, and economical, and they must meet the needs of the architect's client.

Architects advise the client on building sites and prepare cost analysis and land-use studies. Architects participate in getting construction bids, negotiating the building contract, monitoring the progress of construction to assure specified standards for quality of work, and meeting time schedules.

Training programs are varied. One program is postgraduate. Another combines a pre-professional undergraduate degree with a graduate degree. The quickest and most popular way to get a license is to earn the 5-year bachelor's degree in architecture. However, because courses are specialized, these courses may not transfer easily to other degree programs if a person loses interest in the field. Typical courses include architectural history and theory; building design, including technical and legal aspects; professional practice; mathematics; the physical sciences; and liberal arts.

Although architects design buildings, their duties require engineering, managerial, and supervisory skills. Visual orientation–to conceptualize and understand spatial relationships–is an essential ability. Artistic or drawing ability helps but is not critical. The key is that architects must be able to visually communicate their ideas to clients. Creative as well as written and oral communication abilities are important. Also needed is the flexibility to work independently or as part of a team of engineers, urban planners, interior designers, or landscape architects. Most architects have proficiency and sophistication in computer-aided design and drafting (CADD).

Artistic, combined with scientific, interests highlight architecture. As well as creative interests, the field demands specificity, preciseness, practicality, and application of theory and standards. Highly developed abilities, combined with keen interest in the field, will help candidates deal with this competitive field.

Architects thrive on prestige and the recognition by others of their creative efforts. Architects are persuasive, and they definitely attempt to influence their clients to their own way of thinking. Architects are designers who work with their minds and are seen by others as intellectually bright. A high salary, variety, and diversion are important to them.

People in this field have rich imaginations and are naturally curious and intuitive. Other characteristics include being independent and having high energy for projects they create. However, architects often move on to something new without finishing the first project. The field itself is also in flux because styles and preferences change. This change requires the architect to keep up with trends and learn new skills, such as using new building materials or applying new construction technologies. Architects dislike routine; therefore, they may appear impatient at times. Some also may be quick to act, which results in making mistakes that others may view as careless. However, architects as a group are seen as bright and smart.

Where Do Architecture Graduates Work?

Architects are more likely to work in the private, for-profit sector of the economy than most other college graduates. They are quite entrepreneurial, with more than 1 in 4 working in their own business as their primary source of income. About 56 percent of architects work in wage and salary jobs, usually in engineering or architectural service firms or in the construction industry. Few opportunities exist for architects in the nonprofit sector. About 10 percent of architects work for a government agency—most often at the local level.

FIGURE 1

Percentage Distribution of Employed Persons with Only a Bachelor's Degree in Architecture/Environmental Design, by Major Sector of Economic Activity

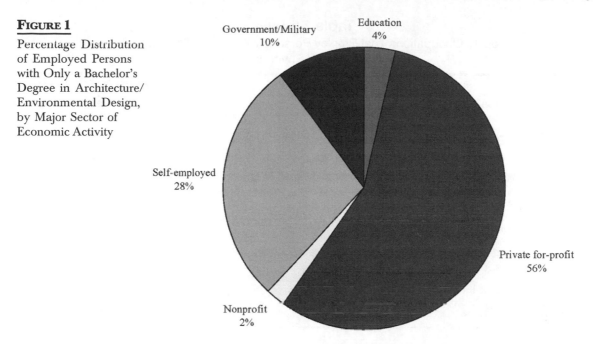

Government/Military 10%

Education 4%

Self-employed 28%

Private for-profit 56%

Nonprofit 2%

Occupations

Unlike many other majors at the undergraduate level, a clear relationship exists between the architecture major and the labor market. One-half of all persons who graduate with a bachelor's degree in architecture eventually become employed as architects after college. However, women who earn architecture degrees are somewhat less likely to work as professional architects than their male counterparts, although 38 percent of women with a bachelor's degree in architecture work as architects. Women with an architecture degree are somewhat more likely to work as artists and writers or in other creative fields than are their male counterparts.

Most graduates with an architecture degree at the bachelor's degree level are employed in jobs that are related to architecture. Only 15 percent of graduates work in jobs unrelated to the field. Of those working in jobs outside of the field, promotion and pay are the two most frequently cited reasons for working in another field.

Table 1

Top 10 Occupations That Employ Persons with Only a Bachelor's Degree in Architecture and Environmental Design

Top 10 Occupations	PERCENT OF EMPLOYED		
	All	Men	Women
Architects	51.8	54.7	38.5
Top- and mid-level managers, executives, administrators	13.0	13.7	9.5

(continued)

Table 1 (continued)

Top 10 Occupations That Employ Persons with Only a Bachelor's Degree
in Architecture and Environmental Design

Top 10 Occupations	PERCENT OF EMPLOYED		
	All	Men	Women
Sales occupations, including retail	4.1	3.4	7.0
Insurance, securities, real estate, business services	2.9	2.6	4.2
Drafting, including computer drafting	2.5	2.0	4.7
Other management-related occupations	2.2	2.4	1.4
Construction trades, miners, well drillers	2.2	2.7	0.0
Artists, broadcasters, writers, editors, entertainers, public relations specialists	2.1	1.1	6.6
Civil engineers, including architectural and sanitary	2.0	1.8	2.6
All other engineers	1.6	1.6	1.5

▶ One-half of all persons with a bachelor's degree in architecture are employed as architects, although men are more likely than women to work as architects.

▶ About 1 in 7 graduates with a bachelor's degree work in managerial and administrative positions. Many of these individuals remain in the building and design industries, but have advanced to more-senior management positions.

▶ About 7 percent of architecture-program graduates at the bachelor's degree level find sales jobs in real estate, insurance, and other sales-related areas.

▶ Some architecture degree holders work as drafters and as civil engineers.

Activities on the Job

Graduates with a bachelor's degree in architecture are heavily engaged in design administration and management activities as a regular part of their work.

▶ Nearly 80 percent of architecture graduates are involved in accounting, finance, and contracting as they oversee design and construction projects.

▶ Design of equipment and work processes are important elements of the work of architects, with 60 percent engaging in these activities on a weekly basis.

▶ Project management and administrative duties are also important tasks undertaken by persons with degrees in architecture. More than 70 percent of these individuals regularly engage in these activities during the workweek.

- A substantial number of persons with a bachelor's degree in architecture are engaged in the design of materials and devices.

- Few architecture graduates are engaged in basic research activities, but 1 in 5 is regularly engaged in some type of applied research.

Salaries

The annual salaries of persons with a bachelor's degree in architecture are above the average of all college graduates employed in full-time jobs. College graduates with a degree in architecture earn an average of $56,100 per year, a rate of pay about 4 percent greater per year than the average pay of all college graduates. Younger architects aged 25 to 29 earn an average of $37,500 per year. The rate of pay for architects grows rapidly up to an average of $66,200 between the ages of 50 and 54. This near-doubling in salary is reflective of the value of the years of work experience that older architects bring to their work. Clearly, the skills and abilities developed on the job by architects over the years are highly valued in the labor market.

- Self-employed architects have the highest salaries of all architects who work in full-time jobs, typically earning about $63,900 per year. They earn about $11,000 more per year than architects employed in a wage or salary job in a private, for-profit firm.

- Architecture graduates who work in educational institutions or government agencies earn about $52,700 per year.

- Bachelor's degree holders in architecture who work in jobs unrelated to their undergraduate major have much lower earnings than those who have jobs related to the major. Graduates employed in jobs related to the major have annual salaries that are more than 25 percent higher than those who work in jobs that are unrelated to the field.

The earnings of persons with a bachelor's degree in architecture differ sharply by the occupation in which they are employed. Graduates with a degree in architecture who are employed as architects earn an average of $58,100, a rate of pay about 7 percent above the average of all college graduates. Those architecture majors who are engaged in real estate and business services have the highest average annual salary of all persons holding this degree. Architecture graduates employed in the drafting occupations have earnings that are well below average.

FIGURE 2

Age/Earnings Profile of Persons with Only a Bachelor's Degree in Architecture and Environmental Design (Full-Time Workers, in 2002 Dollars)

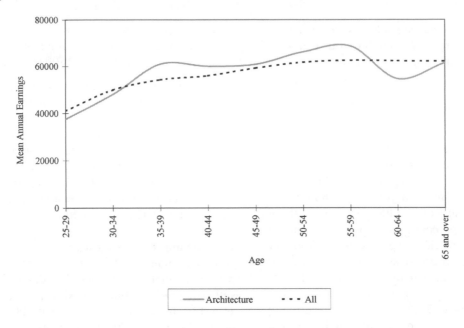

Table 2

Annual Salary of Full-Time Workers with Only a Bachelor's Degree in Architecture and Environmental Design, Top 10 Occupations (in 2002 Dollars)

Earnings in Top 10 Occupations	All	Architecture and Environmental Design
Total	$54,171	$56,096
Architects	$57,929	$58,105
Top- and mid-level managers, executives, administrators	$74,051	$61,635
Sales occupations, including retail	$52,378	$39,841
Insurance, securities, real estate, business services	$68,273	$72,689
Drafting, including computer drafting	$44,348	$39,600
Other management-related occupations	$51,921	$47,032
Construction trades, miners, well drillers	$50,531	$50,615

Earnings in Top 10 Occupations	All	Architecture and Environmental Design
Artists, broadcasters, writers, editors, entertainers, public relations specialists	$52,141	$41,783
Civil engineers, including architectural and sanitary	$61,821	$56,327
All other engineers	$62,544	$58,922

On-the-Job Training

Degree holders in architecture are somewhat less likely than the average college graduate to participate in some type of work-related training during the course of a year. Yet 6 out of 10 persons with a bachelor's degree in the field participate in some type of training activity. Self-employed architects are much less likely to engage in training in the prior year, while those employed by for-profit businesses are much more likely to receive training. Thus, young architects interested in developing skills will find many more training opportunities working for a firm.

▶ Most architects participate in training that is directly related to technical tasks found in their field.

▶ Training in management and supervisory skills is important to architecture graduates, with one-third receiving such training in the prior year.

▶ Architecture majors also frequently receive training in communications skills while on the job.

▶ Those who undergo training are motivated by a desire to improve their technical skills. Few graduates in this field engage in training in order to change jobs or for other motives.

Post-Graduation Activities

Most persons who earn a bachelor's degree do not go on to further education in order to earn an advanced degree. About 80 percent of all persons who receive a bachelor's degree in architecture do not earn an advanced degree. Among those who do earn an advanced degree, most go on to earn a master's degree of some type. Few architecture majors earn doctoral or professional degrees.

▶ Most undergraduates with a degree in architecture who decide to earn a graduate degree continue their education in architecture. About 75 percent of all master's degrees earned by those with a bachelor's degree in architecture are earned in the same field.

▶ An additional 10 percent of master's degrees earned by those with a bachelor's degree in architecture are earned in business.

▶ Only about 1 percent of architecture majors eventually earn a doctoral degree; about half of these are in the architecture field.

▶ A small proportion of architecture graduates earn a degree in law.

About 87 percent of all persons under the age of 65 with a bachelor's degree in architecture are employed, most in full-time jobs. Among those not employed, about one-third are unemployed and actively seeking work. The remaining two-thirds of those architecture majors who are jobless are individuals who are not actively seeking work. A substantial proportion of these individuals retired from work even though they are under the age of 65.

Employment Outlook

The job outlook for the architectural profession is quite strong. Between 2000 and 2010, the number of employed architects is expected to increase by more than 26,000. While overall employment levels are expected to increase by 15.2 percent, the demand for architects is expected to increase by 21 percent, a rate of growth about equal to that of all college graduates. Thus the demand for architects will grow at a rate 40 percent faster than the rate of employment growth projected for the economy as a whole. Creative jobs—such as artists and writers—that employ a substantial number of women architecture graduates are also expected to grow at a rapid rate. Table 3 includes projections of employment growth for those occupations identified in Table 1 as most likely to employ persons who hold a bachelor's degree in architecture.

Table 3

Projected Change in Employment in the Top 10 Occupations That Employ Persons with Only a Bachelor's Degree in Architecture and Environmental Design

Top 10 Occupations	Actual Employment in 2000 (000s)	Projected Employment in 2010 (000s)	Absolute Change (000s)	Percentage Change
Architects	124	150	26	21.0%
Top- and mid-level managers, executives, administrators	10,564	11,834	1,270	12.0%
Sales occupations, including retail	15,513	17,365	1,852	11.9%
Insurance, securities, real estate, business services	1,548	1,726	178	11.5%
Drafting, including computer drafting	213	255	42	19.7%
Other management-related occupations	4,956	5,801	845	17.1%
Construction trades, miners, well drillers	7,451	8,439	988	13.3%
Artists, broadcasters, writers, editors, entertainers, public relations specialists	2,371	2,864	493	20.8%
Civil engineers, including architectural and sanitary	232	256	24	10.3%
All other engineers	253	254	1	0.4%

CHAPTER 30

Chemical Engineering

Chemical engineering is a relatively small specialization. It is surpassed by electrical, mechanical, civil, industrial, and aeronautical engineering. Chemical engineering combines the knowledge of principles of chemistry with engineering in the production and use of chemicals. The work involves designing and developing manufacturing processes and supervising production. A current focus is to plan and test new methods of manufacturing processes to increase industrial output and to use existing resources safely and efficiently.

Chemical is a generic term, so the products addressed in this discussion cut across numerous industries. The chemicals are used to make paper, fertilizers, PVC pipe for plumbing, and printing ink; they are used to produce food; and they are used in the petroleum refining area. Chemical engineers frequently specialize in particular operations such as polymerization or fermentation and in areas such as plastics and pharmaceuticals. Chemical engineers also use electrical and mechanical engineering in their work. Research and development of new chemicals are a part of this field.

Chemical engineers are involved in biomedicines, agricultural chemicals, fibers, and synthetic fuels. Chemical engineers work on ways to reduce acid rain and smog, to recycle and reduce wastes, and to develop new sources of environmentally clean energy.

Common courses studied are organic and physical chemistry, thermodynamics, kinetics, heat transport, process control, advanced mathematics, and state-of-the-art computer-aided design.

Like other engineers, chemical engineers must be skilled in the basic sciences and high-level mathematics. They must also have good analytical reasoning and technical and spatial abilities. Because chemicals change their form—liquid to gas, for example—and different processes use pressure, heat, and cooling, some engineers find the field difficult because of the level of abstraction and computerized mathematical modeling involved.

Chemical engineers are most interested in scientific data and ideas and in their applications. They enjoy the exploration and the analytical and mechanical facets of their studies and work. Machines and manual activities afford the opportunity to satisfy the desire to achieve practical results.

Chemical engineers—because they are among the best paid of engineers—value income, prestige, intellectual stimulation, working with numbers, creativity, research, and the opportunity for change and diversity in their work.

Chemical engineers rely on logic and reasoning in making decisions. Because people are not predictable—a quality that chemical engineers expect in their work—interpersonal relations can be problematic. Chemical engineers are thorough, detail-oriented, persistent, and pragmatic. They prefer well-organized efforts.

Where Do Chemical Engineering Majors Work?

Almost 9 out of 10 employed chemical engineering majors work as wage and salary workers in the private, for-profit sector of the economy. More than 80 percent work in the private, for-profit sector of the economy as wage and salary workers for businesses and corporations, and 7 percent are self-employed in their own incorporated or non-incorporated business or practice. The government sector employs only 9 percent of all chemical engineering majors with only a bachelor's degree. Only 3 percent of employed chemical engineering majors work for educational institutions or for private, nonprofit organizations.

FIGURE 1

Percentage Distribution of Employed Persons with Only a Bachelor's Degree in Chemical Engineering, by Major Sector of Economic Activity

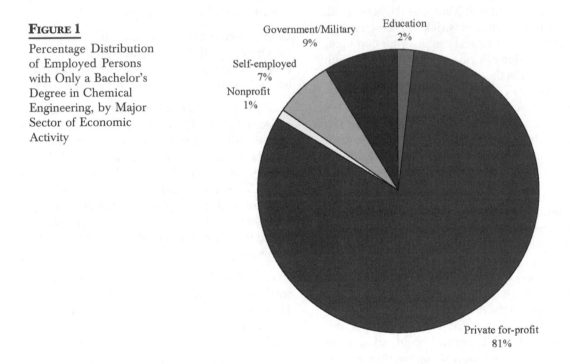

Government/Military 9%

Education 2%

Self-employed 7%

Nonprofit 1%

Private for-profit 81%

Occupations

The rate of related employment is high among chemical engineering majors. Nearly one-half of all employed chemical engineering graduates work in jobs that are closely related to their major. Another 38 percent work in jobs that are somewhat related to their major. Only 14 percent work in jobs that are not related to their undergraduate major field of study. Chemical engineers cite a number of different reasons for working in jobs that are not related to their undergraduate major field of study.

When asked to list the single most important reason for working in an area outside their field, 29 percent chose an unrelated job voluntarily because they wanted to change their career and professional interests. Nearly 18 percent are forced to work outside the field because of a lack of jobs related to chemical engineering. Better pay and promotion opportunities are cited as the most important reasons by 15 percent of chemical engineering majors who work in jobs unrelated to their undergraduate major. Family-related reasons are cited as the most important factor by 12 percent of the graduates.

Chemical engineering majors are concentrated in few occupational areas. Only 3 occupations employ 66 percent of all employed chemical engineering majors. A large proportion—37 percent—are employed as chemical engineers. Another 18 percent are employed in top- to mid-level managerial, executive, and administrative occupations. Nearly 12 percent of chemical engineering graduates are employed in other miscellaneous engineering occupations. Only 3 percent of chemical engineering majors are employed in miscellaneous management occupations, such as management analysts, purchasing agents, inspectors, and other regulatory officers. Between 2 and 3 percent of the graduates are employed in marketing and sales occupations and as chemists.

Table 1
Top 10 Occupations That Employ Persons with Only a Bachelor's Degree in Chemical Engineering

Top 10 Occupations	PERCENT OF EMPLOYED		
	All	Men	Women
Chemical engineers	37.4	39.0	29.5
Top- and mid-level managers, executives, administrators	17.5	19.3	9.0
Other miscellaneous engineers	11.7	10.8	16.1
Other management-related occupations	3.0	3.4	1.2
Sales occupations, including retail	2.5	2.9	0.9
Chemists, except biochemists	2.3	2.0	3.6
Other marketing and sales occupations	2.2	1.8	3.7
Other service occupations, except health	1.3	1.0	2.7
Insurance, securities, real estate, business services	1.1	1.0	1.7
Computer engineers	1.0	0.8	2.0

▶ Only 17 percent of all employed chemical engineering majors are women. Women are less likely than men to be employed as chemical engineers. While 39 percent of male graduates are employed as chemical engineers, only 29 percent of female graduates work in this occupation.

▶ Male chemical engineering majors also are more likely than female graduates to work as top- to mid-level managers, executives, and administrators. Only 9 percent of women are employed in these occupations, versus 19 percent of men.

▶ Sixteen percent of female chemical engineering graduates are employed in other miscellaneous engineering occupations. The proportion of male graduates who choose other miscellaneous engineering occupations is 10 percent.

Activities on the Job

Chemical engineering majors perform a variety of tasks on their jobs.

▶ Nearly 61 percent of chemical engineering majors engage in management and administrative duties on a regular basis; 58 percent regularly perform accounting, finance, and contractual duties as a part of their jobs.

▶ Applied research is performed regularly by one-third of all employed chemical engineering graduates. Nearly one-half are engaged in the design of equipment, processes, structures, and models; 43 percent spend at least some time regularly on their jobs in product development by using knowledge gained from research for the production of materials and devices.

▶ Forty-three percent are engaged in quality/productivity management duties; one-quarter are engaged in sales, purchasing, and marketing activities as a regular part of their jobs.

▶ About 37 percent of employed chemical engineering majors perform computer applications, programming, and systems-development duties regularly.

▶ Thirty-five percent are regularly involved in activities related to employee relations, including recruiting, personnel development, and training.

▶ Few chemical engineering majors are regularly engaged in basic research activities, teaching, and the provision of professional services.

Chemical engineering majors perform a variety of duties regularly on their jobs. However, when asked to rank job duties by the number of typical weekly hours spent on those activities, 21 percent placed management and administrative duties at the top, and 13 percent gave top ranking to the designing of equipment and processes. About 1 in 10 employed chemical engineering graduates spend most of their time during a typical workweek in applying the knowledge gained from research to the development of products and devices. More than 9 percent spend most of their time in a typical week in sales, purchasing, and marketing activities. Another 8 percent selected applied research as the activity on which they spend most of their time during a typical workweek.

Salaries

The average annual salary of full-time chemical engineering majors with only a bachelor's degree is $75,600, a level that is nearly 40 percent higher than the average annual salary of all full-time employed college graduates. Like most college graduates, the salary of chemical engineering majors increases with age. This increase indicates that they get more productive and can earn higher salaries as they spend more time on the job. The rate of increase—by age—in the annual salary of chemical engineering majors is much steeper than the rate of increase in the average salary of all college graduates. This rate of increase implies that the productivity of chemical engineering majors rises more rapidly with age than the productivity of all college graduates. Within all age groups, the average annual salary of chemical engineering majors is considerably higher than the average annual salary of all college graduates.

> The annual average salary of chemical engineering majors between the ages of 25 and 29 is $58,200. Graduates between the ages of 30 and 34 earn an average of $64,200 annually.

> The average annual salary increases at a rapid pace as chemical engineering graduates get older. The average annual salary of graduates from 40 to 44 years old is $85,200, and the salary of graduates from 55 to 59 years old is $89,500 per year.

> Access to jobs that are closely related to their undergraduate major field of study is associated with a sizable earnings premium among chemical engineering majors who are employed in full-time jobs. The average annual salary of graduates who work in jobs that are closely related to their major field of study is $81,400. Graduates whose jobs are somewhat related to their major earn

$74,700 per year. The average annual salary of chemical engineering graduates whose jobs are unrelated to their major is $53,500, a level that is less than two-thirds of the salary of their counterparts with closely related jobs.

> The two sectors that are predominant employers of chemical engineering majors also pay them the highest annual salary. Graduates employed in the private, for-profit sector earn $78,000 annually. Self-employed chemical engineering majors have the second-highest salary of all sectors in the economy. Working in their own incorporated or non-incorporated business or practice results in an average annual salary of $74,000 among chemical engineering majors. Government employees earn an average annual salary of $58,100.

The average annual earnings of chemical engineering majors are much higher than the average earnings of all college graduates in most of the 10 occupations that are predominant employers of chemical engineering graduates. When employed as chemical engineers, chemical engineering graduates earn an average salary of $76,300. The average annual salary of graduates employed in top- to mid-level management, executive, and administrative occupations is $104,200. The salary for employment in other miscellaneous engineering occupations among chemical engineering majors is $66,900. The 3 percent who are employed in management-related occupations earn an average salary of $81,100.

FIGURE 2

Age/Earnings Profile of Persons with Only a Bachelor's Degree in Chemical Engineering (Full-Time Workers, in 2002 Dollars)

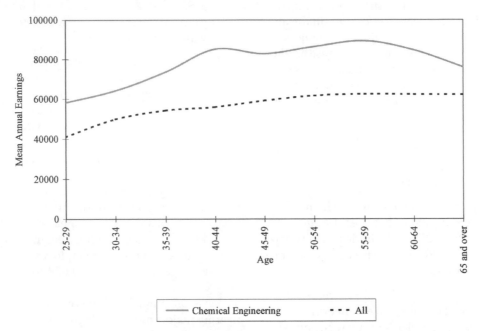

Table 2

Annual Salary of Full-Time Workers with Only a Bachelor's Degree in Chemical Engineering, Top 10 Occupations (in 2002 Dollars)

Earnings in Top 10 Occupations	All	Chemical Engineering
Total	$54,171	$75,579
Chemical engineers	$74,384	$76,311
Top- and mid-level managers, executives, administrators	$74,051	$104,246
All other engineers	$62,544	$66,933
Other management-related occupations	$51,921	$81,076
Sales occupations, including retail	$52,378	$55,697
Chemists, except biochemists	$53,934	$46,381
Other marketing and sales occupations	$58,208	$62,249
Other service occupations, except health	$39,984	$32,697
Insurance, securities, real estate, business services	$68,273	$44,078
Computer engineers	$66,859	$71,287

On-the-Job Training

The career potential of a job is closely associated with the amount of work-related training on the job. Work-related training is regarded as an investment by firms because it makes workers more productive. Firms that invest in their work force are more likely to offer pay increases and promotions to match the increasing productivity of their workers. Firms that do not invest in their workers are relatively less likely to offer pay increases and promotions. The rate of training among employed chemical engineering majors is higher than the rate for all college graduates. Three-quarters of all employed chemical engineering majors reported some type of work-related training on their jobs during the past year. The training rate among all college graduates is 68 percent.

- Of those chemical engineering majors who received some training in the past year, 76 percent received technical training in their occupational field.

- Fewer than 38 percent received training to improve their general professional skills, such as public speaking and business writing.

- Forty-six percent of the training recipients received management or supervisory training.

Nearly 93 percent of chemical engineering majors who participated in some work-related training did so to improve their occupational skills and knowledge. About 54 percent are required or expected by their employers to undergo training. Increased opportunity for promotion, advancement, and salary increases is the reason for 49 percent of chemical engineering majors to participate in work-related training. Almost 35 percent are engaged in training activities to learn skills for a recently acquired position.

Post-Graduation Activities

After graduating with a bachelor's degree, 42 percent of chemical engineering majors proceed to earn a postgraduate degree: about 30 percent earn a master's degree, 9 percent graduate with a doctorate, and 4 percent earn a professional degree.

- Out of the master's degrees, 39 percent are earned in the field of business administration and management, and 34 percent are earned in chemical engineering. About 15 percent earn a master's degree in other major or miscellaneous engineering fields.

- Among those who earn doctoral degrees, 60 percent major in chemical engineering, 15 percent major in physical sciences, and 10 percent earn their doctoral degrees in other miscellaneous engineering fields.

- Fifty-eight percent of all professional degrees of graduates with an undergraduate degree in chemical engineering are in the field of law. Another 39 percent of degrees are earned in health-related fields.

Out of all the chemical engineering graduates who are under the age of 65, 89 percent are employed. Only 2 percent are officially unemployed; that is, they are not employed and are actively seeking employment. The remaining 9 percent are out of the labor force; that is, they are not employed and are not seeking employment. Retirement is the reason for labor force withdrawal among two-thirds of non-elderly chemical engineering majors who are out of the labor force. More than 22 percent withdraw because of family responsibilities, and 18 percent do not want or need to work. Chronic illness or permanent disability is the reason for 8 percent of the labor force withdrawals among chemical engineering majors, and 7 percent of the withdrawals are the result of enrollment in school.

Employment Outlook

According to the projections by the U.S. Bureau of Labor Statistics, employment in occupations that require at least a bachelor's degree is expected to grow faster than employment in other sectors of the American labor market. Between 2000 and 2010, the U.S. economy is projected to add 22.2 million jobs, yielding an employment growth rate of 15.2 percent. The employment growth projections in the top 10 occupations that are most likely to employ chemical engineering graduates are presented in Table 3.

▶ The demand for chemical engineering occupations is expected to grow by only 3 percent between 2000 and 2010.

▶ The demand for computer engineering occupations, including hardware and software computer engineers, that employ only 1 percent of chemical engineering majors is expected to increase by 90 percent between 2000 and 2010.

▶ Employment in top- to mid-level managerial, executive, and administrative occupations—the second-largest employer of chemical engineering majors—is projected to grow at a somewhat below-average rate of 12 percent. This area will produce 1.27 million additional jobs between 2000 and 2010.

Table 3
Projected Change in Employment in the Top 10 Occupations That Employ Persons with Only a Bachelor's Degree in Chemical Engineering

Top 10 Occupations	Actual Employment in 2000 (000s)	Projected Employment in 2010 (000s)	Absolute Change (000s)	Percentage Change
Chemical engineers	33	34	1	3.0%
Top- and mid-level managers, executives, administrators	10,564	11,834	1,270	12.0%
All other engineers	253	254	1	0.4%
Other management-related occupations	4,956	5,801	845	17.1%
Sales occupations, including retail	15,513	17,365	1,852	11.9%
Chemists, except biochemists	92	110	18	19.6%
Other marketing and sales occupations	621	758	137	22.1%
Other service occupations, except health	9,652	11,287	1,635	16.9%
Insurance, securities, real estate, business services	1,548	1,726	178	11.5%
Computer engineers	757	1,436	679	89.7%

CHAPTER 31

Civil Engineering

Civil engineers design and supervise the construction of roads, buildings, bridges, tunnels, airports, water supply, and sewage systems. People can still see today the results of the earliest practitioners in this field: the Egyptian pyramids, the Roman Forum, and the aqueducts. Developed geographic areas that have already experienced industrial growth and expansion may have less demand for civil engineers. Engineers move from place to place as projects begin and end. Many projects are government related. In addition, a number of civil engineers assume management functions as top engineers. Specialties include structural, water resources, environmental, construction, transportation, and manufacturing.

Civil engineers analyze reports, maps, drawings, blueprints, tests, and aerial photography on soil composition, terrain, hydrological characteristics, and topographical and geological data to plan and design projects. They calculate costs and determine the feasibility of projects based on analysis of collected data, application of engineering techniques, and mathematical analysis. Civil engineers are involved in preparing modifications to reports and in writing specifications, construction schedules, and environmental impact studies. They also make on-site inspections and monitor progress to ensure conformance to plans, specifications, and safety standards.

The civil engineering curriculum follows a core of basic sciences and high-level mathematics. The disciplines covered include structural, environmental, transportation planning, and geotechnological engineering. Courses include structural mechanics, fluid mechanics, and environmental science.

The required courses and the solutions to problem-oriented examples used in instruction require analytical reasoning, logical application of theoretical principles, and creativity. The ability to adapt to new projects, work in groups, communicate, and write reports are additional requirements.

Civil engineers like to study science and mathematics, and they prefer to see concrete manifestations of their work. They are doers and thinkers with an acute sense of observation. Where mechanical and electrical engineers can focus on the project immediately in front of them, civil engineers are not afraid of the physical size or scope of a project. For example, civil engineers are not afraid of building a bridge across a very broad expanse of water versus working on an electrical switch.

Civil engineers value the use of imagination to discover new ideas, a high income, intellectual thought and reasoning, outside work, status, and variety.

The practical orientation of civil engineers will soon reveal a business orientation and a preference for organization, which enables them to achieve goals. They enjoy realism, memory for details, objectivity, cause-effect logical thinking, and a willingness to be critical. Because civil engineers often work beside bulldozer operators and crane operators, these engineers tend to be "down to earth" in their communications with others.

Where Do Civil Engineering Majors Work?

About 63 percent of all employed civil engineering majors work as wage and salary workers in the private, for-profit sector of the economy. One-half work in the private, for-profit sector of the economy as wage and salary workers for businesses and corporations, and 13 percent are self-employed in their own incorporated or non-incorporated business or practice. The government sector employs more than one-third of all civil engineering majors with a bachelor's degree. The remaining 3 percent work for educational institutions or for private, nonprofit organizations.

The rate of related employment is quite high among civil engineering majors. More than 63 percent of all employed civil engineering graduates work in jobs that are closely related to their major. Another 27 percent work in jobs that are somewhat related to their major. Only 10 percent are employed in jobs that are not related to their undergraduate major field of study. The latter group of civil engineering majors cite a number of different reasons for working in jobs that are not related to their undergraduate major field of study.

When asked to list the single most important reason for working in an area outside their field, 29 percent chose an unrelated job voluntarily because they wanted to change their career and professional interests. Better pay and promotion opportunities are the main factors in the decision of 19 percent of civil engineering majors who work outside their field. Nearly 14 percent are forced to work outside the field because of a lack of jobs related to civil engineering. General working conditions are cited as the most important factor by 10 percent of civil engineering graduates working outside their field.

FIGURE 1

Percentage Distribution of Employed Persons with Only a Bachelor's Degree in Civil Engineering, by Major Sector of Economic Activity

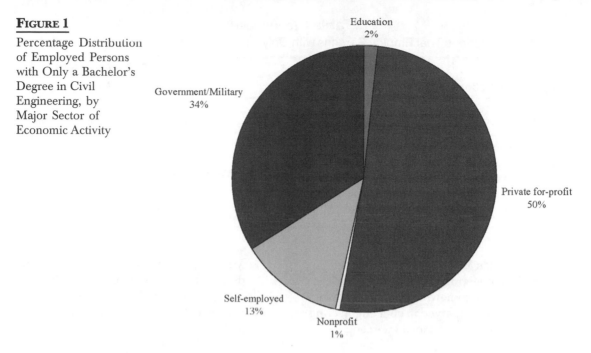

Education
2%

Government/Military
34%

Private for-profit
50%

Self-employed
13%

Nonprofit
1%

Occupations

Civil engineering majors are concentrated in very few occupational areas. More than one-half are employed in civil engineering occupations. One-fifth are employed in top- to mid-level managerial, executive, and administrative occupations. Another 6 percent are employed in miscellaneous engineering occupations, and almost 4 percent work in other management-related occupations. Just the top two occupations employ more than 7 out of 10 civil engineering majors.

Table 1

Top 10 Occupations That Employ Persons with Only a Bachelor's Degree in Civil Engineering

Top 10 Occupations	PERCENT OF EMPLOYED		
	All	Men	Women
Civil engineers, including architectural and sanitary	52.5	52.2	57.4
Top- and mid-level managers, executives, administrators	19.0	19.6	9.9
Other miscellaneous engineers	5.5	5.3	9.2
Other management-related occupations	3.6	3.6	2.8
Construction trades, miners, well drillers	3.1	3.3	0.0

(continued)

Table 1 (continued)
Top 10 Occupations That Employ Persons with Only a Bachelor's Degree in Civil Engineering

Top 10 Occupations	PERCENT OF EMPLOYED		
	All	Men	Women
Insurance, securities, real estate, business services	1.5	1.6	0.0
Sales occupations, including retail	1.2	1.2	1.4
Aeronautical, aerospace, and astronautical engineers	1.1	1.1	1.0
Mechanical engineers	0.9	0.9	1.1
Other marketing and sales occupations	0.8	0.8	0.9

▶ Fewer than 7 percent of all employed civil engineering majors are women. Women are somewhat more likely than men to be employed in civil engineering occupations: 57 versus 52 percent.

▶ Male civil engineering majors are twice as likely as female graduates to work as top- to mid-level managers, executives, and administrators. Only 10 percent of women are employed in these occupations versus 20 percent of men.

▶ Female civil engineering majors are more likely than male graduates to secure jobs in other miscellaneous engineering occupations.

Activities on the Job

Civil engineering majors perform a variety of tasks on their jobs.

▶ Slightly fewer than three-quarters of employed civil engineering majors spend part of a typical workweek in managerial and administrative duties and in accounting, finance, and contractual activities.

▶ More than 45 percent are engaged in the design of equipment, processes, structures, and models; 44 percent regularly engage in the management of quality and efficiency of the production process.

▶ Four out of 10 employed civil engineering majors perform computer applications, programming, and systems-development duties regularly. Another 40 percent are regularly involved in employee-relations activities, including recruiting, personnel development, and training.

▶ One-quarter are engaged in sales, purchasing, and marketing activities as a regular part of their jobs, and one-quarter provide professional services—such as health care, financial, or legal services—as a regular part of their jobs.

▶ One-fifth of all employed civil engineering majors regularly participate in applied research activities, and another one-fifth utilize findings from research for the production of materials and devices.

▶ Few civil engineering majors are regularly engaged in basic research activities and teaching.

Civil engineering majors perform a variety of duties regularly on their jobs. When asked to rank job duties by the number of weekly hours spent on those activities, a third placed management and administrative duties at the top, and 17 percent gave top ranking to the designing of equipment and processes.

Salaries

The average annual salary of full-time civil engineering majors with only a bachelor's degree is $66,100, a level that is nearly 22 percent higher than the average annual salary of all full-time employed college graduates. As with most college graduates, the salary of civil engineering majors increases with age. This increase indicates that they get more productive and can earn higher salaries as they spend more time on the job. The rate of increase in the annual salary—by age—of civil engineering majors is somewhat steeper than the rate of increase in the average salary of all college graduates. This increase implies that their productivity rises more rapidly with age than the increase in the productivity of all college graduates. Within all age groups, the average annual salary of civil engineering majors is somewhat higher than the average annual salary of all college graduates.

▶ The annual average salary of civil engineering majors between the ages of 25 and 29 is $47,000. Graduates between the ages of 30 and 34 earn $56,400 annually.

▶ The salary rises to $62,000 among graduates between the ages of 35 and 39, followed by another increase to $73,500 among graduates between the ages of 40 and 44.

▶ After this age, the salary increases at a moderate pace as civil engineering graduates get older. The average annual salary of graduates between the ages of 50 and 54 is $74,200 per year.

▶ The average annual salary of civil engineering majors who work in jobs that are closely related to their major field of study is $66,500. The annual average salary of graduates whose jobs are somewhat related to their undergraduate major field of study is $69,300. Civil engineering graduates whose jobs are unrelated to their major earn an annual average salary of $53,100.

▶ Civil engineering graduates who are employed in the private sector by for-profit businesses and corporations earn more than their counterparts employed in other sectors of the economy. Their average annual salary is $71,400. Government sector employees with a bachelor's degree in civil engineering earn an average annual salary of $61,500. Self-employed civil engineering graduates earn an average of $60,000.

FIGURE 2

Age/Earnings Profile of Persons with Only a Bachelor's Degree in Civil Engineering
(Full-Time Workers, in 2002 Dollars)

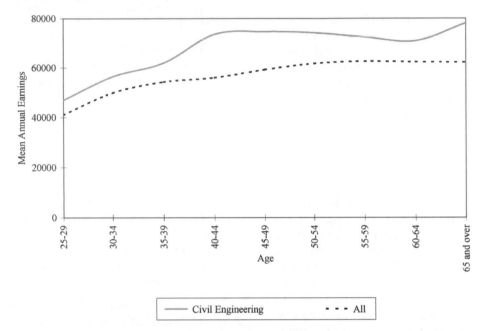

The average annual earnings in three out of the top four occupations that employ more than three-quarters of all civil engineering graduates is higher than the annual average earnings of all college graduates who are employed in those occupations. The average annual salary of civil engineering majors employed in top- to mid-level management, executive, and administrative occupations is $86,600, which is $12,600 more than the average earnings of all college graduates employed in that occupation. Graduates employed in civil engineering occupations earn $62,900. Those who are employed in other miscellaneous engineering occupations earn $62,400, and the average remuneration of the few civil engineering majors who work in management-related occupations is $63,900 per year.

Table 2

Annual Salary of Full-Time Workers with Only a Bachelor's Degree
in Civil Engineering, Top 10 Occupations (in 2002 Dollars)

Earnings in Top 10 Occupations	All	Civil Engineering
Total	$54,171	$66,126
Civil engineers, including architectural and sanitary	$61,821	$62,956
Top- and mid-level managers, executives, administrators	$74,051	$86,653

Earnings in Top 10 Occupations	All	Civil Engineering
Other miscellaneous engineers	$62,544	$62,427
Other management-related occupations	$51,921	$63,947
Construction trades, miners, well drillers	$50,531	$60,061
Insurance, securities, real estate, business services	$68,273	$39,237
Sales occupations, including retail	$52,378	$44,753
Aeronautical, aerospace, and astronautical engineers	$68,111	$73,133
Mechanical engineers	$64,905	$70,672
Other marketing and sales occupations	$58,208	$43,459

On-the-Job Training

The career potential of a job is closely associated with the amount of work-related training on the job. Work-related training is regarded as an investment by firms because it makes workers more productive. Firms that invest in their work force are more likely to offer pay increases and promotions to match the increasing productivity of their workers. Firms that do not invest in their workers are relatively less likely to offer pay increases and promotions. The proportion of employed civil engineering majors who engage in some type of work-related training is the same as the training rate among all college graduates. Two-thirds of all employed civil engineering majors reported some type of work-related training on their jobs during the past year.

▶ Of those civil engineering majors who received some training in the past year, 79 percent received technical training in their occupational field.

▶ Fifty-two percent of the recipients received management or supervisory training.

▶ Fewer than 27 percent received training to improve their general professional skills, such as public speaking and business writing.

Nearly 94 percent of civil engineering majors who participate in some work-related training do so to improve their occupational skills and knowledge. About 55 percent are required or expected by their employers to undergo training. Increased opportunity for promotion, advancement, and salary increases is the reason for 48 percent of civil engineering majors to participate in work-related training. Little more than one-quarter are engaged in training activities to learn skills for a recently acquired position. Less than one-fifth of all civil engineering majors who received some training cite licensing or certification as one of the reasons they attended training activities during the past year.

Civil engineering majors cite a variety of reasons for their participation in work-related training activities. When asked to identify the most important reason, nearly 70 percent cite the need to acquire further skills and knowledge in their occupational field, and 12 percent state that their employer required or expected employees to participate in work-related training activities.

Post-Graduation Activities

After graduating with a bachelor's degree, 32 percent of civil engineering majors proceed to earn a postgraduate degree: 27 percent earn a master's degree, 4 percent graduate with a doctorate, and only 1 percent earn a professional degree.

▶ Fifty-three percent of the master's degrees are earned in civil engineering, 22 percent are earned in the field of business administration and management, and 14 percent are earned in other miscellaneous engineering fields.

▶ Among those who earn doctoral degrees, 65 percent major in civil engineering and 20 percent major in other miscellaneous engineering fields.

▶ Sixty-two percent of all professional degrees of persons with a bachelor's degree in civil engineering are in the field of law. Another 22 percent are earned in health-related fields.

Out of all civil engineering graduates under the age of 65, 91 percent are employed. Only 3 percent are officially unemployed; that is, they are not employed and are actively seeking employment. The remaining 6 percent are out of the labor force; that is, they are not employed and are not seeking employment. Retirement is the reason for labor force withdrawal among 65 percent of civil engineering majors who are out of the labor force. Fewer than 12 percent withdraw because of family responsibilities, and 12 percent do not want or need to work. Chronic illness or permanent disability resulted in 10 percent of the labor force withdrawals among civil engineering majors, and 5 percent of the withdrawals were the result of enrollment in school.

Employment Outlook

According to the projections by the U.S. Bureau of Labor Statistics, employment in occupations that require at least a bachelor's degree is expected to grow faster than employment in other sectors of the American labor market. Between 2000 and 2010, the U.S. economy is projected to add 22.2 million jobs, yielding an employment growth rate of 15.2 percent. The employment growth projections in the top 10 occupations that are most likely to employ civil engineering graduates are presented in Table 3.

▶ The demand for civil engineering occupations is expected to grow by only 10 percent between 2000 and 2010. This growth rate was much smaller than the projections for the previous decade. Decreased environmental regulations at the federal, state, and local levels translate into a smaller need for civil engineers in the planning, execution, and monitoring of requirements of various environmental regulations.

▶ Employment in top- to mid-level managerial, executive, and administrative occupations—the second-largest employer of civil engineering majors—is projected to grow at a below-average rate of 12 percent. This growth will result in 1.27 million additional jobs between 2000 and 2010.

▶ Employment in other miscellaneous engineering occupations—the third-largest employer of civil engineering majors—is expected to remain constant over the next decade.

Table 3

Projected Change in Employment in the Top 10 Occupations That Employ
Persons with Only a Bachelor's Degree in Civil Engineering

Top 10 Occupations	Actual Employment in 2000 (000s)	Projected Employment in 2010 (000s)	Absolute Change (000s)	Percentage Change
Civil engineers, including architectural and sanitary	232	256	24	10.3%
Top- and mid-level managers, executives, administrators	10,564	11,834	1,270	12.0%
Other miscellaneous engineers	253	254	1	0.4%
Other management-related occupations	4,956	5,801	845	17.1%
Construction trades, miners, well drillers	7,451	8,439	988	13.3%
Insurance, securities, real estate, business services	1,548	1,726	178	11.5%
Sales occupations, including retail	15,513	17,365	1,852	11.9%
Aeronautical, aerospace, and astronautical engineers	50	57	7	14.0%
Mechanical engineers	221	251	30	13.6%
Other marketing and sales occupations	621	758	137	22.1%

CHAPTER 32

Computer Systems Engineering

Computer engineering is working with the hardware and software aspects of systems design and development. Its emphasis is on the building of prototypes; however, considerable overlap occurs with computer scientists who emphasize the theoretical and also the application of theory. Computer engineering generally applies theories and principles of science and mathematics to the design of hardware, software, networks, and processes to solve technical problems. Computer systems engineers design new computing devices or computer-related equipment, systems, or software. Computer hardware engineers design, develop, test, and supervise the manufacture of chips, device controllers, and storage capacity units.

Both hardware and software engineers may work on hardware device drivers and software packages that act as go-betweens for computer peripherals, such as modems, printers, and the computer. However, software engineers usually design and develop software systems for control and automation of manufacturing, business, and management processes. They are also called

software developers when they design software applications for customers. Software developers also work on analyzing and solving programming problems.

Educational programs can include course work in computer architecture, design of digital logic machines and circuits, hardware and software microprocessor interfaces, robotics, structure of large-scale computer systems, algorithms and data structure, software design and development, operating systems design, computer communication networks, compiler design, calculus, and physics.

The interests of computer systems engineers are heavily influenced by the power and versatility of the computer. Computers have the capacity to empower the creativity of individuals in unique ways. Computer technology even creates a cultural identity of "techies" among those involved. Some even claim that the computer has an addictive power. So this engineering specialty builds on scientific and technical interests to produce applications. Those involved

333

enjoy being imaginative, independent, and critical. They realize that their work can create a worldwide change in how many activities are done. As with all engineering areas, some will prefer to enter management positions and thus leave the technical aspects of the field.

Computer systems engineers value the intellectual stimulation of working with their minds. They achieve success through applying research findings and using mathematics to produce new technology. Developing and designing systems can also challenge theory as one works on the "cutting edge" in a discovery process. Receiving financial rewards is an important goal, as is enjoying the recognition and prestige of working in this highly visible computer field.

Engineers rely on facts, they study what worked before, and they prefer situations where the outcomes are immediate. They seek logical results by reflecting and analyzing their observations. They tend to be thorough and orderly. This style often translates into dependable behavior. They tend to be independent, individualistic, and decisive.

Where Do Computer Systems Engineering Majors Work?

A large majority of computer systems engineering majors work in the private, for-profit sector as wage and salary workers for businesses and corporations or in a self-employed position in their own incorporated or non-incorporated business. More than 80 percent work in the private, for-profit sector for businesses and corporations, and 4 percent of computer systems engineering graduates are self-employed. The government sector employs 8 percent of all computer systems engineering majors with a bachelor's degree. Educational institutions employ 4 percent, and the remaining 2 percent work for private, nonprofit organizations.

Almost all computer systems engineering graduates are employed in jobs that are either closely or somewhat related to their undergraduate major field of study. More than 70 percent of all employed computer systems engineering graduates work in jobs that are closely related to their major. Another 24 percent work in jobs that are somewhat related to their major. Only 6 percent are employed in jobs that are not related to their undergraduate major field of study. Most of the latter group of computer systems engineering graduates cite three main reasons for working outside their field of study: 40 percent could not find jobs in the computer systems engineering field, 15 percent wanted to change careers and professional interests, and 12 percent worked outside their field for better pay and promotion opportunities.

FIGURE 1

Percentage Distribution of Employed Persons with Only a Bachelor's Degree in Computer Systems Engineering, by Major Sector of Economic Activity

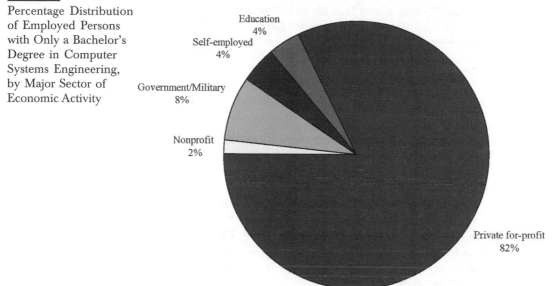

Education
4%

Self-employed
4%

Government/Military
8%

Nonprofit
2%

Private for-profit
82%

Occupations

Computer systems engineering majors are concentrated in very few occupational areas. Nearly one-half are employed as computer engineers; 11 percent work as computer systems analysts; another 11 percent are employed as computer programmers; and more than 6 percent are employed in top- to mid-level managerial, executive, and administrative occupations. These four occupations employ 76 percent of all employed computer systems engineering graduates. Most occupations in the list of top 10 predominant employers of computer systems engineering majors are in the computing or engineering field.

Table 1

Top 8 Occupations That Employ Persons with Only a Bachelor's Degree in Computer Systems Engineering

	PERCENT OF EMPLOYED		
Top 8 Occupations	**All**	**Men**	**Women**
Computer engineers	46.6	48.7	35.0
Computer systems analysts	11.4	11.1	12.9
Computer programmers	11.2	7.5	31.7
Top- and mid-level managers, executives, administrators	6.3	6.8	3.5

(continued)

Table 1 (continued)

Top 8 Occupations That Employ Persons with Only a Bachelor's
Degree in Computer Systems Engineering

Top 8 Occupations	PERCENT OF EMPLOYED		
	All	Men	Women
Electrical and electronics engineers	4.5	5.0	1.6
Other computer and information science occupations	3.6	3.7	3.1
Electrical, electronics, industrial, and mechanical technicians and technologists	2.5	2.9	0.0
Information systems scientists and analysts	2.3	2.7	0.0

Although females constitute only 15 percent of employed computer systems engineering majors, their occupational employment is quite different from that of their male counterparts.

- While almost one-half of male graduates are employed in the computer engineering occupation, only 35 percent of women work as computer engineers.

- Women are slightly more likely to work as systems analysts than men. Out of all employed female computer systems engineering majors, 13 percent work as computer systems analysts; 11 percent of men work as computer systems analysts.

- The biggest disparity in the occupational employment among male and female computer systems engineering majors is in the computer programming occupation. While only about 8 percent of men work as computer programmers, 32 percent of female graduates work as computer programmers.

- The disparity between male and female occupational employment also exists in the high-level managerial occupations, which employ 7 percent of male graduates and only about 4 percent of female graduates.

- Five percent of male computer systems engineering majors work as electrical and electronics engineers. Only 2 percent of female graduates are employed in these occupations.

Activities on the Job

Although they perform a variety of duties, the activities of most computer systems engineering majors on their jobs are focused on certain tasks.

- Nine out of 10 employed computer systems engineering majors perform computer applications, programming, and systems-development duties as a regular part of their job.

- More than one-half of employed computer systems engineering majors are engaged in the design of equipment, processes, and structures on a daily basis.

- Forty-six percent spend part of a typical workweek in managerial and administrative duties, and more than 30 percent regularly engage in accounting, finance, and contractual activities.

- Thirty-six percent of all employed computer systems engineering majors regularly undertake applied research activities, and 41 percent utilize findings from research for the production of materials and devices.

- Twenty-nine percent regularly perform managerial duties to oversee the quality and efficiency of the production process.

- One-fifth report that they are regularly involved in employee-relations activities, including recruiting, personnel development, and training.

- Few computer systems engineering majors are regularly engaged in basic research activities and teaching.

Computer systems engineering majors perform a variety of duties regularly on their jobs. When asked to rank job duties by the number of weekly hours spent on those activities, 58 percent place computer applications, programming, and systems-development duties at the top. About 8 percent spend most of their time on management and administrative duties. The designing of equipment and processes is given top ranking by 7 percent of computer systems engineering majors. Another 7 percent spend most of their time at work in the production of materials and devices.

Salaries

The average annual salary of full-time computer systems engineering majors with only a bachelor's degree is $70,100, a level that is 29 percent higher than the average annual salary of all full-time employed college graduates. The field of computer systems engineering is a relatively new field and is composed of many younger people. The median age of graduates is between 30 and 35 years. The average age of all college graduates is 44. In addition to the age difference between computer systems engineering majors and all college graduates, another distinguishing characteristic of this field is the rapidly changing skill requirements. The functions performed by older persons who are employed in the field of computer systems engineering may be different from those performed by their younger counterparts.

- The field of computer systems engineering is dynamic and is characterized by high entry wages. The average annual salary of graduates between the ages of 25 and 29 years is $58,000, which is $16,900—or 41 percent—higher than the average annual salary of all college graduates in that age range.

- Graduates between the ages of 30 and 34 earn $74,500, a level that is $24,700—or 49 percent—more than the salary of all college graduates in that age range.

- Because of the dynamic nature of the field, the age earnings profile of computer systems engineering graduates in older age groupings does not represent the age/earnings profile that today's graduates can expect over their working lives.

- The average annual salary of computer systems engineering majors who work in jobs that are closely related to their major field of study is $71,100. Those engineering majors whose jobs are somewhat related to their undergraduate major earn an average annual salary of $59,300. Very few computer systems engineering graduates are employed in jobs that are not related to their undergraduate major field of study.

◗ The annual average salary of computer systems engineering graduates who are employed in the private sector by for-profit businesses and corporations is $70,300. Government sector employees with a bachelor's degree in computer systems engineering earn a much lower average annual salary of $48,800.

The average annual salary of computer systems engineering majors who are employed as computer engineers is $75,700. Graduates who work as computer systems analysts earn an average salary of $53,100, and the average earnings of graduates employed full-time in computer programming occupations is $58,300 per year.

Employment of graduates in the top- to mid-level managerial, executive, and administrative occupations is associated with average annual earnings of $69,000. Computer systems engineering graduates who work in computer engineering and computer programming earn more than the average for all college graduates employed in those occupations. The average annual salary of computer systems engineering graduates employed in top- to mid-level managerial occupations and in computer systems analyst occupations is lower than the average salary of all college graduates employed in these occupations.

FIGURE 2

Age/Earnings Profile of Persons with Only a Bachelor's Degree in Computer Systems Engineering (Full-Time Workers, in 2002 Dollars)

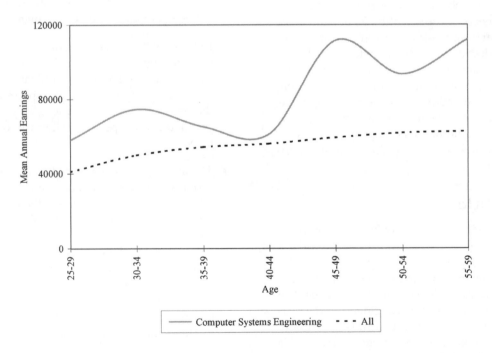

Table 2
Annual Salary of Full-Time Workers with Only a Bachelor's Degree in Computer Systems Engineering, Top 8 Occupations (in 2002 Dollars)

Earnings in Top 8 Occupations	All	Computer Systems Engineering
Total	$54,171	$70,084
Computer engineers	$66,859	$75,664
Computer system analysts	$59,818	$53,095
Computer programmers	$55,715	$58,261
Top- and mid-level managers, executives, administrators	$74,051	$68,961
Electrical and electronics engineers	$66,404	$63,242
Other computer and information science occupations	$54,228	$58,729
Electrical, electronics, industrial, and mechanical technicians and technologists	$49,128	$44,230
Information systems scientists and analysts	$60,005	$54,235

On-the-Job Training

The career potential of a job is closely associated with the amount of work-related training on the job. Work-related training is regarded as an investment by firms because it makes workers more productive. Firms that invest in their work force are more likely to offer pay increases and promotions to match the increasing productivity of their workers. Firms that do not invest in their workers are relatively less likely to offer pay increases and promotions. The rapidly evolving field of computer systems engineering requires graduates to "be on their toes" and to engage in work-related training even at a young age. Therefore, despite their younger average age, the proportion of employed computer systems engineering majors who engage in some type of work-related training is the same as the training rate among all college graduates, who tend to be older. Two-thirds of all employed computer systems engineering majors report some type of work-related training on their jobs annually.

- Of those computer systems engineering majors who receive some training, 88 percent receive technical training in their occupational field.

- Thirty-four percent of the training recipients participate in management or supervisory training.

- Fewer than 27 percent receive training to improve their general professional skills, such as public speaking and business writing.

About 93 percent of computer systems engineering majors who participate in some work-related training cite the need to improve their occupational skills and knowledge as one of the reasons to acquire work-related training. Increased opportunity for promotion, advancement, and salary increases is one of the reasons to partici-pate in work-related training for 57 percent of computer systems engineering majors. Fewer than one-half engage in training activities to learn skills for a recently acquired position, and 43 percent are required or expected by their em-ployers to undergo training.

When asked to identify the most important rea-son to participate in work-related training, more than 62 percent cite the need to acquire further skills and knowledge in their occupational field; 11 percent undertake training to upgrade their skills for a newly acquired position. In addition, 10 percent are required or expected to partici-pate in work-related training activities, and an-other 10 percent identify increased salary and better promotion opportunities as the most im-portant reason for participating in work-related training.

Post-Graduation Activities

After graduating with a bachelor's degree, 35 percent of computer systems engineering ma-jors proceed to earn a postgraduate degree: 32 percent earn a master's degree, and 3 percent graduate with a doctorate.

▶ A large majority of the master's degrees are earned in fields that are closely re-lated to their undergraduate major: 35 percent of the master's degrees are earned in computer systems engineering, 24 percent are earned in other miscella-neous engineering fields, and another 18 percent are earned in the computer- and information-sciences field. About 19 percent—or most of the remaining master's degrees—are earned in the field of business administration and manage-ment.

▶ Among those who earn doctoral degrees, 52 percent major in computer systems engineering, 38 percent major in the computer and information-sciences field, and the remaining 10 percent are split evenly between other miscellaneous engineering fields and mathematics.

Out of all computer systems engineering gradu-ates, 92 percent are employed. Only 3 percent are officially unemployed; that is, they are not employed and are actively seeking employment. The remaining 5 percent are out of the labor force; that is, they are not employed and are not seeking employment. A large part of the labor force withdrawals (62 percent) among computer systems engineering majors stems from family-related reasons. Another 22 percent cite the lack of desire or the lack of a need to work as the reason for their labor force withdrawal.

Employment Outlook

According to the projections by the U.S. Bureau of Labor Statistics, employment in occupations that require at least a bachelor's degree is ex-pected to grow faster than employment in other sectors of the American labor market. Between 2000 and 2010, the U.S. economy is projected to add 22.2 million jobs, which will yield an employment growth rate of 15.2 percent. The employment growth projections in the top 10 occupations that are most likely to employ com-puter systems engineering graduates are pre-sented in Table 3. Projected employment growth in some of these occupations considerably out-paces the overall growth of employment in the U.S. economy.

▶ The demand for computer engineering occupations is expected to nearly double between 2000 and 2010. The number of computer engineering jobs is expected to increase from 757,000 in 2000 to 1.44 million in 2010.

▶ Employment of computer systems analysts—the second-largest employer of computer systems engineering majors—is projected to increase by 60 percent between 2000 and 2010.

▶ Computer programming occupations—the third major employer of computer systems engineering majors—are projected to add 95,000 jobs between 2000 and 2010. This increase will yield a growth rate of 16 percent.

▶ Miscellaneous computer and information science occupations are projected to grow by 61 percent, from 203,000 jobs in 2000 to 326,000 jobs in 2010.

Table 3

Projected Change in Employment in the Top 8 Occupations That Employ Persons with Only a Bachelor's Degree in Computer Systems Engineering

Top 8 Occupations	Actual Employment in 2000 (000s)	Projected Employment in 2010 (000s)	Absolute Change (000s)	Percentage Change
Computer engineers	757	1,436	679	89.7%
Computer systems analysts	431	689	258	59.9%
Computer programmers	585	680	95	16.2%
Top- and mid-level managers, executives, administrators	10,564	11,834	1,270	12.0%
Electrical and electronics engineers	288	319	31	10.8%
Other computer and information science occupations	203	326	123	60.6%
Electrical, electronics, industrial, and mechanical technicians and technologists	519	582	63	12.1%
Information systems scientists and analysts	28	39	11	39.3%

CHAPTER 33

Electrical and Electronics Engineering

Electrical and electronics engineers design new technologies and products, write performance requirements, develop maintenance schedules, and supervise the manufacture of electrical and electronics equipment. Like other engineers, they test equipment, solve operating problems, and estimate the time and costs of engineering projects. The major areas in which people work are power generation, transmission, and distribution; communications, including the exploding wireless area; and computer electronics and electrical equipment manufacturing. Electrical and electronics engineering is foundational to all manufacturing, so it cuts across many areas, such as industrial robot-control systems.

Electrical engineering is the largest engineering specialty. It is a cyclical field affected by the impact of defense spending, such as in aviation electronics. A prime motivating force in the field is industry's drive to remain competitive in the world market. Electrical engineers also want to be involved in research and development, especially with computers and communications

equipment. Specific examples of technologies where electrical engineers have had primary roles are integrated circuitry, satellite communications, pacemakers, and microprocessors.

Course work in this field includes circuits and systems, electromagnetic field theory, digital systems, calculus, chemistry, and physics.

Electrical and electronics engineers are interested in both the scientific and technical areas of their field. They need technical and mechanical skills in order to relate theoretical procedures to practical applications. Some areas of electronics involve higher involvement in scientific interests. In these areas, people are often in technical positions and concentrate on developmental work. Electrical and electronics engineers enjoy being imaginative, independent, and critical. They identify themselves as scientists.

Electrical and electronics engineers value the intellectual stimulation of working with their minds. They achieve this goal through applying research findings and by using numbers to calculate probable outcomes. For some, the opportunity for creative endeavors and varied projects is a motivational tool. Some electrical engineers are content with less diversity in their work and enjoy using their hands in the production phase of this field. Important goals include receiving prestige and financial rewards.

Electrical and electronics engineers painstakingly accumulate their data. This process contributes to their dependability. By reflecting on and analytically studying their observations, they arrive at logical conclusions based on the facts. Because they make judgments so often in their work, they may appear to be determined and resistant to change. They can be very independent, individualistic, and driven once they have made a decision.

Where Do Electrical and Electronics Engineering Majors Work?

Nearly 85 percent of all employed electrical and electronics engineering majors work as wage and salary workers in the private, for-profit sector of the economy, either for businesses and corporations or as self-employed workers in their own business. More than three-quarters work in the private, for-profit sector of the economy as wage and salary workers for businesses and corporations, and 8 percent are self-employed in their own business. The government sector employs 12 percent of all electrical and electronics engineering majors with a bachelor's degree.

The rate of related employment is quite high among electrical and electronics engineering majors. Almost 55 percent of all employed electrical and electronics engineering graduates work in jobs that are closely related to their major. Another 34 percent work in jobs that are somewhat related to their major. Only 11 percent are employed in jobs that are not related to their undergraduate major field of study. The latter group of electrical and electronics engineering majors cite a number of different reasons for working in jobs that are not related to their undergraduate major field of study. One-half cite better pay and promotion opportunities as one reason for working outside their undergraduate field of study. The same proportion said that a change in career and professional interests is a factor that influenced their decision to work outside their field of study. Nearly 40 percent of electrical and electronics engineering majors are forced to work outside their major field of study because they are unable to find jobs related to electrical and electronics engineering. About the same proportion cite job location as one of the reasons for working outside their field of study.

When asked to list the single most important reason for working in an area outside their field, nearly one-quarter cite their inability to find jobs that are not related to their undergraduate major. About 21 percent choose an unrelated job voluntarily because they want to change their career and professional interests. Better pay and promotion opportunities are important factors in the decision of 18 percent of electrical and electronics engineering majors who work outside their field.

FIGURE 1

Percentage Distribution of Employed Persons with Only a Bachelor's Degree in Electrical and Electronics Engineering, by Major Sector of Economic Activity

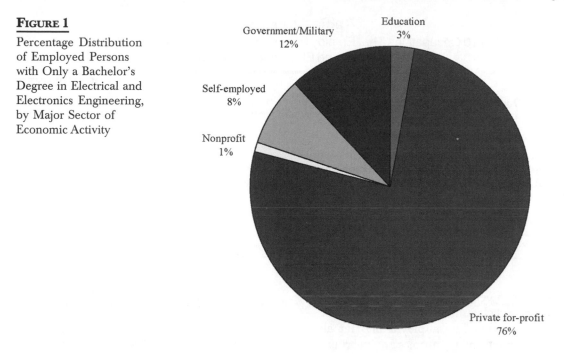

Government/Military
12%

Education
3%

Self-employed
8%

Nonprofit
1%

Private for-profit
76%

Occupations

Electrical and electronics engineering majors are concentrated in very few occupational areas. More than 70 percent are employed in four occupations: 44 percent are employed as electrical or electronics engineers; 13 percent are employed in top- to mid-level managerial, executive, and administrative occupations; another 10 percent are employed in miscellaneous engineering-related jobs such as computer engineers; and 4 percent work in other miscellaneous engineering occupations.

Table 1

Top 10 Occupations That Employ Persons with Only a Bachelor's Degree in Electrical and Electronics Engineering

Top 10 Occupations	PERCENT OF EMPLOYED		
	All	Men	Women
Electrical and electronics engineers	44.1	44.4	38.6
Top- and mid-level managers, executives, administrators	12.9	13.5	3.2
Computer engineers	10.0	9.6	17.3
Other miscellaneous engineers	4.3	4.2	4.9
Other management-related occupations	2.6	2.6	1.3

(continued)

345

Table 1 (continued)
Top 10 Occupations That Employ Persons with Only a Bachelor's Degree in Electrical and Electronics Engineering

Top 10 Occupations	PERCENT OF EMPLOYED		
	All	Men	Women
Sales occupations, including retail	2.5	2.4	4.0
Other marketing and sales occupations	1.9	1.9	1.9
Electrical, electronics, industrial, and mechanical technicians and technologists	1.8	1.7	3.3
Computer programmers	1.8	1.8	2.3
Aeronautical, aerospace, and astronautical engineers	1.8	1.8	1.3

▶ Only 5 percent of all employed electrical and electronics engineering majors are women. The employment of female electrical and electronics engineering majors is somewhat less concentrated than their male counterparts. Women are somewhat less likely than men to be employed as electrical and electronics engineers. While 44 percent of men are employed in this occupation, only 39 percent of females secure jobs as electrical and electronics engineers.

▶ Male electrical and electronics engineering majors are more likely than female graduates to work as top- to mid-level managers, executives, and administrators. While 14 percent of male graduates are employed in these occupations, only 3 percent of women are employed in these managerial occupations.

▶ Female electrical and electronics engineering majors are considerably more likely than male graduates to secure jobs in computer engineering occupations: 17 percent versus 10 percent.

Activities on the Job

Electrical and electronics engineering majors perform a variety of tasks on their jobs.

▶ More than 60 percent of employed electrical and electronics engineering majors perform computer applications, programming, and systems-development duties regularly.

▶ About 54 percent are engaged in the design of equipment, processes, structures, and models. The same proportion regularly engage in managerial and administrative duties at their jobs.

▶ One-half of all employed electrical and electronics engineering majors also perform duties in accounting, finance, and contracts during a typical workweek.

▶ Just less than 40 percent are engaged in the design of equipment, processes, structures, and models.

▶ Three out of 10 perform managerial duties related to overseeing the quality and efficiency of the production process.

And the same proportion engage in employee-relations activities, including recruiting, personnel development, and training. An equal proportion also regularly engage in applied research activities at their jobs.

▶ Few electrical and electronics engineering majors are regularly engaged in basic research activities and teaching.

Electrical and electronics engineering majors perform a variety of duties regularly on their jobs. When asked to rank job duties by the number of weekly hours spent on those activities, 20 percent place computer applications, programming, and systems-development duties at the top; 16 percent spend most of their time designing equipment and processes; and another 16 percent give top ranking to their managerial and administrative duties.

Salaries

The average annual salary of full-time electrical and electronics engineering majors with only a bachelor's degree is $69,000, a level that is nearly 27 percent higher than the average annual salary of all full-time employed college graduates. Like most college graduates, the salary of electrical and electronics engineering majors increases with age. This increase indicates that they get more productive and can earn higher salaries as they spend more time on the job. The rate of increase in the annual salary as the engineer gets older is somewhat steeper than the rate of increase in the average salary of all college graduates. This increase implies that productivity rises more rapidly with age than the increase in the productivity of all college graduates. Within all age groups, the average annual salary of electrical and electronics engineering majors is higher than the average annual salary of all college graduates.

▶ The annual average salary of electrical and electronics engineering majors between the ages of 25 and 29 is $52,700. Graduates between the ages of 30 and 34 earn $63,800 annually.

▶ The salary rises to $67,900 among graduates between the ages of 35 and 39, followed by another increase to $75,200 among those 40 to 44 years old.

▶ After peaking at a level of $78,700 for those 45 to 49 years old, the average annual salary gradually declines.

Access to jobs related to their undergraduate field of study is associated with a sizable earnings premium among electrical and electronics engineering majors. The average annual salary of graduates who work in jobs that are closely related to their major field of study is $71,500. The annual average salary of graduates whose jobs are somewhat related to their undergraduate major field of study is $69,400. Electrical and electronics engineering graduates whose jobs are unrelated to their major earn an annual average salary of $53,400.

Electrical and electronics engineering graduates who are employed in the private sector by for-profit businesses and corporations earn more than their counterparts employed in other sectors of the economy. Their average annual salary is $70,600. Government sector employees with a bachelor's degree in electrical and electronics engineering earn an average annual salary of $65,600. Self-employed graduates earn an average annual salary of $66,100.

The average annual earnings of electrical and electronics engineering majors in the top 10 occupations that employ them are higher than the annual average earnings of all college graduates who are employed in those occupations. The average annual salary of majors employed as electrical and electronics engineers is $67,300.

Electrical and electronics engineering graduates who work in top- to mid-level management, executive, and administrative occupations earn an annual salary of $92,600, which is $18,500– or 25 percent–higher than the average earnings of all college graduates employed in that occupation. Computer engineers and other miscellaneous engineering occupations pay higher salaries to electrical and electronics engineering majors than to all college graduates employed in those engineering occupations.

FIGURE 2

Age/Earnings Profile of Persons with Only a Bachelor's Degree in Electrical and Electronics Engineering (Full-Time Workers, in 2002 Dollars)

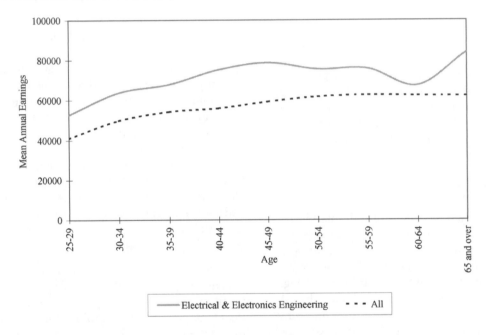

Table 2

Annual Salary of Full-Time Workers with Only a Bachelor's Degree in Electrical and Electronics Engineering, Top 10 Occupations (in 2002 Dollars)

Earnings in Top 10 Occupations	All	Electrical and Electronics Engineering
Total	$54,171	$68,977
Electrical and electronics engineers	$66,404	$67,333
Top- and mid-level managers, executives, administrators	$74,051	$92,629
Computer engineers	$66,859	$68,898
All other engineers	$62,544	$69,870

Earnings in Top 10 Occupations	All	Electrical and Electronics Engineering
Other management-related occupations	$51,921	$66,751
Sales occupations, including retail	$52,378	$61,544
Other marketing and sales occupations	$58,208	$90,256
Electrical, electronics, industrial, and mechanical technicians and technologists	$49,128	$50,303
Computer programmers	$55,715	$67,095
Aeronautical, aerospace, and astronautical engineers	$68,111	$73,577

On-the-Job Training

The career potential of a job is closely associated with the amount of work-related training on the job. Work-related training is regarded as an investment by firms because it makes workers more productive. Firms that invest in their work force are more likely to offer pay increases and promotions to match the increasing productivity of their workers. Firms that do not invest in their workers are less likely to offer pay increases and promotions. The proportion of employed electrical and electronics engineering majors who engage in some type of work-related training is about the same as the training rate among all college graduates. Two-thirds of all employed electrical and electronics engineering majors report some type of work-related training on their jobs during the past year.

- Of those electrical and electronics engineering majors who received some training in the past year, 82 percent received technical training in their occupational field.

- Thirty-eight percent of the training recipients received management or supervisory training.

- Fewer than 29 percent received training to improve their general professional skills, such as public speaking and business writing.

Nearly 93 percent of electrical and electronics engineering majors who participate in some work-related training do so to improve their occupational skills and knowledge. More than one-half are required or expected by their employers to undergo training. Increased opportunity for promotion, advancement, and salary increases is the reason to participate in work-related training among nearly one-half of electrical and electronics engineering majors. One-third are engaged in training activities to learn skills for a recently acquired position. And 10 percent of electrical and electronics engineering majors who received some training cite licensing or certification as one of the reasons they attended training activities during the past year.

Electrical and electronics engineering majors cite a variety of reasons for their participation in work-related training activities. When asked to identify the most important reason, nearly 70 percent cite the need to acquire further skills and knowledge in their occupational field. And 11 percent state that their employer required or expected employees to participate in work-related training activities.

Post-Graduation Activities

After graduating with a bachelor's degree, 35 percent of electrical and electronics engineering majors proceed to earn a postgraduate degree: 29 percent earn a master's degree, 5 percent graduate with a doctorate, and only 2 percent earn a professional degree.

▶ One-half of the master's degrees are earned in electrical and electronics engineering, 27 percent are earned in the field of business administration and management, and 6 percent of all master's degrees are earned in the field of computer and information sciences.

▶ Among those who earn doctoral degrees, 63 percent major in electrical and electronics engineering, 10 percent major in miscellaneous engineering fields, 8 percent major in computer and information sciences, and 7 percent major in physical sciences.

▶ Ten percent of all professional degrees are in the field of law. Another 26 percent are earned in health-related fields.

Out of all electrical and electronics engineering graduates under the age of 65, 89 percent are employed. Only 4 percent are officially unemployed; that is, they are not employed and are actively seeking employment. The remaining 7 percent are out of the labor force; that is, they are not employed and are not seeking employment. Retirement is one of the reasons for labor force withdrawal among 61 percent of electrical and electronics engineering majors who are out of the labor force. Fewer than 9 percent withdraw because of family responsibilities, and 13 percent do not want or need to work. Chronic illness or permanent disability resulted in 11 percent of the labor force withdrawals among non-elderly electrical and electronics engineering graduates, and 12 percent of the withdrawals are the result of enrollment in school.

Employment Outlook

According to the projections by the U.S. Bureau of Labor Statistics, employment in occupations that require at least a bachelor's degree is expected to grow faster than employment in other sectors of the American labor market. Between 2000 and 2010, the U.S. economy is projected to add 22.2 million jobs. This increase will yield an employment growth rate of 15.2 percent. The employment growth projections in the top 10 occupations that are most likely to employ electrical and electronics engineering graduates are presented in Table 3.

▶ Between 2000 and 2010, the demand for electrical and electronics engineering occupations is expected to grow by 31,000 jobs, yielding a growth rate of 11 percent.

▶ Employment in top- to mid-level managerial, executive, and administrative occupations—the second-largest employer of electrical and electronics engineering majors—is projected to grow at a rate of 12 percent. This growth will result in 1.27 million additional jobs between 2000 and 2010.

▶ Computer engineering occupations—the third-largest employer of electrical and electronics engineering majors—are expected to grow by 90 percent between 2000 and 2010 with the addition of 679,000 jobs.

Table 3
Projected Change in Employment in the Top 10 Occupations That Employ
Persons with Only a Bachelor's Degree in Electrical and Electronics Engineering

Top 10 Occupations	Actual Employment in 2000 (000s)	Projected Employment in 2010 (000s)	Absolute Change (000s)	Percentage Change
Electrical and electronics engineers	288	319	31	10.8%
Top- and mid-level managers, executives, administrators	10,564	11,834	1,270	12.0%
Computer engineers	757	1,436	679	89.7%
All other engineers	253	254	1	0.4%
Other management-related occupations	4,956	5,801	845	17.1%
Sales occupations, including retail	15,513	17,365	1,852	11.9%
Other marketing and sales occupations	621	758	137	22.1%
Electrical, electronics, industrial, and mechanical technicians and technologists	519	582	63	12.1%
Computer programmers	585	680	95	16.2%
Aeronautical, aerospace, and astronautical engineers	50	57	7	14.0%

CHAPTER 34

Industrial Engineering

Industrial engineering is the study that determines the most effective ways for an organization to use the basic components of production—people, machines, materials, information, and energy—to make or process a product. Industrial engineers link management and operations. Industrial engineers are more concerned with increasing productivity through the management of people, organizational policies, procedures, and technology than are engineers in other specialties, who generally work more with products or processes.

The main function of industrial engineers is to make a high-quality product as efficiently as possible. They do this by carefully studying the product and its requirements of design, manufacturing, and information systems, and they use mathematical analysis and modeling methods, such as operations research, to seek the best solutions to meet the requirements. They develop management-control systems to aid in financial planning and cost analysis, they design production planning and control systems to coordinate activities and monitor quality control, and they design or improve systems for the physical distribution of goods and services. Industrial engineers conduct surveys to find plant locations with the best combinations of raw materials, transportation, and costs. They also develop wage and salary administration systems and job evaluation programs.

Courses taken by industrial engineers are production engineering, work management, plant layout, work measurement, labor law, cost analysis, and statistics.

Industrial engineers are interested in business first and then in scientific and technical areas, with a hands-on focus on how something is done. By the time they are employed, industrial engineers learn to have a strong business orientation rather than a scientific focus, as a mechanical or an electrical engineer would have. As with many engineering specialties, the field demands a skill and interest in knowing how operations are performed.

The priorities of industrial engineers include making a good salary, being recognized in a leadership position, having prestige within the organization, being stimulated by problem solving, and enjoying the variety of different tasks to study and make recommendations.

A characteristic of industrial engineers includes self-confidence, which comes from collecting facts and observing actual operations. While appearing good natured, they follow proven logic and reasoning—based on their keen sense of observation—rather than following their feelings.

They examine each step of an operation and know who is supposed to do what. They are critical and systematic. They can be seen as very mechanical, impersonal, and impatient when they are confronted with excuses for poor performance. They are very demanding and tough, and they enjoy being the boss.

Where Do Industrial Engineering Majors Work?

A large majority of all employed industrial engineering majors work as wage and salary workers in the private, for-profit sector of the economy. As many as 7 out of 10 work in the private, for-profit sector of the economy as wage and salary workers for businesses and corporations, and 16 percent are self-employed in their own incorporated or non-incorporated business or practice. The government sector employs 8 percent of all industrial engineering majors with a bachelor's degree. Educational institutions employ 5 percent of industrial engineering graduates with only a bachelor's degree.

FIGURE 1

Percentage Distribution of Employed Persons with Only a Bachelor's Degree in Industrial Engineering, by Major Sector of Economic Activity

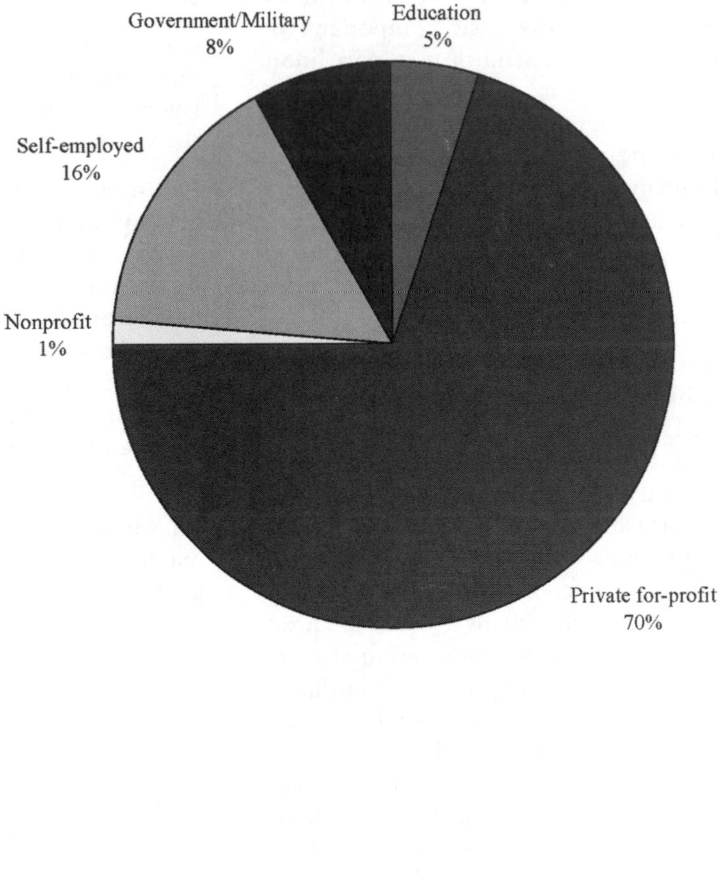

Government/Military 8%

Education 5%

Self-employed 16%

Nonprofit 1%

Private for-profit 70%

Occupations

Industrial engineering majors have a strong preference for business and management, and they gravitate toward jobs that are more management oriented. Relative to other engineering graduates, fewer industrial engineering graduates are employed in jobs that are closely related to their undergraduate major field of study. Only 35 percent are employed in jobs that are closely related to industrial engineering. A somewhat higher proportion, 45 percent, are employed in jobs that are somewhat related to their undergraduate major. One-fifth are employed in jobs that are not related to their undergraduate major field of study. Little more than one-half of the latter group of industrial engineering graduates cite their decision to change their career and profession as one of the reasons for working in a job that is not related to their undergraduate major field of study. One-half found better pay and promotion opportunities outside their undergraduate major field of study. About 44 percent cite a better working environment as one of the reasons to work outside their field of study, and 37 percent work outside their major field of study for family-related reasons. The location of jobs influenced 33 percent in their decision to work in areas that are unrelated to their undergraduate major, and 24 percent were forced to work outside the industrial engineering field because they were unable to find jobs related to their field.

When asked to list the single most important reason for working in an area outside their field, 28 percent voluntarily chose an unrelated job because of better pay and promotion opportunities, and 21 percent said they wanted to change their career and professional interests. Family-related reasons were the main factor in the decision of 15 percent of industrial engineering majors who worked outside their field, and 14 percent were forced to work outside the field because of their inability to find a job related to industrial engineering. Only 6 percent considered working conditions to be the most important reason for taking a job outside their major field of study.

Industrial engineering majors, unlike graduates from other engineering fields, are concerned with increasing productivity through the management of people, organizational policies, procedures, and technology. In contrast, engineers in other specialties generally work more with products or processes. This characteristic is manifested in their occupational attachment. More than one-fifth of industrial engineering majors are employed in top- to mid-level managerial, executive, and administrative occupations. Another 10 percent are employed in miscellaneous management-related occupations, such as management analysts, purchasing agents, inspectors, and other regulatory officers; 18 percent are employed as industrial engineers; and 11 percent work in other engineering occupations. A total of 10 percent work in occupations in the areas of marketing, sales, insurance, finance, and real estate.

Table 1
Top 10 Occupations That Employ Persons with Only a Bachelor's Degree in Industrial Engineering

Top 10 Occupations	PERCENT OF EMPLOYED		
	All	Men	Women
Top- and mid-level managers, executives, administrators	20.6	21.6	13.4
Industrial engineers	18.0	16.9	25.6
Other management-related occupations	9.5	9.2	11.3
Other miscellaneous engineers	7.2	7.8	3.0
Sales occupations, including retail	4.9	5.6	0.0
Mechanical engineers	3.8	3.9	2.8
Insurance, securities, real estate, business services	3.0	3.1	2.4
Miscellaneous computer and information science occupations	2.6	2.3	4.6
Other marketing and sales occupations	2.4	0.9	12.5
Teachers, secondary school	2.4	2.7	0.0

▶ Only 13 percent of all employed industrial engineering majors are women. More than one-quarter of employed female graduates work as industrial engineers, whereas only 17 percent of men choose to work in that occupation.

▶ Male industrial engineering majors are more likely than female graduates to work as top- to mid-level managers, executives, and administrators. Only 13 percent of women are employed in these occupations versus 22 percent of men.

▶ Nearly 13 percent of female graduates are employed in other marketing and sales occupations. In contrast, fewer than 1 percent of male industrial engineering graduates work in these occupations.

▶ Employment among male graduates also is more concentrated in mechanical and other miscellaneous occupations than women; 12 percent of men work in these occupations compared to only 6 percent of women.

Activities on the Job

Industrial engineering majors perform a variety of tasks on their jobs.

▶ A little more than 70 percent of industrial engineering graduates regularly engage in accounting, finance, and contractual duties; 65 percent spend part of a typical workweek in managerial and administrative duties.

▶ One-half regularly perform managerial duties to oversee the quality and efficiency of the production process.

▶ Forty-five percent of employed industrial engineering majors perform computer applications, programming, and systems-development duties regularly; 40 percent regularly engage in the design of equipment, processes, structures, and models.

▶ Thirty-five percent are regularly involved in employee-relations activities, including recruiting, personnel development, and training; the same proportion engage in utilizing findings from research for the production of materials and devices.

▶ One-fifth of employed industrial engineering majors regularly undertake applied research activities.

▶ Few employed industrial engineering graduates regularly engage in basic research activities, teaching, and providing professional services.

When asked to rank job duties by the number of weekly hours spent, one-fourth place management and administrative duties at the top, and 12 percent give top ranking to the sales, purchasing, and marketing activities. About 11 percent spend the majority of their time during a typical workweek on computer applications, programming, and systems-development duties.

Salaries

The average annual salary of full-time industrial engineering majors with only a bachelor's degree is $68,400, a level that is nearly 26 percent higher than the average annual salary of all full-time employed college graduates. As for most college graduates, the average annual salary of industrial engineering majors increases with age. This increase indicates that they get more productive and therefore can earn higher salaries as they spend more time on the job. The rate of increase in the annual salary as the engineers age is much steeper than the rate of increase in the average salary of all college graduates. This increase implies that their productivity rises more rapidly with age than the increase in the productivity of all college graduates. Within all age groups, the average annual salary of industrial engineering majors is much higher than the average annual salary of all college graduates.

▶ The annual average salary of industrial engineering majors between the ages of 25 and 34 is $52,700. Graduates between the ages of 35 and 39 earn $72,300 annually.

▶ The salary rises to $76,100 among graduates between the ages of 40 and 44. The annual average salary of age groups older than this shows a certain amount of fluctuation, which is a result of small numbers of individuals in some of these groups combined with a few individuals with very high salaries.

Caution: The average salary in these groups is not reflective of true average salaries of industrial engineering graduates in these age groups.

▶ The average annual salary of industrial engineering majors who work in jobs that are closely related to their major field of study is $69,600. The annual average salary of graduates whose jobs are somewhat related to their undergraduate major field of study is somewhat lower at $66,800. The one-fifth of industrial engineering majors who are employed in jobs that are unrelated to their major earn an annual average salary of $70,200. The unrelated occupations in which industrial engineering graduates are employed include high-level managerial, executive, administrative, and sales occupations and occupations that deal with insurance,

FIGURE 2

Age/Earnings Profile of Persons with Only a Bachelor's Degree in Industrial Engineering (Full-Time Workers, in 2002 Dollars)

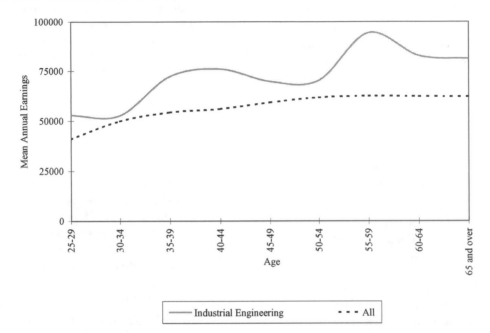

real estate, and stocks and bonds transactions. As noted earlier, industrial engineering graduates employed in these occupations have higher salaries than other occupations.

▶ Self-employed industrial engineering graduates who work full-time earn an average annual salary of $84,100. Most of these high salaries are associated with self-employed graduates with an incorporated business or practice. The annual average salary of industrial engineering graduates who are employed in the private sector by for-profit businesses and corporations is $68,700 per year. Government sector employees with a bachelor's degree in industrial engineering earn an average annual salary of $61,000. Educational institutions pay

full-time employed industrial engineering graduates with only a bachelor's degree an annual salary of only $40,100.

The average annual earnings of industrial engineering majors in most of the 10 occupations that are predominant employers of graduates is higher than the annual average earnings of all college graduates who are employed in those 10 occupations. The average annual salary of industrial engineering majors employed in top- to mid-level management, executive, and administrative occupations is $87,500, which is $13,400 more than the average earnings of all college graduates employed in that occupation. Male graduates are more likely to be employed in these occupations. The annual average salary of industrial engineering graduates employed as industrial engineers is much lower, at $56,700. This occupation is also the top employer of

Table 2

Annual Salary of Full-Time Workers with Only a Bachelor's Degree in
Industrial Engineering, Top 10 Occupations (in 2002 Dollars)

Earnings in Top 10 Occupations	All	Industrial Engineering
Total	$54,171	$68,411
Top- and mid-level managers, executives, administrators	$74,051	$87,494
Industrial engineers	$59,290	$56,713
Other management-related occupations	$51,921	$74,303
All other engineers	$62,544	$75,559
Sales occupations, including retail	$52,378	$79,803
Mechanical engineers	$64,905	$59,908
Insurance, securities, real estate, business services	$68,273	$96,978
Miscellaneous computer and information science occupations	$54,228	$73,478
Other marketing and sales occupations	$58,208	$73,224
Teachers, secondary school	$40,355	$38,347

female industrial engineering graduates. Employment in other management-related occupations is associated with an annual average salary of $74,300. Those who are employed in other miscellaneous engineering occupations earn $75,600, and the average remuneration of the industrial engineering majors who work in sales occupations and in occupations involving the insurance, real estate, and securities exchange is $79,800 and $97,000, respectively.

On-the-Job Training

The career potential of a job is closely associated with the amount of work-related training on the job. Work-related training is regarded as an investment by firms because it makes workers more productive. Firms that invest in their work force are more likely to offer pay increases and promotions to match the increasing productivity of their workers. Firms that do not invest in their workers are relatively less likely to offer pay increases and promotions. The proportion of employed industrial engineering majors who engage in some type of work-related training is about the same as the training rate among all college graduates. Two-thirds of all employed industrial engineering majors reported some type of work-related training on their jobs during the past year.

▶ Of those industrial engineering majors who received some training in the past year, 76 percent received technical training in their occupational field.

▶ Forty-six percent of the recipients received management or supervisory training.

▶ Fewer than 28 percent received training to improve their general professional skills, such as public speaking and business writing.

Nearly 93 percent of industrial engineering majors who participate in some work-related training do so to improve their occupational skills and knowledge. Increased opportunity for promotion, advancement, and salary increases is the reason for 47 percent of industrial engineering majors to participate in work-related training. Likewise, 47 percent of employers require them to undergo training. One-third are engaged in training activities to learn skills for a recently acquired position. Fewer than one-fifth of all industrial engineering majors who received some training cite licensing or certification as one of the reasons they attended training activities during the past year.

Although a variety of reasons motivate industrial engineering graduates to undergo training, the most important reason for their decision to go through work-related training is to sharpen their occupational skills and knowledge. Nearly two-thirds cite this as the main reason to acquire work-related training. About 12 percent consider employer requirement to be the main reason for their involvement in work-related training activities.

Post-Graduation Activities

After graduating with a bachelor's degree, 30 percent of industrial engineering majors proceed to earn a postgraduate degree: 26 percent earn a master's degree, only 2 percent earn a professional degree, and 1 percent earn a doctoral degree.

▶ Fifty-four percent of the master's degrees are earned in business administration and management; one-fifth are earned in

the field of industrial engineering. Other majors and miscellaneous engineering fields are chosen as the major field of study for their master's degree by 5 percent of industrial engineering majors, and another 5 percent graduated with a master's degree in one of the physical sciences.

▶ Among those who earn doctoral degrees, 44 percent major in industrial engineering, 17 percent major in computer and information sciences, and 16 percent major in other areas or miscellaneous engineering fields.

▶ Most professional degrees of industrial engineering majors are earned in either law (65 percent) or the health professions (21 percent).

Out of all industrial engineering graduates under the age of 65, 87 percent are employed. Only 4 percent are officially unemployed; that is, they are not employed and are actively seeking employment. The remaining 9 percent are out of the labor force; that is, they are not employed and are not seeking employment. Retirement is the reason for labor force withdrawal among 55 percent of industrial engineering majors who are out of the labor force. Fewer than 18 percent withdraw because of family responsibilities, and 16 percent do not want or need to work. Chronic illness or permanent disability resulted in 14 percent of the labor force withdrawals among industrial engineering majors.

Employment Outlook

According to the projections by the U.S. Bureau of Labor Statistics, employment in occupations that require at least a bachelor's degree is expected to grow faster than employment in other sectors of the American labor market. Between 2000 and 2010, the U.S. economy is projected to add 22.2 million jobs, which will yield an employment growth rate of 15.2 percent. The employment growth projections in the 10 occupations that are most likely to employ industrial engineering graduates are presented in Table 3.

- Employment in top- to mid-level managerial, executive, and administrative occupations—the second-largest employer of industrial engineering majors—is projected to grow at a rate of 12 percent. This growth will result in 1.27 million additional jobs between 2000 and 2010.

- The demand for industrial engineers is projected to increase by only 7,000 jobs, representing a growth rate of less than 5 percent.

- The demand for other management-related occupations is projected to increase by 845,000 jobs, or 17 percent, between 2000 and 2010, whereas employment in sales occupations is projected to grow 12 percent, a rate below the rate of growth of total employment in the U.S. economy between 2000 and 2010.

Table 3

Projected Change in Employment in the Top 10 Occupations That Employ
Persons with Only a Bachelor's Degree in Industrial Engineering

Top 10 Occupations	Actual Employment in 2000 (000s)	Projected Employment in 2010 (000s)	Absolute Change (000s)	Percentage Change
Top- and mid-level managers, executives, administrators	10,564	11,834	1,270	12.0%
Industrial engineers	154	161	7	4.5%
Other management-related occupations	4,956	5,801	845	17.1%
All other engineers	253	254	1	0.4%
Sales occupations, including retail	15,513	17,365	1,852	11.9%
Mechanical engineers	221	251	30	13.6%
Insurance, securities, real estate, business services	1,548	1,726	178	11.5%
Miscellaneous computer and information science occupations	203	326	123	60.6%
Other marketing and sales occupations	621	758	137	22.1%
Teachers, secondary school	1,113	1,314	201	18.1%

Mechanical Engineering

Mechanical engineers design and develop power-producing machines, such as internal combustion engines, steam and gas turbines, and jet and rocket engines. They use computers not only to form preliminary designs for systems or devices but also to perform calculations that will predict the behavior of the design and to collect and analyze performance data. They also design and develop power-using machines, such as refrigeration and air-conditioning equipment, robots, machine tools, material handling systems, and industrial production equipment. They can specialize in applied mechanics, design engineering, heat transfer, power plant engineering, pressure vessels and piping, plant maintenance, construction, and underwater technology.

Mechanical engineering is the broadest specialization within the engineering field. It cuts across many interdependent concentrations, such as electrical and aeronautical engineering. Mechanical engineers design the tools needed by other engineers to do their work. Mechanical engineers also are involved in developing new technologies. This collaboration requires them to work as part of a team. Most are employed in manufacturing, including defense work, which can create cycles in job availability. Mechanical engineers can spend considerable time in

factories or production areas outside—not in clean, quiet offices.

Beyond the general engineering foundation courses taken by all engineers, special courses in mechanical engineering include machine design, mechanical vibration, power engineering, kinematics, physical metallurgy, and mechanics.

Mechanical engineers combine practical and technical skills with analytical and intellectual pursuits. The application focus may determine whether the individual is an engineer or a technologist. The engineer is required to be more involved than the technologist in mental and analytical questions and to be more broadly focused in seeking solutions that cut across other disciplines.

Mechanical engineers value work that requires research and a high level of creativity. They like to use their imagination, they like to be inventive, and they like to be well paid for their efforts. They desire to do things they want and to be recognized as having attained high achievement. They enjoy being independent as well as being in situations where they experience variety and diversity by doing different things. They enjoy mental challenges.

Technical, mechanical, and manual skills are involved in mechanical engineering. Mechanical engineers are precise and methodical, and they follow rational principles. They are goal oriented, not easily distracted, and well organized, and they prefer to assume responsibility and control.

Mechanical engineers trust their ability to collect needed information and then use their proven logic skills to process the observations. These traits give the mechanical engineer the appearance of someone who is impersonal and not influenced by the feelings of others. This pattern "works" for mechanical engineers because they often are employed in places where other workers have similar characteristics. However, once someone they respect makes "the problem" known to them about their interpersonal style, they make efforts to compensate for their very analytical thinking in social situations.

Where Do Mechanical Engineering Majors Work?

Three-quarters of all employed mechanical engineering graduates work as wage and salary workers in the private, for-profit sector of the economy for businesses and corporations. Another 10 percent work in the private, for-profit sector of the economy as self-employed workers in their own incorporated or non-incorporated business or practice. The government sector employs 11 percent of all mechanical engineering majors with only a bachelor's degree, and educational institutions employ only 2 percent of mechanical engineering graduates.

FIGURE 1

Percentage Distribution of Employed Persons with Only a Bachelor's Degree in Mechanical Engineering, by Major Sector of Economic Activity

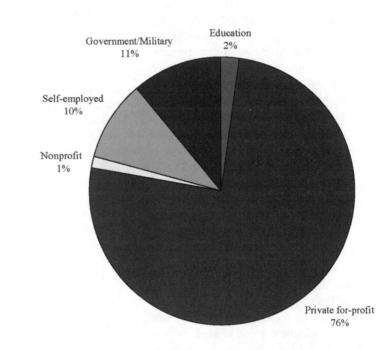

Government/Military
11%

Education
2%

Self-employed
10%

Nonprofit
1%

Private for-profit
76%

Occupations

Little less than one-half of employed mechanical engineering majors work in jobs that are closely related to their undergraduate major. Nearly 39 percent are employed in jobs that are somewhat related to their major, and the remaining 12 percent work in jobs that are not related to their major. Mechanical engineering majors identify a variety of reasons for working outside their major field of study. For 52 percent of the graduates, one of the reasons to work outside their field is better pay and promotion opportunities. The same proportion indicates a change in their career interests after graduation as one of the reasons to seek employment outside their field. About 2 in 5 prefer the working conditions in jobs that are not related to mechanical engineering. One-third are employed outside their field because of the preferred location of the job, and 3 out of 10 are forced to work outside their field because of a lack of jobs related to engineering. One-fifth cite family-related reasons for working in unrelated jobs.

Although graduates offer numerous reasons for working in unrelated jobs, a change in career interests is offered by 26 percent as the most important reason. Better pay and promotion opportunities are the most important reason to 18 percent, and 13 percent indicate a lack of related jobs as the most important reason for employment in unrelated jobs. About 11 percent consider working conditions as the most important reason, 8 percent offer family-related reasons, and another 8 percent say job location is the most important reason for working in a job that is not related to their undergraduate major field of study.

Like most engineering majors, the employment of mechanical engineering graduates is concentrated in a few occupations. In fact, more than 80 percent are employed in just 10 occupations. Nearly 46 percent are employed as mechanical engineers, the occupation for which they were trained in their undergraduate education. Like other engineering majors, some mechanical engineering graduates are very likely to be employed in top- to mid-level managerial, executive, and administrative occupations: 16 percent are employed in these occupations. Nearly 13 percent are employed in other engineering occupations, including aerospace, industrial, computer, and other miscellaneous engineering positions.

Table 1

Top 10 Occupations That Employ Persons with Only a Bachelor's Degree in Mechanical Engineering

Top 10 Occupations	PERCENT OF EMPLOYED		
	All	Men	Women
Mechanical engineers	45.7	45.5	49.2
Top- and mid-level managers, executives, administrators	16.0	16.6	5.2
Other miscellaneous engineers	6.0	5.5	15.0
Aeronautical, aerospace, and astronautical engineers	3.8	3.8	3.9
Sales occupations, including retail	2.9	2.9	1.0

(continued)

Table 1 (continued)

Top 10 Occupations That Employ Persons with Only a Bachelor's
Degree in Mechanical Engineering

Top 10 Occupations	PERCENT OF EMPLOYED		
	All	Men	Women
Other management-related occupations	2.5	2.4	4.5
Industrial engineers	1.7	1.8	1.1
Other marketing and sales occupations	1.5	1.6	0.0
Insurance, securities, real estate, business services	1.4	1.5	0.0
Computer engineers	1.3	1.2	2.3

▶ Only 5 percent of all employed mechanical engineering majors are women. These women are very likely to be employed as either mechanical engineers (49 percent) or in other engineering occupations. Nearly 72 percent are employed in one of the five engineering occupations listed in Table 1.

▶ Male mechanical engineering majors also are very likely to find employment in engineering occupations. Nearly 46 percent work in mechanical engineering occupations, and a total of 58 percent work in one of the five engineering occupations listed above.

▶ Male graduates are more likely than females to work as top- to mid-level managers, executives, and administrators. Only 5 percent of women are employed in these occupations versus 17 percent of men.

Activities on the Job

Mechanical engineering majors perform a variety of tasks on their jobs.

▶ Given their high rates of employment in mechanical and other engineering occupations, it is not surprising that 60 percent are regularly engaged in the design of equipment, processes, structures, and models at their jobs.

▶ The same proportion spends some time during every workweek in managerial and administrative duties. Accounting, finance, and contractual duties are performed regularly by 65 percent of employed mechanical engineering graduates.

▶ Two-fifths of employed mechanical engineering graduates are engaged in computer applications, programming, and systems-development duties. Another two-fifths utilize findings from research for the production of materials and devices, or they use managerial duties to oversee the quality and efficiency in the production process.

▶ Much like other engineering graduates, few employed mechanical engineering graduates regularly engage in basic research activities, teaching, and providing professional services.

When asked to rank job duties by the number of weekly hours spent on those activities, mechanical engineers ranked equipment- and process-design duties and managerial and administrative duties as their top priority. One-quarter spend most of their time in designing equipment, processes, structures, and models. Another 22 percent spend most of their work time on managerial and administrative duties. Nearly 10 percent spend most of their time at work in utilizing findings from research for the production of materials and devices; 7 percent spend the majority of their time during a typical workweek on computer applications, programming, and systems-development duties; and 12 percent give top ranking to sales, purchasing, and marketing activities.

Salaries

The average annual salary of full-time mechanical engineering majors with only a bachelor's degree is $68,800, a level that is 27 percent higher than the average annual salary of all full-time employed college graduates. As with most college graduates, the salary of mechanical engineering majors increases with age. This increase indicates that the engineers get more productive and therefore can earn higher salaries as they spend more time on the job. As the engineers get older, the rate of increase in the annual salary is much steeper than the rate of increase in the average salary of all college graduates. This increase implies that their productivity rises more rapidly with age than the increase in the productivity of all college graduates. Within all age groups, the average annual salary of mechanical engineering majors is much higher than the average annual salary of all college graduates.

▶ The annual average salary of mechanical engineering majors between the ages of 25 and 29 is $49,900. Graduates between the ages of 30 and 34 earn $59,600 annually.

▶ The salary rises to $64,500 among graduates between the ages of 35 and 39, continues to rise to $73,100 among graduates between the ages of 40 to 44, and peaks at $85,300 between the ages of 50 and 54.

▶ The average annual salary of mechanical engineering majors who work in jobs that are closely related to their major field of study is $70,400. The annual average salary of graduates whose jobs are somewhat related to their undergraduate major field of study is somewhat lower at $69,400. Employment in jobs that are not related to their undergraduate majors results in a sizable reduction in the average annual salaries of mechanical engineering majors. Those who are employed in unrelated jobs earn $60,300. Nearly 9 out of 10 mechanical engineering majors, however, are employed in jobs that are closely or somewhat related to their major.

▶ Self-employed mechanical engineering graduates who work full-time earn an average annual salary of $73,000. Most of these high salaries are associated with self-employed graduates with an incorporated business or practice, who account for 56 percent of all full-time self-employed mechanical engineering graduates. The annual average salary of mechanical engineering graduates who are employed in the private sector by for-profit businesses and corporations is $69,400 per year. Government sector employees with a bachelor's degree in mechanical engineering earn an average annual salary of $63,800.

FIGURE 2

Age/Earnings Profile of Persons with Only a Bachelor's Degree in Mechanical Engineering (Full-Time Workers, in 2002 Dollars)

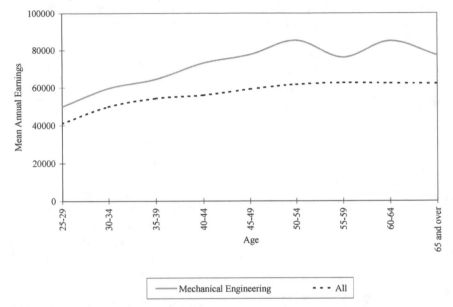

The average annual earnings of mechanical engineering majors in 9 out of 10 occupations that are predominant employers of graduates are higher than the annual average earnings of all college graduates who are employed in those occupations. The average annual salary of mechanical engineering majors employed as mechanical engineers is $65,300. Those who are employed in top- to mid-level management, executive, and administrative occupations earn an average annual salary of $89,600, which is 21 percent more than the average annual earnings of all college graduates employed in that occupation. Male graduates are more likely to be employed in these occupations.

Table 2

Annual Salary of Full-Time Workers with Only a Bachelor's Degree in Mechanical Engineering, Top 10 Occupations (in 2002 Dollars)

Earnings in Top 10 Occupations	All	Mechanical Engineering
Total	$54,171	$68,806
Mechanical engineers	$64,905	$65,333
Top- and mid-level managers, executives, administrators	$74,051	$89,626
All other engineers	$62,544	$65,223

Earnings in Top 10 Occupations	All	Mechanical Engineering
Aeronautical, aerospace, and astronautical engineers	$68,111	$68,437
Sales occupations, including retail	$52,378	$68,494
Other management-related occupations	$51,921	$70,005
Industrial engineers	$59,290	$62,504
Other marketing and sales occupations	$58,208	$69,790
Insurance, securities, real estate, business services	$68,273	$70,186
Computer engineers	$66,859	$63,514

On-the-Job Training

The career potential of a job is closely associated with the amount of work-related training on the job. Work-related training is regarded as an investment by firms because it makes workers more productive. Firms that invest in their work force are more likely to offer pay increases and promotions to match the increasing productivity of their workers. Firms that do not invest in their workers are less likely to offer pay increases and promotions. The proportion of employed mechanical engineering majors who engage in some type of work-related training is about the same as the training rate among all college graduates. Two-thirds of all employed mechanical engineering majors reported some type of work-related training on their jobs during the past year.

- Of those mechanical engineering majors who received some training in the past year, 78 percent received technical training in their occupational field.

- Forty-five percent of the training recipients received management or supervisory training.

- Thirty-one percent received training to improve their general professional skills, such as public speaking and business writing.

Mechanical engineering majors offer numerous reasons for participating in work-related training activities. Nearly 93 percent of mechanical engineering majors who participate in some work-related training do so to improve their occupational skills and knowledge. More than one-half of mechanical engineering graduates are required to undergo work-related training. Increased opportunity for promotion, advancement, and salary increases are the reasons for 48 percent of mechanical engineering majors to participate in work-related training. About 3 out of 10 employed mechanical engineering graduates are engaged in training activities to learn skills for a recently acquired position.

Out of this variety of reasons to acquire work-related training, just under two-thirds of employed mechanical engineering graduates consider improvement of occupational skills and knowledge to be the most important reason for engaging in training. The main reason 11 percent of employed mechanical engineering graduates acquire training is because it is required by their employer; 9 percent report increased pay and promotion opportunities as their motivating force to acquire training.

Post-Graduation Activities

After graduating with a bachelor's degree, 30 percent of mechanical engineering majors proceed to earn a postgraduate degree: 25 percent earn a master's degree; 3 percent earn a doctoral degree; and 2 percent earn a professional degree.

▶ Four out of 10 master's degrees are earned in the field of mechanical engineering. One-third are earned in business management and administration, and another 17 percent are earned in other miscellaneous engineering fields.

▶ Among the few who earn a doctoral degree, 80 percent major in an engineering field: 60 percent choose mechanical engineering, and the remaining 20 percent choose other engineering fields.

▶ Most professional degrees of mechanical engineering majors are earned in law (65 percent). Another 30 percent are split between other professions and mechanical engineering.

Out of all mechanical engineering graduates under the age of 65, 92 percent are employed. Only 3 percent are officially unemployed; that is, they are not employed and are actively seeking employment. The remaining 5 percent are out of the labor force; that is, they are not employed and are not seeking employment. Retirement is the reason for labor force withdrawal among 68 percent of mechanical engineering majors who are out of the labor force. Fewer than 15 percent do not need or want to work, and 1 in 10 labor force withdrawals among mechanical engineering majors is attributable to chronic illness or permanent disability.

Employment Outlook

According to the projections by the U.S. Bureau of Labor Statistics, employment in occupations that require at least a bachelor's degree is expected to grow faster than employment in other sectors of the American labor market. Between 2000 and 2010, the U.S. economy is projected to add 22.2 million jobs, which will yield an employment growth rate of 15.2 percent. The employment growth projections in the top 10 occupations that are most likely to employ mechanical engineering graduates are presented in Table 3.

▶ The mechanical engineering occupation is projected to add 30,000 jobs between 2000 and 2010. This increase will yield an employment growth rate of 14 percent.

▶ Employment in top- to mid-level managerial, executive, and administrative occupations—the second-largest employer of mechanical engineering majors—is projected to grow at a rate of 12 percent. This increase will result in 1.27 million additional jobs between 2000 and 2010.

▶ With the exception of other marketing and sales occupations, miscellaneous management-related occupations, and computer-engineering occupations, the demand for the remaining occupations in Table 3 is projected to grow at a lower rate than growth of overall employment in the U.S. economy. The projected employment in the computer engineering occupation is expected to nearly double between 2000 and 2010.

Table 3

Projected Change in Employment in the Top 10 Occupations That
Employ Persons with Only a Bachelor's Degree in Mechanical Engineering

Top 10 Occupations	Actual Employment in 2000 (000s)	Projected Employment in 2010 (000s)	Absolute Change (000s)	Percentage Change
Mechanical engineers	221	251	30	13.6%
Top- and mid-level managers, executives, administrators	10,564	11,834	1,270	12.0%
Other miscellaneous engineers	253	254	1	0.4%
Aeronautical, aerospace, and astronautical engineers	50	57	7	14.0%
Sales occupations, including retail	15,513	17,365	1,852	11.9%
Other management-related occupations	4,956	5,801	845	17.1%
Industrial engineers	154	161	7	4.5%
Other marketing and sales occupations	621	758	137	22.1%
Insurance, securities, real estate, business services	1,548	1,726	178	11.5%
Computer engineers	757	1,436	679	89.7%

Humanities and Social Sciences

CHAPTER 36

Anthropology and Archaeology

A nthropology and archaeology are both social sciences with a historical focus. People working in these areas have similar abilities, interests, values, and personality patterns.

Anthropology

Anthropology is the study of the origin and behavior of humans and their physical, social, and cultural development. Anthropologists study the way of life, remains, language, or physical characteristics of people in various parts of the world. Some anthropologists compare the customs, values, and social patterns of different cultures. A person usually specializes in one region of the world and has a particular focus. Sociocultural anthropologists do comparative studies and examine the evolution of customs, cultures, and social lives of groups in settings from nonindustrialized societies to those of modern urban areas. Linguistic anthropologists study the role of language in various cultures.

Anthropologists gather and analyze data on the human physique; social customs; and artifacts, such as weapons, tools, pottery, and clothing. They apply anthropological data and techniques to the solution of problems in industrial relations, race and ethnic relations, social work, political administration, education, and public health. Physical anthropology is the study of the meanings and causes of human physical differences and their effects on culture, heredity, and environment. Physical anthropologists observe and measure bodily variations and physical attributes of existing human types, often using skeletal remains in museums. These anthropologists study physical and physiological adaptations to differing environments, hereditary characteristics of living populations, and nutrition. They also examine growth patterns, sexual differences, and aging phenomena of human groups.

Educational courses may include peoples and cultures; cultures of the world; language and communication; stones and bones; prehistory of the New World; individual and culture; human origins; cultural survival; and myth and religion.

Archaeology

Archaeology involves the systematic recovery and examination of material evidence, such as tools and pottery remaining from past human cultures, to determine the history, customs, and living habits of earlier civilizations. Archaeologists reconstruct a record of extinct cultures, especially preliterate ones. To determine age and cultural identity, archaeologists study, classify, and interpret artifacts, architectural features, and types of structures recovered by excavation. Archaeologists establish the chronological sequence of development of each culture from simpler to more advanced levels. A person usually specializes in a specific civilization, such as Egyptian or the Colombian history of the Americas.

Educational course work may include archaeological science; archaeological recording; illustration and publication; archaeometry; archaeological method and theory; osteoarchaeology; zooarchaeology; geoarchaeology; biblical archaeology; history and archaeology of the ancient Near East; Syro-Palestinian pottery; problems in the archaeology of Bronze and Iron Age Levant; Greek art and archaeology; coinage; politics and economy in the Greek World; and archaeology of ancient China and South America.

Anthropologists and archaeologists use a high degree of abstract conceptualization in their work. Good reading and language skills are prerequisites. Because this field predominantly deals with data and doesn't have much involvement with people, it relies on scientific theories to solve problems. To a lesser extent, numerical skills are necessary, but the logic and reasoning abilities required in high mathematics are the ones that enhance scientific ability. Well-developed spatial skills are required, especially for archaeology.

People considering anthropology and archaeology may at first be confused by their inclusion in the broad category of social sciences. These majors usually do not attract people with high social interests. Anthropologists and archaeologists are researchers and, in fact, share similar interests with people who work in labs or engineering. Although anthropologists and archaeologists deal with ideas, their work is also concrete, meticulous, and manual, as in the case of reconstructing artifacts such as pottery. They also need organizational skills that are used in planning a search or "dig."

Values supported by these fields include independence and variety, as well as the obvious ones of the search to discover new facts or hypotheses, intellectual stimulation, and creative insight. Anthropologists and archaeologists decide for themselves what areas to pursue, what their goals are, and how they plan to achieve their goals. Since the social sciences are multidisciplinary, these workers can also choose those with whom they want to work. The nature of the field is expansive, so the work offers the opportunity for a great deal of variety and diversion.

People in this field have rich imaginations and are naturally curious and intuitive. Others may perceive these workers as unrealistic, particularly when they avoid paying attention to facts or ignore viewpoints that are at odds with their ideas. Anthropologists and archaeologists enjoy dealing in possibilities and have broad interests. Many who are persuasive enjoy teaching, creating in others a fascination with their own ideas. These workers tend to dislike details, are independent, and have a high energy for projects they create, although they may move on to something new without finishing the first project.

Where Do Anthropology and Archaeology Graduates Work?

Anthropology and archaeology graduates are employed in all five sectors of the economy. About 40 percent work in the private, for-profit sector for businesses and corporations, and 18 percent are self-employed. Anthropology and archaeology graduates are fond of teaching; educational institutions employ 23 percent, often as teachers in elementary or secondary schools and as postsecondary teachers. The government sector employs 12 percent of anthropology and archaeology graduates, and 7 percent find employment in the nonprofit sector of the economy, working for tax-exempt or charitable organizations.

Anthropology and archaeology graduates do not learn skills in the classroom that can be readily applied in the labor market. A graduate degree in the field can sharpen their skills and increase the likelihood of finding jobs in their major field of study. Even then, jobs that utilize the skills of anthropology and archaeology are not numerous. Those who have just a bachelor's degree in the field frequently find employment in jobs that are not related to their undergraduate field of study. In fact, 58 percent of all employed anthropology and archaeology graduates work in jobs that are not related to their major field of study, while 22 percent consider their jobs to be somewhat related to their undergraduate field of study. Only 20 percent report that their employment is closely related to their major.

A large proportion of anthropology and archaeology graduates work in jobs unrelated to their major. Various factors underlie the decision to work in such jobs. Pay and promotion opportunities and the lack of jobs in their field are the most commonly cited reasons. When asked to select the most important reason for employment outside their major field of study, 29 percent of the graduates choose better pay and promotion opportunities, and 19 percent find the lack of jobs in their field as the most important factor in their employment decision. Only 20 percent rank a change in their career interests as the top reason, and 11 percent consider family-related reasons as the most important factor influencing their employment choice in an unrelated job. The general working environment is the top-ranking factor for 12 percent of graduates working in unrelated jobs, and only 3 percent consider job location as the most important factor underlying their decision to work in an unrelated job.

FIGURE 1

Percentage Distribution of Employed Persons with Only a Bachelor's Degree in Anthropology and Archaeology, by Major Sector of Economic Activity

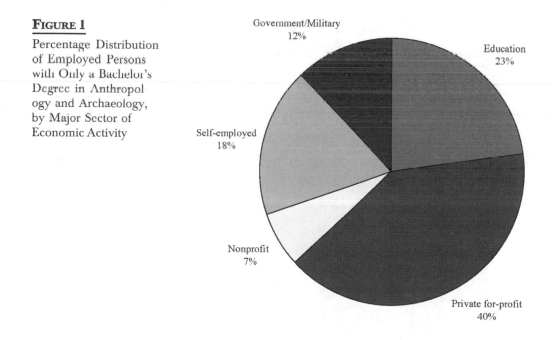

Government/Military
12%

Education
23%

Self-employed
18%

Nonprofit
7%

Private for-profit
40%

Occupations

The employment of anthropology and archaeology graduates is spread across many different occupations. No single occupation employs a majority of graduates. Only 55 percent are employed in the top 10 occupations that are predominant employers of these graduates. Top- to mid-level executive, administrative, and managerial occupations are the top employer of anthropology and archaeology graduates, employing only 8 percent of the graduates. The high degree of abstract conceptualization in their work requires anthropology and archaeology majors to possess good reading and language skills. These skills allow some graduates to gain access to jobs as broadcasters, writers, and editors. These occupations are the second-largest employer of anthropology and archaeology graduates, with 7 percent of all employed graduates working in these occupations. Clerical and administrative support occupations employ 6 percent, and nearly 10 percent work in sales occupations and in miscellaneous marketing occupations. The top 10 employers of anthropology and archaeology graduates also include such management-related occupations as management analysts; purchasing agents; regulatory officers; insurance, finance, and real estate occupations; transportation occupations; and miscellaneous social scientist occupations.

Table 1
Top 10 Occupations That Employ Persons with Only a Bachelor's Degree in Anthropology and Archaeology

Top 10 Occupations	PERCENT OF EMPLOYED		
	All	Men	Women
Top- and mid-level managers, executives, administrators	8.2	15.6	4.1
Artists, broadcasters, writers, editors, entertainers, public relations specialists	6.8	5.0	7.8
Teachers, elementary school	6.6	3.1	8.5
Other administrative (e.g., record clerks, telephone operators)	5.6	3.1	7.0
Other management-related occupations	5.6	6.0	5.4
Sales occupations, including retail	5.5	2.0	7.5
Insurance, securities, real estate, business services	4.6	3.1	5.4
Transportation and material-moving occupations	4.4	9.4	1.7
Other marketing and sales occupations	4.1	1.2	5.6
Other social scientists	3.9	8.4	1.4

Only 36 percent of all employed anthropology and archaeology graduates are men. The occupational employment patterns of male and female anthropology and archaeology graduates are somewhat different.

- Male graduates are more likely than female graduates to work as top-level executives, administrators, and managers: 16 percent of all employed male graduates work in these occupations, compared to only 4 percent of employed female graduates.

- Transportation occupations employ 9 percent of male anthropology and archaeology graduates and only 2 percent of female graduates.

- Male graduates also are more likely than female graduates to work as social scientists. While 8 percent of males work in these occupations, only 1 percent of female graduates find employment in these occupations.

- Female anthropology and archaeology graduates are somewhat more likely than male graduates to work as writers, editors, and broadcasters—8 percent versus 5 percent.

- Sales and marketing occupations are more likely to employ female anthropology and archaeology graduates than male graduates. A larger proportion of female graduates work in clerical and administrative support occupations compared to their male counterparts.

Activities on the Job

The activities in which anthropology and archaeology graduates spend most of their time at work are as diverse as the occupations in which they are employed.

- Seventeen percent spend most of their workweek in sales, purchasing, and marketing activities. As noted earlier, sales and marketing occupations employ nearly 10 percent of the graduates.

- Thirteen percent report that they spend most hours during a typical work week in providing professional services such as consulting services.

- Another 13 percent say that management and administrative duties take up most of their time at work.

- One in 10 employed anthropology and archaeology graduates works as a teacher. About one-quarter of all employed graduates state that they regularly spend at least 10 hours per week in teaching activities.

- Seven percent spend most of their time at work in accounting, finance, and contractual duties.

- Six percent of employed anthropology and archaeology graduates spend a major portion of their typical workweek in computer applications, programming, and systems-development activities.

- Five percent are engaged for most of their time at work in employee-relations activities, including recruiting, personnel development, and training activities; another 5 percent spend most of their typical workweek in applied research activities.

Salaries

The average annual salary of anthropology and archaeology graduates who have only a bachelor's degree and are employed full-time is $45,800, a level that is only 84 percent of the average annual salary of all full-time employed college graduates. The salary of anthropology and archaeology graduates increases, although slowly, with age, indicating that they get more productive and therefore can earn somewhat higher salaries as they spend more time on the job. However, the average salary of anthropology and archaeology graduates remains well below the average salary of all college graduates in each age range. In fact, as they get older, the gap between the average salary of anthropology and archaeology graduates and that of all college graduates widens.

▶ The annual average salary of anthropology and archaeology graduates between the ages of 25 and 34 is $43,400. Graduates between the ages of 35 and 44 earn $45,100 annually.

▶ The average salary of anthropology and archaeology graduates peaks at $48,200 for those who are between the ages of 45 and 54.

The average annual salary of anthropology and archaeology graduates who work in jobs that are closely related to their major field of study is higher than the average annual salary of those who are employed in jobs that are somewhat related to their major. However, graduates who work in jobs that are unrelated to their major earn a higher average annual salary than both groups of graduates with closely or somewhat related jobs. Closely related jobs pay full-time employed anthropology and archaeology graduates $43,300 annually. Graduates employed in somewhat related jobs earn $39,600 per year, and those whose jobs are unrelated to their undergraduate major field of study earn an average annual salary of $49,000.

Anthropology and archaeology graduates who are employed by businesses and corporations in the private, for-profit sector of the economy earn more than those employed in other sectors of the economy. The annual average salary of full-time employed anthropology and archaeology graduates in this sector is $54,800. The private, nonprofit sector pays full-time employed anthropology and archaeology graduates an average salary of $45,800 per year. Employment of graduates in full-time jobs in the education sector yields an average annual salary of $39,300. Self-employed anthropology and archaeology graduates earn $37,100 per year, and those who work in the government sector earn an average salary of $36,000.

The average salary of all college graduates and anthropology and archaeology graduates in each of the top 10 occupations that are predominant employers of anthropology and archaeology graduates is presented here.

FIGURE 2

Age/Earnings Profile of Persons with Only a Bachelor's Degree in Anthropology and Archaeology (Full-Time Workers, in 2002 Dollars)

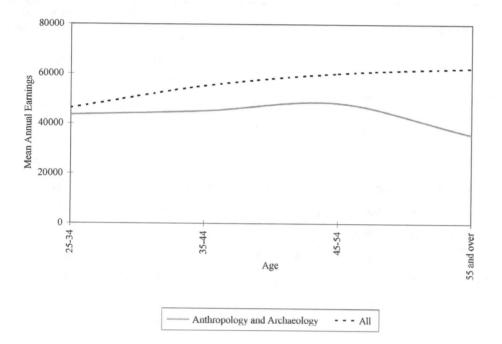

- The average annual salary of anthropology and archaeology graduates employed in insurance, finance, and real estate occupations is $75,200. Although these occupations are not related to their major field of study, access to these jobs results in a high level of earnings among graduates.

- Another relatively high-paying occupation is in the top- to mid-level executive, administrative, and managerial area. Anthropology and archaeology graduates employed in these occupations earn $56,200 per year.

- Elementary school teachers with a bachelor's degree in anthropology and archaeology earn $45,600 per year.

- The average salary of anthropology and archaeology graduates employed in management-related occupations is $41,300 per year; the salary in clerical and administrative support occupations is $34,100 per year.

- Employment in the broadcasting, writing, and editing occupations yields a below-average salary of $31,400 per year.

Table 2
Annual Salary of Full-Time Workers with Only a Bachelor's Degree
in Anthropology and Archaeology, Top 10 Occupations (in 2002 Dollars)

Earnings in Top 10 Occupations	All	Anthropology and Archaeology
Total	$54,171	$45,775
Top- and mid-level managers, executives, administrators	$74,051	$56,234
Artists, broadcasters, writers, editors, entertainers, public relations specialists	$52,141	$31,387
Elementary school teachers	$39,167	$45,638
Other administrative (e.g., records clerks, telephone operators)	$34,547	$34,140
Other management-related occupations	$51,921	$41,260
Sales occupations, including retail	$52,378	$39,593
Insurance, securities, real estate, business services	$68,273	$75,239
Transportation and material-moving occupations	$64,088	$45,374
Other marketing and sales occupations	$58,208	$79,248
Other social scientists	$47,262	$37,278

On-the-Job Training

The career potential of a job is closely associated with the amount of work-related training on the job. Work-related training is regarded as an investment by firms because it makes workers more productive. Firms that invest in their workforce are more likely to offer pay increases and promotions to match the increasing productivity of their workers. Firms that do not invest in their workers are less likely to offer pay increases and promotions. The incidence of work-related training among anthropology and archaeology graduates is much lower than the rate of participation in work-related training among all college graduates. While 68 percent of all college graduates acquire some kind of work-related training during a year, only 57 percent of anthropology and archaeology majors annually engage in work-related training.

▶ Of those anthropology and archaeology graduates who receive some work-related training during the year, 66 percent receive technical training in the occupations in which they are employed.

▶ Twenty-seven percent of the training recipients participate in management or supervisory training.

▶ Forty-three percent receive training to improve their general professional skills, such as public speaking and business writing.

Although various reasons underlie the decision of anthropology and archaeology graduates to participate in work-related training activities, workshops, or seminars, three reasons stand out as most commonly cited by graduates. These reasons are a desire to improve skills and knowledge in the occupational area of their employment, mandatory training requirements of the employer, and increased opportunities for advancement in the form of a higher salary and a promotion.

When asked to identify the most important reason to acquire training, 68 percent of anthropology and archaeology graduates who undergo training identify the need to improve their occupational skills and knowledge. Only 1 in 10 reports a mandatory training requirement by the employer as the most important factor underlying their involvement in work-related training; according to another 10 percent of the training participants, the most important reason to acquire work-related training is to secure a salary increase and a promotion. Only 5 percent cite the necessity to learn skills for a newly acquired position, and another 5 percent rank the need to obtain a professional license or certificate as the number one reason for their participation in work-related training activities.

Post-Graduation Activities

Postgraduate schooling is widespread among anthropology and archaeology graduates. Of all graduates with a bachelor's degree in anthropology and archaeology, 46 percent proceed to earn a postgraduate degree: 29 percent earn a master's degree, 7 percent earn a doctoral degree, and 10 percent earn a professional degree.

- Twenty-seven percent of all master's degrees earned by undergraduate anthropology and archaeology majors are in the field of anthropology and archaeology; 15 percent are earned in education; 11 percent are earned in health sciences; and 5 percent each are earned in public affairs, other social sciences, and business administration and management.

- Just more than one-half of the doctoral degrees earned by anthropology and archaeology undergraduate majors are earned in the field of anthropology and archaeology. About 11 percent are earned in psychology, and the rest are spread across various fields of study, including education, health, social sciences, physical sciences, and business.

- Sixty-three percent of the professional degrees of undergraduate anthropology and archaeology majors are concentrated in the field of law, and another 30 percent of the degrees are earned in the health professions.

Of all anthropology and archaeology graduates under the age of 65, 76 percent are employed. About 6 percent are officially unemployed; in other words, they are not employed and are actively seeking employment. The remaining 18 percent are out of the labor force; that is, they are not employed and are not seeking employment. Four main reasons underlie the labor force withdrawal of anthropology and archaeology graduates: 43 percent cite family responsibilities as the reason for labor force withdrawal, and 24 percent lack the desire or the need to work. Postgraduate schooling among anthropology and archaeology majors is responsible for 17 percent of the labor force withdrawals. Because of a chronic illness or a disabling condition, 16 percent are unable to participate in the labor force.

Employment Outlook

According to the projections by the U.S. Bureau of Labor Statistics, employment in occupations that require at least a bachelor's degree is expected to grow faster than employment in other sectors of the American labor market. Between 2000 and 2010, the U.S. economy is projected

to add 22.2 million jobs, yielding an employment growth rate of 15.2 percent. The employment growth projections in the top 10 occupations that are most likely to employ anthropology and archaeology graduates are presented here.

▶ The fastest growth in demand is projected in miscellaneous marketing and sales occupations and the occupations of editor, broadcaster, and writer. Total employment in these occupations is projected to grow by about 22 percent and 21 percent, respectively, between 2000 and 2010. These two occupations also represent the highest and the lowest salary occupations for anthropology and archaeology graduates. Sales and marketing occupations pay above-average salaries to these graduates, while the occupations of editor, broadcaster, and writer pay below-average salaries to full-time employed anthropology and archaeology graduates.

▶ The largest employer of anthropology and archaeology graduates—upper-level executive, administrative, and managerial occupations—is projected to add 1.27 million jobs between 2000 and 2010. This represents an employment growth rate of nearly 12 percent. This occupation is more likely to employ male than female anthropology and archaeology graduates.

▶ The demand for management-related jobs is projected to grow at 17 percent, while employment of personnel in the finance, insurance, and real estate occupations is projected to grow by 178,000 jobs, or 12 percent, between 2000 and 2010.

Table 3
Projected Change in Employment in the Top 10 Occupations That Employ Persons with Only a Bachelor's Degree in Anthropology and Archaeology

Top 10 Occupations	Actual Employment in 2000 (000s)	Projected Employment in 2010 (000s)	Absolute Change (000s)	Percentage Change
Top- and mid-level managers, executives, administrators	10,564	11,834	1,270	12.0%
Artists, broadcasters, writers, editors, entertainers, public relations specialists	2,371	2,864	493	20.8%
Elementary school teachers	1,532	1,734	202	13.2%
Other administrative (e.g., records clerks, telephone operators)	16,911	18,522	1,611	9.5%
Other management-related occupations	4,956	5,801	845	17.1%
Sales occupations, including retail	15,513	17,365	1,852	11.9%
Insurance, securities, real estate, business services	1,548	1,726	178	11.5%
Transportation and material-moving occupations	10,088	11,618	1,530	15.2%
Other marketing and sales occupations	621	758	137	22.1%
Other social scientists	15	17	2	13.3%

CHAPTER 37

Communications

This major includes people who write, edit, translate, and report factual information. They use their language skills and knowledge of special writing techniques to communicate facts. Those in communications find employment with radio and television stations, newspapers, and publishing firms, and in organizations where they work as public relations specialists.

People in communications have similar abilities and interests. Their talents include the effective use of oral and written language and the expression of content simply and clearly. Although speech writing may be referred to as ghost writing, most people in communications are not secretive introverts. They enjoy assuming a promoting and influencing role, they like projecting themselves in front of others, and they feel comfortable in public. They also enjoy working with people.

A communications major satisfies several values. One is the enjoyment of dealing creatively with diverse activities, which provide intellectual challenges and the opportunity to use one's mind. Another value is the prestige that comes with public recognition and personal contact with which people in other majors may be uncomfortable. A third value may be the desire for fame and riches; if riches do not come, the experience of seeking fame may be sufficiently satisfying.

Communications workers are outgoing, energetic, and enthusiastic. This energized style enables them to act quickly and to improvise. Some workers who are focused on business matters are organized, practical, and pragmatic. Those who are perceived as pragmatic may appear to be people-oriented but may have set priorities and may, at times, seem insensitive to the feelings of others.

Public relations specialists prepare and disseminate information that keeps targeted groups informed about policies, activities, and accomplishments; the information may be directed to the general public, private-interest groups such as employees or consumers, or stockholders of organizations. However, public relations specialists also keep management aware of feedback about the public's attitudes and concerns. In the case of politics, these specialists are very involved with political campaigns.

This field requires the preparation of press releases and communication with people in the media who might print or broadcast these materials. Public relations specialists set up, plan, and attend speaking engagements as well as represent organizations at community meetings. They also present films or deliver presentations to interested parties who may or may not be part of a public relations program. Their work involves doing research, writing, preparing and distributing materials, maintaining contacts, and responding to inquiries. In government, this person may be referred to as a press secretary, information officer, or public affairs specialist. Most often these specialists are in large cities.

A common public relations sequence of courses includes public relations principles and techniques; public relations management and administration, including organizational development; writing that emphasizes news releases, proposals, annual reports, scripts, speeches, and related items; visual communications, including desktop publishing and computer graphics; and research, emphasizing social science research and survey design and implementation. Courses in advertising, sociology, and creative writing also are helpful, as is familiarity with word processing and other computer applications. Specialties are offered in public relations for business, government, or nonprofit organizations.

The ability to write and speak well is essential for public relations specialists. They must have research skills and then express the important thoughts clearly and simply. They are doers who possess a creative flair. Good judgment, problem solving, and decision making are part of their job. The abilities to lead and to persuade (to influence others' thinking) are definite skills used to get the intended results and outcomes.

Television newscasters and radio announcers, who often are called disc jockeys, are part of the communications field. Beginners usually start at small stations and move up as they "prove" themselves. Announcers at small stations may be called upon to do all of the following: select and introduce recorded music; present news, sports, weather, and commercials, often chitchatting with their audience to fill in time blocks; research and prepare written scripts; write up news reports and commercials; and operate control boards. Large stations permit specialization: news anchors introduce videotaped news segments or live reports from reporters in the field; weathercasters or meteorologists report information they have gathered from weather services; and sportscasters select the coverage, write, and report sporting news and events.

Educational courses may include radio news gathering and writing; television newswriting;

television news production; fundamentals of sports reporting; advertising; copywriting; sound recording; listening to music; history of music; and history of jazz.

Announcing requires a pleasant and well-controlled voice, good pacing, excellent pronunciation, and proper English usage. Television announcers usually appear neat and make a good visual presentation. A well-rounded and broad education enables announcers to deal with a diversity of topics with verbal facility and possibly a "glib tongue." Computer literacy is required because stories are created and edited on the computer.

Where Do Communications Majors Work?

Graduates with bachelor's degrees in communications are most likely to work as wage and salary employees in private, for-profit firms, with only a small proportion working in the nonprofit area for charities, foundations, and nonprofit interest groups. Nearly 1 in 6 graduates of communications programs are self-employed. This statistic reflects a growing trend in the communications field: producers, directors, writers, and on-air personalities are hired on a temporary contract basis to complete particular assignments and then move on to complete other work at entirely different organizations. This industry is among the largest employers of these so-called contingent workers who are contracted to engage in specific tasks, usually for short periods of time. Educational institutions, particularly colleges and universities, also employ communications graduates in the public relations and marketing departments to support various college publications, such as alumni magazines. Government agencies, along with elected officials, also employ communications majors to provide public relations and speechwriting support.

FIGURE 1

Percentage Distribution of Employed Persons with Only a Bachelor's Degree in Communications, by Major Sector of Economic Activity

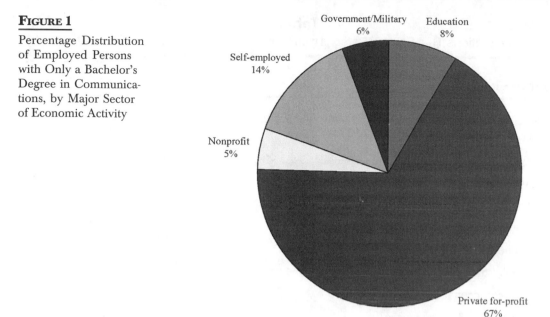

Government/Military
6%

Education
8%

Self-employed
14%

Nonprofit
5%

Private for-profit
67%

Occupations

Access to jobs that are more closely related to the communications degree is somewhat limited in this highly competitive field. Fewer than 1 in 3 persons with a degree in the communications field report that they work in a job closely tied to their undergraduate degree. Only about 18 percent of communications majors report that they work as broadcasters, writers, and public relations specialists or in similar types of creative positions in the field. However, a substantial number of graduates report that they work in jobs that are somewhat related to the field;

for example, about 1 in 6 were involved in sales and marketing positions, whereas about 13 percent had managerial or administrative positions often in the communications sector. It is important to note that more than 3 in 10 graduates of communications programs had jobs unrelated to their undergraduate major. These positions included secretarial and clerical jobs and unrelated finance and accounting jobs. Those working outside the field said the lack of job opportunities, poor pay and promotion potential, and poor working conditions were important reasons why they were employed in unrelated jobs.

Table 1
Top 10 Occupations That Employ Persons with Only a Bachelor's Degree in Communications

Top 10 Occupations	PERCENT OF EMPLOYED		
	All	Men	Women
Artists, broadcasters, writers, editors, entertainers, public relations specialists	17.6	18.9	16.1
Top- and mid-level managers, executives, administrators	12.6	16.2	8.5
Sales occupations, including retail	8.3	8.6	7.9
Insurance, securities, real estate, business services	8.2	7.8	8.6
Other marketing and sales occupations	8.1	8.4	7.7
Other management-related occupations	6.2	5.7	6.8
Other administrative (e.g., records clerks, telephone operators)	3.8	2.2	5.5
Other service occupations, except health	3.5	2.6	4.5
Secretaries, receptionists, typists	2.6	0.1	5.5
Accountants, auditors, other financial specialists	2.4	1.4	3.6

▶ Men and women communications majors are about equal in their ability to find work in creative writing and editing positions.

▶ Men are nearly twice as likely as women to work in high-paying positions as top- or mid-level managers.

▶ The rate of employment of female communications graduates in clerical positions is three times higher than the rate among their male counterparts. Nearly 1 in 6 women with a degree in communications work in a clerical occupation.

▶ skill requirements of persons entering this career field.

▶ Managerial and administrative tasks, along with employee-relations tasks, also are important duties of persons with degrees in communication.

▶ Little research is conducted by graduates with degrees in this field.

▶ Computer skills, including the development of computer applications, are an important activity undertaken by communications program graduates.

Activities on the Job

▶ Persons with a degree in communications are most likely to spend a good part of their workweek engaged in a marketing or sales activity. Sales and marketing skills are a major part of the

Salaries

Communications majors have annual salaries that are below those of the average graduate with a bachelor's degree. The average communications graduate with a bachelor's degree earns $48,900, whereas the average college graduate earns $54,200, representing an earnings deficit of about 10 percent per year for the communications major. Young communications majors between the ages of 25 and 29 have average annual earnings of $37,500 per year. Communications careers are characterized by a substantial amount of skill development on the job, most often through informal learning by observing others and quite often by simply doing the tasks. The impact of this on-the-job learning is illustrated in Figure 2, showing that the earnings of communications majors grow sharply with age and years of work experience. By ages 50 to 55, the earnings of communications majors increase to $72,000, more than doubling the annual earnings in inflation-adjusted terms.

Although self-employment offers a certain amount of career anxiety, its economic rewards are substantial. Self-employed communications majors earn an average of $61,000 per year, representing an earnings premium of 25 percent relative to the average earnings of all communications majors. Graduates of communications programs who work in educational institutions have earnings of only $36,100 annually. Graduates of communications programs who are employed in jobs that are closely related to their field of study have substantially higher earnings than other communications graduates.

The earnings of persons with a bachelor's degree in communications vary systematically by occupation. Those employed in creative occupations such as writer, artist, and public relations specialist have above-average salaries, earning $49,900 per year. The highest pay is found among those communications majors who are employed in managerial and administrative positions. The annual salaries of communications majors employed in occupations that don't generally require a college degree, such as secretarial and clerical positions, are quite low.

FIGURE 2

Age/Earnings Profile of Persons with Only a Bachelor's Degree in Communications (Full-Time Workers, in 2002 Dollars)

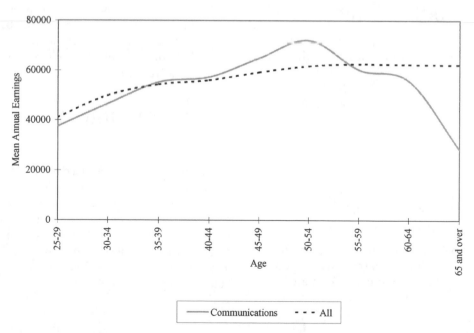

Table 2

Annual Salary of Full-Time Workers with Only a Bachelor's Degree
in Communications, Top 10 Occupations (in 2002 Dollars)

Earnings in Top 10 Occupations	All	Communications
Total	$54,171	$48,907
Artists, broadcasters, writers, editors, entertainers, public relations specialists	$52,141	$49,897
Top- and mid-level managers, executives, administrators	$74,051	$62,885
Sales occupations, including retail	$52,378	$47,080
Insurance, securities, real estate, business services	$68,273	$59,803
Other marketing and sales occupations	$58,208	$53,540
Other management-related occupations	$51,921	$45,221
Other administrative (e.g., records clerks, telephone operators)	$34,547	$32,249
Other service occupations, except health	$39,984	$40,668
Secretaries, receptionists, typists	$32,246	$32,284
Accountants, auditors, other financial specialists	$57,382	$37,963

On-the-Job Training

Many of the skills used by graduates of communications programs are learned through informal, on-the-job training activities. However, over the course of a year, about two-thirds of all employed persons with a degree in communications will engage in some type of classroom training activity to improve their job-related skills.

▶ Most often the training that communications majors participate in is to enhance a specific professional skill, such as writing copy, marketing, or art.

▶ Forty percent participate in training to enhance their personal communication skills, including public speaking and business writing.

▶ Most communications majors who receive this training are motivated by a desire to increase their professional skills and improve their chance for career advancement.

Post-Graduation Activities

Most individuals who earn a degree in communications do not go on to complete a program of study leading to an advanced degree. Only about 18 percent of communications majors eventually earn a graduate degree of some sort; three-quarters of these earn a master's degree, about 10 percent earn a doctorate, and 15 percent earn a professional degree.

- Individuals with a bachelor's degree in communications who complete a master's program often earn the degree outside the communications field. Three-quarters of all master's degrees awarded to persons with an undergraduate degree in communications are in fields unrelated to the major. Only 1 in 5 earns a master's degree in education, and 17 percent go on to earn a degree in business.

- While relatively few communications majors go on to earn a doctorate, about one-half of those who do earn a doctorate complete their studies in the communications field. About one-sixth of those with doctorates earn them in education.

- Most of those who earn a professional degree earn it in the field of law. Few earn a degree in medicine.

The employment rate of persons with a bachelor's degree in communications is nearly 90 percent. Most work in full-time positions, and those who do not almost always prefer part-time work; that is, they voluntarily choose to work on a part-time basis. Of those remaining without employment, about 7 of 10 choose not to work, most often because of family responsibilities. About 3 percent of all communications majors are classified as unemployed.

Employment Outlook

According to the most recent projections by the U.S. Bureau of Labor Statistics, the employment outlook for college graduates suggests continued strong demand. However, the job outlook for any given undergraduate major field of study depends on the kinds of occupations in which graduates from that major are employed. Communications majors are employed in a set of occupations that present a mixed picture of future job prospects.

- Employment in sales and marketing occupations is expected to increase by 22 percent over the projection period between 2000 and 2010. This rate of increase is 7 percentage points higher than the average rate of job growth (15.2 percent) expected in the economy as a whole.

- Employment for communications majors in the creative occupations of artist, broadcaster, writer, and public relations specialist is expected to increase by nearly 21 percent through 2010, representing the second-highest rate of increase among the top 10 occupations that employ communications majors.

- Employment in top-level managerial occupations; sales occupations; and insurance, securities, and real estate occupations (the second , third , and fourth-largest employers of communications graduates with a bachelor's degree) is projected to grow by about 12 percent between 2000 and 2010, a rate of growth that is 3 percentage points lower than the overall projected rate of job growth in the U.S. economy.

Table 3

Projected Change in Employment in the Top 10 Occupations That
Employ Persons with Only a Bachelor's Degree in Communications

Top 10 Occupations	Actual Employment in 2000 (000s)	Projected Employment in 2010 (000s)	Absolute Change (000s)	Percentage Change
Artists, broadcasters, writers, editors, entertainers, public relations specialists	2,371	2,864	493	20.8%
Top- and mid-level managers, executives, administrators	10,564	11,834	1,270	12.0%
Sales occupations, including retail	15,513	17,365	1,852	11.9%
Insurance, securities, real estate, business services	1,548	1,726	178	11.5%
Other marketing and sales occupations	621	758	137	22.1%
Other management-related occupations	4,956	5,801	845	17.1%
Other administrative (e.g., records clerks, telephone operators)	16,911	18,522	1,611	9.5%
Other service occupations, except health	9,652	11,287	1,635	16.9%
Secretaries, receptionists, typists	4,980	5,501	521	10.5%
Accountants, auditors, other financial specialists	2,115	2,481	366	17.3%

CHAPTER 38

Dramatic Arts

This broad entertainment field covers majors in theater, the arts, drama, drama literature, and cinematology. Individuals studying in these majors may aspire to be an actor or actress, comedian, stage director, news or sports announcer, director, production assistant, or producer. The performance media are likewise diversified, including theater, film, television, and radio. Two interests commonly shared among members of this group are expressing ideas and creating images for audiences. Actors and actresses entertain and communicate with people through their portrayal and interpretation of roles. Although some people may never have seen a play on stage, everyone has watched actors and actresses performing in movies or on television.

The business management side of dramatic arts is the focus of directors and producers whose backgrounds may differ from those of actors and actresses. Directors interpret plays or scripts. They also audition and select cast and crew members. Directors use their knowledge of acting, voice, and movement to achieve the best possible performance. They typically will approve the scenery, costumes, choreography, and music. Producers are entrepreneurs. They select scripts of playwrights or scriptwriters, arrange financing, and decide on the size and content of the production and its budget. They hire directors, principal cast members, and key production staff. They negotiate contracts with artistic personnel's booking managers. Producers coordinate activities for writers, directors, and managers.

The field of dramatic arts involves experiential learning. However, most people enter drama curricula to enhance their chances in this highly competitive field. Courses include communications, stage speech and movement, directing, playwriting, play production, set design, history of drama, and acting. Opportunities for participating in dramatic productions, announcing, and being in front of audiences are constantly sought after. No specific training requirements are necessary for directors and producers.

Several abilities are needed in dramatic arts: being able to perform before an audience with poise and self-confidence; interpreting roles and expressing ideas and emotions through gestures, facial expressions, and voice inflections; understanding the script author's ideas and demonstrating to others methods of moving or speaking to convey these ideas to an audience; speaking clearly and loudly; and memorizing dialogue and responding to clues promptly. Although not an ability, physical appearance is often a factor in being accepted for certain roles.

The interests of those in dramatic arts are definitely in the entertainment field and typically include a liking for literary, artistic, and musical activities. Outgoing and extroverted, those in dramatic arts want to work with or in front of people.

Creativity and imagination are hallmark values of those in the dramatic arts. A cluster of rewards—prestige, public attention, and recognition—also go along with this field. Especially those who succeed are recognized and noticed by the public. Because of this field's glamorous image, even an association with it brings prestige. Directors and producers value leadership and, when successful, are rewarded with generous salaries. Actors, however, have the reputation of accepting sporadic work and varied roles, often resulting in the perception that they lead independent lifestyles.

People in dramatic arts enjoy being trendsetters and innovators. Their ideas provide energy, and they thrive in going from one project to another. Routine is problematic for them; they prefer to be versatile. They have good interpersonal skills,

focusing on the feelings of others, which helps them connect or resonate with others. They are perceived as friendly and warm individuals.

Where Do Dramatic Arts Majors Work?

Finding a job closely related to the field of dramatic arts is difficult. Graduates of dramatic arts programs at the undergraduate level don't generally work in jobs in the field, instead finding employment across key segments of the American economy. Usually persons with a bachelor's degree in dramatic arts work as wage and salary workers in for-profit businesses and corporations. Often dramatic arts graduates are self-employed, usually as consultants rather than as small business owners. Of those with an undergraduate degree in dramatic arts, 1 in 4 works in an educational institution, frequently as an elementary or secondary school teacher. Few dramatic arts majors work in a government agency or for a nonprofit charitable foundation.

FIGURE 1

Percentage Distribution of Employed Persons with Only a Bachelor's Degree in Dramatic Arts, by Major Sector of Economic Activity

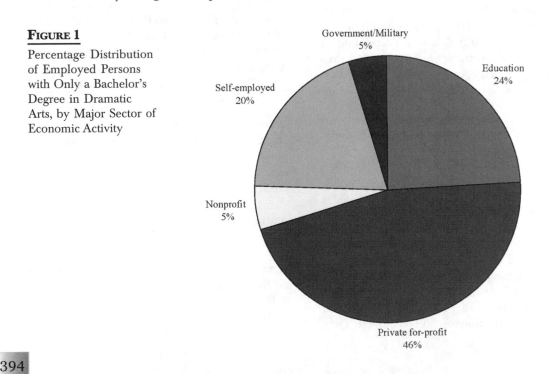

Government/Military 5%

Education 24%

Self-employed 20%

Nonprofit 5%

Private for-profit 46%

Occupations

Most dramatic arts majors work in jobs that are not closely related to their undergraduate fields of study. Those who work in jobs related to the field are most often employed in creative occupations such as artist, entertainer, writer, and broadcaster. Still, only 1 in 5 dramatic arts majors works in these positions. About 8 percent of those with bachelor's degrees in the field are employed as secondary school teachers, with many of them reporting that their work is closely related to the dramatic arts. These individuals often work as arts and theater teachers and as drama coaches at the high school level. Only 1 in 4 dramatic arts majors works in sales jobs. About one-third of those involved in sales work in high-level jobs related to securities, insurance, and real estate.

A major problem for graduates of dramatic arts programs is that not only are they frequently employed in jobs outside their major, but also they often work in positions that do not even require a college degree of any type. A look at the data in Table 1 reveals that a minimum of 20 percent of all majors in this field work as secretaries and clerks, in low-level service occupations (such as janitors and parking lot attendants), and in food preparation and service jobs. Typically these jobs do not require a college degree and generally have salaries that are well below the average of all bachelor's degree holders. Those employed in jobs outside the field say poor pay and promotion opportunities and limited availability of jobs related to dramatic arts are the two primary reasons why they are employed in jobs unrelated to the field.

Table 1

Top 10 Occupations That Employ Persons with Only a Bachelor's Degree in Dramatic Arts

Top 10 Occupations	PERCENT OF EMPLOYED		
	All	Men	Women
Artists, broadcasters, writers, editors, entertainers, public relations specialists	19.8	22.8	17.4
Top- and mid-level managers, executives, administrators	8.5	10.3	7.1
Teachers, secondary school	8.1	5.7	10.1
Secretaries, receptionists, typists	7.1	4.4	9.4
Sales occupations, including retail	6.1	4.7	7.2
Other administrative (e.g., records clerks, telephone operators)	5.0	3.8	6.0
Other service occupations, except health	5.0	3.8	6.0
Other marketing and sales occupations	3.2	3.5	2.9
Food preparation and service occupations	3.2	4.5	2.1
Other management-related occupations	3.1	2.5	3.6

- Men with undergraduate degrees in dramatic arts are about 30 percent more likely than women with the same degree to work in creative positions such as artist and writer.

- Women with a degree in dramatic arts are much more likely than their male counterparts to be employed as secondary teachers: 10 percent of women with an undergraduate degree in the field work as teachers, while only 6 percent of men are employed as secondary school teachers.

- Women with a degree in dramatic arts are substantially more likely than men to be employed in jobs that do not require a college degree. Nearly one-quarter of women with degrees in this field work outside the college labor market, compared to only 1 in 6 men.

Activities on the Job

- Typically the job duties of graduates of most dramatic arts programs include routine administrative tasks related to accounting, finance, and contracts.

- Because a high fraction of majors work in sales-related positions and marketing, sales-related duties are an important part of the responsibilities of graduates from this major.

- Teaching duties are a major part of the job responsibilities for many graduates from this field, not only for those involved in secondary education but also for those employed in the creative fields of art, writing, and entertainment.

- Supervisory and employee relations tasks are key job duties of about one-half of the graduates from this field.

Salaries

The annual salaries of those employed in full-time jobs with a bachelor's degree in dramatic arts are quite low compared to the earnings of graduates with undergraduate degrees in other major fields of study. Dramatic arts majors earn $41,600 per year, whereas the average person with a bachelor's degree has an annual salary of $54,200; dramatic arts majors earn about 23 percent less per year than the average college graduate. Although the earnings of graduates from this field do increase over their working lives, the size of their earnings deficit relative to the average college graduate remains large. Between the ages of 25 and 29, graduates in dramatic arts earn $32,200. Over the next 25 years, annual salaries increase to nearly $49,700 per year. This increase in earnings suggests that on-the-job training is important for dramatic arts majors, who must rely on the workplace rather than the classroom to acquire the skills valued by employers. The earnings of majors vary somewhat based on the sector of the economy in which they are employed. Salaries are highest for those working in private, for-profit businesses and corporations. Those working in educational institutions have average salaries of only $33,700, a low rate of pay even by that industry's standards.

FIGURE 2

Age/Earnings Profile of Persons with Only a Bachelor's Degree in Dramatic Arts
(Full-Time Workers, in 2002 Dollars)

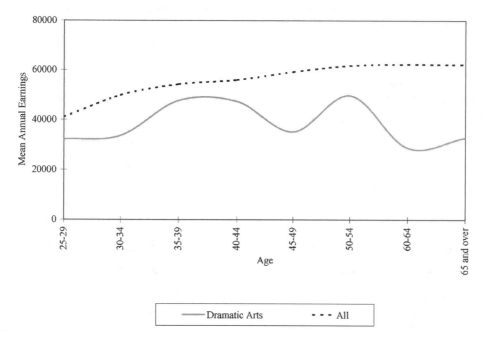

The availability of jobs that utilize the skills learned in college is an important determinant of the earnings of dramatic arts majors. While only 20 percent of majors work as artists, entertainers, etc., their annual salaries average $49,500 per year, a rate of pay 20 percent higher than the average of all graduates in the dramatic arts field. Those who work in management and administrative positions earn $63,000, a salary level that is well above the earnings of the average dramatic arts majors. Those majors with low earnings are employed in jobs that do not use skills learned within the major and that do not usually employ college graduates. Majors who work as secretaries earn only $29,500 per year; majors working as clerks earn $32,500. Those employed in low-level service jobs earn $29,800; those employed in food preparation jobs earn only $25,300 per year. In part the earnings of dramatic arts majors are low because of their relatively poor success in getting jobs that utilize college-level skills.

Table 2

Annual Salary of Full-Time Workers with Only a Bachelor's Degree
in Dramatic Arts, Top 10 Occupations (in 2002 Dollars)

Earnings in Top 10 Occupations	All	Dramatic Arts
Total	$54,171	$41,580
Artists, broadcasters, writers, editors, entertainers, public relations specialists	$52,141	$49,526
Top- and mid-level managers, executives, administrators	$74,051	$63,015
Teachers, secondary school	$40,355	$41,623
Secretaries, receptionists, typists	$32,246	$29,496
Sales occupations, including retail	$52,378	$42,036
Other administrative (e.g., records clerks, telephone operators)	$34,547	$32,473
Other service occupations, except health	$39,984	$29,768
Other marketing and sales occupations	$58,208	$36,530
Food preparation and service occupations	$29,506	$25,304
Other management-related occupations	$51,921	$36,733

On-the-Job Training

Informal on-the-job learning is critical to the long-term career development of persons who earn degrees in dramatic arts. Access to jobs in which employers invest in general skills and in job-specific skills is essential to long-term labor market success for majors in this field. The likelihood of participating in work-based training activities varies considerably among dramatic arts majors, depending on the occupation in which they are employed. For example, about three-quarters of those employed in sales-related occupations participate in work-based training seminars and workshops, while fewer than one-half of those employed in jobs that do not require a college degree receive this type of training.

▶ Most often the training received by graduates in dramatic arts is related to the development of specific occupational skills. For example, those employed in marketing and sales positions usually participate in sales-related training programs and activities.

▶ Development of writing and public speaking skills is also an important part of the work-based training activities of those majors who are employed in college labor market jobs.

▶ Most of those who participate in training are motivated by the desire to acquire job-specific skills that in many instances may lead to enhanced opportunities for advancement.

Post-Graduation Activities

About one-third of all dramatic arts majors who complete an undergraduate program of study go on to eventually earn an advanced degree. Most of these individuals decide to earn a master's degree. More than 1 in 4 graduates earn a master's degree, about 2 percent earn a doctorate, and an additional 2 percent earn a professional degree.

- Among those who earn a master's degree, one-half continue their studies in the dramatic arts field. About 1 of 6 earn a master's degree in education, and about 6 percent earn a business degree.

- Dramatic arts majors who earn a doctorate stay in the field about one-third of the time. Other areas in which they earn doctorates include psychology, communications, and languages.

- While only a small number of dramatic arts majors earn a professional degree, most who do earn a professional degree study law. Virtually no dramatic arts majors complete a medical education.

About 8 of 10 dramatic arts majors are employed after graduation. However, nearly 1 of 4 who are employed work in part-time positions. This rate of part-time employment is double that of the average college graduate. Among those who are jobless, about 3 in 10 are involuntarily unemployed and actively seeking work. The rest who choose not to work say are not participating in the labor market primarily because of family responsibilities.

Employment Outlook

According to employment projections of the U.S. Bureau of Labor Statistics, the employment situation of graduates of dramatic arts programs is not likely to improve markedly over the coming years. Projections of job growth in occupations that are most likely to employ the graduates of dramatic arts programs suggest a relatively slow growth in the job prospects for graduates in the major.

- Employment as artist or entertainer, and in other creative occupational fields, is expected to increase by 21 percent between 2000 and 2010, a rate of growth equal to the expected rate of increase in the overall demand for bachelor's degree holders and well above the 15.2 percent increase forecast in overall employment levels in the American economy.

- Most of the other occupations that employ majors from this field are expected to have slower rates of employment growth through 2010. The sales occupations are expected to increase by 12 percent in retail sales occupations to 22 percent in miscellaneous marketing and sales occupations over the projection period, while the demand for secondary school teachers will increase by 18 percent.

- These developments suggest that in general the increase in demand for graduates from dramatic arts will be slower than the increase in demand for college graduates. Dramatic arts majors will likely continue to have difficulty in the labor market in the future and will more likely work in part-time positions, be unemployed, and work in jobs that do not require a college degree.

Table 3

Projected Change in Employment in the Top 10 Occupations That
Employ Persons with Only a Bachelor's Degree in Dramatic Arts

Top 10 Occupations	Actual Employment in 2000 (000s)	Projected Employment in 2010 (000s)	Absolute Change (000s)	Percentage Change
Artists, broadcasters, writers, editors, entertainers, public relations specialists	2,371	2,864	493	20.8%
Top- and mid-level managers, executives, administrators	10,564	11,834	1,270	12.0%
Teachers, secondary school	1,113	1,314	201	18.1%
Secretaries, receptionists, typists	4,980	5,501	521	10.5%
Sales occupations, including retail	15,513	17,365	1,852	11.9%
Other administrative (e.g., records clerks, telephone operators)	16,911	18,522	1,611	9.5%
Other service occupations, except health	9,652	11,287	1,635	16.9%
Other marketing and sales occupations	621	758	137	22.1%
Food preparation and service occupations	10,140	11,717	1,577	15.6%
Other management-related occupations	4,956	5,801	845	17.1%

CHAPTER 39

English Language, Literature, and Letters

English is a subject or a course of study. As a course of study, it does not convert directly to an occupation, as do most other majors, such as accounting for accountants and art for artists. English is a language and, like other languages, is a foundational ability.

The study of English also involves literature. The study of literature typically is divided by country, such as English or American literature; by time period; or by type of literature, such as poetry and novels. Some people study literature to critically examine authors' expressive styles or they study, as models, the great works of accepted masters to develop their own creative writing. Others view creative writing as a more unique individualistic expression.

Many English majors continue their appreciation for this field by becoming teachers; these individuals should also explore the education major. Others studying English use it as a preparatory step to writing. The occupations of writer and editor are described here. For other writing occupations, consider the journalism major.

Writers and Editors

Writers develop original fiction and nonfiction for books, magazines, trade journals, newspapers, technical reports, company newsletters, radio and television broadcasts, movies, and advertisements. The following are illustrative writing and editing occupations.

Newswriters prepare news items for newspapers or news broadcasts on information supplied by reporters or wire services. Columnists analyze news and write commentaries based on personal knowledge and experience. Editorial writers write comments to stimulate public opinion in accordance with their publication's viewpoint. Copywriters write advertising for promotional purposes to sell products or services. Technical writers take technical and scientific information and make it understandable to nontechnical audiences; this information may be presented as assembly instructions, operating manuals, catalogs, and parts lists. Unlike other writers whose work may be assigned by an editor, novelists have a freedom in what they write and where they work, such as at home. But writers in general follow a process of collecting information, either by interview or research, and then organizing, writing, rewriting, and shaping the information for the best delivery or organization for a specific purpose or publication.

Editors select and prepare material for publication or broadcast and supervise writers. They review, rewrite, and edit writers' work. The primary duties of an editor include planning the content of books, magazines, or newspapers and supervising their preparation. Editors decide what will appeal to readers. They hire and assign staff, plan budgets, and negotiate contracts—in other words, they are managers. In a broadcasting firm this person is called a program director.

Entrants to editorial jobs often have titles as editorial assistant, copy assistant, or production assistant. They review copy for errors in grammar, punctuation, and spelling. They check manuscripts for readability, style, and agreement with editorial policy. They add and rearrange sentences to improve clarity, and they delete incorrect and unnecessary material. Editorial assistants do research for writers and verify facts, dates, and statistics. Assistants also may arrange page layouts of articles, photographs, and advertising. They may compose headlines, prepare copy for printing, and proofread printer's galleys. Some editorial assistants read and evaluate manuscripts submitted by freelance writers or answer letters about published or broadcast material. Production assistants on small newspapers or in radio stations clip stories that come over the wire services' printers, answer phones, and make photocopies.

Abilities include good clear writing and using correct grammar. But writers have visions they want to share. They also perceive themselves to have teaching ability and social ability. They work well with people and have a goal to keep people well informed. Editors have definite leadership qualities, which they execute when deciding which areas to highlight and what to provide readers. Computer proficiency and familiarity with electronic publishing are becoming basic skills.

Writers and editors have artistic interests such as art, music, and drama in addition to literary interests. The literary interests are closely related to an interest in analyzing, examining, and researching material. In general, writers have social interests. Editors also have a liking for business activities.

Benefits include working with the mind, creativity, variety and diversion, and a good income, which some do not get. Identifying topics and issues, researching them, and then seeking the best way to write them up is a mental challenge. Imagination is needed to discover new untold stories. And, following the saying "old news is stale news," writers and editors are constantly searching for material. In the discovery process they have all their sensory capacities functioning and thus know when it is time to delve further or move on.

Personal characteristics include curiosity, possessing a broad range of knowledge, self-motivation, and perseverance. Often events that writers are covering are surrounded by confusion, yet they still must produce a coherent piece of writing. Writers and editors constantly are making judgments in deciding what to write. Their work requires tact and the ability to encourage others to participate with them in the creation of a story. Working under pressure is fairly typical, and thus writing is stressful. Being a self-motivator and self-starter is important because some writers and editors work at home on a fee-for-service basis or as freelancers. These writers need self-discipline and self-promotion to get additional work, and they need to avoid distractions that are atypical of an office environment.

Where Do English Majors Work?

The employment of English majors is spread across the five sectors of the economy. Fewer than one-half work in the private, for-profit sector for businesses and corporations. Another 14 percent work in the private, for-profit sector as self-employed workers in their own business or practice. Nearly 3 of 10 English majors work in the education sector of the economy, hired mainly as teachers. Another 10 percent work in the government sector, and 7 percent work in the nonprofit sector of the economy for tax-exempt or charitable organizations.

Not many English majors work in jobs that are related to their major. The reason is that English is not an occupation but an ability that provides a foundation on which other occupational skills can be developed. Only 30 percent of the graduates work in jobs that are closely related to their major. Another 30 percent say their jobs are somewhat related to their major. The remaining 40 percent work in jobs that are not at all related to their undergraduate major.

Various factors underlie the decision of English majors to work in jobs that are unrelated to their major. More than one-half do so because of better pay and promotion opportunities outside their field. A little less than one-half indicate that the reason for working in an unrelated job is the working conditions, such as hours, equipment, or general working environment. The same proportion report that one of the reasons they choose to work outside their field is their desire to change career and professional interests. A little less than 30 percent of English graduates who work in unrelated jobs do so because of family-related reasons, and another 30 percent are unable to find related jobs.

FIGURE 1

Percentage Distribution of Employed Persons with Only a Bachelor's Degree in English, by Major Sector of Economic Activity

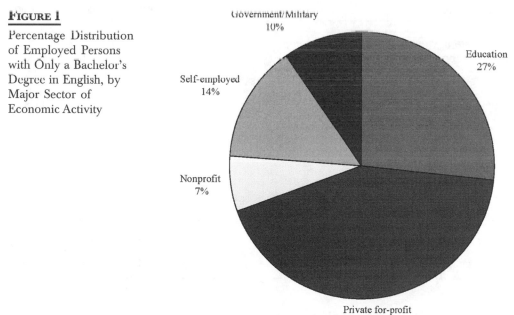

Government/Military 10%

Education 27%

Self-employed 14%

Nonprofit 7%

Private for-profit 42%

The most important reason for employment outside their major field of study among English majors is better pay and promotion opportunities. Slightly more than one-quarter consider that to be the most important reason. About 23 percent consider a change in their career and professional interests to be the number one reason for working in unrelated jobs. Almost one-third are distributed evenly between family-related reasons, non-availability of related jobs, and the overall working environment as the most important factors influencing their decision to work outside their undergraduate major field.

Occupations

Employment among English majors is dispersed across a variety of occupations. Artists, broadcasters, writers, editors, entertainers, and public relations specialist occupations employ 11 percent of all employed English majors. Another 11 percent are employed in top- to mid-level managerial, executive, and administrative occupations, and an equal proportion are employed as teachers in secondary schools. Occupations that involve insurance, stocks and bonds, real estate transactions, and business services employ 6 percent of English graduates. English majors also are employed in secretarial jobs; sales occupations; management-related occupations as accountants, management analysts, financial specialists, and purchasing agents; elementary school teaching; clerical jobs; and miscellaneous service occupations.

Table 1
Top 10 Occupations That Employ Persons with Only a Bachelor's Degree in English

	PERCENT OF EMPLOYED		
Top 10 Occupations	**All**	**Men**	**Women**
Artists, broadcasters, writers, editors, entertainers, public relations specialists	10.7	11.5	10.3
Top- and mid-level managers, executives, administrators	10.6	17.3	7.0
Teachers, secondary school	10.6	9.0	11.4
Insurance, securities, real estate, business services	5.9	10.0	3.7
Secretaries, receptionists, typists	5.1	1.4	7.1
Sales occupations, including retail	4.9	6.3	4.2
Other management-related occupations	4.8	5.5	4.5
Other administrative (e.g., records clerks, telephone operators)	4.8	2.0	6.2
Teachers, elementary school	3.5	1.1	4.7
Other service occupations, except health	3.2	4.4	2.6

- Men constitute 35 percent of all employed English graduates. Male English majors are somewhat more likely than female English majors to work as artists, broadcasters, writers, editors, entertainers, and public relations specialists—12 percent versus 10 percent.

- Men also are more likely to work in top- to mid-level managerial and administrative jobs and in occupations involving insurance, securities, real estate, and business services.

- Women are more likely than men to be employed in secretarial, administrative/clerical, and teaching occupations.

Activities on the Job

The diversity in the occupational attachment of English majors is reflected in the breadth of duties they perform on their jobs.

- Although 81 percent of all employed English graduates perform accounting, finance, and contractual duties as a regular part of their jobs, only 8 percent spend most of their time in a typical workweek performing these duties. Many English majors perform these duties as a part of their jobs, but very few spend most of their time in performing them.

- Forty-eight percent of employed English majors perform management and administrative duties regularly, and 13 percent spend most of their time during a typical workweek in performing these duties.

- One-third of all employed English majors engage in teaching activities. Most of those who do engage in teaching activities spend more time in teaching than any other activity. Nearly 21 percent of employed English graduates spend most of their typical workweek on teaching activities.

- Another one-third of employed English majors perform sales, purchasing, and marketing duties regularly at their jobs. About 14 percent spend most hours during a week in performing these duties.

- Engaging in computer applications, programming, and systems-development activities is reported by one-third of all employed English graduates. However, only 7 percent spend most of their time on these activities.

- Another 31 percent regularly engage in employee-relations activities, including recruiting, personnel development, and training. Only 5 percent conduct these duties during most of their working time.

- One-fourth of all employed English majors regularly provide professional services, and 1 in 10 graduates report that they spend most of their time in the provision of professional services.

Salaries

The average annual salary of English graduates who have only a bachelor's degree and are employed full-time is $48,900, a level that is 90 percent of the average annual salary of all full-time employed college graduates. As for most college graduates, the salary of English majors increases with age, indicating that they get more productive and therefore can earn higher salaries as they spend more time on the job. However, at different ages, English majors earn lower salaries than all college graduates.

▶ The annual average salary of English majors between the ages of 25 and 29 is $36,000. Graduates between the ages of 30 and 34 earn $47,300 annually.

▶ Average annual earnings of English graduates increase at a moderate pace as they get older. The average annual salary of English majors between 35 and 39 who are employed full-time is $47,800. The average salary of those between 40 and 44 is $50,000 per year. The salary peaks between the ages of 50 and 54, with an average salary of $55,900.

▶ The average annual salary of English majors who work in jobs that are closely related to their major field of study is lower than the average annual salary of those who are employed in jobs that are somewhat related to their major— $46,000 versus $52,000. Graduates whose jobs are closely related are employed in teaching occupations that generally pay lower salaries than some of the jobs in the communications sector and in upper-level managerial and sales jobs that are somewhat related to the undergraduate major of English and are generally associated with higher salaries. Many English majors who are employed in unrelated jobs typically work in clerical, secretarial, and low-end sales and service sector jobs.

▶ English graduates who work in the private, for-profit sector for corporations and businesses earn an average salary of $56,200. Self-employed English graduates operating their own incorporated or non-incorporated business earn an average annual salary of $50,200. The government sector pays English graduates who are employed full-time an average annual salary of $43,900. The annual average remuneration of English graduates with full-time jobs in the private, nonprofit sector is $42,500. English majors who are employed by educational institutions earn only $38,800 per year, a level that is lower than the average salary of English majors employed in other sectors of the economy.

There are sizable variations in the average annual salary of English graduates depending on the occupation in which they are employed. The average annual salary of English majors is 90 percent of the average salary of all college graduates. In 6 of the top 10 occupations that are predominant employers of English majors, the salary of all college graduates exceeds that of English majors.

▶ English majors employed in business services, insurance, securities, and real estate occupations earn an average salary of $75,400, which is higher than the average salary of graduates working in the top 10 occupations that are predominant employers of English graduates.

▶ The annual salary of those who are in top- and mid-level managerial, executive, and administrative occupations is $70,700.

▶ Employment as broadcasters, writers, editors, and other entertainment and public relations occupations pays English majors $58,600 annually.

▶ Those who are employed as teachers at the elementary and secondary level, respectively, earn $42,500 and $38,700.

FIGURE 2

Age/Earnings Profile of Persons with Only a Bachelor's Degree in English
(Full-Time Workers, in 2002 Dollars)

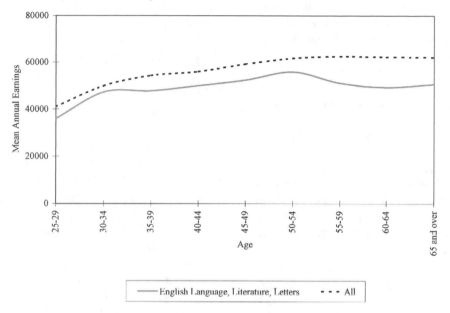

Table 2

Annual Salary of Full-Time Workers with Only a Bachelor's Degree in
English, Top 10 Occupations (in 2002 Dollars)

Earnings in Top 10 Occupations	All	English Language, Literature, and Letters
Total	$54,171	$48,890
Artists, broadcasters, writers, editors, entertainers, public relations specialists	$52,141	$58,583
Top- and mid-level managers, executives, administrators	$74,051	$70,706
Teachers, secondary school	$40,355	$38,691
Insurance, securities, real estate, business services	$68,273	$75,419
Secretaries, receptionists, typists	$32,246	$33,654
Sales occupations, including retail	$52,378	$41,134
Other management-related occupations	$51,921	$48,508
Other administrative (e.g., records clerks, telephone operators)	$34,547	$33,777
Teachers, elementary school	$39,167	$42,528
Other service occupations, except health	$39,984	$36,342

On-the-Job Training

The career potential of a job is closely associated with the amount of work-related training on the job. Work-related training is regarded as an investment by firms because it makes workers more productive. Firms that invest in their workforce are more likely to offer pay increases and promotions to match the increasing productivity of their workers. Firms that do not invest in their workers are relatively less likely to offer pay increases and promotions. Employed English majors are somewhat less likely to receive work-related training, compared to all employed college graduates. Whereas 68 percent of all employed college graduates received some work-related training, 63 percent of English majors received training on the job during the past year.

- Of those English majors who receive some training, 70 percent receive technical training in their occupational field.

- Thirty-seven percent receive training to improve their general professional skills, such as public speaking and business writing.

- Twenty-eight percent of recipients who receive training participate in management or supervisory training.

Of those English majors who participate in some work-related training, 93 percent do so to improve their occupational skills and knowledge. Nearly one-half are required or expected by their employers to undergo training. Increased opportunity for promotion, advancement, and salary increases are the reasons that 40 percent of English majors participate in work-related training; 29 percent cite the need to learn skills for a newly acquired position as one of the reasons for their participation in work-related training. When asked to identify the most important reason to acquire training, 65 percent of English majors who undergo training choose the need

to improve their occupational skills and knowledge. Another 12 percent report mandatory training requirements by the employer as the most important factor for their involvement in work-related training.

Post-Graduation Activities

Nearly 45 percent of English graduates with a bachelor's degree proceed to earn a post-graduate degree: 33 percent earn a master's degree, 5 percent graduate with a doctorate, and fewer than 6 percent earn a professional degree.

- Only 26 percent of the master's degrees are earned in English. Education is the major field of choice among 31 percent of master's degree earners, and another 9 percent of English graduates earn a master's degree in business management and administrative services. Master's degrees earned by English majors also included majors in psychology (4 percent) and communications (3 percent).

- Doctoral degrees among English majors are, for the most part, concentrated in English and education; 47 percent of the doctoral degrees are earned in English, and 16 percent are earned in education.

- Eight of 10 professional degrees of English majors are in the field of law. Most of the remaining professional degrees are earned in the health professions.

Of all English graduates under the age of 65, 80 percent are employed. Only 3 percent are officially unemployed; in other words, they are not employed and are actively seeking employment. The remaining 17 percent are out of the labor force; that is, they are not employed and are not seeking employment. Family responsibilities are cited as the reason for labor force withdrawal among 42 percent of this group of English graduates, and another 41 percent voluntarily withdrew from the labor force because they did not want or need to work.

Employment Outlook

According to the projections by the U.S. Bureau of Labor Statistics, employment in occupations that require at least a bachelor's degree is expected to grow faster than employment in other sectors of the American labor market. Between 2000 and 2010, the U.S. economy is projected to add 22.1 million jobs, yielding an employment growth rate of 15 percent. The employment growth projections in the top 10 occupations that are most likely to employ English graduates are mixed.

- The demand for artists, broadcasters, entertainers, and public relations specialists is expected to grow by 21 percent. Between 2000 and 2010, these occupations are expected to add 493,000 jobs. These occupations employ 11 percent of English graduates.

- Elementary and secondary school teaching occupations together employ 14 percent of all English majors. The current demographic surge in the elementary school–age population is expected to increase the future demand for secondary school teachers by 18 percent between 2000 and 2010. Over the same period, elementary school teachers will see only a 13 percent increase in employment.

- The total employment in upper-level managerial/administrative and insurance/securities occupations, which employ many English majors and pay them above-average salaries, is projected to increase at rates below the average for all occupations. Employment in top- to mid-level management and administrative occupations is projected to grow by 12 percent, adding 1.27 million jobs between 2000 and 2010. Insurance, securities, real estate, and business services occupations are projected to add 178,000 jobs over the same time period, also yielding an employment growth rate of about 12 percent.

Table 3

Projected Change in Employment in the Top 10 Occupations That Employ Persons with Only a Bachelor's Degree in English

Top 10 Occupations	Actual Employment in 2000 (000s)	Projected Employment in 2010 (000s)	Absolute Change (000s)	Percentage Change
Artists, broadcasters, writers, editors, entertainers, public relations specialists	2,371	2,864	493	20.8%
Top- and mid-level managers, executives, administrators	10,564	11,834	1,270	12.0%
Teachers, secondary school	1,113	1,314	201	18.1%
Insurance, securities, real estate, business services	1,548	1,726	178	11.5%

(continued)

Table 3 (continued)
Projected Change in Employment in the Top 10 Occupations That Employ Persons with Only a Bachelor's Degree in English

Top 10 Occupations	Actual Employment in 2000 (000s)	Projected Employment in 2010 (000s)	Absolute Change (000s)	Percentage Change
Sales occupations, including retail	15,513	17,365	1,852	11.9%
Other management-related occupations	4,956	5,801	845	17.1%
Other administrative (e.g., records clerks, telephone operators)	16,911	18,522	1,611	9.5%
Teachers, elementary school	1,532	1,734	202	13.2%
Other service occupations, except health	9,652	11,287	1,635	16.9%

CHAPTER 40

Foreign Languages and Literature

This is not one major, but many—such as Arabic, Chinese, French, German, Italian, Portuguese, Russian, and Spanish, as well as the classics. The study of language is about communication and includes the knowledge of a language's culture, history, and literature. The purpose of studying a language is more than to foster communication, for today, where great cities of the world become small villages because of telecommunication and satellites, language is an aid to international relations and a foundation for business.

Although proficiency in speaking, reading, and writing a language is basic, context is equally important to the linguist. Linguistics is a specialization itself. Similar to the liberal arts orientation, the study of each language involves an examination of the people who speak the language, their way of communicating, and the culture of the countries in which the language is spoken. Knowing the language's composition is only part of developing communication proficiency; the literature and the history of the country are also used by college departments of language to convey the cultural context necessary to communicate accurately in either spoken or written form. Just as women's studies often uses significant female innovators and leaders to help convey modern-day perspectives and changes, the study of the literary masterpieces of a language gives insights into historic periods of development.

The course work in a foreign language, therefore, focuses on proficiency in using the language, reading its literature, and studying its history and geography.

Linguistic ability involves memory and visual and auditory discrimination skills. Some people learn certain languages in a more visual manner that requires precise sight memory. For example, learning-disabled students frequently have difficulty in discriminating between *d* and *b* and between *p* and *q;* this difficulty would give them trouble in learning a foreign language because its instruction emphasizes reading. Auditory discrimination of sounds is another important ability, and inflection in tonal sound is also helpful. As in any language, the use of accurate grammar, punctuation, spelling, and sentence structure is important, as is reading ability. The selection of the correct word is important to convey accurately the correct message.

Language majors have literary interests, including both reading and speaking. The focus of oral communication is on the people who are communicating. Because the context in which a person communicates is important to a full understanding of the meaning of a message, appreciation of varying situations is essential.

An intellectual value is embedded in the study and use of languages, for oral and written communication involve working with the mind. Language thus provides a means of self-expression. With various ways and styles of communicating, people with strong communication skills have the means to influence others.

Obviously this is a field in which individuals appreciate the skill of expressing themselves effectively. Good conversationalists usually have good insights about interpersonal relations. Linguists often appreciate imaginative ideas, which can energize them, whereas routine activities and paying attention to details can undo their visions. Linguists truly believe in their intuitions and can become absorbed in what they do, which may create problems in other dimensions of their lives.

Where Do Foreign Languages and Literature Majors Work?

The employment of graduates of foreign languages and literature programs is mainly concentrated in the private, for-profit sector and the education sector of the economy. Businesses and corporations in the private, for-profit sector employ 44 percent of foreign languages and literature graduates, and 9 percent are self-employed, bringing the total private, for-profit sector employment to 53 percent. More than 3 of 10 foreign languages and literature graduates work in the education sector of the economy, hired mostly as secondary and elementary school teachers. The government sector employs 10 percent, and 6 percent work in the nonprofit sector of the economy for tax-exempt or charitable organizations.

FIGURE 1

Percentage Distribution of Employed Persons with Only a Bachelor's Degree in Foreign Languages and Literature, by Major Sector of Economic Activity

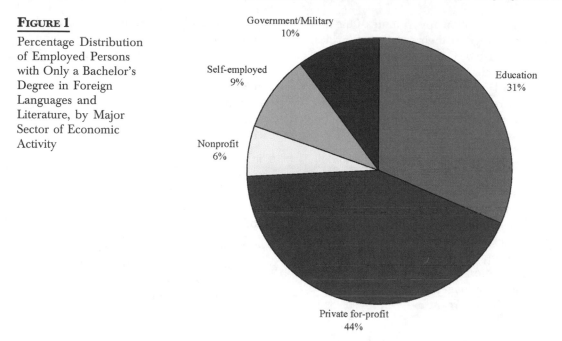

Government/Military
10%

Self-employed
9%

Education
31%

Nonprofit
6%

Private for-profit
44%

Occupations

Not many foreign languages and literature majors work in jobs that are related to their major. Their undergraduate education provides them with the ability to communicate in a foreign language and with the knowledge of the cultural, historical, and geographical characteristics of the country in which the language is spoken. The direct use of the ability to communicate in a foreign language is limited to few jobs in the economy. Most jobs that place a preference on or require the knowledge of a foreign language also require the prospective employee to perform tasks that require additional skills and abilities. Only 27 percent of the graduates work in jobs that are closely related to their major, and fewer than one-fifth are employed in jobs that are somewhat related to their undergraduate major. The remaining 54 percent work in jobs that are not related to their undergraduate major.

Foreign languages and literature graduates offer a variety of reasons for their employment in jobs that are unrelated to their major. One-half do so because of better pay and promotion opportunities outside their field, and one-half cite a desire to change their profession as one of the reasons for their job choice outside the field of foreign languages. A little less than one-half indicate that working conditions such as hours, equipment, and general working environment are a factor in their decision to work in an unrelated job, and 42 percent work in unrelated jobs because of the location of jobs. Nearly 40 percent are forced to work in unrelated jobs because of a lack of jobs that are related to their field of study, and 31 percent cite family-related reasons for their employment choice.

When asked to identify the most important reason for employment outside their major field of study, one-quarter of all foreign languages and literature graduates who work in unrelated jobs cite pay and promotion opportunities. One-fifth consider a change in their career and professional interests to be the number one reason for working in unrelated jobs. Nearly 16 percent are unable to find jobs in their field, and 12 percent rank family-related reasons as the number one factor underlying their decision to work in unrelated jobs.

Employment among foreign languages and literature majors is dispersed across a variety of occupations. One should expect this employment pattern because of the high rate of employment in jobs that are unrelated to their major. Secondary school teaching occupations employ the largest proportion of graduates—15 percent. The second-largest employer of these graduates is upper-level managerial and administrative jobs, in which 8 percent are employed. Sales occupations and secretarial occupations each employ 7 percent of foreign languages and literature graduates; 6 percent work in clerical jobs; 5 percent are employed in miscellaneous management-related jobs as management analysts, purchasing agents, or regulatory officers; and 4 percent are employed as elementary school teachers.

A little more than three-quarters of all employed foreign languages and literature graduates are women. The occupational employment patterns of male and female graduates are not very different.

▶ Males are somewhat more likely than female graduates to be employed as secondary school teachers—17 percent versus 14 percent.

Table 1
Top 10 Occupations That Employ Persons with Only a Bachelor's Degree in Foreign Languages and Literature

Top 10 Occupations	PERCENT OF EMPLOYED		
	All	Men	Women
Teachers, secondary school	14.8	16.6	14.2
Top- and mid-level managers, executives, administrators	8.4	7.7	8.7
Sales occupations, including retail	7.1	7.4	7.0
Secretaries, receptionists, typists	6.7	1.8	8.3
Other administrative (e.g., records clerks, telephone operators)	6.0	5.0	6.3
Other management-related occupations	4.6	1.9	5.4
Insurance, securities, real estate, business services	4.4	2.1	5.1
Teachers, elementary school	4.0	1.5	4.8
Other service occupations, except health	3.9	3.8	3.9
Other marketing and sales occupations	3.5	2.6	3.8

- Female graduates are more likely than males to be employed as elementary school teachers—5 percent versus 2 percent.

- Women also are more likely to work in secretarial occupations: 8 percent of women are employed in these occupations, compared to less than 2 percent of men.

Activities on the Job

The diversity in the occupational employment of foreign languages and literature majors is reflected in the breadth of duties they perform on their jobs.

- About 36 percent regularly engage in teaching activities at work, and one-quarter typically spend most of their time at work in teaching activities.

- Forty-three percent of employed foreign languages and literature graduates regularly perform management and administrative duties at work, and 13 percent spend most of their time during a typical workweek in performing these duties.

- Sales, purchasing, and marketing activities are regularly performed by 26 percent of all employed foreign languages and literature graduates, and 12 percent consider these duties to be a major part of their jobs.

- The majority of the workweek of 9 percent of foreign languages and literature graduates is spent in providing professional services such as financial services, and another 9 percent consider computer applications, programming, and systems-development duties as a major part of their job.

- Another 9 percent of all employed foreign languages and literature graduates spend most of their time in a typical workweek performing accounting, finance, and contractual duties.

Salaries

The average annual salary of foreign languages and literature graduates who have only a bachelor's degree and are employed full-time is $46,500, a level that is 14 percent lower than the average annual salary of all full-time employed college graduates. As with most college graduates, the salary of foreign languages and literature majors increases with age, although at a slow pace, indicating that they get more productive and therefore can earn higher salaries as they spend more time on the job. However, within different age groups, foreign languages and literature graduates earn lower salaries than all college graduates. Additionally, because the rate of increase in the average salary of foreign languages graduates is slower than the rate of all college graduates as they age, the age/earnings profiles of the two groups of graduates diverge as they age.

- The annual average salary of foreign languages and literature majors between the ages of 25 and 29 is $39,000, increasing to $46,500 between the ages of 40 and 44. The salary peaks between the ages of 45 and 49 at $49,900.

The average annual salary of foreign languages and literature majors who work in jobs that are either closely related or not related to their major field of study is lower than the salary of those who are employed in jobs that are somewhat related to their undergraduate major. Graduates whose jobs are closely related earn $40,900 annually, and those whose jobs are not related earn $49,900 per year. A number of graduates with

FIGURE 2

Age/Earnings Profile of Persons with Only a Bachelor's Degree in Foreign Languages and Literature (Full-Time Workers, in 2002 Dollars)

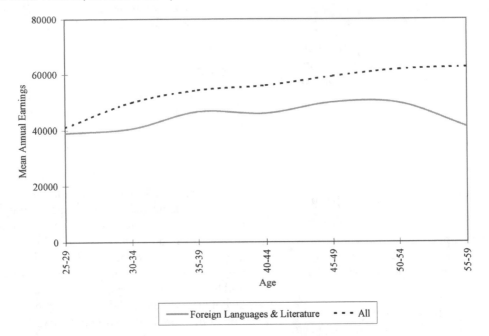

closely related jobs are employed in teaching occupations that generally pay lower salaries. Foreign languages and literature graduates whose jobs are somewhat related to their major earn an average salary of $51,500 per year.

Foreign languages and literature graduates who work in the government sector earn higher salaries than their counterparts employed in other sectors of the economy. These graduates earn an average salary of $52,100 per year. Employment in the private, for-profit sector for corporations and businesses results in an average annual salary of $49,000, and self-employed graduates earn $46,400 per year. Full-time employment in the education sector among foreign languages and literature graduates yields an annual salary of $40,100, a level that is somewhat higher than the annual average remuneration of graduates with full-time jobs in the private, nonprofit sector, which is $39,000.

There are sizable variations in the average annual salary of foreign languages and literature graduates, depending on the occupation in which they are employed. The average annual salary of foreign languages and literature majors is only 86 percent of the average salary of all college graduates. In one-half of the top 10 occupations that are predominant employers of foreign languages and literature majors, the salary of all college graduates exceeds the salary of foreign languages and literature majors.

- ▶ Foreign languages and literature majors employed in upper-level administration and management jobs and those who work in miscellaneous management-related jobs earn $60,400 and $57,900, respectively, per year. These two occupations are the highest-paying among the top 10 employers of foreign languages and literature graduates.

Table 2

Annual Salary of Full-Time Workers with Only a Bachelor's Degree in Foreign Languages and Literature, Top 10 Occupations (in 2002 Dollars)

Earnings in Top 10 Occupations	All	Foreign Languages and Literature
Total	$54,171	$46,502
Teachers, secondary school	$40,355	$44,513
Top- and mid-level managers, executives, administrators	$74,051	$60,337
Sales occupations, including retail	$52,378	$46,222
Secretaries, receptionists, typists	$32,246	$33,415
Other administrative (e.g., records clerks, telephone operators)	$34,547	$42,526
Other management-related occupations	$51,921	$57,909
Insurance, securities, real estate, business services	$68,273	$54,894
Teachers, elementary school	$39,167	$40,825
Other service occupations, except health	$39,984	$56,443
Other marketing and sales occupations	$58,208	$48,105

▶ Secondary and elementary school teachers with bachelor's degrees in foreign languages and literature earn $44,500 and $40,800, respectively.

▶ The annual average salary of graduates employed in clerical and administrative occupations is $42,500. The lowest-paying occupation among the top 10 employers of foreign languages and literature graduates is in the secretarial field–$33,400 per year.

On-the-Job Training

The career potential of a job is closely associated with the amount of work-related training on the job. Work-related training is regarded as an investment by firms because it makes workers more productive. Firms that invest in their workforce are more likely to offer pay increases and promotions to match the increasing productivity of their workers. Firms that do not invest in their workers are relatively less likely to offer pay increases and promotions. Employed foreign languages and literature majors are somewhat less likely to receive work-related training compared to all employed college graduates. Whereas 68 percent of all employed college graduates receive some work-related training, 63 percent of foreign languages and literature graduates participate in work-related training during a year.

▶ Of those foreign languages and literature majors who receive some work-related training, 69 percent received technical training in their occupational field.

▶ Thirty-three percent received training to improve their general professional skills, such as public speaking and business writing.

▶ Twenty-six percent of the training recipients received management or supervisor training.

Of those foreign languages and literature majors who participate in work-related training, 90 percent do so to improve their occupational skills and knowledge. Nearly 55 percent are required or expected by their employers to undergo training. Increased opportunity for promotion, advancement, and salary increases is the reason for 42 percent of foreign languages and literature majors to participate in work-related training, and 27 percent cite the need to learn skills for a newly acquired position as one of the reasons for their participation in work-related training. When asked to identify the most important reason to acquire training, 61 percent of foreign languages and literature majors who undergo training choose the need to improve their occupational skills and knowledge. About 15 percent report mandatory training requirement by the employer, and 8 percent consider better pay and promotion opportunities as the most important factor for their involvement in work-related training.

Post-Graduation Activities

Of those foreign languages and literature graduates with a bachelor's degree, 45 percent proceed to earn a postgraduate degree: 34 percent earn a master's degree, 6 percent graduate with a doctorate, and 5 percent earn a professional degree.

▶ Only 28 percent of the master's degrees are earned in foreign languages and literature. Another 28 percent choose education as the major field of choice for their master's degree. About 13 percent of the master's degrees are earned in business management and administration services, and 6 percent are earned in English language and literature.

▶ Doctoral degrees among foreign languages and literature majors are for the most part concentrated in foreign languages, education, and English. One-half of the doctoral degrees are earned in foreign languages and literature, 11 percent are earned in education, and 8 percent are earned in English.

▶ More than 90 percent of all professional degrees of undergraduate foreign languages and literature majors are in the field of law. Most of the remaining professional degrees are earned in health-related fields.

Of all foreign languages and literature graduates under the age of 65, 78 percent are employed. Only 4 percent are officially unemployed; in other words, they are not employed and are actively seeking employment. The remaining 18 percent are out of the labor force; that is, they are not employed and are not seeking employment. Family responsibilities are cited as the reason for labor force withdrawal among 46 percent of this group of foreign languages and literature graduates, and another 36 percent voluntarily withdraw from the labor force because they do not want or need to work.

Employment Outlook

According to the projections by the U.S. Bureau of Labor Statistics, employment in occupations that require at least a bachelor's degree is expected to grow faster than employment in other sectors of the American labor market. Between 2000 and 2010, the U.S. economy is projected to add 22.2 million jobs, yielding an employment growth rate of 15.2 percent. The employment growth projections in the top 10 occupations that are most likely to employ foreign languages and literature graduates are presented here.

▶ Employment in top- to mid-level management and administrative occupations is projected to grow by 12 percent, adding 1.3 million jobs between 2000 and 2010.

▶ Elementary and secondary school teaching occupations together employ 19 percent of all foreign languages and literature majors. The current demographic surge in the elementary school–age group of the population is expected to increase the future demand for secondary school teachers by 18 percent between 2000 and 2010. Over the same time period, elementary school teachers will see a 13 percent increase in employment.

▶ Employment in secretarial occupations that employ more than 8 percent of foreign languages and literature graduates is projected to grow by 10 percent over the decade.

Table 3

Projected Change in Employment in the Top 10 Occupations That Employ Persons with Only a Bachelor's Degree in Foreign Languages and Literature

Top 10 Occupations	Actual Employment in 2000 (000s)	Projected Employment in 2010 (000s)	Absolute Change (000s)	Percentage Change
Teachers, secondary school	1,113	1,314	201	18.1%
Top- and mid-level managers, executives, administrators	10,564	11,834	1,270	12.0%
Sales occupations, including retail	15,513	17,365	1,852	11.9%
Secretaries, receptionists, typists	4,980	5,501	521	10.5%
Other administrative (e.g., records clerks, telephone operators)	16,911	18,522	1,611	9.5%
Other management-related occupations	4,956	5,801	845	17.1%
Insurance, securities, real estate, business services	1,548	1,726	178	11.5%
Teachers, elementary school	1,532	1,734	202	13.2%
Other service occupations, except health	9,652	11,287	1,635	16.9%
Other marketing and sales occupations	621	758	137	22.1%

CHAPTER 41

Geography

Geography can be viewed as either a physical science or a social science, depending on an institution's or faculty's orientation. Although geography is the analysis of distributions of physical and cultural phenomena on local, regional, continental, and global scales, the specializations offer meaningful descriptions of the work.

Economic geographers study the distribution of resources and economic activities. Political geographers are concerned with the relationship of geography to political phenomena, and cultural geographers study the geography of cultural phenomena. Physical geographers study the variations in climates, vegetation, soil, and landforms, along with their implications for human activity. Urban and transportation geographers study cities and metropolitan areas. Regional geographers study the physical, economic, political, and cultural characteristics of regions, ranging in size from a congressional district to entire continents. Medical geographers study health-care delivery systems, epidemiology (the study of the causes and control of epidemics), and the effect of the environment on health.

In schools geography is taught as a social science. An emphasis is on the comparative location of different countries and the relation of their people to those from another country. Oftentimes a descriptive approach is used to understand various cultures, including ethnic distributions, political organizations, and economic activities. Geographers can also consult with governments or international organizations on economic exploitation of regions and on determinations of ethnic and natural boundaries between nations.

From a physical science perspective, geographers conduct research on physical and climatic aspects of regions and landforms and survey soils, plants, and animals within an area. Geographers integrate their findings with other specialties such as geology, oceanography, meteorology, and biology. Some geographers construct and draw maps.

Educational course work may include economic geography; resource management; cultural and political geography; cartography and air photos; environmental issues, such as ecosystems, resources, and energy; air and water quality engineering; various regional geography courses; computer skills; and mathematical and quantitative research methods.

Abilities vary depending on the specialization. For a physical science orientation, individuals will need advanced mathematics and science courses requiring a physics background; therefore, understanding technical and scientific information and using numbers to solve problems are required. Understanding spatial relations and recognizing shapes and sizes are needed in mapmaking or photo interpretation. Language skills and making judgments from data are required for decision making. Thinking from a global perspective, instead of analyzing from concrete evidence that is immediately available, is a skill that some individuals may not yet have developed.

The interests of geographers, especially those with a physical science perspective, are scientific, involving the exploration and analysis of natural and social phenomena. Geographers have a technical and practical orientation. After they have studied and organized their data, they like to become confident and feel comfortable defending their opinions. Geographers have interests similar to those of civil engineers, who also are able to "see the big picture" and often work at field sites.

The values of geographers include a research orientation, working with one's mind, and possibly analyzing computer data. They enjoy the variety that the field offers and the possible creative explanations and solutions they devise. Geographers value the prestige afforded by the type of problems they work with or bestowed by the organization for which they work.

The person oriented to the physical sciences is logical, analytical, and decisive. These scientists prefer things not to be complex but kept factual, clearly stated, and accurate. Because these scientists are very self-confident in their conclusions, some can appear stubborn. The person oriented to the social sciences tends to be concerned with people, has interpersonal relationship skills, and has an enthusiastic and positive approach to life. The social scientist involves others and motivates them. Whereas the physical scientist tolerates routine, the social scientist may get bored with it; subsequently, details may be left undone or overlooked, which can be problematic.

Where Do Geography Majors Work?

Geography majors have an above-average likelihood of being employed in the government sector. Nearly 3 of 10 work for the government. In contrast, 11 percent of all college graduates are government employees. About 46 percent of geography majors work for businesses and corporations in the private, for-profit sector; 8 percent are self-employed in their own business or practice. Educational institutions employ 14 percent of geography graduates, and the remaining 3 percent work for the private, nonprofit sector in tax-exempt or charitable organizations.

FIGURE 1

Percentage Distribution of Employed Persons with Only a Bachelor's Degree in Geography, by Major Sector of Economic Activity

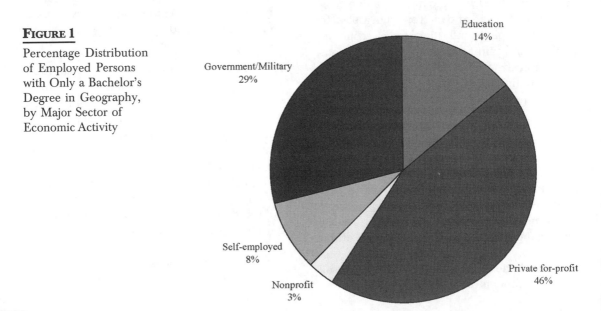

Occupations

Only 20 percent of geography majors work in jobs that are closely related to their undergraduate major. Another 29 percent are employed in jobs that are somewhat related to their major. The remaining 50 percent report that their jobs are not at all related to their undergraduate major.

Although geography majors list numerous reasons for their employment in jobs that are unrelated to their major, three-quarters cite as a factor better pay and promotion opportunities outside their field in their decision to work in unrelated jobs. A change in career interest is a factor in the decision of 54 percent of geography majors working in unrelated jobs, and another 55 percent are influenced by job location. About 44 percent cite as a factor a better working environment outside their field, and 41 percent are unable to find related jobs.

When asked to list the most important factor that influenced their decision to work in unrelated jobs, 43 percent of geography majors cite pay and promotion opportunities. One fifth say they chose to work in another field because of a change in their career interests. The most important reason indicated by 8 percent of those who are employed in an unrelated job is the lack of available jobs in the field of geography. According to another 8 percent of geography graduates working in unrelated jobs, family-related reasons force them to work outside their major field.

Geography majors are employed in a wide variety of occupations. The top 10 occupations account for only 56 percent of all employed graduates. More than one-fifth of all employed geography graduates work in managerial occupations; these include top- to mid-level managerial and executive occupations and other miscellaneous management-related occupations such as management analysts, purchasing agents, inspectors, and other regulatory officers. About 14 percent work in top- to mid-level managerial and administrative occupations, and 7 percent are employed in other miscellaneous management-related occupations. Surveying and mapping occupations employ more than 6 percent, and another 6 percent are employed in sales occupations. The remaining occupations in the list of the top 10 employers of geography majors employ between 3.5 and 4.5 percent of the graduates.

Table 1

Top 10 Occupations That Employ Persons with Only a Bachelor's Degree in Geography

Top 10 Occupations	PERCENT OF EMPLOYED		
	All	Men	Women
Top- and mid-level managers, executives, administrators	14.0	16.4	8.1
Other management-related occupations	7.2	6.8	8.2
Surveying and mapping	6.3	8.0	2.3
Sales occupations, including retail	5.8	6.9	3.0
Other service occupations, except health	4.6	3.7	6.9
Other administrative (e.g., records clerks, telephone operators)	4.1	1.9	9.4

(continued)

Table 1 (continued)
Top 10 Occupations That Employ Persons with Only a Bachelor's Degree in Geography

	PERCENT OF EMPLOYED		
Top 10 Occupations	**All**	**Men**	**Women**
Protective-service occupations	3.6	5.0	0.0
Construction trades, miners, well drillers	3.5	3.6	3.5
Postsecondary professors	3.4	3.3	3.5
Civil engineers, including architectural and sanitary	3.3	3.3	3.5

▶ Males make up 70 percent of all employed geography graduates and are twice as likely as women to be employed in top- to mid-level managerial, executive, and administrative jobs—16 percent versus 8 percent.

▶ Male geography graduates also are more likely than women to work in surveying and mapping occupations and sales occupations.

▶ The employment of female majors is more concentrated than males in administrative/clerical and service sector occupations.

▶ Protective-service occupations employ 5 percent of male graduates and none of the female geography graduates.

Activities on the Job

The diversity in the occupational employment of geography majors is reflected in the breadth of duties they perform on their jobs.

▶ Although 70 percent of all employed geography graduates perform accounting, finance, and contractual duties as a regular part of their jobs, only 5 percent spend most of their time in a typical workweek performing these duties.

Many geography majors perform these duties as a part of their jobs, but very few spend most of their time in performing them.

▶ The top employer of geography majors is high-level managerial and administrative occupations. Hence, it is not surprising to find that 55 percent of employed geography majors perform management and administrative duties regularly, and 21 percent spend most of their time during a typical workweek in performing these duties. A much higher proportion of geography majors perform managerial and administrative functions rather than accounting, finance, and contractual duties as a major part of their jobs.

▶ Computer applications, programming, and systems-development duties are regularly performed by 40 percent of employed geography majors. For 10 percent of the graduates, these duties take up most of their time during a typical workweek.

▶ Another 40 percent of employed geography majors perform employee-relations duties, including recruiting, personnel development, and training; but only 5 percent spend a major part of their workweek in these activities.

▶ More than one-third of the graduates regularly engage in sales, purchasing, and marketing activities, and 11 percent consider these duties to be a major part of their job. One-third regularly engage in managerial duties to oversee the quality and efficiency of the production process, but only 3 percent consider those duties to be the main part of their job.

▶ Teaching takes up most of the time during a typical workweek for 11 percent of geography graduates; 24 percent perform teaching functions as a regular part of their job.

▶ Just more than one-fifth of employed geography majors regularly engage in providing professional services such as financial, legal, and health services; 7 percent spend most of their time at work in these activities.

▶ Few geography majors regularly engage in basic or applied research, product development, and equipment-design activities.

Salaries

The average annual salary of geography graduates who have only a bachelor's degree and are employed full-time is $50,400, a level that is 93 percent of the average annual salary of all full-time employed college graduates. As with most college graduates, the salary of geography majors increases with age, indicating that they get more productive and therefore can earn higher salaries as they spend more time on the job. However, the average annual salary of geography majors is lower than the average salary of all college graduates in every age group presented in Figure 2.

▶ The annual average salary of geography majors between the ages of 25 and 29 is $36,800. Graduates between the ages of 30 and 34 earn $45,400 annually.

▶ The average annual earnings of geography graduates increase as they get older at about the same rate as that of all college graduates. The average annual salary of geography majors between the ages of 35 and 39 who are employed full-time is $49,100, and those between the ages of 40 and 44 earn $53,500 per year.

▶ The annual average salary continues to increase and peaks at a level of $59,200 among graduates between the ages of 50 and 54.

▶ The average annual salary of geography majors who work in jobs that are closely related to their major field of study is much lower than for those who are employed in jobs that are somewhat related or not related to their major. Graduates who work in closely related jobs earn $39,700 per year. Those who work in jobs that are somewhat related to their major earn $53,700, and graduates with unrelated jobs earn an average annual salary of $52,800. Many graduates whose jobs are somewhat related or unrelated to their undergraduate major are employed in high-level managerial, administrative, and sales jobs that are associated with higher salaries than the average salary of geography majors in surveying and mapping occupations, postsecondary teaching, or civil engineering occupations. Other college graduates (mainly civil engineering majors) who work in civil engineering occupations earn a much higher salary than geography majors employed as civil engineers.

▶ Geography majors who work for businesses and corporations in the private, for-profit sector earn $55,000 per year. This salary is higher than salaries of geography majors employed in other sectors of the economy. Graduates who work in their own business or practice earn $51,900 per year. The government sector pays geography graduates who are employed full-time an average annual salary of $50,100. The average annual remuneration of geography graduates employed by educational institutions is only $35,400.

The average annual salary of geography majors employed in each of the top 10 occupations is lower than the salary of all college graduates employed in those occupations. There are sizable variations in the annual average salary within the group of geography graduates.

▶ The highest annual earnings are among geography graduates employed in top- to mid-level managerial jobs–$69,400 annually. Employment of geography majors in sales occupations pays an average annual salary of $49,800.

▶ The annual average remuneration in management-related occupations is $48,700; employment in construction trades and protective-service occupations pays an annual salary of $47,900 and $46,800, respectively.

▶ Clerical/administrative, service, and postsecondary teaching occupations are low-paying occupations that pay even lower salaries to geography majors.

▶ The average annual salary of geography majors employed as civil engineers is $38,800. This salary is much lower than the $61,800 salary of all college graduates who work in civil engineering occupations. Most of the graduates in the latter group are civil engineering majors who are trained specifically for civil engineering occupations and earn higher salaries for higher productivity attributable to their better job-related skills. Geography majors, however, are not trained to master the same skills as their civil engineering counterparts.

FIGURE 2

Age/Earnings Profile of Persons with Only a Bachelor's Degree in Geography (Full-Time Workers, in 2002 Dollars)

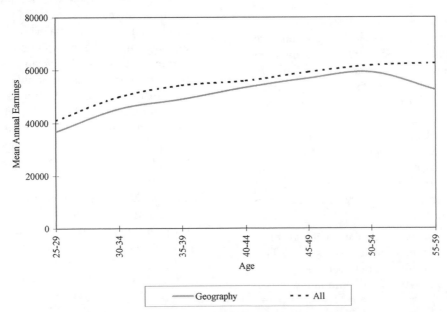

Table 2
Annual Salary of Full-Time Workers with Only a Bachelor's Degree in Geography, Top 10 Occupations (in 2002 Dollars)

Earnings in Top 10 Occupations	All	Geography
Total	$54,171	$50,428
Top- and mid-level managers, executives, administrators	$74,051	$69,357
Other management-related occupations	$51,921	$48,669
Surveying and mapping	$45,232	$43,774
Sales occupations, including retail	$52,378	$49,760
Other service occupations, except health	$39,984	$37,617
Other administrative (e.g., records clerks, telephone operators)	$34,547	$34,130
Protective-service occupations	$49,130	$46,778
Construction trades, miners, well drillers	$50,531	$47,933
Postsecondary professors	$42,234	$37,353
Civil engineers, including architectural and sanitary	$61,821	$38,787

On-the-Job Training

The career potential of a job is closely associated with the amount of work-related training on the job. Work related training is regarded as an investment by firms because it makes workers more productive. Firms that invest in their workforce are more likely to offer pay increases and promotions to match the increasing productivity of their workers. Firms that do not invest in their workers are relatively less likely to offer pay increases and promotions. Employed geography majors are somewhat more likely to participate in work-related training than all employed college graduates. More than 7 of 10 geography majors receive training, compared to 68 percent of all employed college graduates.

▶ Of those geography majors who received some training in the past year, 89 percent received technical training in the occupation in which they are employed.

▶ One-third of the training recipients receive management or supervisor training.

▶ One-quarter receive training to improve their general professional skills, such as public speaking and business writing.

Numerous reasons underlie the decision of geography majors to acquire work-related training. Four factors are commonly cited by many training recipients: 1) a desire to improve occupational skills and knowledge, 2) mandatory training requirements of the employer, 3) increased opportunities for promotion and salary increases, and 4) the need to learn skills for a newly acquired position. More than 90 percent of geography graduates participate in work-related training to improve their occupational skills and knowledge. Nearly 54 percent are required or expected by their employers to undergo training. Increased opportunity for promotion, advancement, and salary increases is the reason for 51 percent of geography majors to participate in work-related training. One-third of training recipients cite the need to learn skills for a newly acquired position as one of the reasons for their participation in work-related training. Fewer than one-fifth of geography majors participating in training activities do so to acquire a professional license or certificate.

When asked to identify the most important reason to acquire training, 70 percent of geography majors who undergo training identify the need to improve their occupational skills and knowledge. Another 11 percent report mandatory training requirements by the employer as the most important factor for their involvement in work-related training. According to 8 percent, the most important factor is to improve their opportunities for a salary increase and promotion. And 1 in 20 considers the need to obtain a professional license or certificate as the main factor in influencing their decision to undergo work-related training.

Post-Graduation Activities

One-third of geography graduates with a bachelor's degree proceed to earn a postgraduate degree: 28 percent earn a master's degree, 2 percent graduate with a doctorate, and 2 percent earn a professional degree.

▶ Nearly one-quarter of the master's degrees are earned in education, and one-fifth of master's degree recipients choose geography as their major field of study. Business management and administrative services are the major field of study for 16 percent of all the master's degrees earned by undergraduate geography majors. Only 1 in 10 master's degrees is earned in one of the social sciences or in history.

▶ Doctoral degrees among undergraduate geography majors are mainly concentrated in geography (57 percent) or in one of the social sciences or history (19 percent).

▶ Eighty-five percent of the professional degrees earned by undergraduate geography graduates are in law, and 12 percent are in public affairs.

Of all geography graduates under the age of 65, 89 percent are employed. Only 4 percent are officially unemployed; in other words, they are not employed and are actively seeking employment. The remaining 7 percent are out of the labor force; that is, they are not employed and are not seeking employment. More than one-half of the labor force withdrawals among geography majors are attributable to the lack of a desire or need to work. One-quarter of geography graduates who are out of the labor force cite family responsibilities as a reason for their withdrawal. One-fifth are retired, and 13 percent are unable to participate in the labor force because of a chronic illness or disability.

Employment Outlook

According to the projections by the U.S. Bureau of Labor Statistics, employment in occupations that require at least a bachelor's degree is expected to grow faster than employment in other sectors of the American labor market. Between 2000 and 2010, the U.S. economy is projected

to add 22.2 million jobs, yielding an employment growth rate of 15.2 percent. The employment growth projections in the top 10 occupations that are most likely to employ geography graduates are presented here.

▶ The largest employer of geography majors, high-level managerial and administrative occupations, is projected to add more than 1.3 million jobs between 2000 and 2010, yielding an employment growth rate of 12 percent.

▶ Employment in management-related occupations is expected to grow by 17 percent.

▶ Employment growth rates that are well above the average for all occupations and for college graduates are projected for postsecondary professors and protective-service occupations.

▶ Surveying and mapping and clerical/administrative occupations are projected to grow at below-average rates.

Table 3

Projected Change in Employment in the Top 10 Occupations That Employ Persons with Only a Bachelor's Degree in Geography

Top 10 Occupations	Actual Employment in 2000 (000s)	Projected Employment in 2010 (000s)	Absolute Change (000s)	Percentage Change
Top- and mid-level managers, executives, administrators	10,564	11,834	1,270	12.0%
Other management-related occupations	4,956	5,801	845	17.1%
Surveying and mapping	65	71	6	9.2%
Sales occupations, including retail	15,513	17,365	1,852	11.9%
Other service occupations, except health	9,652	11,287	1,635	16.9%
Other administrative (e.g., records clerks, telephone operators)	16,911	18,522	1,611	9.5%
Protective-service occupations	3,087	3,896	809	26.2%
Construction trades, miners, well drillers	7,451	8,439	988	13.3%
Postsecondary professors	1,344	1,659	315	23.4%
Civil engineers, including architectural and sanitary	232	256	24	10.3%

CHAPTER 42

History

Historians are social scientists who study all aspects of human society. They use research as a basic activity to provide insights that help others understand the different ways in which individuals and groups make decisions, exercise power, and respond to change. History develops a greater understanding and appreciation of today's cultures and civilizations. Social sciences are interdisciplinary in nature. Specialists in one discipline often find that their research overlaps work being done in another field.

Historians research, analyze, and interpret the past. They use many sources of information in their research, including government and institutional records, newspapers and other periodicals, photographs, interviews, films, and unpublished manuscripts such as personal diaries and letters. Historians usually specialize in a specific country or region; a particular time period; or a particular field, such as social, intellectual, political, or diplomatic history. Biographers collect detailed information on individuals. Genealogists trace family histories. Other historians help study and preserve archival materials, artifacts, and historic buildings and sites.

Students have the opportunity to specialize in history, and typically a wide range of course work is offered. Courses may include Western civilization; African civilization; and Asian, Middle Eastern, Latin American, European, or United States history (all with designated time periods). Focus can be on specific countries such as China, Japan, or Southeast Asia; Third World countries; the history of religion; or women.

Language, social, and teaching abilities characterize historians. They tend to be excellent readers and possess good memories. Intellectual curiosity and creativity are fundamental personal traits for historians as they seek new information about people, things, and ideas. They think logically and, in writing, work methodically and systematically.

Historians primarily have social interests along with organizational and scientific interests—that is, seeking more definitive understandings through research. Many historians prefer teaching as a field, for it allows them to arrange, construct, and interpret events for others as they imagine them to have occurred. They enjoy reading and appreciate the fact that their field permits use of diverse methodologies to collect and assemble data.

Historians value organization and working independently. Variety and diversion are important to them. They prefer to entertain different perspectives of events while committed to objectivity and openmindedness. They gain satisfaction by working with their minds and through their appreciation for researching topics.

Generally historians are friendly and enthusiastic, but they can get absorbed in their own thoughts. Although they are quick to respond to those in need of help, they can find themselves getting over-involved and taking on too

FIGURE 1

Percentage Distribution of Employed Persons with Only a Bachelor's Degree in History, by Major Sector of Economic Activity

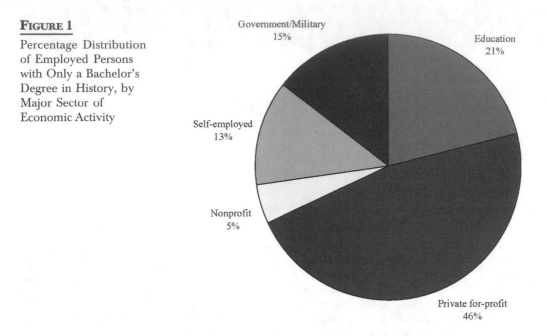

Government/Military
15%

Education
21%

Self-employed
13%

Nonprofit
5%

Private for-profit
46%

much to do. A personality characteristic of some who enter this field is the belief that they are capable of doing anything that interests them.

Where Do History Majors Work?

History majors with a bachelor's degree are employed across the spectrum of the American economy. They are more likely than many other college graduates with degrees in other fields to work in private, for-profit firms, with more than 4 of 10 working for private businesses and corporations. Frequently history majors work in the education sector; most of these work as teachers. About 15 percent are employed by a federal, state, or local government organization. A fairly substantial proportion of persons with an undergraduate degree in history are self-employed, either operating their own business or serving in a consulting capacity. History majors who run their own companies have the highest earnings of all graduates from this field of study.

Occupations

The overwhelming majority of history majors are employed in jobs that are not closely related to their undergraduate field of study. About 13 percent of employed persons with only a bachelor's degree in history work in managerial or administrative occupations; another 16 percent work in various sales, marketing, insurance, securities, and real estate sales occupations. Many of those history majors who report that they are employed in jobs related to their major work as either secondary or elementary school teachers. History majors with jobs that are closely related to their undergraduate field earn substantially less than those who are employed in unrelated jobs. However, only those persons employed in unrelated occupations that require a college degree of some type have solid earnings experiences. Those history majors employed in jobs that do not require a college degree generally have inferior employment opportunities and earnings experiences relative to those who are employed in college labor market jobs.

▶ Men with an undergraduate degree in history are much more likely than women to work in managerial or administrative positions, as well as in high-level, sales-related jobs in insurance, real estate, and securities.

▶ Women are much more likely than men to work as teachers, particularly as elementary school teachers.

▶ About 6 percent of women with a history degree work in non-college labor market jobs.

Activities on the Job

▶ Persons with an undergraduate degree in history often have managerial and supervisory duties as a major component of their employment.

▶ About 1 in 3 employed history majors with a bachelor's degree are involved in the development or use of computer applications on the job.

▶ Accounting, contracting, and finance duties are a part of the job duties of most history majors.

▶ History bachelor's degree holders undertake little basic or applied research while on the job.

Table 1
Top 10 Occupations That Employ Persons with Only a Bachelor's Degree in History

Top 10 Occupations	PERCENT OF EMPLOYED		
	All	Men	Women
Top- and mid-level managers, executives, administrators	12.7	15.5	7.3
Teachers, secondary school	8.9	8.2	10.4
Sales occupations, including retail	6.8	7.9	4.8
Insurance, securities, real estate, business services	6.5	8.4	2.9
Other management-related occupations	6.2	6.0	6.5
Artists, broadcasters, writers, editors, entertainers, public relations specialists	4.8	4.6	5.1
Other administrative (e.g., records clerks, telephone operators)	4.5	3.5	6.4
Teachers, elementary school	4.2	2.0	8.5
Accountants, auditors, other financial specialists	3.8	4.1	3.2
Other marketing and sales occupations	3.0	2.6	3.7

FIGURE 2

Age/Earnings Profile of Persons with Only a Bachelor's Degree in History
(Full-Time Workers, in 2002 Dollars)

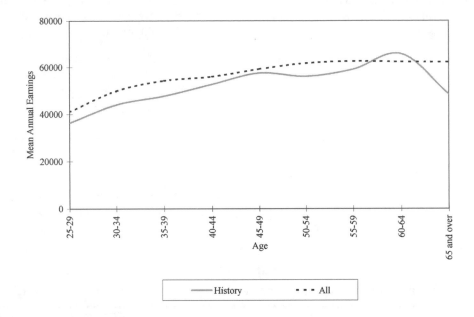

Salaries

Salaries of the typical college graduate with a degree in history are somewhat below those of the average college graduate at the bachelor's degree level. Salaries for history majors average $51,500 per year, a figure that is $2,700, or about 5 percent, below that of the salary of the average employed person with a bachelor's degree. Younger graduates of history programs earn salaries that average about $37,400 per year. By ages 45 to 49, the earnings of history majors increase to $57,500. As history majors acquire skills through both on-the-job learning and formal training, the value of these work experiences raises their earnings in the labor market. History majors who work for private, for-profit firms earn an average of $55,500, and self-employed history majors who own their businesses earn an average of $73,100 per year. In contrast, majors employed by educational organizations earn on average only $39,800 per year. Majors who work in jobs closely related to their major earn substantially lower annual salaries than those working in jobs not closely related to the field.

The highest-paying jobs for graduates of history programs are in the managerial and administrative areas. Employment in this occupational group (where 1 in 7 history majors works) pays an annual salary of $74,700 for full-time work. History majors who work in insurance, securities, and real estate sales positions also have high annual salaries. The earnings of those who go into the teaching profession are substantially lower than in other occupations that frequently employ graduates of history programs. Teachers' wages are set by contracts that usually base compensation on seniority and highest degree earned. Little differences exist in the earnings of teachers by undergraduate major field of study. History majors who work in jobs that

Table 2
Annual Salary of Full-Time Workers with Only a Bachelor's Degree in History, Top 10 Occupations (in 2002 Dollars)

Earnings in Top 10 Occupations	All	History
Total	$54,171	$51,483
Top- and mid-level managers, executives, administrators	$74,051	$74,659
Teachers, secondary school	$40,355	$41,682
Sales occupations, including retail	$52,378	$45,259
Insurance, securities, real estate, business services	$68,273	$71,993
Other management-related occupations	$51,921	$51,130
Artists, broadcasters, writers, editors, entertainers, public relations specialists	$52,141	$51,364
Other administrative (e.g., records clerks, telephone operators)	$34,547	$35,585
Teachers, elementary school	$39,167	$38,840
Accountants, auditors, other financial specialists	$57,382	$54,820
Other marketing and sales occupations	$58,208	$57,439

do not usually require a college degree earn below-average wages. Those who work in clerical and secretarial positions earn an average of $35,600.

On-the-Job Training

Graduates of history programs participate in work-related workshops and seminars less often than majors in other fields, so informal on-the-job learning is an even more important method of skills acquisition for majors in this field. Over the course of a year, about 60 percent of employed history program graduates participate in some type of training activity.

▶ Most often history majors participate in training designed to enhance their occupationally specific skills, whether in secondary teaching or real estate sales.

▶ A substantial amount of training is devoted to the development of writing and public speaking skills.

Post-Graduation Activities

About one-half of all history majors continue their education beyond the bachelor's degree level and earn an advanced degree. About 30 percent of those with a bachelor's degree complete a master's degree program, and approximately 4 percent earn a doctorate. History is an important educational pathway to the study of law; about 1 in 9 history majors eventually earn a law degree.

▶ Most history majors who go on to earn a master's degree do not continue their studies in history. Only 16 percent of master's degrees earned by those with a bachelor's degree in history are in history. More than one-quarter of all master's degrees earned by this group are in education, and about 13 percent are in business.

▶ Among history majors who earn a doctorate, about 40 percent are in some type of history specialty. An additional 26 percent earn their degree in education.

About 85 percent of persons with a bachelor's degree in history are employed, usually in full-time positions. Only 3 of 100 history majors are involuntarily unemployed. Most of those who are jobless do not work because of family responsibilities, or they simply have no job desire.

Employment Outlook

Employment in occupations that employ persons with bachelor's degrees is expected to grow more slowly than the overall demand for college graduates through 2010. The U.S. Bureau of Labor Statistics projects that the demand for persons with a bachelor's degree will increase by 22.2 percent between 2000 and 2010. Only two of the occupations in which most history majors work are expected to grow at this pace. More rapid job growth is expected in creative positions (such as writers and artists) that employ historians, as well as in marketing and sales jobs, where a sizable proportion of history degree holders work.

Table 3
Projected Change in Employment in the Top 10 Occupations That Employ Persons with Only a Bachelor's Degree in History

Top 10 Occupations	Actual Employment in 2000 (000s)	Projected Employment in 2010 (000s)	Absolute Change (000s)	Percentage Change
Top- and mid-level managers, executives, administrators	10,564	11,834	1,270	12.0%
Teachers, secondary school	1,113	1,314	201	18.1%
Sales occupations, including retail	15,513	17,365	1,852	11.9%
Insurance, securities, real estate, business services	1,548	1,726	178	11.5%
Other management-related occupations	4,956	5,801	845	17.1%
Artists, broadcasters, writers, editors, entertainers, public relations specialists	2,371	2,864	493	20.8%
Other administrative (e.g., records clerks, telephone operators)	16,911	18,522	1,611	9.5%
Teachers, elementary school	1,532	1,734	202	13.2%
Accountants, auditors, other financial specialists	2,115	2,481	366	17.3%
Other marketing and sales occupations	621	758	137	22.1%

CHAPTER 43

Journalism

Journalists gather information and prepare stories that inform the public about local, state, national, and international events. Journalists present points of view on current events, reporting about politics and politicians; those whose power affects others; and celebrities such as movie, musical, and sports figures. Areas highlighted are foreign affairs, consumer affairs, health, sports, theater, business, social events, religion, and science.

Journalists gather information by researching documents, observing, and talking with and interviewing people. Later they organize the material, establish a focus, and write their stories. Reporters take notes and may take photographs or videos. Newswriters write the stories submitted by the reporter. Live stories are reported by radio and TV reporters. News correspondents operate in large U.S. and foreign cities to report news and interest pieces there. Beginners usually start at small publications where they cover all the following: take photographs, write headliners, lay out pages, edit wire service copy, write editorials, solicit advertisements, and perform general office work. Some journalists move to other communications jobs such as advertising and public relations if journalism proves to be too hectic or stressful or the pay is insufficient.

About three-fourths of the courses in a typical curriculum are in liberal arts, and the rest are in journalism. Journalism courses include introduction to the mass media, basic reporting, copyediting, history of journalism, and press law and ethics. Broadcasting students take courses in producing newscasts and production. Newspaper- and magazine-oriented students specialize in news-editorial journalism. Liberal arts courses taken are English (especially writing courses), political science, economics, history, psychology, speech, and business. Foreign language and computer courses are key skill courses.

Abilities include writing, speaking, and using correct grammar. Journalists have interpersonal skills and are able to convince and influence others. They also exhibit leadership qualities and are recognized for getting things moving. Word-processing skills are a prerequisite, with computer graphics and desktop publishing skills being helpful. Recall that most beginning journalists start with small publications, so news photography may be part of the job.

The primary interest of journalists is literary, but usually not limited to only one of the arts. A person with artistic interests usually likes art, music, drama, literature, and entertainment. Analytical and research interests are also enjoyed by journalists. They like involvement with people. Journalists enjoy variety in their work because the content shifts daily with the news.

Journalists value doing many different tasks. They seek opportunities to use their imagination, develop new insights, and discover previously unknown information. Journalists enjoy working with their minds and take pride in their own intellectual knowledge. They take on a difficult task with a goal to succeed and expect to be acknowledged when they achieve the goal. Journalists see their work as important, and some achieve public recognition.

Personal characteristics may show this group to act first and then later fill in the facts. Journalists can have a quick wit. They can be argumentative and make a case even for things they do not truly accept. Journalists are smart, enabling them to change subjects frequently and easily. Their sharp minds and possibly surface relations with many keep them on the move.

Where Do Journalism Majors Work?

Although a large proportion of journalism graduates work in the private, for-profit sector for businesses and corporations or as self-employed persons in their own business or practice, more than one-fifth are dispersed across educational institutions, the government, and the private, nonprofit sector of the economy. About 64 percent work in the private, for-profit sector for businesses and corporations, and 14 percent are self-employed in their own business or practice.

The education sector and the private, nonprofit sector each employ 8 percent of journalism graduates. The remaining 6 percent work for the government.

Journalism majors have a high likelihood of working in a job that is closely or somewhat related to their undergraduate major. About 47 percent are employed in jobs that are closely related to their major, 27 percent work in jobs that are somewhat related to their major, and the remaining 26 percent are employed in unrelated jobs.

Journalism majors offer many reasons for working outside their field; the most important reason is better pay and promotion opportunities, with 30 percent citing this reason. About 20 percent consider the lack of jobs in their field to be the number one reason for working in an unrelated job. Another one-fifth cite a change in their career and professional interest as the most important factor to influence their decision to work in jobs that are not related to their major field of study. Family-related factors are cited by only 9 percent as the most important influence on their choice of an unrelated job.

FIGURE 1

Percentage Distribution of Employed Persons with Only a Bachelor's Degree in Journalism, by Major Sector of Economic Activity

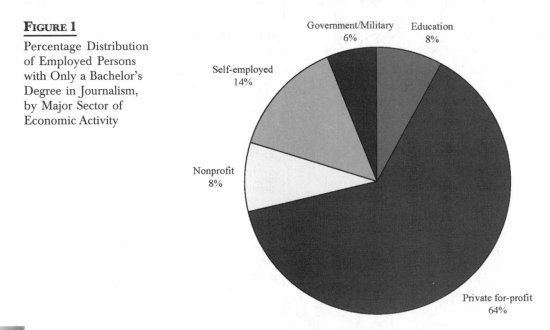

Table 1
Top 10 Occupations That Employ Persons with Only a Bachelor's Degree in Journalism

Top 10 Occupations	PERCENT OF EMPLOYED All	Men	Women
Artists, broadcasters, writers, editors, entertainers, public relations specialists	36.8	35.6	37.9
Top- and mid-level managers, executives, administrators	12.1	15.7	8.6
Other management-related occupations	7.0	8.3	5.7
Other marketing and sales occupations	6.6	5.3	7.8
Sales occupations, including retail	5.1	8.4	1.9
Other administrative (e.g., record clerks, telephone operators)	4.3	2.1	6.4
Insurance, securities, real estate, business services	4.1	4.8	3.5
Secretaries, receptionists, typists	2.8	0.1	5.3
Personnel, training, labor-relations specialists	2.5	2.2	2.9
Accountants, auditors, other financial specialists	1.6	1.3	1.9

Occupations

More than one-third of employed journalism graduates are employed as artists, broadcasters, writers, editors, entertainers, and public relations specialists. About 12 percent work in top- to mid-level managerial and administrative occupations, and 7 percent work in miscellaneous management occupations such as management analysts, purchasing agents, inspectors, and other regulatory officers. Another 7 percent are employed in miscellaneous marketing and sales occupations. The rest are dispersed across a variety of occupations.

- Men constitute 49 percent of all employed journalism graduates. Male journalism majors are somewhat less likely than female journalism majors to work as artists, broadcasters, writers, editors, entertainers, and public relations specialists–36 percent versus 38 percent.
- Men are much more likely than women journalism graduates to work in top- to mid-level managerial and administrative jobs.
- Women, however, are more likely than men to be employed in secretarial and administrative/clerical occupations.

Activities on the Job

The occupational employment patterns of journalism majors are reflected in the types of duties they perform on their jobs.

- One-fifth of all employed journalism graduates spend most of their workweek performing sales, purchasing, and marketing duties.
- Sixteen percent spend most of their time during a typical workweek performing management and administrative duties.

▶ Engagement in computer applications, programming, and systems-development activities is reported by 37 percent of all employed journalism graduates. However, only 6 percent spend most of their time on these activities.

▶ Although 79 percent of all employed journalism graduates perform accounting, finance, and contractual duties as a regular part of their jobs, only 4 percent spend most of their time in a typical workweek performing these duties. Many journalism majors perform these duties as a part of their jobs, but very few spend most of their time in performing them.

▶ Another 40 percent regularly engage in employee-relations activities, including recruiting, personnel development, and training, but only 4 percent conduct these duties during most of their working time.

Salaries

The average annual salary of journalism graduates who have only a bachelor's degree and are employed full-time is $52,500, a level that is 3 percent lower than the average annual salary of all full-time employed college graduates. As with most college graduates, the salary of journalism majors increases with age, indicating that they get more productive and therefore can earn higher salaries as they spend more time on the job. The annual average salary of journalism majors less than 35 is below the average salary of all college graduates. After the age of 35, the average salary of journalism majors moderately exceeds the average salary of all college graduates in subsequent age groups.

▶ The average annual salary of journalism majors between the ages of 25 and 29 is $35,300. Graduates between the ages of 30 and 34 earn $45,500 annually.

▶ Average annual earnings of journalism graduates increase at a moderate pace as they get older. The average annual salary of journalism majors between the ages of 35 and 39 who are employed full-time is $55,900, and the average salary for those between the ages of 40 and 44 is $59,900 per year. The salary peaks between the ages of 45 and 49 at $66,300 and remains in that range until age 65.

The average annual salary of journalism majors who work in jobs that are closely related to their major field of study is higher than the average salary of their counterparts who work in jobs that are either somewhat or not related to their undergraduate major field of study. The average salary of journalism majors in closely related jobs is $56,900; those employed in jobs that are somewhat related to journalism earn $52,000, and employment in unrelated jobs yields an annual salary of only $44,200.

Self-employed journalism graduates operating their own incorporated or non-incorporated business earn an average annual salary of $59,800. Journalism graduates who work in the private, for-profit sector for corporations and businesses earn an average salary of $54,900. The annual average remuneration of journalism graduates with full-time jobs in the private, nonprofit sector is $46,300. The government sector pays an average annual salary of $44,800 and journalism majors who are employed by educational institutions earn only $37,700 per year.

There are sizable variations in the average annual salary of journalism graduates, depending on the occupation in which they are employed. In 6 of the top 10 occupations that are predominant employers of journalism majors, the salary of all college graduates exceeds that of journalism majors.

▶ The annual salary of journalism majors who work in top- and mid-level managerial, executive, and administrative occupations is $77,300.

▶ Those who are employed in personnel, training, and labor-relations specialist jobs earn an average annual salary of $54,200.

▶ As broadcasters, writers, editors, and personnel in other entertainment occupations and as public relations specialists, journalism majors earn $53,000 annually.

▶ Of the top 10 occupations that are predominant employers of journalism graduates, secretarial and clerical jobs pay the lowest salaries.

FIGURE 2

Age/Earnings Profile of Persons with Only a Bachelor's Degree in Journalism (Full-Time Workers, in 2002 Dollars)

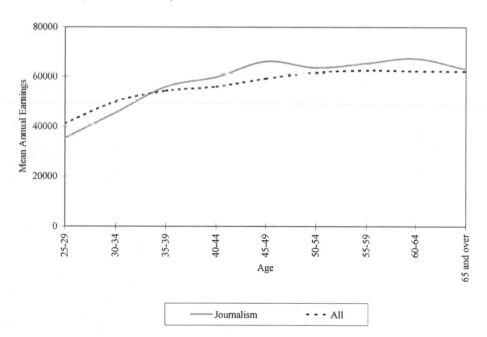

Table 2
Annual Salary of Full-Time Workers with Only a Bachelor's Degree in Journalism, Top 10 Occupations (in 2002 Dollars)

Earnings in Top 10 Occupations	All	Journalism
Total	$54,171	$52,500
Top- and mid-level managers, executives, administrators	$74,051	$77,325
Personnel, training, and labor relations specialists	$51,577	$54,205
Artists, broadcasters, writers, editors, entertainers, public relations specialists	$52,141	$53,049
Other marketing and sales occupations	$58,208	$51,220
Insurance, securities, real estate, business services	$68,273	$50,662
Accountants, auditors, other financial specialists	$57,382	$49,707
Other management-related occupations	$51,921	$48,233
Sales occupations, including retail	$52,378	$47,379
Secretaries, receptionists, typists	$32,246	$34,581
Other administrative (e.g., records clerks, telephone operators)	$34,547	$30,322

On-the-Job Training

The career potential of a job is closely associated with the amount of work-related training on the job. Work-related training is regarded as an investment by firms because it makes workers more productive. Firms that invest in their workforce are more likely to offer pay increases and promotions to match the increasing productivity of their workers. Firms that do not invest in their workers are relatively less likely to offer pay increases and promotions. Employed journalism majors are less likely to receive work-related training, compared to all employed college graduates. Whereas 68 percent of all employed college graduates receive some work-related training, 59 percent of journalism majors receive training on the job during a year.

▶ Of those journalism majors who receive some training, 65 percent receive technical training in their occupational field.

▶ Forty-three percent receive training to improve their general professional skills, such as public speaking and business writing.

▶ Thirty-seven percent of the training recipients participate in management or supervisor training.

Journalism graduates cite a number of reasons for participating in work-related training. When asked to identify the most important reason to acquire training, 61 percent who undergo training choose the need to improve their occupational skills and knowledge. Another 13 percent report a mandatory training requirement by the employer as the most important factor for their involvement in work-related training, and 11 percent place improved pay and promotion opportunities as the number one factor.

Post-Graduation Activities

Only 17 percent of journalism graduates with a bachelor's degree proceed to earn a post-graduate degree: 13 percent earn a master's degree, 1 percent earn a doctorate, and 3 percent earn a professional degree.

- Only 22 percent of the master's degrees are earned in journalism. Education is the major field of choice among 21 percent of master's degree earners, and another 11 percent of journalism graduates earn a master's degree in communications. About 9 percent earn a master's degree in business management and administrative services; another 9 percent proceed from a bachelor's degree in journalism to a master's degree in language, linguistics, and literature, including English and foreign languages.

- Twenty-three percent of all doctoral degrees among journalism majors are earned in psychology, and another 22 percent are earned in the field of language, linguistics, and literature, including English and foreign languages. Only 15 percent of graduates with a doctoral degree major in journalism, and 11 percent choose to graduate with a doctorate in education.

- Almost all (96 percent) professional degrees of journalism majors are in the field of law.

Of all journalism graduates under the age of 65, 89 percent are employed. Only 3 percent are officially unemployed; in other words, they are not employed and are actively seeking employment. The remaining 8 percent are out of the labor force; that is, they are not employed and are not seeking employment. Family responsibilities are cited as the reason for labor force withdrawal among 31 percent of this group of journalism graduates, and another 24 percent voluntarily withdrew from the labor force because they did not want or need to work. About 29 percent retired, and 12 percent withdrew to attend school.

Employment Outlook

According to the projections by the U.S. Bureau of Labor Statistics, employment in occupations that require at least a bachelor's degree is expected to grow faster than employment in other sectors of the American labor market. Between 2000 and 2010, the U.S. economy is projected to add 22.2 million jobs, yielding an employment growth rate of 15.2 percent. The employment growth projections in the top 10 occupations that are most likely to employ journalism graduates are mixed.

- The demand for artists, broadcasters, entertainers, and public relations specialists is expected to grow by 21 percent. Between 2000 and 2010, these occupations are expected to add 493,000 jobs.

- Employment in top- to mid-level management and administrative occupations is projected to grow by 12 percent, adding 1.3 million jobs between 2000 and 2010.

- Management-related jobs are projected to grow by 17 percent, a pace somewhat above the average of all occupations, whereas marketing occupations, which employ 7 percent of journalism majors, are expected to grow by 22 percent over the decade.

Table 3

Projected Change in Employment in the Top 10 Occupations That
Employ Persons with Only a Bachelor's Degree in Journalism

Top 10 Occupations	Actual Employment in 2000 (000s)	Projected Employment in 2010 (000s)	Absolute Change (000s)	Percentage Change
Artists, broadcasters, writers, editors, entertainers, public relations specialists	2,371	2,864	493	20.8%
Top- and mid-level managers, executives, administrators	10,564	11,834	1,270	12.0%
Other management-related occupations	4,956	5,801	845	17.1%
Other marketing and sales occupations	621	758	137	22.1%
Sales occupations, including retail	15,513	17,365	1,852	11.9%
Other administrative (e.g., records clerks, telephone operators)	16,911	18,522	1,611	9.5%
Insurance, securities, real estate, business services	1,548	1,726	178	11.5%
Secretaries, receptionists, typists	4,980	5,501	521	10.5%
Personnel, training, and labor relations specialists	490	578	88	18.0%
Accountants, auditors, other financial specialists	2,115	2,481	366	17.3%

CHAPTER 44

Legal Studies and Pre-Law

The education of most lawyers takes seven years of full-time study after high school graduation. The typical pattern is to take four years of undergraduate study in a pre-law major and then three years in law school. While there is no recommended pre-law major, commonly taken courses are English, foreign language, public speaking or communications, government, philosophy, history, political science, economics, business, mathematics, and computer science. The purpose of these courses is to help a person communicate, define problems, collect information, establish facts, and draw valid conclusions.

All lawyers, also called attorneys, interpret the law and apply it to specific situations. In the United States, attorneys act as both advocates and advisors. As advocates, they represent one of the opposing parties as either the prosecutor or the defense attorney in criminal or civil trials by presenting evidence that supports their position or client in court. As advisors, lawyers counsel their clients about their legal rights and obligations and suggest particular courses of action in business and personal matters.

The legal specialization determines the detailed aspects of a lawyer's job; the amount of time spent in court also depends on the specialization. In criminal law, defense attorneys represent individuals who have been charged with crimes, arguing their cases in law courts. Prosecutors work for various levels of federal or state government, upholding laws against those who violate them. In civil law, lawyers assist clients with litigation, wills, trusts, contracts, mortgages, real estate titles, and property leases.

Many legal specializations exist, such as bankruptcy, probate, international and intellectual property, and copyright law. Some lawyers work on business activities for corporations, others work in many capacities for the government, and still others function as attorney generals or district attorneys.

In the practice of law, an important skill is to influence the opinions and decisions of others. Lawyers need to win others' respect and confidence in order to convince them to take certain actions. Using the imagination and being able to demonstrate new ways to do or say something are helpful skills. The ability to search for and discover new facts and develop ways to apply them is required. The need to use computer software packages to research the legal literature is increasing. To reach conclusions, lawyers use perseverance and logical reasoning in their analysis of complex legal issues. During undergraduate education, a person develops skills in analytical thinking, communication and public speaking, and relationships (understanding and working with all kinds of people). Lawyers must be able to read and listen carefully to identify important details that could help a client win a case. Specialized courses require the use of judgment in knowing how to conduct a case or deal with a problem in different areas of law. Contracts, real estate, probate, and tax work require additional numerical skills and the ability to think with numbers to reach solutions.

Lawyers like to be involved in business and organizational pursuits. Being verbally persuasive, they like having the opportunity to lead. Lawyers have concerns about the well-being of others. They have a breadth of interests.

Practicing lawyers value work that requires a high level of mental activity. They enjoy doing many tasks that offer diversion, doing something of perceived importance, and succeeding at something they view as difficult. They also enjoy being paid well for their efforts.

In general, lawyers are quick, energetic, enthusiastic, frank, and assertive. They think logically, seek answers and reasons, and enjoy challenges. They are independent and tend to avoid repetitive and boring activities. Typically they could be good at doing a number of different things. They are usually good company and may be outspoken.

Where Do Legal Studies/Pre-Law Majors Work?

Most employed legal studies/pre-law graduates– 71 percent–work in the private, for-profit sector of the economy. Although a majority of these for-profit workers are employed in wage and salary jobs for businesses and corporations, a fairly large proportion of legal studies/pre-law graduates are self-employed in their own for-profit businesses. Another one-quarter are employed in the public sector. The remaining legal studies/pre-law graduates are employed in educational institutions and nonprofit organizations.

Only 31 percent of legal studies/pre-law graduates work in jobs that are closely related to their major field of study. Another 31 percent report working in jobs that are somewhat related to their major field of study. The remaining graduates work in jobs that are unrelated to their major. One-third of this group reported pay and promotion opportunities as the main reason for taking a job that is unrelated to their major field of study. About 1 in 6 decided to change their career, and another 1 in 6 said they could not find a job related to their undergraduate major field of study.

FIGURE 1

Percentage Distribution of Employed Persons with Only a Bachelor's Degree in Legal Studies/Pre-Law, by Major Sector of Economic Activity

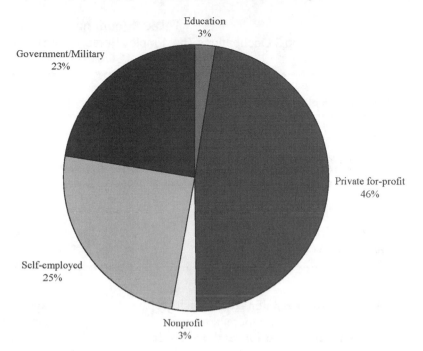

Education 3%

Government/Military 23%

Private for-profit 46%

Nonprofit 3%

Self-employed 25%

Occupations

Those legal studies/pre-law graduates who enter the labor market after a bachelor's degree work in a variety of occupations. The breadth of their undergraduate course work is reflected in the variety of occupations in which they are employed. More than one-fifth of legal studies/pre-law graduates are employed as top- or mid-level managers or in other management-related occupations. Another one-fifth are employed in jobs that are more related to their area of expertise as legal studies/pre-law majors, as security personnel in protective-service occupations, and as legal service providers in social service occupations. Pre-law graduates also are employed in administrative, accounting, finance, insurance, sales, and marketing occupations.

Table 1

Top 9 Occupations That Employ Persons with Only a Bachelor's Degree in Legal Studies/Pre-Law

| | PERCENT OF EMPLOYED | | |
Top 9 Occupations	All	Men	Women
Top- and mid-level managers, executives, administrators	13.1	19.7	4.6
Other management-related occupations	9.2	9.5	8.8
Other administrative (e.g., records clerks, telephone operators)	7.5	3.6	12.4

(continued)

447

Table 1 (continued)
Top 9 Occupations That Employ Persons with Only a Bachelor's
Degree in Legal Studies/Pre-Law

	PERCENT OF EMPLOYED		
Top 9 Occupations	**All**	**Men**	**Women**
Lawyers, paralegal occupations	7.5	9.2	5.3
Accountants, auditors, other financial specialists	6.1	5.0	7.5
Insurance, securities, real estate, business services	5.7	7.4	3.6
Protective-service occupations	5.2	9.2	0.0
Sales occupations, including retail	4.9	4.0	6.0
Social workers	4.2	3.2	5.4

▶ Men with a bachelor's degree in legal studies/pre-law are more likely than women to work as top- and mid-level managers, administrators, and executives. One-fifth of male graduates work as top- and mid-level managers, compared to only 5 percent of female graduates.

▶ Women are more concentrated in administrative positions such as record clerks and telephone operators. Only 3.5 percent of male graduates work in administrative occupations, compared to 12.5 percent of female graduates.

Activities on the Job

The occupational employment of legal studies/pre-law graduates is also reflected in the activities that they perform on their jobs during a typical week.

▶ More than 80 percent perform accounting, finance, and contractual duties as a regular part of their jobs.

▶ Managerial and administrative duties are regularly performed by more than 60 percent of graduates.

▶ Less than one-half are engaged in the provision of professional services as a daily part of their jobs.

▶ Slightly less than 2 in 5 graduates are regularly engaged in an assortment of computer applications, including programming and information processing.

▶ More than 3 in 10 graduates report that their daily job duties include employee-relations and personnel matters. A similar proportion are regularly involved in sales, purchasing, and marketing activities.

▶ One-fifth of all legal studies/pre-law graduates regularly engage in product development activities.

▶ Slightly more than 10 percent report that they perform basic or applied research or undertake teaching as a regular part of their weekly employment activities.

Salaries

Legal studies/pre-law graduates who are employed in full-time positions earn an average annual salary of $54,200, the same level as all bachelor's degree holders. As for most college graduates, the salary of legal studies/pre-law graduates increases with age, indicating that they get more productive and therefore earn higher salaries as they spend more time on the job. At different ages, pre-law graduates earn about the same as all college graduates.

▶ Legal studies/pre-law graduates between the ages of 25 and 29 who are employed in full-time jobs earn $37,100. Graduates between the ages of 45 and 49 earn $77,000.

Legal studies/pre-law graduates who are employed in full-time jobs that are closely related to their major field of study earn more—$61,500—

than those who are employed in jobs unrelated to their undergraduate major. Because of the diversity in their undergraduate course work, many legal studies/pre-law graduates consider managerial, administrative, and high-level sales and marketing jobs as related to their classroom training. These jobs pay above-average salaries.

Graduates who are self-employed, operating their own incorporated or non-incorporated business, earn an annual average salary of $67,800, which is higher than the annual average salary of legal studies/pre-law graduates employed in other sectors of the economy.

The average annual salary of full-time employed legal studies/pre-law graduates varies widely by occupation. In 6 of the 9 occupations in which legal studies/pre-law graduates are most likely to be employed, their annual average salary is higher than that of all college graduates.

FIGURE 2

Age/Earnings Profile of Persons with Only a Bachelor's Degree in Legal Studies and Pre-Law (Full-Time Workers, in 2002 Dollars)

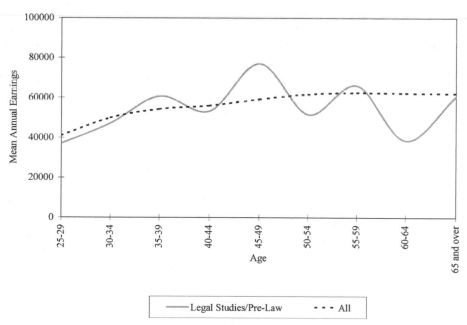

Table 2
Annual Salary of Full-Time Workers with Only a Bachelor's Degree in Legal Studies/Pre-Law, Top 9 Occupations (in 2002 Dollars)

Earnings in Top 9 Occupations	All	Legal Studies/Pre-Law
Total	$54,171	$54,234
Top- and mid-level managers, executives, administrators	$74,051	$77,266
Other management-related occupations	$51,921	$53,392
Other administrative (e.g., records clerks, telephone operators)	$34,547	$25,762
Lawyers, paralegal occupations	$68,248	$82,533
Accountants, auditors, other financial specialists	$57,382	$43,451
Insurance, securities, real estate, business services	$68,273	$80,547
Protective-service occupations	$49,130	$38,808
Sales occupations, including retail	$52,378	$59,308
Social workers	$36,371	$40,448

On-the-Job Training

Work-related training is an important indicator of long-term career potential in a job. Firms that invest in their workers at high rates are much more likely to offer pay increases and promotions than firms that do not invest in their workers. More than 60 percent of legal studies/pre-law graduates say that they participate in some work-related training activity during a year.

▶ Three-fourths of legal studies/pre-law graduates who receive some training are engaged in technical training in their occupation.

▶ Nearly 40 percent receive general professional training to improve their communication skills in public speaking and general writing.

▶ One-third receive training to sharpen their managerial and supervisory skills.

More than one-half of all who were engaged in a work-related training activity say that the main reason they attended the training activity is to increase their occupational skills and knowledge. One-fifth of those who received training did so because their employer required or expected them to undergo training.

Post-Graduation Activities

Nearly one-half—47 percent—of all legal studies/pre-law graduates with a bachelor's degree proceed to earn a professional degree. Another 10 percent earn a master's degree, and 2 percent go on to earn a doctoral degree.

▶ Of all the pre-law/legal graduates who earn a professional degree, 88 percent choose law as their major field of study.

▶ Seventy percent of the doctoral degrees of legal studies/pre-law graduates are in the field of law, and about 22 percent earn their doctorate in education, psychology, or a social science.

▶ The major fields of study of the master's degree of legal studies/pre-law graduates are mainly distributed across law, business, and the social sciences: 30 percent of the master's degrees are earned in law, 23 percent are earned in business administration, and 11 percent are earned in the social sciences.

About 83 percent of legal studies/pre-law graduates who are under the age of 65 and have only a bachelor's degree are employed. More than 90 percent of the employed graduates have full-time jobs with a typical workweek of 35 hours or more. About 6 percent of legal studies/pre-law graduates are not employed but are seeking employment, and the remaining 11 percent are neither working nor looking for work. The latter group—11 percent—choose to withdraw from the labor force because of family responsibilities, because of chronic sickness or a disabling condition, or because they do not desire or need to work. A small fraction of labor force withdrawals among legal studies/pre-law graduates occur because of retirement.

Employment Outlook

The U.S. Bureau of Labor Statistics projects employment in occupations that require at least a bachelor's degree to grow faster than employment in other sectors of the American labor market. Between 2000 and 2010, the U.S. economy is projected to add 22.2 million jobs, yielding an employment growth rate of 15.2 percent.

▶ The fastest employment growth rate of the 9 predominant employers of legal studies/pre-law graduates is among social workers. The demand for social workers will grow at a rate that is more than two times faster than the average rate of growth of all jobs in the economy. The employment in this occupation is expected to grow by 141,000—or 30 percent—between 2000 and 2010.

▶ Protective-service occupations, which mainly employ male legal studies/pre-law graduates, are expected to add 809,000 jobs, yielding a growth rate of 26 percent.

▶ Employment in top- and mid-level management and administrative occupations, a top employer of all legal studies/pre-law graduates (particularly men), is expected to grow by 12 percent, adding 1.3 million jobs between 2000 and 2010.

▶ Administrative and clerical occupations, the main employer of female legal studies/pre-law graduates, are expected to add 1.6 million jobs, yielding a growth rate of only 10 percent between 2000 and 2010.

Table 3
Projected Change in Employment in the Top 9 Occupations That Employ
Persons with Only a Bachelor's Degree in Legal Studies/Pre-Law

Top 9 Occupations	Actual Employment in 2000 (000s)	Projected Employment in 2010 (000s)	Absolute Change (000s)	Percentage Change
Top- and mid-level managers, executives, administrators	10,564	11,834	1,270	12.0%
Other management-related occupations	4,956	5,801	845	17.1%
Other administrative (e.g., records clerks, telephone operators)	16,911	18,522	1,611	9.5%
Lawyers, paralegal occupations	1,076	1,291	215	20.0%
Accountants, auditors, other financial specialists	2,115	2,481	366	17.3%
Insurance, securities, real estate, business services	1,548	1,726	178	11.5%
Protective-service occupations	3,087	3,896	809	26.2%
Sales occupations, including retail	15,513	17,365	1,852	11.9%
Social workers	468	609	141	30.1%

CHAPTER 45

Liberal Arts and General Studies

For many people this major is a philosophy of what education should be—the training of the mind to analyze, to be a critical thinker, to communicate orally and in writing, and to be an educated person characterized by breadth of knowledge. Today the support of a liberal arts education is a reaction to college having become "vocational training" in some people's minds. A liberal arts education upholds the belief in the tradition of obtaining a broad base of knowledge that allows students to develop proficiency in basic skills; to be exposed to methods of inquiry in the various subjects and disciplines in the arts and humanities, social sciences, natural sciences, and mathematics; and to become acquainted with ideas in Western culture, with differing views in non-Western cultures, and with the major issues and problems facing contemporary society. Many companies and professional schools, including medicine, value the benefits and problem-solving skills nurtured by a liberal arts tradition—provided a student has taken the prescribed prerequisite courses. Some colleges and universities honor this tradition by requiring a core liberal arts curriculum or a general studies component within their programs.

The following is a sample liberal arts curriculum with some illustrative courses. Each student has considerable freedom to choose from among these academic fields.

- Basic Skills: English; Mathematics; Foreign Language Proficiency.

- Methods of Inquiry: Introduction to Science; Introduction to Art; Women's Studies—Images, Myths, and Reality; Culture of the World; Fiction; Drama; Geology of Oceans and Coasts; Principles of Microeconomics.

- The Western Cultural Heritage: African-American History; European Economic Development; Music as Self-Expression; Understanding the Bible.

- Alternative Cultures and Societies: Rural Workers in the Third World; American Urban History; Eastern Religions;

Contemporary Japanese and Cultural Society; Economic Issues in Minority Communities; Modern African Civilization.

▶ Theoretical Perspectives and Changes: Ethics–East and West; Sociology of the Family; Film Theory; Economics of Developing Nations.

▶ Current Issues in Perspective: Philosophical Problems of Law and Justice; Gender Politics; Computers and Society; Science, Technology, and Public Policy; Contemporary Revolutionary Politics; Crisis and Conflict in Black Africa; Water–Planning for the Future.

The values, interests, and abilities required in a liberal arts education involve exposure to a breadth of knowledge, intellectual stimulation, and the desire to communicate about an inquiry. Individual characteristics follow these personal goals, in addition to postponing for the moment concrete and practical skill development in a specific field of concentration.

Where Do Liberal Arts/ General Studies Majors Work?

The breadth of the educational experiences of liberal arts/general studies graduates is reflected in the diversity of their employment. Fewer than one-half of the graduates work for businesses and corporations in the private, for-profit sector of the economy, and 16 percent are self-employed in their own business or practice. One-fifth work in the education sector of the economy, and 12 percent work in the government sector of the economy.

Given the diversity of the educational experiences of these graduates, it naturally follows that most liberal arts/general studies graduates do not work in jobs that are closely related to their undergraduate major. In fact, only 26 percent do so, and 30 percent work in jobs that are somewhat related to their field. The remaining 44 percent work in jobs that are not at all related to their undergraduate major.

Liberal arts/general studies graduates offer various reasons for their employment in jobs unrelated to their undergraduate major field of study. When asked to select the most important factor influencing their decision to work in an unrelated job, 31 percent say better pay and promotion opportunities lured them away from jobs related to their major. One-fifth cite a change in their career and professional interests as the most important factor influencing their decision to work outside their major field of study. More than 11 percent cite family-related reasons, and another 8 percent state their inability to find jobs related to liberal arts/general studies as the most important reason for their employment shift outside their field.

FIGURE 1

Percentage Distribution of Employed Persons with Only a Bachelor's Degree in Liberal Arts/ General Studies, by Major Sector of Economic Activity

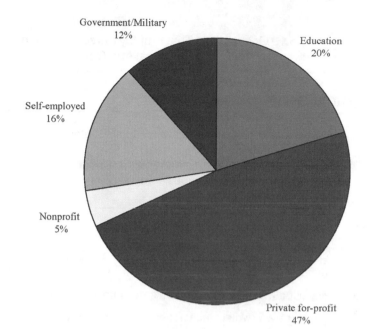

Government/Military 12%

Education 20%

Self-employed 16%

Nonprofit 5%

Private for-profit 47%

Occupations

The education of graduates who major in liberal arts/general studies does not prepare them for any particular profession or vocation. Rather, this education provides exposure to the subject matter of a broad array of disciplines and provides a foundation of critical thinking and problem-solving skills on which the graduates can proceed to build the practical skills needed in specific fields. Graduates are employed in diverse occupations. Several different occupations are included in the list of the top 10 employers of liberal arts/general studies graduates. This

list includes occupations in management, teaching, insurance and finance, sales, marketing, communications and broadcasting, public relations, and accounting. One-tenth of these graduates work in executive, administrative, and managerial jobs; 9 percent work as elementary school teachers. The next largest employer of these graduates is insurance, securities, real estate, and business service occupations, representing 8 percent of the graduates. Management-related occupations and sales occupations each employ 6 percent. Less than 5 percent work in marketing and sales, secretarial, clerical, mass communications, and accounting occupations.

Table 1
Top 10 Occupations That Employ Persons with Only a Bachelor's Degree
in Liberal Arts/General Studies

Top 10 Occupations	PERCENT OF EMPLOYED		
	All	Men	Women
Top- and mid-level managers, executives, administrators	10.2	15.2	6.1
Teachers, elementary school	8.8	1.0	15.1
Insurance, securities, real estate, business services	7.9	9.4	6.7
Other management-related occupations	6.4	6.9	6.0
Sales occupations, including retail	6.4	8.9	4.4
Other marketing and sales occupations	4.5	5.8	3.4
Secretaries, receptionists, typists	4.5	0.6	7.6
Other administrative (e.g., records clerks, telephone operators)	4.4	6.2	2.9
Artists, broadcasters, writers, editors, entertainers, public relations specialists	4.0	4.5	3.6
Accountants, auditors, other financial specialists	3.0	2.0	3.7

▶ Men, who constitute 45 percent of all employed liberal arts/general studies graduates, are twice as likely as women to work in executive, administrative, and managerial occupations. More than 15 percent of male graduates work in these occupations, compared to only 6 percent of women.

▶ Men also are more likely than women to work in insurance, securities, real estate, and business services occupations–9 percent versus 7 percent.

▶ Sales and marketing occupations more frequently employ male liberal arts/general studies graduates than female graduates.

▶ Women, however, are considerably more likely than men to be employed in elementary school teaching. Whereas 15 percent of female graduates work in this occupation, only 1 percent of men choose to teach in elementary schools.

▶ Women also are much more likely than men to work in secretarial jobs. Nearly 8 percent of female graduates work as secretaries, typists, and receptionists, compared to only one-half percent of men.

Activities on the Job

The activities in which liberal arts/general studies majors engage at work are as diverse as their undergraduate curriculum and their post-graduation occupational employment.

▶ Seventeen percent spend most of their time at work on sales, purchasing, marketing activities, and management and administrative duties.

▶ Sixteen percent consider teaching to be their major activity at work.

▶ One in 10 employed liberal arts/general studies graduates spends most of their time at work in providing professional services in the form of human services such as counseling, legal services, and health services.

▶ Eight percent of employed liberal arts/general studies graduates spend most of their time at work in performing computer applications, programming, and systems-development duties.

▶ Five percent of the graduates consider accounting, finance, and contractual duties to consume most of their time at work.

▶ Another 5 percent of the graduates spend most of their time at work in employee-relations activities, including recruiting, personnel development, and training.

Salaries

The average annual salary of liberal arts/general studies graduates who have only a bachelor's degree and are employed full-time is $52,200, a level that is 4 percent lower than the average annual salary of all full-time employed college graduates. The shape of the age/earnings profile of liberal arts/general studies graduates is very similar to that of all college graduates, but the average salary of these graduates in each age group is at a somewhat lower level than the average salary of all college graduates in the age groups. This age/earnings profile implies that most graduates get more productive as they age.

▶ The average annual salary of liberal arts/general studies graduates between the ages of 25 and 29 is $40,000. Between the ages of 30 and 34, the annual average salary rises to $47,800, followed by another small increase to $48,200 for graduates between the ages of 35 and 39.

▶ The salary continues to rise until it peaks at $63,700 for those between the ages of 50 and 54.

The annual average salary of liberal arts/general studies graduates is little affected by whether their jobs are related to their undergraduate major field of study. Closely related jobs pay an annual average salary of $53,100 per year. The annual average earnings of graduates employed in jobs that are somewhat related and of those whose jobs are unrelated to their undergraduate major field of study are $51,900. Because liberal arts/general studies graduates do not learn any profession- or vocation-specific job skills in the classroom, the relationship of the duties that they perform on the job and their annual salary is not strong.

Self-employed liberal arts/general studies graduates earn a higher average salary than graduates working in other sectors of the economy. The annual average salary of self-employed liberal arts/general studies majors who work full-time in their business or practice is $61,700. Those who work for businesses or corporations in the private, for-profit sector of the economy earn an annual average salary of $53,900. The government sector pays an annual average salary of $48,900 to liberal arts/general studies graduates who work full-time. As for most other college graduates from different majors, the education sector, which pays $41,400 to full-time employed liberal arts/general studies graduates, is the lowest-paying sector in the economy.

FIGURE 2

Age/Earnings Profile of Persons with Only a Bachelor's Degree in Liberal Arts/General Studies (Full-Time Workers, in 2002 Dollars)

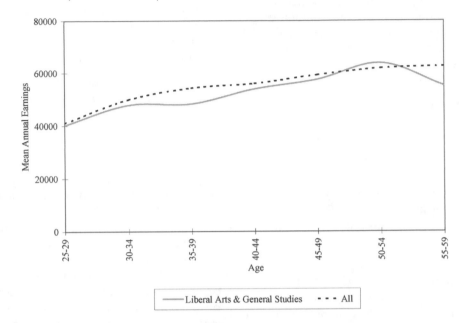

Although the annual average salary of liberal arts/general studies graduates is 4 percent lower than the salary of all college graduates, in 7 of the 10 occupations that are predominant employers of liberal arts/general studies graduates, the salary of these graduates exceeds the salary of all college graduates employed in these occupations. The average salary of liberal arts/general studies graduates and all college graduates in each of these 10 occupations is presented here.

▶ The highest earnings of liberal arts/general studies graduates are in marketing and sales occupations. In this group of occupations, the annual salary of graduates is $77,600; this group is more likely to employ male than female liberal arts/general studies graduates.

▶ Graduates employed in accounting and financial occupations earn the

second-highest salary of $68,900 per year. Only 3 percent are employed in this group.

▶ Graduates employed in the arts, communications, and public relations occupations earn the third-highest salary of $59,800.

▶ The top employer of liberal arts/general studies graduates—executive, administrative, and managerial occupations—pays these graduates an annual average salary of $66,400. This group employs more male liberal arts/general studies graduates.

▶ The lowest earnings of liberal arts/general studies graduates are in the elementary school teacher occupation. This occupation mostly employs female liberal arts graduates and pays an average annual salary of $41,000.

Table 2
Annual Salary of Full-Time Workers with Only a Bachelor's Degree in Liberal Arts/General Studies, Top 10 Occupations (in 2002 Dollars)

Earnings in Top 10 Occupations	All	Liberal Arts/General Studies
Total	$54,171	$52,203
Top- and mid-level managers, executives, administrators	$74,051	$66,413
Teachers, elementary school	$39,167	$41,045
Insurance, securities, real estate, business services	$68,273	$57,882
Other management-related occupations	$51,921	$54,099
Sales occupations, including retail	$52,378	$46,741
Other marketing and sales occupations	$58,208	$77,633
Secretaries, receptionists, typists	$32,246	$49,402
Other administrative (e.g., records clerks, telephone operators)	$34,547	$44,111
Artists, broadcasters, writers, editors, entertainers, public relations specialists	$52,141	$59,753
Accountants, auditors, other financial specialists	$57,382	$68,945

On-the-Job Training

The career potential of a job is closely associated with the amount of work-related training on the job. Work-related training is regarded as an investment by firms because it makes workers more productive. Firms that invest in their workforce are more likely to offer pay increases and promotions to match the increasing productivity of their workers. Firms that do not invest in their workers are relatively less likely to offer pay increases and promotions. Of liberal arts/general studies graduates, 63 percent engage in some type of work-related training during a year. The rate of participation in training is 68 percent among all college graduates.

▶ Of those liberal arts/general studies graduates who receive some training, 71 percent receive technical training in the occupation in which they are employed.

▶ Twenty-eight percent of the training recipients receive management or supervisor training.

▶ Thirty-six percent receive training to improve their general professional skills, such as public speaking and business writing.

Although numerous reasons underlie the decision of liberal arts/general studies majors to participate in work-related training activities, workshops, or seminars, four factors stand out. They are a desire to improve skills and knowledge in the occupational area of their employment, mandatory training requirements of the employer, the need to obtain a professional license or certificate, and increased opportunities for advancement in the form of a promotion and higher salary.

When asked to identify the most important reason to acquire training, 62 percent of liberal arts/general studies majors who undergo training identify the need to improve their occupational skills and knowledge. Another 15 percent report a mandatory training requirement by the employer as the most important factor for involvement in work-related training. According to 8 percent, the most important factor is to obtain a professional license or certificate. Finally, 7 percent rank an improvement in their opportunities for a salary increase and promotion as the number one factor in influencing their decision to participate in work-related training.

Post-Graduation Activities

Of those liberal arts/general studies graduates with a bachelor's degree, 38 percent proceed to earn a postgraduate degree: 24 percent earn a master's degree, 3 percent graduate with a doctorate, and another 11 percent earn a professional degree.

- One-quarter earn their master's degree in business management and administrative services. Another one-quarter choose education as the major field of study for their master's degree. The rest are dispersed across many different major fields.

- Only 3 percent of liberal arts/general studies graduates earn a doctorate. One-fifth of these degrees are earned in psychology, 15 percent in law, and another 15 percent in education. The rest are spread across many different major fields.

- Seven of 10 professional degrees among undergraduate liberal arts/general studies majors are earned in law, and 1 in 4 is earned in the health professions.

Of all liberal arts/general studies graduates under the age of 65, 81 percent are employed. Only 3 percent are officially unemployed; in other words, they are not employed and are actively seeking employment. The remaining 15 percent are out of the labor force; that is, they are not employed and are not seeking employment. Many of the labor force withdrawals among liberal arts/general studies graduates are attributable to family responsibilities and lack of a need or desire to work. Nearly 55 percent cite family responsibilities as one of the reasons for their labor force withdrawal. Another 36 percent voluntarily withdrew from the labor force because they did not have the need or desire to work. Of these non-elderly liberal arts/general studies graduates, 13 percent cite retirement as the reason for their labor force withdrawal.

Employment Outlook

According to the U.S. Bureau of Labor Statistics, employment in occupations that require at least a bachelor's degree is expected to grow faster than employment in other sectors of the American labor market. Between 2000 and 2010, the U.S. economy is projected to add 22.2 million jobs, yielding an employment growth rate of 15.2 percent. The employment growth projections in the top 10 occupations that are most likely to employ liberal arts/general studies graduates are presented here.

- The largest employer of liberal arts/ general studies majors—executive, administrative, and managerial occupations—is projected to add more than 1.3 million jobs between 2000 and 2010, yielding an employment growth rate of 12 percent. Twice as many male liberal arts/general studies graduates as female graduates are employed in this occupation. This group includes high-paying jobs.

- The demand for elementary school teachers is projected to grow by 13 percent. This is a low-paying occupation, employing mostly female liberal arts/ general studies graduates.

- Employment is projected to grow by one-fifth in art, broadcasting, mass media, and public relations occupations. This group employs about 4 percent of liberal arts/general studies graduates and pays high salaries to these graduates.

- Another rapidly growing area among the top 10 employers of liberal arts/general studies graduates is marketing and sales occupations. The employment in this area is expected to increase by 22 percent. These occupations are associated with the highest salaries among liberal arts/general studies graduates and employ a higher proportion of male than female liberal arts/general studies graduates.

Table 3

Projected Change In Employment In the Top 10 Occupations That Employ Persons with Only a Bachelor's Degree in Liberal Arts/General Studies

Top 10 Occupations	Actual Employment in 2000 (000s)	Projected Employment in 2010 (000s)	Absolute Change (000s)	Percentage Change
Top- and mid-level managers, executives, administrators	10,564	11,834	1,270	12.0%
Teachers, elementary school	1,532	1,734	202	13.2%
Insurance, securities, real estate, business services	1,548	1,726	178	11.5%
Other management-related occupations	4,956	5,801	845	17.1%
Sales occupations, including retail	15,513	17,365	1,852	11.9%
Other marketing and sales occupations	621	758	137	22.1%
Secretaries, receptionists, typists	4,980	5,501	521	10.5%
Other administrative (e.g., records clerks, telephone operators)	16,911	18,522	1,611	9.5%
Artists, broadcasters, writers, editors, entertainers, public relations specialists	2,371	2,864	493	20.8%
Accountants, auditors, other financial specialists	2,115	2,481	366	17.3%

CHAPTER 46

Music and Dance

Many people are interested in music and dance for recreational purposes. As a source of employment, however, these fields are very competitive. Musicians play musical instruments, sing, compose, arrange, or conduct groups in instrumental or vocal performances. Dancers perform modern ballet or folk, ethnic, tap, and jazz dances. Many people get involved in music-related occupations, such as music therapist; songwriter; music teacher; booking agent; music store worker; disc jockey; and, for some with technical knowledge, sound and audio technician and instrument repairer. Because of the strenuous physical requirements, dancers leave the field at an early age.

Specialization is common among musicians, such as playing in a band, a rock group, or a jazz group. They typically focus on such specific instruments as string, brass, woodwind, percussion, piano, or electronic synthesizers. Some musicians learn related instruments, such as trombone and trumpet. Singers are classified by the type of music they sing, such as rock, reggae, folk, rap, country and western, or opera, or by their voice range, such as soprano, contralto, tenor, baritone, or bass.

Composers create original music, from popular songs to symphonies and operas. They transcribe their ideas into musical notation using harmony, rhythm, melody, and tonal structure. Use of computers to compose and edit music is becoming common. Arrangers transcribe and adapt musical compositions to a particular style for bands, choral groups, or individuals. Conductors lead musical groups. They audition and select musicians, choose the music that complements their talents, and direct rehearsals to achieve the desired sound.

Dancers express ideas, stories, rhythm, and sound with their bodies. Most perform as a group. Many dancers sing and act as well as dance; for example, they may work in opera, musicals, television, music videos, and commercials.

Although few dance routines are written down, most collegiate programs offer courses in ballet and classical techniques, dance composition, dance history, and movement analysis. Dancing and music require instruction, and practice generally begins at an early age. Formal course work includes musical theory, music interpretation, and composition.

Finger and motor coordination are necessary for playing instruments, as well as the ability to recognize music symbols for interpreting music properly. Also important is being able to hear and recognize tonal and harmonic balance, rhythm, and tempo. Singers need to know the qualities of various musical instruments and to understand how they relate in orchestrations and arrangements for desired effects. Performing with poise and self-confidence before an audience is either an innate ability or one to be perfected.

Skill in dancing requires understanding dance steps and memorizing dance routines. Ability is needed to move with grace and rhythm and to coordinate body movements to music and to the movements of other dancers. Exercise, practice, and excellent physical condition are necessary. Dancers express such emotions as joy, sorrow, or excitement by the way they move their arms, legs, and body.

Artistic interests characterize those in music and dance. While singers may be more inclined to linguistic expression, dancers express bodily and athletically the flow and rhythm of music. Instrumental musicians can be very involved in technical equipment for the acoustical enhancement of their instruments. Music and dance are meant to be heard and seen; thus, performers enjoy creatively projecting themselves and their expressions to others.

Opportunities exist for satisfying many values through music and dance. One can get attention and recognition by performing in public, and the work is both varied and creative. Yet differences exist between the two areas of dance and music: Dancing demands physical activity that some enjoy, while music permits an independence that enables the performer to decide how to play or sing a selection.

The preceding descriptions that include both practicing routines and creative endeavors suggest different personality types within these fields. Consider a group of dancers or musicians striving as perfectionists to get "it" right. This drive demands concentration, persistence, and an appreciation of working harmoniously. With new songs and styles constantly appearing, music encourages individuality. This phenomenon creates an openness for experimenting and competing for audiences to accept a novel approach.

Where Do Music Majors Work?

Of employed music majors, 54 percent work as wage and salary workers in the private, for-profit sector of the economy. Although a majority of music majors employed in the private, for-profit sector work as wage and salary workers for businesses or corporations, a fairly large proportion are self-employed in their own business or professional practice. Educational institutions employ nearly one-third of all music majors. And 1 in 10 music majors is employed in the private, nonprofit sector of the economy for tax-exempt or charitable organizations.

Only 45 percent of music majors work in jobs that are closely related to their major field of study. Another 12 percent report working in jobs that are somewhat related to their major. The remaining 43 percent work in jobs that are not at all related to music. Of those music graduates who work in unrelated jobs, 30 percent do so because of better opportunities for promotion and higher salaries in unrelated jobs. Nearly one-fifth work outside their major because they are unable to find jobs in their field of study. Another one-fifth changed their professional and career interests, and 14 percent cited family-related reasons for their decision to work in an area outside their field of study.

FIGURE 1

Percentage Distribution of Employed Persons with Only a Bachelor's Degree in Music, by Major Sector of Economic Activity

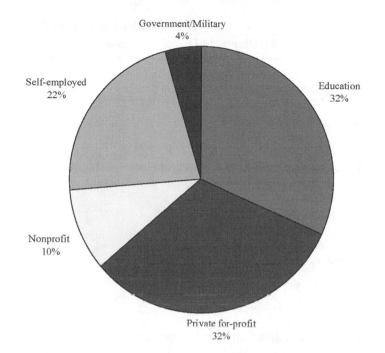

Government/Military 4%

Education 32%

Self-employed 22%

Nonprofit 10%

Private for-profit 32%

Occupations

Employed music majors work in a variety of occupations. One-quarter of all employed music majors are employed as teachers: 10 percent work as elementary school teachers, 10 percent as secondary school teachers, and 5 percent as postsecondary professors. No other single occupation employs a large majority of music majors. About 12 percent are employed as artists, broadcasters, writers, editors, entertainers, and public relations specialists. Other predominant employers of music majors are management-related occupations: 5 percent are employed in personnel management, training, and labor-relations occupations, and another 5 percent are employed in other miscellaneous management-related occupations such as management analysts, purchasing agents, inspectors, and other regulatory officers. About 5 percent are employed in sales occupations, including retail sales.

Table 1

Top 10 Occupations That Employ Persons with Only a Bachelor's Degree in Music

Top 10 Occupations	PERCENT OF EMPLOYED		
	All	Men	Women
Artists, broadcasters, writers, editors, entertainers, public relations specialists	12.2	16.4	9.3
Teachers, secondary school	10.3	14.3	7.6

(continued)

Table 1 (continued)

Top 10 Occupations That Employ Persons with Only a Bachelor's Degree in Music

| | PERCENT OF EMPLOYED | | |
Top 10 Occupations	All	Men	Women
Teachers, elementary school	10.0	4.6	13.8
Personnel, training, and labor relations specialists	5.3	2.6	7.2
Other management-related occupations	5.3	7.7	3.7
Postsecondary professors	5.1	4.5	5.5
Sales occupations, including retail	5.0	6.2	4.1
Top- and mid-level managers, executives, administrators	4.9	6.3	4.0
Secretaries, receptionists, typists	4.2	0.0	7.1
Other administrative (e.g., records clerks, telephone operators)	3.3	1.3	4.8

▶ More male than female music majors work as artists, broadcasters, writers, editors, entertainers, and public relations specialists–16 percent versus 9 percent.

▶ Whereas 14 percent of male music majors are employed as secondary school teachers, only 8 percent of female music majors have jobs as secondary school teachers.

▶ Female music majors are more likely than their male counterparts to be employed as elementary school teachers. While 14 percent of female music graduates are employed as elementary school teachers, only 5 percent of men who are music graduates work as teachers in elementary schools.

▶ Female music majors are also more likely than male music majors to work as personnel, training, and labor-relations specialists, whereas males are more inclined to work in other management-related jobs, such as management analysts, financial specialists, and purchasing agents.

▶ Women who major in music also are more likely to work in secretarial and administrative/clerical occupations.

Activities on the Job

▶ Given the high concentration of music majors in teaching occupations, it is hardly surprising to find that 53 percent are regularly engaged in teaching activities on their jobs. Not only do a large fraction of music majors regularly engage in teaching activities on their jobs, but also a sizable proportion spend most of their typical week in teaching activities. Nearly 37 percent of employed music graduates spend most of their typical workweek on teaching activities.

▶ Although 86 percent of all employed music graduates perform accounting, finance, and contractual duties as a regular part of their jobs, only 8 percent spend most of their time performing these duties in a typical workweek.

Many music majors perform these duties as a part of their jobs, but very few spend most of their time in performing them.

▶ Forty percent of music graduates regularly perform managerial and administrative duties as a part of their employment.

▶ About 30 percent of all employed music graduates regularly engage in computer applications, programming, and systems-development activities. Another 30 percent regularly perform employee-relations activities, including recruiting, personnel development, and training.

▶ About one-fifth of music majors regularly engage in sales, purchasing, and marketing activities.

▶ Fewer than 1 in 5 spend a part of their typical workweek in providing professional services.

▶ Less than 15 percent of music majors engage in basic or applied research, and fewer than 10 percent regularly perform product-development and equipment-design activities in their jobs.

Salaries

The average annual salary of music graduates who have only a bachelor's degree and are employed full-time is $41,300, a level that is only 76 percent of the average annual salary of all full-time employed college graduates. As with most college graduates, the salary of music majors increases with age, indicating that they get more productive and therefore can earn higher salaries as they spend more time on the job. However, at different ages, music majors earn considerably lower salaries than the average for all college graduates.

▶ The average annual salary of music majors between the ages of 25 and 29 is only $28,000. Graduates between the ages of 30 and 34 earn $40,200 annually.

▶ Average annual earnings of music graduates increase at a moderate pace as they get older. The average annual salary of music majors between the ages of 50 and 54 is $47,400.

▶ The average annual salary of music majors who work in jobs that are closely related to their major field of study is only $39,000. Graduates whose jobs are somewhat related to their major earn $46,300 per year. The average annual salary of music majors whose jobs are unrelated to the major is $41,700. Many music graduates whose jobs are closely related to their majors are employed in teaching occupations.

▶ The average annual salary of music majors who are employed by educational institutions is $38,000, a level that is lower than salaries of music majors in other sectors of the economy. Music graduates employed in the private, nonprofit sector earn $38,300, which is slightly more than teachers earn. The private, for-profit sector pays an average annual salary of $43,900 to music majors who are employed full-time. Self-employed music graduates operating their own incorporated or non-incorporated business earn an average annual salary of $43,600.

FIGURE 2

Age/Earnings Profile of Persons with Only a Bachelor's Degree in Music
(Full-Time Workers, in 2002 Dollars)

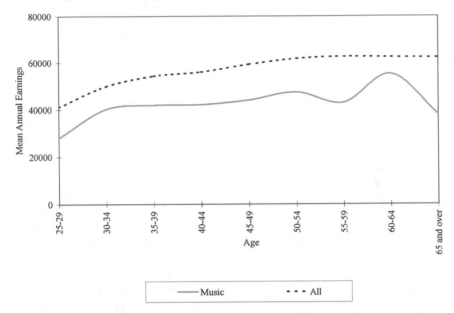

The average annual salary of music graduates varies widely by occupation. The average annual salary of music majors is much lower than the salary of all college graduates. In 8 of the top 10 occupations that are predominant employers of music graduates, the salary of all college graduates exceeds that of music majors. The average annual salary of music majors who secure jobs in broadcasting and entertainment occupations is $51,000. Those who are employed as teachers at the elementary, secondary, or post-secondary level earn $38,200, $36,100, and $34,200, respectively, per year. Access to jobs in top- to mid-level managerial and administrative occupations and in personnel, training, and labor relations occupations is associated with higher annual earnings among music majors.

Table 2

Annual Salary of Full-Time Workers with Only a Bachelor's Degree
in Music, Top 10 Occupations (in 2002 Dollars)

Earnings in Top 10 Occupations	All	Music
Total	$54,171	$41,265
Artists, broadcasters, writers, editors, entertainers, public relations specialists	$52,141	$50,999

Earnings in Top 10 Occupations	All	Music
Teachers, secondary school	$40,355	$36,114
Teachers, elementary school	$39,167	$38,247
Personnel, training, and labor relations specialists	$51,577	$54,108
Other management-related occupations	$51,921	$36,369
Postsecondary professors	$42,234	$34,249
Sales occupations, including retail	$52,378	$41,032
Top- and mid-level managers, executives, administrators	$74,051	$56,927
Secretaries, receptionists, typists	$32,246	$32,127
Other administrative (e.g., records clerks, telephone operators)	$34,547	$38,257

On-the-Job Training

The career potential of a job is closely associated with the amount of work-related training on the job. Work-related training is regarded as an investment by firms because it makes workers more productive. Firms that invest in their workforce are more likely to offer pay increases and promotions to match the increasing productivity of their workers. Firms that do not invest in their workers are relatively less likely to offer pay increases and promotions. The likelihood of receiving work-related training is lower among music majors compared to all college graduates. Whereas 68 percent of all employed college graduates receive some work-related training, only 59 percent of music majors receive training on the job during a year.

- Of those music majors who receive some training, 72 percent receive technical training in their occupational field.

- Thirty-one percent receive training to improve their general professional skills, such as public speaking and business writing.

- One-quarter of the training recipients participate in management or supervisor training.

Of those music majors who participate in some work-related training, 93 percent do so to improve their occupational skills and knowledge. About 46 percent are required or expected by their employers to undergo training. More opportunity for promotion, advancement, and salary increases is the reason for 41 percent of music majors to participate in work-related training.

Post-Graduation Activities

Nearly 44 percent of music graduates with a bachelor's degree proceed to earn a postgraduate degree. Of those with a bachelor's degree, 37 percent earn a master's degree, 5 percent graduate with a doctorate, and fewer than 2 percent earn a professional degree.

- More than 6 of 10 master's degrees are earned in music; 17 percent of music graduates earn a master's degree in education.

- A similar choice of major field of study is observed among music majors who earn doctoral degrees. Two-thirds of the doctoral degrees are earned in the field of music. About 17 percent graduate with doctoral degrees in education.

- Among the few music majors who earn professional degrees, 64 percent choose law as their major field of study; 22 percent earn their professional degrees in health-related fields.

Of all music graduates under the age of 65, 84 percent are employed. Only 1.7 percent are officially unemployed; in other words, they are not employed and are actively seeking employment. The remaining 14 percent are out of the labor force; that is, they are not employed and are not seeking employment. Family responsibilities are the reason for labor force withdrawal among 41 percent of this group of music graduates. Of those music majors who are out of the labor force, 37 percent do not need or want to work. One-quarter of labor force withdrawals of music majors are attributable to retirement.

Employment Outlook

According to the U.S. Bureau of Labor Statistics, employment in occupations that require at least a bachelor's degree is expected to grow faster than employment in other sectors of the American labor market. Between 2000 and 2010 the U.S. economy is projected to add 22.2 million jobs, yielding an employment growth rate of 15.2 percent. The employment growth projections in the top 10 occupations that are most likely to employ music graduates are mixed.

- The demand for artists, broadcasters, entertainers, and public relations specialists is expected to grow by 21 percent. Between 2000 and 2010, these occupations are expected to add 493,000 jobs. These occupations employ 12 percent of music graduates.

- Teaching occupations employ 25 percent of all music majors. The current demographic surge in the elementary school–age population is expected to increase the future demand for secondary school teachers by 18 percent between 2000 and 2010. Over the same time period, elementary school teachers will see only a 13 percent increase in employment. These projections suggest slower employment growth for female music graduates, who are more likely to be employed as elementary school teachers. Male music graduates, however, are more likely to be employed as secondary school teachers. The demand for postsecondary professors is projected to grow by 23 percent between 2000 and 2010.

- Employment in personnel, training, and labor-relations specialist occupations, as well as in management-related occupations, is projected to grow in the 17- to 18-percent range.

- Employment in management and sales occupations is projected to add jobs at the comparatively slow pace of 12 percent between 2000 and 2010.

- Secretarial and administrative/clerical occupations are projected to grow at below-average rates.

Table 3
Projected Change in Employment in the Top 10 Occupations
That Employ Persons with Only a Bachelor's Degree in Music

Top 10 Occupations	Actual Employment in 2000 (000s)	Projected Employment in 2010 (000s)	Absolute Change (000s)	Percentage Change
Artists, broadcasters, writers, editors, entertainers, public relations specialists	2,371	2,864	493	20.8%
Teachers, secondary school	1,113	1,314	201	18.1%
Teachers, elementary school	1,532	1,734	202	13.2%
Personnel, training, and labor relations specialists	490	578	88	18.0%
Other management-related occupations	4,956	5,801	845	17.1%
Postsecondary professors	1,344	1,659	315	23.4%
Sales occupations, including retail	15,513	17,365	1,852	11.9%
Top- and mid-level managers, executives, administrators	10,564	11,834	1,270	12.0%
Secretaries, receptionists, typists	4,980	5,501	521	10.5%
Other administrative (e.g., records clerks, telephone operators)	16,911	18,522	1,611	9.5%

CHAPTER 47

Philosophy

Philosophy is speculation about existence and the inquiry, analysis, and interpretation of reality. Philosophy is described as the search to know and to understand what is of basic value and importance in life. The scope of philosophy is the relationship between humanity and nature and between the individual and society.

Religion is the systematic study of organized systems of beliefs, worship, practices, rituals, and ethical values that center on a way of life. Religious beliefs—not limited to Buddhist, Christian, Jewish, or Moslem—usually focus on a divine, superhuman power or powers to be obeyed and worshipped as the creator(s) and ruler(s) of the universe.

Theology is technically the study and description of God, but theology can also be the study of religious doctrines expounded by a particular religion or denomination.

While there are philosophers and teachers of religion and theology, the most common occupation associated with religion is member of the clergy or Imam. As religious and spiritual leaders, clergy are teachers and interpreters of their traditions and faith. They organize and lead regular religious services and officiate at special ceremonies, including confirmations, weddings, and funerals. Clergy may lead worshipers in prayer; administer sacraments; deliver sermons; and read from sacred texts such as the Bible, Talmud, or Koran. When not conducting worship services, clergy organize, supervise, and lead religious education programs for their congregations. Clergy often visit the sick or bereaved to provide comfort. They also counsel persons who are seeking religious or moral guidance and those who are troubled by family or personal problems. Clergy may work to expand the membership of their congregations and solicit donations to support their congregations' activities and facilities.

The educational requirements for philosophy may include ancient philosophy, history of modern philosophy, introduction to logic, symbolic logic, theory of knowledge, metaphysics, moral philosophy, existentialism, Chinese and Indian philosophy, aesthetics, and philosophy of science.

The educational requirements for entry into theology and the clergy and Imam vary greatly, requiring specific information from a particular denomination. Course work for Protestant ministers, Jewish rabbis, and Catholic priests have similarities and focus on the Bible or sacred scripture; dogma and canon law; theology; church history or Jewish history; public speaking or preaching; community services; and religious education.

Clergy members have social, language, and teaching abilities. These are used for religious education, proselytizing, and motivating people to remain committed to religion (persuasive ability also helps for this last purpose). While different leadership styles exist, clergy members direct, manage, and supervise many activities associated with their ministries. Most obvious to many members of religious communities are the skills in providing social services and often the zealous belief or passion an individual expresses on behalf of his or her religious convictions.

Of foremost importance to clergy members of most religions is their selection of a way of life. A commitment is expected about how one leads his or her personal life beyond the more visual aspects of "the career," such as preaching. Interests for clergy members are primarily social, followed by what may be described as enjoying the breadth of focus afforded by a liberal arts education. Organizational and persuasive interests are also important.

Clergy members and Imams value working with people, working with one's mind, and having variety and diversion. Limitless are the issues and practical problems that community members bring to their clerical leaders to solve; thus, having a creative mind is helpful. Leadership and a sense of achievement are also afforded to religious leaders.

Clergy members are people-oriented individuals who reach out to others and who are comfortable dealing with the feelings of others. For these reasons, pastoral counseling, dealing with community concerns, and trying to resolve the issues of others bring clergy members personal satisfaction. They are committed and loyal to their convictions. They believe and trust others, often ignoring facts that can put them in awkward positions.

Where Do Philosophy Majors Work?

One-third of all employed philosophy graduates work in the private, nonprofit sector, mostly as clergy and other religious workers in churches, synagogues, mosques, and temples. Another 31 percent of employed philosophy majors are employed as wage and salary workers for businesses and corporations operating in the private, for-profit sector of the economy. About 15 percent work in the for-profit sector of the economy as self-employed workers in their own business or practice. Educational institutions employ 14 percent of all employed philosophy majors. The remaining 8 percent work in the government sector.

Only 36 percent of philosophy majors work in jobs that are closely related to their major field of study. Another 21 percent report working in jobs that are somewhat related to their major. The remaining 42 percent work in jobs that are not at all related to the field of philosophy. Graduates cite numerous reasons for their employment in an unrelated job. The most important reason cited by 23 percent of graduates who work in unrelated jobs is better opportunities for promotion and higher salaries. One-fifth report the decision to change their career as the most important factor influencing their employment decision. Family-related reasons are the most important factor for working in jobs unrelated to the field of philosophy among 16 percent of the group. About 9 percent cite the general working environment as the number one reason for their decision to work outside the field. Another 8 percent are unable to find jobs that are related to their undergraduate field of study.

FIGURE 1

Percentage Distribution of Employed Persons with Only a Bachelor's Degree in Philosophy, by Major Sector of Economic Activity

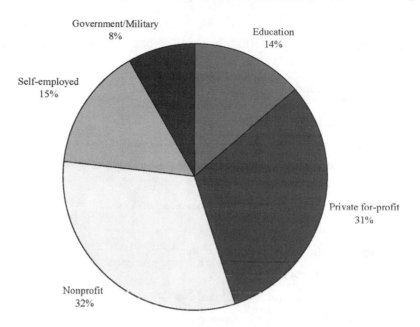

Government/Military 8%

Education 14%

Self-employed 15%

Private for-profit 31%

Nonprofit 32%

Occupations

Employed philosophy majors work in a variety of occupations, although they are fairly concentrated in religious occupations. Three out of ten employed philosophy graduates work as clergy and as other religious workers. These jobs are closely related to the undergraduate education of philosophy majors. Another 1 in 10 philosophy graduates is employed in an executive, administrative, or managerial position. Many of these jobs are within the field of philosophy; they are administrative jobs within religious or educational institutions. Nearly 5 percent work as writers, editors, broadcasters, and public relations specialists. As noted, numerous reasons such as pay and promotion opportunities, as well as a change in career interests, motivate philosophy majors to accept jobs that are unrelated to their undergraduate major. Many of the jobs in the remaining 7 of the top 10 predominant occupations that employ philosophy graduates fall in the category of unrelated jobs. Insurance, stocks and bonds, real estate, and business services occupations employ 5 percent of philosophy graduates. Another 4 percent work in sales occupations. In addition, philosophy majors work in construction, secretarial, clerical, management-related, and labor-relations occupations.

Table 1

Top 10 Occupations That Employ Persons with Only a Bachelor's Degree in Philosophy

| | PERCENT OF EMPLOYED | | |
Top 10 Occupations	All	Men	Women
Clergy, other religious workers	29.6	35.9	5.5
Top- and mid-level managers, executives, administrators	10.4	11.3	6.8
Artists, broadcasters, writers, editors, entertainers, public relations specialists	4.7	3.1	10.7
Insurance, securities, real estate, business services	4.5	4.9	3.2
Sales occupations, including retail	4.2	3.8	5.3
Construction trades, miners, well drillers	3.2	3.7	1.2
Secretaries, receptionists, typists	2.7	0.1	12.8
Other management-related occupations	2.7	3.1	1.4
Other administrative (e.g., records clerks, telephone operators)	2.4	1.4	6.1
Personnel, training, and labor relations specialists	2.3	2.1	3.1

Almost 80 percent of employed philosophy graduates with only a bachelor's degree are males. Male philosophy graduates and female philosophy graduates tend to work in different occupations.

- Men are more than 6 times more likely than women to be employed as clergy and other religious workers. Nearly 36 percent of men work in these occupations, compared to only 5.5 percent of women. The preference of many major religions for male clergy is largely responsible for this gender difference in employment patterns of philosophy graduates.

- Male philosophy graduates also are more likely than female graduates to be employed in administrative and managerial positions. About 11 percent of employed male philosophy graduates work as executives, administrators, or managers, compared to 7 percent of female graduates.

- Writing, editing, broadcasting, and public relations jobs are more likely to employ female philosophy graduates; 11 percent of employed female graduates work in these jobs, compared to only 3 percent of male philosophy graduates.

- Sharp differences in the male and female employment of philosophy graduates are also observed in secretarial and clerical occupations. About 13 percent of female graduates work as secretaries, receptionists, and typists, compared to almost no employed male graduates. Clerical occupations employ more than 6 percent of women but only 1 percent of male philosophy graduates.

Activities on the Job

▶ Nearly 60 percent of employed philosophy graduates regularly engage in managerial and administrative duties at work. About 17 percent spend most of their time at work performing these duties. These activities follow from their concentration in the clergy and in religious, administrative, and managerial occupations. Administrative duties are quite common among clergy members.

▶ About 4 of 10 philosophy graduates regularly engage in teaching duties, and 12 percent spend most of their time in performing these duties.

▶ Philosophy graduates also provide professional services, mainly in the form of counseling and guidance services for marital, health, financial, and religious problems. About 12 percent of employed philosophy graduates spend most of their time in these duties at work.

▶ One-quarter regularly engage in marketing and sales activities, and more than 1 in 10 graduates spend most of their workweek in performing these duties.

▶ Employee-relations activities such as recruiting, training, and labor relations regularly engage 38 percent of all employed philosophy graduates; 6 percent consider these duties to be a major part of their jobs.

▶ Computer applications, programming, and systems-development activities are performed regularly by 26 percent of all employed philosophy graduates, and 6 percent consider these activities to be a major part of their jobs.

▶ Few philosophy graduates spend a major portion of their workweek in accounting and contractual activities or in basic and applied research.

Salaries

The average annual salary of philosophy graduates who have only a bachelor's degree and are employed full-time is $42,900, a level that is only 79 percent of the average annual salary of all full-time employed college graduates. As for most college graduates, the salary of philosophy graduates increases with age, indicating that they get more productive and therefore can earn higher salaries as they spend more time on the job. However, at different ages, philosophy majors earn considerably lower salaries than the average for all college graduates.

▶ The average annual salary of philosophy majors between the ages of 25 and 29 and between 30 and 34 is about $33,600. This salary increases to $39,800 between the ages of 35 and 40 and peaks at $47,200 for those between 40 and 54.

▶ As philosophy graduates age further, their salaries decline. Graduates between the ages of 55 and 64 earn $42,600, and pre-retirement graduates over the age of 65 earn an average annual salary of $39,200.

The average annual salary of philosophy graduates who work in jobs that are closely related to their major field of study is lower than the salary of their counterparts who work in jobs that are somewhat related or not related to their undergraduate major field of study. Closely related jobs tend to be religious worker and clergy member, which are generally associated with lower salaries, compared to occupations in which philosophy graduates use just some of their major-related skills on the job and consider the job to be somewhat related to their undergraduate major. Some of these occupations include high-level administrative occupations in religious organizations or educational institutions and also broadcasting and writing occupations that pay philosophy graduates higher salaries than those earned by all full-time employed philosophy graduates. Graduates working in closely related jobs earn $37,100 per year, whereas those whose jobs are somewhat related to their undergraduate major earn $48,700 annually.

Occupations that typically are reported by philosophy graduates as unrelated to their major pay either very high or very low salaries. On the high salary end are insurance, stocks and bonds, real estate, and other financial sector jobs.

At the other end of the salary spectrum are clerical and secretarial jobs. The net effect is an average annual salary of $45,300 among graduates who work in unrelated jobs. This salary is higher than the salary in closely related jobs but lower than the salary earned by graduates whose jobs are somewhat related to their major.

The private, for-profit sector pays a higher average salary to philosophy majors than other sectors of the economy. The self-employment segment of the private, for-profit sector of the economy pays an average salary of $50,800 per year. Those who are employed by businesses and corporations in the private, for-profit sector earn $47,300 per year. The government sector pays full-time employed philosophy graduates an average annual salary of $45,600. Graduates employed by educational institutions earn $38,600 annually.

FIGURE 2

Age/Earnings Profile of Persons with Only a Bachelor's Degree in Philosophy
(Full-Time Workers, in 2002 Dollars)

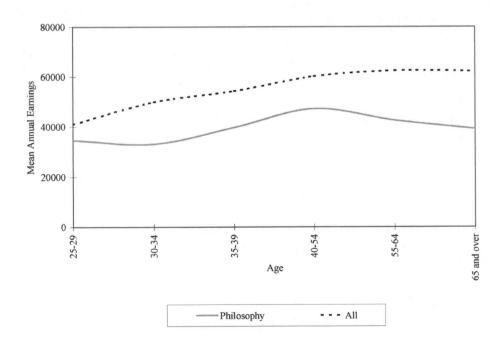

The average annual salary of philosophy graduates varies widely by occupation. In 8 of the top 10 occupations that are predominant employers of philosophy graduates, the salary of all college graduates exceeds that of philosophy majors. The remaining two occupations pay only a slightly higher salary to philosophy majors than to all college graduates.

▶ The highest salary of philosophy majors within the top 10 occupations is in upper-level executive, administrative, and managerial occupations. Graduates in these occupations earn $64,500 per year. These occupations employ more male than female philosophy graduates.

▶ Employment of philosophy graduates in insurance, securities, real estate, and business services occupations yields an average annual salary of $60,800. These occupations employ mostly male philosophy graduates.

▶ Broadcasting, writing, and public relations jobs, which employ more female than male philosophy graduates, pay an annual salary of $54,000.

▶ Employment of philosophy graduates in management-related jobs such as management analyst, purchasing agent, and regulatory officer and in labor relations jobs is associated with an above-average salary.

▶ A large number of philosophy graduates are employed as clergy and other religious workers. This occupation has one of the lowest salaries of the top 10 employers of philosophy majors. The average salary in this occupation is $34,400. Only clerical occupations pay a lower salary than clergy and other religious workers. The secretarial field, which employs almost no male philosophy graduates, is low-paying.

Table 2
Annual Salary of Full-Time Workers with Only a Bachelor's Degree in Philosophy, Top 10 Occupations (in 2002 Dollars)

Earnings in Top 10 Occupations	All	Philosophy
Total	$54,171	$42,865
Clergy, other religious workers	$34,519	$34,371
Top- and mid-level managers, executives, administrators	$74,051	$64,501
Artists, broadcasters, writers, editors, entertainers, public relations specialists	$52,141	$54,060
Insurance, securities, real estate, business services	$68,273	$60,836
Sales occupations, including retail	$52,378	$39,646
Construction trades, miners, well drillers	$50,531	$39,822
Secretaries, receptionists, typists	$32,246	$35,511
Other management-related occupations	$51,921	$45,213
Other administrative (e.g., records clerks, telephone operators)	$34,547	$30,470
Personnel, training, and labor relations specialists	$51,577	$45,130

On-the-Job Training

The career potential of a job is closely associated with the amount of work-related training on the job. Work-related training is regarded as an investment by firms because it makes workers more productive. Firms that invest in their workforce are more likely to offer pay increases and promotions to match the increasing productivity of their workers. Firms that do not invest in their workers are relatively less likely to offer pay increases and promotions. A little more than 6 of 10 employed philosophy graduates receive work-related training. Whereas 68 percent of all employed college graduates received some work-related training, 63 percent of philosophy majors receive training on the job more than one year.

▶ Of those philosophy majors who receive some training, 68 percent receive technical training in their occupational field.

▶ Thirty-five percent receive training to improve their general professional skills, such as public speaking and business writing.

▶ Thirty-six percent of the training recipients participate in management or supervisor training.

Of those philosophy majors who participate in some work-related training, 93 percent do so to improve their occupational skills and knowledge. About 44 percent are required or expected by their employers to undergo training. More opportunity for promotion, advancement, and salary increases is the reason for 28 percent of philosophy majors to participate in work-related training. One-quarter state that one of the reasons to participate in work-related training is to learn skills for a newly acquired position.

When asked to identify the most important factor influencing the decision to participate in work-related training, 69 percent want to improve skills and knowledge in their current occupation, and 14 percent are required by their employer to undergo training. Only 4 percent of philosophy graduates consider higher salary or increased promotion opportunity as the main reason to participate in training.

Post-Graduation Activities

Post-graduation schooling rates are high among philosophy graduates. Nearly 52 percent of philosophy graduates with a bachelor's degree proceed to earn a postgraduate degree. Of the philosophy majors with a bachelor's degree, 35 percent earn a master's degree, 9 percent graduate with a doctorate, and 8 percent earn a professional degree.

▶ Fifty-five percent of the master's degrees are earned in philosophy, 14 percent are earned in education, and 9 percent are earned in psychology.

▶ More than 60 percent of the doctoral degrees of undergraduate philosophy majors are earned in philosophy. Another one-tenth of the doctoral degrees are in the field of psychology. Other social sciences account for 8 percent of the graduates with doctoral degrees. Doctoral degrees in education are earned by 5 percent of the graduates, and another 5 percent major in the field of languages and literature.

▶ Fifty-four percent of the professional degrees of undergraduate philosophy majors are earned in law, and 3 of 10 earn professional degrees in philosophy. Another 12 percent earn professional degrees in the health professions.

Of all philosophy graduates under the age of 65, 85 percent are employed. Only 2 percent are officially unemployed; in other words, they are not employed and are actively seeking employment. The remaining 13 percent are out of the labor force; that is, they are not employed and are not seeking employment. Family responsibilities are the reason for labor force withdrawal among 38 percent of this group of philosophy graduates, and 34 percent are out of the labor force because they do not need or want to work. About 15 percent have chronic illness or a disabling condition, and another 15 percent are retired.

Employment Outlook

According to the U.S. Bureau of Labor Statistics, employment in occupations that require at least a bachelor's degree is expected to grow faster than employment in other sectors of the American labor market. Between 2000 and 2010, the U.S. economy is projected to add 22.2 million jobs, yielding an employment growth rate of 15.2 percent. The employment growth projections in the top 10 occupations that are most likely to employ philosophy graduates are mixed.

- Clergy and other religious occupations are projected to add nearly 45,000 jobs between 2000 and 2010, yielding a growth rate of 15 percent. More than one-third of male philosophy graduates are employed in these occupations. These occupations are the second-lowest-paying occupations of the top 10 employers of philosophy graduates.

- Employment in top- to mid-level management and administrative occupations is projected to grow by 12 percent. This occupation mainly employs male graduates and has the highest salary of the top 10 employers of philosophy graduates.

- The demand for artists, broadcasters, entertainers, and public relations specialists is expected to grow by 21 percent. Between 2000 and 2010, these occupations are expected to add 493,000 jobs. These occupations are predominantly employers of female philosophy graduates.

- Jobs associated with the other predominant employers of female philosophy graduates, secretarial and clerical occupations, are projected to grow at below-average rates of about 10 percent. The rapid spread in the use of computers, electronic mail, and other digital communication devices and automation techniques is expected to result in a small rate of growth of employment in these occupations.

Table 3
Projected Change in Employment in the Top 10 Occupations That Employ Persons with Only a Bachelor's Degree in Philosophy

Top 10 Occupations	Actual Employment in 2000 (000s)	Projected Employment in 2010 (000s)	Absolute Change (000s)	Percentage Change
Clergy, other religious workers	293	338	45	15.4%
Top- and mid-level managers, executives, administrators	10,564	11,834	1,270	12.0%

(continued)

Table 3 (continued)
Projected Change in Employment in the Top 10 Occupations That Employ Persons with Only a Bachelor's Degree in Philosophy

Top 10 Occupations	Actual Employment in 2000 (000s)	Projected Employment in 2010 (000s)	Absolute Change (000s)	Percentage Change
Artists, broadcasters, writers, editors, entertainers, public relations specialists	2,371	2,864	493	20.8%
Insurance, securities, real estate, business services	1,548	1,726	178	11.5%
Sales occupations, including retail	15,513	17,365	1,852	11.9%
Construction trades, miners, well drillers	7,451	8,439	988	13.3%
Secretaries, receptionists, typists	4,980	5,501	521	10.5%
Other management-related occupations	4,956	5,801	845	17.1%
Other administrative (e.g., records clerks, telephone operators)	16,911	18,522	1,611	9.5%
Personnel, training, and labor relations specialists	490	578	88	18.0%

CHAPTER 48

Political Science, Government, and International Relations

Three interconnected fields are offered in some institutions as three distinct majors: political science, government, and international relations. In some colleges they may be combined and called political science. Some colleges consider this field as composed of four distinct subfields: political philosophy and theory, American government, comparative politics, and international relations.

Political science is the study of the origin, development, and operation of political systems and public policy. Political scientists conduct research on a wide range of subjects, such as relations between the United States and other countries, the institutions and political life of nations, the politics of small towns or a major metropolis; and the decisions of the U.S. Supreme Court. In studying such topics as public opinion, political decision making, ideology, and public policy, political scientists analyze the structure and operation of governments and various political entities. Depending on the topic under study, a political scientist may conduct a public opinion survey, analyze election results, analyze public documents, or interview public officials.

A person majoring in American government studies the main components of the federal government—the presidency, the Congress, and the judicial system—as well as state, county, and local governments. Politics, the election process, political parties, interest groups, think tanks, and the media are analyzed. This field includes domestic and foreign affairs, as well as varied substantive areas such as transportation, civil rights, education, energy, and the environment.

International relations or international affairs may have a perspective that fits a specific institution's goals or the unique expertise of its faculty. This major introduces a variety of theoretical approaches to international politics and economics. In addition to studying comparative politics, international economics, and American foreign policy, students examine major issues such as international war and peace, change and continuity, balance of power assessment, the political utility of military force, and European/North American/South American governmental differences and Pacific Rim/Asian/Western/African/European/Middle Eastern political differences and issues that foster international cooperation and conflict. The primary objective of the field is to develop an understanding of international affairs and economics, issues and dilemmas facing countries, foreign policy instruments, and processes by which countries make policy decisions to reconcile disparate and incompatible goals.

Educational course work for political science may include introduction to politics, American ideology, interest groups and public policy, science technology and public policy, religion and politics, modern political thought, civil liberties, legislative politics, urban politics, and American social welfare policy.

Educational course work in government may include introduction to American government, intergovernmental relations, American national security policy, United States foreign policy, American constitutional law, the American presidency, parties and elections, legislative process, and state and local government. Many political science and government students often intern

with a member of Congress, an elected public servant, or a federal or state government agency.

Course work in international relations may include politics and government, international relations, comparative political systems, politics and China/Japan/Black Africa/Middle East/Latin America/Modern Russia/Northern Ireland/Europe/Eastern Europe/Arab-Israel issues, bureaucratic and organizational politics, comparative modern economic systems, American foreign policy, international relations theories, international economics, and international security issues.

One of the abilities required in these fields is "catching on" quickly to understand and analyze connections and associations between diverse material and information. For example, political scientists compare the merits of various forms of government, and a government major analyzes large amounts of data on the federal budget. There is fluidity to the field, so adaptability is needed as new laws or different interpretations of existing legislation appear; different elected officials push for new policies; and local, state, national, or international events occur that bring about the need for change. So a continuous need exists for critical thinking to make decisions based on new facts and figures. Communication skills are essential, as is the ability to speak authoritatively.

Those who work in these fields are people-oriented. Their interests, however, are more focused on leading and influencing others than on humanitarian concerns. These workers appreciate and understand the value of bureaucracy and organization. While they have good interpersonal skills, they realize that results will come from group activities that involve convincing, negotiating, and compromising. Political science, government, and international relations offer a context for intellectual pursuit in which the scientific method of analysis and inquiry plays a major role.

The values associated with these fields are primarily intellectual, with a research orientation. Those in these fields enjoy working with their minds to seek new or creative analyses of situations, problems, or issues. There is opportunity for variety, as the topics and public priorities change. Because individuals often work closely with a policymaker or person with political power, prestige is associated with the work.

People in this field generally dislike detailed work. They enjoy being curious, being innovators, and doing original thinking or exploring possibilities. Many are excellent speakers and come across as intelligent and convincing. Others are quite independent and appear stubborn and committed to proving their ideas or viewpoints.

Where Do Political Science Majors Work?

College graduates with degrees in political science work in a fairly broad array of work settings and sectors of the economy. While a major in political science is commonly thought of as a means to prepare for a career in government, the majority of political science graduates with a bachelor's degree work in the for-profit sector of the economy. More than one-half of political science majors with a bachelor's degree work as wage and salary employees in private, for-profit businesses. An additional 13 percent are self-employed, owning businesses and consulting services. Another 1 in 5 political science majors works in federal, state, or local government organizations, including legislative and judicial

FIGURE 1

Percentage Distribution of Employed Persons with Only a Bachelor's Degree in Political Science, by Major Sector of Economic Activity

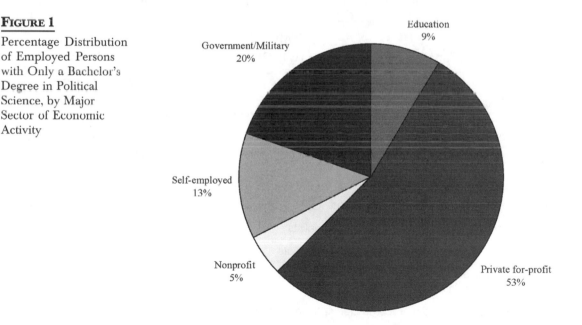

Education
9%

Government/Military
20%

Self-employed
13%

Nonprofit
5%

Private for-profit
53%

bodies; in the executive agencies such as federal and state departments of labor and justice; and in local government. Almost 1 in 10 political science majors work in the education sector, most often as elementary or secondary school teachers. Relatively few graduates with a bachelor's degree in political science are employed in nonprofit charities and research foundations.

Occupations

Political science majors with a bachelor's degree are seldom employed in jobs that are closely related to their field. Instead, the majority of majors work in jobs that are unrelated to political science. Those employed in jobs unrelated to political science say that better pay and promotion opportunities, changing career interests, and an inability to find a job related to the field are major reasons why they work in unrelated jobs. A high proportion of political science majors become employed as managers and administrators. More than 1 in 5 majors at the bachelor's degree level work in management or administration. Various sales jobs are also important sources of employment for majors from this field of study. About 1 of 6 political science majors work in insurance, stocks and bonds, real estate, and sales occupations, many in high-paying positions. Unlike some other majors, most political science majors who are employed in a job unrelated to their field of study are still employed in a job that generally requires a college degree, although not in a specific major. Access to college labor market jobs is a key element to the long-term labor market success of graduates from this major. Those majors who fail to become employed in a job that requires a college degree have much lower earnings.

Table 1

Top 10 Occupations That Employ Persons with Only a Bachelor's Degree in Political Science

Top 10 Occupations	PERCENT OF EMPLOYED		
	All	Men	Women
Top- and mid-level managers, executives, administrators	21.1	24.9	13.3
Insurance, securities, real estate, business services	8.5	9.4	6.5
Sales occupations, including retail	8.4	10.1	5.0
Other management-related occupations	7.0	6.4	8.3
Accountants, auditors, other financial specialists	4.9	5.4	3.9
Personnel, training, and labor relations specialists	4.4	3.1	7.0
Artists, broadcasters, writers, editors, entertainers, public relations specialists	4.0	3.0	6.1
Other administrative (e.g., records clerks, telephone operators)	3.7	2.2	6.8
Other marketing and sales occupations	3.1	3.6	2.0
Protective-service occupations	3.0	4.1	0.7

▶ Women with political science degrees are more likely to work in personnel and training staff positions, as writers and other creative staff, and in non-college labor market clerical and administrative positions.

▶ Men with a bachelor's degree in political science are twice as likely than women to be employed in managerial and administrative positions.

Activities on the Job

▶ Managerial and administrative tasks are among the most important job duties undertaken by majors from this field of study. These tasks are wide-ranging, depending on the specific area in which the individual is employed, but can include such issues as employee supervision and relations, contracting, and finance.

▶ Sales and marketing activities are also an important job duty for graduates with a political science degree.

▶ About one-third of all political science majors report that they are regularly involved in the development and/or use of computer applications.

▶ Few political science majors at the bachelor's degree level spend much of their workweek on either applied or basic research activities.

Salaries

College degrees in the social science fields are generally thought to lead to jobs that pay below-average salaries, yet the annual salaries of political science majors are actually above the average for college graduates. Moreover, as the data in the following chart reveals, the size of the earnings advantage of political science majors increases with years of work experience. Majors between the ages of 25 and 29 earn about $40,900 per year. By ages 55 to 59 the mean annual salary of persons with a bachelor's degree in political science rises to $76,600. Those political science majors who work in the private, for-profit sector have much higher earnings than those employed in education, government, or nonprofit organizations. Those working for private firms and corporations earn an average of $59,800, while self-employed political science graduates earn an average of $62,400. Political science majors who work for government agencies earn about $54,100 per year (in 2002 dollars). Unsurprisingly, there is little connection between the earnings of political science majors and the degree to which their job is related to their undergraduate major. Securing a job that is related to the political science field does not necessarily result in higher earnings. Instead, access to a job that requires a college degree is the key to high earnings for graduates from this field of study.

College graduates who earn a bachelor's degree in political science earn $57,000 per year, about $2,800 more per year annually than the average person with a bachelor's degree. The highest-paying jobs for majors are in the managerial and administrative area, where the annual salary averages $76,200 per year. High annual salaries are also earned by those majors who have jobs related to the sale of insurance, stocks and bonds, and other financial instruments and real estate. The annual salaries of majors are much lower when they work in clerical positions and other jobs that generally do not require a college diploma.

FIGURE 2

Age/Earnings Profile of Persons with Only a Bachelor's Degree in Political Science
(Full-Time Workers, in 2002 Dollars)

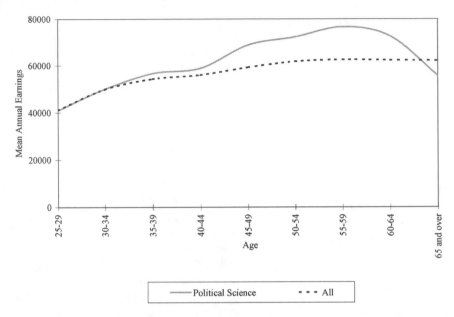

Table 2

Annual Salary of Full-Time Workers with Only a Bachelor's Degree in Political Science, Top 10 Occupations (in 2002 Dollars)

Earnings in Top 10 Occupations	All	Political Science
Total	$54,171	$56,971
Top- and mid-level managers, executives, administrators	$74,051	$76,244
Insurance, securities, real estate, business services	$68,273	$68,315
Sales occupations, including retail	$52,378	$54,020
Other management-related occupations	$51,921	$54,135
Accountants, auditors, other financial specialists	$57,382	$46,792
Personnel, training, and labor relations specialists	$51,577	$50,936
Artists, broadcasters, writers, editors, entertainers, public relations specialists	$52,141	$58,082
Other administrative (e.g., records clerks, telephone operators)	$34,547	$36,237
Other marketing and sales occupations	$58,208	$60,592
Protective-service occupations	$49,130	$59,997

On-the-Job Training

Political science majors enter the labor market with few occupationally specific skills, so on-the-job learning is essential for long-term advancement. Many of the skills used on the job are developed simply by observing or learning by doing. However, participation in work-based training programs such as seminars and workshops is also an important way that political science majors develop occupational skills. Nearly two-thirds of political science majors participated in some type of training activity in the last year.

▶ Management and supervisory training is an important element of training received by majors.

▶ Developing communication skills such as writing and public speaking are a key goal for those who participate in training from this field of study.

Post-Graduation Activities

Political science majors are very likely to earn a graduate degree at some point after graduation from college. In fact, 1 of 2 majors eventually earns an advanced degree. About one-fifth of all political science majors who earn a bachelor's degree go on to earn a master's degree. Another 4 percent earn a doctorate. A major pathway to law school and the legal profession is through the undergraduate political science major. One-quarter of all those with a bachelor's degree in the field earn a law degree.

▶ The most popular graduate field of study for political science majors is business; 1 in 4 master's degrees is earned in the business area by political science majors who go on to earn a master's degree.

▶ Many undergraduates continue their education in political science or the related field of public administration. About 16 percent of those who earn a master's degree complete their studies in some aspect of political science, while an additional 12 percent earn their degree in public administration.

▶ More than 40 percent of those who earn doctorates continue their studies in political science. About 1 of 7 earn a doctorate in education.

The employment rate of those with an undergraduate diploma in political science is about 87 percent, most of whom work in full-time positions. Another 4 percent are involuntarily unemployed. The remaining 9 percent have no job desire and are not actively seeking employment.

Employment Outlook

Opportunities in occupations that employ a substantial number of political science majors at the bachelor's degree level will grow at a pace above the average for the economy as a whole, but below the average rate of growth in demand for persons with a bachelor's degree.

▶ The demand for workers in managerial and administrative occupations will increase by 12 percent between 2000 and 2010, adding 1.3 million positions over the 10-year period.

▶ Growth in the high-level sales occupations in insurance and securities is also projected to increase by 12 percent, adding more than 178,000 workers over the projection period.

▶ Creative jobs such as broadcaster and writer that substantial numbers of political science majors hold will grow at a pace well above the overall rate of new job creation for the economy as a whole and at about the same rate for jobs that employ persons with a bachelor's degree.

Table 3

Projected Change in Employment in the Top 10 Occupations
That Employ Persons with Only a Bachelor's Degree in Political Science

Top 10 Occupations	Actual Employment in 2000 (000s)	Projected Employment in 2010 (000s)	Absolute Change (000s)	Percentage Change
Top- and mid-level managers, executives, administrators	10,564	11,834	1,270	12.0%
Insurance, securities, real estate, business services	1,548	1,726	178	11.5%
Sales occupations, including retail	15,513	17,365	1,852	11.9%
Other management-related occupations	4,956	5,801	845	17.1%
Accountants, auditors, other financial specialists	2,115	2,481	366	17.3%
Personnel, training, and labor relations specialists	490	578	88	18.0%
Artists, broadcasters, writers, editors, entertainers, public relations specialists	2,371	2,864	493	20.8%
Other administrative (e.g., records clerks, telephone operators)	16,911	18,522	1,611	9.5%
Other marketing and sales occupations	621	758	137	22.1%
Protective-service occupations	3,087	3,896	809	26.2%

CHAPTER 49

Sociology

One of the most recognized social sciences is sociology. Sociologists study human society and social behavior by examining the groups and social institutions that people form, as well as various social, religious, political, and business organizations. Sociologists study also the behavior and interaction of groups, trace their origin and growth, and analyze the influence of group activities on individual members. These professionals are concerned with the characteristics of social groups, organizations, and institutions; the ways that individuals are affected by each other and by the groups to which they belong; and the effect of social traits such as sex, age, and race on a person's daily life. The results of sociological research aid educators, lawmakers, administrators, and others interested in resolving social problems and formulating public policy.

The specializations are quite varied. Criminologists research the relationship between criminal law and social order to understand the causes of crime and the behavior of criminals. Penologists study the punishment for crime, the control and prevention of crime, the management of penal institutions, and the rehabilitation of criminal offenders. Rural sociologists study rural communities in contrast with urban communities, as well as problems brought about by the impact of scientific and industrial revolutions on the rural way of life. Social ecologists research the interrelations between physical environments and technology on the distribution of people and their activities. Urban sociologists study the origin, growth, structure, and demographic characteristics of cities and social patterns, along with the distinctive problems that result from the urban environment, such as social problems and racial discrimination rooted in the failure of society to achieve its collective purposes. Medical sociologists research social factors affecting health care, including the definition of illness, patient and practitioner behavior, social epidemiology, and the delivery of health care. Demographers conduct surveys and experiments to study human populations and trends.

Educational course work may include American society, social inequality, urban social problems, violence in the family, sociology of prejudice, gender in a changing society, sociology of work, sociology of poverty, aging and society, sociology of health, race and ethnic relations, community analysis, social deviance, social policy, and interventions.

The abilities of sociologists include understanding and using the theories and research methods of social sciences. Being able to analyze and interpret information is an important skill. An expectation is to be able to collect and organize detailed research notes into a logical presentation, as the outcome of sociologists' work is written reports of findings. Good written and oral communication skills are needed, especially the latter for conducting interviews. Computer skills for data processing and analysis are expected.

Like all scientists, sociologists have analytical and problem-solving interests. Because the focus of the field is mostly on formal organizations and families, sociologists enjoy studying group behavior. Their people orientation reflects a concern for the welfare of others, but through indirect contacts such as policies and ideas instead of working in direct service relations such as teaching or counseling.

Sociologists have intellectual and research values. In social research, the topics examined usually are quite varied, and the field allows for use of novel methods of analysis. However, the issues studied require a considerable amount of thought and reasoning, along with searching for new approaches to analyze and interpret information.

People in this field are imaginative. They are energetic and comfortable in using their own ideas to guide their beliefs instead of relying fully on the data. They can be idealists. Their inquisitiveness leads them to explore many things. Other people are attracted to sociologists because they try hard to understand individuals without making judgments about them. It is this quality that enables sociologists to discover new factual relationships within the social problems they are attracted to study.

Where Do Sociology Majors Work?

Sociology majors at the bachelor's degree level are employed across all the major sectors of the American economy. However, relative to college graduates in other fields, they are much more likely to work in government organizations or nonprofit foundations. About 37 percent of sociology majors are employed by private, for-profit organizations, largely in jobs unconnected to their major. While only about 11 percent of college graduates work in a government job, 1 in 4 persons with a bachelor's degree in sociology is employed by a federal, state, or local government agency. About 6 percent of all college graduates work in the nonprofit sector, while 10 percent of sociology majors work for a charitable or nonprofit research organization. Interestingly, sociology majors are about as likely as the average college graduate to be self-employed. However, they are usually engaged as self-employed consultants rather than as the owners of companies.

FIGURE 1

Percentage Distribution of Employed Persons with Only a Bachelor's Degree in Sociology, by Major Sector of Economic Activity

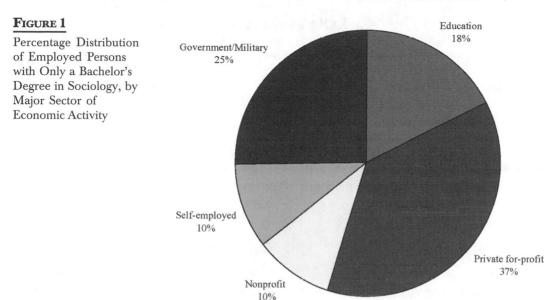

Government/Military 25%

Education 18%

Self-employed 10%

Nonprofit 10%

Private for-profit 37%

Occupations

Employment in jobs related to the major field of study is unusual for undergraduates with a degree in sociology. Sociology majors work in a variety of occupations. About 1 of 8 work in managerial or administrative positions, while an equal proportion work in sales-related jobs, including high-level insurance, real estate, and stocks and bonds sales positions. About 10 percent of sociology majors with a bachelor's degree are employed in some aspect of social work. Fewer than one-quarter of all sociology majors work in jobs that they believe are closely related to their undergraduate major. However, little earnings difference exists between those in closely related jobs and those in jobs unrelated to the field.

Table 1

Top 10 Occupations That Employ Persons with Only a Bachelor's Degree in Sociology

Top 10 Occupations	PERCENT OF EMPLOYED		
	All	Men	Women
Top- and mid-level managers, executives, administrators	13.9	21.5	8.6
Social workers	10.0	6.1	12.6
Other administrative (e.g., records clerks, telephone operators)	5.7	4.6	6.5
Other management-related occupations	5.7	5.2	6.1
Sales occupations, including retail	5.2	5.9	4.8
Other marketing and sales occupations	4.1	2.8	5.0

(continued)

Table 1 (continued)

Top 10 Occupations That Employ Persons with Only a Bachelor's Degree in Sociology

Top 10 Occupations	PERCENT OF EMPLOYED		
	All	Men	Women
Secretaries, receptionists, typists	4.1	0.4	6.7
Personnel, training, and labor relations specialists	4.1	4.2	4.0
Insurance, securities, real estate, business services	3.7	4.8	3.0
Accountants, auditors, other financial specialists	3.5	3.3	3.6

▶ Men with a bachelor's degree in sociology are much more likely than women with a degree in the field to work in higher-level managerial and administrative positions.

▶ Women with a degree in sociology are twice as likely as men with a degree in the field to be employed in low-paying social work jobs.

▶ While few men with a degree in sociology work in clerical positions, nearly 7 percent of women hold jobs in these non-college labor market occupations.

Activities on the Job

▶ Graduates of sociology programs engage in fairly diverse job duties within the range of occupations in which they are employed.

▶ Management and supervisory activities are an important part of the work of many graduates of this major.

▶ Many sociology majors use sales and marketing skills on their jobs.

▶ Teaching is also an important function for many graduates of this major.

Salaries

While the average annual salary of sociology majors at the bachelor's degree level is below the average salary of bachelor's degree holders in general, the salaries are not nearly as low as often attributed to graduates in this field. Sociology graduates earn an average of $47,800 per year, an annual rate of pay about 12 percent less than the pay of the average college graduate. Young sociology majors between the ages of 25 and 29 earn about $36,000 per year. By ages 45 to 49 their earnings increase to $53,000 per year, a pay rate 47 percent higher than that of young sociology majors. The increase in the salaries of majors as they age is an indication of the way that employers value on-the-job learning and work experience. Sociology majors enter the labor market after college with few occupationally specific skills. Instead, they must acquire those skills in the workplace, through informal, on-the-job learning by observation; learning by doing; and participation in work-based training programs. As skills and productivity increase with years of work experience, salaries increase proportionately.

The earnings of sociology majors vary considerably by major field of study. Those employed in private, for-profit businesses earn an average salary of $53,800, while those working in a government job earn $46,600. Sociology majors employed in educational and nonprofit organizations have average earnings of only $38,700 per year.

FIGURE 2

Age/Earnings Profile of Persons with Only a Bachelor's Degree in Sociology (Full-Time Workers, in 2002 Dollars)

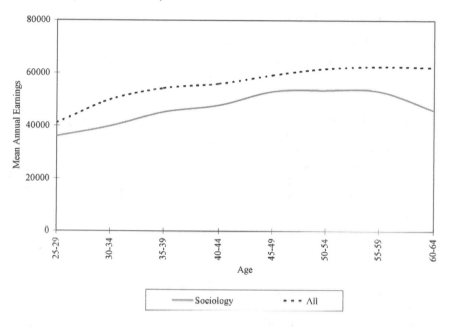

Table 2

Annual Salary of Full-Time Workers with Only a Bachelor's Degree in Sociology, Top 10 Occupations (in 2002 Dollars)

Earnings in Top 10 Occupations	All	Sociology
Total	$54,171	$47,810
Top- and mid-level managers, executives, administrators	$74,051	$69,481
Social workers	$36,371	$38,113
Other administrative (e.g., records clerks, telephone operators)	$34,547	$36,148
Other management-related occupations	$51,921	$48,923
Sales occupations, including retail	$52,378	$45,695
Other marketing and sales occupations	$58,208	$46,280

(continued)

Table 2 (continued)
Annual Salary of Full-Time Workers with Only a Bachelor's Degree in Sociology, Top 10 Occupations (in 2002 Dollars)

Earnings in Top 10 Occupations	All	Sociology
Secretaries, receptionists, typists	$32,246	$31,625
Personnel, training, and labor relations specialists	$51,577	$53,176
Insurance, securities, real estate, business services	$68,273	$50,861
Accountants, auditors, other financial specialists	$57,382	$47,415

Sociology majors employed in managerial and administrative jobs have relatively high annual salaries. Majors working in these jobs earn an average of $69,500 per year. In contrast, those with jobs in social work who have direct contact with clients earn an average pay of only $38,100 per year. Sociology majors employed in sales-related positions receive annual pay of $45,700.

On-the-Job Training

Developing skills on the job is an important part of the long-term career development of graduates of sociology programs. Most of this skill development is accomplished through informal on-the-job learning. But formal work-based classroom training is an equally important way that majors from this field acquire skills valued at work. Of majors from the field, 70 percent participate in job-related workshops and seminars as part of their professional development over the course of a year.

- Management and supervisory training is a key training activity undertaken by graduates in this field.

- Nearly 70 percent of all those who participate in training are involved in developing an occupational skill that is related to their jobs, which may be in sales, marketing, or social services.

Post-Graduation Activities

More than one-third of all sociology majors continue their education beyond the bachelor's degree level and earn graduate or professional degrees of some type. About 28 percent of sociology graduates eventually earn a master's degree, and about 4 percent go on to earn a doctorate. Slightly more than 4 percent earn a professional degree after graduation from college.

- Only a small proportion of those who earn an undergraduate degree in sociology continue study in this field at the master's degree level. Only 7 percent of those who earn a master's degree continue in sociology. Nearly one-quarter earn a master's degree in education. Substantial numbers also earn master's degrees in psychology and business.

- More than 40 percent of all doctorates awarded to those with an undergraduate degree in sociology are in sociology. Education and psychology together account for about 25 percent of all the doctorates awarded to undergraduates from this field.

▶ About three-quarters of those who earn a professional degree study law, and 1 in 6 earns a medical doctor's degree.

The employment rate of sociology graduates is relatively low. Only 77 percent of all majors under the age of 65 are employed. About 4 percent of all non-elderly (under the age of 65) sociology majors are involuntarily unemployed and actively seeking work. About 18 percent of sociology majors are not seeking a job, most often because of family responsibilities.

Employment Outlook

The overall rate of increase in the demand for workers in occupations that are most likely to employ graduates from the sociology field will increase at a slower rate than the overall demand for workers with a bachelor's degree. Between 2000 and 2010, employment of bachelor's degree holders is expected to increase by about 21 percent, while job growth rates for most occupations that employ sociology majors are projected to grow at a rate substantially below this. The largest exception to this is in the social work field. Total employment in social work is expected to increase by more than 141,000 jobs, or about 30 percent over this period. Strong job growth is forecast in marketing occupations as well.

Table 3
Projected Change in Employment in the Top 10 Occupations That Employ Persons with Only a Bachelor's Degree in Sociology

Top 10 Occupations	Actual Employment in 2000 (000s)	Projected Employment in 2010 (000s)	Absolute Change (000s)	Percentage Change
Top- and mid-level managers, executives, administrators	10,564	11,834	1,270	12.0%
Social workers	468	609	141	30.1%
Other administrative (e.g., records clerks, telephone operators)	16,911	18,522	1,611	9.5%
Other management-related occupations	4,956	5,801	845	17.1%
Sales occupations, including retail	15,513	17,365	1,852	11.9%
Other marketing and sales occupations	621	758	137	22.1%
Secretaries, receptionists, typists	4,980	5,501	521	10.5%
Personnel, training, and labor relations specialists	490	578	88	18.0%
Insurance, securities, real estate, business services	1,548	1,726	178	11.5%
Accountants, auditors, other financial specialists	2,115	2,481	366	17.3%

CHAPTER 50

Visual Arts

Depending on the purpose for creating the art, visual arts can be categorized as either graphic art or fine art. Graphic artists use their skills and ideas in commercial interests, as in advertising and design or in working for corporations, retail stores, or publishing companies. Fine artists typically create art to satisfy their own need for self-expression; they may display their art in museums and art galleries, with some of their work sold to private collectors. Most individuals in the visual arts are unable to earn a full-time living unless they are exceptional.

Graphic art is used in creating packaging, promotional displays, and sales brochures; visual designs for corporate reports and literature; and distinctive logos for products or companies. Graphic artists are responsible for the layout and design of magazines, newspapers, and journals, as well as graphics for television and the Internet.

Fine art involves different forms. Painters generally work in two dimensions. Painters depict real objects or project varied feelings or thoughts through color, perspective, and shading techniques. Sculptors design in three dimensions. They mold or join materials such as clay, glass, plastic, or metal, or they cut and carve forms from plaster, wood, or stone. Printmakers create printed images from designs cut into wood, stone, or metal. Designs can be engraved in wood or metal, etched in metal by acid, or made as inkjet or laser prints from computers.

Many people work in a variety of visual art professions. Some of these are described here.

Illustrators paint or draw pictures for books, magazines, films, and such paper products as greeting cards, wrapping paper, stationery, and calendars. Illustrators also create "story boards" used in the making of television commercials and movies.

Art directors or visual journalists decide how to present text in an eye-appealing and organized manner, using photographs or other artwork, such as cartoons, in magazines and newspapers.

Photographers work with stills (portraits), videos of special events such as weddings, or photojournalism. News photographers demonstrate the role that technology plays in the visual arts; for example, digital cameras use electronic memory rather than a film negative to record an image, which then can be transmitted immediately by computer modem and telephone lines. Visual communication is entrenched in our society, as we experience it daily.

Designers make up another large group of visual artists. They may specialize in such areas as industrial equipment (industrial designers); automobiles; clothing (fashion designers); furniture (furniture designers); fabrics, upholstery, and rugs (textile designers); and interiors of homes, restaurants, retail stores, office space, and buildings (interior designers). After hearing a client's needs, designers first communicate their ideas by sketches and then make models, prototypes, or detailed illustrations drawn to scale. These models, typically developed with computer-aided industrial design, enable decision makers to have a clear idea of the final product. Design is not a static field. Fashion trends are constantly changing. Knowledge of new products, textiles, and fabrics creates demands to keep abreast of many different manufacturers' products and consumers' acceptability of these newer developments.

Most programs in art and design provide training in computer design techniques; this training is especially critical for those entering commercial art. The educational course work tends to be very practical and, of course, corresponds to the specializations described here.

Artistic ability varies, whether it be the talent to draw, paint, photograph, or sculpt. A person's skills are assessed, captured, and displayed by a "portfolio," a collection of samples of one's work. Others use the portfolio technique to evaluate a person's ability. Such samples show ability and technique in eye-hand precision; color usage; vision; and the use of oils, watercolors, acrylics, pastels, pen, and pencil. Artistic ability also needs planning and organization to deliver and communicate ideas and feelings. Some might claim the creative and expressive skills to be a persuasive intent. Additional abilities are spatial—to see differences in size, shape, and form and to visualize relationships; mechanical—to work with equipment and to understand how things come together to produce the best images; and manual—to coordinate use of the hands with creative intellectual thought.

The interests of artists vary depending on the areas in which they work. Besides a predominant liking for art, those in commercial fields like the applications of business, which can offer a hectic and challenging pace that coincides with creative interests. Graphic artists are technologically oriented. Fine artists, however, have a more focused interest in art and a more intellectual approach to the field without the business and technological interests.

Visual artists obviously value creative imagination and the logical correlate of independence, which permits self-expression. Variety and diversion are sought, with routine generally not tolerated. While expressions of feelings are afforded, the visual arts offer opportunities for a high level of mental activity. There is also appreciation for concrete creations. Opportunities for recognition and high achievement are available and pursued. People are accepting of flexible work schedules.

Personality characteristics can range from ingenuity and boldness to concern and sensitivity about one's work, whether in reaction to praise or criticism. While a commonality exists in bringing forth the expansion of ideas, personal style can be either the projection of exuberant self-enthusiasm or the preference for a quiet reserve. Although intellectually bright, visual artists frequently express themselves not through academics but rather from a desire to be imaginative and independent. Visual artists need self-discipline to start projects on their own because many work as freelancers; they also need to budget their time, be problem solvers, and meet deadlines. Designers need sales ability, persistence, and adaptability because styles and fashion can change quickly, requiring openness to new ideas.

Where Do Visual Arts Graduates Work?

The employment of visual arts graduates is spread across the five sectors of the economy. Fewer than one-half work in the private, for-profit sector for businesses and corporations. Self-employment is common among arts majors who value independence so that they can maximize individual expression. More than one-fifth are self-employed in their own business or practice. Another 18 percent of arts graduates find employment in educational institutions, working as elementary or secondary school teachers. About 6 percent work in the government sector, and 5 percent find employment in the nonprofit sector of the economy, working for tax-exempt or charitable organizations.

Arts majors have to be exceptionally good at what they do to be able to earn a full-time living with a job in their field. Therefore, it is not surprising that many arts majors work in jobs that are unrelated to their major. Only 38 percent of the graduates work in jobs that are closely related to the visual arts. Another 24 percent say that their jobs are somewhat related to their major. The remaining 38 percent work in jobs that are not at all related to their undergraduate major.

Why do arts graduates work in unrelated jobs? A number of factors underlie this decision, although pay and promotion opportunities and the lack of jobs in their field are the most commonly cited reasons. When asked to pick the most important reason for employment outside their major field of study, 23 percent of the arts graduates find the lack of jobs in their field as the most important factor in their decision, and 21 percent pick better pay and promotion opportunities as the number one reason for their employment in an unrelated job. About 17 percent rank a change in their career interests as the top reason, and 14 percent consider family-related reasons as the most important factor influencing the employment choice in an unrelated job. The general working environment is the top-ranking factor for only 8 percent of arts graduates working in unrelated jobs.

FIGURE 1

Percentage Distribution of Employed Persons with Only a Bachelor's Degree in Visual Arts, by Major Sector of Economic Activity

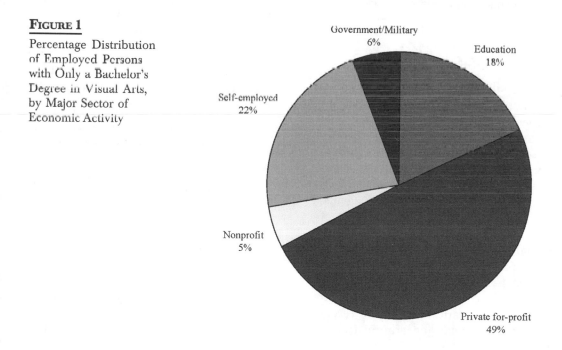

Government/Military 6%

Education 18%

Self-employed 22%

Nonprofit 5%

Private for-profit 49%

Table 1
Top 10 Occupations That Employ Persons with Only a Bachelor's Degree in Visual Arts

Top 10 Occupations	PERCENT OF EMPLOYED		
	All	Men	Women
Artists, broadcasters, writers, editors, entertainers, public relations specialists	25.4	29.0	23.1
Top- and mid-level managers, executives, administrators	7.5	8.2	7.1
Sales occupations, including retail	6.2	5.5	6.7
Other administrative (e.g., records clerks, telephone operators)	5.2	5.0	5.4
Other management-related occupations	4.4	3.7	4.9
Teachers, elementary school	4.0	2.3	5.1
Secretaries, receptionists, typists	4.0	0.4	6.3
Teachers, secondary school	3.9	5.2	3.1
Other marketing and sales occupations	3.4	3.0	3.7
Precision production occupations	2.9	4.9	1.6

Occupations

Two-thirds of all employed arts graduates are concentrated in the top 10 occupations that are predominant employers of these graduates. One-quarter of the graduates work in art and entertainment occupations; 8 percent are in high-level executive, administrative, and managerial occupations. Management-related occupations such as management analysts, purchasing agents, and regulatory officers employ 4 percent of the majors. One-tenth of the arts graduates work in sales and marketing occupations, and 8 percent are employed as elementary or secondary school teachers. Slightly more than 9 percent of arts graduates work in administrative support occupations as secretaries, typists, and receptionists and in clerical and administrative occupations.

Only 40 percent of all employed arts graduates are men. The occupational employment patterns of male arts graduates and female arts graduates are different.

▶ Male arts graduates are more likely than female arts graduates to work as artists in the arts and entertainment occupations: 29 percent of men are employed in these occupations, compared to 23 percent of female graduates.

▶ Male arts graduates also are somewhat more likely than female arts graduates to work as top-level executives, administrators, and managers. Slightly more than 8 percent of all employed male graduates work in these occupations, compared to 7 percent of employed female graduates.

- Male arts graduates are more likely than female arts graduates to work as secondary school teachers, whereas females are more likely than males to be employed as elementary school teachers.

- Female arts graduates are more concentrated in sales and marketing occupations than are male arts majors.

- Female arts graduates also are much more likely than their male counterparts to work as secretaries, typists, and receptionists.

Activities on the Job

The activities on which arts graduates spend most of their time at work reflect their employment patterns in different occupations.

- About 13 percent spend most of their workweek in sales, purchasing, and marketing activities. As noted, sales and marketing occupations employ 10 percent of the graduates.

- About 12 percent spend most of their time at work in teaching activities. About one-quarter of all employed graduates state that they regularly spend at least some time in teaching activities.

- Management and administrative duties take up most of the time at work among 12 percent of employed arts graduates.

- Most arts programs provide training in computer design techniques. Various forms of fine art such as art design, illustration, sculpting, and even painting require the use of computers. One-quarter of all employed arts graduates work in various art and entertainment occupations. Therefore, it is not surprising to find that 35 percent of employed arts graduates regularly engage in computer applications, programming, and

systems-development activities; 8 percent spend most of their time at work in these activities.

- About 7 percent spend most of their typical workweek in accounting, finance, and contractual duties.

- Only 5 percent consider designing of models and structures to be the main part of their job. An equal proportion spend most of their time in providing professional services such as consulting. A little less than 5 percent spend most of their typical workweek in developing products based on the findings of applied research activities.

Salaries

The average annual salary of visual arts graduates who have only a bachelor's degree and are employed full-time is $43,600 in 2002-dollar terms, a level that is 20 percent lower than the average annual salary of all full-time employed college graduates. The average salary of visual arts graduates increases just slightly with age and remains well below the average salary of all college graduates in each age range. Since the average salary of all college graduates increases with age and the salary of visual arts graduates remains somewhat flat after an initial increase, their salary deficit relative to the salary of all college graduates increases with age.

- The average annual salary of visual arts graduates between the ages of 25 and 29 is $33,500. Graduates between the ages of 30 and 34 earn $44,700 annually, and the average salary for those between the ages of 35 and 39 is $44,600.

- The average annual salary of arts graduates increases slightly to $46,700 between the ages of 40 and 44. The average salary of arts graduates between the ages of 45 and 49 peaks at $47,000.

Although the average annual salary of arts majors who work in jobs that are closely related to their major field of study is higher than the salary of those who are employed in jobs that are somewhat related or unrelated to their major, the differences in salary among these groups are moderate. Closely related jobs pay full-time employed arts graduates $44,600 annually. Graduates employed in somewhat related jobs earn $41,500 per year, and those whose jobs are unrelated to their undergraduate major field of study earn an average annual salary of $41,100.

Self-employed visual arts graduates earn more than their counterparts employed in other sectors of the economy. The average annual salary of full-time self-employed arts graduates is $51,100. Arts graduates working in the private, for-profit sector for businesses and corporations earn $42,400 per year, the same as arts graduates who work in the government sector. Private, nonprofit, full-time jobs pay arts graduates $37,400 per year. The average salary of visual arts graduates working in educational institutions is $36,000 per year.

Visual arts graduates possess skills that are not readily marketable. Therefore, they often find employment in jobs that are unrelated to their field, and these jobs are frequently low-paying. Except for in the teaching occupations, the average salary of arts graduates in the top 10 occupations is lower than the salary of all college graduates employed in those occupations. The average salary of all college graduates and visual arts graduates in the top 10 occupations that are predominant employers of visual arts graduates is presented here.

- The highest average salary of visual arts graduates in the 10 occupations is in high-level executive, administrative, and managerial occupations. Graduates employed in these occupations earn $57,100 per year. These occupations are more likely to employ male than female graduates.

- The average salary of arts graduates employed in management-related occupations is $47,400 per year; the salary in miscellaneous marketing and sales occupations is the third highest of the top 10 occupations for this major, or $44,900.

- Full-time employed secondary school teachers with a bachelor's degree in arts earn $42,600 per year; those who are elementary school teachers earn $40,400 per year.

- Employment in secretarial, clerical, and administrative support occupations is associated with an average salary of $31,800 per year among visual arts graduates.

FIGURE 2

Age/Earnings Profile of Persons with Only a Bachelor's Degree in Visual Arts
(Full-Time Workers, in 2002 Dollars)

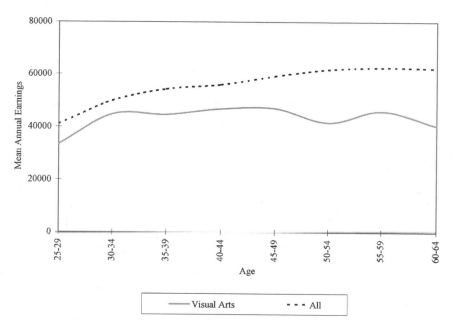

Table 2

Annual Salary of Full-Time Workers with Only a Bachelor's Degree
in Visual Arts, Top 10 Occupations (in 2002 Dollars)

Earnings in Top 10 Occupations	All	Visual Arts
Total	$54,171	$43,559
Artists, broadcasters, writers, editors, entertainers, public relations specialists	$52,141	$45,804
Top- and mid-level managers, executives, administrators	$74,051	$57,116
Sales occupations, including retail	$52,378	$40,243
Other administrative (e.g., records clerks, telephone operators)	$34,547	$31,683
Other management-related occupations	$51,921	$47,441
Teachers, elementary school	$39,167	$40,359
Secretaries, receptionists, typists	$32,246	$31,797
Teachers, secondary school	$40,355	$42,618
Other marketing and sales occupations	$58,208	$44,903
Precision production occupations	$39,328	$33,766

On-the-Job Training

The career potential of a job is closely associated with the amount of work-related training on the job. Work-related training is regarded as an investment by firms because it makes workers more productive. Firms that invest in their workforce are more likely to offer pay increases and promotions to match the increasing productivity of their workers. Firms that do not invest in their workers are relatively less likely to offer pay increases and promotions. The incidence of work-related training among visual arts graduates is substantially lower than the rate of participation in work-related training among all college graduates. While 68 percent of all college graduates acquire some kind of work-related training during a year, only 52 percent of arts majors annually engage in work-related training.

▶ Of those arts graduates who receive some work-related training during the year, 70 percent receive technical training in the occupation in which they are employed.

▶ One-fourth of the training recipients receive management or supervisory training.

▶ One-third receive training to improve their general professional skills, such as public speaking and business writing.

Although numerous reasons underlie the decision of arts graduates to participate in work-related training activities, workshops, or seminars, four reasons are most commonly cited by graduates. Included among these are a desire to improve skills and knowledge in the occupational area of their employment, mandatory training requirements of the employer, increased opportunities for advancement in the form of a higher salary and promotion, and the need to learn skills for a newly acquired position. Nearly

93 percent of visual arts graduates who participate in work-related training do so to improve their occupational skills and knowledge. Another 47 percent list an employer requirement as one of the reasons for participation in work-related training. More opportunity for promotion and salary increases is one of the reasons to acquire training among 46 percent of the training recipients. About 23 percent cite the need to learn skills for a newly acquired position as one of the factors that underlie the decision to engage in training. Another 18 percent cite the need for training to acquire a professional license or certificate.

When asked to identify the most important reason to acquire training, 65 percent of visual arts graduates who undergo training identify the need to improve their occupational skills and knowledge. Another 12 percent report a mandatory training requirement by the employer as the most important factor underlying their involvement in work-related training. According to 6 percent of the training participants, the most important reason is a salary increase and promotion. Another 6 percent rank the need to obtain a professional license or certificate as the number one reason for participation in work-related training activities. Slightly less than 5 percent rank the necessity to learn skills for a newly acquired position as the number one reason to acquire training.

Post-Graduation Activities

Of all graduates with a bachelor's degree in visual arts, 25 percent proceed to earn a postgraduate degree: 22 percent earn a master's degree, 1 percent earn a doctoral degree, and 2 percent earn a professional degree.

▶ Nearly one-half of all master's degrees earned by undergraduate visual arts majors are in the field of visual arts.

About 19 percent are earned in education, 5 percent are earned in other arts fields, such as dramatic arts, and 4 percent are earned in business administration and management.

▶ The doctoral degrees earned by visual arts undergraduate majors are spread across the fields of visual arts, education, health professions, social sciences, and psychology.

▶ The professional degrees of undergraduate visual arts majors are concentrated in the field of law and in the health professions.

Of all visual arts graduates under the age of 65, 78 percent are employed. Only 4 percent are officially unemployed; in other words, they are not employed and are actively seeking employment. The remaining 18 percent are out of the labor force; that is, they are not employed and are not seeking employment. Two main reasons underlie the labor force withdrawal of visual arts graduates: 50 percent cite family responsibilities as the reason for labor force withdrawal, and 31 lack the desire or the need to work. Additionally, 11 percent are retired, and the same proportion has a chronic illness or a disabling condition. Another 10 percent cite school enrollment as one of the reasons for labor force withdrawal.

Employment Outlook

According to the U.S. Bureau of Labor Statistics, employment in occupations that require at least a bachelor's degree is expected to grow faster than employment in other sectors of the American labor market. Between 2000 and 2010, the U.S. economy is projected to add 22.2 million jobs, yielding an employment growth rate of 15.2 percent. The employment growth projections in the top 10 occupations that are most likely to employ visual arts graduates are presented in Table 3.

▶ The fastest growth in demand is projected in the miscellaneous marketing and sales occupations. These occupations are projected to add 137,000 jobs, representing a growth rate of 22.1 percent over the 2000–2010 projections period. These occupations employ only 3 percent of all visual arts graduates with a bachelor's degree.

▶ Arts and entertainment occupations, which include artists, editors, broadcasters, and entertainers, are projected to add 493,000 jobs between 2000 and 2010, yielding a 21 percent growth rate. One out of four visual arts graduates is employed in these occupations. However, these occupations are more likely to employ male than female visual arts graduates.

▶ The demand for secondary school teachers continues to be high due to the surge in numbers of school-aged children and the demand for smaller class sizes. The Bureau of Labor Statistics projects the need for an additional 201,000 secondary school teachers between 2000 and 2010, representing a growth of 18 percent over the projections period. The demand for elementary school teachers is projected to increase by 202,000, from 1.532 million in 2000 to 1.734 million in 2010, a growth rate of 13 percent over the projections period.

▶ Employment in management-related occupations is projected to grow at above-average rates, with an additional 845,000 jobs between 2000 and 2010, representing a growth rate of 17 percent over the projections period.

▶ The second-largest employer of visual arts graduates—upper-level executive, administrative, and managerial occupations—is projected to add 1.27 million jobs between 2000 and 2010. This figure represents an employment growth rate of 12 percent, which is somewhat lower than the projection of overall job growth in the U.S. economy over the same time period.

▶ Employment in administrative support and secretarial occupations is projected to grow at below-average rates. Widespread use of computers has eroded the demand for personnel in these occupations. These occupations are more likely to employ female than male visual arts graduates.

Table 3
Projected Change in Employment in the Top 10 Occupations That Employ Persons with Only a Bachelor's Degree in Visual Arts

Top 10 Occupations	Actual Employment in 2000 (000s)	Projected Employment in 2010 (000s)	Absolute Change (000s)	Percentage Change
Artists, broadcasters, writers, editors, entertainers, public relations specialists	2,371	2,864	493	20.8%
Top- and mid-level managers, executives, administrators	10,564	11,834	1,270	12.0%
Sales occupations, including retail	15,513	17,365	1,852	11.9%
Other administrative (e.g., records clerks, telephone operators)	16,911	18,522	1,611	9.5%
Other management-related occupations	4,956	5,801	845	17.1%
Teachers, elementary school	1,532	1,734	202	13.2%
Secretaries, receptionists, typists	4,980	5,501	521	10.5%
Teachers, secondary school	1,113	1,314	201	18.1%
Other marketing and sales occupations	621	758	137	22.1%
Precision production occupations	13,060	13,811	751	5.8%

Natural Sciences

CHAPTER 51

Animal Food Sciences

Animal food scientists develop better, more efficient ways of producing and processing meat, poultry, eggs, and milk. Specialists such as dairy scientists, poultry scientists, and animal breeders study genetics, nutrition, reproduction, growth, and development of domestic farm animals. Some animal food scientists inspect and grade livestock, purchase livestock, or work in technical sales or marketing. Others work as extension agents for government agencies, performing educational and consultative roles in bringing farmers and ranchers the latest research and new developments to assist in addressing specific local problems. This educational outreach system has helped the United States secure preeminence worldwide in the field of agriculture.

While dairy scientists conduct research in selecting, breeding, feeding, and managing cattle, the poultry scientist does the same with poultry. The latter additionally focuses on increasing the efficiency of production and improving the quality of poultry products. These goals are achieved by developing improved practices in incubation, brooding, feeding, rearing, housing, artificial insemination, and disease and parasite prevention and control. Similarly, dairy scientists carry out experiments to determine the effects of different kinds of feed on the quantity, quality, and nutritive value of milk; dairy scientists also study the physiology of reproduction and lactation.

Despite this field's being a relatively small one in terms of employment, each state has a land-grant college that offers agricultural science degrees, which include animal food science offerings such as animal husbandry. The curriculum covers communications, economics, business, and physical and life sciences courses. Specific courses may include animal breeding, reproductive physiology, nutrition, and meat and muscle biology.

The abilities required for animal food science include scientific, mathematical, and mechanical skills, as well as a business sense. Animal food scientists use manual dexterity, whether for working hands-on with animals or machinery. A salient feature of graduates is their leadership and interpersonal skills. As noted earlier, they can be disseminators of information, and, because of a consultative function of disseminating current knowledge, they are constantly involved in new learning.

In terms of interests, a combination of likes emerges, with animal food scientists primarily enjoying science but also liking applications and technology. A people and business orientation also fits those who work in this field.

Animal food scientists value the opportunity to have diversity in their work, be independent and do what they want, seek high achievement, and expect to receive a good salary. Animal food scientists feel it is important to use their minds in their work.

Studies have highlighted three personality characteristics of those working in the animal food sciences: being independent, working alone, and possessing a sense of community. The independence may reflect the reality of rural living. One quickly learns to be able to do various tasks and repair many different things when living in a rural area. And people involved in animal food sciences usually are friendly people who come together with a strong sense of community.

Where Do Animal Food Science Majors Work?

Most animal food science majors work in the private, for-profit sector of the economy. A large proportion of graduates of animal food science programs become self-employed; more than 1 in 4 animal food science majors operate their own businesses after graduation. Many of these self-employed individuals operate their own farms or their own wholesaling or retailing organizations. Fewer than one-half of animal food science majors work in wage and salary positions for a business or corporation. Relatively few majors from this field work in nonprofit organizations.

Occupations

Men who earn bachelor's degrees in animal food science are quite likely to be employed in agriculture-related occupations. More than 1 in 5 men with a college degree in this field work in an agricultural occupation. In contrast, women who earn an animal food science degree are much less likely to work in an agriculture-related field. Instead, women are more likely to work in the health professions or in management-related jobs such as accountant or personnel manager. About two-thirds of animal food science majors work

FIGURE 1

Percentage Distribution of Employed Persons with Only a Bachelor's Degree in Animal Food Sciences, by Major Sector of Economic Activity

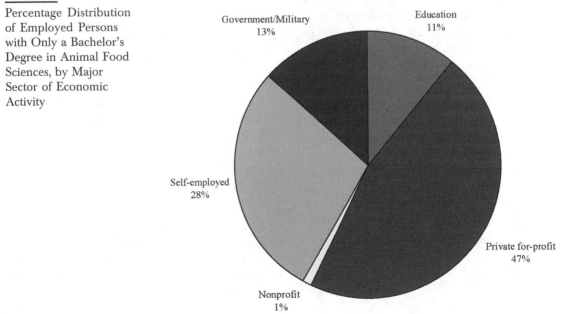

Government/Military
13%

Education
11%

Self-employed
28%

Nonprofit
1%

Private for-profit
47%

in jobs that are related in some way to their undergraduate field of study. About one-third work in jobs that are unrelated to animal food science studies. Those who work in occupations unrelated to the field most often say that they choose to work in another field because of the comparatively poor working conditions they observe in jobs related to animal studies. One-quarter of those who work outside the field say they cannot find a job related to the major.

▶ About 1 in 5 animal food science majors work in a managerial or an administrative position, although men are somewhat more likely than women to report employment in these occupations.

▶ Only about 7 percent of animal food science majors work as agricultural scientists, although a sharp difference in employment in this occupation exists between men and women. About 18 percent of men with an undergraduate degree in animal food science work as agricultural/food scientists, while fewer than 3 percent of women with a degree in this field work in that occupation.

▶ Sales occupations, including retail sales, employ about 6 percent of all graduates of this field who work in full-time jobs.

Table 1
Top 10 Occupations That Employ Persons with Only a Bachelor's Degree in Animal Food Sciences

Top 10 Occupations	PERCENT OF EMPLOYED		
	All	Men	Women
Agriculture, forestry, fishing, and related occupations	16.8	22.6	3.7
Top- and mid-level managers, executives, administrators	13.3	17.1	4.9
Insurance, securities, real estate, business services	6.3	9.1	0.0
Sales occupations, including retail	6.2	5.6	7.5
Other management-related occupations	5.9	4.1	10.1
Accountants, auditors, other financial specialists	5.6	5.9	5.0
Construction trades, miners, well drillers	3.5	5.1	0.0
Health technologists and technicians	3.3	0.7	9.3
Registered nurses, pharmacists, therapists, physician assistants	3.2	0.0	10.3
Agricultural and food scientists	3.0	3.6	1.7

Activities on the Job

Animal food science majors working in full-time jobs engage in a number of different tasks while at work.

- Accounting, finance, and contractual issues are topics that most graduates from this major deal with over the course of the workweek.

- Providing professional services in the occupation in which the graduate is employed, such as a position in health or agricultural science, is also a major activity that consumes a substantial number of hours during the workweek.

- A substantial proportion of graduates engage in production- and operations-related activities, but few graduates are involved in the design of equipment or production processes.

- About 1 in 3 graduates of this field are engaged in the development of computer applications of some type.

- The majority of graduates in this field are regularly involved in personnel and human resource issues over the course of the workweek.

- Relatively few persons with a bachelor's degree in animal food science are regularly involved in either applied or basic research on the job.

Salaries

The annual salaries of animal food science majors are well below the average salaries of all college graduates. Persons with only a bachelor's degree in animal food science had an average annual salary in 2002 dollars of $46,400, an annual rate of pay that was about 15 percent less than the average salary of the average college graduate. Animal food science majors between the ages of 25 and 29 have earnings that average $33,100. However, as the data in Figure 2 reveals, the earnings of graduates with degrees in this field increase with age. The earnings of animal food science majors peak between ages 50 and 54, when annual salaries average $59,600 per year. Much of the increase in earnings of graduates from this field of study occurs as they develop more years of work experience. While not necessarily valuing older workers more than younger ones, employers pay more salary to older workers because they value the skills and abilities developed through years of work experience.

- Animal food science majors employed in private sector wage and salary jobs have the highest earnings of all graduates with degrees in this field. These majors earn about 8 percent more than the average graduate employed in a full-time job.

- Self-employed graduates also have a substantial earnings advantage relative to the average graduates within the field.

- Graduates who work in educational institutions have earnings that are 17 percent below the average of all full-time employed graduates with a degree in animal food sciences.

- Animal food science majors employed in jobs unrelated to their field have higher annual salaries than those who work in jobs that are closely related to the field. Those employed in jobs that are unrelated to the field earn 20 percent more per year than those who work in a job closely related to the major.

The earnings of animal food science majors vary considerably among the occupations in which they are most likely to be employed. Table 2 reveals that those graduates employed in stocks and bonds, futures and commodities, real estate,

FIGURE 2

Age/Earnings Profile of Persons with Only a Bachelor's Degree in Animal Food Sciences
(Full-Time Workers, in 2002 Dollars)

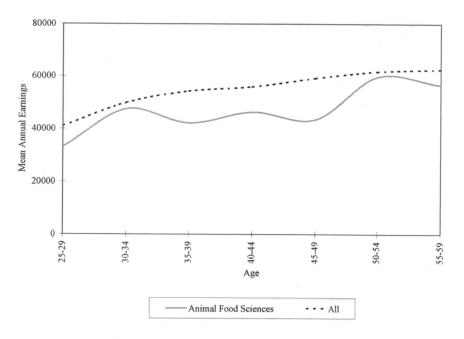

and other types of sales occupations have the highest salaries of all animal food science majors. Graduates who work in agriculture and related occupations have earnings that are quite low, with annual salaries that average only $32,200.

Table 2

Annual Salary of Full-Time Workers with Only a Bachelor's Degree
in Animal Food Sciences, Top 10 Occupations (in 2002 Dollars)

Earnings in Top 10 Occupations	All	Animal Food Sciences
Total	$54,171	$46,402
Agriculture, forestry, fishing, and related occupations	$45,437	$32,246
Top- and mid-level managers, executives, administrators	$74,051	$58,548
Insurance, securities, real estate, business services	$68,273	$71,998
Sales occupations, including retail	$52,378	$69,773

(continued)

Table 2 (continued)
Annual Salary of Full-Time Workers with Only a Bachelor's Degree
in Animal Food Sciences, Top 10 Occupations (in 2002 Dollars)

Earnings in Top 10 Occupations	All	Animal Food Sciences
Other management-related occupations	$51,921	$35,970
Accountants, auditors, other financial specialists	$57,382	$46,079
Construction trades, miners, well drillers	$50,531	$48,200
Health technologists and technicians	$42,774	$47,182
Registered nurses, pharmacists, therapists, physician assistants	$53,508	$33,147
Agricultural and food scientists	$49,124	$34,915

On-the-Job Learning

The career potential of a job is closely associated with the amount of work-related training on the job. Work-related training is regarded as an investment by firms because it makes workers more productive. Firms that invest in their workforce are more likely to offer pay increases and promotions to match the increasing productivity of their workers. Firms that do not invest in their workers are relatively less likely to offer pay increases and promotions. The incidence of work-related training among animal food sciences graduates is about the same as the participation rate in work-related training among all college graduates. While 68 percent of all college graduates acquire some kind of work-related training during a year, about 7 of 10 persons with a degree in animal food science say that they received work-related training of some type during the prior year. Self-employed graduates of animal food science programs were as likely as persons holding wage and salary jobs to engage in some type of work-related training during the prior year.

▶ More than 8 of 10 animal food science majors who participate in some type of training report that the training is designed to improve some specific skill related to their current job duties.

▶ Unlike majors in other fields of study, few of these majors are trained in the communications area. Fewer than 1 in 5 majors say they received any training in business writing or public speaking.

▶ Managerial and supervisor training is generally not provided to graduates with degrees in this field.

Post-Graduation Activities

A relatively high proportion of animal food science majors go on to complete a graduate degree after finishing their undergraduate program. About 17 percent of all persons who earned a bachelor's degree in animal food science subsequently earn a master's degree of some type. Nearly 5 percent eventually earn a doctorate. About 12 percent of bachelor's degree holders in animal food science earn a professional degree of some type.

- Of those who earn a master's degree, 28 percent earn one in animal food science. An additional 22 percent earn a master's degree in another area of agricultural science.

- Business is also a major area in which a number of animal food science majors earn a master's degree; 1 in 5 master's degrees earned by animal food science majors is in business.

- Among those who earn a doctorate, more than one-third continue their studies in animal food science, about 30 percent earn a doctorate in a field related to biological sciences, and about one-sixth earn a doctorate in a health-related area.

- Virtually all of the animal food science majors who earn a professional degree earn it in the health field, either in medicine or veterinary medicine. Few animal food science majors go on to earn a professional degree in law.

About 90 percent of persons with only a bachelor's degree in animal food science are employed. Among those not working, about one-third are still actively looking for work. The remaining two-thirds are persons who have decided not to actively participate in the labor market; the majority of this group indicate that they do not want to work because they have retired, even though they have not reached age 65.

Employment Outlook

The long-term job prospects for most college graduates are expected to remain strong through 2010. The projections produced by the U.S. Bureau of Labor Statistics suggest that those industries and occupations most likely to hire college graduates will expand at an above-average pace. The data included in Table 3 includes projections of employment change between 2000 and 2010 for those occupations identified as most likely to employ persons who hold a bachelor's degree in animal food science.

- More than 1 in 5 men with a bachelor's degree in animal food science work in agriculture and related occupations. Bureau of Labor Statistics projections suggest slow growth in the demand for workers in this occupational area. The projected rate of growth in demand for workers in this occupation is less than one-fourth of the projected overall rate of job growth in the nation.

- One in 6 animal food science majors works in a management or administrative position. The demand for workers in this area is projected to grow, albeit more slowly than the rate of growth projected for all occupations. Between 2000 and 2010, managerial and administrative positions are projected to increase by 1.27 million, or 12 percent.

- About 1 in 5 women with degrees in animal food science work as health professionals or health technicians. These occupations are expected to grow at a rapid pace through 2010.

Table 3

Projected Change in Employment in the Top 10 Occupations That Employ
Persons with Only a Bachelor's Degree in Animal Food Sciences

Top 10 Occupations	Actual Employment in 2000 (000s)	Projected Employment in 2010 (000s)	Absolute Change (000s)	Percentage Change
Agriculture, forestry, fishing, and related occupations	1,429	1,480	51	3.6%
Top- and mid-level managers, executives, administrators	10,564	11,834	1,270	12.0%
Insurance, securities, real estate, business services	1,548	1,726	178	11.5%
Sales occupations, including retail	15,513	17,365	1,852	11.9%
Other management-related occupations	4,956	5,801	845	17.1%
Accountants, auditors, other financial specialists	2,115	2,481	366	17.3%
Construction trades, miners, well drillers	7,451	8,439	988	13.3%
Health technologists and technicians	2,192	2,773	581	26.5%
Registered nurses, pharmacists, therapists, physician assistants	2,908	3,698	790	27.2%
Agricultural and food scientists	17	19	2	11.8%

CHAPTER 52

Biology and Life Sciences

Advances in the knowledge of basic life processes, especially at the genetic and molecular levels, are the driving forces in the field of biotechnology. Such specializations as microbiology, microchemistry, and biophysics have become large enough to be separate majors. This development has blurred classifications in the study of biology, but often majors continue to use traditional names of concentration areas. For example, biological scientists who do biomedical research typically are referred to as medical scientists.

Aquatic biologists examine various types of water life, such as plankton, clams, shrimp, or lobsters. Specialization in saltwater species is designated as marine biology. Aquatic biologists investigate the conditions of water–its salinity, temperature, acidity, light, and oxygen content–to determine its relationship with aquatic life.

Botanists study the development, physiology, heredity, environment, distribution, anatomy, and economic value of plants for application to forestry, horticulture, and pharmacology. Botany also includes the study of the behavior of chromosomes and reproduction and of the biochemistry of plants and plant cells. Botanists investigate environments and plant communities and the effect of rainfall, temperature, climate, soil, and elevation on plant growth from seed to mature plants.

Physiologists research the cellular structure and organ systems of plants and animals. Physiologists study growth, respiration, and glands and their relationship to bodily functions, excretion, movement, and reproduction under normal and abnormal conditions.

Zoology is the study of reptiles, frogs, fish, sponges, birds, and mammals. Zoologists also examine these creatures' habits, diseases, relationship to the environment, genetics, growth, and development.

Most colleges and universities offer programs in biological sciences, which are sometimes called life sciences. These institutions approach educational course work in general biology from a research and development perspective. Specialization often occurs in advanced degrees. Typical courses may include principles of biology, environment and population biology, genetics, cell physiology, biochemistry, and general microbiology, as well as mathematics, physics, and chemistry.

Biology requires good academic ability to handle the heavy load of science and mathematics courses. Biologists use logic and scientific thinking in their analyses, and they apply methodologies to make judgments. Recognition of differences in size, form, color, and texture is important. Finger dexterity, coordinated use of eyes and manual movement, and the ability to use laboratory and scientific equipment are all requirements. The ability to withstand prolonged periods of concentration is often required for performance.

The interests of biologists are predominantly scientific and technological, with an interest in the liberal arts. The scientific interests are more in the life sciences. The liberal arts interests can include the humanities as well as social sciences, which foster a wide human perspective. Biologists also are interested in laboratory work or field applications. They are interested in scientific applications related to living beings versus the inanimate applications of physics and chemistry.

Biologists value options that satisfy creative and intellectual pursuits. The field of biology provides prestige, variety, and an appreciation for research values, as well as the opportunity for receiving a good salary.

Where Do Biology Majors Work?

Persons with a bachelor's degree in biology are employed across key segments of the American economy. Unlike the graduates from many other fields of study, fewer than one-half of all biology bachelor's degree holders work as wage and salary employees at for-profit businesses and corporations. Instead, many biology majors work in educational institutions as teachers. About 1 in 8 biology majors work in a government organization. An additional 8 percent work in nonprofit foundations and research organizations. A surprisingly large number of biology majors are self-employed. About 12 percent operate their own business or consulting service.

FIGURE 1

Percentage Distribution of Employed Persons with Only a Bachelor's Degree in Biology, by Major Sector of Economic Activity

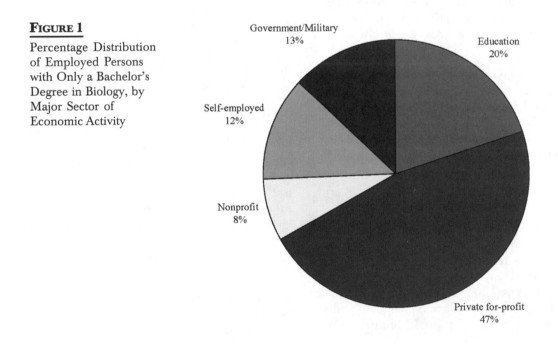

Government/Military 13%

Education 20%

Self-employed 12%

Nonprofit 8%

Private for-profit 47%

Table 1
Top 10 Occupations That Employ Persons with Only a Bachelor's Degree in Biology

Top 10 Occupations	PERCENT OF EMPLOYED		
	All	Men	Women
Health technologists and technicians	10.3	4.6	17.4
Top- and mid-level managers, executives, administrators	9.5	14.1	4.0
Biological scientists	7.7	5.6	10.2
Sales occupations, including retail	6.3	7.8	4.4
Teachers, secondary school	5.9	5.5	6.4
Other management-related occupations	3.8	4.7	2.8
Registered nurses, pharmacists, therapists, physician assistants	3.6	2.3	5.3
Insurance, securities, real estate, business services	3.3	4.2	2.2
Other marketing and sales occupations	3.2	3.5	3.0
All other engineers	2.5	3.4	1.4

Occupations

Employment at the bachelor's degree level in occupations that are closely related to the undergraduate major field of study is more difficult to achieve for biology majors than other undergraduate specialties. Health technology and technician jobs are the single largest occupation in which biology degree holders are employed. This occupational area includes such jobs as medical and laboratory technician and radiological technician. An additional 10 percent of biology degree holders work in managerial and professional positions often related to the undergraduate major. An additional 8 percent work as biological scientists, and about 3 percent work in other medical professions as therapists and clinicians. More than 1 in 3 employed persons who have a bachelor's degree in biology work in jobs that are unrelated to the undergraduate major field of study. Sales and management-related jobs, including human resources management, are some of the occupations that employ these individuals.

- Women with a bachelor's degree in biology are about four times more likely to work as health technologists than their male counterparts.

- Men with a bachelor's degree in biology are much more likely than women to be employed as either managers and administrators or biological scientists.

- Both men and women are equally likely to work as elementary or secondary school teachers.

Activities on the Job

- Biology majors spend the greatest part of their workweek delivering a set of professional services that characterize their current jobs. Such services may include the delivery of laboratory analysis of biological substances or the provision of various health care services.

▶ Applied research is an important part of the job for many graduates with a biology degree. However, basic research tasks are undertaken much less often.

▶ Teaching is an important part of the job for many biology graduates. Teaching can include peer education and training activities or teaching at the elementary or secondary school level.

▶ Administrative duties also are an important part of the tasks undertaken by biology graduates. These duties include employee relations, purchasing, accounting, finance, and record-keeping activities.

Salaries

Biology majors have annual salaries of $51,000 per year on average, a rate of pay that is about 6 percent below the annual salary rate of all college graduates in 2002 dollars. Biology bachelor's degree holders aged 25 to 29 have earnings of $40,800 per year. This wage increases to $56,300 by ages 45 to 49, reflecting the increase in skills and abilities that additional years of work experience bring to individuals. This experience makes them more productive and thus more valuable to their employers. Biology graduates who work in the private, for-profit sector as wage and salary employees have annual salaries of $54,400 per year. However, those graduates who are self-employed have annual earnings that average $64,800 per year. Those who work in nonprofit or educational organizations earn only about $41,500 per year, while those in government jobs earn $46,700.

In many fields of study, access to jobs that are related to the undergraduate major leads to higher earnings after graduation. However, this case is not true for biology majors. Those majors employed in jobs that are not related to their major field of study have annual salaries that are about the same as those working in jobs that are related to the field.

The earnings of employed biology majors vary sharply by occupation. Those employed as health technologists and technicians—the single largest occupation in which majors find work—earn about $43,200 per year. Biological scientists earn $43,500 on an annual basis. Biology majors employed in managerial and administrative positions have annual salaries that are well above average at $67,300.

FIGURE 2

Age/Earnings Profile of Persons with Only a Bachelor's Degree in Biology
(Full-Time Workers, in 2002 Dollars)

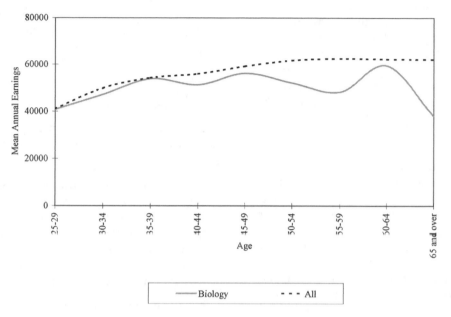

Table 2

Annual Salary of Full-Time Workers with Only a Bachelor's Degree
in Biology, Top 10 Occupations (in 2002 Dollars)

Earnings in Top 10 Occupations	All	Biology
Total	$54,171	$51,041
Health technologists and technicians	$42,774	$43,178
Top- and mid-level managers, executives, administrators	$74,051	$67,332
Biological scientists	$42,794	$43,542
Sales occupations, including retail	$52,378	$56,801
Teachers, secondary school	$40,355	$38,553
Other management-related occupations	$51,921	$54,058
Registered nurses, pharmacists, therapists, physician assistants	$53,508	$47,421
Insurance, securities, real estate, business services	$68,273	$60,588
Other marketing and sales occupations	$58,208	$61,130
All other engineers	$62,544	$56,890

On-the-Job Training

The career potential of a job is closely associated with the amount of work-related training on the job. Work-related training is regarded as an investment by firms because it makes workers more productive. Firms that invest in their workforce are more likely to offer pay increases and promotions to match the increasing productivity of their workers. Firms that do not invest in their workers are relatively less likely to offer pay increases and promotions. The incidence of work-related training among biology graduates is about the same as the participation rate in work-related training among all college graduates. While 68 percent of all college graduates acquire some kind of work-related training during a year, about two-thirds of employed biology graduates engage in a job-oriented training program during a year. Those employed in jobs that are related to the field are substantially more likely to participate in work-related workshops and seminars than persons employed in jobs that are unrelated to the biology major.

▶ Most of the training is associated with the development of specific professional skills related to the job, such as learning new lab techniques or procedures or learning new methods of conducting treatments or therapies.

▶ About one-third of the training participants receive instruction in managerial or supervisory areas. About one-fourth participate in training designed to improve communications skills.

▶ While training provides participants with new skills, many believe that such skill development will lead to advancement or a new position.

Post-Graduation Activities

The majority of biology majors earn some type of advanced degree after completing their undergraduate education. In fact, a higher proportion of those who major in biology go on to an advanced degree of some type than almost any other undergraduate major field of study. More than 1 in 5 biology bachelor's degree holders eventually earn a master's degree. About 7 percent earn a doctorate, and 25 percent earn a professional degree.

▶ Among those who earn a master's degree, one-quarter choose to study education in preparation for a teaching career. About 27 percent earn a master's degree in biology or a related biological science field, while 13 percent earn a master's degree in a health-related field.

▶ Clearly the majority of those who earn a master's degree build on their undergraduate education in biology. However, this is not the only pathway open to undergraduate majors at the master's level. More than 10 percent of biology majors who earn a master's degree study business at the graduate level. Others earn degrees in such fields as physics, mathematics, and engineering.

▶ More than two-thirds of biology majors who earn a doctorate study some biological sciences discipline. Health and education are also areas in which those with biology undergraduate degrees eventually earn doctoral degrees.

▶ At the professional level, virtually all those who earn a degree study medicine. Nearly 1 in 4 persons who earn a biology degree at the undergraduate level go on to earn a professional degree in medicine. A small proportion of professional degrees earned by biology majors is in the field of law.

About 84 percent of those with a bachelor's degree are employed, although about one-sixth of those working hold part-time positions usually because they choose to work part-time. Of those who are not employed, almost all have chosen not to work. Fewer than 2 percent of all those with a biology degree are unemployed and actively seeking work. About 1 in 5 of those not working are full-time students. However, many biology majors choose not to work in order to meet family responsibilities at home.

Employment Outlook

The demand for students with biology degrees is expected to remain relatively strong through 2010. Employment in 6 out of the top 10 occupations that employ biology graduates is projected to grow at a rate faster than the overall projected growth in the U.S. economy.

▶ Employment in the health technologists field is expected to grow by more than one-quarter through 2010, a rate of growth well above the national average

for all occupations and about the same rate of expansion as the demand for persons who hold a bachelor's degree. Similarly high rates of employment growth are projected for health professionals such as nurses, pharmacists, therapists, and physician assistants.

▶ The demand for biological scientists is projected to increase by 21 percent between 2000 and 2010. Nearly 8 percent of all biology graduates are employed as biological scientists.

▶ Management-related occupations and marketing and sales occupations, both important areas of employment for biology majors, are respectively projected to grow by 18 and 22 percent over the projections period.

▶ The growth in the number of school-age children is projected to keep the demand for secondary school teachers strong during the first decade of the 21st century. The demand for secondary school teachers is projected to increase by 18 percent between 2000 and 2010. Nearly 6 percent of all biology majors are employed as secondary school teachers.

Table 3
Projected Change in Employment in the Top 10 Occupations That Employ Persons with Only a Bachelor's Degree in Biology

Top 10 Occupations	Actual Employment in 2000 (000s)	Projected Employment in 2010 (000s)	Absolute Change (000s)	Percentage Change
Health technologists and technicians	2,192	2,773	581	26.5%
Top- and mid-level managers, executives, administrators	10,564	11,834	1,270	12.0%
Biological scientists	73	88	15	20.5%

(continued)

Table 3 (continued)

Projected Change in Employment in the Top 10 Occupations That Employ Persons with Only a Bachelor's Degree in Biology

Top 10 Occupations	Actual Employment in 2000 (000s)	Projected Employment in 2010 (000s)	Absolute Change (000s)	Percentage Change
Sales occupations, including retail	15,513	17,365	1,852	11.9%
Teachers, secondary school	1,113	1,314	201	18.1%
Other management-related occupations	4,956	5,801	845	17.1%
Registered nurses, pharmacists, therapists, physician assistants	2,908	3,698	790	27.2%
Insurance, securities, real estate, business services	1,548	1,726	178	11.5%
Other marketing and sales occupations	621	758	137	22.1%
All other engineers	253	254	1	0.4%

CHAPTER 53

Chemistry

All physical things, whether occurring naturally or artificially, are composed of chemicals. Chemists in basic research and development investigate the properties, composition, and structure of matter and the laws that govern the combination of elements and reactions of substances. In applied work, chemists create new products and processes, or they improve existing ones, such as plastics. In manufacturing, chemists specify the ingredients, mixing times, and temperatures for each stage in a production process. They monitor automated processes in the production of paint, and they conduct tests to assure that products meet prescribed standards.

Chemists often specialize in a subfield. Analytical chemists determine the structure, composition, and nature of substances, and they develop analytical techniques. For example, they identify the presence and concentration of chemical pollutants in air, water, and soil. Organic chemists study the chemistry of the vast number of carbon compounds. They have developed many commercial products, such as drugs and plastics. Inorganic chemists study compounds consisting mainly of elements other than carbon, such as those in electronics components. Physical chemists study the physical characteristics of atoms and molecules and investigate how chemical reactions work. Their research may result in new and better energy sources.

A chemistry curriculum includes biology, mathematics, and physics courses, as well as analytical, organic, inorganic, and physical chemistry. Computer skills that enable modeling and simulations are necessary to operate the computerized laboratory equipment.

Scientific, mathematical, and analytical thinking are critical abilities for chemists. Also, technical and manual skills are required to work in labs and with laboratory equipment. Because chemists often work on interdisciplinary teams, understanding the language and terminology of other disciplines is essential, and so is having knowledge of business, marketing, and economics. Leadership ability is important in situations that require chemists to supervise other staff. Good oral and written communication is necessary for report writing.

Beyond enjoying science and mathematics, chemists must like to work with their hands while building apparatus and performing scientific experiments. They enjoy mental challenges, working independently, and the satisfaction of developing practical solutions. Outcomes are achieved by perseverance, curiosity, and the ability to concentrate on detail.

Chemists value intellectual stimulation, where they expend a considerable amount of thought and reasoning. They search for new facts and ways to apply them. The use of mathematics is an integral part of this research. Chemists view themselves as creative in their work. The prestige of the field is a motivational force. The work and projects they are given are varied. Chemists expect to be paid well.

Chemists are serious and committed people. They are steadfast in their thinking. They often initiate projects independently and stay with them until completion. They have personal motivation, they can concentrate and follow logic, and they are thorough. Chemists enjoy being original in their pursuits, and they take pride in calling on their personal wealth of knowledge to solve problems.

Where Do Chemistry Majors Work?

Slightly less than 65 percent of persons who hold a bachelor's degree in chemistry work for private, for-profit businesses. About 1 out of 10 are self-employed as consultants to other organizations or as independent business owners. Chemistry majors also work in educational institutions and in the government. The educational sector employs 12 percent of chemistry majors, and another 11 percent work in the government. Few chemistry majors are employed in nonprofit charities or research foundations. The earnings of chemistry majors working in the private sector are much higher than those employed in education, government, or nonprofit organizations.

FIGURE 1

Percentage Distribution of Employed Persons with Only a Bachelor's Degree in Chemistry, by Major Sector of Economic Activity

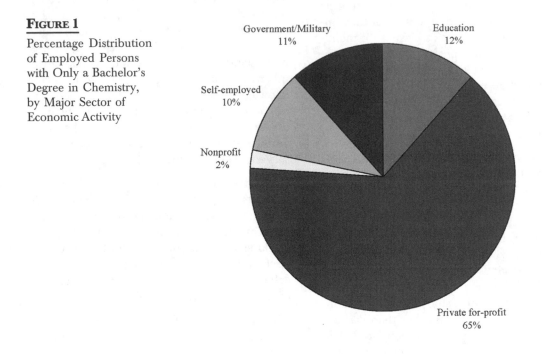

Government/Military 11%

Education 12%

Self-employed 10%

Nonprofit 2%

Private for-profit 65%

Occupations

Graduates of chemistry programs at the undergraduate level are generally employed in jobs that are connected to the major field of study. More than 70 percent work in jobs related to chemistry, and the majority of these persons view their current job as closely related to the field of chemistry. About one-quarter of all persons who earn a degree in chemistry are employed as chemists. However, most of those who are not employed as chemists do not work in a scientific occupation. Approximately 1 in 6 chemistry majors work in high-level managerial and administrative positions that are often related in some degree to the undergraduate field of study. Some chemistry majors are employed in engineering occupations, including chemical engineering. Nearly 30 percent of chemistry majors work in jobs unrelated to their undergraduate majors. Most often these individuals work in jobs outside of their major because of changes in their career aspirations. Those employed in jobs unrelated to the major have annual salaries that are close to the salaries in jobs related to chemistry.

Table 1
Top 10 Occupations That Employ Persons with Only a Bachelor's Degree in Chemistry

Top 10 Occupations	PERCENT OF EMPLOYED		
	All	Men	Women
Chemists, except biochemists	23.8	25.2	20.4
Top- and mid-level managers, executives, administrators	16.3	19.9	7.2
Sales occupations, including retail	6.2	7.5	3.0
Other management-related occupations	4.6	3.7	6.9
Miscellaneous engineers	2.9	3.1	2.5
Insurance, securities, real estate, business services	2.8	2.7	3.1
Other marketing and sales occupations	2.7	3.0	2.0
Biological scientists	2.6	1.4	5.7
Health technologists and technicians	2.6	1.4	5.7
Teachers, secondary school	2.3	2.2	2.4

- One-quarter of men with a bachelor's degree in chemistry work in the chemist occupation; only one-fifth of women with chemistry degrees are employed in the chemist occupation.

- Men are much more likely to become employed as managers and administrators than are women with a degree in chemistry. Men are more than two and one-half times more likely to be employed in high-level management positions than their female counterparts.

- Women with degrees in chemistry are spread out across a variety of occupations that are somewhat less connected to the chemistry major.

Activities on the Job

- Basic research activities are an important part of the job duties of many graduates of chemistry programs. Unlike most other employed persons with only a bachelor's degree, basic research is an important part of the work of chemistry program graduates.

- Employee supervision and overall managerial responsibilities are also key job duties of many chemistry degree holders.

- Substantial proportions of those who hold a degree in chemistry develop or utilize computer applications on the job.

Salaries

The annual salaries of persons with a bachelor's degree in chemistry are well above the salaries of the average college graduate. The annual salary averages $61,600 per year, about 14 percent more per year than the $54,200 earned by the average bachelor's degree holder in 2002-dollar terms. Annual salaries for young chemistry majors are quite high. Those between the ages of 25 and 29 earn $48,100 per year, a rate of pay well above that of other young bachelor's degree holders. Over time, the earnings of chemistry graduates increase. The skills and knowledge developed as a result of years of work experience result in higher productivity and higher wages as chemistry majors age. By the ages of 50 to 54, the average annual salary of a person with only a chemistry degree rises to $71,400.

- Chemistry graduates who work as employees of private, for-profit corporations have annual salaries of $64,900. Those employed by educational institutions earn much less. Their annual salaries average only $41,800.

- Graduates employed in jobs that are closely related to the field of study have no earnings advantage compared to those who work in jobs that are unrelated to the field.

The annual salary of persons with a degree in chemistry varies considerably by the occupation in which they work. Majors who proceed to managerial and administrative positions earn more than $81,800 per year, well above the average rate of pay for chemistry majors employed full-time. Those employed as chemists have annual salaries of $56,400 per year. Those employed in occupations that are not closely related to the field also have relatively high salaries. The earnings of persons with a degree in chemistry who work in insurance, real estate, and securities sales are more than $74,700 per year. Chemistry majors who are employed as biological scientists or in health technology fields have earnings that are well below the average for the major.

FIGURE 2

Age/Earnings Profile of Persons with Only a Bachelor's Degree in Chemistry
(Full-Time Workers, in 2002 Dollars)

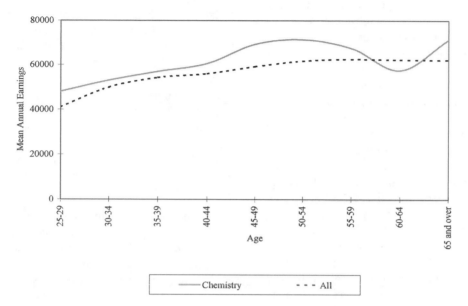

Table 2

Annual Salary of Full-Time Workers with Only a Bachelor's Degree
in Chemistry, Top 10 Occupations (In 2002 Dollars)

Earnings in Top 10 Occupations	All	Chemistry
Total	$54,171	$61,619
Chemists, except biochemists	$53,934	$56,357
Top- and mid-level managers, executives, administrators	$74,051	$81,839
Sales occupations, including retail	$52,378	$62,267
Other management-related occupations	$51,921	$67,463
Miscellaneous engineers	$62,544	$73,294
Insurance, securities, real estate, business services	$68,273	$74,684
Other marketing and sales occupations	$58,208	$66,094
Biological scientists	$42,794	$42,191
Health technologists and technicians	$42,774	$47,913
Teachers, secondary school	$40,355	$38,654

On-the-Job Training

The career potential of a job is closely associ-ated with the amount of work-related training on the job. Work-related training is regarded as an investment by firms because it makes work-ers more productive. Firms that invest in their workforce are more likely to offer pay increases and promotions to match the increasing pro-ductivity of their workers. Firms that do not in-vest in their workers are relatively less likely to offer pay increases and promotions. The inci-dence of work-related training among chemis-try graduates is lower than the participation rate in work-related training among all college graduates. While 68 percent of all college gradu-ates acquire some kind of work-related training during a year, fewer than two-thirds of all chem-istry majors participate in workshops or semi-nars that are designed to improve their work-based skills. Chemistry majors are less likely than the average college graduate to en-gage in professional training activities over the course of the year. Persons employed in private, for-profit firms are considerably more likely to participate in work-based training than those who work in education or who are self-employed.

▶ More than three-quarters of those who participate in training are developing additional professional skills related to the job in which they are employed.

▶ Nearly 40 percent receive training in employee supervision or related management-skills areas.

▶ Few chemistry majors participate in training to maintain an occupational license or certification. Often employers require or expect staff to participate in training to develop their skills. How-ever, many see training as an opportu-nity to advance their careers.

Post-Graduation Activities

Relatively high proportions of chemistry ma-jors continue their formal education after col-lege and earn an advanced degree of some type. Only 44 percent of chemistry graduates do not earn an advanced degree; 56 percent of those who earn a bachelor's degree in chemistry even-tually earn a graduate or professional degree. A very high fraction of those with an undergradu-ate degree in chemistry earn doctoral or profes-sional degrees (usually in medicine); more than one-third of all chemistry majors earn a doctor-ate or a medical doctor's degree.

▶ One out of 3 degree holders who earn a master's degree continues their studies in chemistry. One-fifth earn their master's degree in business, and an additional 10 percent earn their master's degree in education. About 10 percent branch out into health and biological sciences at the master's degree level.

▶ Two-thirds of the doctoral degrees earned are in the field of chemistry, and an additional 20 percent are in biologi-cal sciences.

▶ Few chemistry majors earn a professional degree in law. More than 13 percent of all persons who earn a bachelor's degree go on to complete a doctor of medicine degree. Chemistry at the undergraduate level is an important pathway to the study of medicine.

About 83 percent of persons with only a bachelor's degree are employed, most in full-time positions. About 3 out of 100 chemistry degree holders are officially unemployed; that is, they are not employed and are actively seek-ing work. Most unemployed chemistry majors decided that they did not want to work. A substantial proportion have taken early retirement, while others remain at home to meet family responsibilities.

Employment Outlook

Overall demand for college graduates is expected to increase at a relatively rapid pace (22.2 percent) between 2000 and 2010. The demand for chemists is expected to grow by 18 percent over the projections period, a rate of growth that is slower than the demand for all college graduates but faster than the rate of growth of overall employment in the U.S. economy (15.2 percent). Management and sales occupations that employ a substantial share of college graduates with degrees in chemistry are expected to grow at a rate that is faster than the overall projected growth in employment but slower than the average rate of growth of employment for those with a bachelor's degree.

Table 3

Projected Change in Employment in the Top 10 Occupations That Employ Persons with Only a Bachelor's Degree in Chemistry

Top 10 Occupations	Actual Employment in 2000 (000s)	Projected Employment in 2010 (000s)	Absolute Change (000s)	Percentage Change
Chemists, except biochemists	92	110	18	19.6%
Top- and mid-level managers, executives, administrators	10,564	11,834	1,270	12.0%
Sales occupations, including retail	15,513	17,365	1,852	11.9%
Other management-related occupations	4,956	5,801	845	17.1%
Miscellaneous engineers	253	254	1	0.4%
Insurance, securities, real estate, business services	1,548	1,726	178	11.5%
Other marketing and sales occupations	621	758	137	22.1%
Biological scientists	73	88	15	20.5%
Health technologists and technicians	2,192	2,773	581	26.5%
Teachers, secondary school	1,113	1,314	201	18.1%

CHAPTER 54

Forestry and Environmental Sciences

Currently most foresters and conservationists work for state and federal governments, managing public forests and parks. The number of these workers will decline, however, with the U.S. Forest Service's de-emphasis on timber programs. To reflect this trend, private industry's role in lumber and paper production will be highlighted in this discussion of forestry.

Foresters work with local forest owners and inventory the type, amount, and location of the timber. They develop an appraisal of the timber's value, negotiate the purchase, and write a contract for the sale. Afterward, they subcontract with loggers or pulpwood cutters for tree removal, aid in road layout, and monitor the contract's specifications and environmental requirements.

Foresters consider the business economics balanced with the environmental impact on natural resources ecosystems. They determine how best to conserve wildlife habitats, creek beds, and water and soil quality while complying with regulations. They supervise the planting and growing of new trees; choose and prepare the site; and use controlled burning, bulldozers, or herbicides to clear weeds, brush, and logging debris. Foresters advise on the type, number, and placement of trees to be planted, monitoring their growth and determining the best time for harvesting. If these professionals detect signs of disease or harmful insects, they decide the treatment to prevent the infestation of healthy trees.

Range managers (also called range conservationists, range ecologists, or range scientists) manage, improve, and protect rangelands to maximize their use without damaging the environment. Rangelands contain many natural resources, including grass and shrubs for animal grazing, wildlife habitats, water from vast watersheds, recreation facilities, and valuable mineral and energy resources. Range managers help ranchers attain optimum livestock production by determining the number and kind of animals to graze, the grazing system to use, and the best season for grazing. At the same time, however, range managers work to maintain soil stability and vegetation for other uses, such as wildlife habitats and outdoor recreation.

Soil conservationists provide technical assistance to farmers and ranchers concerned with the conservation of soil, water, and related natural resources. They develop programs designed to get the most productive use of land without damaging it. Conservationists visit areas with erosion problems, find the source of the problem, and help landowners and managers develop management practices to combat the problem and implement revegetation of disturbed sites.

Foresters and conservation scientists often specialize in one area, such as forest resource management, urban forestry, wood technology, or forest economics.

A forestry curriculum stresses science, mathematics, communications, computer science, forest economics, business administration, wetland analysis, water and soil quality, and wildlife conservation. An experiential component may be required. Range management course work combines plant, animal, and soil sciences with ecology and resource management. Additional courses are in economics, computer science, forestry, hydrology, agronomy, and wildlife and recreation. Few colleges offer programs in soil conservation.

Science, mathematics, and computer skills are required in forestry and conservation work. Increasingly, technology is being applied as aerial photographs are used for mapping large forest areas and land use, which requires spatial ability. Much of the business practice of a company is learned on the job. Interpersonal skills are needed, whether for use in timber sales or in providing consultation to forest owners, farmers, or ranchers. And specific skills are required in applying scientific principles in practical ways, such as rotating crops so that farm soil remains fertile, treating trees with the proper chemicals to prevent the spread of disease, or feeding cattle to produce prime quality beef.

The interests of foresters and conservation scientists follow an applied scientific orientation, stressing practical uses of natural resources. These professionals enjoy the outdoors, are mechanically inclined and physically strong, are willing to walk long distances in densely wooded areas to carry out their work, and work long hours to put out fires. Most work in southeastern and western states and Alaska.

As a group, they value the independence of making decisions on their own, variety, working with their minds, status gained within their community, outside work, and high achievement.

These workers enjoy privacy and solitude and are thoughtful in interpersonal exchanges. They are analytic thinkers, logical, objective, and practical. Forests grow, are damaged, die, and are regenerated, providing foresters and conservationists a time perspective within a continuum. They are keen observers and possess a strong memory for details.

Where Do Environmental Sciences Graduates Work?

The employment of a majority of environmental sciences graduates is split between the government sector and the private, for-profit sector of the economy. About 40 percent of the graduates work for businesses and corporations in the private, for-profit sector, particularly in the timber and paper industry and with farmers and ranchers. About 38 percent of the graduates find employment in the government sector, frequently managing public parks and forests. Only 12 percent of environmental sciences graduates are self-employed in their own business or practice, and 6 percent work in the education sector. Only 4 percent work in the nonprofit sector of the economy.

FIGURE 1

Percentage Distribution of Employed Persons with Only a Bachelor's Degree in Environmental Sciences, by Major Sector of Economic Activity

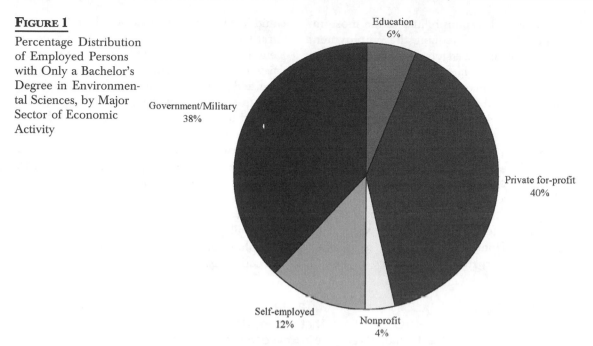

Education 6%

Government/Military 38%

Private for-profit 40%

Self-employed 12%

Nonprofit 4%

More than 6 in 10 environmental sciences graduates work in a job that is closely related or somewhat related to their undergraduate major field of study. About 35 percent are employed in jobs that are closely related to their major field, and 27 percent say their job is somewhat related to environmental sciences. The remaining graduates consider the duties that they perform at work to be unrelated to their major field of study.

Why do environmental sciences graduates work in unrelated jobs? A variety of factors underlie this employment decision. About 62 percent of environmental sciences majors who work in unrelated jobs cite pay and promotion opportunities as one of the factors underlying their employment decision. Cutbacks in the federal government budget, particularly in the area of public lands management, have reduced the number of jobs available to environmental sciences graduates. About 60 percent report the lack of jobs in the field as one of the reasons for working in a job that is not related to their field. Employment in the field of environmental

sciences is often located in the southwestern and western states and in Alaska; thus, these graduates are restricted in the places where they can find jobs related to their major. Consequently, 53 percent of graduates working in unrelated jobs cite job location as one of the factors influencing their employment decision. About 45 percent of graduates working in unrelated jobs cite the overall working environment as a factor in their employment decision, and the same proportion voluntarily work in unrelated jobs to change their career track. More than one-third cite family-related responsibilities for their employment choice.

When asked to select the most important reason for employment outside their major field of study, 26 percent choose better pay and promotion opportunities as the number one reason for their employment in an unrelated job. Another 25 percent find the lack of jobs in their field as the most important factor in their decision. About 17 percent rank a change in their career interests as the top reason, and 13 percent consider family-related responsibilities as the most important factor influencing the employment choice in an unrelated job. The general working environment is a factor for 5 percent of environmental sciences graduates working in unrelated jobs, and job location is selected as the number one reason by another 5 percent.

Occupations

Of all employed environmental sciences graduates, 64 percent are concentrated in the top 10 occupations that are predominant employers of these graduates. Often their jobs involve management of public lands, farms, or ranches. About 15 percent are employed in top- to mid-level executive, managerial, and administrative occupations. Another 11 percent are employed as forestry and conservation scientists; 6 percent work in agriculture, forestry, fishing, and related occupations. Sales and marketing occupations employ 9 percent of the graduates. About 6 percent work in mining and drilling occupations, and another 6 percent work as biological scientists. Only 5 percent work in protective-service occupations, mainly as park rangers. Another 4 percent work in other management-related occupations, usually as regulatory officers and management analysts. A small proportion, less than 3 percent, find employment in miscellaneous engineering occupations.

Table 1
Top 10 Occupations That Employ Persons with Only a Bachelor's Degree in Environmental Sciences

Top 10 Occupations	PERCENT OF EMPLOYED		
	All	Men	Women
Top- and mid-level managers, executives, administrators	15.0	17.0	6.2
Forestry and conservation scientists	11.3	12.6	5.7
Agriculture, forestry, fishing, and related occupations	6.0	6.5	3.7
Sales occupations, including retail	5.8	5.1	9.0
Biological scientists	5.6	5.2	7.5
Construction trades, miners, well drillers	5.2	6.4	0.0
Protective-service occupations	4.5	5.4	0.4
Other management-related occupations	4.4	5.1	1.5
Other marketing and sales occupations	3.4	2.6	7.2
Miscellaneous engineers	2.8	2.6	3.9

Of all employed environmental sciences graduates, 80 percent are men. The occupational employment patterns of male and female environmental sciences graduates are quite different; only 45 percent of female environmental sciences graduates are employed in the top 10 occupations, compared to 69 percent of male graduates. Several of the top 10 occupations are in the field of environmental sciences or are somewhat related to the field, indicating that female graduates are more likely to find employment outside the field.

▶ Male graduates are more concentrated than female graduates in top- to mid-level executive, administrative, and managerial occupations. While 17 percent of employed male graduates work in these occupations, only 6 percent of female graduates find jobs in these occupations.

▶ Males are twice as likely as females to work as forestry and environmental scientists. About 13 percent of male graduates are employed in these occupations, compared to 6 percent of female environmental sciences graduates.

▶ Men with bachelor's degrees in environmental sciences also are more likely than females to find employment in agriculture, forestry, fishing, mining, drilling, protective-service, and management-related occupations.

▶ Female graduates, however, are more likely than male graduates to work in sales and marketing occupations and as biological scientists.

Activities on the Job

The activities in which environmental sciences graduates spend most of their time at work are reflective of their employment patterns in different occupations.

▶ Twenty-two percent spend most of their typical workweek in management and administrative duties, and more than 60 percent spend at least 10 hours per week in performing these duties at work.

▶ Twelve percent of employed environmental sciences graduates spend most of their typical workweek in sales, purchasing, and marketing activities. As noted, sales and marketing occupations employ 9 percent of these graduates.

▶ Nine percent spend a major part of their typical workweek in providing professional services such as managerial or consulting services.

▶ Twelve percent spend most of their time at work in teaching activities. About one-quarter of all employed graduates state that they regularly spend at least some time in teaching activities.

▶ Applied research activities take up most of the time at work among 6 percent of employed environmental sciences graduates, and 5 percent perform computer applications, programming, and systems-development activities most of the time at their job.

Salaries

The average annual salary of environmental sciences graduates who have only a bachelor's degree and are employed full-time is $48,500, a level that is 11 percent lower than the average annual salary of all full-time employed college graduates. The salary of environmental sciences graduates increases with age, indicating that they get more productive and therefore can earn higher salaries as they spend more time on the job. The average salary of environmental sciences graduates is below the salary of all college graduates in most age groups.

▶ The average annual salary of environmental sciences graduates between the ages of 25 and 29 is $32,500. Graduates between the ages of 30 and 34 earn $40,100 annually. The average salary of those between the ages of 35 and 39 is $48,400.

▶ The average annual salary of environmental sciences graduates increases to $52,200 between the ages of 45 and 49 and peaks at $65,900 between the ages of 50 and 54.

The average annual salary of environmental sciences graduates who work in jobs that are closely related to their major field of study is about the same as the average salary of their counterparts who are employed in somewhat related jobs, and it is higher than the salary of those who are employed in jobs that are not related to their undergraduate major field of study. Closely related jobs pay full-time employed environmental sciences graduates $45,200 annually. Graduates employed in jobs that are somewhat related to their undergraduate major earn $45,500 per year, and those whose jobs are unrelated to their undergraduate major field of study earn an average annual salary of $40,700.

Environmental sciences graduates who are employed by businesses and corporations in the private, for-profit sector of the economy earn more than their counterparts employed in other sectors of the economy. The average annual salary of full-time environmental sciences graduates in this sector is $45,800. Self-employed graduates earn an average salary of $44,700 per year. Environmental sciences graduates who work in the government sector earn an average salary of $42,900 per year, and the education sector pays these graduates an average annual salary of $36,800. Full-time jobs in the private, nonprofit sector yield an average salary of only $31,700 per year.

Forestry and conservation scientist and biological scientist occupations pay environmental sciences graduates a somewhat higher salary than the average salary of all college graduates employed in these occupations. In the remaining 8 of the top 10 occupations, the average salary of environmental sciences graduates is lower than or equal to the average salary of all college graduates employed in these occupations.

▶ The highest average salary of environmental sciences graduates out of the 10 occupations is in high-level executive, administrative, and managerial occupations. Graduates employed in these occupations earn $61,100 per year. This area is considerably more likely to employ male than female environmental sciences graduates.

▶ The average salary of environmental sciences graduates employed in management-related occupations is $48,700 per year. The salary in sales occupations is the third highest out of the top 10 occupations—$47,800 per year.

▶ Foresters and conservation scientists with a bachelor's degree in environmental sciences earn $47,000 per year. The average salary of graduates employed in agriculture, forestry, and fishing occupations is $44,100 per year.

▶ The salary of biological scientists is lower relative to other occupations, and the lowest salary of all 10 occupations is earned by graduates who are employed in miscellaneous marketing and sales occupations—$40,600. This group employs 7 percent of female graduates and only 3 percent of their male counterparts.

FIGURE 2

Age/Earnings Profile of Persons with Only a Bachelor's Degree in Environmental Sciences (Full-Time Workers, in 2002 Dollars)

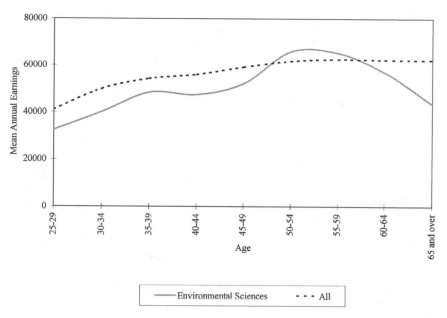

Table 2

Annual Salary of Full-Time Workers with Only a Bachelor's Degree in Environmental Sciences, Top 10 Occupations (in 2002 Dollars)

Earnings in Top 10 Occupations	All	Environmental Sciences
Total	$54,171	$48,456
Top- and mid-level managers, executives, administrators	$74,051	$61,120
Forestry, conservation scientists	$44,501	$47,002
Agriculture, forestry, fishing, and related occupations	$45,437	$44,080
Sales occupations, including retail	$52,378	$47,755
Biological scientists	$42,794	$43,542
Construction trades, miners, well drillers	$50,531	$46,923
Protective-service occupations	$49,130	$44,291
Other management-related occupations	$51,921	$48,664
Other marketing and sales occupations	$58,208	$40,577
Miscellaneous engineers	$62,544	$50,160

On-the-Job Training

The career potential of a job is closely associated with the amount of work-related training on the job. Work-related training is regarded as an investment by firms because it makes workers more productive. Firms that invest in their workforce are more likely to offer pay increases and promotions to match the increasing productivity of their workers. Firms that do not invest in their workers are relatively less likely to offer pay increases and promotions. The incidence of work-related training among environmental sciences graduates is much higher than the participation rate in work-related training among all college graduates. While 68 percent of all college graduates acquire some kind of work-related training during a year, 77 percent of environmental sciences majors engage in work-related training during a year.

- Of those environmental sciences graduates who receive some work-related training, 80 percent receive technical training in the occupation in which they are employed.

- Thirty-five percent of the training recipients participate in management or supervisor training.

- Twenty-nine percent receive training to improve their general professional skills, such as public speaking and business writing.

Although numerous reasons underlie the decision of environmental sciences graduates to participate in work-related training activities, workshops, or seminars, graduates most commonly cite four reasons. Included among these are a desire to improve skills and knowledge in the occupational area of their employment, a mandatory training requirement of the employer, increased opportunities for advancement in the form of a higher salary and promotion, and the need to obtain a professional license or certificate.

When asked to identify the most important reason to acquire training, 60 percent of environmental sciences graduates who undergo training identify the need to improve their occupational skills and knowledge. Another 14 percent report a mandatory training requirement by the employer as the most important factor underlying their involvement in work-related training. According to 9 percent of the training participants, the most important reason is the need to obtain a professional license or certificate, and 8 percent rank pay and promotion opportunities as the number one reason for their participation in work-related training activities. Slightly less than 5 percent rank the necessity to learn skills for a newly acquired position as the number one reason to acquire training.

Post-Graduation Activities

Of all graduates with a bachelor's degree in environmental sciences, 24 percent proceed to earn a postgraduate degree: 19 percent earn a master's degree, 3 percent earn a doctoral degree, and 2 percent earn a professional degree.

- Thirty-seven percent of all master's degrees earned by undergraduate environmental sciences majors are in the field of environmental sciences. About 13 percent of the degrees are earned in business, and 11 percent graduate with a master's degree in education. Another 7 percent choose to earn a master's degree in agricultural sciences and biological sciences, respectively.

- Thirty percent of the doctoral degrees are earned in environmental sciences, 26 percent in biological sciences, 13 percent in social sciences, and 12 percent in education.

▶ Sixty-four percent of the professional degrees of undergraduate environmental sciences majors are earned in the field of law, and the remaining 36 percent are earned in the health professions.

Of all environmental sciences graduates under the age of 65, 92 percent are employed. Only 1 percent are officially unemployed; in other words, they are not employed and are actively seeking employment. The remaining 7 percent are out of the labor force; that is, they are not employed and are not seeking employment. Two main reasons underlie the labor force withdrawal of environmental sciences graduates: 37 percent report that they are retired, and 20 percent cite family responsibilities as the reason for labor force withdrawal. Additionally, 9 percent do not have the need or desire to work, and the same proportion have a chronic illness or a disabling condition. Finally, 4 percent cite school enrollment as one of the reasons for their labor force withdrawal.

Employment Outlook

According to the U.S. Bureau of Labor Statistics, employment in occupations that require at least a bachelor's degree is expected to grow faster than employment in other sectors of the American labor market. Between 2000 and 2010, the U.S. economy is projected to add 22.2 million jobs, yielding an employment growth rate of 15.2 percent. Employment in occupations that require at least a bachelor's degree is projected to increase by 22 percent. The employment growth projections in the top 10 occupations that are most likely to employ environmental sciences graduates are presented in Table 3.

▶ The demand for biological scientists is projected to increase by 21 percent, from 73,000 jobs in 2000 to 88,000 jobs in 2010.

▶ The fastest growth in demand is projected in protective-service occupations. With an additional 809,000 jobs, the demand for these occupations is projected to grow by more than 26 percent between 2000 and 2010. The earnings of environmental sciences majors employed in these occupations are somewhat lower than the earnings of all environmental sciences majors. These occupations are significantly more likely to employ male than female graduates from this major field of study.

▶ Above-average growth is also projected in miscellaneous marketing and sales occupations. Between 2000 and 2010, employment in these occupations is projected to increase by 137,000, or 22 percent. Unfortunately, environmental sciences graduates employed in these occupations earn less than those employed in the remaining 9 occupations. These occupations are more likely to employ female graduates.

▶ Erosion of environmental protection laws has led to a slowdown in the projected increase in the demand for employment in environmental sciences and forestry occupations. Between 2000 and 2010, employment in these occupations, which are the second-largest employer of environmental sciences graduates, is projected to increase by just 2,000 jobs, or by 7 percent. Projections for the previous period (1996–2006) had estimated the demand for personnel in these occupations to grow by 19 percent.

▶ The largest employer of environmental sciences graduates—upper-level executive, administrative, and managerial occupations—is projected to add 1.27 million jobs between 2000 and 2010. This employment growth rate is an increase of 12 percent.

▶ Employment in occupations that are the third-largest employer of environmental science graduates is projected to increase by only 4 percent, from 1.43 million in 2000 to 1.48 million in 2010.

▶ Management-related occupations are projected to add 845,000 jobs, representing a growth rate of 17 percent over the projections period.

Table 3
Projected Change in Employment in the Top 10 Occupations That Employ Persons with Only a Bachelor's Degree in Environmental Sciences

Top 10 Occupations	Actual Employment in 2000 (000s)	Projected Employment in 2010 (000s)	Absolute Change (000s)	Percentage Change
Top- and mid-level managers, executives, administrators	10,564	11,834	1,270	12.0%
Forestry, conservation scientists	29	31	2	6.9%
Agriculture, forestry, fishing, and related occupations	1,429	1,480	51	3.6%
Sales occupations, including retail	15,513	17,365	1,852	11.9%
Biological scientists	73	88	15	20.5%
Construction trades, miners, well drillers	7,451	8,439	988	13.3%
Protective-service occupations	3,087	3,896	809	26.2%
Other management-related occupations	4,956	5,801	845	17.1%
Other marketing and sales occupations	621	758	137	22.1%
Miscellaneous engineers	253	254	1	0.4%

CHAPTER 55

Geology and Geophysics

Geology and geophysics are closely related fields, but there are many differences. Graduates of these programs are often known as geoscientists. Geologists study the composition, structure, and history of the earth's crust. They seek to find out how rocks are formed and what has happened to them since their formation. Geophysicists use the principles of physics and mathematics to study not only the earth's surface but also its internal composition; ground and surface waters; atmosphere; oceans; and magnetic, electrical, and gravitational forces. Both fields are applied to the exploration of natural resources and include such specific activities as designing landfill sites, preserving water supplies, and approving hazardous waste disposal.

The subdisciplines help differentiate the varied types of work that geoscientists perform. Petroleum geologists explore for oil and gas deposits by studying and mapping the subsurfaces of oceans and land. Mineralogists analyze and classify minerals and precious stones according to composition and structure. Paleontologists study fossils found in geological formations to trace the evolution of plant and animal life and the geologic history of the earth. Oceanographers study and map the ocean flow by using sensing devices aboard ships or underwater research crafts. Hydrologists examine the distribution, circulation, and physical properties of underground and surface water. They study the form and intensity of precipitation, its rate of infiltration into the soil and movement through the earth, and its return to the ocean and atmosphere.

The curriculum for all geoscientists covers mineralogy, paleontology, stratigraphy, structural geology, and geologic methods. When the goal of employment is environmental or regulatory work, course work includes hydrology, hazardous waste management, environmental legislation, chemistry, fluid mechanics, or geologic logging.

Scientific and technical abilities are essential to obtain knowledge of the field and to use the specialized equipment. Spatial skill is needed for comprehending maps, geologic structures, and the layout of sites. Computer skills are necessary for constructing models and data processing. Oral and written proficiency is needed in report writing and communicating findings. General memory, paying attention to detail, and working independently characterize many workers.

Geologists have scientific interests, which include analytical thinking and a research orientation in traditional core subjects such as chemistry, mathematics, and physics. A technical orientation will fit the laboratory and field exploration aspects of this field.

FIGURE 1

Percentage Distribution
of Employed Persons
with Only a Bachelor's
Degree in Geology, by
Major Sector of
Economic Activity

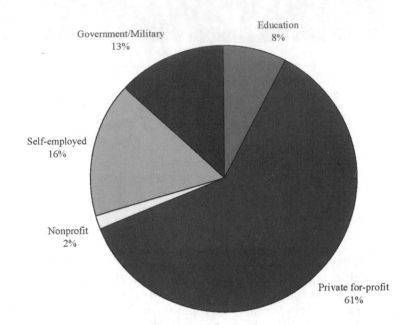

Government/Military
13%

Education
8%

Self-employed
16%

Nonprofit
2%

Private for-profit
61%

Geoscientists have a need for discovery through their imagination, curiosity, and study. Mental stimulation is important to them, but they are often stimulated more by working with data than with people. They value the opportunity for variety. They also value the recognition that their work affords them within their respective communities. Geoscientists tend to be quiet and can function easily without a lot of people contact. To others, they may seem impersonal, idea-oriented, and very objective in their interactions and opinions. Their analytical and careful approach in understanding things reflects their basic values.

Where Do Geology Majors Work?

More than 6 out of 10 employed geology graduates work for businesses and corporations in the private, for-profit sector. Another 16 percent work as self-employed workers in their own business or practice. More than one-fifth of all employed geology majors are employed by the government and the education sector. About 13 percent work for the government, and 8 percent are employed by educational institutions.

Not many geology majors work in jobs that are related to their major. Only one-third work in jobs that are closely related to their major field of study. Another 30 percent work in jobs that are somewhat related to their undergraduate major. The undergraduate curriculum of geology majors includes instruction in various science fields, particularly physics, mathematics, and chemistry. These skills enable geologists to get jobs in scientific fields that may not be closely related to their major. The remaining 36 percent of all employed geology majors work in jobs that are not at all related to their undergraduate major field of study.

Geology majors list numerous reasons for their employment in jobs that are unrelated to their major. More than one-half cite one or more of the following reasons for working outside their major field: better pay or promotion opportunities, job location, a change in their career interest, and a lack of available jobs that are related to their major. Almost 45 percent are turned away from working in related jobs because of such working conditions as hours of work, equipment at work, or the overall work environment. And 3 out of 10 also cite family-related reasons for their employment choice in an unrelated field.

Geology majors listed numerous reasons for working in an unrelated field. However, the single most important reason indicated by 35 percent of those who are employed in an unrelated job is the lack of available jobs in the field of geology. One-fifth chose to work in another field because of a change in their career interests. According to 16 percent of geology graduates working in unrelated jobs, the most important reason is availability of better pay and promotion opportunities outside the field.

Occupations

Geology majors are employed in a variety of occupations that span across scientific, technical, and business fields. Nearly 30 percent are employed as geologists and earth scientists. A top- to mid-level managerial, executive, or administrative occupation is second in the list of top 10 occupations that employ geology majors. About 12 percent of geology majors are employed in these occupations. Each of the remaining 8 out of the top 10 occupations employs less than 5 percent of working geology graduates. Occupations that involve insurance, stocks and bonds, real estate transactions, and business services employ 5 percent of geology graduates. The remaining occupations include scientific and technical occupations, such as miscellaneous engineering occupations, construction trades, miners and well diggers, engineering technologists and technicians, and computer programmers. Also included within the list of top 10 occupations are sales and services occupations and secondary school teachers.

Table 1
Top 10 Occupations That Employ Persons with Only a Bachelor's Degree in Geology

Top 10 Occupations	PERCENT OF EMPLOYED		
	All	Men	Women
Geologists, including earth scientists	29.1	29.5	25.9
Top- and mid-level managers, executives, administrators	12.3	13.0	7.8
Insurance, securities, real estate, business services	5.2	5.2	5.1
Miscellaneous engineers	4.1	3.9	5.8
Sales occupations, including retail	3.9	3.5	6.3
Other service occupations, except health	3.2	3.3	2.1
Teachers, secondary school	3.1	3.0	3.8
Construction trades, miners, well drillers	2.9	3.3	0.0
Miscellaneous engineering technologists and technicians	2.4	2.5	1.5
Computer programmers	2.1	2.1	1.7

▶ Men—who constitute more than 85 percent of all employed geology graduates—are slightly more likely than women to be employed as geologists and earth scientists.

▶ Upper-level managerial and administrative occupations are more likely to employ male geology graduates than female graduates: 13 percent versus 8 percent.

▶ Female geology majors are more likely than their male counterparts to be employed in miscellaneous engineering occupations, in sales occupations, and as teachers.

▶ Out of the top 10 employers of geology majors, 41 percent of male graduates are employed in scientific, engineering, and technical occupations versus only 35 percent of employed female geology graduates.

Activities on the Job

The diversity in the occupational employment of geology majors is reflected in the breadth of duties that they perform on their jobs.

▶ Although 69 percent of all employed geology graduates perform accounting, finance, and contractual duties as a regular part of their jobs, only 5 percent spend most of their time in a typical week performing these duties. Many geology majors perform these duties as a part of their jobs, but very few spend a majority of their time in performing them.

▶ The second major employer of geology majors is high-level managerial and administrative occupations. Hence, it is not surprising to find that 52 percent of employed geology majors perform management and administrative duties on a regular basis, and 13 percent spend a majority of their time during a typical week in performing these duties. A much higher proportion of geology majors perform managerial and administrative functions rather than accounting, finance, and contractual duties as a major part of their jobs.

▶ Computer applications, programming, and systems development are performed by 41 percent of employed geology majors on a regular basis. Nine percent report that these duties take up a majority of their time during a typical week.

▶ Fourteen percent of employed geology graduates engage intensively in applied research activities.

▶ Thirty-eight percent of employed geology majors regularly perform managerial duties to oversee the quality and efficiency of the production process, but only 4 percent consider these duties to constitute a major part of their jobs.

▶ About one-third of employed geology majors perform employee-relations duties, including recruiting, personnel development, and training. Only 3 percent spend a major part of their workweek in these activities.

▶ Sales, purchasing, and marketing duties are regularly performed by 32 percent, and 9 percent spend most of their time in performing these duties.

▶ Although one-quarter regularly engage in providing financial, legal, and health services, only 9 percent spend most of their time at work in these activities.

One-fifth of employed geology majors regularly engage in designing equipment and processes, and another one-fifth utilize research findings to produce materials and devices. However, only 2 to 3 percent spend the majority of their time in these tasks.

Fewer than one-fifth of geology graduates engage in teaching and basic research duties on their jobs. Only 6 percent spend most of their time in teaching duties, and 3 percent consider basic research to be the main part of their job.

Salaries

The average annual salary of geology graduates who are employed full-time is $58,400, a level that is nearly 8 percent higher than the average annual salary of all full-time employed college graduates. Like most college graduates, the salary of geology majors increases with age. This trend indicates that they get more productive and therefore can earn higher salaries as they spend more time on the job. The average annual salary of geology majors increases at a faster pace as they age, and the average salary exceeds that of all college graduates in all age groups.

The average annual salary of geology majors between the ages of 25 and 29 is $47,100. Graduates between the ages of 30 and 34 earn $47,200 annually.

The average annual earnings of geology graduates increase more rapidly as they get older. This increase widens the gap between their salary and that of all college graduates. The average annual salary of full-time geology graduates who are 35 to 39 years old is $58,300; those who are 40 to 44 years old earn $59,100 per year.

The average annual salary continues to increase to $64,900, $70,500, and $73,800, respectively, among geology graduates who are 45 to 49, 50 to 54, and 55 to 59 years old. The salary of full-time employed geology graduates peaks at $80,300 between the ages of 60 and 64.

The average annual salary of geology majors who work in jobs that are closely related to their major field of study is lower than those who are employed in jobs that are somewhat related to their major: $60,400 versus $61,900. Many graduates whose jobs are somewhat related to their undergraduate major are employed in high-level managerial, administrative, and sales jobs that are associated with higher salaries than the average salary of geologists and earth scientists whose jobs are closely related to their major. The average annual salary of full-time employed geology majors who are employed in unrelated jobs is $53,100.

Self-employed geology majors earn higher salaries than their counterparts employed in other sectors of the economy. Their annual average salary is $82,700. Almost 46 percent of all full-time, self-employed geology majors work in their own business as geologists, including earth scientists who serve as managers or administrators of their business. Another 13 percent work in their own insurance, securities, real estate, and business services business, and 12 percent work in their own business in sales occupations. Graduates who work for businesses and corporations in the private, for-profit sector earn an average salary of $55,000. The government sector pays geology graduates who are employed full-time an average annual salary of $49,800. The average annual salary of geology graduates employed by educational institutions is $46,400.

In 6 out of 10 top occupations that employ geology graduates, their average annual salary is higher than the salary of all college graduates. Within the group of geology majors, there are sizable variations in their average annual salary by the occupation in which they are employed.

▶ Graduates employed in sales occupations and those working in construction trades, including miners and well drillers, earn more than $77,600 annually.

▶ The average annual salary of geologists employed in high-level managerial and administrative occupations is $66,700.

▶ Employment of geology majors in insurance, securities, real estate, and business services occupations is associated with an average annual salary of $64,400.

▶ Graduates employed as geologists and earth scientists earn $58,600 per year, and those employed in miscellaneous engineering occupations earn $52,800.

▶ Employment in service, teaching, and engineering technician/technologist occupations among geology majors is associated with an average salary between $41,300 and $42,300.

FIGURE 2

Age/Earnings Profile of Persons with Only a Bachelor's Degree in Geology
(Full-Time Workers, in 2002 Dollars)

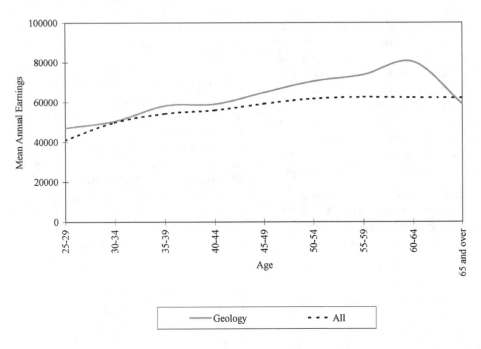

Table 2
Annual Salary of Full-Time Workers with Only a Bachelor's Degree in Geology, Top 10 Occupations (in 2002 Dollars)

Earnings in Top 10 Occupations	All	Geology
Total	$54,171	$58,393
Geologists, including earth scientists	$58,489	$58,561
Top- and mid-level managers, executives, administrators	$74,051	$66,729
Insurance, securities, real estate, business services	$68,273	$64,404
Miscellaneous engineers	$62,544	$52,789
Sales occupations, including retail	$52,378	$78,462
Other service occupations, except health	$39,984	$41,810
Teachers, secondary school	$40,355	$41,261
Construction trades, miners, well drillers	$50,531	$77,643
Miscellaneous engineering technologists and technicians	$47,416	$42,309
Computer programmers	$55,715	$62,508

On-the-Job Training

The career potential of a job is closely associated with the amount of work-related training on the job. Work-related training is regarded as an investment by firms because it makes workers more productive. Firms that invest in their work force are more likely to offer pay increases and promotions to match the increasing productivity of their workers. Firms that do not invest in their workers are relatively less likely to offer pay increases and promotions. Employed geology majors are just as likely as all employed college graduates to participate in work-related training. Almost 68 percent of all employed geology graduates receive some work-related training during a year.

▶ Of those geology majors who receive some training, 82 percent receive technical training in their occupational field.

▶ Thirty percent of the training recipients participate in management or supervisory training.

▶ Twenty-three percent receive training, such as public speaking and business writing, to improve their general professional skills.

Geology majors who receive work-related training offer numerous reasons for acquiring training. Eighty-eight percent participate in work-related training to improve their occupational skills and knowledge. More than one-half are required or expected by their employers to undergo training. Increased opportunity for promotion, advancement, and salary increases is the reason for 43 percent of geology majors to participate in work-related training; 29 percent cite the need to learn skills for a newly acquired position as one of the reasons for their participation in work-related training; and 23 percent participate in training to obtain a professional license or certificate.

When asked to identify the most important reason to acquire training, 59 percent of geology majors who undergo training identify the need to improve their occupational skills and knowledge. Another 12 percent report mandatory training requirements by the employer as the most important factor for their involvement in work-related training. About 1 in 10 consider the need to obtain a professional license or certificate as the main factor to influence their decision to undergo work-related training.

Post-Graduation Activities

Almost 4 out of 10 geology graduates with a bachelor's degree proceed to earn a postgraduate degree: 29 percent earn a master's degree, 9 percent graduate with a doctorate, and 2 percent earn a professional degree.

- Nearly 60 percent of the master's degrees are earned in geology, and 9 percent are earned in business management and administrative services. Six percent of master's degrees earned by geology majors are in the field of environmental sciences and other conservation and renewable natural resources fields.

- More than 80 percent of the doctoral degrees among undergraduate geology majors are earned in geology.

- Half of the professional degrees earned by undergraduate geology graduates are in the health fields, and one-third are in law.

Out of all geology graduates under the age of 65, 86 percent are employed. Only 4 percent are officially unemployed; that is, they are not employed and are actively seeking employment. The remaining 10 percent are out of the labor force; that is, they are not employed and are not seeking employment. About 45 percent of geology majors who withdraw from the labor force are retired. Postgraduate education activity among geology majors is the reason for 27 percent of the labor force withdrawal. Another 22 percent withdraw due to family responsibilities, and 10 percent lack the desire or need to work.

Employment Outlook

According to the projections by the U.S. Bureau of Labor Statistics, employment in occupations that require at least a bachelor's degree is expected to grow faster than employment in other sectors of the American labor market. Between 2000 and 2010, the U.S. economy is projected to add 22.2 million jobs, yielding an employment growth rate of 15.2 percent. The employment growth projections in the top 10 occupations that are most likely to employ geology graduates are presented in the following list and in Table 3:

- The demand for geologists and earth scientists is expected to grow by 20 percent. Between 2000 and 2010, these occupations are expected to add 5,000 jobs. These occupations employ 29 percent of geology graduates.

- The second-largest employer of geology majors—high-level managerial and administrative occupations—is projected to add more than 1.27 million jobs between 2000 and 2010, yielding an employment growth rate of 12 percent.

▶ Between 2000 and 2010, 178,000 additional jobs are projected in the insurance, securities, real estate, and business services occupations.

▶ Employment in non-health-services, secondary school teacher, and computer programming occupations is projected to increase by 16 to 18 percent. These occupations together employ 8 percent of all geology graduates with a bachelor's degree.

Table 3

Projected Change in Employment in the Top 10 Occupations That
Employ Persons with Only a Bachelor's Degree in Geology

Top 10 Occupations	Actual Employment in 2000 (000s)	Projected Employment in 2010 (000s)	Absolute Change (000s)	Percentage Change
Geologists, including earth scientists	25	30	5	20.0%
Top- and mid-level managers, executives, administrators	10,564	11,834	1,270	12.0%
Insurance, securities, real estate, business services	1,548	1,726	178	11.5%
Miscellaneous engineers	253	254	1	0.4%
Sales occupations, including retail	15,513	17,365	1,852	11.9%
Other service occupations, except health	9,652	11,287	1,635	16.9%
Teachers, secondary school	1,113	1,314	201	18.1%
Construction trades, miners, well drillers	7,451	8,439	988	13.3%
Miscellaneous engineering technologists and technicians	519	582	63	12.1%
Computer programmers	585	680	95	16.2%

CHAPTER 56

Microbiology and Biochemistry

Biologists and those in the life sciences have a preference for practicality, and they possess a matter-of-fact thinking style. They are dependable doers who often achieve by overcoming distractions. They are seen by others as intelligent, well informed, skilled at reasoning, and quick at reaching solutions. While some biologists are quiet and reserved, others are outgoing and imaginative.

Microbiology

Microbiologists investigate the growth and characteristics of microscopic organisms, such as bacteria, algae, or fungi. Medical microbiologists study the relationships between organisms and disease or the effect of antibiotics on microorganisms. Other microbiologists specialize in the environment; food; agriculture; virology, which is the study of viruses; or immunology, which is the study of mechanisms that fight infections. Many microbiologists use biotechnology to study cell production and human disease.

Microbiologists conduct bench research by using cellular, biochemical, or molecular techniques that are directed at discovering therapeutic agents, such as those that prevent or reverse insulin resistance in noninsulin-dependent diabetics. Microbiologists develop cell-based assays to assess the effects of lead components. Cell/molecular biology is a sub-specialty of microbiology. Cell/molecular biologists participate in the discovery of new molecules that inhibit growth/metastasis of tumors, and they are responsible for cloning/transfecting cells with suspected molecules to study results.

Scientific, computer, and mathematical skills are essential in this field, as is critical thinking. As a bench scientist, manual ability is also critical in the performance of the laboratory work involved. Leadership ability also is necessary because teams work on these projects. The scientist must be able to get projects started and to be organized so that goals are reached. Lastly, having well-developed language skills to communicate findings and write reports is highly rated.

A microbiologist's interests are that of a serious laboratory scientist. Microbiologists enjoy ideas, but they also have a wide range of interests. People nurture these diverse likes through liberal arts courses in the humanities and social sciences. Their likes definitely would be considered intellectual.

Microbiologists value creativity—the search to find new ways to do something. They have great confidence in their own minds, and they have the knowledge to accomplish their goals. They are motivated by the self-perceived importance of their work, which they know is difficult, and they seek success and the recognition of high achievement.

Biochemistry

Biochemists study the chemical composition of living things and the complex chemical combinations and reactions involved in metabolism, reproduction, growth, and heredity. Much of the work in biotechnology is done by biochemists and molecular biologists because this technology involves understanding the complex chemistry of life.

Biochemists perform laboratory assays. They develop protocols that use well-controlled and reproducible procedures on how to optimize cell-culture processes under the supervision of a supervisor with an advanced degree. Biochemists analyze, evaluate, and interpret test results. Documentation is critical, especially for validation purposes; thus, biochemists use mathematics and statistics. Their work can involve modern synthetic methods and techniques.

Biochemists need to be capable in science and mathematics, as well as with computer skills. Communicating well with assistants is important, and so is possessing language skills to write reports that include observations and documentation. Biochemists have good laboratory skills to design experiments, and they are detailed record keepers and accurate data-entry keyers. They may schedule their own activities. Their work demands sophistication in statistics. In research and development work, they need to develop goals with a team and work from the objectives developed.

A biochemist's interests are more like those of a chemist, but in the biological area; thus, the scientific interests are more technologically focused. Biochemists enjoy working with things and ideas. But they gain satisfaction in the humanitarian involvement of their work, which improves healing for others.

Biochemists value high achievement and success in doing something of importance. They enjoy the mental stimulation of working with their minds. They look for variety and diversion to satisfy their creative bent. Their laboratory and research work fits with their preference for independence.

Biophysics

Biophysicists study the physical principles of living cells and organisms and their electrical and mechanical energy. Biophysicists investigate the dynamics of seeing and hearing, the transmission of electrical impulses along nerves and muscles, and the damage to cells and tissues caused by X rays and nuclear particles. They examine the manner in which characteristics of plants and animals are carried forward through successive generations. They also examine the absorption of light by chlorophyll in photosynthesis or by pigments of the eye involved in vision. Biophysicists analyze functions of electronics and human brains. They also study the spatial configuration of submicroscopic molecules as proteins by using an X-ray or electron microscope. Specializations within this major may include the use of radiation and nuclear particles for cancer treatment or the use of atomic isotopes to discover transformation of substances in cells.

Education courses may include molecular biophysics and biophysical chemistry, membrane function, cell biology, function of neural systems, chemical biology, molecular and cellular immunology, population genetics, principles of genetic analysis, structure and function of proteins, nucleic acids, molecular mechanisms of gene control, and microbiology. Prerequisite courses would be in chemistry, biochemistry, physics, advanced mathematics, and biology.

Biophysics is a very demanding academic field. Students entering the program usually are excellent students and are equally proficient at the highest levels in language, mathematics, and science. People in the field are quick to figure things out. They are well read, as well as being very capable in mathematics, statistics, and computer usage. They have excellent spatial ability and are proficient in their fine motor skills so that they can use the equipment required by the laboratory work.

Biophysicists are interested in scientific, technical, and mechanical things. They also are good organizers and planners. Biophysicists must be good at conceptualizing, processing sophisticated data, and operating high-technology equipment. A person entering this major should like laboratory work.

Values associated with biophysics include independence, which is required to do a type of research that is challenging and demanding. A tolerance for doing detailed and repetitive bench laboratory work is accepted because of the mental challenge and opportunity for the use of creative talents. The laboratory work also demands physical stamina to satisfy personal goals for high achievement.

Where Do Microbiology/ Biochemistry Majors Work?

Bachelor's degree holders in microbiology/biochemistry are likely to find employment across all major sectors of the American economy. The majority of graduates in these fields work in wage and salary jobs for private, for-profit businesses. Nearly 1 in 5 microbiology/biochemistry majors who earned a bachelor's degree work for educational institutions at the primary, secondary, and university levels, with an additional 9 percent of the majors working for the government or military. About 8 percent of graduates from this major work in not-for-profit organizations, such as charities or research organizations.

FIGURE 1

Percentage Distribution of Employed Persons with Only a Bachelor's Degree in Microbiology/Biochemistry, by Major Sector of Economic Activity

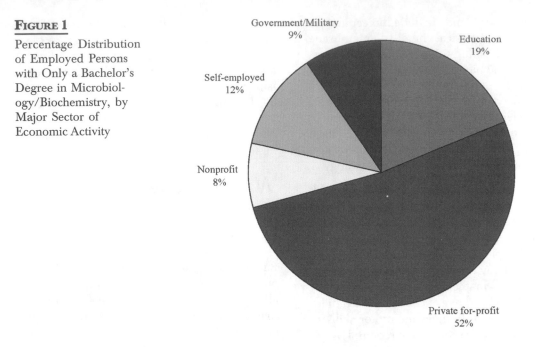

Government/Military
9%

Education
19%

Self-employed
12%

Nonprofit
8%

Private for-profit
52%

Occupations

The occupational areas most likely to employ persons who earn a bachelor's degree in microbiology/biochemistry are the health technologist and health technician areas. About 17 percent of all employed microbiology/biochemistry bachelor's degree holders work in these occupational areas. The biological scientists and chemist occupations employ an additional 17 percent of graduates of these majors. Nearly three-quarters of microbiology/biochemistry majors with a bachelor's degree are employed in jobs that are related to their undergraduate field of study. About one-quarter work in jobs that are unrelated to the undergraduate major. Those who work in jobs not related to the major do so because they see greater pay and promotion opportunities in unrelated jobs and because working conditions are superior outside of the field. Many of these individuals also have changed their career interests over time.

Table 1

Top 10 Occupations That Employ Persons with Only a Bachelor's Degree in Microbiology/Biochemistry

	PERCENT OF EMPLOYED		
Top 10 Occupations	**All**	**Men**	**Women**
Health technologists and technicians	17.4	9.8	25.8
Top- and mid-level managers, executives, administrators	13.4	17.0	9.5
Biological scientists	12.9	8.9	17.3

Top 10 Occupations	PERCENT OF EMPLOYED		
	All	Men	Women
Sales occupations, including retail	7.0	12.4	1.2
Chemists, except biochemists	4.6	4.1	5.1
Medical scientists (excluding practitioners)	4.2	2.3	6.3
Insurance, securities, real estate, business services	2.8	2.2	3.4
Other marketing and sales occupations	2.8	5.3	0.0
Teachers, secondary school	2.4	4.0	0.6
Protective-service occupations	2.3	4.4	0.0

▶ One in 4 women who earn a bachelor's degree in microbiology/biochemistry is employed as a health technologist or technician, while fewer than 1 in 10 men with bachelor's degrees in this field work as health technicians.

▶ About 13 percent of all graduates work in managerial and administrative positions, but men are nearly twice as likely as women to work in these occupations.

▶ About 13 percent of microbiology/biochemistry bachelor's degree holders are employed as biological scientists. The field of biological sciences is more likely to employ female than male graduates. While 9 percent of male microbiology/biochemistry graduates work as biological scientists, the share of female graduates working in this occupation is 17 percent.

Activities on the Job

Persons with bachelor's degrees in microbiology/biochemistry have a diverse set of job tasks and responsibilities ranging from administration and management to teaching and research.

▶ Microbiology/biochemistry bachelor's degree holders spend a substantial amount of time engaged in providing the professional services for which they were trained in the biological sciences. These professional services include many activities associated with the delivery of health care and support.

▶ Basic and applied research is an important component of the jobs of many bachelor's degree holders in the microbiology/biochemistry fields.

▶ As in most professional jobs, workers engage in administrative tasks revolving around accounting, finance, and contractual topics on a weekly basis.

> ◗ About one-third of bachelor's degree holders in this field are involved in the development and use of various types of computer applications.

Salaries

The annual salaries of persons with a bachelor's degree in microbiology/biochemistry are below that of the average for all bachelor's degree holders in the nation. Annual salaries for persons with a degree in microbiology or biochemistry average $49,500, while the earnings of all college graduates average about $54,200 per year. Thus microbiology/biochemistry graduates earn about 9 percent less per year than other college graduates. Younger graduates aged 25 to 29 have earnings that average about $38,100 per year. The earnings of graduates from this field of study increase with age. By age 40 to 44, the annual salary of bachelor's degree holders in this field of study increases to more than $65,000 per year. Additional years of work experience and the knowledge developed through on-the-job learning lead to this increase in earnings over time.

FIGURE 2

Age/Earnings Profile of Persons with Only a Bachelor's Degree in Microbiology/Biochemistry (Full-Time Workers, in 2002 Dollars)

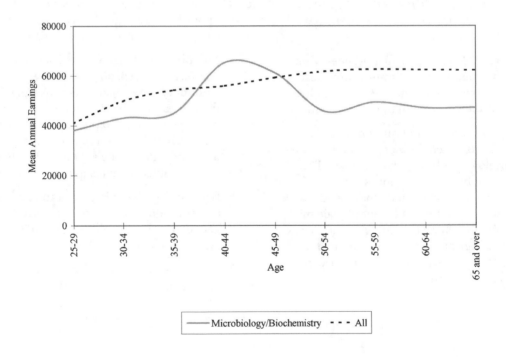

▶ Microbiology/biochemistry bachelor's degree holders who work in private, for-profit business organizations have annual salaries that are about 10 percent higher than the average of all employed persons with a degree in this major.

▶ While a substantial proportion of microbiology/biochemistry graduates work in the education sector, their earnings are relatively low. Those who work in educational institutions have annual salaries that are 25 percent below the average earnings of majors with degrees in this field.

▶ There appears to be little relationship between the salary levels of graduates and the degree to which their jobs are related to the field of study. Microbiology/biochemistry majors who work in jobs closely related to their field of study have no earnings advantage relative to those graduates employed in jobs unrelated to the field.

Microbiology/biochemistry majors who work as health technologists earn about $45,500 per year, a rate of pay nearly $2,700 more per year than bachelor's degree holders in other major fields of study employed in the same occupation. However, majors in this field who work as biological scientists earn somewhat less than the average pay of other college graduates employed in that field. Majors in this field who switch to jobs as managers and administrators have high earnings. Those microbiology/biochemistry majors who work in managerial and administrative positions have earnings that are almost 50 percent higher than the average earnings of graduates with bachelor's degrees in these fields.

Table 2

Annual Salary of Full-Time Workers with Only a Bachelor's Degree in Microbiology/Biochemistry, Top 10 Occupations (in 2002 Dollars)

Earnings in Top 10 Occupations	All	Microbiology/Biochemistry
Total	$54,171	$49,524
Health technologists and technicians	$42,774	$45,520
Top- and mid-level managers, executives, administrators	$74,051	$73,084
Biological scientists	$42,794	$40,862
Sales occupations, including retail	$52,378	$44,451
Chemists, except biochemists	$53,934	$53,921
Medical scientists (excluding practitioners)	$55,111	$64,090
Insurance, securities, real estate, business services	$68,273	$37,011
Other marketing and sales occupations	$58,208	$43,209
Teachers, secondary school	$40,355	$42,273
Protective-service occupations	$49,130	$53,542

On-the-Job Training

The career potential of a job is closely associated with the amount of work-related training on the job. Work-related training is regarded as an investment by firms because it makes workers more productive. Firms that invest in their workforce are more likely to offer pay increases and promotions to match the increasing productivity of their workers. Firms that do not invest in their workers are relatively less likely to offer pay increases and promotions. The overwhelming majority of microbiology/biochemistry majors engage in some type of training designed to enhance their productivity on the job. More than 70 percent received some type of training during the prior year. Persons in management and management-related occupations are most likely to participate in some type of training.

- Technical training directly related to the professional activities of microbiology/biochemistry majors is the predominant form of training received by these majors.

- Management and supervisory training is also a major training activity undertaken by graduates from these majors.

- About one-quarter of those who undergo some type of training do so in order to meet occupational license or certification requirements.

- Most of those who engage in training do so simply to expand their skills and abilities.

Post-Graduation Activities

Graduate education is an important long-term career pathway for persons who earn an undergraduate degree in either microbiology or biochemistry. Nearly one-half of all persons who earn a degree in either of these fields go on to earn an advanced degree of some type. Graduates with degrees in this field are more likely to earn an advanced degree than almost any other undergraduate major. More than 1 in 6 earn a master's degree, 12 percent earn a doctoral degree, and 1 in 5 earns a professional degree.

- One-quarter of those who earn a master's degree continue in the fields of microbiology or biochemistry. An additional 8 percent earn a master's degree in other biological sciences.

- One-sixth earn their master's degree in a health-related field.

- Fifteen percent of graduates in the microbiology/biochemistry fields earn a degree in business.

- Nearly 60 percent of those who go on to earn a Ph.D. continue their studies in microbiology/biochemistry. Another 25 percent earn a doctorate in another biological specialty.

- Among those who earn a professional degree, virtually all go on to pursue a medical degree, although a few majors from these undergraduate programs choose to earn a law degree.

About 87 percent of microbiology/biochemistry majors under the age of 65 are employed, and 9 out of 10 of these individuals work in full-time jobs. Most part-timers are voluntarily employed in these jobs; part-time schedules help them meet family obligations. Among those not working, fewer than 2 percent are officially classified as unemployed; that is, they are not employed and are actively seeking employment. Most of those not working have voluntarily chosen not to work. Many of these individuals have chosen to stay at home to meet family responsibilities.

Employment Outlook

The future demand for many of the occupations that employ graduates from microbiology/biochemistry appears to be relatively strong. Projections of employment produced by the U.S. Bureau of Labor Statistics indicate rapid growth in a number of occupational areas in which graduates from microbiology/biochemistry programs are often employed. The data in Table 3 includes are projections of employment change between 2000 and 2010 for those occupations identified as most likely to employ persons with a bachelor's degree in microbiology/biochemistry.

▶ The health technologist and technician occupation employs a substantial proportion of all graduates from this major. Employment in this occupation is expected to grow by more than 26 percent, adding 581,000 jobs between 2000 and 2010.

▶ Employment in the biological scientist occupation is also expected to increase by nearly 21 percent through 2010.

▶ Employment in the chemist occupation is expected to grow by nearly 20 percent between 2000 and 2010, a rate of growth somewhat above the average of overall employment levels in the economy.

▶ Employment growth in the medical scientist occupations and protective-service occupations is projected to be more than 26 percent. Nearly 7 percent of all microbiology/biochemistry graduates with a bachelor's degree are employed in these occupations.

Table 3
Projected Change in Employment in the Top 10 Occupations That
Employ Persons with Only a Bachelor's Degree in Microbiology/Biochemistry

Top 10 Occupations	Actual Employment in 2000 (000s)	Projected Employment in 2010 (000s)	Absolute Change (000s)	Percentage Change
Health technologists and technicians	2,192	2,773	581	26.5%
Top- and mid-level managers, executives, administrators	10,564	11,834	1,270	12.0%
Biological scientists	73	88	15	20.5%
Sales occupations, including retail	15,513	17,365	1,852	11.9%
Chemists, except biochemists	92	110	18	19.6%
Medical scientists (excluding practitioners)	37	47	10	27.0%
Insurance, securities, real estate, business services	1,548	1,726	178	11.5%
Other marketing and sales occupations	621	758	137	22.1%
Teachers, secondary school	1,113	1,314	201	18.1%
Protective-service occupations	3,087	3,896	809	26.2%

CHAPTER 57

Physics and Astronomy

Physics is the exploration and identification of the basic principles governing the structure and behavior of matter, the generation and transfer of energy, and the interaction of matter and energy. Physicists design and perform experiments with lasers, telescopes, and mass spectrometers. They attempt, through observation and analysis, to discover the laws that describe the forces of nature such as gravity, electromagnetism, and nuclear interactions. In laboratories they seek ways to apply physical laws and theories to problems in nuclear energy, electronics, optics, materials, communications, aerospace technology, navigation equipment, and medical instrumentation. Applied research builds on basic research as solid-state physics leading to the development of transistors and integrated circuits used in computers. Physicists also design research equipment. This equipment, too, has well-recognized uses. Lasers are used in surgery. Microwaves become ovens, and physicists' measuring devices analyze blood or the chemical content of food.

Astronomy is a subfield of physics. Astronomers use physics and mathematics to learn about the fundamental nature of the universe, including the sun, moon, planets, stars, and galaxies. Astronomers are researchers who analyze large quantities of data from observatories and satellites. These professionals spend only a few weeks each year making observations of the heavens with optical or radio telescopes.

Typical courses in the physics curriculum include mechanics, electromagnetics, optics, thermodynamics, atomic physics, and quantum mechanics. Social sciences course work such as economics and computer technology is typically required. Some universities may recommend engineering course work to prepare for bachelor entry-level positions such as technicians in laboratories.

In physics and astronomy, scientific, mathematical, and computer abilities are important. The field requires an imaginative mind. The abilities to plan, record, analyze, and produce oral and written reports are requirements that are often provided to others with non-physics backgrounds. Manual, technical, and spatial skills are used in performing research. Many of these professionals work in teams; thus, interpersonal skills are helpful.

The interests of physicists focus on ideas and data. They like science, research, and probing the unknown. Laboratory work is enjoyed. Some laboratory work does not allow for a great deal of socialization; however, interpersonal skills will be needed if any activity involves teamwork.

People in this field value research, working with their minds, and variety. They enjoy solving practical problems by using their analytical skills.

Physicists and astronomers have inquisitive minds, combined with perseverance. They have stick-to-itiveness qualities. They rely on imaginative minds. Astronomers, for example, rarely make observations by looking directly through a telescope because electronics-detecting and enhanced photographic equipment can "see" more than the human eye. Physicists are independent, meaning mostly that they can work by themselves, concentrating on and confident in their own abilities to solve problems.

Where Do Physics Majors Work?

Nearly 6 of 10 employed physics graduates work for businesses and corporations in the private, for-profit sector. Another 10 percent who work in the private, for-profit sector are self-employed in their own business or practice. The government sector employs 15 percent of physics graduates, and 13 percent work for educational institutions. Only 3 percent work in the private, nonprofit sector for tax-exempt or charitable organizations.

Nearly three-quarters of all employed physics graduates work in jobs that are either closely related or somewhat related to their major field of study. Most are employed in jobs that are somewhat related to their field of study. Only 29 percent consider their employment to be closely related to their major field of study, whereas 44 percent state that their employment is somewhat related to their major field of study. The undergraduate curriculum of physics majors includes instruction in other scientific fields,

particularly in computer technology and engineering. These skills enable physics graduates to secure employment in fields that may not be closely related to their undergraduate major. The rest of all employed physics graduates—27 percent—work in jobs that are not at all related to their undergraduate major field of study.

Physics majors who work in unrelated jobs list numerous reasons for their employment decision. Better pay and promotion opportunities are one of the reasons among 55 percent for working in an unrelated job. Nearly one-half voluntarily work in an unrelated job because of a desire to change careers, and 46 percent cite their inability to find a related job as one of the reasons to work outside their major field of study. One-third work in unrelated jobs because of the better overall working environment in those jobs compared to related jobs. Nearly one-fifth cite family-related reasons as one of the factors in the decision to work in an unrelated job.

Although physics majors working in unrelated jobs listed various reasons for their field of employment, the two most important reasons are a change in career interests and better pay and promotion opportunities. More than 25 percent cite a change in career interest, and another 25 percent report better pay and promotion opportunities as the most important reason for their employment in an unrelated job. About one-fifth cite their inability to find a related job as the number one reason for working in an unrelated job. Slightly more than 1 in 10 consider the overall working environment to be the most important reason for their employment in an unrelated job, and 7 percent consider family-related reasons to be the most important factor for working in an unrelated job.

FIGURE 1

Percentage Distribution of Employed Persons with Only a Bachelor's Degree in Physics, by Major Sector of Economic Activity

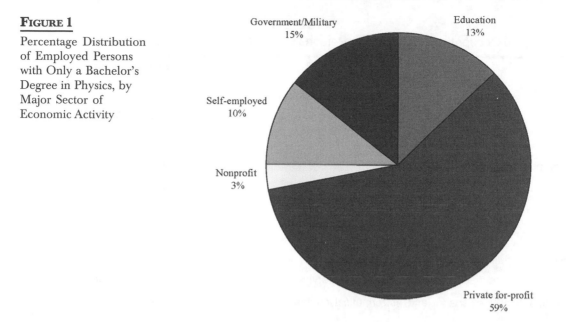

Government/Military
15%

Education
13%

Self-employed
10%

Nonprofit
3%

Private for-profit
59%

Occupations

The employment of physics graduates is somewhat concentrated in a few occupations. The top 10 occupations employ 58 percent of physics graduates. Many of these 10 predominant employers of physics graduates are in managerial, computer, and engineering fields. Of the top 10 occupations, 4 are engineering occupations, employing more than one-fifth of all employed physics graduates. These include 9 percent who are employed in electrical and electronics engineering, 5 percent in computer engineering, 3 percent in aerospace engineering, and 4.5 percent in other miscellaneous engineering occupations. Top- to mid-level managerial, executive, and administrative occupations employ 13 percent, 6 percent are employed as computer programmers, and 5 percent are employed as computer systems analysts. Only 6 percent of all employed physics graduates with only a bachelor's degree are employed as physicists and astronomers. Also included in the list of the top 10 employers of physics graduates are insurance, securities, real estate, and business services occupations, as well as secondary school teacher occupations.

Table 1

Top 10 Occupations That Employ Persons with Only a Bachelor's Degree in Physics

Top 10 Occupations	PERCENT OF EMPLOYED		
	All	Men	Women
Top- and mid-level managers, executives, administrators	12.8	13.7	3.0
Electrical and electronics engineers	8.8	9.3	3.1
Computer programmers	6.3	5.9	10.3
Physicists and astronomers	6.1	6.5	1.2
Computer engineers	5.4	5.8	1.2
Computer systems analysts	4.6	4.8	1.5
All other engineers	4.5	4.8	1.6
Insurance, securities, real estate, business services	3.5	3.8	0.0
Aeronautical, aerospace, and astronautical engineers	3.0	2.9	3.1
Teachers, secondary school	2.8	2.8	3.5

Men constitute more than 92 percent of all employed physics graduates. The employment patterns of male and female physics graduates are quite different. Men are more than twice as likely as women to be employed in one of the top 10 occupations. While 60 percent of men are employed in the top 10 occupations, only 29 percent of women work in them. As noted, these occupations are mostly in engineering, high-level management, and computers. Male and female employment is also very different within the group of top 10 occupations.

▶ Upper-level managerial and administrative occupations are considerably more likely to employ male physics graduates than women—14 percent versus 3 percent.

▶ Nearly 23 percent of men work in engineering occupations, compared to only 9 percent of female physics graduates.

▶ Female physics graduates also are much less likely than their male counterparts to be employed as computer systems analysts or as physicists and astronomers.

▶ Only 1 occupation among the top 10– computer programmer–employs a considerably larger proportion of female physics graduates than male physics graduates: 10 percent of female graduates are employed in this occupation, compared to 6.5 percent of male graduates.

Activities on the Job

The activities that physics graduates perform on the job are reflective of the occupations in which they are employed.

▶ Nearly 60 percent of all employed physics graduates perform computer applications, programming, and systems-development duties as a regular part of their jobs, and more than 21 percent spend most of their time in a typical workweek performing these duties. As noted, more than one-fifth of all employed physics graduates work in computer occupations.

▶ The other major employer of physics majors is high-level executive, managerial, and administrative occupations. Hence, it is not surprising to find that 49 percent of employed physics majors regularly perform management and administrative duties and 14 percent spend most of their time during a typical workweek in performing these duties. A much higher proportion of physics majors perform managerial and administrative functions rather than accounting, finance, and contractual duties as a major part of their jobs.

▶ Fewer than one-quarter of all employed physics graduates regularly perform sales, purchasing, and marketing duties, and 9 percent consider these duties to constitute a major part of their jobs.

▶ Physics graduates also design and develop products and equipment. Almost 45 percent of employed physics majors regularly engage in the designing of equipment and processes. Another 37 percent regularly use research findings to produce materials and devices in their jobs.

▶ More than one-third of employed physics graduates regularly engage in applied research, and 7 percent spend a major part of their time at work in this activity.

▶ Fewer than one-fifth engage regularly in teaching activities, and 5 percent spend most of their work time in teaching.

▶ Eleven percent regularly engage in providing professional services such as financial services, and 5 percent spend most of their time at work in these activities.

▶ About one-third of employed physics majors regularly perform employee-relations duties, including recruiting, personnel development, and training. Only 4 percent spend a major part of their workweek in these activities.

▶ Only 3 percent of physics graduates spend most of their time in basic research. Another 3 percent consider accounting, finance, and contractual duties to be a major part of their employment activities.

Salaries

The average annual salary of physics graduates who have only a bachelor's degree and are employed full-time is $69,600, a level that is nearly 30 percent higher than the average annual salary of all full-time employed college graduates. Like the salary of most college graduates, the salary of physics majors increases with age, indicating that they get more productive and therefore can earn higher salaries as they spend more time on the job. The average annual salary of physics majors increases at a faster pace as they age, and the average salary exceeds the average salary of all college graduates in every age range.

▶ The average annual salary of physics majors between the ages of 25 and 34 is $51,600.

- The average annual earnings of physics graduates increase rapidly as they get older, widening the gap between their salary and that of all college graduates. Graduates between the ages of 35 and 44 earn an average of $70,500 annually. The average annual salary of physics majors between the ages of 45 and 54 who are employed full-time is $75,900, and those between the ages of 55 and 64 earn $89,000 per year.

The average annual salary of physics majors who work in jobs that are closely related to their major field of study is somewhat lower than the salary of those who are employed in jobs that are somewhat related to their major–$73,300 versus $75,600. However, both of these groups of physics graduates earn considerably higher salaries than those who work in unrelated jobs. This last group earns an average annual salary of $55,300. Many graduates whose jobs are somewhat related to their undergraduate major are employed in high-level managerial and administrative occupations that are associated with very high salaries. The average salary of physics graduates employed in these occupations is $95,400 per year.

Physics graduates who are employed in the private, for-profit sector for businesses and corporations, or as self-employed workers in their own business or practice, earn higher salaries than those employed in the government or education sectors of the economy. The average annual salary of physics graduates who work for businesses and corporations in the private, for-profit sector is $73,800. Full-time self-employed physics graduates earn $72,800 per year. The government sector pays physics graduates who

are employed full-time an average annual salary of $63,100. The average annual remuneration of physics graduates employed by educational institutions is $49,500.

In all of the top 10 top occupations that employ physics graduates, the average annual salary is higher than the salary of all college graduates. Within the group of physics majors, the average annual salary varies somewhat by the occupation in which these graduates are employed.

- Graduates employed in top- to mid-level executive, managerial, and administrative occupations earn more than $95,400 annually.

- The almost 7 percent of physics graduates who are employed in the insurance, securities, real estate, and business services occupations and in aerospace engineering earn more than $79,000 per year.

- The other three engineering occupations in the list of the top 10 employers pay an average salary between $68,900 and $71,500 per year.

- Computer programmers with a bachelor's degree in physics earn more than $68,000 per year. This occupation is a major employer of female physics graduates, employing more than 10 percent of these graduates.

- Graduates employed as physicists and astronomers earn $66,500 per year, and the average annual pay of computer systems analysts with a bachelor's degree in physics is $60,700.

FIGURE 2

Age/Earnings Profile of Persons with Only a Bachelor's Degree in Physics
(Full-Time Workers, in 2002 Dollars)

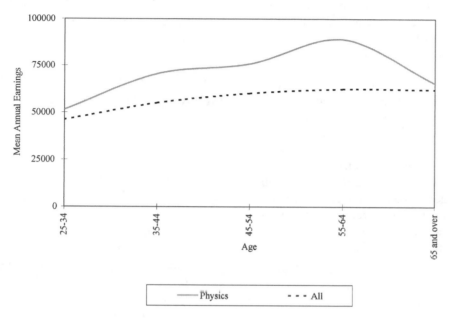

Table 2

Annual Salary of Full Time Workers with Only a Bachelor's Degree in Physics,
Top 10 Occupations (in 2002 Dollars)

Earnings In Top 10 Occupations	All	Physics
Total	$54,171	$69,612
Top- and mid-level managers, executives, administrators	$74,051	$95,394
Electrical and electronics engineers	$66,404	$68,878
Computer programmers	$55,715	$67,955
Physicists and astronomers	$65,246	$66,490
Computer engineers	$66,859	$71,500
Computer systems analysts	$59,818	$60,720
All other engineers	$62,544	$71,120
Insurance, securities, real estate, business services	$68,273	$82,707
Aeronautical, aerospace, and astronautical engineers	$68,111	$79,181
Teachers, secondary school	$40,355	$73,699

On-the-Job Training

The career potential of a job is closely associated with the amount of work-related training on the job. Work-related training is regarded as an investment by firms because it makes workers more productive. Firms that invest in their workforce are more likely to offer pay increases and promotions to match the increasing productivity of their workers. Firms that do not invest in their workers are relatively less likely to offer pay increases and promotions. Employed physics majors are somewhat less likely than all employed college graduates to participate in work-related training. Whereas 68 percent of all employed college graduates receive some work-related training during the year, the proportion of physics graduates who participate in work-related training during the year is 62 percent.

▶ Of those physics majors who receive some training during a year, 77 percent receive technical training in their occupational field.

▶ Thirty-eight percent of the training recipients participate in management or supervisor training.

▶ Twenty-six percent receive training to improve their general professional skills, such as public speaking and business writing.

Physics majors who receive work-related training offer numerous reasons for acquiring training. When asked to identify the most important reason to acquire training, 68 percent of physics majors who undergo training identify the need to improve their occupational skills and knowledge. Another 13 percent report a mandatory training requirement by the employer as the most important factor for their involvement in work-related training. Increased opportunity for a promotion and a higher salary is the most important factor influencing training decisions among 8 percent of employed graduates who acquire training. Only 3 percent consider license or certification requirements or the need to learn skills for a newly acquired position as the most important reason for their participation in work-related training.

Post-Graduation Activities

More than 6 of 10 physics graduates with a bachelor's degree proceed to earn a postgraduate degree: 32 percent earn a master's degree, 25 percent earn a doctorate, and 4 percent earn a professional degree.

▶ One-third of the master's degrees are earned in physics, 19 percent in engineering fields, 16 percent in the field of business management and administrative services, and 8 percent in education. About 6 percent of the master's degrees of undergraduate physics majors are earned in other physical sciences such as chemistry and geology, 5 percent are earned in computer and information sciences, and another 5 percent are earned in mathematics.

▶ More than 60 percent of the doctoral degrees among undergraduate physics majors are earned in physics, 11 percent in engineering, 7 percent in other physical sciences, and 5 percent in biology and other life sciences.

▶ Nearly 56 percent of the professional degrees earned by undergraduate physics graduates are in health professions, and 40 percent are in the field of law.

Of all physics graduates under the age of 65, 88 percent are employed. Only 5 percent are officially unemployed; in other words, they are not employed and are actively seeking employment.

The remaining 8 percent are out of the labor force; that is, they are not employed and are not seeking employment. Nearly 70 percent of physics graduates under the age of 65 who withdraw from the labor force report that they are retired, and 18 percent suffer from a chronic illness or disabling condition. Postgraduate educational activity among physics majors is one of the reasons for 7 percent of the labor force withdrawal. About 5 percent withdraw because of family responsibilities, and 2 percent have no desire or need to work.

Employment Outlook

According to the U.S. Bureau of Labor Statistics, employment in occupations that require at least a bachelor's degree is expected to grow faster than employment in other sectors of the American labor market. Between 2000 and 2010, the U.S. economy is projected to add 22.2 million jobs, yielding an employment growth rate of 15.2 percent. The employment growth projections in the top 10 occupations that are most likely to employ physics graduates are presented in Table 3.

▶ The area of high-level managerial and administrative occupations is projected to add 1.27 million jobs between 2000 and 2010, yielding an employment growth rate of 12 percent.

▶ The demand for electrical and electronics engineers is projected to grow at a rate of 11 percent, adding 31,000 jobs between 2000 and 2010. Computer engineering employment is projected to almost double over the same period. The employment in aerospace engineering occupations is projected to grow at a slightly below-average rate of 14 percent, and the demand for other miscellaneous engineering occupations is projected to remain almost unchanged over the projections period.

▶ Approximately 258,000 additional computer systems analyst jobs are projected to result in a 60 percent growth in employment in this occupation by the year 2010. The demand for computer programmers is projected to increase by 16 percent.

▶ Between 2000 and 2010, the demand for physicists and astronomers is projected to increase by 10 percent.

Table 3
Projected Change in Employment in the Top 10 Occupations That Employ
Persons with Only a Bachelor's Degree in Physics

Top 10 Occupations	Actual Employment in 2000 (000s)	Projected Employment in 2010 (000s)	Absolute Change (000s)	Percentage Change
Top- and mid-level managers, executives, administrators	10,564	11,834	1,270	12.0%
Electrical and electronic engineers	288	319	31	10.8%
Computer programmers	585	680	95	16.2%
Physicists and astronomers	10	11	1	10.0%
Computer engineers	757	1,436	679	89.7%
Computer systems analysts	431	689	258	59.9%
All other engineers	253	254	1	0.4%
Insurance, securities, real estate, business services	1,548	1,726	178	11.5%
Aeronautical, aerospace, and astronautical engineers	50	57	7	14.0%
Teachers, secondary school	1,113	1,314	201	18.1%

CHAPTER 58

Plant Food Sciences

Agricultural scientists often work with biological scientists and researchers in the application of biotechnological advances to agriculture. Agricultural scientists work in three general areas: basic or applied research; management or administration of marketing or production operations in companies that produce food products or agricultural chemicals, supplies, and machinery; and consulting for business firms or government. This section focuses on food science, plant science, and soil science.

Food science or technology helps meet consumer demand for healthful, safe, palatable, and convenient food products. These scientists use their knowledge of chemistry and microbiology to develop new or better ways of preserving, processing, packaging, storing, and delivering foods. Some scientists are involved in researching new food sources; analyzing food content to determine levels of vitamins, fats, sugar, or protein; or discovering substitutes for harmful or undesirable additives. In private industry, the scientists may work in test kitchens to investigate new processing techniques. In government, the scientists enforce regulations, inspect food processing, and ensure that sanitation, safety, quality, and waste-management standards are met.

Plant science covers a group of specialties. Agronomy is the study of crop production. Agronomists want to discover the best methods of planting, cultivating, and harvesting to get the most efficient yields and quality. Agronomists examine the effects of various climates and soils on such crops as cotton, corn, tobacco, or cereal grains. Plant breeders develop and select varieties through crossbreeding, mutating, and hybridization to improve crop yield; size; nutritional quality; maturity; and resistance to frost, drought, disease, and insects. Plant breeders use principles of genetics and knowledge of plant growth. The study of entomology aids in the control and elimination of agricultural and forest pests. Entomologists develop new and improved pesticides and biological methods, which include the use of natural enemies to control pests. Entomologists are involved in preventing importation and spread of injurious insects.

Soil scientists study the best soil types for growing different plants. These scientists conduct clinical analyses on the microorganism content of soil to determine microbial reactions and chemical and mineralogical relationships to plant growth. The scientists investigate responses of specific soil types to tillage; fertilization; nutrient transformations; crop rotation; environmental consequences; gas, water, or heat flow; and industrial-waste control practices.

All states have a land-grant college that offers agricultural science degrees. The general curriculum includes communications, economics, business, physical science, and life science courses. Students studying food science take courses, for example, in food chemistry, food analysis, food microbiology, and food-processing operations. Students in plant and soil science take courses in plant pathology, soil chemistry, entomology, plant physiology, biochemistry, and molecular biology.

Those interested in this field need scientific and mathematical abilities as well as business sense. Agricultural scientists use logic and scientific thinking in their analyses, and they apply methodologies to make judgments. The ability to recognize differences in size, form, color, and texture is important. Finger dexterity, eye/hand coordination, and the ability to use laboratory and scientific equipment are requirements. Those involved in management or administration are expected to develop budgets, to communicate orally and in writing, and to lead others.

People in this field should like science. Food technologists—similar to biologists—have more of a people orientation than a technical focus. Agronomists, animal breeders, entomologists, and soil scientists are more technologically oriented and have more similarities with those in the physical sciences than those in the life sciences.

Agricultural scientists value the opportunity to be independent, have variety, work with their mind, gain high achievement, and earn a good salary. These scientists value being practical and view themselves as "doers."

Overall, agricultural scientists generally are realistic and practical, and they possess an excellent memory for detail. They do care about ideas and learning. Everyone is not just concerned solely with applications—consider, for example, the intellectual field of genetics. However, agricultural scientists are doers. They will make a judgment as quickly as they have collected and observed enough to bring closure to a decision; then they will plan an operation or organize an activity.

Where Do Plant Food Sciences Majors Work?

Nearly 60 percent of all plant science graduates with only a bachelor's degree are employed in the private, for-profit sector of the economy. An additional 11 percent of plant science majors are self-employed; they operate their own for-profit businesses. The remaining plant science graduates work in government, educational organizations, and nonprofit organizations, including charities and public interest groups.

FIGURE 1

Percentage Distribution of Employed Persons with Only a Bachelor's Degree in Plant Food Sciences, by Major Sector of Economic Activity

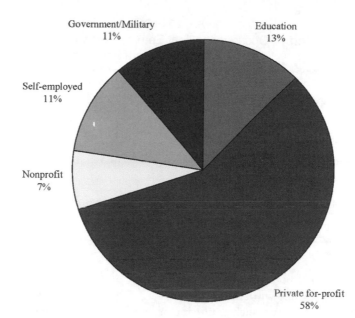

Government/Military
11%

Education
13%

Self-employed
11%

Nonprofit
7%

Private for-profit
58%

Occupations

Although many plant science majors work in jobs with titles that don't readily identify them as plant scientists, most graduates in this field report that they work in jobs related to plant science, sometimes in managerial or sales positions. Often graduates in these programs are employed as health professionals or technologists and technicians. Only about one-quarter of all plant science graduates work in jobs that are not related to their undergraduate major. Family responsibilities, limited pay, and limited promotional opportunities are the most frequently cited reasons for working in an unrelated job.

Table 1

Top 10 Occupations That Employ Persons with Only a Bachelor's Degree in Plant Food Sciences

Top 10 Occupations	PERCENT OF EMPLOYED		
	All	Men	Women
Top- and mid-level managers, executives, administrators	19.8	22.6	18.7
Registered nurses, pharmacists, therapists, physician assistants	19.4	1.2	26.8
Agricultural and food scientists	7.4	18.5	2.9
Sales occupations, including retail	6.3	4.7	6.9
Other marketing and sales occupations	3.9	6.0	3.0

(continued)

Table 1 (continued)
Top 10 Occupations That Employ Persons with Only a Bachelor's Degree in Plant Food Sciences

| | PERCENT OF EMPLOYED | | |
Top 10 Occupations	All	Men	Women
Other management-related occupations	3.8	1.9	4.6
Insurance, securities, real estate, business services	3.6	5.4	2.8
Health technologists and technicians	3.4	0.0	4.8
Other administrative (e.g., records clerks, telephone operators)	3.3	0.5	4.5
Personnel, training, and labor relations specialists	2.4	3.5	2.0

▶ More than 1 in 4 women with a degree in plant science work in one of the health professions, such as nursing or physical therapy. Relatively few women with degrees in the plant science field find work as food scientists.

▶ Men who earn undergraduate degrees in plant science are most likely to work in managerial or administrative positions or as agricultural or food scientists.

▶ A substantial portion of both men and women with degrees in this field find work as managers and administrators.

▶ Quality control and productivity management activities are regularly undertaken by 40 percent of employed plant science majors.

▶ Computer applications, programming, and systems-development activities are a regular part of work for 30 percent of employed majors in this field.

▶ Few graduates with a bachelor's degree in plant science are regularly involved in either basic- or applied-research activities.

Activities on the Job

Plant science majors working in full-time jobs perform a variety of tasks over the course of their workweek.

▶ Eighty percent are involved in accounting, contractual, or financial issues as a regular part of their weekly work activities.

▶ Sixty percent are involved in personnel and management issues over the course of a typical workweek.

Salaries

In 2002, plant food science majors with a bachelor's degree earned an average of $50,800 a year in a full-time job, compared to the average salary of $54,200 among all college graduates. As for most college graduates, the earnings of plant science majors rise with age. Therefore, as these individuals become more productive on the job, their earnings increase. This increase reflects their greater contributions to production. However, at most age levels, full-time plant science majors have earnings that are below those of the average college graduate with a bachelor's degree.

FIGURE 2

Age/Earnings Profile of Persons with Only a Bachelor's Degree in Plant Food Sciences
(Full-Time Workers, in 2002 Dollars)

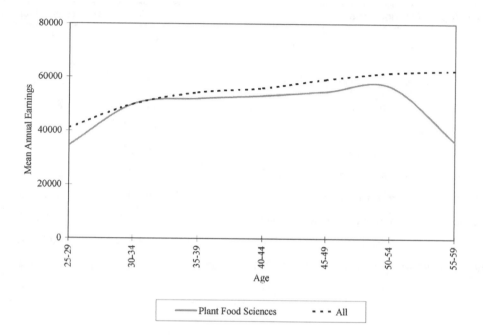

- On average, 25- to 29-year-old plant science majors employed in full-time jobs earn $34,600 per year.

- By ages 50–54, the average earnings for a plant science major with a bachelor's degree increase to $56,700 per year.

- Plant science majors employed in jobs unrelated to their undergraduate major field of study report higher earnings than graduates employed in jobs related to the field.

- Plant science graduates who work in the private, for-profit sector or in government organizations have annual salaries that are about one-quarter higher than those employed by nonprofit agencies or educational institutions.

The earnings of plant science majors vary sharply by occupation; however, within any occupational area, plant science graduates usually have lower salaries than the average college graduate employed in that occupation. Exceptions to this observation include high-level sales positions in stocks, bonds, futures and commodities, real estate, and pharmaceutical sales and agricultural and food scientist positions. Table 2 compares the earnings of plant science majors to all workers who have a bachelor's degree for the occupations in which plant science majors are most frequently employed.

Table 2

Annual Salary of Full-Time Workers with Only a Bachelor's Degree
in Plant Food Sciences, Top 10 Occupations (in 2002 Dollars)

Earnings in Top 10 Occupations	All	Plant Food Sciences
Total	$54,171	$50,840
Top- and mid-level managers, executives, administrators	$74,051	$54,968
Registered nurses, pharmacists, therapists, physician assistants	$53,508	$47,716
Agricultural and food scientists	$49,124	$52,972
Sales occupations, including retail	$52,378	$47,580
Other marketing and sales occupations	$58,208	$65,323
Other management-related occupations	$51,921	$51,402
Insurance, securities, real estate, business services	$68,273	$99,379
Health technologists and technicians	$42,774	$34,230
Other administrative (e.g., records clerks, telephone operators)	$34,547	$26,821
Personnel, training, and labor relations specialists	$51,577	$54,810

On-the-Job Learning

On-the-job learning is an important indicator of the long-term career potential of a job. Firms that invest in their workers at high rates are much more likely to offer pay increases and promotions than firms that fail to make such investments. Persons with a bachelor's degree in plant science are quite likely to have engaged in some type of job-related training during the past year. Nearly three-fourths of all employed plant science majors received training in the past year.

▸ Most often, the training received by plant science majors is related to a specific technical aspect of their current job.

▸ Managerial and supervisory training is also a major training investment. More than 45 percent of plant science majors had this type of training in the past year.

▸ Firms also make substantial investments in the communications skills of plant science majors. One-third of these majors have been to training that has developed either public speaking or writing skills.

Most persons receive training to develop and maintain skills that are needed for their current job. About one-third of all those who receive training believe that it increases their chances for promotion on the job.

Post-Graduation Activities

About one-quarter of all persons who earn an undergraduate degree in plant science go on to earn an advanced degree of some type. About

20 percent earn a master's degree, and 3 percent earn a doctorate. Few plant science majors go on to earn a professional degree in law or medicine.

▶ Of those plant science majors who earn a master's degree, about one-half receive their advanced degree in the plant sciences field, with an additional one-sixth earning degrees in health-related fields.

▶ Business and education fields are also popular choices for plant science majors who choose to earn a master's degree.

▶ One-half of all plant science majors who earn a doctoral degree continue to specialize in plant science. Most others who earn a doctorate do so in the biological or health sciences.

About 85 percent of plant science majors are employed, with fewer than 2.5 percent officially classified as unemployed; in other words, they are not employed and are actively seeking employment. Among the remainder, most people choose to withdraw voluntarily from the work force. About one-half of those not participating in the labor force choose to remain at home to meet family responsibilities.

Employment Outlook

The U.S. Bureau of Labor Statistics expects that employment growth in occupations that require a bachelor's degree or above will be among the most rapid of any sector of the American labor market. Between 2000 and 2010, total employment in the United States will likely increase by about 22.2 million jobs, or by about 15.2 percent. The forecasts for occupations that are the predominant employers of graduates of plant science undergraduate programs are substantially more optimistic.

▶ More than 1 in 4 women with a bachelor's degree in plant science are employed in a health profession. Employment in such fields as nursing, pharmacy, and counseling is expected to grow sharply in the future. Similarly, health technology careers, such as radiation technologists, are expected to increase at a rapid pace. Both sets of occupations are projected to increase employment by 26 percent to 27 percent. The projected rate of growth of employment in these occupations is 75 percent greater than the average for all occupations.

▶ Management and administrative jobs also employ a substantial number of plant science graduates. This field is projected to grow at a slightly below-average rate. Management opportunities will add an additional 1.27 million positions, accounting for a 12 percent growth rate through 2010.

▶ The demand for agricultural and food scientists will also grow at a below-average rate for all jobs in the economy. Total employment in this occupation is expected to increase by 12 percent through 2010.

Table 3

Projected Change in Employment in the Top 10 Occupations That Employ
Persons with Only a Bachelor's Degree in Plant Food Sciences

Top 10 Occupations	Actual Employment in 2000 (000s)	Projected Employment in 2010 (000s)	Absolute Change (000s)	Percentage Change
Top- and mid-level managers, executives, administrators	10,564	11,834	1,270	12.0%
Registered nurses, pharmacists, therapists, physician assistants	2,908	3,698	790	27.2%
Agricultural and food scientists	17	19	2	11.8%
Sales occupations, including retail	15,513	17,365	1,852	11.9%
Other marketing and sales occupations	621	758	137	22.1%
Other management-related occupations	4,956	5,801	845	17.1%
Insurance, securities, real estate, business services	1,548	1,726	178	11.5%
Health technologists and technicians	2,192	2,773	581	26.5%
Other administrative (e.g., records clerks, telephone operators)	16,911	18,522	1,611	9.5%
Personnel, training, and labor relations specialists	490	578	88	18.0%

Technology

CHAPTER 59

Computer Science

Computer science prepares students for the broad career title of computer scientist. This career consists of a wide range of professionals who design computers and the software that runs them. Computer scientists develop information technologies and develop and adapt principles for applying computers to new uses. Additionally, at a less-theoretical level of expertise is computer programming. Programming involves writing, testing, and maintaining the detailed directions and steps computers must execute to perform their functions.

Computer science is distinguished by the higher level of theoretical expertise and innovation applied to complex problems, as well as the creation or application of new technology. Computer scientists can be theorists, researchers, or inventors. They may work at an academic institution on theory, hardware, or language design. Others working in industry typically apply theory, develop specialized languages or information technologies, or design programming tools and knowledge-based systems.

Systems analysts who often specialize—for example, in financial or engineering systems—enable computer technology to solve and meet an organization's needs. These analysts study the goals of managers to understand the steps involved in the task and break down a process into programmable procedures. Solutions may include planning and developing new computer systems or devising ways to apply existing systems to additional operations. Analysts specify the information to be entered into the system, design the processing steps, and format the output to meet the users' needs. Analysts prepare specifications for hardware and software, flowchart diagrams, and structure charts for computer programmers to follow in implementing the system.

The role of computer programmers is changing with advances in technology, languages, and programming tools; however, programmers often are categorized differently within organizations from the personnel who are into more theoretical applications. Computer programs direct the computer on what to do, what information to identify and access, how to process it, and what equipment to use. Programs can be of different complexity, depending on whether a program is a simple accounting function or one for building a complex mathematical model. Programs are written in different languages, and most programmers know more than one programming language. Programmers' skills also vary depending on the systems on which they work, such as the Internet, World Wide Web, or mainframe. Some programmers have much wider responsibilities than those described here and are programmer-analysts, performing a combined role that integrates systems-analyst functions.

The educational pathway in this field is varied. In general, the future entrants into computer and information sciences will be different from current workers because of having more educational training. Course work will focus on learning programming skills, usually in more than one language, and using common software packages and information systems. Systems analysts can come either from computer science programs or, for example, from accounting, finance, or engineering programs. That is, this is a skills-based field, so the programming and language experience, the technology one has experienced, and the practical applications one has worked with are all considered factors by an employer who is viewing a person's appropriate training and background.

The abilities of computer and information scientists involve thinking logically and making constant decisions. They often must deal with a number of tasks simultaneously and be able to concentrate and pay close attention to detail. Although many work independently, they often work in teams on large projects. These professionals must be able to communicate effectively with computer personnel such as programmers and managers, as well as with users or other staff who have no technical computer background. The field has experienced tremendous growth; thus, many individuals have been promoted to leadership positions requiring these abilities as well as organizational skills. Most difficult in this fast-growing field is the dual need to perform one's work while simultaneously doing the continual study necessary to keep up-to-date with new technology.

The likes of computer and information scientists begin with scientific or technological interests. This field is generally an applied one.

Satisfaction can be gained from concrete applications and uses, whether in technology, business, or engineering. A systems orientation involves liking interaction with people, observing operations, and possessing knowledge of available hardware and software. Interpersonal skills are needed to fully understand the goals, processes, and desired outcomes of users in order to deliver a satisfactory systems solution. Programmers will be involved in work that continually demands thoroughness and attention to detail.

The values within computer and information sciences tend to be common but may be prioritized differently by those in varied roles. All prefer to work with their minds, with computer science professionals desiring this more, as well as the opportunity to be creative. Computer science is a high-paying field, which is attractive to many. Having challenging work and doing something that is important is also valued. Some view the opportunity for variety and diversity within the field as desirable.

Those in computer and information sciences are generally not impulsive. Their work style tends to be thorough and systematic. They project patience and perseverance in order to get it "right," complete a task, or pursue something they value. They project self-confidence because in their own minds they have carefully studied and analyzed something with the expectation that a logical outcome and result will follow. While highly practical, they may be seen as insensitive to the feelings of others.

Where Do Computer Science Majors Work?

A large majority of computer science graduates work in the private, for-profit sector of the economy for businesses and corporations or are self-employed in their own business or consulting practice. Businesses and corporations in the private, for-profit sector employ about 78 percent, and 5 percent are self-employed. Nearly 1 in 10 employed computer science graduates work in the government sector. The education sector employs only 5 percent of these graduates, and 3 percent work in the private, non-profit sector for tax-exempt or charitable organizations.

Classroom training in the field of computer science is more applicable in the labor market than the classroom instruction in many other fields of study. Widespread and increasing use of computers in every sector of the economy provides computer science graduates many employment opportunities within their field of expertise. Three-quarters of all employed graduates work in jobs that are closely related to their field, and another 18 percent are employed in jobs that are somewhat related to their undergraduate major field of study. Only 7 percent of computer science graduates are employed in jobs that are not related to their field of study.

Why do computer science graduates work in jobs that are not related to their undergraduate major field of study? The few—7 percent—graduates in this category offer a variety of reasons for their employment choice. General working conditions, including the hours of work and the overall working environment, are a factor in the decision to work in unrelated jobs among 45 percent of the graduates. Another 45 percent voluntarily choose to work in unrelated jobs because they want to change their career path—away from the field of computer science. About 42 percent cite pay and promotion opportunities as one of the reasons for working in an unrelated job. Another 42 percent of all computer science graduates working in jobs that are not related to their field report the lack of jobs in the field as one of the factors underlying their employment choice; this indication may mean that these graduates have failed to become skilled in new technologies. One-quarter cite family-related reasons for choosing to work in an unrelated job.

FIGURE 1

Percentage Distribution of Employed Persons with Only a Bachelor's Degree in Computer Science, by Major Sector of Economic Activity

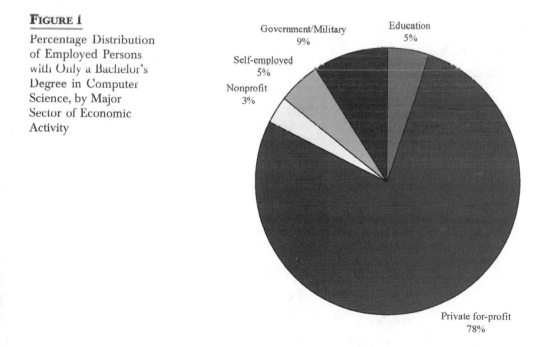

Government/Military
9%

Education
5%

Self-employed
5%

Nonprofit
3%

Private for-profit
78%

When asked to select the most important factor influencing their choice to work in an unrelated job, 28 percent cite pay and promotion opportunities. Another 22 percent are forced to work outside their field because of a lack of related jobs, and 19 percent report a change in career and professional interest. About 14 percent cite family-related reasons, and 7 percent report that the most important factor that influenced their employment in an unrelated job is the overall work environment.

Occupations

The employment of computer science graduates is very concentrated in a few occupations. The top 3 occupations employ 63 percent of the graduates, and the top 10 occupations employ 9 of 10 graduates. Computer science graduates are mainly employed in two broad types of occupations: computer-related occupations and managerial and administrative occupations. Another 28 percent are employed as computer programmers, 23 percent work as computer systems analysts, and 12 percent work as computer engineers. About 14 percent work in other computer and information science occupations. Only 8 percent of the graduates are employed in top- to mid-level executive, administrative, and managerial occupations. Another 2 percent work as accountants, auditors, and financial specialists. Finally, 2 percent work in other management-related occupations such as management analysts, purchasing agents, and regulatory occupations.

Table 1

Top 10 Occupations That Employ Persons with Only a Bachelor's Degree in Computer Science

Top 10 Occupations	PERCENT OF EMPLOYED		
	All	Men	Women
Computer programmers	27.5	27.0	28.6
Computer systems analysts	22.9	21.5	25.9
Computer engineers	12.4	13.5	10.0
Top- and mid-level managers, executives, administrators	8.1	10.2	3.7
Information systems scientists and analysts	6.1	6.1	6.1
Other computer and information science occupations	5.6	5.5	5.9
Computer scientists, except systems analysts	2.3	2.7	1.4
Accountants, auditors, other financial specialists	2.0	2.0	2.1
Other management-related occupations	1.7	1.9	1.2
Other administrative (e.g., record clerks, telephone operators)	1.4	0.8	2.5

Nearly 7 of 10 computer science graduates are men. The occupational employment patterns of male and female graduates are quite similar. Females are somewhat less concentrated than their male counterparts in the top 10 occupations. While 91 percent of male graduates work in the top 10 occupations, 87 percent of female graduates find employment in these occupations.

▶ The one area with the largest difference in employment of male and female computer science graduates is high-level managerial occupations. While 10 percent of male computer science graduates work in upper-level executive, administrative, and managerial occupations, only 4 percent of female graduates find employment in these occupations.

▶ Male graduates are somewhat more likely than female graduates to work as computer engineers.

▶ Female computer science graduates are slightly more likely than male graduates to work as computer systems analysts and computer programmers

Activities on the Job

The activities of computer science graduates on the job are reflective of their occupational employment.

▶ Ninety-one percent of all employed computer science graduates regularly perform computer applications, programming, and systems-development duties at work; 66 percent spend most of their time at work in these activities. This result is to be expected given the heavy concentration of their employment in computer-related occupations.

▶ Forty-three percent of the graduates spend at least 10 hours during the workweek in performing management and administrative tasks, and 9 percent who consider management and administration to be a major part of their jobs spend most of their time at work in performing these duties.

▶ Fifteen percent of employed computer science graduates regularly engage in sales, purchasing, and marketing activities; 3 percent spend most of their time during a typical week in performing these duties.

▶ Three percent each spend most of their workweek in performing the following activities: design of processes and equipment; development of products from results of applied research; or accounting, financial, and contractual duties and applied research.

▶ Only 2 percent spend most of their time at work in employee-relations activities, including recruiting, personnel development, and training. Another 2 percent of computer science graduates spend most of their time during a typical workweek in providing professional services such as computer consulting services and financial services.

Salaries

The average annual salary of computer science graduates who have only a bachelor's degree and are employed full-time is $58,800, a level that is nearly 9 percent higher than the average annual salary of all full-time employed college graduates. Like the salary of most college graduates, the salary of computer science graduates increases with age, indicating that they get more productive and therefore can earn higher salaries as they spend more time on the job. The field of computer science is largely composed of younger persons. Very few persons in the field are over the age of 45, and the number above the age of 55 is quite small. The rapid pace of change in the field indicates that the skills of older computer science graduates are quite different from the skills acquired by their younger counterparts in the classroom. Thus, although more mature graduates earn a degree in the field of computer science, their qualifications are different from their younger counterparts. The average annual salary of computer science majors increases at a faster pace as they age, and their average salary exceeds the average salary of all college graduates except those over the age of 45.

> ▶ The average annual salary of computer science graduates between the ages of 25 and 29 is $50,400. Between the ages of 30 and 34, the average annual salary rises to $57,300, followed by another increase to $65,900 for those between the ages of 35 and 39.

> ▶ The average salary of computer science graduates between the ages of 40 and 44 peaks at $72,300 per year.

Securing employment in a job that is closely related or somewhat related to their undergraduate major is associated with sizable salary advantages among computer science graduates. The average annual salary of graduates who work in closely related jobs is $58,300. Graduates with employment in jobs that are somewhat related to their major earn $59,300 per year. In contrast, the average salary of graduates employed full-time in a job that is not related to their field of study is only $43,300.

Computer science graduates who are self-employed in their own business or practice earn a higher average salary–$65,700–than graduates working in other sectors of the economy. Graduates who work for businesses and corporations in the private, for-profit sector of the economy earn $59,000 per year. The government sector pays computer science graduates an average annual salary of $51,800. As for most other college graduates from different majors, the educational sector pays full-time employed computer science graduates $44,600 per year, making education the lowest-paying employment sector.

The average salary of computer science graduates and all college graduates in each of these 10 occupations is presented in Table 3.

> ▶ The highest earnings of computer science graduates are in the top- to mid-level managerial and administrative occupations. The average salary of computer science graduates in these occupations–$81,400–is 10 percent higher than the average salary of all college graduates employed in these occupations. These occupations are more likely to employ male than female computer science graduates.

> ▶ Graduates working as computer scientists (except computer systems analysts) earn $66,900 per year. This occupation is more likely to employ male than female graduates.

> ▶ Computer engineering occupations pay computer science graduates $62,700 per year, and graduates employed in miscellaneous computer and information science occupations earn an average salary of $57,100 annually.

FIGURE 2

Age/Earnings Profile of Persons with Only a Bachelor's Degree in Computer Science (Full-Time Workers, in 2002 Dollars)

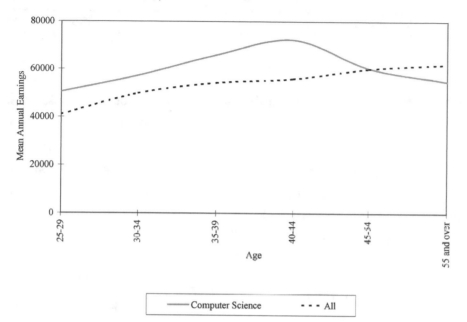

▶ Computer science graduates employed as computer systems analysts, the second-largest employer of these graduates, earn $58,700 per year. Computer programmers with a degree in computer science earn an average annual salary of $54,300.

▶ The average remuneration of computer science graduates employed in management-related occupations such as management analysts, purchasing agents, or regulatory officers is $56,900 per year.

▶ The lowest average salary of computer science graduates out of the top 10 occupations is in clerical jobs. The annual salary of graduates in this occupation is only $29,700 per year. However, this occupation employs slightly more than 1 percent of computer science graduates.

Table 2

Annual Salary of Full-Time Workers with Only a Bachelor's Degree in Computer Science, Top 10 Occupations (in 2002 Dollars)

Earnings in Top 10 Occupations	All	Computer Science
Total	$54,171	$58,848
Computer programmers	$55,715	$54,279

(continued)

Table 2 (continued)
Annual Salary of Full-Time Workers with Only a Bachelor's Degree
in Computer Science, Top 10 Occupations (in 2002 Dollars)

Earnings in Top 10 Occupations	All	Computer Science
Computer systems analysts	$59,818	$58,713
Computer engineers	$66,859	$62,741
Top- and mid-level managers, executives, administrators	$74,051	$81,383
Information systems scientists and analysts	$60,005	$60,950
Other computer and information science occupations	$54,228	$57,100
Computer scientists, except systems analysts	$64,834	$66,860
Accountants, auditors, other financial specialists	$57,382	$49,435
Other management-related occupations	$51,921	$56,872
Other administrative (e.g., records clerks, telephone operators)	$34,547	$29,687

On-the-Job Training

The career potential of a job is closely associated with the amount of work-related training on the job. Work-related training is regarded as an investment by firms because it makes workers more productive. Firms that invest in their workforce are more likely to offer pay increases and promotions to match the increasing productivity of their workers. Firms that do not invest in their workers are relatively less likely to offer pay increases and promotions. The rate of participation in work-related training during a year among employed computer science graduates is 70 percent, which is slightly higher than the 68-percent training participation rate of all college graduates.

▶ Of those computer science graduates who receive some training during the year, 90 percent receive technical training in the occupation in which they are employed.

▶ Thirty percent of the training recipients participate in management or supervisor training.

▶ Twenty-nine percent receive training to improve their general professional skills, such as public speaking and business writing.

Although numerous reasons underlie the decision of computer science majors to participate in work-related training activities, workshops, or seminars, four factors are most commonly cited. Included among these are a desire to improve skills and knowledge in the occupational area of their employment, increased opportunities for advancement in the form of a promotion and a higher salary, mandatory training requirements of the employer, and the need to acquire skills for a new position.

When asked to select the most important reason to acquire training, 71 percent of computer science majors who undergo training identify the need to improve their occupational skills and knowledge. About 9 percent report a mandatory training requirement by the employer as the most important factor for their involvement in work-related training. Another 9 percent rank improvement in their opportunities for a salary increase and promotion as the number one factor in influencing their decision to participate in work-related training. According to 8 percent, the most important factor for their involvement in training is the need to learn skills for a recently acquired position.

Post-Graduation Activities

Only 17 percent of computer science graduates with a bachelor's degree proceed to earn a post-graduate degree: 16 percent earn a master's degree, and 1 percent earn a doctoral degree.

- Forty-six percent earn their master's degree in the field of computer science, 29 percent earn a master's degree in business, and 9 percent earn a master's degree in an engineering field.

- Nearly 64 percent of all doctoral degrees of undergraduate computer science majors are earned in computer science. The remaining doctoral degrees are spread across mathematics, engineering, and the social sciences.

Of all computer science graduates under the age of 65, 92 percent are employed. Only 3 percent are officially unemployed; in other words, they are not employed and are actively seeking employment. The remaining 5 percent are out of the labor force; that is, they are not employed and are not seeking employment. Many of the labor force withdrawals among computer science graduates are attributable to family responsibilities and a lack of the need or desire to work. Nearly 69 percent cite family responsibilities as one of the reasons for labor force withdrawal. Another 27 percent cite a lack of the need or desire to work as the reason for their labor force withdrawal.

Employment Outlook

According to the U.S. Bureau of Labor Statistics, employment in occupations that require at least a bachelor's degree is expected to grow faster than employment in other sectors of the American labor market. Between 2000 and 2010, the U.S. economy is projected to add 22.2 million jobs, yielding an employment growth rate of 15.2 percent. The employment growth projections in the top 10 occupations that are most likely to employ computer science graduates are presented here.

- Employment in 8 of the top 10 occupations that hire computer science graduates is projected to grow at an above-average rate between 2000 and 2010.

- The demand for computer engineers is projected to increase by nearly 90 percent between 2000 and 2010. Employment in this occupation is expected to grow by 679,000 jobs over the projections period, reaching 1.44 million by 2010.

- A growth of 60 percent is projected in the computer systems analyst occupations and miscellaneous computer and information science occupations.

- The demand for computer programmers will grow at a rate slightly above the national average. With an additional 95,000 jobs, employment of computer programmers is expected to increase 16 percent over the projections period.

▶ The fourth-largest employer of computer science graduates—upper-level executive, administrative, and managerial occupations—is projected to add 1.27 million jobs between 2000 and 2010, yielding an employment growth rate of 12 percent. More than twice as many male computer science graduates as females are employed in these occupations. In addition, these jobs are associated with the highest salary among computer science graduates.

Table 3
Projected Change in Employment in the Top 10 Occupations That Employ Persons with Only a Bachelor's Degree in Computer Science

Top 10 Occupations	Actual Employment in 2000 (000s)	Projected Employment in 2010 (000s)	Absolute Change (000s)	Percentage Change
Computer programmers	585	680	95	16.2%
Computer systems analysts	431	689	258	59.9%
Computer engineers	757	1,436	679	89.7%
Top- and mid-level managers, executives, administrators	10,564	11,834	1,270	12.0%
Information systems scientists and analysts	28	39	11	39.3%
Other computer and information science occupations	203	326	123	60.6%
Computer scientists, except systems analysts	28	39	11	39.3%
Accountants, auditors, other financial specialists	2,115	2,481	366	17.3%
Other management-related occupations	4,956	5,801	845	17.1%
Other administrative (e.g., records clerks, telephone operators)	16,911	18,522	1,611	9.5%

CHAPTER 60

Data and Information Processing

This major trains people to be computer systems managers who will direct and plan programming, computer operation, and data processing and will coordinate the specifications for computer hardware, systems design, and software needs of an organization. This major helps a student analyze the computer and data information requirements of an organization, including the assignment, scheduling, and reviewing of the work of systems analysts, computer programmers, and computer operators. People study the personnel and computer hardware requirements with the objective to evaluate equipment alternatives and to make recommendations about purchasing decisions. Because of the broad scope of this field, managers must have the technical knowledge that allows them to understand and guide the work of subordinates and to explain the work in nontechnical terms to other managers. Some academic advisors suggest that a person wanting to pursue this field take a dual major such as accounting or computer operations and include systems analyst training.

The goal of this major is to examine how management information technology is used to identify and solve an organization's information-related problems. Programs typically build on the historical development of large and powerful computers that carry out organization-wide tasks such as database management. Then the focus is on "end-user computing," which deals with direct linkage of workers and user-friendly computer facilities. Increasingly, familiarization with networking workstations and PC configurations will be needed.

Educational requirements vary but usually involve courses in data operations, information resources, purchasing and materials management, business systems integration, and telecommunications and networks. Programming, quantitative models, and decision analysis are additional courses, plus the management requirements for a business degree. This program may be referred to as management information systems.

The abilities required of management information specialists (MIS) include logic, decision-making skills, and scientific and quantitative thinking and reasoning to solve complex problems. Knowledge of structural components of computer technology and programming are prerequisites. Oral and written communication abilities are necessary to deal with the many people doing information-related work. Organization and coordination skills are needed any time that one is working with an organizational system.

People in this field are interested in analytical thinking and in working with their minds and ideas. These workers appreciate the role and practicality of machines and have a preference for autonomy and directing others. Management information specialists blend a hybrid of technological and business orientations.

Values in this field include the satisfaction of creating a better solution to a complex issue. Usually people in the field have a research orientation and take pride in their logic and ability to develop answers. They also realize their skills and uniqueness and thus want to be well paid.

The computer nerd is the wrong image for people in the MIS field. MIS employees very likely can be outgoing, or they can be serious and less people-oriented. They are smart and enjoy using their minds to seek creative solutions. But they also can be very independent, practical, logical, and stubborn, with persistence and stick-to-itiveness to a task.

Where Do Data and Information Processing Graduates Work?

Businesses and corporations in the private, for-profit sector of the economy employ more than 70 percent of persons who graduate in the field of data and information processing. About 12 percent of all employed data and information processing graduates work in the government sector, and educational institutions employ 7 percent. The rate of self-employment among these graduates is low. Only 4 percent are self-employed in their own business or practice, and 5 percent work for private, nonprofit organizations.

Data and information processing graduates possess skills and knowledge that are directly applicable in the labor market. Many firms require data and information processing services. The extent of the practical application of these graduates' skills enables many of them to find jobs in their field. Nine-tenths of employed graduates work in jobs that are related to their undergraduate major field of study. About 66 percent work in jobs that are closely related to their major, and another 23 percent consider their jobs to be somewhat related to their undergraduate major. Only 10 percent of data and information processing graduates work in jobs that are not related to their undergraduate major.

The economic recession of 2001 had a powerful adverse impact on the employment of computer and information systems professionals. Job losses in the information industry in key geographic areas—including Boston's Route 128; the northern Virginia area; Denver, Colorado; the Research Triangle in North Carolina; Austin, Texas; and the Silicon Valley region of California—began an extended period of job loss in the nation. Unemployment and underemployment of information technology workers rose sharply, reversing the long-term labor-shortage conditions that had characterized these labor markets in the 1980s and 1990s. As the national economy recovers, growth in the demand for college graduates with strong IT backgrounds is expected to recover. However, firms will increasingly send more routine IT functions overseas for processing and analysis. Known as "offshoring," this practice may reduce the rapid pace of growth in demand for IT professionals.

FIGURE 1

Percentage Distribution of Employed Persons with Only a Bachelor's Degree in Data and Information Processing, by Major Sector of Economic Activity

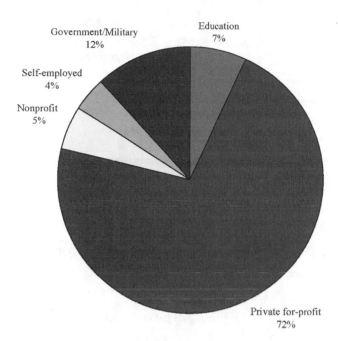

Government/Military
12%

Education
7%

Self-employed
4%

Nonprofit
5%

Private for-profit
72%

Why do 10 percent of data and information processing graduates work in unrelated jobs? They cite a variety of reasons for their employment in unrelated jobs. About 13 percent consider better pay and promotion opportunities outside their field as one of the reasons to work in those jobs. Another 39 percent are unable to find jobs that are related to their major field of study. About 21 percent work in unrelated jobs to change their career track, and another 21 percent cite job location as one of the reasons underlying their employment choice. About 15 percent are forced to work in unrelated jobs because of family-related reasons, and 8 percent cite general working conditions—such as hours of work, equipment at work, and the general working environment—as one of the factors that influence their decision.

When asked to select the most important reason for employment outside their major field of study, 30 percent of the graduates report that they are unable to find a job in their field, and 23 percent point to better pay and promotion opportunities. About 14 percent consider a change in career track as the most important factor to influence their decision to work in an unrelated job, and 8 percent consider job location as the top-ranking factor in their employment choice outside the field of data and information processing.

Occupations

The employment of data and information processing graduates is concentrated in a few occupations. Two-thirds are employed in only 4 occupations, and the top 10 occupations account for nearly 90 percent of all employed data and information processing graduates. Employment of data and information processing graduates is mainly concentrated in computer-related, managerial, and management-related occupations. About 68 percent are employed in computer-related occupations: programmers, computer systems analysts, information systems analysts, miscellaneous computer and information science

Table 1
Top 10 Occupations That Employ Persons with Only a Bachelor's Degree in Data and Information Processing

Top 10 Occupations	PERCENT OF EMPLOYED		
	All	Men	Women
Computer programmers	22.0	21.7	22.7
Computer systems analysts	20.4	17.8	24.9
Information systems scientists and analysts	16.3	17.7	14.0
Top- and mid-level managers, executives, administrators	8.5	11.3	4.0
Other computer and information science occupations	6.1	5.0	7.9
Other administrative (e.g., records clerks, telephone operators)	4.9	3.8	6.7
Other management-related occupations	3.9	4.7	2.5
Computer engineers	3.3	5.1	0.4
Insurance, securities, real estate, business services	1.9	1.3	2.7
Accountants, auditors, other financial specialists	1.4	0.3	3.3

occupations, and computer engineering occupations. About 9 percent are employed as top- to mid-level executives, managers, and administrators, and 4 percent work in management-related occupations such as management analysts and regulatory officers.

About 63 percent of employed data and information processing graduates are men. The occupational employment patterns of male and female data and information processing graduates are somewhat different.

- Female graduates are more likely than males to work as computer systems analysts. One-quarter of employed female graduates work in this occupation, compared to 18 percent of their male counterparts.

- Female graduates also are more likely than male graduates to work in clerical and administrative support occupations—7 percent versus 4 percent.

- Male graduates are much more likely than female graduates to work as top- to mid-level executives, administrators, and managers. Nearly 11 percent of all employed male graduates work in these occupations, compared to only 4 percent of employed female graduates.

- Men with a bachelor's degree in data and information processing also are more likely than female graduates to work as information systems scientists—18 versus 14 percent.

- The occupation of computer engineering also is more likely to hire male than female data and information processing graduates. While 5 percent of male graduates are employed as computer engineers, only 0.4 percent of their female counterparts work in this occupation.

Activities on the Job

The activities in which data and information processing graduates engage at work are closely related to the occupation in which they are employed.

- Eighty-six percent of all employed data and information processing graduates regularly spend time at work in computer applications, programming, and systems-development activities, while 59 percent spend a major part of their typical workweek in performing computer application duties.

- While 45 percent of employed data and information processing graduates report that they spend at least 10 hours per week in management and administration duties at work, 8 percent indicate that they spend most of their time at work on these activities.

- Only 5 percent of the graduates spend most of their time at work on sales, purchasing, and marketing activities.

- Applied research is the main activity at work among 4 percent of employed data and information processing graduates. Another 4 percent spend most of their workweek on accounting, finance, and contractual duties.

Salaries

The average annual salary of data and information processing graduates who have only a bachelor's degree and are employed full-time is $52,100, a level that is only 4 percent lower than the average annual salary of all full-time employed college graduates. Like the salary of most college graduates, the salary of data and information processing graduates increases with age, indicating that they get more productive and therefore can earn higher salaries as they spend more time on the job. Within each age range, the average salary of data and information processing graduates is quite close to the average salary of all college graduates in those age groups.

- The average annual salary of data and information processing graduates between the ages of 25 and 29 is $43,300. Graduates between the ages of 30 and 34 earn $52,500 annually.

- The average annual salary of data and information processing graduates increases to $58,400 between the ages of 35 and 39. The average annual salary of data and information processing graduates peaks between the ages of 45 to 49 at $65,800 per year.

The average annual salary of data and information processing graduates who work in jobs that are related to their major field of study is considerably higher than the salary of graduates who work in jobs that are not related to their undergraduate major. Closely related jobs pay full-time employed data and information processing graduates $54,700 annually. Graduates employed in somewhat related jobs earn $47,400 per year, and those whose jobs are unrelated to their undergraduate field earn $46,100 per year.

FIGURE 2

Age/Earnings Profile of Persons with Only a Bachelor's Degree in Data and Information Processing (Full-Time Workers, in 2002 Dollars)

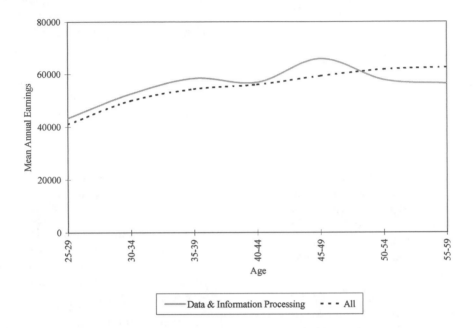

Earning an average salary of $53,700 annually, data and information processing graduates who work in the private, for-profit sector of the economy for businesses and corporations have a higher salary than those who are employed in other sectors of the economy. The remuneration of data and information processing graduates in the government sector is $46,600 per year. The average salary of data and information processing graduates employed in the education sector is $45,200 per year.

The average annual salary of data and information processing graduates in most of the top 10 occupations that are their predominant employers is below the salary of all college graduates employed in those occupations. The average annual salary of data and information processing graduates and all college graduates in the top 10 occupations is presented here.

▶ Data and information processing graduates employed in high-level executive, administrative, and managerial occupations earn an average annual salary of $68,300. This group is a predominant employer of male graduates.

▶ Another predominant employer of male data and information processing graduates—computer engineering—pays graduates an annual average salary of $57,600.

▶ Information systems scientists with a bachelor's degree in data and information processing earn an average annual salary of $55,400. Their counterparts who are employed as computer systems analysts earn $54,000 per year. Graduates employed as computer programmers earn an average salary of $50,800 annually.

Table 2
Annual Salary of Full-Time Workers with Only a Bachelor's Degree
in Data and Information Processing, Top 10 Occupations (in 2002 Dollars)

Earnings in Top 10 Occupations	All	Data and Information Processing
Total	$54,171	$52,146
Computer programmers	$55,715	$50,754
Computer systems analysts	$59,818	$54,042
Information systems scientists and analysts	$60,005	$55,433
Top- and mid-level managers, executives, administrators	$74,051	$68,258
Other computer and information science occupations	$54,228	$54,483
Other administrative (e.g., records clerks, telephone operators)	$34,547	$36,085
Other management-related occupations	$51,921	$52,208
Computer engineers	$66,859	$57,597
Insurance, securities, real estate, business services	$68,273	$43,416
Accountants, auditors, other financial specialists	$57,382	$45,346

▶ The average salary of data and information processing graduates employed in management-related occupations such as management analysts, purchasing agents, and regulatory officers is $52,200 per year.

▶ Clerical and administrative occupations pay data and information processing graduates the lowest salary of the top 10 occupations–$36,100 per year.

On-the-Job Training

The career potential of a job is closely associated with the amount of work-related training on the job. Work-related training is regarded as an investment by firms because it makes workers more productive. Firms that invest in their workforce are more likely to offer pay increases and promotions to match the increasing productivity of their workers. Firms that do not invest in their workers are relatively less likely to offer pay increases and promotions. The incidence of work-related training among data and information processing graduates is slightly higher than the rate of participation in work-related training among all college graduates. While 68 percent of all college graduates acquire some kind of work-related training during a year, nearly 71 percent of data and information processing graduates annually engage in work-related training.

▶ Of those data and information processing graduates who receive some training during the year, 93 percent receive technical training in the occupation in which they are employed.

- Thirty-one percent of the training recipients participate in management or supervisory training.

- Twenty-seven percent receive training to improve their general professional skills, such as public speaking and business writing.

Although numerous reasons underlie the decision of data and information processing graduates to participate in work-related training activities, workshops, or seminars, four factors are most commonly cited. Included among these are a desire to improve skills and knowledge in the occupational area of their employment, increased opportunities for advancement in the form of a higher salary and promotion, mandatory training requirements of the employer, and the need to learn new skills for a newly acquired position. About 94 percent of data and information processing graduates participate in work-related training to improve their occupational skills and knowledge. Increased opportunity for promotion and a higher salary is one of the reasons to acquire training among 66 percent of all data and information processing graduates who receive work-related training. About 55 percent list employer requirements as one of the reasons for their participation in work-related training. Little more than 40 percent cite the need to learn skills for a newly acquired position as one of the factors that underlie their decision to engage in training.

When asked to select the most important reason to acquire training, 67 percent of data and information processing graduates who undergo training identify the need to improve their occupational skills and knowledge. According to 13 percent of the training participants, the most important reason to participate in training activities is advancement within the firm in the form of a salary increase or promotion. About 11 percent report mandatory training requirements by the employer as the most important

factor underlying their involvement in work-related training. The need to learn skills for a newly acquired position is the number one reason to acquire training among 6 percent of data and information processing graduates who participate in training activities.

Post-Graduation Activities

Of all graduates with a bachelor's degree in data and information processing, only 7 percent proceed to earn a postgraduate degree, all of whom earn a master's degree.

- Fifty-seven percent of all master's degrees earned by undergraduate data and information processing majors are in the field of business administration and management. Only 10 percent of the degrees are in data and information processing, and 22 percent of the master's degrees are earned in other computer and information science fields. Only 7 percent of the master's degrees of undergraduate data and information processing majors are in the field of education.

Of all data and information processing graduates under the age of 65, 91 percent are employed. Only 2 percent are officially unemployed; in other words, they are not employed and are actively seeking employment. The remaining 6 percent are out of the labor force; that is, they are not employed and are not seeking employment. The main reason underlying the labor force withdrawal of data and information processing graduates is family responsibilities; nearly 60 percent cite this reason for their labor force withdrawal. Additionally, one-fifth of labor force withdrawals among data and information processing graduates are attributable to school enrollment. Although not many graduates proceed to earn formal post-graduate degrees, enrollment in courses and programs that are not necessarily a part of a formal degree curriculum is quite common among data and information processing graduates in order to keep current with technological developments. Another 1 in 10 reports that they do not have the need or the desire to work, and 8 percent have a chronic illness or a disabling condition that prevents their participation in the labor market.

Employment Outlook

According to the U.S. Bureau of Labor Statistics, employment in occupations that require at least a bachelor's degree is expected to grow faster than employment in other sectors of the American labor market. Between 2000 and 2010, the U.S. economy is projected to add 22.2 million jobs, yielding an employment growth rate of 15.2 percent. Growth in the demand for college graduates is expected to average around 20 percent over the same time period. The employment growth projections in the top 10 occupations that are most likely to employ data and information processing graduates are presented here.

- Between 2000 and 2010, the demand for computer engineers, computer systems analysts, and miscellaneous computer and information science occupations is projected to slow from its tremendous pace of the 1990s. Employment growth is expected to be most rapid in computer engineering occupations, which are projected to increase by nearly 90 percent. The occupation of computer systems analysts is projected to add 258,000 jobs, yielding a growth rate of 60 percent. Miscellaneous computer and information science occupations are expected to increase by 60 percent over the decade.

- The demand for computer programmers is projected to increase at a below-average rate. Between 2000 and 2010, the U.S. economy is projected to increase by 16 percent, a growth rate well below that projected for demand for bachelor's degree holders. Technological change and the transfer of some computer programming functions to overseas installations may further dampen growth in this occupation.

- The demand for personnel in upper-level managerial occupations and in insurance, finance, and real estate occupations is projected to increase at a rate of about 12 percent between 2000 and 2010.

- Employment projections for other management-related occupations, such as management analysts, purchasing agents, and regulatory officers, are similar to those for overall employment. Total jobs in these occupations are projected to increase by 17 percent.

- Between 2000 and 2010, the employment in clerical and administrative support occupations is projected to grow by only 10 percent.

The outlook for information technology workers is less clear as the slowdown in the information industry has diminished demand for workers with management information skills. The recession of 2001 caused sharp increases in unemployment and underemployment of workers in these fields. Technological change and the "offshoring" of many IT functions suggest the possibility of slower overall growth in demand for workers in these fields than currently forecast.

Table 3

Projected Change in Employment in the Top 10 Occupations That Employ
Persons with Only a Bachelor's Degree in Data and Information Processing

Top 10 Occupations	Actual Employment in 2000 (000s)	Projected Employment in 2010 (000s)	Absolute Change (000s)	Percentage Change
Computer programmers	585	680	95	16.2%
Computer systems analysts	431	689	258	59.9%
Information systems scientists and analysts	28	39	11	39.3%
Top- and mid-level managers, executives, administrators	10,564	11,834	1,270	12.0%
Other computer and information science occupations	203	326	123	60.6%
Other administrative (e.g., records clerks, telephone operators)	16,911	18,522	1,611	9.5%
Other management-related occupations	4,956	5,801	845	17.1%
Computer engineers	757	1,436	679	89.7%
Insurance, securities, real estate, business services	1,548	1,726	178	11.5%
Accountants, auditors, other financial specialists	2,115	2,481	366	17.3%

Electrical and Electronics Engineering Technology

Electrical and electronics technology curricula include the design, development, testing, and manufacture of electrical and electronics equipment, such as radios, radar, sonar, television, industrial and medical measuring or control devices, navigational equipment, and computers. Electrical and electronics technicians may work in product evaluation and testing, using measuring and diagnostic devices to adjust, test, and repair equipment.

Electrical and electronics engineering technology is also applied to a wide variety of systems such as communications and process controls. Electromechanical engineering technicians combine fundamental principles of mechanical engineering technology with knowledge of electrical and electronic circuits to design, develop, test, and manufacture electrical and computer-controlled mechanical systems.

Educational course work may include college algebra, trigonometry, physics, electric circuits, microprocessors, digital electronics, circuit analysis, communication systems, energy conversion, control engineering, power systems, engineering analysis, electricity and electronics, distributed systems, and related laboratory courses.

Engineering technicians are independent; they can work without someone watching over them and giving directions. The freedom that they desire is obtained through working with numbers, machines, and equipment. These technicians enjoy the variety and diversion that work provides. They also cite satisfaction gained from being able to do important or difficult work very well, affording them a sense of high achievement.

Where Do Electrical and Electronics Engineering Technology Majors Work?

A large majority of all employed electrical and electronics engineering technology graduates work in the private, for-profit sector of the economy. Of these employed graduates, 8 of 10 work for businesses and corporations in the private, for-profit sector. Another 6 percent who work in the private, for-profit sector are self-employed in their own business or practice. The government sector employs 10 percent of electrical and electronics engineering technology graduates, and only 3 percent work for educational institutions. The private, nonprofit sector employs only 1 percent of these graduates.

The applied nature of the classroom training of electrical and electronics engineering technology graduates gives them better access to jobs that are related to their major field of study. More than 90 percent of all employed electrical and electronics engineering technology graduates work in jobs that are either closely or somewhat related to their major field of study. About 47 percent are employed in jobs that are closely related to their field of study, and 44 percent consider their employment to be somewhat related to their major field of study. The remaining 9 percent of all employed electrical and electronics engineering technology graduates are employed in jobs that are not at all related to their undergraduate major field of study.

Although each electrical and electronics engineering technology graduate lists numerous reasons for the field in which they are employed, when asked to identify the most important reason for their employment in an unrelated job, nearly 35 percent cite pay and promotion opportunities, and 22 percent cite a desire to change their career track. More than 11 percent choose family-related reasons, and another 11 percent list the lack of related jobs as the most important reason underlying their employment choice. Only 3 percent each rank job location and working conditions as the number one reason for working in an unrelated job.

FIGURE 1

Percentage Distribution of Employed Persons with Only a Bachelor's Degree in Electrical and Electronics Engineering Technology, by Major Sector of Economic Activity

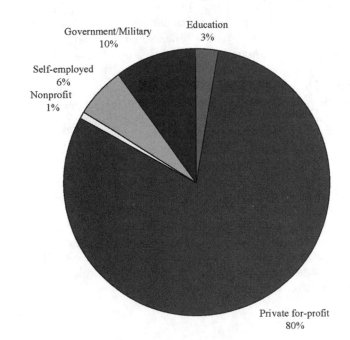

Government/Military 10%

Education 3%

Self-employed 6%

Nonprofit 1%

Private for-profit 80%

Occupations

The employment of electrical and electronics engineering technology graduates is concentrated in a few occupations. The top 2 occupations employ 40 percent of the graduates, and nearly 60 percent work in only 4 occupations. The top 10 occupations employ 77 percent of electrical and electronics engineering technology graduates. Many of these 10 predominant employers of electrical and electronics engineering technology graduates span the engineering, technology, managerial, and computer fields. In fact, 3 of the top 10 occupations are engineering occupations that employ 39 percent of all employed electrical and electronics engineering technology graduates. These include 28 percent who are employed as electrical and electronics engineers, 8 percent who work as computer engineers, and 3 percent who work in other miscellaneous engineering occupations. Top- to mid-level managerial, executive, and administrative occupations employ 11 percent of the graduates, and more than 12 percent are employed as electrical and electronics technicians and technologists. Little more than 4 percent work as mechanics and repairers. Only 5 percent work as either computer systems analysts (3 percent) or computer programmers (2 percent).

Table 1

Top 10 Occupations That Employ Persons with Only a Bachelor's Degree in Electrical and Electronics Engineering Technology

Top 10 Occupations	PERCENT OF EMPLOYED		
	All	Men	Women
Electrical and electronics engineers	27.9	28.7	12.7
Electrical, electronics, industrial, and mechanical technicians and technologists	12.4	12.3	14.6
Top- and mid-level managers, executives, administrators	11.0	11.2	8.2
Computer engineers	7.6	7.6	7.8
Mechanics, repairers	4.1	4.3	0.0
Sales occupations, including retail	3.7	3.9	0.0
All other engineers	3.1	3.1	4.1
Computer systems analysts	2.9	2.9	4.4
Other management-related occupations	2.3	2.0	6.2
Computer programmers	2.2	2.4	0.0

Men constitute nearly 95 percent of all employed electrical and electronics engineering technology graduates. The employment patterns of male and female graduates are quite different. Men are more likely than women to be employed in one of the top 10 occupations. While 78 percent of men are employed in the top 10 occupations, only 58 percent of women work in them. As noted, these occupations are mostly engineering, managerial, technical, and computer occupations.

▶ Electrical and electronics engineering occupations are considerably more likely to employ male electrical and electronics engineering technology graduates than their female counterparts—29 percent versus 13 percent.

▶ Men also are more likely than women to work in top- to mid-level executive, managerial, and administrative occupations. While 11 percent of male graduates work in these occupations, 8 percent of female electrical and electronics engineering technology graduates are employed in these occupations.

▶ Female graduates are somewhat more likely than male graduates to be employed as technicians and technologists—15 percent versus 11 percent. Women with degrees in electrical and electronics engineering technology also are more likely than their male counterparts to work in management-related occupations such as management analysts, purchasing agents, and regulatory officers.

Activities on the Job

The activities that electrical and electronics engineering technology graduates perform on the job are reflective of the occupations in which they are employed.

▶ Nearly 60 percent of all employed electrical and electronics engineering technology graduates perform computer applications, programming, and systems-development duties as a regular part of their job; 19 percent spend most of their time in a typical workweek performing these duties.

▶ One-half of all employed graduates report that they regularly perform management and administrative duties, and 15 percent spend most of their time during a typical workweek in performing these duties.

▶ Electrical and electronics engineering technology graduates also design and develop products and equipment. One-half of employed graduates regularly engage in the design of equipment and processes, and 13 percent spend most of their time performing these tasks. Another 35 percent regularly use research findings to produce materials and devices in their jobs, and 6 percent consider these duties to be the main part of their job.

▶ Little more than one-quarter of all employed electrical and electronics engineering technology graduates regularly perform sales purchasing and marketing, and 9 percent consider these duties to constitute a major part of their jobs.

▶ More than one-quarter of employed electrical and electronics engineering technology graduates regularly engage in applied research, and 5 percent spend a major part of their time at work in this activity.

▶ About 35 percent regularly perform managerial duties to oversee the efficiency and quality of the production process, although only 3 percent spend most of their work time in these activities.

- Only 2 percent each spend most of their time in performing teaching and accounting/financial/contractual duties and in providing professional services such as financial or legal services.

- Very few employed electrical and electronics engineering technology graduates perform employee-relations duties, such as recruiting and personnel development, or engage in basic research activities.

Salaries

The average annual salary of electrical and electronics engineering technology graduates who have only a bachelor's degree and are employed full-time is $57,900, a level that is nearly 7 percent higher than the average annual salary of all full-time employed college graduates. Like the salary of most college graduates, the salary of electrical and electronics engineering technology graduates increases with age, indicating that they get more productive and therefore can earn higher salaries as they spend more time on the job. The average annual salary of electrical and electronics engineering technology graduates somewhat exceeds the salary of all college graduates in every age range.

- The average annual salary of electrical and electronics engineering technology graduates between the ages of 25 and 29 is $43,300. Graduates between the ages of 30 and 34 earn $52,900 annually. The average annual salary of graduates between the ages of 35 and 39 is $58,600, with a further increase to $59,400 among those between 40 and 44.

Graduates between the ages of 45 and 54 earn $70,500 per year, and the average annual salary of those between the pre-retirement ages of 55 and 64 is $73,000.

- The average annual salary of electrical and electronics engineering technology graduates who work in jobs that are related to their major field of study is somewhat higher than the salary of graduates who are employed in jobs that are not related to their major. Graduates working in closely related jobs earn $57,800 per year, and the salary of those who are employed in jobs that are somewhat related to their major is a little higher—$58,600 per year. Fewer than 1 in 10 electrical and electronics engineering technology graduates work in jobs that are unrelated to their undergraduate major field of study, and they earn an average annual salary of $55,300.

- Self-employment in a business or practice is associated with a higher average annual salary than employment in other sectors of the economy among electrical and electronics engineering technology graduates. Full-time self-employed graduates earn $63,000 per year. The majority who are employed in the private, for-profit sector for businesses and corporations earn $58,000 per year. Government sector employees with a bachelor's degree in electrical and electronics engineering technology also earn $58,000 per year. The average annual remuneration of graduates employed by educational institutions is only $46,900.

FIGURE 2

Age/Earnings Profile of Persons with Only a Bachelor's Degree in Electrical and Electronics Engineering Technology (Full-Time Workers, in 2002 Dollars)

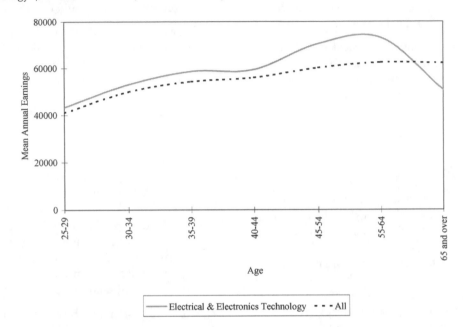

Only 3 of the top 10 occupations that employ electrical and electronics engineering technology graduates pay them an average annual salary that is higher than the average salary of all college graduates. These three occupations—top- to mid-level managers, mechanics and repairers, and sales occupations—employ one-fifth of all working electrical and electronics engineering technology graduates. Within the group of electrical and electronics engineering technology graduates, the average annual salary varies somewhat depending on the occupation in which they are employed.

▶ Graduates employed in top- to mid-level executive, managerial, and administrative occupations earn $78,200 annually.

▶ Graduates employed as electrical and electronics engineers earn $60,400 per year.

▶ The average annual salary of electrical and electronics engineering graduates who are in sales occupations and those employed as computer engineers and computer systems analysts ranges between $56,100 and $59,800.

▶ Electrical and electronics technician and technologist occupations—the second-largest employer—pay these graduates an average annual salary of $47,500 per year. Among the top 10 occupations that are predominant employers of electrical and electronics engineering technology graduates, this amount is the lowest average salary.

Table 2
Annual Salary of Full-Time Workers with Only a Bachelor's Degree in Electrical and Electronics Engineering Technology, Top 10 Occupations (in 2002 Dollars)

Earnings in Top 10 Occupations	All	Electrical and Electronics Engineering Technology
Total	$54,171	$57,927
Electrical and electronics engineers	$66,404	$60,435
Electrical, electronics, industrial, and mechanical technicians and technologists	$49,128	$47,465
Top- and mid-level managers, executives, administrators	$74,051	$78,214
Computer engineers	$66,859	$58,976
Mechanics, repairers	$41,011	$49,448
Sales occupations, including retail	$52,378	$56,143
All other engineers	$62,544	$51,500
Computer systems analysts	$59,818	$59,756
Other management-related occupations	$51,921	$49,256
Computer programmers	$55,715	$54,590

On-the-Job Training

The career potential of a job is closely associated with the amount of work-related training on the job. Work-related training is regarded as an investment by firms because it makes workers more productive. Firms that invest in their workforce are more likely to offer pay increases and promotions to match the increasing productivity of their workers. Firms that do not invest in their workers are relatively less likely to offer pay increases and promotions. Employed electrical and electronics engineering technology graduates are somewhat less likely than all employed college graduates to participate in work-related training. Whereas 68 percent of all employed college graduates receive some work-related training during the year, the proportion of electrical and electronics engineering technology graduates who participate in work-related training during a year is 65 percent.

- Of those electrical and electronics engineering technology graduates who participate in training, 84 percent receive technical training in their occupational field.

- Thirty-eight percent of the training recipients participate in management or supervisor training.

- Twenty-nine percent receive training to improve their general professional skills, such as public speaking and business writing.

Electrical and electronics engineering technology graduates who receive work-related training offer numerous reasons for acquiring training. More than 94 percent participate in work-related training to improve their occupational skills and knowledge. Nearly 53 percent are required or expected by their employers to undergo training. More opportunity for promotion, advancement, and salary increases is the reason for 55 percent of electrical and electronics engineering technology graduates to participate in work-related training, and 40 percent cite the need to learn skills for a newly acquired position as one of the reasons for their participation in work-related training.

When asked to identify the most important reason to acquire training, 66 percent of electrical and electronics engineering technology graduates who undergo training identify the need to improve their occupational skills and knowledge. Another 13 percent report a mandatory training requirement by the employer as the most important factor for their involvement in work-related training. More opportunity for a promotion and a salary increase is the most important factor influencing the decision to acquire training among 11 percent of employed graduates. Nearly 6 percent consider the need to learn skills for a newly acquired position as the most important reason for their participation in work-related training.

Post-Graduation Activities

One-fifth of all electrical and electronics engineering technology graduates with a bachelor's degree proceed to earn a postgraduate degree: 16 percent earn a master's degree, 2 percent graduate with a doctorate, and another 2 percent earn a professional degree.

- Nearly 29 percent of the master's degrees are earned in electrical and electronics engineering technology, and 25 percent are earned in engineering. Another 20 percent are earned in the field of business management and administrative services, and 10 percent each are earned in the fields of computer science and education.

- Electrical and electronics engineering technology is the field of choice among 40 percent of the graduates with a doctoral degree, and one-fifth of the doctoral degrees are earned in one of the physical sciences. About 15 percent earn a doctorate in mathematics, and 12 percent earn one in public affairs.

- More than one-half of the professional degrees earned by undergraduate electrical and electronics engineering technology graduates are in the field of law, 24 percent are in the health professions, and 20 percent are in engineering fields.

Of all electrical and electronics engineering technology graduates under the age of 65, 92 percent are employed. Only 5 percent are officially unemployed; in other words, they are not employed and are actively seeking employment. The remaining 3 percent are out of the labor force; that is, they are not employed and are not seeking employment. The small number of electrical and electronics engineering technology graduates under the age of 65 who are out of the labor force give three main reasons for their labor force withdrawal. Nearly 55 percent are retired, 29 percent have a chronic illness or a disabling condition, and 10 percent are enrolled in school.

Employment Outlook

According to the U.S. Bureau of Labor Statistics, employment in occupations that require at least a bachelor's degree is expected to grow faster than employment in other sectors of the American labor market. The demand for college graduates is expected to rise by about 21 percent between 2000 and 2010. Over that same time period the U.S. economy is projected to add 22.2 million jobs, yielding an overall employment growth rate of 15.2 percent. The employment growth projections in the top 10 occupations that are most likely to employ electrical and electronics engineering technology graduates are presented here. The outlook for electrical engineering technicians is mixed. Projected losses in the nation's manufacturing sector mean slow growth in many of the traditional sources of employment for graduates in this field of study. Demand for workers in this major is more likely to grow rapidly in occupations that apply mathematical skills, such as computer systems engineers.

▶ Slow growth is projected for electrical and electronics engineers between 2000 and 2010. Employment in this occupation is expected to increase by just 11 percent. Computer hardware engineer employment, however, is expected to increase by nearly 90 percent over the same time period.

▶ Employment in the electrical and electronics technician and technologist occupations is projected to grow by 12 percent between 2000 and 2010.

▶ High-level managerial and administrative occupations are projected to add more than 1.2 million jobs between 2000 and 2010, yielding an employment growth rate of 12 percent.

▶ The demand for mechanics and repairers is projected to grow at a rate of 11 percent between 2000 and 2010, somewhat below the projected growth of employment in the United States.

▶ Growth in computer engineering employment is projected to slow from its very rapid pace during the last decade, with employment projected to rise by about 24 percent, and the demand for other miscellaneous engineering occupations is projected to grow at 9 percent.

▶ Additionally, about 258,000 computer systems analyst jobs are projected to be created between 2000 and 2010, increasing demand by 60 percent over the decade.

Table 3
Projected Change in Employment in the Top 10 Occupations That Employ Persons with Only a Bachelor's Degree in Electrical and Electronics Engineering Technology

Top 10 Occupations	Actual Employment in 2000 (000s)	Projected Employment in 2010 (000s)	Absolute Change (000s)	Percentage Change
Electrical and electronics engineers	288	319	31	10.8%
Electrical, electronics, industrial, and mechanical technicians and technologists	519	582	63	12.1%
Top- and mid-level managers, executives, administrators	10,564	11,834	1,270	12.0%
Computer engineers	757	1,436	679	89.7%

(continued)

Table 3 (continued)
Projected Change in Employment in the Top 10 Occupations That Employ
Persons with Only a Bachelor's Degree in Electrical and Electronics Engineering Technology

Top 10 Occupations	Actual Employment in 2000 (000s)	Projected Employment in 2010 (000s)	Absolute Change (000s)	Percentage Change
Mechanics, repairers	5,820	6,482	662	11.4%
Sales occupations, including retail	15,513	17,365	1,852	11.9%
All engineers	1,465	1,603	138	9.4%
Computer systems analysts	431	689	258	59.9%
Other management-related occupations	4,956	5,801	845	17.1%
Computer programmers	585	680	95	16.2%

CHAPTER 62

Industrial Production Technology

This area covers several different facets of production and construction. Chemical engineering technology prepares people to be employed in industries that produce pharmaceuticals, chemicals, and petroleum products. Chemical engineering technicians work in laboratories as well as processing plants. They help develop new chemical products and processes, test processing equipment and instrumentation, monitor quality, and operate chemical manufacturing facilities.

Civil engineering technology prepares people to help civil engineers plan and build highways, buildings, bridges, dams, and wastewater treatment systems, as well as perform related surveys and studies. Some civil engineering technicians inspect water and wastewater treatment systems to ensure that pollution control requirements are met. Others estimate construction costs and specify materials to be used. Some may even prepare drawings or perform land-surveying duties.

Industrial engineering technology is the study of the time, motion, methods, and speed involved in the performance of maintenance, production, and clerical operations to establish standard production rates with the goal to improve efficiency. The engineering technician prepares charts, graphs, and diagrams to illustrate workflow, routing, floor layouts, material handling, and machine utilization. To determine the time involved and fatigue rate, this technician observes workers as they operate equipment or perform tasks. The technician recommends revisions of methods of operation or material handling and suggests alterations in equipment layout to increase production or improve standards. The engineering technician may assist in planning work assignments in accordance with worker performance, machine capacity, production schedules, and anticipated delays.

Educational courses in these areas may include production planning and control, automated manufacturing and robotics, occupational safety and health, quality control, industrial processes, materials processing, hazardous waste management, cost estimating and bidding, engineering material science, engineering drawing, designing and planning, and computers in industrial technology and industrial electronics. Students also take mathematics, computer, and physics courses.

The study of engineering technology requires knowledge and the use of high-level mathematics and geometry. Technologists need eye, hand, and finger coordination to operate machines, adjust instruments, and use measuring tools. Drawing and sketching involve finger dexterity. Technicians perform detailed work with great accuracy. Judgment is required in analyzing data to make decisions. The ability to direct the activities of others is called for in setting up equipment such as seismographic recording instruments to gather data about oil-bearing rock layers. Technologists need skills to use computer and software packages and to write technical reports in clear language.

Where Do Industrial Production Technology Majors Work?

A large majority of all employed industrial production technology graduates work in the private, for-profit sector of the economy. Three-quarters of employed graduates work for businesses and corporations in the private, for-profit sector; another 10 percent are self-employed in their own business or practice. The government sector employs 7 percent of industrial production technology graduates, and only 5 percent work for educational institutions. The private, nonprofit sector employs only 3 percent of these graduates.

Of all employed industrial production technology graduates, 83 percent work in jobs that are either closely or somewhat related to their major field of study. About 43 percent are employed in jobs that are closely related to their field of

FIGURE 1

Percentage Distribution of Employed Persons with Only a Bachelor's Degree in Industrial Production Technology, by Major Sector of Economic Activity

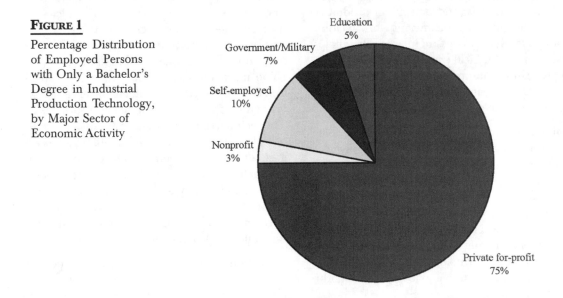

study, and 40 percent consider their employment to be somewhat related to their major field of study. The remaining 17 percent of all employed industrial production technology graduates are employed in jobs that are not at all related to their undergraduate major field of study.

Industrial production technology graduates who work in unrelated jobs list numerous reasons for their employment decision. Pay and promotion opportunities are one of the reasons influencing the decision of 51 percent of employed industrial production technology graduates to work in an unrelated job. One-half voluntarily work in an unrelated job because of the working conditions, such as the hours of work, equipment, and the overall working environment. The desire to change their career track is one of the reasons among 35 percent of jobholders for working in an unrelated job. More than one-quarter work in an unrelated job because they are unable to find jobs related to their major field of study, and 17 percent cite family-related reasons as one of the factors in their decision to work in an unrelated job.

Although each industrial production technology graduate lists numerous reasons for the field in which they are employed, when asked to identify the most important reason for their employment in an unrelated job, nearly 31 percent cite pay and promotion opportunities, and 18

percent consider a desire to change their career track as the number one reason. Nearly 17 percent rank working conditions as the number one reason for working in an unrelated job, and 13 percent list the lack of related jobs as the most important reason underlying their employment choice. Family-related factors are the number one reason for 11 percent of those who work in unrelated jobs. Although 44 percent cite job location as one of the factors underlying their decision to work in unrelated jobs, only 6 percent rate job location as the number one reason for their employment decision.

Occupations

The top 10 occupations employ 63 percent of industrial production technology graduates. About 28 percent work in managerial occupations. Of these, 23 percent work in top- to mid-level executive, administrative, and managerial occupations, and another 5 percent work in management-related occupations such as cost analysts and estimators, purchasing agents, and regulatory officers. Nearly 13 percent secure employment in engineering occupations. About 11 percent are employed as technicians, technologists, and other precision production occupations, including those in construction trades. Little more than 7 percent of the graduates secure employment in sales occupations.

Table 1
Top 10 Occupations That Employ Persons with Only a Bachelor's Degree in Industrial Production Technology

Top 10 Occupations	PERCENT OF EMPLOYED		
	All	Men	Women
Top- and mid-level managers, executives, administrators	22.8	23.8	2.3
Sales occupations, including retail	7.4	7.8	0.0
Industrial engineers	6.5	6.6	4.7

(continued)

Table 1 (continued)
Top 10 Occupations That Employ Persons with Only a Bachelor's Degree
in Industrial Production Technology

	PERCENT OF EMPLOYED		
Top 10 Occupations	**All**	**Men**	**Women**
Other management-related occupations	5.3	4.8	15.9
Electrical, electronics, industrial, and mechanical technicians and technologists	4.1	3.9	7.6
Precision production occupations	3.7	3.8	0.0
All other engineers	3.4	3.5	1.8
Mechanical engineers	3.3	3.4	0.0
Protective-service occupations	3.2	2.6	13.6
Construction trades, miners, well drillers	2.9	3.1	0.0

Men constitute 95 percent of all employed industrial production technology graduates. The employment patterns of male and female graduates are quite different. Men are more likely than women to be employed in one of the top 10 occupations. While 63 percent of men are employed in the top 10 occupations, only 46 percent of women work in them.

▶ Men are considerably more likely than women to work in top- to mid-level executive, managerial, and administrative occupations. While 24 percent of male graduates work in these occupations, only 2 percent of female industrial production technology graduates are employed in these occupations.

▶ Women with degrees in industrial production technology are more likely than their male counterparts to work in management-related occupations such as cost analysts and estimators, purchasing agents, and regulatory officers; 16 percent of women work in these occupations, compared to only 5 percent of men.

▶ Protective-service occupations are more likely to employ female than male industrial production technology graduates. While 14 percent of female graduates work in these occupations, only 3 percent of males are employed in protective-service occupations.

Activities on the Job

The activities that industrial production technology graduates perform on the job are reflective of the occupations in which they are employed.

▶ Sixty-two percent of all employed industrial production technology graduates regularly perform managerial and administrative duties at work, and 22 percent spend most of their typical workweek in performing these tasks.

▶ Fifteen percent of employed industrial production technology graduates spend most of their workweek in production, operations, and maintenance activities.

618

▶ Little more than 40 percent of all employed industrial production technology graduates regularly perform sales purchasing and marketing, and 12 percent consider these duties to constitute a major part of their jobs.

▶ Industrial production technology graduates also design and develop products and equipment. About 40 percent of employed graduates regularly engage in the design of equipment and processes, and 10 percent spend most of their time in performing these tasks. Another 38 percent regularly use research findings to produce materials and devices in their jobs, and 6 percent consider these duties to be the main part of their jobs.

▶ Forty percent of all employed industrial production technology graduates perform computer applications, programming, and systems-development duties as a regular part of their jobs, and 8 percent spend a major part of a typical workweek in performing these duties.

▶ About 57 percent regularly perform managerial duties to oversee the quality and efficiency of the production process, although 7 percent spend most of their work time in these activities.

▶ About 46 percent of employed industrial production technology graduates perform employee-relations duties such as recruiting and personnel development or engage in basic research activities; 5 percent spend a major portion of their typical workweek in performing these duties.

▶ Although 70 percent of the graduates regularly perform accounting, finance, and contractual duties at work, only 4 percent report that these duties take up a major portion of their typical workweek.

▶ Few industrial production technology graduates engage in teaching, applied research, or basic research activities.

Salaries

The average annual salary of industrial technology graduates who have only a bachelor's degree and are employed full-time is $57,700, a level that is nearly 7 percent higher than the average annual salary of all full-time employed college graduates. Like the salary of most college graduates, the salary of industrial production technology graduates increases with age, indicating that they get more productive and therefore can earn higher salaries as they spend more time on the job. The average annual salary of graduates exceeds the salary of all college graduates in most age ranges.

▶ The average annual salary of industrial production technology graduates between the ages of 25 and 34 is $47,900. Graduates between the ages of 35 and 44 earn $58,600 annually. The average salary peaks at $68,000 among graduates between the ages of 45 and 54. Those in the pre-retirement group between the ages of 55 and 64 earn an average salary of $61,300 per year.

▶ The average annual salary of industrial production technology graduates who work in jobs that are closely related to their major field of study is $56,400, a level that is somewhat lower than the salary of graduates who are employed in jobs that are somewhat related or unrelated to their undergraduate major field of study. Graduates working in somewhat related jobs earn $58,400 per year, and the average annual salary of industrial production technology graduates working in jobs that are unrelated to their major is $59,200.

▶ Industrial production technology graduates who work for businesses and corporations in the private, for-profit sector of the economy earn more than those who are employed in other sectors of the economy. The average salary of this group of graduates is $59,500 per year. Self-employed graduates who work in their own business or practice earn $47,000 per year. The government sector pays industrial production graduates who work in full-time jobs an average annual salary of $48,400. Employment in the education sector on a full-time basis is associated with an average salary of $38,100 per year.

In 4 of the top 10 occupations that employ industrial production technology graduates, the average annual salary is noticeably higher than the salary of all college graduates. These include upper-level managerial, sales, technician and technologist, and precision production occupations. The average annual salary of industrial production technology graduates employed in two of the remaining six occupations (management-related and protective-service occupations) is only $500 to $600 (or 1 percent) more than that of all college graduates working in these occupations. The salary of these majors in the remaining four occupations (of the top 10) is lower than that of all college graduates.

FIGURE 2

Age/Earnings Profile of Persons with Only a Bachelor's Degree in Industrial Production Technology (Full-Time Workers, in 2002 Dollars)

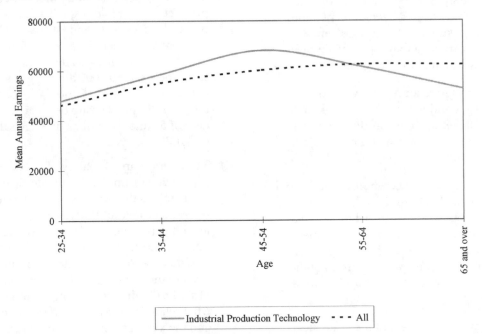

▶ Graduates employed in top- to mid-level executive, managerial, and administrative occupations earn $74,900 annually.

▶ Sales occupations pay industrial production technology graduates an average annual salary of $71,400.

▶ Graduates employed as mechanical engineers earn $61,000 per year. Those employed in miscellaneous engineering occupations earn an average annual salary of $54,100.

▶ Graduates employed in management-related occupations and those who are employed as technicians and technologists have median salaries between $51,300 and $52,400 per year.

▶ The average annual salary of graduates who are employed in protective-service occupations is $49,800 per year, and a job in precision production is associated with an average salary of $44,900 per year among industrial production technology graduates.

Table 2
Annual Salary of Full-Time Workers with Only a Bachelor's Degree in Industrial Production Technology, Top 10 Occupations (in 2002 Dollars)

Earnings in Top 10 Occupations	All	Industrial Production Technology
Total	$54,171	$57,672
Top- and mid-level managers, executives, administrators	$74,051	$74,882
Sales occupations, including retail	$52,378	$71,413
Industrial engineers	$59,290	$57,923
Other management-related occupations	$51,921	$52,447
Electrical, electronics, industrial, and mechanical technicians and technologists	$49,128	$51,269
Precision production occupations	$39,328	$44,923
All other engineers	$62,544	$54,112
Mechanical engineers	$64,905	$61,038
Protective-service occupations	$49,130	$49,788
Construction trades, miners, well drillers	$50,531	$45,035

On-the-Job Training

The career potential of a job is closely associated with the amount of work-related training on the job. Work-related training is regarded as an investment by firms because it makes workers more productive. Firms that invest in their workforce are more likely to offer pay increases and promotions to match the increasing productivity of their workers. Firms that do not invest in their workers are relatively less likely to offer pay increases and promotions. Employed industrial production technology graduates are somewhat less likely than all employed college graduates to participate in work-related training. Whereas 68 percent of all employed college graduates receive some work-related training during the year, the proportion of industrial production technology graduates who participate in work-related training during the year is 65 percent.

▶ Of those industrial production technology graduates who receive some training, 82 percent receive technical training in their occupational field.

▶ Forty-four percent of the training recipients receive management or supervisor training.

▶ Twenty-seven percent receive training to improve their general professional skills, such as public speaking and business writing.

Industrial production technology graduates who receive work-related training offer numerous reasons for acquiring training. Nearly 94 percent report the need to improve their occupational skills and knowledge as one of the factors underlying their decision to acquire work-related training. About 55 percent of training recipients undergo training because the employer requires it. More opportunity for promotion, advancement, and salary increases is a reason among 43 percent of graduates who acquire some training during a year. One-third cite the need to learn skills for a newly acquired position as one of the reasons for participation in work-related training. Finally, 15 percent cite the need to obtain a professional license or certificate as a factor underlying their decision to acquire work-related training.

When asked to identify the most important reason to acquire training, 66 percent of industrial production technology graduates who undergo training identify the need to improve their occupational skills and knowledge. Another 15 percent report a mandatory training requirement by the employer as the most important factor for their involvement in work-related training. More opportunity for a promotion and salary increase is the most important factor influencing training decisions among 7 percent of employed graduates who acquire training. Another 5 percent consider the need to learn skills for a newly acquired position as the most important reason for their participation in work-related training. Finally, 5 percent rank the need to obtain a professional license or certificate as the most important reason for participation in work-related training activities.

Post-Graduation Activities

Only 15 percent of all industrial production technology graduates with a bachelor's degree proceed to earn a postgraduate degree. Almost all of the degrees earned by these graduates are master's degrees.

▶ Nearly 23 percent of the master's degrees are earned in industrial production technology, 45 percent are earned in the field of business management and administrative services, and 10 percent are earned in education.

Of all industrial production technology graduates under the age of 65, 92 percent are employed. Only 3 percent are officially unemployed; in other words, they are not employed and are actively seeking employment. The remaining 5 percent are out of the labor force; that is, they are not employed and are not seeking employment. The small numbers of industrial production technology graduates under the age of 65 who are out of the labor force give three main reasons for their labor force withdrawal. Nearly 54 percent are retired, 17 percent have a chronic illness or a disabling condition, and 17 percent are enrolled in school.

Employment Outlook

According to the U.S. Bureau of Labor Statistics, employment in occupations that require at least a bachelor's degree is expected to grow faster than employment in other sectors of the American labor market. Between 2000 and 2010, the U.S. economy is projected to add 22.2 million jobs, yielding an employment growth rate of 15.2 percent. The employment growth projections in the top 10 occupations that are most likely to employ industrial production technology graduates are presented here.

▶ High-level managerial and administrative occupations are projected to add nearly 1.3 million jobs between 2000 and 2010, yielding an employment growth rate of 12 percent.

▶ Employment in the industrial technician and technologist occupations and sales occupations is projected to increase between 10 and 12 percent over the decade.

▶ Industrial engineering occupations are projected to grow by only 5 percent over the projection period 2000 to 2010.

▶ Protective-service occupations are projected to add 809,000 jobs as homeland security becomes a key national priority, yielding a demand growth rate of 26 percent.

▶ Between 2000 and 2010, the demand for mechanical engineers is projected to increase by 14 percent.

Table 3

Projected Change in Employment in the Top 10 Occupations That Employ Persons with Only a Bachelor's Degree in Industrial Production Technology

Top 10 Occupations	Actual Employment in 2000 (000s)	Projected Employment in 2010 (000s)	Absolute Change (000s)	Percentage Change
Top- and mid-level managers, executives, administrators	10,564	11,834	1,270	12.0%
Sales occupations, including retail	15,513	17,365	1,852	11.9%
Industrial engineers	154	161	7	4.5%
Other management-related occupations	4,956	5,801	845	17.1%

(continued)

Table 3 (continued)
Projected Change in Employment in the Top 10 Occupations That Employ
Persons with Only a Bachelor's Degree in Industrial Production Technology

Top 10 Occupations	Actual Employment in 2000 (000s)	Projected Employment in 2010 (000s)	Absolute Change (000s)	Percentage Change
Electrical, electronics, industrial, and mechanical technicians and technologists	519	582	63	12.1%
Precision production occupations	13,060	13,811	751	5.8%
All other engineers	1,456	1,603	138	9.4%
Mechanical engineers	221	251	30	13.6%
Protective-service occupations	3,087	3,896	809	26.2%
Construction trades, miners, well drillers	7,451	8,439	988	13.3%

CHAPTER 63

Mechanical Engineering Technology

Mechanical engineering technicians work with engineers to design, develop, test, and manufacture industrial machinery, mechanical parts, and other equipment. These technicians may assist in the testing of a guided missile or in the planning and design of an electric power generation plant. They make sketches and rough layouts, record data, make computations, analyze results, and write reports. When planning production, mechanical engineering technicians prepare layouts and drawings of the assembly process and of parts to be manufactured. They estimate labor costs, equipment life, and plant space needed. Some test and inspect machines and equipment in manufacturing departments or work with engineers to eliminate production problems.

Their work may involve the reviewing of project instructions and blueprints to ascertain test specifications; procedures; test equipment required; the nature of identified technical problems and possible solutions, such as parts redesign; the substitution of materials or parts; or the rearrangement of parts or subassemblies. They may devise, fabricate, and assemble new or modified mechanical components or assemblies of products. They may set up prototypes and test apparatus such as a control console, recording equipment, and cables in accordance with specifications; they then operate the controls of test apparatus and prototypes to observe and record test results. Afterward, they may recommend design and material changes to reduce cost and production time.

Educational courses may include mechanics, stress analysis, mechanical design, thermodynamics, materials, measurement and analysis laboratory, heat transfer, refrigeration and air conditioning, fluid dynamics, and related labs. Students also take advanced mathematics, computer, and physics courses.

Engineering technicians are quiet, hardworking, and conscientious. They are people who pay attention to detail and are logical thinkers. They like to lead predictable lives that mirror the logic they use in their jobs. They rely on their memory and analysis of current facts to make judgments and decisions.

FIGURE 1

Percentage Distribution of Employed Persons with Only a Bachelor's Degree in Mechanical Engineering Technology, by Major Sector of Economic Activity

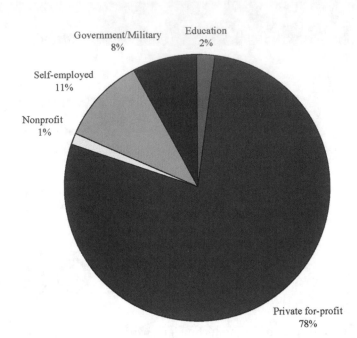

Government/Military
8%

Education
2%

Self-employed
11%

Nonprofit
1%

Private for-profit
78%

Where Do Mechanical Engineering Technology Majors Work?

Most graduates of mechanical engineering technology programs at the bachelor's degree level work as wage and salary employees in private, for-profit businesses and corporations. An additional 11 percent are self-employed individuals operating their own businesses or consulting services. Few college graduates with a bachelor's degree in mechanical engineering technology are employed in educational or nonprofit organizations. About 8 percent work for a government agency.

Occupations

About one-third of the graduates of mechanical engineering technology programs at the bachelor's degree level report that they are employed as mechanical engineers. An additional 7 percent are employed in some other type of related engineering capacity, and about 3 percent work as aeronautical engineers. Thus, more than 4 in 10 graduates of mechanical engineering technology programs at the bachelor's degree level work in a job with an engineer title. Nearly 85 percent of employed graduates work in jobs that are related to their undergraduate major. Those employed in jobs unrelated to their major are outside the field primarily because they developed interests in another area. However, a substantial number working outside the field report that they could not find suitable employment related to mechanical engineering technology. Those working outside the field have earnings well below those with jobs related to their major.

Table 1

Top 10 Occupations That Employ Persons with Only a Bachelor's Degree in Mechanical Engineering Technology

Top 10 Occupations	PERCENT OF EMPLOYED		
	All	Men	Women
Mechanical engineers	31.4	32.3	14.0
Top- and mid-level managers, executives, administrators	15.9	16.8	0.0
All other engineers	6.8	6.9	4.9
Sales occupations, including retail	5.6	5.7	2.8
Mechanics, repairers	4.1	4.3	0.0
Electrical, electronics, industrial, and mechanical technicians and technologists	3.6	3.6	3.7
Aeronautical, aerospace, and astronautical engineers	3.4	3.6	0.0
Transportation and material-moving occupations	3.3	3.5	0.0
Agriculture, forestry, fishing, and related occupations	3.0	3.2	0.0
Other management-related occupations	2.9	2.1	19.0

▶ Men with an undergraduate degree in mechanical engineering technology are more than twice as likely as women with the same degree to be employed as mechanical engineers.

▶ Fewer than 1 in 5 women with a degree in mechanical engineering technology have an engineering job title, compared to more than 40 percent of men.

▶ Women with a degree in mechanical engineering are often employed in management-related occupations, including accounting, finance, and human resources. Few women have access to management or administrative positions.

Activities on the Job

▶ Mechanical engineering technology graduates are engaged in job tasks that are associated with designing equipment, designing processes, and overseeing production operations, particularly in regard to quality control.

▶ Mechanical engineering technology graduates are also involved in a number of purchasing decisions made by producers, where they apply their technical knowledge in the acquisition of materials used in various production technologies.

▶ Some applied research is undertaken by graduates from this field of study, but little basic research is undertaken by these individuals.

▶ Development of computer applications is undertaken by about 1 in 3 employed persons with a bachelor's degree in mechanical engineering technology.

Salaries

The annual salaries of persons with only a bachelor's degree in mechanical engineering technology are well above the mean salaries of all employed bachelor's degree holders. While the average person with a bachelor's degree earns $54,200 per year, those with a degree in this field earn $62,200, or about 15 percent more per year than the average college graduate. Those mechanical engineering technology graduates who work in the private, for-profit sector have annual salaries of about $65,000 per year, a rate of pay more than one-quarter higher than that of their counterparts who work in jobs in the government sector. Graduates between the ages of 25 and 29 earn about $45,500 per year. Annual salaries keep increasing in inflation-adjusted terms through ages 50 to 55, and the average salary peaks at about $82,500 per year in 2002 dollars. Mechanical engineering technology graduates who work in jobs related to their field of study earn 45 percent more per year than those employed in jobs unrelated to the major field. Clearly, finding employment in a job that requires the skills learned as an undergraduate is an essential element of success in this field.

FIGURE 2

Age/Earnings Profile of Persons with Only a Bachelor's Degree in Mechanical Engineering Technology (Full-Time Workers, in 2002 Dollars)

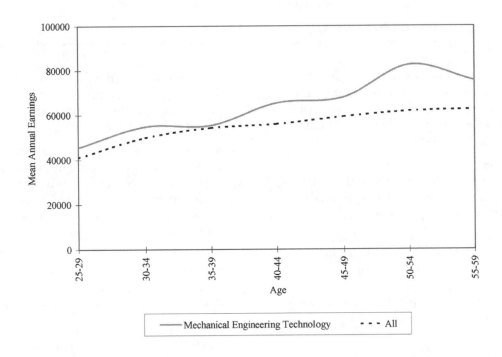

Table 2
Annual Salary of Full-Time Workers with Only a Bachelor's Degree in
Mechanical Engineering Technology, Top 10 Occupations (in 2002 Dollars)

Earnings in Top 10 Occupations	All	Mechanical Engineering Technology
Total	$54,171	$62,242
Mechanical engineers	$64,905	$64,396
Top- and mid-level managers, executives, administrators	$74,051	$82,191
All other engineers	$62,544	$66,183
Sales occupations, including retail	$52,378	$56,650
Mechanics, repairers	$41,011	$46,831
Electrical, electronics, industrial, and mechanical technicians and technologists	$49,128	$48,784
Aeronautical, aerospace, and astronautical engineers	$68,111	$62,998
Transportation and material-moving occupations	$64,088	$46,526
Agriculture, forestry, fishing, and related occupations	$45,437	$35,598
Other management-related occupations	$51,921	$55,368

Mechanical engineering technology graduates who are employed in engineering job titles have earnings in the mid-$60,000 range. Those working with the mechanical engineering job title earn $64,400 per year, while those working as aerospace engineers have an annual salary of $63,000. Graduates working in other engineering occupations earn $66,200. Employment in managerial and administrative jobs means higher pay for mechanical engineering technology graduates who are able to move into these positions, earning salaries that average $82,200 per year in 2002 dollars. Those employed in sales jobs, mechanic and repairer positions, management-related occupations, and other jobs unrelated to the field have annual salaries that are well below those of the average earnings of graduates in this field.

On-the-Job Learning

Mechanical engineering technology graduates are somewhat less likely than other college graduates to participate in a job-related training activity over the course of a year, although nearly 7 of 10 did report such training activity in the past year.

▶ About 80 percent of all those who received training over the course of the year were trained in some specific activity related to the professional field. Such training could encompass a wide variety of topics, including quality management, training in a specific process of equipment used in production, or training on the use of new materials or production techniques.

▶ About 40 percent received training in managerial or supervisory areas, suggesting that many graduates in this degree field have supervisory responsibilities as part of their regular job duties.

▶ Nearly 9 of 10 persons who receive training do so to acquire a specific set of skills or competencies directly related to their job.

Post-Graduation Activities

▶ Most persons who earn a degree in mechanical engineering technology do not continue their education in order to earn an advanced degree. Only 1 in 5 persons with a bachelor's degree in this field eventually goes on to earn an advanced degree of some type.

▶ Most of those who are awarded an advanced degree earn a master's degree of some type. More than 40 percent of these individuals earn a master's degree in business. Only about 1 in 3 earn a master's degree in some engineering field. Nearly 1 in 10 go on to earn a master's in education.

▶ Less than 3 percent of all graduates at the bachelor's degree level continue their formal schooling past the master's degree level. Most of the individuals who earn a doctorate of some type usually do so in an engineering field. Very few undergraduate majors from this field earn a professional degree in either law or medicine.

Of those with a degree in this field, 90 percent are employed, most in full-time jobs. Among those who are jobless, about 40 percent are unable to find suitable work. The remaining persons not working have decided that they do not want to work. Interestingly, unlike those in many other fields, almost none of these individuals chose not to work because of family responsibilities. Instead, most of those under the age of 65 who are voluntarily jobless have decided to take an early retirement.

Employment Outlook

While the employment outlook for college graduates in general remains bright over the coming years, slower growth is expected for those occupations that employ graduates of mechanical engineering technology programs. The number of employed persons with a bachelor's degree is expected to increase by almost 21 percent between 2000 and 2010, yet the number of persons employed as mechanical engineers is expected to increase by only 14 percent, according to the U.S. Bureau of Labor Statistics. The projected rate of increase in the demand for aeronautical engineer employment is expected to increase 14 percent through 2010.

▶ The demand for managers and administrators that employ mechanical engineering technology graduates will be well below average. The rate of growth in this area is expected to be sluggish compared to the economy as a whole, and considerably slower than the average for all college graduates.

▶ Management-related jobs, which employ a relatively high proportion of women with degrees in mechanical engineering technology, will grow at a slightly higher rate than the overall job growth in the nation between 2000 and 2010.

Table 3

Projected Change in Employment in the Top 10 Occupations That Employ
Persons with Only a Bachelor's Degree in Mechanical Engineering Technology

Top 10 Occupations	Actual Employment in 2000 (000s)	Projected Employment in 2010 (000s)	Absolute Change (000s)	Percentage Change
Mechanical engineers	221	251	30	13.6%
Top- and mid-level managers, executives, administrators	10,564	11,834	1,270	12.0%
All engineers	1,465	1,603	138	9.4%
Sales occupations, including retail	15,513	17,365	1,852	11.9%
Mechanics, repairers	5,820	6,482	662	11.4%
Electrical, electronics, industrial, and mechanical technicians and technologists	519	582	63	12.1%
Aeronautical, aerospace, and astronautical engineers	50	57	7	14.0%
Transportation and material-moving occupations	10,088	11,618	1,530	15.2%
Agriculture, forestry, fishing, and related occupations	1,429	1,480	51	3.6%
Other management-related occupations	4,956	5,801	845	17.1%

INDEX

A

abilities, assessing, 21–22
  career-related, 23–24
  information, collecting, 32–33
  information, organizing, 33–40
    action plan, establishing, 39–40
    goals, setting, 33–34
    majors, examining options, 35–37
    priorities, determining, 34–35
    risks, assessing, 37–39
  reality testing, 24–25
  self-assessing, 22–25
Ability Explorer, 25
accounting, 177–183
  activities on the job, 180
  employment outlook, 182–183
  occupations, 179–180
  on-the-job training, 182
  postgraduation activities, 182
  salaries, 180–182
  workplaces, 178–179
activities on the job
  accounting, 180
  aerospace, aeronautical, and astronautical engineering, 302
  animal food sciences, 514
  anthropology and archaeology, 379
  applied mathematics, operations research, and statistics, 189
  architecture and environmental design, 310–311
  audiology and speech pathology, 78
  biology and life sciences, 521–522
  chemical engineering, 318
  chemistry, 530
  civil engineering, 326–327
  communications, 388
  computer science, 589
  computer systems engineering, 336–337
  criminal justice and criminology, 86
  data and information processing, 599
  dramatic arts, 396
  economics, 198–199
  electrical and electronics engineering, 346–347

electrical and electronics engineering technology, 608–609
elementary teacher education, 257
English language, literature, and letters, 405
financial management, 209
foreign languages and literature, 415
forestry and environmental sciences, 539
general business, 219
general mathematics, 228–229
geography, 424–425
geology and geophysics, 548–549
health and medical technology, 94
history, 433
home economics: dietetics, food, and nutrition, 104–105
industrial engineering, 356–357
industrial production technology, 618–619
journalism, 439–440
legal studies and pre-law, 448
liberal arts and general studies, 456–457
marketing, 238
mathematics and science teacher education, 266–267
mechanical engineering, 366–367
mechanical engineering technology, 627
medical preparatory programs, 115
microbiology and biochemistry, 559–560
music and dance, 466–467
nursing, 123
parks, recreation, fitness, and leisure studies, 133
pharmacy, 141
philosophy, 477
physical education and coaching, 274
physical therapy, 148
physics and astronomy, 568–569
plant food sciences, 578
political science, government, and international relations, 487
psychology, 157–158
public administration, 246–247
secondary teacher education, 282–283
social work, 168–169
sociology, 494

special education, 292–293
visual arts, 503
aerospace, aeronautical, and astronautical
  engineering, 299–306
  activities on the job, 302
  employment outlook, 305–306
  occupations, 301–302
  on-the-job training, 304–305
  postgraduation activities, 305
  salaries, 302–304
  workplaces, 300
American workers, 6–13
  literacy, 8–9
animal food sciences, 511–518
  activities on the job, 514
  employment outlook, 517–518
  occupations, 512–513
  on-the-job training, 516
  postgraduation activities, 516–517
  salaries, 514–516
  workplaces, 512
anthropology and archaeology, 375–384
  activities on the job, 379
  employment outlook, 383–384
  occupations, 378–379
  on-the-job training, 382–383
  postgraduation activities, 383
  salaries, 379–382
  workplaces, 376–377
applied mathematics, operations research,
  and statistics, 185–194
  activities on the job, 189
  employment outlook, 193–194
  occupations, 187–189
  on-the-job training, 191–192
  postgraduation activities, 192–193
  salaries, 189–191
  workplaces, 186–187
archaeology, see anthropology and
  archaeology
architecture and environmental design, 307–314
  activities on the job, 310–311
  employment outlook, 314
  occupations, 309–310
  on-the-job training, 313
  postgraduation activities, 313
  salaries, 311–313
  workplaces, 308–309
artistic ability, 23–24

artistic personality type, 25–27
arts, entertainment, and media interests, 28
astronautical engineering, see aerospace,
  aeronautical, and astronautical engineering
astronomy, see physics and astronomy
audiology and speech pathology, 75–82
  activities on the job, 78
  employment outlook, 81–82
  occupations, 77–78
  on-the-job training, 80
  postgraduation activities, 80
  salaries, 78–80
  workplaces, 76–77

B

Barron's, 53
behavioral and medical sciences, 73–174
biochemistry, see microbiology and biochemistry
biology and life sciences, 519–526
  activities on the job, 521–522
  employment outlook, 525–526
  occupations, 521
  on-the-job training, 524
  postgraduation activities, 524–525
  salaries, 522–523
  workplaces, 520–521
biophysics, 556–557
blue collar vs. white collar, 51–52
business and administration, 175–251
business detail interests, 28
business personality type, 26–27

C

career choices, 1–72
  abilities, interests, and values, 21–40
    assessing, 21–22
    career-related, 23–24
    information, collecting, 32–33
    information, organizing, 33–40
    personal values, 35
    personality types, 25–27
    reality testing, 24–25
    self-assessing abilities, 22–25
    self-assessing interests, 25–30
    self-assessing values, 30–32
    work values, 31
  economics of, 41–72
    blue collar vs. white collar, 51–52

earnings of college graduates, 67–72
economic environment, 48–52
employment experiences of college
   graduates, 62–67
graduate study, 55–59
high school vs. college graduate earnings,
   43–48
higher education as investment, 42–48
information required, 52–55
labor market for college graduates, 55–62
manufacturing and service industries, 49–50
pre-college decisions, 3–20
   alcohol use, 4
   basic skills, 4, 6–13
   child bearing, 3, 11–12
   costs of college, 17–20
   drug use, 4
   educational goals, 4, 15–16
   occupational skills, 4, 16–17
   parental involvement, 4–6
   work and school, 4, 13–15
The Career Decision-Making System Revised, 31
chemical engineering, 315–322
   activities on the job, 318
   employment outlook, 322
   occupations, 317–318
   on-the-job training, 321
   postgraduation activities, 321–322
   salaries, 318–320
   workplaces, 316
chemistry, 527–533
   activities on the job, 530
   employment outlook, 533
   occupations, 529–530
   on-the-job training, 532
   postgraduation activities, 532–533
   salaries, 530–531
   workplaces, 528
civil engineering, 323–331
   activities on the job, 326–327
   employment outlook, 330–331
   occupations, 325–326
   on-the-job training, 329–330
   postgraduation activities, 330
   salaries, 327–329
   workplaces, 324–325
clerical ability, 23–24
coaching, *see* physical education and coaching
college as investment, 1, 4–6

college graduates
   earnings of, 67–72; *see also* entries for
      individual majors
   employment experiences, 62–67
   graduate study, 55–59
   labor market for, 55–62
   labor market participation, 59–62
communications, 385–392
   activities on the job, 388
   employment outlook, 391–392
   occupations, 387–388
   on-the-job training, 390
   postgraduation activities, 390–391
   salaries, 388–390
   workplaces, 386–387
community personal value, 35
computer science, 585–594
   activities on the job, 589
   employment outlook, 593–594
   occupations, 588–589
   on-the-job training, 592–593
   postgraduation activities, 593
   salaries, 589–592
   workplaces, 586–588
computer systems engineering, 333–341
   activities on the job, 336–337
   employment outlook, 340–341
   occupations, 335–336
   on-the-job training, 339–340
   postgraduation activities, 340
   salaries, 337–339
   workplaces, 334–335
construction, mining, and drilling interests, 28
costs of college, 17–20
   earnings missed while attending, 17
   financial aid, 17–18
   tuition, 17–20
crafts personality type, 26–27
creativity work value, 31
criminal justice and criminology, 83–90
   activities on the job, 86
   employment outlook, 89–90
   occupations, 85–86
   on-the-job training, 88–89
   postgraduation activities, 89
   salaries, 86–88
   workplaces, 84–85

D

dance, *see* music and dance
data and information processing, 595–604
   activities on the job, 599
   employment outlook, 603–604
   occupations, 597–599
   on-the-job training, 601–602
   postgraduation activities, 602–603
   salaries, 599–601
   workplaces, 596–597
decisions, pre-college, 3–20
   alcohol use, 4
   basic skills, 4, 6–13
   child bearing, 3, 11–12
   costs of college, 17–20
   drug use, 4
   educational goals, 4, 15–16
   occupational skills, 4, 16–17
   parental involvement, 4–6
   work and school, 4, 13–15
dramatic ability, 23–24
dramatic arts, 393–400
   activities on the job, 396
   employment outlook, 399–400
   occupations, 395–396
   on-the-job training, 398
   postgraduation activities, 399
   salaries, 396–398
   workplaces, 394
dropouts, 7–8, 12, 15–16

E

economic environment for graduates, 48–52
economics, 195–204
   activities on the job, 198–199
   employment outlook, 203–204
   higher education as investment, 42–48
   high school vs. college graduate earnings,
      43–48
   occupations, 197–198
   on-the-job training, 201–202
   postgraduation activities, 202
   salaries, 199–201
   workplaces, 196–197
education, 253–296
education and social service interests, 28
educational goals, setting, 15–16

electrical and electronics engineering, 343–351
   activities on the job, 346–347
   employment outlook, 350–351
   occupations, 345–346
   on-the-job training, 349
   postgraduation activities, 350
   salaries, 347–349
   workplaces, 344–345
electrical and electronics engineering
   technology, 605–614
   activities on the job, 608–609
   employment outlook, 612–614
   occupations, 607–608
   on-the-job training, 611–612
   postgraduation activities, 612
   salaries, 609–611
   workplaces, 606
elementary teacher education, 255–261
   activities on the job, 257
   employment outlook, 260–261
   occupations, 257
   on-the-job training, 259
   postgraduation activities, 259–260
   salaries, 258–259
   workplaces, 256–257
employment outlook
   accounting, 182–183
   aerospace, aeronautical, and astronautical
      engineering, 305–306
   animal food sciences, 517–518
   anthropology and archaeology, 383–384
   applied mathematics, operations research,
      and statistics, 193–194
   architecture and environmental design, 314
   audiology and speech pathology, 81–82
   biology and life sciences, 525–256
   chemical engineering, 322
   chemistry, 533
   civil engineering, 330–331
   communications, 391–392
   computer science, 593–594
   computer systems engineering, 340–341
   criminal justice and criminology, 89–90
   data and information processing, 603–604
   dramatic arts, 399–400
   economics, 203–204
   electrical and electronics engineering, 350–351
   electrical and electronics engineering
      technology, 612–614

elementary teacher education, 260–261

English language, literature, and letters, 409–410

financial management, 213–214

foreign languages and literature, 419

forestry and environmental sciences, 543–544

general business, 223–224

general mathematics, 232–234

geography, 428–429

geology and geophysics, 552–553

health and medical technology, 98–99

history, 436

home economics: dietetics, food, and nutrition, 109–110

industrial engineering, 360–361

industrial production technology, 623–624

journalism, 443–444

legal studies and pre-law, 451–452

liberal arts and general studies, 460–461

marketing, 241

mathematics and science teacher education, 270

mechanical engineering, 370–371

mechanical engineering technology, 630–631

medical preparatory programs, 118–119

microbiology and biochemistry, 563

music and dance, 470–471

nursing, 126–127

parks, recreation, fitness, and leisure studies, 137–138

pharmacy, 143–144

philosophy, 480–481

physical education and coaching, 277

physical therapy, 151–152

physics and astronomy, 573–574

plant food sciences, 581–582

political science, government, and international relations, 489–490

psychology, 162–163

public administration, 250–251

secondary teacher education, 286–287

social work, 173–174

sociology, 497

special education, 296

visual arts, 507–508

employment trends, 7

engineering, 297–371

English language, literature, and letters, 401–410
   activities on the job, 405
   employment outlook, 409–410
   occupations, 404–405
   on-the-job training, 408
   postgraduation activities, 408–409
   salaries, 405–407
   writers and editors, 401–403
   workplaces, 403–404

environment personal value, 35

environmental design, *see* architecture and environmental design

environmental sciences, *see* forestry and environmental sciences

F

family personal value, 35

financial aid, 10–11

financial management, 205–214
   activities on the job, 209
   employment outlook, 213–214
   occupations, 207–208
   on-the-job training, 212
   postgraduation activities, 212–213
   salaries, 209–211
   workplaces, 206–207

foreign languages and literature, 411–419
   activities on the job, 415
   employment outlook, 419
   occupations, 413–415
   on-the-job training, 417–418
   postgraduation activities, 418
   salaries, 415–417
   workplaces, 412–413

forestry and environmental sciences, 535–544
   activities on the job, 539
   employment outlook, 543–544
   occupations, 538–539
   on-the-job training, 542
   postgraduation activities, 542–543
   salaries, 539–541
   workplaces, 536–538

G

general business, 215–224
   activities on the job, 219
   employment outlook, 223–224
   occupations, 217–219
   on-the-job training, 222
   postgraduation activities, 222–223
   salaries, 219–221
   workplaces, 216–217

general management and support interests, 28
general mathematics, 225–234
    activities on the job, 228–229
    employment outlook, 232–234
    occupations, 226–228
    on-the-job training, 231–232
    postgraduation activities, 232
    salaries, 229–231
    workplaces, 226
general studies, *see* liberal arts and general studies
geography, 421–429
    activities on the job, 424–425
    employment outlook, 428–429
    occupations, 423–424
    on-the-job training, 427–428
    postgraduation activities, 428
    salaries, 425–427
    workplaces, 422
geology and geophysics, 545–553
    activities on the job, 548–549
    employment outlook, 552–553
    occupations, 547–548
    on-the-job training, 551–552
    postgraduation activities, 552
    salaries, 549–551
    workplaces, 546–547
good salary work value, 31
government, *see* political science, government, and international relations
graduate study, 55–59

H

health and medical technology, 91–99
    activities on the job, 94
    employment outlook, 98–99
    occupations, 93–94
    on-the-job training, 96–97
    postgraduation activities, 97–98
    salaries, 94–96
    workplaces, 92–93
helping others personal value, 35
high achievement work value, 31
high school vs. college graduate earnings, 43–48
higher education as investment, 42–48
history, 431–436
    activities on the job, 433
    employment outlook, 436
    occupations, 432–433
    on-the-job training, 435

postgraduation activities, 435–436
    salaries, 434–435
    workplaces, 432
home economics: dietetics, food, and nutrition, 101–110
    activities on the job, 104–105
    employment outlook, 109–110
    occupations, 103–104
    on-the-job training, 107–108
    postgraduation activities, 108–109
    salaries, 105–107
    workplaces, 102–103
HOPE scholarship tax credit, 18
humanities and social sciences, 373–508

I

independence work value, 31
industrial engineering, 353–361
    activities on the job, 356–357
    employment outlook, 360–361
    occupations, 355–356
    on-the-job training, 359–360
    postgraduation activities, 360
    salaries, 357–359
    workplaces, 354
industrial production interests, 29
industrial production technology, 615–624
    activities on the job, 618–619
    employment outlook, 623–624
    occupations, 617–618
    on-the-job training, 622
    postgraduation activities, 622–623
    salaries, 619–621
    workplaces, 616–617
information processing, *see* data and information processing
interests, assessing, 21–22
    information, collecting, 32–33
    information, organizaing, 33–40
        action plan, establishing, 39–40
        goals, setting, 33–34
        majors, examining options, 35–37
        priorities, determining, 34–35
        risks, assessing, 37–39
    personality types, 25–27
    self-assessing, 25–30
international relations, *see* political science, government, and international relations
interpersonal ability, 23–24

investment decision, 1–71
    abilities, interests, and values, 21–40
        assessing, 21–22
        career-related, 23–24
        information, collecting, 32–33
        information, organizing, 33–40
        personal values, 35
        personality types, 25–27
        reality testing, 24–25
        self-assessing abilities, 22–25
        self-assessing interests, 25–30
        self-assessing values, 30–32
        work values, 31
    economics, 41–72
        blue collar vs. white collar, 51–52
        earnings of college graduates, 67–72
        economic environment, 48–52
        employment experiences of college
            graduates, 62–67
        graduate study, 55–59
        high school vs. college graduate earnings,
            43–48
        higher education as investment, 42–48
        information required, 52–55
        labor market for college graduates, 55–62
        manufacturing and service industries, 49–50
    pre-college decisions, 3–20
        alcohol use, 4
        basic skills, 4, 6–13
        child bearing, 3, 11–12
        costs of college, 17–20
        drug use, 4
        educational goals, 4, 15–16
        occupational skills, 4, 16–17
        parental involvement, 4–6
        work and school, 4, 13–15

J–L

job security work value, 31
journalism, 437–444
    activities on the job, 439–440
    employment outlook, 443–444
    occupations, 439
    on-the-job training, 442–443
    postgraduation activities, 443
    salaries, 440–442
    workplaces, 438

labor market for college graduates, 55–62
languages, *see* English language, literature, and
    letters; foreign languages and literature
law, law enforcement, and public safety
    interests, 29
leadership ability, 23–24
leadership work value, 31
legal studies and pre-law, 445–452
    activities on the job, 448
    employment outlook, 451–452
    occupations, 447–448
    on-the-job training, 450
    postgraduation activities, 450–451
    salaries, 449–450
    workplaces, 446–447
leisure personal value, 35
leisure studies, *see* parks, recreation, fitness,
    and leisure studies
liberal arts and general studies, 453–461
    activities on the job, 456–457
    employment outlook, 460–461
    occupations, 455
    on-the-job training, 459–460
    postgraduation activities, 460
    salaries, 457–459
    workplaces, 454–455
life sciences, *see* biology and life sciences
Lifetime Learning scholarship tax credit, 18
literature, *see* English language, literature, and
    letters; foreign languages and literature
Love 'Em or Lose 'Em: Getting Good People to Stay, 35

M

manual ability, 23–24
manufacturing and service industries, 49–50
marketing, 235–241
    activities on the job, 238
    employment outlook, 241
    occupations, 237–238
    on-the-job training, 240
    postgraduation activities, 240–241
    salaries, 238–240
    workplaces, 236–237
mathematical ability, 23–24
mathematics, *see* applied mathematics, operations
    research, and statistics; general mathematics

mathematics and science teacher education,
263–270
  activities on the job, 266–267
  employment outlook, 270
  occupations, 265–266
  on-the-job training, 269
  postgraduation activities, 269
  salaries, 267–268
  workplaces, 264–266
mechanical ability, 22, 24
mechanical engineering, 363–371
  activities on the job, 366–367
  employment outlook, 370–371
  occupations, 365–366
  on-the-job training, 369
  postgraduation activities, 370
  salaries, 367–369
  workplaces, 364
mechanical engineering technology, 625–631
  activities on the job, 627
  employment outlook, 630–631
  occupations, 626–627
  on-the-job training, 629–630
  postgraduation activities, 630
  salaries, 628–629
  workplaces, 626
mechanics, installers, and repairers interests, 29
medical and health services interests, 29
medical preparatory programs, 111–119
  activities on the job, 115
  employment outlook, 118–119
  occupations, 114–115
  on-the-job training, 117–118
  postgraduation activities, 118
  salaries, 115–117
  workplaces, 113–114
medical technology, *see* health and medical
  technology
microbiology and biochemistry, 555–563
  activities on the job, 559–560
  biochemistry, 556
  biophysics, 556–557
  employment outlook, 563
  microbiology, 555–556
  occupations, 558–559
  on-the-job training, 562
  postgraduation activities, 562
  salaries, 560–561
  workplaces, 557–558

music and dance, 463–471
  activities on the job, 466–467
  employment outlook, 470–471
  occupations, 465–466
  on-the-job training, 469
  postgraduation activities, 469–470
  salaries, 467–469
  workplaces, 464–465
musical or dramatic ability, 23–24

N

A Nation at Risk, 6
natural sciences, 509–582
numerical or mathematical ability, 23–24
nursing, 121–127
  activities on the job, 123
  employment outlook, 126–127
  occupations, 123
  on-the-job training, 126
  postgraduation activities, 126
  salaries, 123–125
  workplaces, 122–123
nutrition, *see* home economics: dietetics, food,
  and nutrition

O

Occupational Outlook Handbook, 33
occupational skills, 15–16
occupations
  accounting, 179–180
  aerospace, aeronautical, and astronautical
    engineering, 301–302
  animal food sciences, 512–513
  anthropology and archaeology, 378–379
  applied mathematics, operations research,
    and statistics, 187–189
  architecture and environmental design,
    309–310
  audiology and speech pathology, 77–78
  biology and life sciences, 521
  chemical engineering, 317–318
  chemistry, 529–530
  civil engineering, 325–326
  communications, 387–388
  computer science, 588–589
  computer systems engineering, 335–336
  criminal justice and criminology, 85–86
  data and information processing, 597–599

dramatic arts, 395–396
economics, 197–198
electrical and electronics engineering, 345–346
electrical and electronics engineering technology, 607–608
elementary teacher education, 257
English language, literature, and letters, 404–405
financial management, 207–208
foreign languages and literature, 413–415
forestry and environmental sciences, 538–539
general business, 217–219
general mathematics, 226–228
geography, 423–424
geology and geophysics, 547–548
health and medical technology, 93–94
history, 432–433
home economics: dietetics, food, and nutrition, 103–104
industrial engineering, 355–356
industrial production technology, 617–618
journalism, 439
legal studies and pre-law, 447–448
liberal arts and general studies, 455–456
marketing, 237–238
mathematics and science teacher education, 265–266
mechanical engineering, 365–366
mechanical engineering technology, 626–627
medical preparatory programs, 114–115
microbiology and biochemistry, 558–559
music and dance, 465–466
nursing, 123
parks, recreation, fitness, and leisure studies, 131–133
pharmacy, 141
philosophy, 475–476
physical education and coaching, 273–274
physical therapy, 147–148
physics and astronomy, 567–568
plant food sciences, 577–578
political science, government, and international relations, 486–487
psychology, 156–157
public administration, 245–246
secondary teacher education, 281–282
social work, 167–168
sociology, 493–494

special education, 291–292
visual arts, 502–503
office operations personality type, 26–27
on-the-job training
accounting, 182
aerospace, aeronautical, and astronautical engineering, 304–305
animal food sciences, 516
anthropology and archaeology, 382–383
applied mathematics, operations research, and statistics, 191–192
architecture and environmental design, 313
audiology and speech pathology, 80
biology and life sciences, 524
chemical engineering, 321
chemistry, 532
civil engineering, 329–330
communications, 390
computer science, 592–593
computer systems engineering, 339–340
criminal justice and criminology, 88–89
data and information processing, 601–602
dramatic arts, 398
economics, 201–202
electrical and electronics engineering, 349
electrical and electronics engineering technology, 611–612
elementary teacher education, 259
English language, literature, and letters, 408
financial management, 212
foreign languages and literature, 417–418
forestry and environmental sciences, 542
general business, 222
general mathematics, 231–232
geography, 427–428
geology and geophysics, 551–552
health and medical technology, 96–97
history, 435
home economics: dietetics, food, and nutrition, 107–108
industrial engineering, 359–360
industrial production technology, 622
journalism, 442–443
legal studies and pre-law, 450
liberal arts and general studies, 459–460
marketing, 240
mathematics and science teacher education, 269
mechanical engineering, 369

mechanical engineering technology, 629–630
medical preparatory programs, 117–118
microbiology and biochemistry, 562
music and dance, 469
nursing, 126
parks, recreation, fitness, and leisure studies, 136–137
pharmacy, 143
philosophy, 480
physical education and coaching, 276
physical therapy, 150–151
physics and astronomy, 572
plant food sciences, 580
political science, government, and international relations, 489
psychology, 160–161
public administration, 249
secondary teacher education, 285–286
social work, 172
sociology, 496
special education, 295
visual arts, 506
operations research, *see* applied mathematics, operations research, and statistics
organizational ability, 23–24
outdoor work value, 31

P

parks, recreation, fitness, and leisure studies, 129–138
  activities on the job, 133
  employment outlook, 137–138
  occupations, 131–133
  on-the-job training, 136–137
  postgraduation activities, 137
  salaries, 133–136
  workplaces, 130–131
personal growth value, 35
persuasive ability, 23–24
pharmacy, 139–144
  activities on the job, 141
  employment outlook, 143–144
  occupations, 141
  on-the-job training, 143
  postgraduation activities, 143
  salaries, 141–143
  workplaces, 140–141
philosophy, 473–482
  activities on the job, 477
  employment outlook, 481–482
  occupations, 475–476
  on-the-job training, 480
  postgraduation activities, 480–481
  salaries, 477–479
  workplaces, 474–475
physical activity work value, 31
physical education and coaching, 271–278
  activities on the job, 274
  employment outlook, 277
  occupations, 273–274
  on-the-job training, 276
  postgraduation activities, 276–277
  salaries, 274–276
  workplaces, 272–273
physical therapy, 145–152
  activities on the job, 148
  employment outlook, 151–152
  occupations, 147–148
  on-the-job training, 150–151
  postgraduation activities, 151
  salaries, 148–150
  workplaces, 146–147
physics and astronomy, 565–574
  activities on the job, 568–569
  employment outlook, 573–574
  occupations, 567–568
  on-the-job training, 572
  postgraduation activities, 572–573
  salaries, 569–571
  workplaces, 566–567
plant food sciences, 575–582
  activities on the job, 578
  employment outlook, 581–582
  occupations, 577–578
  on-the-job training, 580
  postgraduation activities, 580–581
  salaries, 578–580
  workplaces, 576–577
plants and animals interests, 29
political science, government, and international relations, 483–490
  activities on the job, 487
  employment outlook, 189–490
  occupations, 496–487
  on-the-job training, 489
  postgraduation activities, 489
  salaries, 487–488
  workplaces, 485–486

postgraduation activities
  accounting, 182
  aerospace, aeronautical, and astronautical
    engineering, 305
  animal food sciences, 516–517
  anthropology and archaeology, 383
  applied mathematics, operations research,
    and statistics, 192–193
  architecture and environmental design, 313
  audiology and speech pathology, 80
  biology and life sciences, 524–525
  chemical engineering, 321–322
  chemistry, 532–533
  civil engineering, 330
  communications, 390–391
  computer science, 593
  computer systems engineering, 340
  criminal justice and criminology, 89
  data and information processing, 602–603
  dramatic arts, 399
  economics, 202
  electrical and electronics engineering, 350
  electrical and electronics engineering
    technology, 612
  elementary teacher education, 259–260
  English language, literature, and letters,
    408–409
  financial management, 212–213
  foreign languages and literature, 418
  forestry and environmental sciences, 542–543
  general business, 222–223
  general mathematics, 232
  geography, 428
  geology and geophysics, 552
  health and medical technology, 97–98
  history, 435–436
  home economics: dietetics, food, and
    nutrition, 108–109
  industrial engineering, 360
  industrial production technology, 622–623
  journalism, 443
  legal studies and pre-law, 450–451
  liberal arts and general studies, 460
  marketing, 240–241
  mathematics and science teacher education,
    269
  mechanical engineering, 370
  mechanical engineering technology, 630
  medical preparatory programs, 118
  microbiology and biochemistry, 562
  music and dance, 469–470
  nursing, 126
  parks, recreation, fitness, and leisure studies,
    137
  pharmacy, 143
  philosophy, 480–481
  physical education and coaching, 276–277
  physical therapy, 151
  physics and astronomy, 572–573
  plant food sciences, 580–581
  political science, government, and
    international relations, 489
  psychology, 161–162
  public administration, 249–250
  secondary teacher education, 286
  social work, 172–173
  sociology, 496–497
  special education, 295–296
  visual arts, 506–507
pre-law, *see* legal studies and pre-law
prestige work value, 31
psychology, 153–163
  activities on the job, 157–158
  employment outlook, 162–163
  occupations, 156–157
  on-the-job training, 160–161
  postgraduation activities, 161–162
  salaries, 158–160
  workplaces, 155–156
public administration, 243–251
  activities on the job, 246–247
  employment outlook, 250–251
  occupations, 245–246
  on-the-job training, 249
  postgraduation activities, 249–250
  salaries, 247–249
  workplaces, 244–245

R–S

recreation, travel, and other personal services
  interests, 29
risk work value, 31

salaries
  accounting, 180–182
  aerospace, aeronautical, and astronautical
    engineering, 302–304
  animal food sciences, 514–516

anthropology and archaeology, 379–382

applied mathematics, operations research, and statistics, 189–191

architecture and environmental design, 311–313

audiology and speech pathology, 78–80

biology and life sciences, 522–523

chemical engineering, 318–320

chemistry, 530–531

civil engineering, 327–329

communications, 388–390

computer science, 589–592

computer systems engineering, 337–339

criminal justice and criminology, 86–88

data and information processing, 599–601

dramatic arts, 396–398

economics, 199–201

electrical and electronics engineering, 347–349

electrical and electronics engineering technology, 609–611

elementary teacher education, 258–259

English language, literature, and letters, 405–407

financial management, 209–211

foreign languages and literature, 415–417

forestry and environmental sciences, 539–541

general business, 219–221

general mathematics, 229–231

geography, 425–427

geology and geophysics, 549–551

health and medical technology, 94–96

history, 434–435

home economics: dietetics, food, and nutrition, 105–107

industrial engineering, 357–359

industrial production technology, 619–621

journalism, 440–442

legal studies and pre-law, 449–450

liberal arts and general studies, 457–459

marketing, 238–240

mathematics and science teacher education, 267–268

mechanical engineering, 367–369

mechanical engineering technology, 628–629

medical preparatory programs, 115–117

microbiology and biochemistry, 560–561

music and dance, 467–469

nursing, 123–125

parks, recreation, fitness, and leisure studies, 133–136

pharmacy, 141–143

philosophy, 477–479

physical education and coaching, 274–276

physical therapy, 148–150

physics and astronomy, 569–571

plant food sciences, 578–580

political science, government, and international relations, 487–488

psychology, 158–160

public administration, 247–249

secondary teacher education, 283–285

social work, 169–171

sociology, 494–496

special education, 293–295

visual arts, 503–505

sales and marketing interests, 30

science teacher education, see mathematics and science teacher education

scientific ability, 23–24

scientific personality type, 26–27

secondary teacher education, 279–287

   activities on the job, 282–283

   employment outlook, 286–287

   occupations, 281–282

   on-the-job training, 285–286

   postgraduation activities, 286

   salaries, 283–285

   workplaces, 280–281

skills, basic, 6–13

   finances and, 10–11

   rewards for, 8

   social pathologies and, 11–13

social ability, 23–24

social pathologies, 11–13

social personality type, 26–27

social work, 165–174

   activities on the job, 168–169

   employment outlook, 173–174

   occupations, 167–168

   on-the-job training, 172

   postgraduation activities, 172–173

   salaries, 169–171

   workplaces

sociology, 491–497

   activities on the job, 494

   employment outlook, 497

   occupations, 493–494

on-the-job training, 496
postgraduation activities, 496–497
salaries, 494–496
workplaces, 492–493
spatial ability, 23–24
special education, 289–296
    activities on the job, 292–293
    employment outlook, 296
    occupations, 291–292
    on-the-job training, 295
    postgraduation activities, 295–296
    salaries, 293–295
    workplaces, 290–291
speech pathology, *see* audiology and speech
  pathology
spiritual personal value, 35
standard of living personal value, 35
statistics, *see* applied mathematics, operations
  research, and statistics
success, college, 1–71
    abilities, interests, and values, 21–40
      assessing, 21–22
      career-related, 23–24
      information, collecting, 32–33
      information, organizing, 33–40
      personal values, 35
      personality types, 25–27
      reality testing, 24–25
      self-assessing abilities, 22–25
      self-assessing interests, 25–30
      self-assessing values, 30–32
      work values, 31
    economics, 41–72
      blue collar vs. white collar, 51–52
      earnings of college graduates, 67–72
      economic environment, 48–52
      employment experiences of college
        graduates, 62–67
      graduate study, 55–59
      high school vs. college graduate earnings,
        43–48
      higher education as investment, 42–48
      information required, 52–55
      labor market for college graduates, 55–62
      manufacturing and service industries, 49–50
    pre-college decisions, 3–20
      alcohol use, 4
      basic skills, 4, 6–13
      child bearing, 3, 11–12

costs of college, 17–20
drug use, 4
educational goals, 4, 15–16
occupational skills, 4, 16–17
parental involvement, 4–6
work and school, 4, 13–15
success, economic, 6–13

T–V

tax credits, 18
technical or mechanical ability, 22, 24
technology, 583–631
transportation interests, 30

US News & World Report, 53

values, assessing, 21–22
    information, collecting, 32–33
    information, organizing, 33–40
      action plan, establishing, 39–40
      goals, setting, 33–34
      majors, examining options, 35–37
      priorities, determining, 34–35
      risks, assessing, 37–39
    personal, 35
    self-assessing, 30–32
    work values, 31
variety work value, 31
visual arts, 499–508
    activities on the job, 503
    employment outlook, 507–508
    occupations, 502–503
    on-the-job training, 506
    postgraduation activities, 506–507
    salaries, 503–505
    workplaces, 500–501

W–Z

work experience as investment, 13–15
work with hands work value, 31
work with mind work value, 31
work with people work value, 31
workplaces
    accounting, 178–179
    aerospace, aeronautical, and astronautical
      engineering, 300
    animal food sciences, 512
    anthropology and archaeology, 376–377

applied mathematics, operations research, and statistics, 186–187

architecture and environmental design, 308–309

audiology and speech pathology, 76–77

biology and life sciences, 520

chemical engineering, 316

chemistry, 528

civil engineering, 324–325

communications, 386–387

computer science, 586–588

computer systems engineering, 334–335

criminal justice and criminology, 84–85

data and information processing, 596–597

dramatic arts, 394

economics, 196–197

electrical and electronics engineering, 344–345

electrical and electronics engineering technology, 606

elementary teacher education, 256–257

English language, literature, and letters, 403–404

financial management, 206–207

foreign languages and literature, 412–413

forestry and environmental sciences, 536–538

general business, 216–217

general mathematics, 226

geography, 422

geology and geophysics, 546–547

health and medical technology, 92–93

history, 432

home economics: dietetics, food, and nutrition, 102–103

industrial engineering, 354

industrial production technology, 616–617

journalism, 438–439

legal studies and pre-law, 446–447

liberal arts and general studies, 454–455

marketing, 236–237

mathematics and science teacher education, 264–265

mechanical engineering, 364

mechanical engineering technology, 626

medical preparatory programs, 113–114

microbiology and biochemistry, 557–558

music and dance, 464–465

nursing, 122–123

parks, recreation, fitness, and leisure studies, 130–131

pharmacy, 140–141

philosophy, 474–475

physical education and coaching, 272–273

physical therapy, 146–147

physics and astronomy, 566–567

plant food sciences, 576–577

political science, government, and international relations, 485–486

psychology, 155–156

public administration, 244–245

secondary teacher education, 280–281

social work, 166–167

sociology, 492–493

special education, 290–291

visual arts, 500–502

writers and editors, 401–403

Occupational Outlook Handbook,

2006-2007 Edition
U.S. Department of Labor

The *OOH*–the most widely used career reference–describes more than 270 major jobs, with summary information on additional jobs. Each job listing discusses the nature of the work, working conditions, job outlook, training and education needed, earnings, related occupations, and additional information sources, making it invaluable for making career decisions, writing resumes, and preparing for interviews. New–a JIST exclusive: *How Educators, Counselors, Librarians, and Business Professionals Can Best Use the* OOH.

ISBN 1-59357-248-4 / Order Code LP-J2484 / **$17.95** Softcover
ISBN 1-59357-247-6 / Order Code LP-J2476 / **$24.95** Hardcover

Exploring Careers, Third Edition

A Young Person's Guide to 1,000 Jobs
Editors at JIST

Engage young people in their futures with this unique volume that organizes 1,000 O*NET jobs into 14 career clusters. Each cluster includes career "clues" to explore, profiles of real workers, skill samplers that list the skills required in certain jobs, and a section describing related jobs. The job descriptions include education and training needed; skills required in math, English, and science; earnings; growth; and yearly openings. Appendixes discuss the relevance of core subjects and give career tips for students.

ISBN 1-56370-488-9 / Order Code LP-J4889 / **$29.95**

Best Jobs for the 21st Century, Third Edition

Michael Farr with database work by Laurence Shatkin, Ph.D.

This data-packed reference is ideal for students, teachers, working people, and anyone interested in career planning and job advancement. It contains 65 lists of jobs with the best pay, fastest growth, and most openings in numerous categories.

The second part of the book describes more than 500 jobs with fast growth, many openings, or high pay–all based on the latest O*NET data from the U.S. Department of Labor.

ISBN 1-56370-961-9 / Order Code LP-J9619 / **$19.95**